CAMDEN TOWN 5

Erarbeitet von
Stephanie Claussen
Pamela Hanus
Kerstin Klemm
Christoph Reuter
Sylvia Wauer

Berater der Fachredaktion Gymnasium
Prof. Dr. Konrad Schröder

Fachliche Beratung
Helmut Bier
Roswitha Henseler
Ute Seemann
Ulrike Selz
Günther Sommerschuh
Prof. Dr. Karin Vogt

Materialien für Schülerinnen und Schüler
- Workbook 5 mit Audio-CD (ISBN 978-3-425-**73425**-5)
- Vocab Practice 5 (ISBN 978-3-425-**73445**-3)
- BiBox – Digitale Unterrichtsmaterialien für Schüler 5
    - Schüler-Einzellizenz (WEB-425-**30019**)
    - Basis-Einzellizenz (WEB-425-**30059**)

Materialien für Lehrkräfte
- Lehrerfassung zum Schülerband 5
  (ISBN 978-3-425-**73505**-4)
- Workbook 5 mit Löser und Audio-CD
  (ISBN 978-3-425-**73515**-3)
- Teacher's Manual 5 (ISBN 978-3-425-**73525**-2)
- Vorschläge für Lernerfolgskontrollen 5
  (ISBN 978-3-425-**73535**-1)
- Audio-CD 5 mit DVD für Lehrkräfte (ISBN 978-3-425-**73575**-7)
- BiBox – Digitale Unterrichtsmaterialien für Lehrer 5
    - Lehrer-Einzellizenz (WEB-425-**73394**)
    - Lehrer-Einzellizenz auf DVD-ROM (ISBN 978-3-425-**73372**-2)
    - Kollegiumslizenz (WEB-425-**73379**)
- Kopiervorlagen 5 (ISBN 978-3-425-**73555**-9)
- Differenzieren und Individualisieren 5 (ISBN 978-3-425-**71121**-8)

Fördert individuell – passt zum Schulbuch

Optimal für den Einsatz im Unterricht mit *Camden Town Gymnasium*! Den Kompetenzstand feststellen, Stärken erkennen und Defizite durch individuelle Fördermaterialien ausgleichen. Direkt und online auf Basis der aktuellen Bildungsstandards und Lehrplananforderungen.

www.diesterweg.de/diagnose

---

westermann GRUPPE

© 2017 Bildungshaus Schulbuchverlage
Westermann Schroedel Diesterweg Schöningh Winklers GmbH, Braunschweig
www.diesterweg.de

Das Werk und seine Teile sind urheberrechtlich geschützt. Jede Nutzung in anderen als den gesetzlich zugelassenen Fällen bedarf der vorherigen schriftlichen Einwilligung des Verlages.

Hinweis zu § 52a UrhG: Weder das Werk noch seine Teile dürfen ohne Einwilligung gescannt und in ein Netzwerk eingestellt werden. Dies gilt auch für Intranets von Schulen und sonstigen Bildungseinrichtungen. Für Verweise (Links) auf Internet-Adressen gilt folgender Haftungshinweis: Trotz sorgfältiger inhaltlicher Kontrolle wird die Haftung für die Inhalte der externen Seiten ausgeschlossen. Für den Inhalt dieser externen Seiten sind ausschließlich deren Betreiber verantwortlich. Sollten Sie daher auf kostenpflichtige, illegale oder anstößige Inhalte treffen, so bedauern wir dies ausdrücklich und bitten Sie, uns umgehend per E-Mail davon in Kenntnis zu setzen, damit beim Nachdruck der Verweis gelöscht wird.

Druck A^2 / Jahr 2018
Alle Drucke der Serie A sind im Unterricht parallel verwendbar.

Redaktion: James Gough, Lucas Mees, Dr. Heike Michaelis, Thorsten Schimming
Layout: Druckreif! Sandra Grünberg, Braunschweig
Illustrationen: Ulf Marckwort, Kassel
Umschlaggestaltung: blum design und kommunikation, Hamburg
Druck und Bindung: westermann druck GmbH, Braunschweig

ISBN 978-3-425-**73405**-7

Wegweiser durch Camden Town

Kapitelteil

Aufbau der *Themes* 1–5

obligatorisch	A	Hier wird jeweils ein Unterthema des *Themes* behandelt.
	B	
	C	
fakultativ	Personal Trainer	Übungsteil zum Trainieren und Wiederholen
	Intercultural photo page	Fotos und landeskundliche Informationen (in *Theme* 2, 4, 5)
	Optional	Literaturauszüge, Sachtexte

Differenzierung und Individualisierung

- ❖ **Extra** — Fakultative zusätzliche Aufgabe
- ❖ **Choose** — Aufgabe mit Wahlmöglichkeiten
- ❖ **Can you do it?** — Aufgabe mit Hilfestellung
- ❖ **A4 Target task** — Offene Aufgabe, die differenzierte Ergebnisse hervorbringen kann

Die fakultativen Teile *Personal Trainer*, *Intercultural photo page* und *Optional* eignen sich für einen differenzierenden und individualisierenden Einsatz im Unterricht.

Kompetenzen

- Jedes Kapitel trainiert mehrere Kompetenzen (siehe Inhaltsverzeichnis).
- In den *target tasks* werden eine oder mehrere Kompetenzen intensiv trainiert. *Target tasks* sind umfangreichere Aufgaben, die Ergebnisse vorhergehender Übungen aufnehmen und einbinden.
- Auf den *Skills pages* befinden sich unterstützende Lern- und Arbeitstechniken zu allen Kompetenzen.
- Die Checklisten am Ende der Kapitel bieten eine Rückschau auf die Kompetenzen des jeweiligen Kapitels.

Anhang

Skills pages	Lern- und Arbeitstechniken
Language in Focus (LiF)	Grammatikanhang zum Nachschlagen
Words	*Wordbanks* (thematische Wortschatzsammlungen) und Wortlisten

Symbole

👥 / 👥	Partnerarbeit/Gruppenarbeit
🎧 S 3, L 1/6	Der Hörtext ist auf der Schüler-CD (Track 3) und auf der Lehrer-CD (CD1, Track 6).
🎥	Das Video zu der Aufgabe befindet sich auf der DVD.
( )	Sprachmittlung
● P3	Hierzu gibt es eine Übung (P3) auf den Personal-Trainer-Seiten.
📖 WB B3, p. 25	Hierzu gibt es eine Aufgabe im Workbook (Aufgabe B3 auf Seite 25).
● Reading, p. 136	Auf Seite 136 befinden sich Hilfen zum Lesen.
● LiF 1R: Tenses, p. 164	Auf Seite 164 befinden sich Hilfen zum Grammatikpensum *tenses*.
● Wordbank Jobs, p. 187	Auf Seite 187 gibt es hilfreiche Wörter und Wendungen zum Thema *jobs*.
❖	Diese Aufgabe eignet sich besonders für Differenzierung/Individualisierung.
🎯 Need help? Look at p. 72.	Um diese Aufgabe zu lösen, findest du Hilfen auf Seite 72.
📄 Portfolio	Das Ergebnis kann im Portfolio-Ordner abgelegt werden.
✂ Project	Projekt
Support ·····	In dieser Box stehen Tipps und sprachliche Hilfen.

To explore the unknown?

Dear student,

Welcome to *Camden Town* 5!

This year, your book has a modular structure. Together with your teacher your class can choose in which order you will work through the five different *Themes*.

Camden Town 5 puts a strong focus on developing the skills you will need for the 'Oberstufe':

➡ All relevant language and general learning skills are systematically trained.
➡ Texts and tasks provide a step-by-step introduction to literary analysis.
➡ *Skills pages* help you develop a solid language learning competency.
  • *Study and communication skills pages* provide study techniques and tips to improve your ability to interact with others in English.
  • *Language skills pages* use tasks to focus on the various functions of English.
➡ Speaking, mediation and intercultural learning are key elements in *Camden Town* 5.
➡ *Target tasks* help you see how much progress you have made.

Remember to look at your *Portfolio pages* from last school year. They will help you set your personal goals for this year.

Enjoy *Camden Town* 5!

Inhalt

Seite	Kommunikative und interkulturelle Kompetenzen	Sprachliche Mittel (**Wortfelder**, Grammatik)	Methodische Kompetenzen (Schwerpunkte)
1	**Knowing me, knowing you**		
10	**A What makes you unique?** (Thema: Identität, Online-Identität) Über Identität sprechen • Die Aussagekraft von Online-Profilen diskutieren • Einem Radiobericht Informationen entnehmen `Target task` Eine Twitter-Diskussion schreiben	**Identität** • **Social Media** R: *Tenses°* • R: *Modal verbs and their substitute forms°*	*Speaking Listening Writing*
12	**B Love is all you need?** (Thema: Anderssein, Beziehungen unter Jugendlichen) Spekulieren • Einem Musikvideo Informationen entnehmen • Einen Songtext erfassen • Über Dating in Deutschland und den USA sprechen • Einen Kommentar verfassen • Einen Romanauszug analysieren `Target task` Eine Geschichte fortschreiben	**Beziehungen** • **Dating** • **Charaktereigenschaften** • **Gefühle** R: *Modal verbs and their substitute forms*	*Viewing Writing Reading Speaking*
19	**C Playing happy families?** (Thema: Familienbeziehungen) Über Erfahrungen sprechen • Erwartungen ausdrücken • Konflikte zwischen Teenagern und Eltern benennen • Gefühle ausdrücken • Spekulationen anstellen • Über Familienmodelle sprechen • Ein Buchcover beschreiben `Target task` Eine Diskussion führen	**Konflikte** • **Beziehungen** R: *The passive°*	*Speaking Listening Writing Reading Viewing*
26	**Personal Trainer:** Training und Wiederholung von Kompetenzen, Wortfeldern und Strukturen		
32	**Optional:** *Will Grayson, Will Grayson* Romanauszüge vergleichen • Eine Zusammenfassung schreiben • Romanauszug mit Perspektivwechsel umschreiben	**Gefühle**	*Reading Writing*
2	**Life through a lens**		
36	**A Every picture tells a story** (Thema: Fotos und ihre Wirkung) Funktion von Fotos benennen • Bearbeitete Bilder analysieren `Target task` Eine Diskussion führen	**Bildbeschreibung** R: *The passive°*	*Speaking Listening*
38	**B To buy or not to buy?** (Thema: Werbung) Eine Antwort auf einen Blogeintrag verfassen • Einen Text mit eigenen Worten zusammenfassen • Über Werbestrategien sprechen • Die eigene Meinung ausdrücken • Aussagen bewerten und ggf. korrigieren • Werbefotos analysieren und kategorisieren • Sich auf ein Ergebnis einigen `Target task` Einen Kommentar verfassen	**Film** • **Werbung** R: *The passive infinitive*	*Speaking Reading Listening Writing*
42	**C Dress to impress** (Thema: Streben nach Luxus-Lifestyle) Ideen für einen Filmanfang sammeln • Filmauszügen Informationen entnehmen • Ein Interview analysieren • Filmische Mittel erkennen • Paraphrasieren • Die Zusammenfassung eines Filmausschnitts vervollständigen `Target task` Einen Filmausschnitt schriftlich zusammenfassen	**Filmische Mittel** *Participle constructions*	*Viewing Reading Speaking Writing*
46	**Personal Trainer:** Training und Wiederholung von Kompetenzen, Wortfeldern und Strukturen		
52	**Intercultural photo page:** *Media* Fotos analysieren • Einen Text für eine Website verfassen	**Medien**	*Reading Listening Writing*
54	**Optional:** *Matched* Über Erwartungen an Teenager sprechen • Gefühle und Stimmungen benennen • Hinweise geben • Ratschläge erteilen	**Gefühle**	*Reading Writing*

Die gelb ausgezeichneten Teile sind als obligatorisch, die rot und grün ausgezeichneten Teile als fakultativ zu behandeln.
° Dieses Pensum befindet sich im Personal Trainer des Kapitels. • R = *revision*

Inhalt

Seite	Kommunikative und interkulturelle Kompetenzen	Sprachliche Mittel (**Wortfelder**, Grammatik)	Methodische Kompetenzen (Schwerpunkte)
	3 Go with the flow		
58	**A In with the in-crowd** (Thema: Jugendgruppierungen in den USA und Deutschland) Rückschlüsse aus Fotos ziehen • Zusammenhänge herstellen • Eine Textanalyse durchführen `Target task` Einen Leitfaden verfassen	Jugendgruppierungen	*Speaking* *Reading* *Writing*
60	**B Popular** (Thema: Streben nach Anerkennung) Vorlieben und Abneigungen ausdrücken • Über Ratschläge diskutieren • Textpassagen zusammenfassen • Eine Zusammenfassung schreiben • Einen Rap analysieren `Target task` Einen Rap schreiben / Forumsbeiträge schreiben und diskutieren	Jugendgruppierungen • Kleidung *Conditional clauses, type 3* • R: *Reported speech*	*Viewing* *Speaking* *Reading* *Writing*
66	**C Under pressure** (Thema: Gruppenzwang) Einer Website Informationen entnehmen • Einem Hörtext Informationen entnehmen und diese als Grundlage für eigene Überlegungen nutzen • Artikeln arbeitsteilig Informationen entnehmen • Inhalte eines Podcasts auf Deutsch wiedergeben `Target task` Eine Unterhaltung / Diskussion führen	Gruppenzwang R: *The passive°* • R: *Reported speech°*	*Speaking* *Listening* *Reading* *Mediation*
70	**Personal Trainer:** Training und Wiederholung von Kompetenzen, Wortfeldern und Strukturen		
76	**Optional:** *The Hacktivists* Szene zusammenfassen • Eine Aussage aus der Perspektive einer Figur formulieren • Eine Charakterisierung schreiben	Charaktereigenschaften	*Reading* *Writing*
	4 One world?		
80	**A What makes you hit the road?** (Thema: Reisen) Über Reiseerfahrungen sprechen • Eine Umfrage durchführen • Bilder beschreiben • Ergebnisse präsentieren `Target task` Eine Collage erstellen	Reisen	*Speaking* *Listening*
82	**B The perfect getaway** (Thema: Reisen und Umweltschutz) Einen Text analysieren • Verschiedene Vorschläge diskutieren • Zeitungsartikel zusammenfassen • Wortfeld anlegen • Kausalzusammenhänge darlegen • Vor- und Nachteile diskutieren `Target task` Einen Erfahrungsbericht verfassen	Reisen • Umweltschutz	*Reading* *Speaking* *Writing*
88	**C Speak English and you'll be understood?** (Thema: Englisch als Weltsprache) Über die Bedeutung von Englisch als Weltsprache sprechen • Statistiken auswerten • Eine Entscheidung begründen • Informationen aus einem deutschen Text auf Englisch wiedergeben `Target task` Eine E-Mail verfassen	Auslandserfahrungen *Gerund or infinitive°* • R: *Relative clauses°*	*Viewing* *Reading* *Speaking* *Mediation* *Writing*
94	**Personal Trainer:** Training und Wiederholung von Kompetenzen, Wortfeldern und Strukturen		
100	**Intercultural photo page:** *Australia* Informationen zu Australien sammeln und auswerten • Eine Entscheidung begründen • Einen Blogeintrag verfassen	Australien	*Viewing* *Listening* *Writing* *Speaking*
102	**Optional:** *Travel writing* Über Reiseziele sprechen • Über einen besonderen Ausflug oder ein Reiseerlebnis schreiben	Reisen	*Reading* *Writing*

Die Angebote in *Camden Town Gymnasium* sind nicht linear abzuarbeiten. Die Auswahl der Übungen und Übungsteile richtet sich nach den Schwerpunkten des schulinternen Curriculums.

Inhalt

Seite	Kommunikative und interkulturelle Kompetenzen	Sprachliche Mittel (**Wortfelder**, Grammatik)	Methodische Kompetenzen (Schwerpunkte)
5	**Great expectations**		
106	**A Jobs, jobs, jobs** (Thema: Jobs, Ferienjobs) Über Ziele für einen Auslandsaufenthalt sprechen • Einer Website mit Stellenanzeigen Informationen entnehmen • Einen deutschen Radiobericht auf Englisch wiedergeben **Target task** Einen Beitrag für eine Radiosendung schreiben	**Auslandsaufenthalt • Jobs** R: *The comparison of adjectives*°	*Speaking* *Reading* *Mediation* *Listening* *Writing*
108	**B Doing a good job** (Thema: Bewerbung) Einem Hörtext Informationen entnehmen • Über Hard / Soft Skills sprechen • Anforderungsprofile für Jobs erstellen • Erste Eindrücke beschreiben • Ein Bewerbungsanschreiben lesen und auf relevante Kriterien prüfen • Ergebnisse diskutieren **Target task** Bewerbung erstellen (Lebenslauf, Anschreiben)	**Jobs • Hard Skills / Soft Skills • Bewerbung** *English equivalents for 'lassen'*	*Listening* *Speaking* *Reading* *Writing*
113	**C Making a difference** (Themen: Internationale Hilfsorganisationen, Bewerbungsgespräch) Über ein Hilfsprojekt sprechen • Layout / Stilmittel eines Flyers untersuchen • Einen Flyer erstellen und präsentieren • Einem Videoclip Informationen entnehmen • Ratschläge erteilen **Target task** Ein Bewerbungsgespräch führen	**Jobs • Bewerbung • Stilmittel**	*Speaking* *Writing* *Viewing* *Listening*
116	**Personal Trainer:** Training und Wiederholung von Kompetenzen, Wortfeldern und Strukturen		
122	**Intercultural photo page:** *The world of work* Über Berufe sprechen • Wortmaterial sammeln • Eine Präsentation halten	**Berufe • Arbeitsalltag**	*Reading* *Speaking* *Listening*
124	**Optional:** *Forty-Five Minutes* Die Atmosphäre eines Dramenauszugs beschreiben • Szenisches Lesen / einen *freeze frame* durchführen	**Bildungssystem**	*Reading* *Speaking*

Die gelb ausgezeichneten Teile sind als obligatorisch, die rot und grün ausgezeichneten Teile als fakultativ zu behandeln.
° Dieses Pensum befindet sich im Personal Trainer des Kapitels. • R = *revision*

Inhalt

Seite	Titel			
	Skills pages (Lern- und Arbeitstechniken)			
	Study and communication skills			
130	Listening			
132	Speaking	132 Preparing and giving a presentation 133 Giving feedback 134 Having a conversation/discussion		
136	Reading	136 Reading techniques and strategies 137 Literary analysis 138 Rhetorical devices		
139	Viewing			
142	Writing	144 Comment 144 Characterization	145 Summary 145 Formal letter	146 Covering letter 147 CV/Résumé
148	Working with dictionaries			
150	Proofreading your texts			
151	Mediation			
153	Methods	1. Think – pair – share 2. Milling around 3. Gallery walk 4. Buzz groups	5. Placemat 6. Bus stop 7. Freeze frame 8. Jigsaw	9. Dramatic reading 10. Four corners 11. Round robin
	Language skills			
155	Varying sentence structure 155 Participles 156 Connectives, conjunctions and adverbs			
157	Varying expression 157 Using synonyms 158 Paraphrasing 159 Style and register			
160	False friends and cultural mistakes			
	Language in Focus (Grammatikanhang)			
162	Grammatical terms			
164	Language in Focus			
	Words (Wortschatzanhang)			
186	Wordbanks	186 Feelings 186 People and relationships 187 Jobs	188 Film 188 Songs 189 Statistics	189 Travel 190 Pictures 191 Texts
192	Word lists	193 Theme 1 201 Theme 2	209 Theme 3 216 Theme 4	224 Theme 5
230	English-German dictionary		265	*Wörter, die im Deutschen und Englischen ähnlich sind*
263	The English alphabet			
263	English sounds		267	Class instructions
264	Names		268	Irregular verbs
270	Quellenverzeichnis			
272	Lösungen			

Die Angebote in *Camden Town Gymnasium* sind nicht linear abzuarbeiten. Die Auswahl der Übungen und Übungsteile richtet sich nach den Schwerpunkten des schulinternen Curriculums.

1 Knowing me, knowing you

What makes you unique?

A1 • P1

a) • Bring in three objects (or photos of them) that show something about you or that matter to you.
  •  Group work (3): Speculate on why the other group members chose their objects and what the objects reveal about them.
  • Explain to the group what your objects mean to you.

> *I wouldn't be the same without my drums. That's why I've included my drumsticks. Playing the drums is a great way to make music and I can also let off some steam when I'm angry. I have brought my mobile …*

b)  Group work (3): Make a list of what might define a person's identity.
Example: *hobbies, the place where you were born, …*

A2

a) Scan the profiles on pages 10/11 and say which social media you are familiar with. List them and add any others that you know.

b) Class survey: Find out how many pupils in your class use these social media. Collect reasons why young people use them.

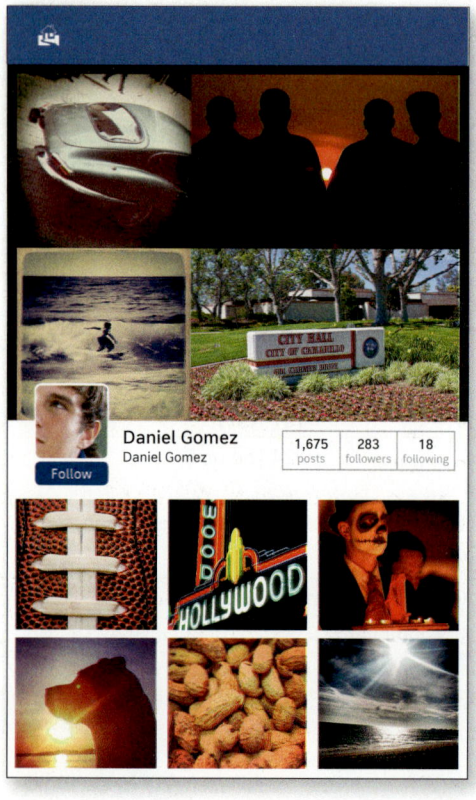

1 What makes you unique?

A3 WB A2, p. 4

a) Compare the profiles. Say which person you would like to contact and why.

b) Find out which aspects of a person's identity are revealed in these profiles.

c) Work with a partner. Discuss to what extent such profiles reveal a user's personality.
• Speaking, p. 134

A4 L 1/1 • Listening, p. 130 WB A1, p. 3, A3, p. 5

a) Listen to a radio report on young people and social media. Decide which of the following statements best sums up what the report is about.
The radio report deals with …
1 what parents should know and do about their children's behaviour online.
2 how teenagers' online behaviour differs from that of adults.
3 how teenagers choose different social media for different purposes.

b) Listen again. Note down aspects that can influence teenagers' online behaviour. Consider, for example, why teenagers choose to use different kinds of social media.
 Compare your notes with a partner's.

c) Compare your own experiences with social media to the experiences mentioned in the report.
● P5, P6

DAGO.COM
ASK WEBSITE FACEBOOK TWITTER YOUTUBE INSTAGRAM SUBMIT

La familia always comes first … Always fun to meet them all. See for yourself in my video of my cousin Julia's quinceañera.

Fashion week – not just the new burger joint uniform, but might be wearing this soon, too … Joining the mariachi band @ Adolfo Camarillo High School.

Went to Universal Studios last Friday as a birthday treat and ended up on stage in the warm-up for the recording of the entertainment show Extra. They needed some strong guys and who would fit the bill better than Señor High School Football himself ;-) Check out the video Dylan made of me …

A5 Target task

 *Need help? Look at p. 26.*

1 Group work (4-5): Write the following tweet at the top of a poster:
"These days, who you are is not important. It's all about how you present yourself online."

2 Now take turns to write tweets in which you express your opinion. Tweets may not be longer than 140 characters. Take into account what you have discussed about a person's identity and presenting yourself online. Remember to keep your tweets short and precise.

3 Put up the posters in the classroom. Read them and choose the Twitter discussion you like best. Explain your choice. • Speaking, p. 134

A | B | C | Personal Trainer | Optional • Skills • LiF • Words

1 Love is all you need?

B1 Viewing: Same Love

a) Speculate on why the photo's title is "Same Love".

Support

The … suggests that this may be … •
The way … makes me think that … •
The photo is open to different interpretations, but I would guess that … •
The fact that … makes me wonder whether the photo is about …

b) Watch the music video for the song *Same Love* by Macklemore and Ryan Lewis featuring Mary Lambert. Find out what the theme of the song is and compare it to your ideas from a).

B2

a) Divide the class in half. One half concentrates on verse 1, the other on verse 3.
With a partner, read your verse carefully and explain what the lyrics express. ● P8

b) Find a pair who worked on the other verse. Present your results to each other.

Support

The phrase "…" suggests that many people still … •
The passage from line … to line … shows that … •
It becomes clear that … •
Boys are supposed to …, but … •
Many … are forced to … •
If we agreed to …, our society might …

Verse 1

When I was in the 3rd grade I thought that I was gay
Cause I could draw, my uncle was,
And I kept my room straight
I told my mom, tears rushing down my face
5   She's like, "Ben you've loved girls since before pre-K[1]"
Trippin'[2], yeah, I guess she had a point, didn't she
A bunch of stereotypes all in my head
I remember doing the math like
"Yeah, I'm good in little league[3]"
10 A preconceived idea of what it all meant
For those who like the same sex had the characteristics
The right-wing conservatives think it's a decision
And you can be cured with some treatment and religion
Man-made rewiring of a predisposition[4] playing God,
15 Ahh no, here we go,
America the brave[5] still fears what we don't know
And God loves all His children, and somehow forgotten
But we paraphrase a book written 35 hundred years ago[6]
I don't know
20 And I can't change, even if I tried, even if I wanted to
My love, my love, my love, she keeps me warm.

[1] pre-K (pre-kindergarten) – *daycare for very young children*
[2] trippin' – *overreacting*
[3] little league – *local baseball leagues for young children*
[4] rewiring of a predisposition – *trying to change a natural condition*

Verse 3

We press play, don't press pause
Progress, march on!
With a veil over our eyes
25 We turn our back on the cause
'Till the day that my uncles can be united by law[7]
Kids are walkin' around the hallway
Plagued by pain in their heart
A world so hateful someone would rather die[8]
30 Than be who they are
And a certificate on paper isn't gonna solve it all
But it's a damn good place to start
No law's gonna change us, we have to change us
Whatever god you believe in,
35 We come from the same one
Strip away the fear, underneath it's all the same love
About time that we raised up
Love is patient, love is kind
Love is patient (not cryin' on Sundays)

[5] America the brave – *the patriotic song 'The Star-Spangled Banner' calls America the "home of the brave"*
[6] a book written 35 hundred years ago – *the Bible, particularly the Old Testament*
[7] can be united by law – *have the right to marry*
[8] someone would rather die – *a reference to the high number of gay teenagers who commit suicide*

Love is all you need? 1

B3 ❖ **Extra: Viewing: Same Love** 📹

Watch the music video again. Describe how the way the video is filmed supports the message of the song. ● *Viewing, p. 139*

B4 ● P10 📖 WB B1, p. 5

For people fighting for more tolerance and rights for gay people and their relationships, *Same Love* became something of an anthem.
Explain why you think this song is likely/not likely to increase tolerance towards gay people.

B5 🎧 S 1, L 1/2 📖 WB B2, p. 6

a) Make a word web with phrases that describe what teenagers do when dating.

b) 👥 Work with a partner. Add more phrases to your word webs.

c) The radio report 'Dating in High School' includes a number of interviews with high school students.
First read the statements **1–9**. Then listen to the report and decide if the statements are true or false.

1 According to statistics, high school couples stand a good chance of staying together for the rest of their lives.
2 Tara says that many students start dating fairly young.
3 Tara thinks that in some situations it is good to bring a date with you.
4 Tara feels under pressure to find a boyfriend and has been looking for one for some time.
5 Lee believes that finding a date is easier for students who are good at sports.
6 Lee has dated friends from his school art club.
7 Katriona is single at the moment.
8 Katriona thinks that a white boy dating a black girl is still seen as a problem by some people.
9 Aaron says that it is completely fine for a white boy to date a black girl these days.

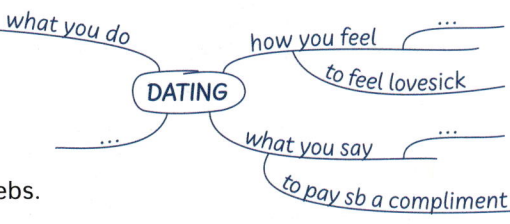
Tara

Lee

Katriona

Aaron

d) Listen again and note down in a few words what made you think that each statement was true/false.
Example:
1 false – only 3% of couples stay together after high school

e) Write a short comment for the radio station's website about dating practices in Germany/at your school. You can use your word web from a).
● *Writing, p. 142*

DATING IN HIGH SCHOOL – Comments:

Stevie_17
I totally agree with what Tara says. I don't see the need to put myself under pressure, and at our school, most students are really relaxed about dating. more …

A | **B** | C | Personal Trainer | Optional • Skills • LiF • Words

13

1 Love is all you need?

B6

a) Carlos, the main character in Alex Sanchez' teenage novel *Getting It*, is 15 years old. Read the beginning of the novel and explain Carlos's problem. • Reading, p. 136   WB B4, p. 8

[…] he broke into a sweat[1] and lost his breath anytime he went near a girl. Like now: He was carrying his tray across Lone Star High's crowded cafeteria, peering out from beneath the frayed hood of his sweatshirt. Ahead of him, a group of golden-skinned beauties garnished their hot
5 dogs at the condiments counter, chatting and giggling.
In the center of the pack stood Roxana Rodriguez. […] She was the girl Carlos yearned for[2].
For her part, however, Roxy didn't seem to even notice Carlos—and since starting high school the previous year he'd yet to summon the nerve[3] to
10 utter a single word to her. But in his secret dreams, the JV[4] cheerleader swarmed all over him.

---

[1] to break into a sweat – *to become very nervous*
[2] to yearn for – *to want something a lot*
[3] to summon the nerve – *to be brave enough*
[4] JV – *short for 'junior varsity', a sports team for younger high school students*

b) Think – pair – share:
1 Write down at least five tips to help solve Carlos's problem.
They can either be funny, serious, or a mixture of the two.
Use modal verbs and look at your word web from B5a) for help.
• Think – pair – share, p. 153   • LiF 8R: Modal verbs, p. 173

> could • might • need to •
> should • had better •
> have to • must • ought to

2 Work with a partner and edit your tips.
You can add new ones.   • Writing, p. 143

3 Group work: Compare your tips. Choose the most helpful one and the funniest one and read them out in class.

c) In order to understand Carlos and his development better, start a character sheet for Carlos. Write down what you find out about him:
- basic information about him (his age, what he does, …),
- his behaviour and his relationships with other people,
- his thoughts and feelings.

Keep your character sheet so you can add more information about Carlos later.   WB B5, p. 8

Carlos
• basic info:
  - 15 years old
  - student at Lone Star High
  - …
• relationships with …:
  - Roxy: …
  - …

Carlos

1 Love is all you need?

B7

Carlos does not talk to his friends about his difficulties in finding a girlfriend because he is afraid that they will make fun of him. One evening, he watches a TV show in which a straight man gets help from gay men to become more attractive to women. As a result, Carlos decides to ask Sal, a gay boy at school, if he could help him as well. Sal needs some time to make up his mind.

a) Buzz groups: Talk about what you think of Carlos's idea.
   • Buzz groups, p. 153

b) Read the next extract from *Getting It* which takes place in the school cafeteria. Explain what makes this an awkward situation for the different characters.

Abruptly, another boy's voice intervened: "Okay, I'll do it."
Carlos sat up, stiff as a Popsicle[1]. Sal loomed over their table, staring directly at him.
5 "On three conditions," Sal continued. "First …" He held up his index finger. "You tell your creep friends here not to give me shit – ever again."
Carlos felt his throat going dry. Didn't Sal realize this was supposed to be a secret?
10 "Second …" Sal added another finger. "It'll cost you six bucks an hour plus expenses. Believe me, I'm letting you off cheap. Start by bringing twenty bucks[2] tomorrow. And most important" – Sal flicked out a third finger – "you help start our school's Gay-
15 Straight Alliance."
With the word "gay" all eyes turned to Carlos. He cringed[3], wanting to crawl beneath the lunch table.
"Now for your first lesson." Sal dabbed a finger across the corner of his own lips. "When you're eating, wipe
20 your mouth."
Embarrassed, Carlos quickly swabbed his mouth with his sweatshirt sleeve, smearing a mustard-yellow line across the olive green.
"Dude, not with your sleeve!" Sal groaned and spun
25 around, shaking his head as he walked away.
When Carlos glanced back at his buds, their eyes were all trained on him.
"What's up with that?" Playboy's face scrunched up as if he'd eaten something sour.
30 "What're you paying him for?" Pulga scowled.
Toro leaned forward, whispering, "Are you friends with him?"
"N-n-no …" Carlos felt like a chicken bone had caught in his throat. "I just, um, asked him to help me with
35 something."

---

[1] Popsicle *(AE) – a sweet, ice-based snack*
[2] buck *(informal, AE) – dollar*
[3] to cringe – *to physically react because you feel embarrassed*

c) Add more points to Carlos's character sheet, and start a character sheet for Sal. Pay particular attention to how Sal feels and the conditions he sets.

d) Decide which of the phrases **A-F** best describe Carlos's friends Playboy, Pulga and Toro. Give reasons for your choice.

A surprised that Carlos and Sal seem close
B make Carlos feel uneasy
C supportive
D relaxed about Carlos and Sal's meeting
E suspicious about Sal and his intentions
F happy for Carlos to get some help

Pulga

Toro

Playboy

e) Comment on how Sal, Carlos and his friends Playboy, Pulga and Toro behave. Say how you feel about them. • Wordbank Feelings, p. 186 • P2

Love is all you need?

B8 📖 WB B6, p. 10

a) When continuing a story, you should base your text on the language and content of the original. 👥 Group work: The two texts A and B both continue the extract from B7, but are not from the original novel. In groups, read both versions, focusing on either the language or content:

Language
1. Check how well the style of writing in versions A and B corresponds to the original. Look at …
   - the use of narrative passages and direct speech,
   - the use of formal/informal language,
   - which characters' thoughts and feelings are presented in greater detail.
2. Note down phrases that seem typical of the characters.
3. Decide which of the two versions fits the original better in terms of language. Note down why you think so.

Content
1. Compare how the characters are presented in versions A and B. Decide how well this corresponds to the original. Use …
   - the character sheet for Carlos as a checklist,
   - your results about Playboy, Pulga and Toro from B7d) and e).
2. Take notes on the key issue in the extract in B7. Check if this is also present in versions A and B.
3. Decide which of the two versions fits the original better in terms of content. Note down why you think so.

A

Carlos felt their eyes on him. When he started to explain to them why Sal had come up to him, he wanted to make it clear that he hadn't turned gay
5 all of a sudden. He just needed help to finally get a girlfriend – and not just any girlfriend, but Roxana, the girl of his dreams.
"Oh, yeah? And the first person you ask for help is the only gay guy at school?" Playboy looked as if
10 he didn't believe a word Carlos had said.
"I'm sorry. I was too afraid to ask you because I thought you would make fun of me," Carlos explained.
"That sounds very gay to me," Playboy replied.
15 Pulga and Toro nervously avoided Carlos's glance, waiting to see how Carlos would react.
"Let us know when Sal has taught you how to find a girlfriend. He'll probably teach you to be his girlfriend!"
20 Playboy wouldn't stop, but Carlos had the feeling that Pulga and Toro felt embarrassed by what Playboy said. As usual, they just didn't seem to have the courage to stand up to Playboy.

B

"With what? Kissing practice?" Playboy looked triumphantly at Pulga and Toro, who exchanged glances.
5 "None of your business." Carlos felt the shock of Sal coming up to him at his table mix with anger over Playboy's remarks. Carlos was thinking hard of a way to make Playboy stop.
"Since when have you got secrets? Is Sal your best
10 buddy now?" Pulga asked with a sharp tone in his voice.
"Nothing has changed. He's going to help me get a girlfriend." Carlos needed all his strength to stay calm.
15 "Just be careful that you aren't his girlfriend in the end!" Playboy could not let go.
Carlos jumped up and clenched his fists, but Toro intervened. "Come on guy, calm down. We can talk about it later."
20 "Yes, tell us about you and Sal on the way home," Playboy nagged him.
Before Carlos could come up with an answer, the bell rang and they all left for their next classes.

b) 👥 Form mixed groups with students who worked on the language and who worked on the content.
1. Present your findings to each other. Note down important points for both language and content.
2. Based on your findings, discuss which of the versions fits the original better. 🔵 Speaking, p. 134
3. Compare the groups' results in class.

Love is all you need?

B9 📖 *WB B3, p. 6*

a) After helping Carlos, Sal expects him to keep his promise to support the Gay-Straight Alliance.
- Read the extract from *Getting It* on pages 17/18 and note down the arguments for and against establishing a Gay-Straight Alliance (GSA).
- Explain which of the arguments you consider most convincing.

arguments for a GSA	arguments against a GSA
A GSA would allow gay and straight students to talk about homophobia.	...
...	

b) Scan the extract and …
- add more points to your character sheets on Sal and Carlos,
- make a character sheet for Mr Harris.

Mr. Harris
- basic info:

Carlos
- basic info:
- 15 years old
- student at Lone St...
- ...

Sal
- basic info:
- ...
- ...

c) Looking back at all the extracts from *Getting It*, discuss the statements below.
● Speaking, p. 134

A Carlos and his friends start to overcome their prejudices.
B Sal demands too much from Carlos in return for helping him.
C High school is a difficult place for someone who is different.

Inside his office, the principal sat behind his metal desk like it was some sort of battle tank, armored with papers. "Hard-Ass Harris," as students called him, was an ex-Army captain with a flattop[1] haircut
5 and a voice that boomed cannonlike through the halls, ordering students to class.
"Take a seat," he now commanded Carlos's group, but there were only four chairs facing his desk.
Carlos seized the opportunity to hang back, hoping to
10 blend into the wall.
But Sal glanced over his shoulder at him. "Come sit up here. I'll stand."
"I'm fine back here," Carlos assured him, and plopped onto the vinyl couch.
15 Sal shot him a peeved look as Mr. Harris braced his hands on top of his desk. "So what's this all about?"
Sal turned to face him. "We want to start a Gay-Straight Alliance."
Mr. Harris's brow furrowed into trenches. "You mean
20 a club for *homosexuals*?" He pronounced the word as if speaking a foreign language.
"No …" Sal's voice resonated with irritation.

"I mean a club where *all students* can talk about homophobia[2] and get support."
25 Carlotta spoke out in agreement. "I'm not gay, but I have friends who are. And I know what it's like to be made fun of."
Vicky followed. "It's hard to feel safe in school when people constantly call you names like 'lesbo[3]' and
30 'dyke[3].'"
"Some students," Espie added more softly, "have gay relatives and no place that feels safe to talk about it."
"That's all well and good." Mr. Harris moved a stack of papers from the right flank[4] of his desk to the left.
35 "But I can't allow a club that condones immorality."
"*Immorality?*" Sal rose up in his seat. "What's immoral is letting people get harassed and not doing anything to stop it." He jabbed his finger like a bayonet[5] toward Mr. Harris. "*That's* immoral!"
40 Carlos watched from the rear, sitting up with interest. He'd come into the meeting secretly kind of hoping the group's application would be denied so that he could avoid getting involved altogether, but now he almost hoped they'd win.

---

[1] flattop – *a typical haircut for American soldiers*
[2] homophobia – *a feeling of fear or hate towards gay people*
[3] lesbo, dyke *(informal)* – *offensive words used to describe gay women*
[4] flank – *side or edge, usually of an army or group of soldiers*
[5] bayonet – *a knife at the end of a gun*

1 Love is all you need?

45 Mr. Harris glowered at Sal. "You're out of line[6], son."

"Mr. Harris?" Carlotta interceded. "I think what Sal is trying to say is, this group will help protect 50 people."

"All day long," Vicky added, "you walk down the hall and hear people say, 'That's so gay,' 'She's 55 so queer.'"

Espie agreed. "You wouldn't let people say racial or religious stuff that way, like 'That's so black' or 'She's so Baptist.'"

"I appreciate your concerns." Mr. Harris said to the 60 girls – and it seemed to Carlos that he shifted the same stack of papers he'd previously moved from the left back to the right. "But I believe a group like this would only be disruptive. I can't allow that."

"Other schools have GSAs," Sal countered. "They're 65 not disruptive."

"What other schools do is their business," Mr. Harris fired back[7]. "I'm responsible for my school. And I say no."

"But you've got to!" Sal shouted.

70 Mr. Harris stood to face him. "Son, I said no. You're dismissed!"

The room fell silent as the girls and Sal stood to leave. But Carlos squirmed in his seat, waiting for someone to correct Mr. Harris. According to the GSA websites 75 he'd originally researched, a school did indeed *have* to allow a GSA, whether the principal liked it or not. Surely Sal knew that – didn't he? Then why wasn't he speaking up?

Carlos clenched his jaw[8], trying to keep quiet. After 80 all, this club was Sal's problem, not his.

---

[6] to be out of line – *to behave in a way that is not appropriate for the situation*

[7] to fire back – *to answer quickly and angrily*
[8] to clench one's jaw – *to force oneself to keep quiet*

B10 Target task  Portfolio  Writing, p. 142 ● P3  Need help? Look at pp. 26/27.

Write an ending for the extract (approximately 200 words).

1 Plan your text. Using your character sheets on Carlos, Sal and Mr Harris, consider …
   • whether or not Carlos will tell Mr Harris that he has to allow a GSA,
   • how Mr Harris would react to Carlos's intervention,
   • how Sal will judge Carlos's contribution to their meeting with Mr Harris.

2 Write your ending. Base your text on the language and content of the original extracts from *Getting It* (see B6, B7 and B9).
   • Read through the extracts to find synonyms for 'said'.
   • Don't forget to mention how characters other than Carlos, Sal and Mr Harris would react to the events in your ending.

3 Work with a partner. Check your partner's text and give feedback by referring to your character sheets and your findings from B8.
   ● Speaking, p. 133

   > • What I liked about your ending was that …
   > • I thought you stayed true to the original by …
   > • It doesn't seem in character for Carlos to …

4 Group work: Read each other's versions.
   Choose the best one in terms of language and content. Present it in class and explain your choice.

Playing happy families?

C1 WB C1, p. 10

a) Four corners: Put up the statements **A-D** about parents and their teenage children in different corners of the classroom.
- Go to the corner with the statement you agree with most.
- Talk about your experiences and expectations. Explain why you chose this statement and not one of the others.
- Take notes on what the other group members say.

Four corners, p. 154

A	Parents should spend as much time as possible with their children.
B	Parents should not interfere with their children's lives once they are twelve years old.
C	Parents should always support their children, even if they commit crimes.
D	Parents should be their children's best friends.

> *As far as I'm concerned … • I would prefer my parents to … •*
> *What I find (un)necessary/most annoying/helpful is … •*
> *In my experience … • For me it's obvious that … • It seems to me that …*

b) In class, first present the views of your groups. Then discuss the statements **A-D**.

Speaking, p. 134

> *Our group agrees that … • What strikes us as a common experience is that … •*
> *What seems most relevant/essential is that … • Our general feeling is that … •*
> *In our view … • According to most members of the group …*

C2 S 2, L 1/3 Listening, p. 130

a) Listen to an extract from a radio report that deals with conflicts between teenagers and their parents. Say which conflicts are mentioned.

b) Work with a partner. Listen to the radio report again.
Partner A: Note down the arguments that are put forward by the teenagers.
Partner B: Note down the parents' arguments.

c) Share your results from b) and think of other typical conflicts between parents and teenagers. Identify and explain the main reasons for these conflicts.

Example: *One of the main reasons why conflicts happen between parents and their teenage children is the question of independence. Teenagers want to be free to make their own decisions, while their parents are worried that …*

1 Playing happy families?

C3 • P4 📖 WB C2, p. 11

👥 Work with a partner. Study the photos on pages 20/21 and say how you think the teenagers feel.
Explain your view by …
- describing the situation shown in the photo and
- referring to body language and facial expressions.

● LiF 1R: Tenses, p. 164   ● Wordbank Feelings, p. 186, Pictures, p. 190

Support

Be sure to use the present progressive to describe the action in the photos.

> The photo shows a mother and daughter … • The two parents in photo … are clearly … •
> Here you can see a father and son who are… • Photo … depicts a teenager who is … •
> In this photo, a family of four are …
>
> They are smiling/laughing, which implies … •
> His body language is tense, which suggests … •
> She is turning away from/avoiding eye contact with … •
> From the look on his face, I can tell that … •
> The mother is gesturing with her hands to show that … •
> The father's stance is very aggressive and he is pointing angrily, so it's clear that … •
> The teenager looks as though he is half asleep … • I think that the teenager feels …,
> because his father's facial expression looks very serious.

1

2

3

5

6

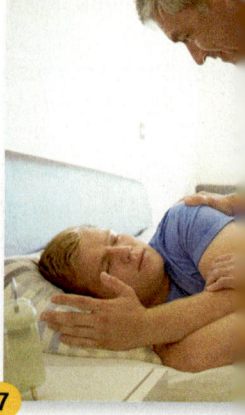
7

Playing happy families?

C4

a) ❖ **Choose:**
👥 Work with a partner. Choose one of the photos. Consider the situation shown in the photo and write a dialogue between two of the people involved.
- Think about the relationship between the people in the photo.
- Imagine what might have happened before the photo was taken.
- Consider the people's roles and make sure the dialogue fits their emotional states.

🔵 *Writing, p. 142* ⚫ *LiF 1R: Tenses, p. 164, 2R: Future tenses, p. 166* ⚫ *Wordbank Feelings, p. 186*

OR:
Pick one of the photos and decide which person you want to be. Write down what is going through your mind.
- Refer to the situation presented in the photo.
- Imagine how the person might be feeling.
- Include references to past events that could affect the present situation.
- Consider what the future might bring and what the person might hope will happen.

🔵 *Writing, p. 142* ⚫ *LiF 1R: Tenses, p. 164, 2R: Future tenses, p. 166* ⚫ *Wordbank Feelings, p. 186*

b) 👥 Group work: Find students who have worked on the same photo as you.
Read your texts to each other and then decide …
- which version is most realistic,
- which version is most creative,
- which version your group thinks reflects the situation shown in the photo best.

Give reasons for your decisions.

4

9

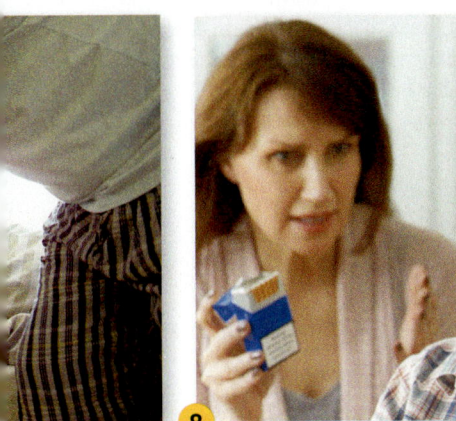

8

1 Playing happy families?

C5 📖 *WB C3, p. 11, C4, p. 12*

a) The novel *The Giver* by Lois Lowry is set in a version of the future. Read this summary of the novel's plot and note down …
- how family life in this future society differs from ours,
- why society has been changed like this.

● *Reading, p. 136*   ● *P7, P9*

b) 👥 Work with a partner. Compare your notes.

Lois Lowry: *The Giver*

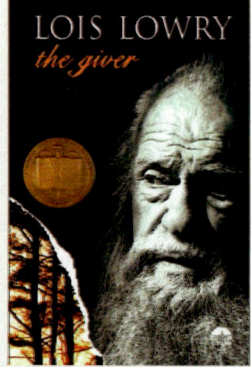

The protagonist of the novel *The Giver*, eleven-year-old Jonas, lives in a futuristic society where 'Sameness' has been established: there are no colours;
5 strong feelings like love and hate, fear and pain have been removed; there is no competition, no prejudice, no conflict and no war since people look very much the same and act in a similar way.

In order to guarantee this polite and happy society the state has eliminated all choice; life is
10 entirely determined by the state; and everything is carefully planned and organized to make life as convenient as possible. The Elders, who represent the state, match partners to be husband and wife, each family unit is assigned two children, a boy and
15 a girl, who come to the family unit when they are one year old. The children are born to Birthmothers and raised in a Nurturing Center with other babies until they are old enough to be part of a family unit. They never meet their natural mothers. When the
20 children leave the family unit, their parents go to a home for elderly people where they live until they are 'released'.

In this society 'release' stands for death, although members of the society do not realize this. Instead,
25 people believe that they are sent Elsewhere, a place outside their society. Apart from old people, unfit Newchildren and those who do not conform to the rules are 'released' as well.

Jonas lives in a family unit of four with his
30 younger sister Lily, his father, who works at the Nurturing Center, and his mother, who has a job at the Department of Justice. Soon there will be the Ceremony of Twelve, a special celebration when
35 twelve-year-olds become adult members of society and are given their job assignment.

Jonas, whose pale blue eyes make him stand out
40 from his friends, feels somewhat uneasy about the Ceremony, and he has no clear idea of what he would like to be. At the Ceremony, Jonas is selected
45 to be the future Receiver of Memory. This is a much honoured position in the peaceful, harmonious society of Sameness; all memories of past wars, of hunger and poverty are suppressed, but they are not completely lost. One person, the Receiver, has to
50 preserve the knowledge to help the state avoid repeating the serious mistakes of the past. He is the only one who can bear the pain.

When Jonas meets the Receiver, a wise old man,
55 he is asked to call him the Giver; soon, a close relationship develops between Jonas and the old man. To pass on all the memories, the Giver places his hands on Jonas' back. Filled with these memories Jonas experiences overwhelming feelings and his
60 world explodes into colour. This is when he realizes how emotionless and empty life in his community really is …

C6 Viewing: *The Giver* 🎥

a) Watch the clip from the film *The Giver*. Use what you know from the plot summary in C5 and say which of the characters and parts of the story you recognize.
● *Viewing, p. 139*

b) Watch the clip again and take notes on how this future society is presented in the film. Work with a partner.
Partner A: Focus on what you see.
Partner B: Focus on what the characters say.

c) Exchange your findings from b) with your partner and say how this vision of the future makes you feel. ● *Speaking, p. 134*

C7

a) Read the extract from the film script for *The Giver* and outline what happens.

b) Analyse how family relations are described in this scene and explain how they differ from family relations in our society. Consider your results from C2 and quote from the text to support your view.
● *Reading, p. 136*

EXT. JONAS' DWELLING - DAY
Father parks his bicycle in a row of bikeports outside the dwelling. Lily rushes over as he unstraps the carrying basket from the back of the bike.

5 **LILY**
Oh, look! He's here! Isn't he cute? Look how tiny he is! And he has funny eyes like yours, Jonas!

Jonas approaches the commotion, glaring at his sister. Father rebukes Lily with his tone:

10 **FATHER**
Lily!

LILY (to Jonas)
I'm sorry for being rude.

JONAS
15 I accept your apology, Lily.

LILY
But look how cute!

Inside the basket lay the precious NEWCHILD, no more than a few months old. The baby has pale,
20 solemn eyes, akin to those of Jonas.

LILY
Maybe he had the same Birthmother as you, Jonas.

INT. JONAS' DWELLING - LIVING AREA - NIGHT
Father places a document filled with text and four 25
lines for signature on the studying desk.

FATHER
We must all sign this pledge promising not to become attached to our temporary guest. My plea for the newchild was accepted by the committee this 30
afternoon.

Father produces a fountain pen and signs on a line.

FATHER (cont'd)
He has been labeled as Uncertain[1], and granted an extra year of nurturing before his Naming and 35
Placement. That is, assuming he is able to reach the special set of weight and maturity standards that the committee has agreed upon.

The rest of the family unit form a queue to add their signatures. 40

FATHER (cont'd)
From now on, the newchild will spend every night with our family unit, so that I may nurture him to the best of my abilities. But we must agree to relinquish him, without protest or appeal, at next year's 45
Ceremony when he is assigned a family.

---

[1] Uncertain – As the baby had not yet gained enough weight for his age, he would normally have been labeled 'Inadequate' and would have been 'released'. Due to a plea by Jonas' father the baby was labeled 'Uncertain' and given an additional year.

A | B | **C** | Personal Trainer | Optional • Skills • LiF • Words

1 Playing happy families?

C8

a) Choose one of the statements below and say what you think about it.
Refer to the way society is organized in *The Giver*.

   A A society without conflict or competition would be a perfect world.
   B A family with members that are chosen to suit each other seems like an ideal family.
   C Personal freedom is essential and should not be limited by the government.
   D Life is easy when all your decisions are made for you.

b) The aim of dystopian fiction is to warn us about dangerous developments in modern society. To do this, dystopian fiction shows us a future society which has become a nightmare as a consequence of these developments.
Explain whether you would consider *The Giver* to be dystopian fiction, taking into account what you have learnt about the society described in C5, C6 and C7. Consider what message *The Giver* might be trying to convey about developments in our own society.

C9 ❖ Extra

Your school's theatre club wants to perform *The Giver* as a play. You are looking at a choice of book covers and have to decide which illustration should be used to advertise the performance.

a) Group work (3): Choose one of the illustrations each and describe it in detail to the members of your group. Explain what different visual elements are used and what they suggest about the plot. ● *Wordbank Pictures, p. 190*

b) In your group discuss the advantages and disadvantages of the different illustrations to decide which one is best suited for your purpose.
● *Speaking, p. 134*

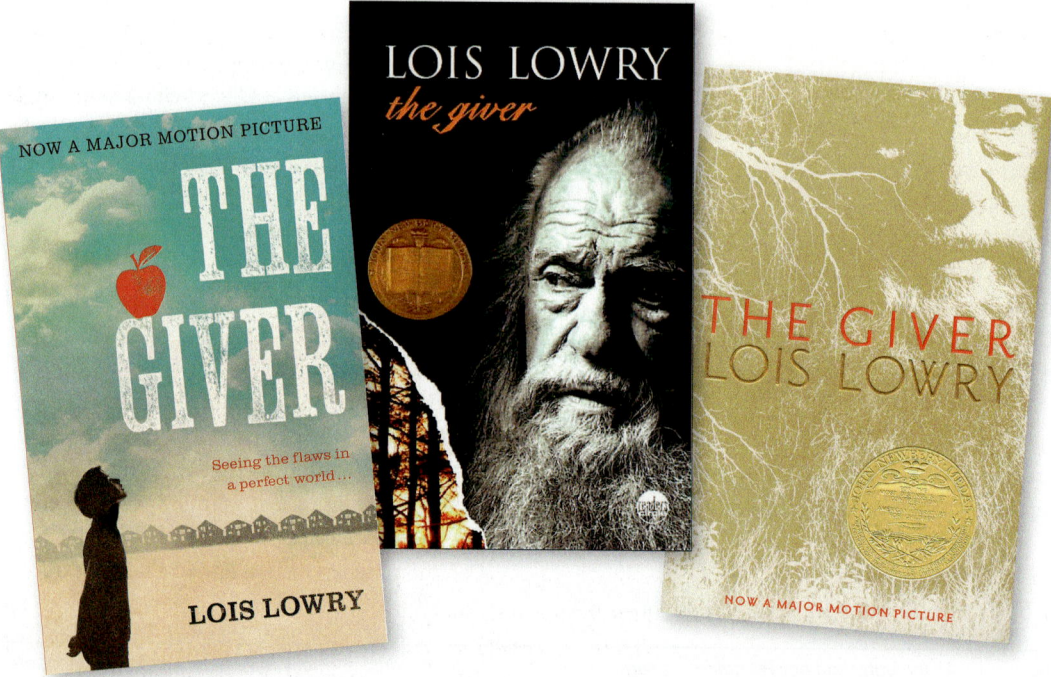

Playing happy families? **1**

C10 Target task 📖 WB C5, p. 12, C6, p. 13   *Need help? Look at p. 28.*

Family life often involves conflicts between children and their parents. In *The Giver* the concept of family is replaced by a 'family unit' of two matched adults and two selected children in order to avoid emotions altogether.
Have a panel discussion about this topic:

> Would it be better to avoid conflicts between parents and children by having 'family units' and a society like the one in *The Giver*, which rejects emotions altogether?

1 Choose two people to prepare for the role of host. The host …
   - introduces the topic,
   - asks the members of the panel to introduce themselves,
   - starts the discussion and keeps it alive,
   - sums up the discussion and closes it.

   Support
   Check page 135 for language support for the role of host.

2 👥 Divide the rest of the class into six groups, each focusing on one of the roles below.
   - Collect ideas about what the respective person might say in the discussion. Think of examples that prove their point.
   - Look back at your results from C2 and consider what you have learnt about the society described in *The Giver*.
   - Anticipate criticism and find arguments to refute it.

Role card: teenager 1
- is supported by parents in difficult situations
- gets guidance from parents
- feels respected as an individual

Role card: teenager 2
- has frequent arguments with parents
- often feels neglected or left alone as parents are busy with their own lives

Role card: teenager 3
- has both positive and negative experiences with parents
- personal choices are taken seriously
- parents are sometimes overprotective

Role card: parent 1
- loves having a big family
- thinks that teenagers need guidelines

Role card: parent 2
- likes his/her children
- is often overworked and struggles to deal with problems
- often has arguments with his/her children

Role card: teacher
- witnesses successes and failures of pupils and the way parents deal with them
- sees negative effects of family problems on pupils

3 Send one representative from each group to form a panel. Then have the panel discussion. Members of the audience can participate in the discussion or act as observers.
   ● *Speaking, p. 134*

4 After the discussion give feedback to the members of the panel.
   ● *Speaking, p. 133*

> *You presented your views/opinion very clearly/convincingly/… •*
> *The discussion was (not) very balanced. • … could have used more … •*
> *Next time you could try to support your view with relevant examples. •*
> *If I were you, I would have used more phrases of agreement/ disagreement to introduce your statements.*

A | B | **C** | Personal Trainer | Optional • Skills • LiF • Words

1 Personal Trainer

Prepare your target task A5:

P1 Words: talking about identity

a) Decide what aspects of a person's identity the following photos illustrate (e.g. age, cultural background) and note them down.

b) Choose four aspects and write statements in which you explain how they affect your identity.

Example: I think the kind of job you have is very important because you spend a lot of time working. All my work comes from school, as I am still a pupil. I spend a lot of time on my homework and at school, and I also meet most of my friends there.

1

2

3

5

6

4

Prepare your target task B10:

P2 Words: relationships and attitudes

a) Combine the verbs on the left with the words on the right to form phrases.

show • meet • give in •
overcome • see • let •
put • turn • be loyal • care

A to sb's demands
B sb down
C against sb
D for sb
E yourself in sb else's shoes

F respect for sb
G to sb
H prejudices against sb
I sb's expectations
J the need to take action

b) Use phrases from a) to complete the following sentences.
1. The bullying of gay teenagers is still a problem at many high schools, but there are more and more students, teachers and principals that **???**.
2. When confronted by a bully, it is important not to **???** and let them get away with bullying.
3. One important step in the fight against bullying is to educate teenagers about what it means to be gay in order to **???**.
4. As in other cases of bullying, it is important to **???** in order to understand what being different really means.
5. If you really **???** your friends, you will support them even if they're different.
6. When your friends are in trouble, don't **???**. Stand up to bullying!

P3 Reading

a) Look at the following terms that can be used to describe the sentence structure and choice of words in a text:

sentence structure:
A participle constructions
B short sentences

choice of words:
C colloquial words
D words with positive/negative connotations
E adjectives and adverbs

Which of the features are shown in the highlighted phrases and words?

When the final bell rang, he trekked slowly toward Roxy's homeroom, his heart galloping ahead of him. Amidst the clamor of students, Roxy stood at the locker with her friends, talking and giggling.
5 Carlos shoved his fists into his jean jacket, fighting the urge to back out. Steeling himself with all his courage, he called out to her, "'S'up?"
Roxy darted a glance at him, briefly nodded, and returned her attention to her friends. As she
10 turned away, Carlos felt his resolve collapse. Maybe this wasn't such a good idea. But he had to do it. He swallowed the lump in his throat and burst out, "Hey, can we talk a sec?"
The words boomed louder than he'd meant,
15 echoing against the metal lockers.
Roxy's group turned instantly silent, peering at him.

"Please?" he quickly added.
Roxy said something to her friends. Then she stepped toward him, her beautiful lips pressed into an irritated line. "What's so important?"
20 "Um ..." Carlos felt the sweat dampening his neck. "Can we go talk somewhere?"
Roxy gave him a hard-jawed look, as if considering. "Look, I've got to get to cheerleading practice. What is it?"
25 Carlos knew what he needed to say and he realized he'd better say it quickly, before he completely lost his nerve. His heart pounded in his chest. He looked straight into her eyes and said it: "I really like you."
30 Sweat drenched his collar as he waited for Roxy's response.

b) Find more examples of the features **A-E** in the text.

c) Write a paragraph about Roxy's response and how Carlos reacts to it. Use some of the features from a).

● *Varying sentence structure, p. 155, Varying expression, p. 159* ● *LiF 7: Participle constructions, p. 170*

1 Personal Trainer

Prepare your target task C10:

P4 Words

1. Write the adjectives for feelings on cards or pieces of paper and make sure you know what they mean. Use a dictionary for help if necessary.
2. 👥 Work with a partner. Turn the cards over, shuffle them and take turns to pick a card. You can either mime the feeling, describe it, or give a reason why you would feel this way. Your partner must guess the feeling.

> *relieved • understood • supported • loved • needed • accepted • special • confident • inspired • motivated • respected • protected*

> *depressed about … • annoyed with … • hurt • misunderstood • lonely • dependent on … • furious about … • unwanted • helpless • frustrated • confused • excluded • neglected*

Extra language training:

P5 Revision: tenses   • LiF 1R: Tenses, p. 164, 2R: Future tenses, p. 166

❖ **Can you do it?**
1. Fill in the verbs in the correct tenses.

Kyla: Three or four years ago, I still `1` (have) my FaceLook profile, but I `2` (take) it down in the last year or so. I `3` (not think) that my photos and personal information `4` (be) really safe there. I guess that's why I `5` (not start) using any other social media in the near future either.

2. You can check your answers on p. 272.
3. You need help?   →   Do a), then b).
   You can do it?   →   Do b).

a) Fill in the verbs in the correct tenses.
   Some words or phrases that signal the use of a certain tense have been underlined.

Zayne: I <u>usually</u> `6` (spend) about two hours a day online. Well, I <u>often</u> `7` (check) my profiles on my mobile during the day as well. I `8` (not do) it in class, though. My best friend Timmy `9` (do) that <u>last year</u> and he `10` (get) into serious trouble for cheating in a test. My favourite social media platform <u>right now</u> `11` (be) PostPix. I guess I `12` (upload) hundreds of photos there <u>so far</u>. What I `13` (like) about it is that it is so easy – I don't have to write any long texts.

b) Fill in the verbs in the correct tenses.

Jennifer: I `14` (love) using Twitter. When I `15` (start) using it a few years ago, I just `16` (write) boring tweets like "Hello from the school bathroom!" My messages `17` (change) a lot since then. I always `18` (try) to tell a little story, play with words or make the tweet interesting in another way. Last year I `19` (delete) my old profile and `20` (set up) a new one – "Tales of a girl geek". So far, my new profile `21` (attract) more than 900 followers. Maybe I `22` (reach) the 1,000 mark at the end of this month! That would be really cool!

P6 Revision: modal verbs and their substitute forms • LiF 8R: Modal verbs, p. 173

a) Make a list of online activities you can do on social media websites. Try to find phrases for as many elements of the picture as possible.

Example: *to share a video with a friend*

b) Write six rules about how to behave online. Use modal verbs and their substitute forms such as *should/can/must/may/might/ be allowed to…*

Example: *You should not tweet anything that others might find offensive because other people can also read what you have written.*

P7 Revision: the passive • Reading • LiF 4R: The passive, p. 168

a) Scan the text about *The Giver* on page 22. Find five passive constructions and write them down. Explain what they reveal about the society of Jonas' world.

b) Based on the information you have gathered about *The Giver*, complete the following sentences using the passive voice.

Example: *1 In the world of 'Sameness' husbands and wives are matched by the Elders.*

1. In the world of 'Sameness' husbands and wives (match) by …
2. When they were one year old, Lily and Jonas (select) for …
3. When their children are old enough to leave home, adults (take) …
4. At the Ceremony, twelve-year-olds (recognize as) … by …
5. The Receiver (trust) with …
6. All memories of the world (transmit) to … by …
7. Jonas' seemingly perfect world (destroy) when …
8. His life (reveal) to be …

1 Personal Trainer

Extra skills training:

P8 **Reading • Writing** • *Varying expression, p. 158*

a) Read verses 1 and 3 of *Same Love* on page 12 and find the lines that go with the following explanations of the lyrics.

1. Lines … to … show that people often think that all gay people act in certain ways.
2. Lines … to … explain that straight people are also expected to behave in certain ways or like certain things.
3. In lines … to …, people say that many Americans are scared of homosexuality and use religion to justify this.
4. According to lines … to …, people are too focused on big goals for the future and ignore problems that affect people right now.
5. Lines … to … suggest that although gay marriage alone won't stop homophobia, it would be an important first step.
6. Lines … to … state that all people are equal, regardless of religion or sexuality.

b) Explain the meaning of these lines from verses 1 and 3 of *Same Love* in your own words.

Verse 1:
"The right-wing conservatives think it's a decision
And you can be cured with some treatment and religion"

Verse 3:
"Kids are walkin' in the hallway
Plagued by pain in their heart
A world so spiteful they would rather die
Than be who they are"

P9 **Reading**

Combine the sentence halves using an appropriate connective.

1. Jonas' world seems perfect
2. All children are raised at a Nurturing Center
3. A Birthmother is a woman
4. The members of a family unit are matched
5. People are 'released'
6. The Elders decide
7. Jonas has no special interests
8. The Receiver knows about all the hardship in the world
9. The wise old man passes on the memories of love and hate
10. The experience of strong feelings makes Jonas realize

because
until
before
but
which
while
so that
who
whereas
when
that

- bears children but never meets them again.
- he is chosen as the Receiver nevertheless.
- profession the members of society will take up.
- they are old enough to live in a family unit.
- the lives they live in this perfect society are empty.
- the citizens of Jonas' world are ignorant of all pain.
- they become too old.
- there are no conflicts or wars.
- their family life is peaceful and harmonious.
- he puts his hands on Jonas' back.

Personal Trainer

P10 Mediation

Read the newspaper article about a Supreme Court decision which deals with the question of same-sex relationships.
Write a message in German about the decision that was taken and how Americans reacted to it.

• Mediation, p. 151

LucaMeier
Gerade habe ich gelesen, was das Oberste Gericht der USA im Juni 2015 entschieden hat. …

26 June 2015

SUPREME COURT RULES IN FAVOR OF GAY MARRIAGE

Same-sex marriage will now be the law everywhere in the United States. The Supreme Court ruled with 5 judges against 4 today that same-sex couples have the right to marry. Thirty-six states and the District of Columbia already recognize that right. Under this decision, the remaining 14 states have to drop their bans on same-sex marriages, which has led to widely different reactions outside the court.

Jim Obergefell, who took the case of gay marriage to the Supreme Court, was aware of the historic moment, "Our love is equal, that the four words etched onto the front of Supreme Court, equal justice under law, apply to us too."

But several religious organizations and conservative politicians criticized the decision. Jennifer Marshall of the Heritage Foundation is not willing to give up her fight for what she believes in, despite the decision by the Supreme Court. "They have issued their decision, but it doesn't end the conversation about what marriage is and why it matters for children, for the future of our society. And we will be continuing to stand for marriage as the union of a man and a woman, and to stand for the freedom to speak and to act consistent with that understanding of marriage."

At the White House, President Obama said that justice had arrived. "This decision affirms what millions of Americans already believe in their hearts. When all Americans are treated as equal, we are all more free. There's so much more work to be done to extend the full promise of America to every American, but today we can say in no uncertain terms that we have made our union a little more perfect."

As news of the Supreme Court decision spread around the US, gay rights activists celebrated in many cities across the country. At least eight states began issuing marriage licenses to same-sex couples.

A | B | C | **Personal Trainer** | Optional • Skills • LiF • Words

1 Optional

John Green, David Levithan: Will Grayson, Will Grayson

O1

Of course, you should not judge a book by its cover. But if you went to a bookshop to find a good read, which of the three books would you want to buy? Explain your choice.

1

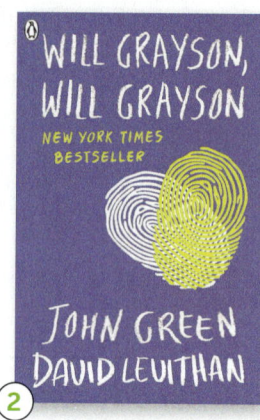
2

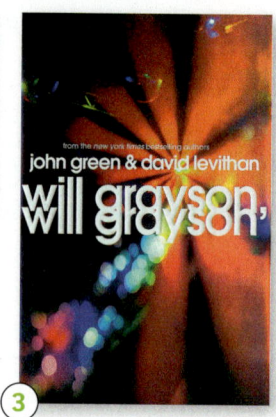
3

O2

The novel *Will Grayson, Will Grayson*, written by the two authors John Green and David Levithan, tells the story of how two boys with the same name meet up by chance in Chicago. In the book, both tell the story from their own point of view.

a) Read the two passages from the beginning of the book and compare the form and the style. Text A is told by one Will Grayson, and in text B the second Will Grayson is the narrator.

● Reading, p. 137   ● Wordbank Texts, p. 191

b) Note down what the two boys reveal about themselves, e.g. by the way they write.

Support
Both extracts are written in the first person, which … •
By writing dialogue in the form of a script, Will II … •
Will I uses … sentence structures, which … • Will I creates emphasis by …

A Will I

Tiny thinks that I am incapable of what humans call emotion because I have not cried since my seventh birthday, when I saw the movie *All Dogs Go to Heaven*. I suppose I should have known from the title
5 that it wouldn't end merrily, but in my defense, I was seven. Anyway, I haven't cried since then. I don't really understand the point of crying. Also, I feel that crying is almost – like, aside from deaths of relatives or whatever – totally avoidable if you follow
10 two very simple rules:
1. Don't care too much. 2. Shut up. Everything unfortunate that has ever happened to me has stemmed from failure to follow one of the rules.

B Will II

i am constantly torn between killing myself and killing everyone around me. those seem to be the two choices. everything else is just killing time.
right now i'm walking through the kitchen to get
5 to the back door.
mom: have some breakfast.
i do not eat breakfast. i never eat breakfast. i haven't eaten breakfast since i was able to walk out the back door without eating breakfast first.
10 mom: where are you going?
school, mom. you should try it some time.
mom: don't let your hair fall in your face like
    that – i can't see your eyes.
but you see, mom, that's the *whole fucking point*.

Optional 1

O3

Will I has gone to Chicago with his friends Tiny and Jane to see their favourite band in a concert but he is not allowed in because he is too young. The concert is in a lonely corner of Chicago and the only other place where he can wait for his friends is a porn shop.
Will II is at the porn shop, too. He is as embarrassed to be there as Will I, but he came to meet a friend, Isaac. Will II has been having very intimate online chats with Isaac for over a year. Isaac has asked Will II to meet him in person for the first time, but has not turned up yet.
When the two Wills find out that they have the same name, they leave the shop. Will I is telling his story to Will II, when both of their phones ring. It's Will I's friend Tiny and Will II's classmate, Maura.

a) Read the extract to find out what problem Will II has and how he reacts to it.

b) Read the extract again and divide it into different parts that show the development of the plot and Will II's understanding of the situation. Find headings for the different parts. ● *Reading, p. 136*

c) Use your headings to write a summary of the extract. ● *Writing, p. 145*

---

maura: what are you doing?
me: oh, hanging out with will grayson.
maura: that's what i thought.
me: what do you mean?
5 maura: where's your mom?
uh-oh. smells like a trap. has maura called my house? has she talked to my mom? pedal motion, backward!
me: am i my mother's keeper? (ha ha ha)
maura: stop lying, will.
10 me: okay, okay. i kinda needed to sneak in on my own. to go to a concert later.
maura: what concert?
fuck! i can't remember which concert o.w.g. [other Will Grayson] said he was going to. and he's still on
15 the phone, so i can't ask.
me: some band you've never heard of.
maura: try me.
me: um, that's their name. 'some band you've never heard of.'
20 maura: oh, i've heard of them.
me: yeah.
maura: i was just reading a review of their album in *spin*.
me: cool.
25 maura: yeah, the album's called 'isaac's not coming, you fucking liar.'
this is not good.
me: that's a pretty stupid name for an album.
what? what what what?
30 maura: give up, will.
me: my password.

maura: what?
me: you totally hacked my password. you've been reading my emails, haven't you?
35 maura: what are you talking about?
me: isaac. how do you know about me meeting up with isaac?
she must have looked over my shoulder when i checked my email at school. she must have seen the
40 keys i typed. she stole my dumb-ass password.
maura: i *am* isaac, will.
me: don't be stupid. he's a guy.
maura: no. he's not. he's a profile. i made him up.
me: yeah, right.
45 maura: i did.
no. no. no. no. no. no. no. no. no. no. no. no. no. no.
me: what?
no please no what no no please no fuck no NO.
maura: isaac doesn't exist. he's never existed.
50 me: you can't –
maura: you're so caught.
I'M so caught?!? what the FUCK.
me: tell me you're joking.
maura: …
55 me: this can't be happening.
other will grayson's finished his conversation and is looking at me now.
o.w.g.: are you okay?
it's hitting. that moment of 'did an anvil really just
60 fall on my head?' has just passed and i am feeling that anvil. oh lord am i feeling that anvil.

A | B | C | Personal Trainer | **Optional** • Skills • LiF • Words

yes, the synapses are conveying the information now.
newsflash: isaac never existed. it was only your friend
posing. it was all a lie. all a lie.
65 me: you. horrendous. bitch.
maura: why is it that girls are never called assholes?
me: i am not going to insult assholes that way. they
    at least serve a purpose.
maura: look, i knew you'd be mad …
70 me: you *KNEW* i would be *MAD*!?!
maura: i was going to tell you.
me: gee, thanks.
maura: but you never told me.
o.w.g.'s looking very concerned now. so i put my hand
75 over the phone for a second and speak to him.
me: i'm actually not okay. in fact, i am probably
    having the worst minute of my life. don't go
    anywhere.
o.w.g. nods.
80 maura: will? look, i'm sorry.
me: …
maura: you didn't actually think he was meeting you
    at a porn store, did you?
me: …
85 maura: it was a joke.
me: …
maura: will?

O4

Now read the final extract.
Describe the roles of Tiny, Will I
and Will II and their feelings.
Use some of these adjectives.
● Wordbank Feelings, p. 186

Support

hopeful • gloomy • desperate • depressing • dejected • hopeless •
hurt • helpless • compassionate • betrayed • friendly • confused •
depressed • frustrated • relieved • comforting • sympathizing •
devastating • positive • understanding • supporting • devastated

> To me … appears to be in a totally …
> situation. He must feel …

> … finds himself in
> an extremely … situation.

> In my view … is completely …
> because …

i have no idea whether i'm talking to him because
he's also named will grayson or because he told me a
little about what's going on with him or because he's
the only person in the world who's willing to listen to
5 me right now. all of my instincts are telling me to curl
up into a tiny ball and roll into the nearest sewer –
but I don't want to do that to o.w.g. i feel he deserves
more than being an eyewitness to my self-
destruction.
10 me: anything like this ever happen to you before?
o.w.g. shakes his head.
o.w.g.: i'm afraid we're in new territory here. my best
    friend tiny was once going to enter me into a
    seventeen magazine's boy of the month contest
15   without telling me, but i don't think that's really
    the same thing.
me: how did you find out?
o.w.g.: he decided he needed someone to proofread
    his entry, so he asked me to do it.
20 me: did you win?
o.w.g.: i told him i'd mail it for him and then filed it
    away. he was really upset that i didn't win … but i
    think it would've been worse if i had.
me: you might have gotten to meet miley cyrus. jane
25   would've died of jealousy.
o.w.g.: i think jane would've died of laughter first.
i can't help it – i imagine isaac laughing, too. and
then i have to kill that image. because isaac doesn't
exist. i feel like i'm going to lose it again.
30 me: why?
o.w.g.: why would jane die laughing?
me: no, why would maura do this?
o.w.g.: i can't honestly say.
maura. isaac. isaac. maura. anvil. anvil. anvil.
35 me: you know what sucks about love?
o.w.g.: what?
me: that it's so tied to truth.
the tears are starting to come back. because that pain
– i know i'm giving it all up. isaac. hope. the future.
40 those feelings. that word. i'm giving it all up, and that
hurts.
o.w.g.: will?
me: i think i need to close my eyes for a minute and
    feel what i need to feel.

45 i shut my eyes, shut my body, try to shut out everything else. i feel o.w.g. stand up. i wish he were isaac, even though i know he's not. i wish maura weren't issac, even though i know she is. i wish i were someone else, even though i know i'll never,
50 ever be able to get away from what i've done and what's been done to me. lord, send me amnesia. make me forget every moment i ever didn't really have with isaac. make me forget that maura exists. this must be what my mother felt when my dad said it
55 was over. i get it now. i get it. the things you hope for the most are the things that destroy you in the end. i hear o.w.g. talking to someone. a murmured recap of everything that's just happened.

i try to calm myself a little, then open my eyes … and
60 see this ginormous guy standing in front of me. when he notices me noticing him, he gives me a broad smile. i swear, he has dimples the size of a baby's head.
ginormous guy: hello there. i'm tiny.
65 he offers his hand. i'm not entirely in a shaking mood, but it's awkward if i just leave him there, so i hold out my hand too. instead of shaking it, though, he yanks me up to my feet.
tiny: did someone die?
70 me: yeah, i did.
he smiles again at that.
tiny: well, then … welcome to the afterlife.

O5

Consider the gesture at the end of the final extract in detail and explain its meaning for Will II.

"he offers his hand. i'm not entirely in a shaking mood, but it's awkward if i just leave him there, so i hold out my hand too. instead of shaking it, though, he yanks me up to my feet."

O6

Group work: Prepare a dramatic reading with the two extracts on pages 33 to 35.
● *Dramatic reading, p. 154*

1. Decide who is going to take which role in the dialogue.
2. Think about the function of the descriptive parts of the text (e.g. lines 45-63, page 35). Discuss how you want to deal with them.
3. Go through the text and decide how it should be spoken. Consider how the two Wills must feel, how Maura feels about Will II's reaction and the impact of Tiny's arrival.
4. Present your reading to the class or to another group and try to express your character's emotions.

O7

Imitate Will I's style to rewrite a part of one of the two extracts on pages 33 to 35 from his point of view.
● *Writing, p. 142*

After this Theme you can …
- ✓ talk about social media
- ✓ write a tweet
- ✓ write a character sheet for a character from a novel
- ✓ analyse a text in terms of language and content
- ✓ write an ending to an extract from a novel
- ✓ give feedback
- ✓ describe a photo by referring to body language and facial expressions
- ✓ have a panel discussion

WB Portfolio-Fragebogen Theme 1

2 Life through a lens

Every picture tells a story

A1

a) Placemat: What role do pictures play in your life? Think of adverts, social media, ... ● *Placemat, p. 153*

b) Name functions that photos can fulfil. Example: *to entertain, to evoke sympathy, ...*

A2 L 1/4   WB A1, p. 21

a) Study the photos on page 37 and pick the one you find most striking. Describe it to a partner and explain why you chose it. Speculate on its function and where it might have been published.
● *Speaking, p. 135*   ● *Wordbank Pictures, p. 190*

b) Speculate on which of the photos on page 37 might have been altered and why.

c) Listen to a radio programme about different ways of altering photos and identify the photos that are mentioned in the programme. Compare the information with your speculations from b).

d) Listen again and note down why the photos were altered. Say which alterations you find acceptable and why. ● P1

A3 WB A2, p. 22

a) This photo was taken at the beginning of the war in Iraq. Study the original photo in the middle and the sections on the left/right and write captions for each of them.

b) Compare your captions with a partner. Discuss how the photo's message has been altered and how this might manipulate public opinion.
● P2

A4 Target task   ◆   WB A3, p. 22   *Need help? Look at pp. 46/47.*

Group work (4): Discuss the use of digitally altered photos and formulate guidelines.

1. Bring photos to class or use the photos on page 37. Select a part of the photo and cover up the rest. Explain to your group how your selection has changed the meaning or effect of the photo.

2. You work for your school magazine. Considering your results from **1**, discuss under what conditions you feel it is acceptable to use digitally altered photos in magazines.
   ● *Speaking, p. 134*

3. Considering the results of your discussion from **2**, formulate guidelines regarding the use of digitally altered photos in your school magazine.

Every picture tells a story

2

1. WAIT A MINUTE I NEED TO POST THIS
2.
3. 
4. LANCÔME PARIS 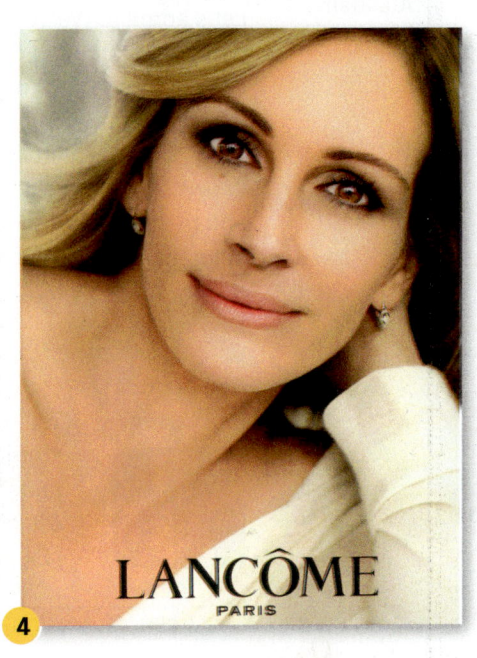
5.
6.

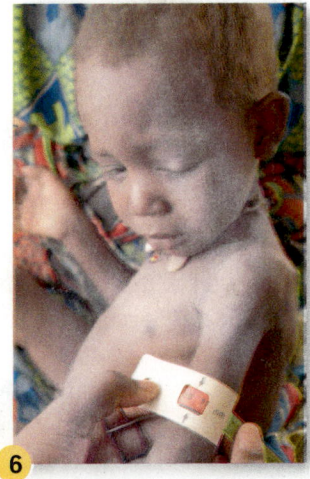

2 To buy or not to buy?

B1

What advertisement (in a magazine, on TV or on the Internet) has made a strong impression on you? Talk about an advertisement you remember well and explain why.

B2 WB B1, p. 23

a) Read the introduction to Alasdair's blog and find a suitable headline for this blog entry.

Seeing the Wood for the trees

Alasdair Wood

13 JUNE, 2017:

So my flatmate Nick has just gone and bought himself a new smartphone. He was convinced he *needed* the latest model. I've seen it on TV – twice as fast, twice as cool, thrice the price!
Let's admit it. We've all fallen victim to advertising campaigns at some point in our lives. Marketing companies have spent years working out how best to convince us to spend our money! It's all about creating a brand that people can trust.
Daily Milk chocolate is the perfect example – everyone in Britain knows there's "a glass and a half" of milk in every chocolate bar and that purple packaging is part of everyone's childhood memories. And who could forget that ad with the gorilla playing the drums? Now that's some successful advertising …

Comments:
Joel Cooper: Tell me about it! I only need to see a fast food ad and my stomach starts to rumble! It just looks so good and I know it'll taste as good as it looks …
It's only food that works for me though, I definitely wouldn't just go and buy a phone because I saw it on TV.

---

b) Post a comment of your own on Alasdair's blog. Say if you have ever "fallen victim" to an advertising campaign and explain why you were tempted to buy something. ● P3

B3 WB B2, p. 24

a) Read the article about advertising strategies on page 39. Summarize in your own words what is said about the strategies 1-5. Say which strategy would have the strongest effect on you and why.
 ● Reading, p. 136, Varying expression, p. 158

b) Work with a partner. Think of examples for at least two of these strategies from adverts you have seen and describe them to your partner.

c) ❖ **Extra:** Think of the advertising strategy you have "fallen victim" to from B2. Say if you have a new understanding of why you were tempted to buy the product and if so, explain what it is.

YOUR GUIDE TO ADVERTISING SUCCESS

1 Emotional Connections

All successful adverts are able to create an emotional connection with their audience. Such adverts typically promise to fulfil the following emotional needs of their audience:
- the need to feel accepted by a group,
- the need to feel accepted by one's self,
- the need to feel attractive,

By showing images associated with wealth, beauty or love, an advert can subtly link its product to positive emotions in the minds of the audience.

Pictures of smiling children and fluffy animals might be less subtle, but they are sure to warm people's hearts – and loosen their wallets.

2 Happy Families

In an age of skyrocketing divorce rates, the idea that you can buy your way into a perfect family life is more tempting than ever before. Some of the most effective adverts are full of images of happy families having a great time together.

The audience is given the clear message that whatever is being advertised, in this case a holiday, is essential for a happy family of their own.

3 Star Power

It's often far easier to borrow someone else's popularity than to build up a brand from nothing. Celebrity endorsements exploit the 'star power' of a celebrity to add a touch of glamour to a product.

With an endorsement from a famous footballer, a product can seem both desirable and exclusive.

4 Peer Pressure

Instead of making their products seem exclusive, some adverts show large groups of people using them. This form of advertising exploits people's fear of being left out, pressuring people to buy something that they otherwise wouldn't want.

Peer pressure in action – anyone who doesn't have the latest smartphone will be left behind.

5 Music

Music can be particularly important for adverts on TV, on the radio or in cinemas, but it can also be relevant for online adverts as well. Music can range from simple jingles – something just catchy enough to stick in people's minds – to an almost cinematic soundtrack that creates a powerful atmosphere for the advert.

2 To buy or not to buy?

B4 • P4

The ASA (Advertising Standards Authority) is a British organization that is responsible for ensuring that advertisements are legal, decent, honest and truthful.

👥 Round robin: Do you think it is important to have an organization that regulates advertising?
In groups of four state your opinion and give reasons.
• Round robin, p. 154

B5 🎧 L 1/5 📖 WB B3, p. 25

a) Read these guidelines from the ASA and say if you agree with them. Give examples.

ASA Advertising and Marketing Guidelines

A. Marketing communications should be legal, decent, honest and truthful.

B. Marketing communications must be prepared with a sense of responsibility to consumers and to society.

C. Marketing communications must not materially mislead or be likely to do so.

D. Marketing communications must not contain anything that is likely to cause serious or widespread offence. Particular care must be taken to avoid causing offence on the grounds of race, religion, gender, sexual orientation, disability or age.

E. Marketing communications must not cause fear or distress without justifiable reason; if it can be justified, the fear or distress should not be excessive. Marketers must not use a shocking claim or image merely to attract attention.

F. Children must not be shown using or in close proximity to dangerous substances or equipment without direct adult supervision.

b) 👥 Group work (4):
Study the adverts on page 41 and discuss which category you would put each photo into:
A should be banned
B could be banned
C should definitely not be banned
Give reasons. • Speaking, p. 134
• LiF 5R: The passive infinitive, p. 169

Support
In my view/opinion the ad violates the rules/should be banned because … •
The presentation of … is offensive/untruthful/inadequate for …/ irresponsible because … •
The ad is (not) likely to offend …/might have a negative influence on …/could be seen as …

c) Listen to a radio interview and note down which ads have been banned and why. Compare your notes with your results from b). Discuss whether you would change your decisions after listening to the interview. • Listening, p. 130, Speaking, p. 134 • P8

To buy or not to buy?

1. You Wouldn't Let Your Child Smoke. Like smoking, eating bacon, sausages and other processed meats is linked to cancer. Go vegan! PETA

2. Maîtrise — For dead straight hair

3. GIRLS THIS SUMMER SHAPE UP OR SHIP OUT — PW

4. SEE CYCLIST. THINK HORSE. Let's all get along — Follow the NICE WAY CODE

5. Unlimited calls, internet & text messages for just £5.99? Now that's a miracle!

B6 Target task ❖ ● P5 📖 WB B4, B5, p. 26 🎯 Need help? Look at pp. 47-49.

Write a comment on the following statement:
"Advertising agencies should not be limited in their choice of pictures or language."

1. Decide what your opinion on the statement is. Find arguments that support your opinion and note them down in a grid. Add arguments that might be used against your position.

Introduction	...	
Main part	pros/arguments for ...	cons/arguments against ...
Conclusion	...	

2. Write your comment:
   - Start with an introductory sentence explaining the importance of the topic.
   - Present your view in the main part. Support it convincingly with your arguments. Include possible counter-arguments and find ways to weaken them.
   - Finish your comment with a statement that sums up your view. ● Writing, p. 144

2 Dress to impress

C1

a) Think – pair – share: Read the headlines below and explain what they reveal about a series of crimes from 2008 and 2009. ● *Think – pair –share, p. 153*

b) Work with a partner. The film *The Bling Ring* was based on the true events referred to in these headlines. Note down some ideas on how you would start the film to attract the viewer's attention. Compare your ideas in class.

> 1 **Going for the Bling: Hollywood Thieves Strike Again!**

> 2 **Teen drama: How the 'bling ring' group used the Internet to break into Hollywood homes**

> 3 **'Bling Ring': Obsession For Fame Gone Too Far**

C2 Viewing: The Bling Ring (1)

a) Watch the opening sequence of *The Bling Ring*. Say if it appeals to you and explain why/why not.

b) Compare the sequence to your ideas for an attractive beginning.

c) Note down what you can tell about the film's plot, main characters and setting. ● *Viewing, p. 139*

d) Compare your notes with a partner's. Then complete the following sentence with the help of your notes.
The extract from the film "The Bling Ring" by director Sofia Coppola, which was released in 2013 and is based on real events, deals with … from …, who …

The Bling Ring cast (left to right):
Katie Chang (Rebecca),
Taissa Farmiga (Sam),
Israel Broussard (Marc),
Claire Julien (Chloe),
Emma Watson (Nicki)

C3 📖 *WB C1, p. 27, C8, p. 30*

Nancy Jo Sales, a US journalist, wrote a book about the real Bling Ring. Read an extract from an interview with her which was published in Forbes magazine.

a) Name the issues that are illustrated by the case of the Bling Ring according to the interview.

b) Read the extract from the interview again and explain the relevance of the following keywords in the context of the film *The Bling Ring*.

> obsession with fame and money and reality TV • self-expression • self-absorption • images of girls and women

c) Identify which of the points mentioned in the interview can be found in the opening sequence of the film *The Bling Ring*.

Dress to impress 2

Forbes: Your book is a much-needed look at our obsession with fame and money and reality TV [...]. When do you think this fixation with celebrity started, and do you see it escalating?

NJS: I think it's escalating because of technology, and because of the obsession with fame and money. [...] There was the birth of the "fashionista" with *Sex and the City* and then *Gossip Girl* – that was a huge thing for this Bling Ring generation. The starlets in the 2000s like Lindsay Lohan and Paris Hilton represent this reckless party girl who is in and out of jail and is never really punished. There were really no consequences and they were really influential, mostly to girls. [...]

Forbes: Do you think technology is changing the way teenagers view the world? Social media can be incredibly helpful, but it also has a darker side.

NJS: We don't really know how the Internet and technology are changing us, or our brains and our attention span. I'm not just placing this on the Millennial generation. We're so very focused on ourselves and on self-promotion. It goes on all day with Facebook and Twitter and Instagram. There's a good side to it too that's creative and funny and it's about self-expression, but it also leads to self-absorption and people focusing on themselves and their image in the world and that is a dangerous thing for a teenager. They are so sensitive about self-image and they're always wondering, "Who am I?" [...]

Forbes: Your book stresses that today's emphasis on fame and money especially affects young girls. You have a daughter – do you talk to her about social media and all of the images of celebrities we're constantly seeing? I would imagine parents have to talk to kids about technology now, just like they would teach them to look both ways before crossing the street.

NJS: My daughter is almost 13 and she's very aware because we talk about these things a lot. It's important, especially if you have a girl. I'm concerned and alarmed about the images of girls and women that are broadcast every single minute. She was reading the news online recently and asked, "Why is Selena Gomez wearing a bikini in a news story?" I think mothers and fathers need to give their kids the awareness to ask. [...]

C4 ❖ **Extra: Viewing: The Bling Ring (1)** 📹 📖 *WB C2, p. 27*

When watching a film there are various ways in which your understanding of the film is influenced.

👥 Jigsaw: In groups of five, watch the opening sequence again and concentrate on one of following five cinematic devices. Look at the skills pages on viewing (pp. 139–141) for support.
A The use of music and sound
B The use of lighting and colour
C The camera movement
D The camera angle
E The field size

Take notes on when and how your cinematic device is used and how it adds to the atmosphere. Exchange results with the rest of your group and add any missing points to your notes.

Now form new groups of five with one person each from A–E. Explain your device to the other members of your group and then take notes on the other devices.

Summarize the atmosphere that is created by the five cinematic devices A–E.
● *Wordbank Film, p. 188*   ● *Viewing, p. 139, Jigsaw, p. 154*

2 Dress to impress

C5 📖 WB C3, p. 28

Read the quotations from reviews of *The Bling Ring* and paraphrase them in your own words. (The highlighting is only relevant for C6.) ● *Varying expression, p. 158*

A Fame, rather than fortune, drives seven teenagers, who are led by a terrifyingly confident girl called Rebecca (Katie Chang). Already hooked on the rush of petty theft – she casually takes purses from cars parked outside a friend's house during a party – Rebecca decides to take it a step further.

B Based on true events, the film follows a gang of wealthy teens fixated on 'celebrity' glamour. They steal luxury goods worth millions of dollars from stars including Paris Hilton and Orlando Bloom by tracking them online. The young thieves easily break into the empty homes and swan around looking for items they have seen their heroes wear.

C Directed by Sofia Coppola, the film tells the story of a group of Los Angeles teenagers who looted the homes of some of their favourite celebrities – Paris Hilton, Lindsay Lohan, Orlando Bloom – stealing over $3 million worth of luxury items. Dubbed the "Bling Ring" by the media they were soon caught, having made no effort to cover their tracks.

Example: **(A)** *The members of the "Bling Ring" want to become famous. Their leader Rebecca enjoys stealing money from parked cars and now wants to do more than that.*

C6 Grammar card: participle constructions ● P7

To make a text more interesting to read, it is important to vary the sentence structure. One way to do this is to use participle constructions. You can use them …
A to shorten relative clauses,
B to shorten adverbial clauses of time/reason,
C to combine two main clauses if the actions in both clauses happen at the same time.
Participles can combine two clauses, provided both clauses have the same subject. A **present participle** (e.g. *looking*) replaces an active clause, a **past participle** (e.g. *looked*) replaces a passive clause.

1 In this sentence, a participle construction is used to shorten an adverbial clause of reason:
   "Already hooked on the rush of petty theft, Rebecca decides to take it a step further."
   → As she is already hooked on the rush of petty theft, Rebecca decides to take it a step further.
   Start a grammar card. Study the highlighted parts of the sentences in C6 and rewrite three of the sentences by replacing the participle construction with a subordinate clause.
   Look at LiF 7 on pages 170-172 for help.

2 Look at the last sentence in review C in C5. The second highlighted part contains a **perfect participle** (*having* + past participle → *having made*). Perfect participles can combine two clauses if the action in one clause takes place before the action in the other. Add this information to your grammar card.

C7 📖 WB C4, p. 28, C5, p. 29

Read the following text about the real Bling Ring. Rewrite the following sentences by replacing the highlighted parts with participle constructions. ● *LiF 7: Participle constructions, p. 170*

In 2008 and 2009 a gang of high school students who lived in wealthy LA suburbs stole more than $3m in clothes, jewellery and art from their celebrity idols. The group, who became known as the "Bling Ring", used gossip websites to plan their thefts. Paris Hilton was particularly careless, as she left a key under her doormat. After they had broken in, the Bling Ring photographed themselves while they tried on designer clothes in Paris's home. Later they bragged to their friends about it and posted their photos on Facebook.

Dress to impress 2

C8 Viewing: The Bling Ring (2)

a) Watch another extract from *The Bling Ring*. Decide which statement describes the message of the extract best. Give reasons for your opinion. • *Viewing, p. 139*

The extract illustrates …
1 … a teenage obsession with celebrities.
2 … wealthy teenagers' lives of boredom and their lack of moral values.
3 … a superficial desire to live like the rich and famous.
4 … an exciting life of thrilling adventures.
5 … teenagers' wishes for respect and popularity among their peers.

b) Copy the grid and watch the extract again. Take notes on what happens in each scene. • P6

scene	content	cinematic devices
A party at a friend's house (0:00–0:47)	…	…
Party scenes and scenes of the group's burglaries (0:48–1:48)	…	…
The burglary at Lindsay Lohan's house (1:49–3:41)	…	…

c) Use your notes to complete the following summary of the extract.

> The extract from **1**, by **2**, deals with how the main characters display **3** *(consider your answer in a) here)*. Arriving at a wealthy friend's house for a party, Rebecca and her friends **4**. While boasting about their latest burglary at **5**, the teenagers **6**. In the following, shots of **7** are mixed with shots that show **8**. The members of the Bling Ring **9** at parties **10**. Besides, it becomes clear how they **11** at celebrity homes, **12**. Subsequently, Rebecca's obsession with Lindsay Lohan is illustrated by **13**. Following a news story about Lindsay Lohan stealing **14**, it is shown how the Bling Ring **15**. At first, Rebecca, Marc and Nicki **16**. While Nicki **17**, Rebecca **18**. Finally, a security camera captures **19**.

d) ❖ **Extra:** Do some Internet research on the real Bling Ring to prepare a short presentation on what these teenagers did and what happened to them after they had been caught by the police.

C9 Target task ❖ Viewing: The Bling Ring (3) 📄 Portfolio
Need help? Look at p. 50.

1 Watch another extract from *The Bling Ring*. While Rebecca has left California to visit her father in Nevada, the members of the Bling Ring are arrested for the burglaries.
Take notes on what happens in this extract, then use your notes to write a summary of the extract. Make sure that you use participle constructions to vary the sentence structure.
You can use the summary in C8 as a model. • *Viewing, p. 139, Writing, p. 145, Varying sentence structure, p. 155*

2 Group work (4): Read the other group members' summaries. Choose the best summary in your group. Consider both the language and content (e.g. clear structure, use of participles).

3 Based on the film extracts you have watched, give the film a rating from 0 to 5 stars. Carry out a class survey to find out what other people thought about the film and discuss the reasons for your ratings. *WB C6, p. 29, C7, p. 30*

2 Personal Trainer

Prepare your target task A4:

P1

a) Copy the grid and sort the verbs according to their connotations.
Then discuss your result with a partner.

> to alter • to enhance • to change • to doctor • to edit •
> to compose • to modify • to retouch • to freshen up •
> to adjust (the brightness and contrast) • to manipulate •
> to correct (the colour) • to improve

positive	neutral	negative
…	…	…

b) Choose the right word to complete the following sentences.
Make sure you use the correct form of the verb.

> Many people 1 their photos to 2 their quality. Bright sunlight might have made half of your photo look too dark, so obviously you would like to 3 . Or there was a strong light which gave the photo a greyish tone, so 4 the colours would help.
> But 5 your holiday snapshots is a different matter to 6 photos that are meant to inform people.
> 7 photos may seem more impressive, but they are not reliable.

P2 Revision: the passive   • LiF 4R: The passive, p. 168

> ❖ **Can you do it?**
> 1. Rewrite the sentences using the passive. Remember to use the correct grammatical form.
>
>   The photo shows the threatening clouds of a thunderstorm.
>   A special effects team designed the cloud for a disaster movie.
>   People have used the photo in posts because they thought it was real.
>
> 2. **You can check your answers on p. 272.**
> 3. **You need help?** → Do a), then b).
>   **You can do it?** → Do b).

a) Use the phrases below to write passive sentences. Remember to use the correct tense.

1 old photos / often / to freshen up.
2 some photos / to take / more than a hundred years ago.
3 some / to keep / in archives / for many years.
4 many of them / to manipulate / by photographers.
5 they / can / to use / as important historical documents.

b) Rewrite the sentences using the passive.
Make sure you use the correct tense.

1 Even two centuries ago photographers documented important historical events.
2 Photographers have always altered photos.
3 They either added people to or deleted them from photos.
4 Photographers and reporters should not doctor their photos of important events.
5 A photo can easily manipulate people.

Prepare your target task B6:

P3 Words: advertising

Match the expressions with the definitions.

1 a short film to promote a product on TV or in cinemas
2 a notice or poster to promote a product, especially in the print media or on the Internet
3 a song or melody that is used to promote a product
4 a panel to display advertising posters in public places, such as alongside motorways or on the sides of buildings
5 a special phrase in advertising or politics formulated to persuade people
6 promotion of goods and services

A advertisement
B slogan
C jingle
D billboard
E commercial
F advertising

P4 Words: adjectives

Copy the grid below. For each adjective write the German translation and find its opposite.

German	(+)	un-	in-	ir-	il-	dis-
…	truthful	…	…	…	…	…
…	reliable	…	…	…	…	…
legal, gesetzlich	legal	–	–	–	illegal	–
…	honest	…	…	…	…	…
…	decent	…	…	…	…	…
…	responsible	…	…	…	…	…
…	adequate	…	…	…	…	…
…	attractive	…	…	…	…	…

P5 Writing: comment

In a comment you express your personal opinion about a statement or topic.
A comment should have a clear structure so that the comment is easy to read and your arguments are easy to follow. Divide your comment into the following three parts:

A Introduction:
An introduction should refer to the topic of the comment and briefly explain its importance. A good introduction should aim to gain the reader's interest. This can be done by using one of the following methods …
- a quotation,
- a rhetorical question,
- a general statement about the importance of the topic nowadays,
- an anecdote, i.e. a brief story about an incident that is relevant to the topic.

B Main part:
The main part of a comment should state your view and support it through the use of different arguments and examples. The main part could also mention arguments against your point of view and then weaken these counter-arguments.

C Conclusion:
A conclusion should summarize your opinion on the topic with a convincing final statement. It may also refer back to the introduction of the comment. A conclusion should not add new information to the comment.

a) Read the following introductions to four different comments.
For each introduction decide whether a quotation, rhetorical question, general statement or an anecdote has been used to gain the reader's interest.

1. In recent years cheap fashion items have changed the way young people shop and, with advertisements offering new ideas to 'shopaholics', we must ask ourselves if we really want this consumerism.

2. When Primark's first store in the United States opened its doors in summer 2015 there were endless queues of young shoppers – many of whom had waited hours for the best bargains. Even several years later we still see crowds of young people leaving the store with bags full of cheap fashion.

3. If advertisements can be believed there are hundreds, if not thousands, of the very latest 'must-have' gadgets and fashion items. But do we really need all the goods that we are encouraged to buy?

4. "It is estimated that six percent of Americans are so-called 'shopaholics'. With retailers ramping up their promotions on TV and even more intensely online, this number is likely to skyrocket in the next few years."

b) Choose two of the four statements **A**-**D**. Note down at least two arguments for each statement and at least two arguments against each statement.

A School in Germany should not start before 9am because research has shown that young people's brains cannot function effectively before that time.

B Chewing gum increases people's concentration, so it should be made obligatory during all school lessons.

C Like in the United States, young people in Germany should be able to get their driver's license at the age of 16.

D It is teachers who need to be able to motivate their students, as students cannot motivate themselves.

c) Look at the following list of useful words and phrases that you can use in the different parts of a comment to help structure your argument.
  ● *LiF 19: The emphatic 'do', p. 185*

A Introduction

> *In recent years the question of … / the topic of … has frequently been discussed / has become more and more important.* • *As more and more cases of … hit the news, it is necessary to discuss whether … / to find a solution for … / to reconsider …* • *"…" is a slogan / a criticism we hear from many politicians / supporters of … / parents. So is it necessary to … / should we really … / does that actually mean …?* • *One of the most urgent problems today concerns …*

B Main part

> ***Making a point:*** *It is clear/undeniable that …* • *Furthermore/Moreover, …* • *We must admit that …* • *Another important aspect is that …* • *… must be considered* • *Considering the fact that …*
> ***Explaining arguments:*** *This does mean …* • *This would probably cause …* • *On the one hand … On the other hand …* • *In contrast to …, …* • *While some may argue that …, in fact …*
> ***Adding new aspects:*** *Others argue that …* • *Another aspect/point/reason put forward is that …*

C Conclusion

> *Finally, it is clear that …* • *To conclude, we do have to accept the fact that …* • *In conclusion …* • *To sum up, it does seem that …* • *Taking all of the arguments into account, we can come to the conclusion that …*

Choose four phrases: one for the introduction, two for the main part and one for the conclusion. Write a mini comment of only four sentences, using the phrases you have chosen to help link your sentences together. You can write your mini comment about one of the statements in b) or you can choose a topic of your own.

2 Personal Trainer

Prepare your target task C9:

P6 Words: reporting verbs to summarize dialogue

When you summarize a film scene, you often need to summarize dialogue. You should avoid lengthy descriptions such as "And then he says … But then she says …". Instead you should summarize it with the help of suitable reporting verbs. Match the definitions with the verbs.

definition		verb
A	to exchange arguments	1 to brag
B	to exaggerate in order to make an impression on someone	2 to offend/insult
C	to fight with words about something	3 to report
D	to say something hurtful that might upset someone	4 to discuss
E	to ask someone about their actions in an angry or threatening way	5 to deny
F	to say that you did not do something	6 to argue over sth
G	to give all the basic information, e.g. the 5 Ws	7 to interrogate
H	to reveal secrets that may cause trouble for others	8 to betray

Extra language training:

P7 Participle constructions • LiF 7: Participle constructions, p. 170

❖ Can you do it?
1. Replace the underlined phrases with a participle construction.
   <u>When they google his name</u>, Rebecca and Mark find out that Orlando Bloom is currently shooting a movie in New York.
   <u>After Rebecca and Mark learnt that Orlando Bloom and Miranda Kerr are out of town</u>, they invite Chloe, Nicki and Sam to break into their house with them.

2. You can check your answers on p. 272.
3. You need help? → Do a), then b).
   You can do it? → Do b).

a) Rewrite these sentences by using a present or past participle to replace the highlighted parts.
   1 The teenagers can easily enter Bloom and Kerr's house as they find the door unlocked.
   2 Inside, Mark finds a box which is filled with thousands of dollars and several Rolex watches.
   3 As she leaves the house, Rebecca takes a rug and a painting with her.
   4 Mark gets angry because he thinks she is going a bit overboard.
   5 Later that night, they go to a party which is thrown by Chloe.
   6 When they see a news report about the burglary at Audrina Patridge's home, they decide to stop breaking into houses for a while.

b) Rewrite the text by replacing the highlighted expressions with participle constructions.

One night, Mark and Rebecca meet and look at celebrity gossip websites. Mark tells Rebecca that Paris Hilton is in Las Vegas at a club opening and then looks up Paris's address online. After Mark has found it online, he agrees when Rebecca suggests they go to her house. She wants to break into it and look around. She correctly guesses that Paris is the type to keep her house keys under her doormat. Mark starts to panic when he actually enters Paris's house, but he quickly becomes distracted when he sees how Paris has decorated her home with pictures of herself. As Mark and Rebecca wander through the house, they find Paris's gigantic dressing rooms. Rebecca takes a bag and begins to stuff it with clothing and jewellery. The two teens take their loot and leave.

Extra skills training:

P8 Mediation ( )

You have found this article and are surprised by the fact that there are evidently different regulations in the EU. You want to know from your Irish friend what the situation is like in Ireland. But first you tell him what you have found out from the article about …
- the Minister for Food and Agriculture's plans,
- the reasons, especially concerning young people,
- the differences across EU countries,
- other ways to reduce smoking. ● *Mediation, p. 151*

Minister will Zigarettenwerbung komplett verbieten

Im Gegensatz zu den meisten EU-Ländern darf in Deutschland im Kino und auf Plakaten noch immer für Tabak geworben werden. Bundeslandwirtschaftsminister Schmidt will dem nun einen Riegel vorschieben.

27.06.2015 – Werbung für Zigaretten, Zigarren und andere Tabakprodukte soll nach dem Willen von Bundeslandwirtschaftsminister Christian Schmidt (CSU) in Deutschland komplett verboten werden. Künftig solle im Kino und auf Plakaten nicht mehr für Tabakprodukte geworben werden dürfen, kündigte Schmidt in der „Bild"-Zeitung an. „Zahlreiche wissenschaftliche Studien belegen, dass eine allgegenwärtige Werbung in der Öffentlichkeit den Einstieg in das Rauchen aktiv fördert." Deutschland sei neben Bulgarien das einzige Land in der Europäischen Union, in dem die Außenwerbung für Zigaretten noch erlaubt sei, sagte der Minister. „Dies konterkariert unsere intensiven Bemühungen in der Tabakprävention gerade bei Kindern und Jugendlichen." Deshalb strebe er ein Verbot der Außenwerbung mit Plakaten sowie der Kinowerbung für Tabakerzeugnisse und elektronische Zigaretten an. Aus dem Drogen- und Suchtbericht 2015 der Bundesregierung geht hervor, dass in Deutschland jedes Jahr etwa 110.000 Menschen an den Folgen des Tabakkonsums sterben. Auch der jüngste Weltdrogenbericht der UN geht auf die Gefahr des Tabakkonsums ein. Wer früh mit Rauchen und Alkohol beginne, neige eher zum Cannabis-Konsum.

„Die Vermeidung von Alkohol und Tabak ist relevant für die Vorbeugung gegen Drogen." Als sehr wirksam hätten sich höhere Preise herausgestellt. Schon eine Preiserhöhung von zehn Prozent für Zigaretten und Alkohol habe nach bisherigen Erkenntnissen einen spürbaren Rückgang beim Konsum zur Folge.

2 Intercultural photo page

Media

1

a) Identify what the photos show about how media work and their role in today's world.

b) Read the text below on media in the US and revise your answer to a) by adding to or changing your initial ideas.

c) Note down for each photo …
- whether you yourself use media in the way presented and/or
- what you think of the media/media industry as it is presented.

The United States of America is the birthplace of many media trends that have spread across the world, thanks to the American talent for innovation and a highly influential entertainment industry. For
5 example, Apple's release of the iPhone started the global success of smartphones; Internet and social media companies, such as Facebook, Twitter and Google, call the US home; and Hollywood blockbusters continue to draw the largest audiences
10 worldwide. Award ceremonies are followed by millions from around the globe and celebrate outstanding achievements and success in film, television and music. They also advance the careers of artists who can then pride themselves on being
15 honored for their work with an Emmy, Grammy or Oscar.
With the growing popularity of online streaming services like Netflix and high-quality TV programs from pay-TV channels such as HBO, US television
20 has once again set a new global trend. In addition, thanks to their nationwide programs broadcast by countless local TV stations, the major US television networks are still responsible for much of the TV abroad as well. But fame and popularity often come
25 at a price due to the ever-growing number of magazines and celebrity websites waiting to be filled with the latest gossip on stars' private lives.
As most of the media companies are profit-oriented businesses, advertising is crucial for financing their
30 programs, which means many shows are frequently interrupted by commercial breaks.
The huge influence of media on daily life cannot be ignored by political parties or politicians either, which is why political candidates – such as those
35 wishing to become the next US president – need to take part and do well in TV debates and talk shows.

2 S 3, L 1/6

Listen to some American exchange students explaining differences they notice between how Germans and Americans use media.
1 Note down in a grid all the differences and similarities that are mentioned.
2 Compare these observations to your notes from task 1c).
Use one colour to highlight any of your points that match the Americans' observations and a different colour to highlight any points that are different.
3 Work with a partner: Compare your results and discuss the Americans' observations.

● Listening, p. 130, Speaking, p. 134

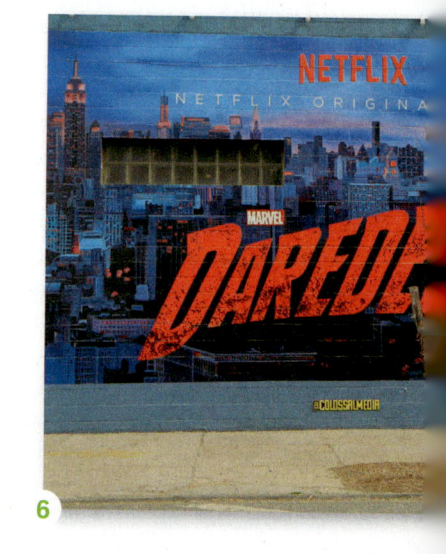

3

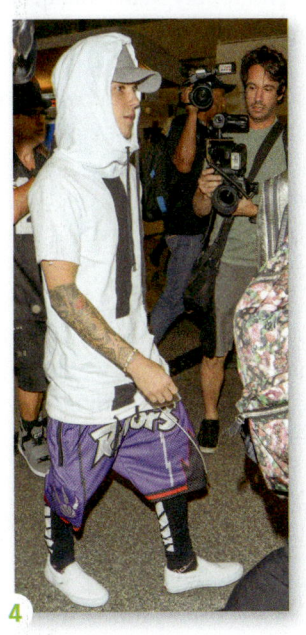

You are asked to help create a website to make exchange students from your US partner high school understand life in Germany better.
Write a short text for the website explaining how German teenagers use media.

• Writing, p. 142

A | B | C | Personal Trainer | **Intercultural photo page** | Optional • Skills • LiF • Words

2 Optional

Ally Condie: Matched

O1

Think – pair – share: Talk about what kind of behaviour society expects of teenagers, e.g. obeying their parents, being good at school, getting involved in politics.
• Think – pair – share, p. 153

O2

a) *Matched* by Ally Condie is a dystopian novel, i.e. a novel set in a future society that has developed in a negative way. Read the following sentence spoken by the teenage protagonist Cassia at the beginning of the novel. Say what teenagers have to do in that society.

"I've waited so long for this: for my Match Banquet. Where I'll see, for the first time, the face of the boy who will be my Match."

b) Read the following key scenes from the beginning of the novel and check if your idea for the quotation in a) proved right.

c) Work with a partner. Talk about …
- how Cassia feels about the ceremony and its relevance for her life,
- how you would feel if you were in her position (Keep your ideas from O1 in mind).

d) Study the extract again to find out more about life in the dystopian society presented in the novel. In order to come to a better understanding of it, start a list with notes on what is different about the society and way of life in *Matched*. • Reading, p. 136

I wait, holding my compact in one hand and my mother's hand in the other. Her palm feels sweaty. For the first time, I realize that she and my father are nervous, too.
5   "Cassia Maria Reyes."
It is my turn.
I stand up, letting go of my mother's hand, and turn toward the screen. I feel my heart pounding and I am tempted to twist my hands the way Lea did, but
10 I hold perfectly still with my chin up and my eyes on the screen. I watch and wait, determined that the girl my Match will see on the screen in his City Hall somewhere out there in Society will be poised and calm and lovely, the very best image of Cassia Maria
15 Reyes that I can present.
But nothing happens.
I stand and look at the screen, and, as the seconds go by, it is all I can do to stay still, all I can do to keep smiling. Whispers start around me. Out of the corner
20 of my eye, I see my mother move her hand as if to take mine again, but then she pulls it back.
A girl in a green dress stands waiting, her heart pounding. Me.
The screen is dark and it stays dark.
That can only mean one thing.   25

CHAPTER 2

The whispers rise soft around me like birds beating their wings under the dome of City Hall. "Your Match is here this evening," the hostess says, smiling. The people around me smile as well, and their murmurs become louder. Our Society is so vast, our Cities so   30 many, that the odds of your perfect Match being someone in your own City are minuscule. It's been many years since such a thing happened here.
These thoughts tumble in my mind, and I close my eyes briefly as I realize what this means, not in   35 abstract, but for me, the girl in the green dress. *I might know my Match.* He might be someone who

goes to the same Second School that I do, someone I see every day, someone –

"Xander Thomas Carrow."

At his table, Xander stands up. A sea of watching faces and white tablecloths, of glinting crystal glasses and shining silver boxes stretches between us.

I can't believe it.

This is a dream. People turn their eyes on me and on the handsome boy in the dark suit and blue cravat. It doesn't feel real until Xander smiles at me. I think, *I know that smile,* and suddenly I'm smiling, too, and the rush of applause and smell of the lilies fully convince me that this is actually happening. Dreams don't smell or sound as strong as this. I break protocol a bit to give Xander a tiny wave, and his smile widens.

The hostess says, "You may take your seats." She sounds glad that we are so happy; of course, we should be. We *are* each other's best Match, after all.

When she brings me the silver box, I hold it carefully. But I already know much of what is inside. Not only do Xander and I go to the same school, we also live on the same street; we've been best friends for as long as I can remember. I don't need the microcard to show me pictures of Xander as a child because I have plenty of them in my mind. I don't need to download a list of favorites to memorize because I already know them. Favorite color: green. Favorite leisure activity: swimming. Favorite recreation activity: games.

"Congratulations, Cassia," my father whispers to me, his expression relieved. My mother says nothing, but she beams with delight and embraces me tightly. Behind her, another girl stands up, watching the screen.

[…]

I sneak another glance at Xander, but there are too many people in my way and I can't see him. Other girls take their turns standing up. The screen lights up for each of them. No one else has a dark screen. I am the only one.

Before we leave, the hostess of the Match Banquet asks Xander and me and our families to step aside and speak with her. "This is an unusual situation," she says, but she corrects herself immediately. "Not unusual. Excuse me. It is merely uncommon." She smiles at both of us. "Since you already know each other, things will proceed differently for you. You will know much of the initial information about each other." She gestures at our silver boxes. "There are a few new courtship guidelines included on your microcards, so you should familiarize yourselves with those when you have an opportunity."

"We'll read them tonight," Xander promises sincerely. I try to keep from rolling my eyes in amusement because he sounds exactly the way he does when a teacher gives him a learning assignment. He'll read the new guidelines and memorize them, as he read and memorized the official Matching material. And then I flush again, as a paragraph from that material flashes across my mind:

If you choose to be Matched, your Marriage Contract will take place when you are twenty-one. Studies have shown that the fertility of both men and women peaks at the age of twenty-four. The Matching System has been constructed to allow those who Match to have their children near this age – providing for the highest likelihood of healthy offspring.

Xander and I will share a Marriage Contract. *We will have children together.*

O3

a) The next day, Cassia looks at the data on the microcard she was given at the ceremony. Read the extract on page 56 and name the moods and feelings she goes through in that situation. Back up your conclusions with sentences from the extract. • *Wordbank Feelings, p. 186*

excited/relieved	"I eat in a hurry, burning my mouth a little, … I'm never really alone (…)" (ll. 123-126) → being alone gives her the chance to do something without her parents watching her
…	…

b) Add more information to the list you started in O2d).

2 Optional

When I ride the air train back to Mapletree Borough, the cottonwood seeds are gone. I want to tell my mother about them, but when I get home she and my father and Bram have already left for their leisure hours. A message for me blinks on the port: *We're sorry to have missed you, Cassia*, it flashes. *Have a good night.*

A beep sounds in the kitchen; my meal has arrived. The foilware container slides through the food delivery slot. I pick it up quickly, in time to hear the sound of the nutrition vehicle trundling along its track behind the houses in the Borough.

My dinner steams as I open it up. We must have a new nutrition personnel director. Before, the food was always lukewarm when it arrived. Now it's piping hot. I eat in a hurry, burning my mouth a little, because I know what I want to do with this rare empty time in this almost-vacant house. I'm never really alone; the port hums in the background, keeping track, keeping watch. But that's all right. I need it for what I'm going to do. I want to look at the microcard without my parents or Bram glancing over my shoulder. I want to read more about Xander before I see him tonight.

When I insert the microcard, the humming takes on a more purposeful sound. The portscreen brightens and my heart beats faster in anticipation, even though I know Xander so well. What has the Society decided I should know about him, the person I'll spend most of my life with?

Do I know everything about him as I think I do, or is there something I've missed?

"Cassia Reyes, the Society is pleased to present you with your Match."

I smile as Xander's face appears on the portscreen immediately following the recorded message. It's a good picture of him. As always, his smile looks bright and real, his blue eyes kind. I study his face closely, pretending that I've never seen this picture before; that I have only had a glimpse of him once, last night at the Banquet. I study the planes of his face, the look of his lips. He *is* handsome. I'd never dared think that he might be my Match, of course, but now that it's happened I am interested. Intrigued. A little scared about how this might change our friendship, but mostly just happy.

I reach up to touch the words *Courtship Guidelines* on the screen but before I do Xander's face darkens and then disappears. The portscreen beeps and the voice says again, "Cassia Reyes, the Society is pleased to present you with your Match."

My heart stops, and I can't believe what I see. A face comes back into view on the port in front of me.

It is not Xander.

O4

Cassia contacts an Official to sort out the confusion about her Match (see O3).
a) Read the extract about Cassia's meeting with an official of the Matching Department.
   ❖ **Choose:** Explain why, according to the Official, Cassia need not be worried.
   Or: Write a text message that the Official could send her superior to inform him/her of what has happened. ● *Writing, p. 142*

b) Read this extract again carefully. Analyse …
   • how Cassia reacts to the information she is given by the Official,
   • how the Official interacts with Cassia. ● *Reading, p. 137*

c) Add more information to the list you started in O2d).

"I'm part of the Matching Department, authorized to deal with information malfunctions," the Official says, noticing my glance. "Fortunately, we don't have much work to do. Since the Matching is so important to the Society, it's very well regulated."

Her words remind me of a paragraph in the official Matching material: *The goal of Matching is twofold: to provide the healthiest possible future citizens for our Society and to provide the best chances for interested citizens to experience successful Family Life. It is of the utmost importance to the Society that the Matches be as optimal as possible.*

"I've never heard of a mistake like this before."
"I'm afraid it does happen now and then. Not

often." She is silent for a moment, and then she asks the question that I do not want to hear: "Did you recognize the other person whose face you saw?"

Suddenly and irrationally I am tempted to lie. I want to say that I have no idea, that I have never seen that face before. I look over at the fountain again and as I watch the rise and fall of the water I know that my pause gives me away. So I answer.

"Yes."

"Can you tell me his name?"

She already knows all of this, of course, so there is nothing to do but tell the truth. "Yes. Ky Markham. That's what was so strange about the whole thing. The odds of a mistake being made, and of a mistake being made with someone else I know –"

"Are virtually nonexistent," she agrees. "That's true. It makes us wonder if the error was intentional, some kind of joke. If we find the person, we will punish them severely. It was a cruel thing to do. Not only because it was upsetting and confusing for you, but also because of Ky."

"Does he know?"

"No. He has no idea. The reason I said it was cruel to use him as part of this prank is because of what he is."

"What he is?" [...]

"This is confidential information, but Ky Markham could never be your Match. He will never be anyone's Match."

"He's chosen to be a Single, then." [...]

She leans closer to me. "No. He's not a Single. Ky Markham is an Aberration."

Ky Markham is an Aberration?

Aberrations live among us; they're not dangerous like Anomalies, who have to be separated from Society. Though Aberrations usually acquire their status due to an Infraction, they are protected; their identities aren't usually common knowledge. Only the Officials in the Societal Classification Department and other related fields have access to such information.

I don't ask my question out loud, but she knows what I am thinking. "I'm afraid so. It's through no fault of his own. But his father committed an Infraction. The Society couldn't overlook a factor like that, even when they allowed the Markhams to adopt Ky. He had to retain his classification as an Aberration, and, as such, was ineligible to be entered in the Matching pool. [...] I don't need to remind you to keep the information about Ky Markham confidential, do I?" she asks mildly, but I hear the iron in her voice. "The only reason I shared it with you was so that you could know without a doubt that he was never intended to be your Match."

"Of course. I won't say anything to anyone."

O5

Later in the novel, Cassia starts to have doubts about the way her society is organized and she says: "(F)irst I believed our Society was perfect. (...) Now I simply don't know."
You are a character in the novel that still knows how today's society functioned. Look at your list (from O2d) with information on the society Cassia lives in and compare it to our society today.
Write an email to Cassia pointing out the dangers and problems you see in her society. Explain to her what you think is wrong about life there.

After this Theme you can …
- ✓ talk about pictures and their role in advertising and the media
- ✓ have a discussion on altered photos and their impact on public opinion
- ✓ analyse advertising strategies
- ✓ comment on advertising standards
- ✓ analyse film scenes
- ✓ use participle constructions to vary sentence structure
- ✓ write a summary of a film extract

📖 *WB Portfolio-Fragebogen Theme 2*

3 Go with the flow

In with the in-crowd

A1

1. Look at the five photos of typical groups in American high schools. Decide which group you would like to join.
2. 👥 Group work: Get together with the other students who have chosen the same group.
   - Tell each other why you chose that photo.
   - Note down what you consider typical of the young people in the photo. Refer to clothes, interests, lifestyle, music etc.
3. Report your results back to the class.

> *I chose/decided on/picked this group because …*
> *I think this group has similar interests/clothes to me, for example …*
> *This group appealed to me most because …*
> *I could not imagine joining any of the other groups because …*

A2 📖 WB A1, A2, p. 39

👤 Read the blog on page 59. Match the photos from A1 to the different high school groups described in the blog and explain your decision to a partner.

> *It seems to me … • It seems likely that … • I assume … • Wouldn't you agree that …?*

A3

Certain rhetorical devices are used in the descriptions to make them more entertaining. Find more examples of the following rhetorical devices from the blog on page 59:
- repetition e.g. "Preps tend to be … and they tend to be …" (ll. 9/10),
- exaggeration e.g. "entire world revolves around sports" (ll. 21/22),
- alliteration e.g. "comfortable, casual clothes" (l. 46).

🔵 *Rhetorical devices, p. 138*

A4

a) Choose the adjective which you think characterizes the tone of the descriptions best.
Give reasons for your choice.

> *serious • light-hearted • humorous • ironic • neutral • critical • matter-of-fact*

3 In with the in-crowd

Cathleen Sankey October 5th, 2016

So there's one question people from outside the USA always ask me: Are high school students divided into groups? Well, it's not exactly like in the movies, but here are the typical, general STEREOTYPES at my high school. But don't forget – the only way to really find out what someone is like is to actually talk to them and get to know them. They can and will surprise you.

Preps or preppies
Why are preps the people we all love to hate? Preps tend to be all-American girls/boys and they tend to be extremely concerned with the way they look. Expect to see people like them on the cover of a Ralph Lauren catalogue! They are outgoing and very involved in activities that call for organizational expertise, such as Student Council. They don't have a problem helping those who are less privileged – as long as it makes them look good. Whenever they need money, they just ask Daddy.

Jocks
Typically these are muscly types, who are sometimes also good-looking. Their entire world revolves around sports and they demand special privileges in return for success on the sports field. What makes jocks so special? They love what they do and are extremely confident, despite the pressure on them. The whole school is counting on them to win that title! Jocks are also not exactly known for their intellectual interests. If they are good athletes, bad grades don't matter because they will go to college on athletic scholarships.

Popular girls/cheerleaders
They will be at the top of the social ladder as far as fashion and looks go. What they lack in brains they make up for in hair products. They'll gladly gossip about anyone in order to make themselves look better. They are very outgoing and must always look like they are in love. Popular girls are involved in almost everything and often get to be cheerleaders. Cruelty is the order of the day with them, as beastliness and bullying are quite common.

Geeks/nerds
While geeks and nerds have been and can be separated into two categories, I'll put them together. They tend to be the people that actually care about their education and they tend to be brainy. As a result they are outside the ranks of popularity. Expect these people to wear comfortable, casual clothes and not spend much time thinking about their physical appearance. Geeks are more likely to have a 'cooler' character than nerds, whereas nerds may be more fanatical about things.

Goths/emos
These types will most often be dressed in dark colors, wearing heavy make-up, and sporting several symbols of all sorts of groups. They love black leather. Hair dyed black or with wild color streaks are typical as well, and lots of tattoos/piercings/chains/metal. – They want to be different and not conform to other people's standards. They are rebels. Expect sarcasm and an "I'm better than you because I'm 'different'" attitude.

b) The tone of a piece of writing will often reveal the author's attitude towards his/her subject. Describe what the author's attitude towards school groups appears to be in the blog.

> *The author appears to approve/ disapprove of ... •*
> *The author seems to have a critical/neutral attitude towards school groups because ...*

c) Work with a partner.
1 First, each partner should note down the different groups of students at your school.
2 Compare your lists and write down the attributes of each group.
3 Discuss to what extent school groups in Germany are similar to those described in A2.

A5 Target task ❖ 📄 Portfolio ● P1, P2, P11 📖 WB A3, p. 40   *Need help? Look at pp. 70/71.*

An American exchange student is going to spend a year at your school. Choose which group from A2 he/she could belong to and think about the problems he/she might face at a German school.
1 Write a survival guide for him/her.
   • Give some friendly advice on how to fit in (you can use your notes from A4c).
   • Include unwritten rules (e.g. for behaviour, clothes) that exist at your school.
   • Use rhetorical devices such as repetition, exaggeration and alliteration to make your text more convincing.
2 Swap guides with a partner and give each other some advice on how to improve your texts.

Writing, p. 142, Rhetorical devices, p. 138, Proofreading, p. 150, Speaking, p. 133

3 Popular

B1 Viewing: A YouTube video 📹 📖 WB B1, p. 41

a) Watch this YouTube video and think of a suitable title for it.

b) Watch the YouTube video again and note down keywords from the tips that the girl gives Eugene.

c) 👥 Work with a partner. Compare your results from b) and add any missing information.

d) Discuss how useful or serious the tips are meant to be. ● Speaking, p. 134

> You can/can't really take any/most of the tips seriously because … • Surely you don't think … •
> The tip about … is quite useful/is meant seriously because … • I really don't believe … •
> In general, I think you can learn a lot about …

B2

👥 Buzz groups: Look at the book cover and read the blurb. Talk about whether or not you would like to read the book. Give reasons.   ● Buzz groups, p. 153

> This book doesn't appeal to me at all because … •
> The concept of this book sounds interesting but/because … •
> The cover would put me off reading this book because … •
> It could be quite exciting to find out … • On the other hand … •
> I prefer to read … • Personally, I find this subject …

Maya is an 8th grader who describes herself as someone at the bottom of the social ladder at 'pretty much the lowest level of people at school who aren't paid to be here'. One day her mother finds a rather dated book from 1952, *Betty Cornell's Teenage Popularity Guide*. She suggests that Maya should follow the advice in the book and write about what happens. Maya embarks on a great experiment and follows Betty's advice on dieting, make-up, fashion etc.

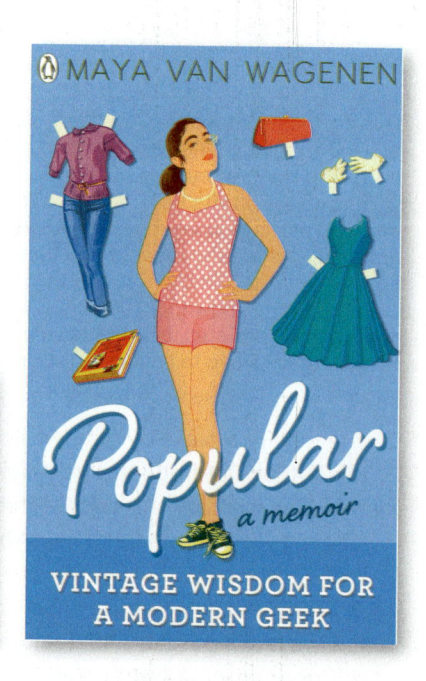

B3

a) One of the last chapters in Betty Cornell's book is about meeting new people and making new friends.
Read the extract on this page and speculate on what Betty's book might have advised Maya to do.   ● Speaking, p. 135

b) Describe in your own words how Kenzie views the consequences of Maya's plan and comment on her reaction.
● Varying expression, p. 158

For this first day, I sit with my regular, Social Outcast group during lunch. I listen politely to another story about how Kenzie's mother is stressing her out.
   "Look, Kenzie, you know how I'm moving next year?" I say when she pauses for breath.
   "Mhm."
   "Well, I want to meet lots of new people before I go. I'm going to sit at different tables, and say "hi" to everyone. You know, make friends."
   "What the hell? You're going to break the status quo! Ruin the social ladder! Destroy all the things that hold this world together!"

Popular 3

B4 📖 WB B2, p. 41

a) Read what happens when Maya puts her plan into action and decide which description best sums up the events. Explain your choice and say why the other descriptions are less appropriate.

This extract from the memoir, *Popular: Vintage wisdom for a modern geek*, by Maya van Wagenen, published in 2014, …

A describes how Maya abandons her social outcast friends.
B describes how Maya tries to act like a popular student.
C describes what happens when Maya plucks up the courage to join the popular group for lunch.

Today is the day. I've been working up to this moment all month long. All year, for that matter. Today I sit with the jocks, the most popular people at our school: the highest of the Volleyball Girls and Football Faction all together at one table. Here goes.

The bell for lunch rings, and I slowly pull myself out of my desk and drag my feet down the hall towards the cafeteria. I can hear the blood pounding against the inside of my skull. My fingers shake as I try to remember everything I've learned, what's truly important in making friends.

I sit down across from a Volleyball Girl.

"Hey, Maya, what's up?" she asks, smacking her neon-pink chewing gum.

"Hey, Cristine, can I sit here today?"

"I guess."

"Thanks."

Carlos Sanchez stumbles in with his buddy Pablo, singing "The Lion Sleeps Tonight". Badly. An onlooker would describe them as drunk, but they did the same thing during third period, so I'm not surprised.

He glances at me. I freeze and force myself to smile, even though I think I'm going to be sick.

"What's up, Maya?" He rejoins the song, then jumps back.

"Holy crap! Since when do *you* sit with *us*?"

I try to stop my voice from shaking.

"I've sat with tons of people." I point to the tables around the lunchroom. The group seems impressed.

A football guy at the end of the table leans forward to see me. "Why?"

I relax a little. "For fun. Anyway, I'm moving to Georgia and –"

"WHAT! YOU'RE MOVING?!" Carlos Sanchez shouts loud enough for the entire cafeteria to hear.

"My dad got a job at a university there."

"But, you make our school look all smart and stuff. And now we're just gonna look dumb!"

Carlos Sanchez will miss me, too! Am I dreaming?

Some of the boys get into an argument about who will miss me most. […]

Someone from the nearby Choir Geek table hears the commotion, looks up, and sees me sitting at the most popular table at school. Her eyes widen, and she pokes one of her friends. They both gawk. One of them mouths, "What the hell?!"

I smile. Soon all the choir girls are staring at me.

I feel like a princess on a float. So I just smile and wave. The whole Popular Table is talking to me, competing, even, for my attention.

As the bell rings on another successful lunch, I get up. One of the Football Faction members leans over to me.

"Don't sit at the gangster table. They're scary."

I'm shocked at his warning. "I already sat with them. They just don't speak much English." He shakes his head and disappears.

When I get into the hall, all the choir girls surround me. "What were you doing?" they ask.

"I've sat with everyone. They weren't too bad."

"But the jocks are terrifying!"

"Maya, you're amazing!"

"You're so brave!"

"You've got some serious balls, man."

Wow, I mean … Wow. I've never been considered brave, or even bold. Now, I have "serious balls".

I practically soar down the hall to my next class, but a question keeps bringing me back to reality: Why is everyone so scared of one another?

b) Read the extract again and note down briefly what happens in each section (1-7).

Example: 1. One day Maya decides to have lunch with the most popular kids at school.
2. When the bell rings, she … and asks Cristine if …

A | **B** | C | Personal Trainer | Optional • Skills • LiF • Words

Popular

B5 ● P10 📖 WB B3, B4, p. 43

Write a summary of the extract from page 61 using your sentences from B4a) and B4b). Make sure you follow the rules for summary writing.

● Writing, p. 145

Checklist: summary

✓ Write an opening sentence to introduce the text (use your sentence from B4a).
✓ Use the present tense.
✓ Use your own words (i.e. find synonyms and paraphrase).
✓ Use formal language.
✓ Do not use direct speech.
✓ Leave out unnecessary details.
✓ Don't give your opinion.
✓ Don't analyse the text.

B6 ● P7

The next day some of the students talked about the incident.
Think about what they might have said/thought and finish their comments.
Before you start, make sure you remember the rules for the conditional, type 3.

● LiF 12R c: Conditional clauses, type 3, p. 177

Example: Lines 1-6: Maya: "I wouldn't have sat with the jocks if I *hadn't been planning it for so long.*"
Lines 7-12: Maya: "If I hadn't been so nervous, I *would have gone to the cafeteria more quickly.*"

1 Lines 14-18: Cristine: "If she hadn't asked me so nicely, I …"
2 Lines 19-22: Maya: "Carlos and Pablo would have seemed drunk to me if I …"
3 Lines 23-39: Carlos: "If she hadn't told me she was leaving, I …"
4 Lines 43-47: Choir member: "I wouldn't have believed Maya would sit with those kids if …"
5 Lines 52-58: Maya: "If he had told me about the gangster table before, I …"
6 Lines 59-68: Maya: "I wouldn't have been so happy to go to my next class if the …"

B7 🎧 L 1/7 📖 WB B5, p. 44, B6, p. 45

a) Listen to the first part of the rap *Parents just don't understand*, written by Will Smith and DJ Jazzy Jeff. Say who and what the rapper is scared of and why.

● Listening, p. 130

b) Say to what extent you can understand his problem.

c) Read the rap on page 63. Note down the rapper's criticisms of the clothes his mother buys him and what counter-arguments she uses.

Example: *The rapper tells his mother that his friends at school laughed at him. – His mother …*

d) This rap is from 1988. Analyse which aspects make it seem dated and/or still up-to-date.

DJ Jazzy Jeff, Will Smith

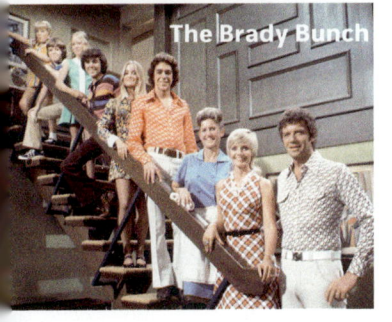

Parents just don't understand

1
You know parents are the same no matter time nor place
They don't understand that us kids are going to make some mistakes
So to you, all the kids all across the land
There's no need to argue, parents just don't understand

5 I remember one year
My mom took me school shopping
It was me, my brother, my mom, oh, my pop[1], and my little sister
All hopped in the car
We headed downtown to the Gallery Mall
10 My mom started bugging[2] with the clothes she chose
I didn't say nothing at first
I just turned up my nose
She said, "What's wrong? This shirt cost $20"
I said, "Mom, this shirt is plaid[3] with a butterfly collar[4]!"

2
The next half hour was the same old thing
My mother buying me clothes from 1963
And then she lost her mind and did the ultimate
I asked her for Adidas and she bought me Zips[5]!
I said, "Mom, what are you doing, you're ruining my rep[6]"
20 She said, "You're only sixteen, you don't have a rep yet"
I said, "Mom, let's put these clothes back, please"
She said, "No, you go to school to learn not for a fashion show"
I said, "This isn't Sha Na Na[7], come on Mom, I'm not Bowzer[8]
Mom, please put back the bell-bottom[9] Brady Bunch[10] trousers
25 But if you don't want to I can live with that but
You gotta put back the double-knit reversible slacks[11]"

She wasn't moved – everything stayed the same
Inevitably the first day of school came
I thought I could get over, I tried to play sick
30 But my mom said, "No, no way, uh-uh, forget it"

3
There was nothing I could do, I tried to relax
I got dressed up in those ancient[12] artifacts[13]
And when I walked into school, it was just as I thought
The kids were cracking up laughing at the clothes Mom bought
35 And those who weren't laughing still had a ball[14]
Because they were pointing and whispering
As I walked down the hall

I got home and told my mom how my day went
She said, "If they were laughing you don't need them,
40 'Cause they're not good friends"
For the next six hours I tried to explain to my mom
That I was gonna have to go through this about 200 more times
So to you all the kids all across the land
There's no need to argue
45 Parents just don't understand

---

[1] pop *(informal, AE)* – *Papa*
[2] to bug *(informal)* – *nerven*
[3] plaid – *kariert*
[4] butterfly collar – *Kragenart*
[5] Zips *(AE)* – *in den 80er-Jahren beliebte Schuhe*
[6] rep (= reputation) – *Ruf*
[7] Sha Na Na – *US-Fernsehshow aus den 70ern von und mit der gleichnamigen Rock'n'Roll-Band*
[8] Bowzer – *ehemaliges Mitglied der Band Sha Na Na*
[9] bell-bottoms *(only pl)* – *Schlaghose(n)*
[10] The Brady Bunch – *US-Sitcom aus den frühen 70ern*
[11] double-knit reversible slacks – *doppelt gestrickte Wendehose*
[12] ancient – *alt, antik*
[13] artifact – *Artefakt; hier: ironisch für „Kunstwerk"*
[14] to have a ball *(informal)* – *sich bestens amüsieren*

3 Popular

B8 ● P8 📖 WB B7, p. 46

The rapper later complains to a friend about shopping with his mother.
Turn these sentences into reported speech.

● LiF 13R: Reported speech, p. 178, 14R: Reported questions, p. 181, 15: Reported imperatives, p. 181

Example: 1 *She asked me what was wrong with that shirt.*

1	She asked me:	"What's wrong with this shirt?"
2	I explained:	"This shirt is old-fashioned."
3	I told her:	"You are ruining my reputation."
4	She answered:	"You're only sixteen. You haven't got a reputation yet."
5	I begged her:	"Put these clothes back."
6	She said:	"No, I won't."
7	She told me:	"You don't go to school for a fashion show."
8	I told my mom:	"I'm feeling really sick."
9	She replied:	"There's no way I believe you. Forget it."
10	Other kids asked me:	"What on earth are you wearing?"
11	I told them:	"My mom has bought me clothes from 1963."
12	I explained to her:	"I will have to go through this about 200 more times."
13	She said:	"If your friends laugh, you don't need them."
14	I said:	"Parents just don't understand."

B9

👥 Group work (3):

a) Each of you should concentrate on one part of the rap.
   Listen to the rap again and note down ...
   - how the rapper achieves a rhythm,
   - the tone of voice he uses,
   - how he relates to the audience.

The rapper stresses ... to convey his emotions. •
The rhythm is achieved by ... •
The rapper exaggerates ... •
By using the phrase ... the rapper addresses the audience directly. •
When his mother speaks, the rapper ...

b) Practise speaking your part of the rap and give each other feedback.
   - Bear in mind that the rap follows a rhythm.
   - Stress certain words (e.g. rhyming words) more than others.
   - Practise using facial expressions (e.g. frustration).
   ● Speaking, p. 133   ● P3

c) Think about how the conflict with the mother could end and write 5–6 more lines of the rap.
   ● Writing, p. 142   ● P4

d) ❖ **Extra:** Perform your version of the rap to the rest of your class.

"My mom has bought me clothes from 1963 ..."

Popular 3

B10 Target task Portfolio P5

Need help? Look at pp. 71/72.

Choose:

a) Write a rap and either make a video clip of it or perform it.
1. Choose one of the topics in this Theme to write about, e.g. different groups at high school, being popular, relationships between teens and parents.
   Use the ideas and vocabulary from the Theme.
2. Pay attention to rhythm and rhyme.
   You may find it easier to write your rap in this rhyme scheme: *When I walked down the hall just the other day,*
   A group of popular kids stood right in my way.
3. Make a video clip or perform your rap live.
   Learn your rap by heart and practise rapping before your performance.
   Pay attention to your movement and facial expressions.
   ● *Writing, p. 142*

OR:

b) Group work (4): Maya posts her question "Why is everyone so scared of one another?" on her social network profile.
1. Write a post answering Maya's question on a piece of paper and pass it to another member of your group.
2. Comment on his/her post and pass it to the next person.
3. When you have all commented on each other's posts, discuss Maya's question.
   ● *Speaking, p. 134*   ● *Wordbank Feelings, People and relationships, p. 186*

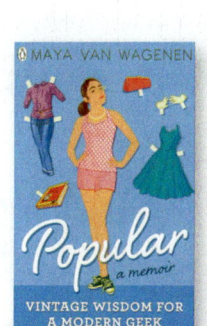

Example:

> **Maya:** Why is everyone so scared of one another?
>
> Answers:
> I guess too many people are just worried about what other people think of them and what they might say about them. So they are extremely careful about what they say and do, especially around certain people. Therefore, it's not surprising that … more …
>
> **Comments**   I think you're absolutely right. And the reason for it is that some kids can be really spiteful. They seem to enjoy making unkind comments about others.

Support

Expressing an opinion:
As far as I can see … •
Personally, … • *Basically, …* •
I would say …

Agreeing:
You're absolutely right. •
That's just how I see it, too. •
That's exactly what I think.

Disagreeing:
I see your point but … •
You don't really mean that, do you? •
I see it differently.

Look at pages 134/135 for more language help.

3 Under pressure

C1 WB C1, p. 47

a) 🎥 Read this page from "The Cool Spot", a website for American teenagers. Tell your partner whether you think the examples of peer pressure are realistic. Explain why/why not.

Support
The examples are quite true to life because … •
I can't imagine that … •
The examples seem quite unrealistic to me because …

b) Think – pair – share: Write down what a person using this website might read after clicking on each of the following links:
- why peer pressure can work,
- how peers pressure,
- spoken vs. unspoken pressure,
- peer pressure can be good, too.

● Think – pair – share, p. 153

| HOME | REALITY CHECK | FACTS ABOUT ALCOHOL | TOO MUCH, TOO SOON, TOO RISKY | MEET YOUR EXPECTATIONS | PEER PRESSURE | THE RIGHT TO RESIST | REAL LIFE |

the cool spot

peer pressure

Your classmates keep asking you to have them over because you have a pool, everyone at school is wearing silly hats so you do too, and your best friend begs you to go running with her/him because you both need more exercise, so you go, too. These are all examples of peer pressure. Don't get it yet?

- introduction
- why peer pressure can work
- how peers pressure
- spoken vs. unspoken pressure
- peer pressure bag of tricks
- peer pressure can be good, too

- **Pressure** is the feeling that you are being pushed toward making a certain choice – good or bad.
- **A peer** is someone in your own age group.
- **Peer pressure** is – you guessed it – the feeling that someone your own age is pushing you toward making a certain choice, good or bad.

3 Under pressure

C2 🎧 L 1/8

a) Listen to a radio show for teenagers and say what the interviewees Mike, Mel, Alison and Corey have in common.

   📖 Listening, p. 130

b) Copy the grid. Then listen again and fill in the information.

Name	Why/How did he/she feel pressured?	What did he/she do as a result of peer pressure?	How does he/she feel about it now?
...	...	...	...

c) 👥 Look at your grid and tell a partner …
   - what, in your opinion, is the most common reason for giving in to peer pressure,
   - what you can imagine people doing/not doing under strong peer pressure.

> Many people give in to peer pressure because … •
> Most people would … if their friends encouraged them. • Despite peer pressure, … •
> For people not to give in to peer pressure, they need to be/have … •
> No matter what their friends said, I don't think people would …

C3 ● P9 📖 WB C2, p. 47

a) 👥 Group work (3): Each group member reads one of the articles on pages 67/68 (A, B or C) from an online magazine for teenagers. Note down …
   - how peer pressure can influence behaviour,
   - tips on how to avoid peer pressure.

   📖 Reading, p. 136

b) Present your information to your group and discuss all your results. Consider the following questions:
   - How realistic are the examples of peer pressure?
   - How useful are the tips on avoiding peer pressure at school?
   - What other tips can you think of?

A | TEEN PROBLEMS — **PEER PRESSURE – Types of peer pressure**

Peer pressure can be present at school or within a broader community. It can affect people of all ages and backgrounds. Peer pressure can affect you in a number of different ways:

5 **Directly.** Peer pressure can be as simple and direct as someone telling you what to do. It might be a good idea to talk to someone you trust if you feel threatened, or if you are being hurt or pressured into something you don't want to do. You could talk to a
10 family member, friend, teacher or counselor. [...]
Indirectly. Peer pressure might not always be obvious to you. It's not uncommon for a group of friends to have particular habits or activities that they do together. But when you're with a different group of
15 friends, it might be unlikely that you do those same things. For example, you might only smoke when you are with certain friends, or you might be more likely to study
20 when you are with other friends.
Individually. Sometimes the pressure comes from you. Feeling different from a group can be
25 hard. Sometimes this happens when people move to a new city or start at a new school or job. This often means having to make new friends and fit into a new environment. To avoid feeling out of place, you might do things to make sure you feel like the rest of
30 the group. When people feel unsure about themselves, they might be more likely to feel the effects of peer pressure.

3 Under pressure

B TEEN PROBLEMS — PEER PRESSURE – Drugs and drink

It is not uncommon for teenagers to experiment with alcohol and drugs. Often peer pressure plays an important role in this. Those teenagers who have already had some experience in taking drugs often try to convince others to try them too. At this age, most adolescents do not think about the consequences of drug-taking, such as the long-term health risks or the fact that it is illegal.

They cannot imagine anything serious happening to them, like drug addiction or a conviction.

It is a known fact that using drugs, smoking or drinking alcohol at an early age can cause serious health problems. Some adolescents find it possible to control these habits but others become dependent. This may cause them to move on to harder drugs, which cause even greater harm. Most teenagers want more than anything to be part of a group. They want to be popular and acknowledged by others. As a result, they may find that they are prepared to behave uncharacteristically. The most popular members of a group have enormous power over the others and may use this to persuade their peers to commit offences such as stealing, drug or alcohol abuse etc.

It is difficult to avoid such pressure as a teenager but it is possible to learn how to cope with it. There are many helplines available to teens with such problems. Here you can find help from trained social workers. It may, however, make more sense to talk to an adult you trust such as a counselor or teacher at school.

C TEEN PROBLEMS — PEER PRESSURE – Dealing with peer pressure

Being an individual means making decisions based on what is best for you. It means taking ownership and responsibility for what you do and how you think. But being an individual also means that you can be a valued part of a comfortable and welcoming group. It might be hard to resist peer pressure and stay an individual. Here are some suggestions that can help you manage peer pressure better.

Value common interests. Hanging out with people who like doing similar stuff may help you avoid a situation where you feel pressured into things you don't want to do. Remember that being seen hanging out in the "cool crowd" might not be as much fun as it looks if you're not comfortable with the decisions that crowd is making.

Say no. Having the strength to say no can be hard, but it can also make you feel good to stick with what you believe in. Explain to people in a calm way why you don't want to be part of something, and you might earn respect from others and gain confidence in yourself.

Try not to judge others. If possible, try not to place judgments on other people's choices. Respecting someone else's choice may help them to respect yours. Remember that you don't have to agree with their actions. Focusing on the reasons why you don't feel happy with the choice might help you to not judge them.

Take action. Taking action against negative peer pressure can be easier when you're more comfortable in your environment. Standing up for yourself and others can be a way to gain that comfort. Both of these are ways in which you might be able to create a positive atmosphere within a group.

Get help in the online forums. Share your struggle and get help and support from others who have been in your shoes.

C4 — S 4-5, L1/9-10 — WB C3, p. 48

You have found a podcast in English about how teenagers experience peer pressure. Work with a partner. One of you listens to Tom's experience, the other one to Linda's. Summarize Tom's/Linda's experience for your partner in German. • Listening, p. 130

Under pressure 3

C5 Target task ❖ ● P6 📖 WB C4, p. 48, C5, p. 49   🎯 *Need help? Look at p. 72.*

👥 Group work (3).

During a Year 9 school trip some of the pupils got very drunk. Two pupils had been persuaded by others to steal vodka from their parents' homes. There was a party late at night, to which most of the class was invited. One girl drank so much that she had to be taken to hospital. After the incident there were several meetings between the pupils, their parents and teachers.

In your group, choose three of the people involved and prepare and act out their conversation about the incident. The conversation should centre on why the incident happened and what could be done to avoid such incidents in the future.

You can choose, for example,
- two pupils and the school counsellor,
- one pupil, one parent, one teacher,
- two pupils and one teacher.

Choose your role.
- Note down ideas to help you with the discussion.
- Use the information from this section on peer pressure and how it can be avoided.
- Use the conversation strategies below for your discussion.

Support
Use these phrases in your conversation:
I was horrified … • *I couldn't think of a way …* •
I didn't want to disappoint my friends because … •
We never expected … • *I can't believe that …* •
How can we trust you after …? •
We thought you were responsible enough to … •
It is your responsibility to … • *We relied on you to …*

● *Speaking, p. 134*   ● *Wordbank People and relationships, p. 186*

---

1 Ways to begin a conversation:
- Ask a question: e.g. *Tell me, Lara …?*
- Give a general greeting: e.g. *I'm sure you are all aware of what happened on the trip.* • *Hopefully, we will be able to shed some light on …*
- Request something: e.g. *I'd like everyone to know that no part of this conversation will be repeated outside this room.*

---

2 Ways to keep up a conversation:
Turn-taking:
- Show you are listening through eye contact and gestures such as nodding.
- Ask follow-up questions: *You said that you didn't like to refuse alcohol. Can you explain why?*
- Ask for clarification: *Are you saying that …?* • *Do you mean …?*
- Do not interrupt when someone else is speaking.

Changing the subject:
- Let the other person know: *There's another point I would like to make.*
- Look for connections: *Speaking of … I just wanted to say …*

---

3 Ways to end a conversation:
Use a phrase that shows you wish to end the conversation: *I think we're all agreed that …* •
After hearing all the main points, it's clear … • *Hopefully we can avoid similar incidents by …*

3 Personal Trainer

Prepare your target task A5:

P1 Words • Reading: giving advice

a) Complete this survival guide. It was sent to a student (and band member) at an American high school who is coming on an exchange to a German school.
Use the following expressions:

> It's not a good idea to … • If I were you, I'd … •
> It might be better if you didn't … • Why not …? •
> People might not understand why … •
> Whatever you do, don't … •
> If you want to be really popular, … •
> A good way to impress people is to …

---

[1] playing in a band is so important to you because we don't have anything similar at our school. We have an orchestra but they don't march around in uniforms. [2] wear your band uniform at school. People aren't very keen on uniforms here. Just wear what everyone else wears – you know, jeans and a T-shirt. Then you won't stand out.
In fact, [3] think of other things to talk about with people when you meet them for the first time. If you talk about your hobbies all the time, you might bore them. [4] find out more about German football teams? That always goes down well. If people think you are interested in Germany, they will want to talk to you. [5] show them that you know something about Germany and German people. It's also a good idea to ask questions.
[6] compare Germany to America all the time. Kids at school are really interested in life in the States, and lots of them would like to go there, but they are also quite proud to be German. They don't want to hear that everything is bigger and better in the States, even if you think it is.
Since you will be in some of our classes, I'd like to give you a few tips on how to behave.
[7] you should help people with their English rather than criticize them. [8] laugh if someone makes a mistake. That won't help you to make friends. However, it's OK to correct the teacher. ☺

---

b) Organize the information in the survival guide into a list of general dos and don'ts.

Dos ✔	Wear what everyone else wears. …
Don'ts ✘	Don't wear your band uniform. …

c) Use your dos and don'ts to check which of the following categories have been covered.
Write one do and one don't for the missing category.

- what to wear
- how to behave in class
- how to get on with people
- how to make a good impression
- what to do in your free time

P2 Rhetorical devices

a) Identify the following rhetorical devices in these sentences: exaggeration, alliteration, repetition. ● *Rhetorical devices, p. 138*
1. Girls love guys who are sporty and strong, but they also want them to be clever in class.
2. I've told you hundreds of times not to talk about people behind their backs.
3. Never tell anyone that you prefer computers to people, and never talk in computer jargon.
4. You're cool, you're funny, you're smart – just show them that!
5. You'll probably discover that some kids love that amazing American accent.
6. Nobody will ever come near you if you wear clothes like that.

b) Rewrite the following sentences. Use one of the rhetorical devices above to emphasize the message of a sentence.
1. Just be yourself and try to be natural.
2. Grades are important, even if some people pretend that they're not.
3. It's OK to be a bit different – but black leather trousers are not a good idea.
4. People won't like you very much if you gossip about them.

Prepare your target task B10:

P3 Words: describing facial expressions and movement

a) Form expressions by matching the verbs and body parts below.

1 to clap	A a face
2 to raise	B your feet
3 to point	C your fingers
4 to roll	D your shoulders
5 to pull	E an eyebrow
6 to shrug	F your eyes
7 to tap	G your finger
8 to shake	H your head
9 to snap	I your hands

b) Use the expressions from a) to say what you would do in the following situations.
Example: You think a performance is good. – *I clap my hands.*
1. You dislike something you have eaten.
2. You don't want to do something.
3. You wish to show somebody something.
4. You disapprove of something.
5. You think someone or something is stupid.
6. You are not sure what to say or do.
7. You wish to get somebody's attention.
8. You want to stress the beat of the music.

P4 Writing: rhyming expressions

a) Match the following rhyming expressions.

1 chewing gum	A anything goes
2 under pressure	B looking dumb
3 casual clothes	C disagree
4 don't you see?	D has to go
5 social ladder	E lose friends fast
6 status quo	F shout out loud
7 social outcast	G dress fresher
8 popular crowd	H doesn't matter

b) Choose two sets of rhymes from a) and write a short rap of four lines.

P5 Words: Best friends?

Use these adjectives to complete the sentences below.

> scared • self-conscious • distressed • annoyed • frightened • dominant • cruel • humiliating • nasty • unsure

Example: *Janice was very **distressed** when she saw the photo that Mandy had posted online. The photo showed her dancing wildly at her friend's house.*

1. Janice didn't realize that her friend could be so ???.
2. They had agreed not to show anyone else the ??? photos that they had taken of each other.
3. Janice was ??? what to do because she was ??? of losing her best friend.
4. On the other hand she was extremely ??? about her friend's actions.
5. Mandy knew how ??? Janice was, particularly in front of some of the boys in her class. Since they all followed her on social media, they would be able to view the photos.
6. She was sure that Sam would make some ??? comments at school the next day.
7. Why was she so ??? of Sam and his friends?
8. The point was that they were the ??? group in the class and if they thought she was stupid, everyone else would, too.

Prepare your target task C5:

P6 Words: the best choice

Choose the word which best fits each sentence.

1. When we realized you were drunk, we were horrific / horrifying / horrified.

2. I never expected / hoped / desired anything like this to happen.

3. What did your friend instruct / tell / order you to do?

4. I thought you were more trusting / trustworthy / trusted.

5. It would have been social suicide not to have drunk / enjoyed / received any alcohol.

6. I didn't call a teacher because I didn't want to make things problematic / difficult / complex for my friends.

7. How do you feel about / wonder about / consider your friends now?

8. I say / estimate / know it was wrong to listen to them.

Extra language training:

P7 **Conditional, type 3** • *LiF 12R c: Conditional clauses, type 3, p. 177*

❖ **Can you do it?**
1. Complete these conditional sentences using the words in brackets.

   If I had stayed at the party until 4am, my parents … (be angry with me)
   My exam results would have been much better if I … (prepare better)

2. **You can check your answers on page 272.**
3. **You need help?** → Do a), then b).
   You can do it? → Do b).

a) Copy and complete the following conditional sentences.

1. If Kenzie (not see) Maya with her own eyes, she wouldn't have believed her.
2. If Josh (be) more considerate, he wouldn't have upset his parents.
3. If the girls (not bully) her, she wouldn't have been so miserable.
4. If the other actors hadn't been so arrogant, Sandy (enjoy) acting in the school play.
5. If the cheerleaders had asked her to join them, she (be) delighted.
6. If Jay hadn't worn the right clothes, the preppies (not accept) him as one of their own.

b) Complete these sentences using the conditional, type 3.

1. If Maya (not act) the way she did, she (stay) in the social outcast group.
2. Many people (try) to talk Maya out of her plan if they (know) that she wanted to destroy the social ladder.
3. If Cristine (tell) Maya to go away, Maya (not be) brave enough to stay.
4. The jocks (not talk) to Maya if she (not speak) to them first.
5. None of the jocks (miss) Maya if she (not sit down) at their table.
6. Maya (not be) the centre of attention among the choir girls if she (not talk) to the jocks.
7. If Maya (not pluck up) enough courage, she (not break) the status quo.
8. If Kenzie (go) with Maya, she (become) just as confident.

3 Personal Trainer

P8 Reported speech • LiF 13R: Reported speech, p. 178

You heard a radio programme about high school groups. Use reported speech to tell a friend what the teenagers said.

Support
Check the rules for backshift of tenses in LiF 13R.

Example: *1 Mark told the radio host that jocks always had a privileged position in high school society.*

Mark:
1 Jocks always have a privileged position in high school society.
2 Being part of a group has helped me become more confident.
3 Preps and nerds will have very different memories of high school.
4 High school has been defined by social groups and stereotypes.

Kim:
5 I don't think that your social group defines your personality.
6 I have been bullied at school because I'm not "popular".
7 My brother is spending a lot of time on his own since he left the art club.
8 I've talked to different groups, and they're all very friendly.

P9 Words: peer pressure

a) Scan the articles on pages 67/68 for words and phrases to talk about peer pressure.
Example: *persuade their peers to …*

b) Organize the words and phrases from a) into a word web. Add more words and phrases, using a dictionary if necessary.

- persuade their peers to …
- forms of peer pressure
- PEER PRESSURE
- how to avoid peer pressure
- gain confidence in yourself

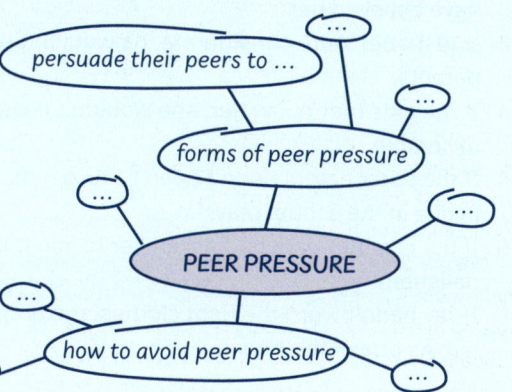

Extra skills training:

P10 Writing: summary

a) Read through this summary. Refer back to the checklist in B5 and make a list of the errors that the author has made when writing the summary. The original extract is on pages 17/18.

b) Write a summary of the extract from O1. Use the checklist from B5 to help you.
• Writing, p. 145

This extract from *Getting It*, by Alex Sanchez, describes a meeting between students – Carlos, Sal, Carlotta, Vicky and Espie – who want to start a GSA and Mr Harris, the principal. At first, the students explain why they think that a GSA is necessary but Mr Harris replies, "I can't allow a club that condones immorality". As a result, Sal begins to lose his temper, which I don't think helps his argument. Although other students try to argue their case calmly, the conflict between Sal and Mr Harris becomes more and more heated. Mr Harris then abruptly dismissed the group. However, Carlos secretly knows that Mr Harris has to allow a GSA.

P11 Mediation • Mediation, p. 151

Your American friend Dan wants to find out about teenage cliques in Germany.
Read this article from an online school magazine and write an email to Dan. Use an appropriate register and don't translate every word – just give him the important information.

Amerikanische Verhältnisse?

Wir kennen sie aus Filmen: Cliquen an amerikanischen High Schools. Doch gibt es sowas auch an deutschen Schulen? In jeder Klasse Grüppchen, klar. Das können Cliquen sein, die auf dem Schulhof zusammen rumhängen und sich auch nach der Schule treffen. Oder es gibt halt die beliebten Leute und die Außenseiter. Aber kann man darüber hinaus Cliquen unterscheiden? Wir versuchen es einfach mal:
Da wären zunächst die *coolen Typen*. Sie sehen gut aus, sind top gestylt und wissen, wie sie sich in Szene setzen müssen. Natürlich haben sie auch das nötige Kleingeld für Markenklamotten. Sie geben in jeder Klasse den Ton an und scheren sich nicht um gute Noten. Die Mädchenherzen fliegen ihnen zu, und darum geht es ihnen ja auch.
Viele coole Typen sind außerdem *Sportler*. Sie spielen in der Schulmannschaft, sei es Handball, Fußball, Basketball. Da es im Sport aber nicht um gutes Aussehen, sondern um Talent geht, sind hier auch Jungs dabei, die nicht zu den Coolen gehören. Und es hat natürlich auch Auswirkungen, wenn einer der „Normalos" auf einmal in der Fußballmannschaft groß auftrumpft. Ob er es so aber schafft, plötzlich zu den Coolen zu gehören? Es ist zumindest möglich. Auch Mädels können eine Sportler-Clique bilden, nur dass die wenigsten Sportler-Mädels in der Klassen-Gesellschaft ganz oben stehen.
Dieser Platz ist reserviert für die *Zicken*. Sie begeistern sich für Shopping, Styling, Make-up, Mode und Jungs. Und man sieht es ihnen an. Sie sind das Pendant zu den coolen Typen, nur dass ihnen ihr Aussehen und Klamotten besonders wichtig sind. Hintenrum wird zwar gelästert was das Zeug hält, aber eigentlich sind sie natürlich BFFs – bis der nächste Zickenkrieg ausbricht. Außerdem gibt es noch die *Musiker*. Sie spielen im Schulorchester oder singen im Chor. Ihre Musik ist allerdings nicht gerade charttauglich, weshalb sie innerhalb ihrer Klassen nicht unbedingt zu den Angesehensten gehören. Sie mögen im Schulalltag sogar eher unscheinbar sein, doch bei ihrem Solo auf der Bühne zeigen sie, was wirklich in ihnen steckt. Und einmal im Jahr geht es auf Chor- oder Orchesterfahrt. Und was da so alles passiert weiß man nur, wenn man selbst mal dabei war.
Gamen, daddeln, zocken, das ist der Lebensinhalt der *Gamer*. Diese Spezies ist in aller Regel männlich und gibt meist nicht viel auf die Klassen-Hierarchie. Der wichtigste Teil ihres Lebens spielt sich eh im Internet und vor dem Rechner ab. In ihrer Parallelwelt sind sie mächtige Helden, die allerlei Abenteuer bestehen, oder eiskalte Elite-Kämpfer, die außerirdische Mutanten zur Strecke bringen.
Natürlich gibt es auch in jeder Klasse die *Außenseiter*. Diese können aber natürlich gleichzeitig auch Sportler, Musiker oder Gamer sein. Oder eben nichts von alledem. Sie zeichnen sich einfach dadurch aus, dass sie von der Mehrheit der Klasse für besonders „uncool" gehalten werden. Das mag daran liegen, dass sie nicht besonders stylish gekleidet sind, dass sie als Streber gelten oder oder oder.
Gibt es diese Cliquen an jeder deutschen Schule? Natürlich nicht! Das wäre ja auch ganz schön langweilig.

3 Optional

Ben Ockrent: The Hacktivists

Beth is a newcomer to the school and Eloise introduces her to her group of friends, the Hacktivists, who meet regularly in a room they have turned into a student-run IT lab. Although they call themselves hackers their activities are entirely harmless ... until their self-elected leader, Archie, is humiliated by the school bully and Beth inspires them to use their IT knowledge to avenge him.

01 Read the beginning of Scene Two and sum up in a few sentences what has just happened.

Scene Two

Music cuts and throwies[1] *are extinguished simultaneous to lights up on* **Archie** *and* **Beth** *facing each other adversarially*

Eloise *enters, followed by* **Mark**, **Steve** *and* **Cath**. *The atmosphere is tense ...*

Beth (understatement) Well, that was embarrassing.

Archie It's his house. He was free to decide who he lets in.

Beth But not to humiliate you.

Archie He didn't humiliate me.

Eloise He made you get down on your knees in front of the entire party and beg you to let us in.

Archie He was just having a laugh. So what? That's fine.

Eloise And did you find it funny?

Archie Yeah, maybe I did, actually.

Eloise You're lying.

Archie Alright then, no. I didn't find it 'funny', exactly –

Cath Then why did you do it?

Hugs *enters, followed by* **Jenny**, **Tania**, **Nisha**, **Seb**, **Pez** *and* **Drew**

Hugs It's all over YouTube.

Steve What is?

Nisha Archie on his knees in front of everyone at the party. Someone filmed it from a window.

Tania They've made it into a song. Used a re-mix of that Madcon song 'Beggin'.

Drew Quite catchy, actually.

Nisha (glancing at her phone) Uh-oh.

Mark What?

Nisha Someone's posted it on Twitter.

Pez What's the hashtag?

Nisha (reading her phone) HashtagMassiveBellEnd[2].

Hugs Amazing.

Archie But I can't have been down on my knees for more than ten seconds!

Jenny They're fairly liberal with the slow-mo.

Cath And the rewinds.

Tania And the freeze-frames.

Archie But why would they do that?

Hugs Cos it's funny?

Nisha It's not funny, Hugs. It's mean.

Pez I could probably hack into the YouTube account and take down the video if you want?

Steve Do it.

Archie No. Leave it up. I don't care.

---

[1] throwie - *Knopfzelle mit Leuchtdiode*

[2] bellend (informal, BE) - *beleidigender britischer Slangausdruck*

Steve Mate, it's probably not even been seen by that many people yet.

Drew *(reading his phone)* Twenty-three thousand, four hundred and nineteen … twenty … twenty-one …

Mark We should stop it now before it starts trending.

Archie Take it down and we make it look like Daniel Cooper's got to us. Don't give him the satisfaction. *(To* **Hugs** *and* **Beth**.*)* You were right. We weren't invited. I accept that. But you know what? I don't care. We're better than him. We're better than all of them.

Beth Then maybe it's about time they found out.

Hugs How?

Beth By teaching this Daniel Cooper a lesson.

Archie Now, hang on a minute –

Beth We agreed. If he didn't let us in we'd start putting this place – all of your talents – to real use. You can't go back on that.

Hugs *(to* **Archie***)* Mate, a deal's a deal.

Archie We said we'd turn this into a real hackerspace. We never said anything about teaching anyone a lesson.

Beth I'm sorry, but can anyone remind me why the Headmaster let you have this place?

Pez Because she wants us to become the next tech giants?

Beth Sorry, tech what?

Eloise Giants.

Beth Oh, giants! Because that's what geeks can be these days. *(To* **Mark**.*)* Can't they, Mogul?

Mark Potentially.

Beth So long as what?

Mark They know what they're doing.

Beth Pez, you said you could take down that video.

Pez So?

Beth So, it sounds to me like you know what you're doing.

Drew *(dismissive)* Cos he knows how to take down a YouTube video?

Seb *(to* **Beth***)* That's easy.

Beth And do you think Daniel Cooper would find that easy?

Drew Probably not.

Seb Definitely not.

Beth And yet he's the one telling you what you can and can not do? How does that make sense?

Steve No one's saying it's fair.

Beth Then it's your job to set things right.

Eloise Can't deny she's got a point.

Hugs I agree.

Archie *(with rising alarm)* No, she doesn't. Okay, yes when the school gave us this place they hoped we'd use it to accomplish something. But not this. We're not going on some vendetta.

Hugs Why not?

Steve Because it's beneath us.

Beth *(correcting him)* Pissing around with LEDs is beneath you. This is justice.

Archie For what? I didn't even want to go to his party in the first place.

Eloise That's not the point anymore.

Archie Alright, then what is the point?

Hugs Freedom.

Beth You said so yourself. That's what hacking is. It's breaking down barriers. Overcoming limitations.

Eloise We were denied access to that party because Daniel Cooper stopped us. He was a barrier to our access.

Steve It was his house. That's private property. It was his choice to make.

3 Optional

125	**Hugs**	And when he made you get down on your knees?	
	Archie	He didn't make me. He asked and I agreed. I was just trying to get us in.	
130	**Beth**	No, Archie. You did that because you were afraid. Now it's his turn to feel fear.	
	Jenny	You can't deny the lad could do with being taught a lesson.	
	Mark	Depends.	
	Beth	On?	
135	**Mark**	What she's got in mind.	

Steve No one's attacking Daniel Cooper!

Mark I'm not saying I'm in. I just want to know what we're talking about.

Beth The course of action is yet to be determined. 140

Mark I mean, in principle.

Hugs Right now the bigger principle is whether, as a collective, we're prepared to keep getting bullied or not. I say not. And I don't seem to be the only one. 145

Archie Very well. Then if it's a decision for the collective we have no choice but to take it to a vote.

O2

a) Copy and complete the grid showing who you think will vote to teach Daniel Cooper a lesson and those who will vote against it.
• *Reading, p. 137*

Name	For or against teaching Daniel Cooper a lesson	Reasons
Archie	against	…
Beth	…	…
Steve	…	…
Hugs	…	…
Eloise	…	…

b) Choose one of the characters and write a short statement from his/her point of view giving the reasons for his/her decision.

c) 👥 Tell a partner how you would vote and why.

O3

Speculate on what the group might do to get their revenge on Daniel.
Read the beginning of Scene Three on page 79 and compare your ideas to what happened.
• *Speaking, p. 135*

O4

Persuaded by Beth, Pez manages to hack into Daniel's medical record at school and manipulate the results of a recent medical examination. After they have let him suffer for a while they send him an anonymous message telling him he is OK. However, they say they are paying him back for his anti-social behaviour.
Compare and comment on the way Archie and Beth react to what was done to Daniel.

O5

Write a short characterization of either Beth or Archie.
• *Writing, p. 144*

Scene Three

*Music cuts and throwies are extinguished. Simultaneously lights go up on **Steve** and **Archie** – the two throwies who couldn't break through.*
***Beth**, **Eloise**, **Mark**, **Hugs**, **Jenny**, **Drew**, **Pez**, **Nisha** and **Seb** sit about the room nearby. A nervous excitement is in the air. Some of them are laughing, perhaps playing an aggressive game of catch[3] with a throwie. They seem empowered.*
***Tania** and **Cath** enter, chucking chocolate bars at the others.*

Cath   Who wants? We've got Wispas, Crunchies, Snickers, M&Ms …

Tania   Dairy Milk, Yorkies, Kit-Kats …

The others scramble to catch the chocolate bars as they're thrown.

Drew   Don't tell me you hacked the vending machine?

Tania   Daniel Cooper's giving them out in the playground.

Seb *(amazed)* For free?

Tania   Got a whole suitcase of them. Just dishing them out to whoever's passing.

Cath   Tania asked him what he was doing and he said 'making amends'.

Mark   Bollocks.

Cath   Seriously. He was well nice to us.

---
[3] playing a game of catch - *zuwerfen spielen*

Tania   Well nice to everyone.

Cath   *(amused)* He looked terrified! Kept glancing around like he thought he was being watched.

Beth *turns triumphantly to **Archie**.*

Archie   *(sarcastic)* Congratulations. You've successfully terrorised Daniel Cooper?

Drew   We hardly terrorised him.

Steve   You made him think his hair was about to fall out.

Tania   And it worked. *(The chocolate.)* Look!

Archie   He thinks he's being watched. He's paranoid.

Eloise   Good. About time he knew what it felt like to be afraid.

Beth   *(to **Archie**)* I'd have thought you'd have come round by now.

Archie   To what? Team Beth?

Beth   To what we're doing. Tell me this hasn't been a first rate example of 'creative problem-solving'?

Archie   It's bullying.

Beth   It's proving a point.

Steve   Which is?

Beth   That we're capable of making a difference.

Archie   We already knew that.

After this Theme you can …
- ✓ identify certain rhetorical devices that are used in a text (repetition, exaggeration, alliteration)
- ✓ write a survival guide for an American exchange student
- ✓ extract information from a video clip
- ✓ write a rap/write a post and comment on other posts
- ✓ talk about peer pressure
- ✓ use reported speech with reporting verbs in the past
- ✓ prepare and have a discussion about an incident on a class trip

WB Portfolio-Fragebogen Theme 3

4 One world?

What makes you hit the road?

A1 • P1, P2   📖 WB A1, A2, p. 57

a) Card survey: Think about what kinds of travel you have experienced. Note down on separate cards …
- why you travelled (e.g. to visit a host family),
- what kind of trip it was (e.g. family holiday),
- how you travelled (e.g. by train),
- where you stayed (e.g. holiday flat).

● *Wordbank Travel, p. 189*

to visit relatives

school exchange

youth hostel

by car   by bus

b) Cluster your cards on the board and briefly explain the notes on your cards as you do so.
   Example: *Most of the time I travel by car or by bus. I have been on a few family holidays to the north of Germany and one school exchange with a school in France. I usually stay with other people – the host family in France and my grandparents or aunts and uncles – when my parents and I go on holiday.*

c) Find out what kinds of travel are most common in your class.

To explore the unknown?

To meet new people?

A2   📖 WB A3, p. 58

a) Jigsaw: The collages A–D on this double page all deal with the question of why people travel. Get into four groups, each focusing on one of the four collages. Take detailed notes on …
- what you can see in the collage,
- the collage's message (refer to the photo(s) and caption, and consider how they are related to each other).   ● *Wordbank Pictures, p. 190*

b) Form groups of four with one expert on each collage.
   Use your notes from a) to present the collages to each other.
- Discuss what the overall message of the collages on this double page could be.

● *Jigsaw, p. 154*

4 What makes you hit the road?

A3 🎧 L 1/11 ● Listening, p. 130

a) Listen to a radio report about recent travel trends. Concentrate on trends **1-3** or **4-6**. For each trend note down …
- what motivates/interests tourists,
- what it means for locals/the local tourist industry.

b) 👥 Work with a partner. Compare your notes with someone who worked on the same trends. Add points you may have missed.

c) 👥 Group work (4): Work together with a pair that worked on the other trends. Present your findings to each other. Note down the points that the other pair make.

d) Think back to your own travel experiences (see A1) and compare them to what is said in the report.

> **Report about recent travel trends**
> 1 development of travelling up to the present
> 2 'deep travel'
> 3 local tourism
> 4 'professional' tourism
> 5 voluntourism
> 6 democratization of travel

appreciate other cultures?   *To de-stress?*

A4 Target task ❖ ● P3

Need help? Look at pp. 94/95.

👥 Group work (4): Prepare a collage about different reasons for travelling.

a) • Choose one of the following questions about why people travel. Is it …
  1 … to get that carefree travel feeling?
  2 … to experience local customs?
  3 … to stay in exotic new places?
  4 … to taste local flavours?
  5 … to try out what you have never done before?
  6 … to be with the people you love?
- Discuss how this question can be interpreted in a positive and in a negative way.
- Create a collage using photos and captions to illustrate your question.
- Prepare cue cards in your group for a three-minute presentation explaining your collage.

b) Gallery walk: Take turns to present your collage and walk around the classroom to learn about the other groups' ideas.

c) Choose the collage that illustrates the different sides of modern travel best. Explain your choice by referring to how well …
- the chosen photos illustrated the question,
- the collage was presented in terms of language and structure,
- the group explained possible interpretations of the question.

● Speaking, p. 132, Gallery walk, p. 153

A | B | C | Personal Trainer | Intercultural photo page | Optional • Skills • LiF • Words

4 The perfect getaway

B1

a) Read this entry from a student website and explain …
- who is writing,
- what the writer is planning,
- what the writer is looking for,
- what problems might occur.

Support your view by referring to the text (give a quotation and the line number).

b) In order to make his text lively and address young people the author of the entry uses …
- colloquial phrases,
- incomplete sentences,
- direct address,
- questions.

Find examples of these strategies in the text and write them down in a grid. ● P4

c) Read the comments that were posted on the student website.
Discuss which holiday suggestion best fits what the six boys are looking for.
● Speaking, p. 134

Q?   **Add Question** | Home | Links | Settings | Log out |

Dave M6 asked: Any suggestions for a holiday abroad for six 16-year-olds?

Hey, guys!
We've made it! Our GCSEs are over and we've got through the exams in one piece. Time for a break, right? Me and a couple of mates want to go on holiday to celebrate our results – or maybe to try and
5 forget them …
So, what're we after? Well, we've already got the go-ahead from our parents so we're definitely going somewhere. We've even convinced 'em to let us go abroad! But where? Let's face it – there can't be that many places that'd be too chuffed about a group of six rowdy teenagers off on a lads' holiday! That's why we're throwing it out to you guys. Can anyone suggest a place that'd take us? It'd be great
10 to stay in a hotel but we can rough it – a youth hostel would be fine. Here's what we're looking for:
- somewhere close to a beach – this is a must!
- warm weather – kinda the point of going abroad ;)
- cool things to do nearby
- cheap – it's not like we're tight or anything, but we don't want to break the bank!

15 Thanks for your help! And if you've got any other tips, let us know.

Answers:

Umbrell@ella: Me and the girls went to Marbella in Spain last year – amazing!!! Flights aren't very cheap if you're going in the school holidays, though :(Stay at a hostel and buy your food at a supermarket to keep costs low. Día and Mercadona were pretty cheap!

20 **t0ny_t1ger:** Denmark? Me and my mates found a great holiday home there – it was proper nice, really peaceful. Copenhagen's not too far away – there are some great clubs there! We had a car, but I guess you could get there by bus.

footballcrazy: Probs easier to stay in Britain … There's plenty of beaches around. Maybe try Devon (cool place, lots to do outdoors) or somewhere on the east coast if you want
25   something cheaper! Weather can still be pretty good in the summer here :p

---

B2

a) Everyone dreams of a holiday in the sun, but there are two sides to every story. Look at the photo, headline, subheadings and first paragraph of the article on page 83. Find out what the article is about and decide if the author's view on the topic is positive or negative. Give reasons.

b) Read the whole article and summarize the text in one or two sentences. ● Reading, p. 136

A Concrete Coastline?
Mediterranean Sea threatened by excessive tourism.

From Greece to Italy, France to Spain, and Turkey to Tunisia, the Mediterranean is surrounded by holiday hotspots. The beautiful coastline, sunny weather and clear, blue sea have always attracted people to the Mediterranean Sea. Today, over 150 million people live along the coast and during the tourist season that number almost doubles.

At the same time the Mediterranean is one of the most diverse natural regions in the world with more than 700 species of dolphins, whales, turtles and fish.

However, this fantastic biodiversity is under threat. Over recent years, the need to protect the Mediterranean's natural wealth has been stressed by environmental organizations, such as WWF Mediterranean and the Union for the Mediterranean.

Speaking on *Our Threatened World*, Lorenzo Imperio from the Union for the Mediterranean explains: "It's becoming harder and harder to ignore the negative effects of the booming tourism industry. The Med's ecosystem is incredibly sensitive and it just can't cope with the pressure caused by so many tourists. The truth is that tourism is the single biggest threat facing the Mediterranean today."

Under Construction

The Mediterranean's popularity is amazing. One in every three tourists heads to the Med, looking for sun, sand and sea. And the numbers show no sign of decline. On the contrary, in 2030 some 350 million visitors are expected – that's more than the entire population of the USA!

With rising numbers of tourists it's no wonder that hotel complexes have been built right across the Med. In Spain, a vast concrete chain of hotels stretches along the entire Costa del Sol, a region so overdeveloped that it's been dubbed Spain's second biggest city.

Of course, this development hasn't been limited to Spain. Hotels cover the coasts of France, Italy and Turkey. In fact, experts warn that by 2020 half of the Mediterranean coastline will be built on as a result of the high demand for hotels and other tourist infrastructure. Even a UN plan to prevent overdevelopment and protect the last areas of natural coastline has failed to stop developers.

Waste not, want not?

And tourism can cause other problems. A typical tourist will use twice as much water each day as the average local; hotels and businesses need millions of litres of water for swimming pools, parks and golf courses. In countries such as Greece, Spain and Tunisia the tourism industry is wasting far too much water in a region that simply doesn't get enough rain.

Another serious consequence of the booming tourism industry is waste. Tourists create huge amounts of sewage and in some areas this goes into the sea after only minimal treatment. This sewage, combined with rubbish left on beaches by lazier tourists, is a major danger for local wildlife.

Of course, the region's natural beauty is also threatened by this pollution – as is the region's economy. Once the beaches are covered with rubbish and the sea is full of sewage, who will want to come to the Med for their holidays? And once the tourists are gone, all the jobs in the tourism industry will be lost.

One might think that there is some cause for hope. After all, green parties have gained support across Europe and environmental awareness is increasing. Yet the situation in the Mediterranean has not improved. Even after campaigns by WWF Mediterranean, just 5% of the coastline has been declared a protected area.

Lorenzo Imperio stresses the need for radical change. "We need to adopt more environmentally sustainable forms of tourism immediately. This is our last chance to protect the Mediterranean before it's too late. If we don't act now, then excessive levels of tourism will leave the Mediterranean Sea as nothing more than a lifeless swimming pool, surrounded by a concrete coastline of empty hotels."

4 The perfect getaway

B3 📖 WB B1, p. 59

a) Scan the article on page 83 for words and phrases relating to the word fields 'holidays' and 'environment'.
  - Find out the meaning of any words that you are unsure about. Use a dictionary if necessary.
    ● *Working with dictionaries, p. 148*
  - Arrange the words and phrases in a graphic organizer. Leave space to add more words later.

b) Outline the problems of mass tourism that are presented in the article.
  👥 Work with a partner. Check your partner's text and give feedback. Then improve your texts.
  ● *Writing, p. 143* ● P5

B4

👥 Group work (4): Organize information on the dangers of mass tourism from the article on page 83 into a flow chart showing causes and effects.

1. Before you start, study this example flow chart on energy consumption and production.
   👥 Use the following expressions to explain it to a partner.

   > *This flow chart illustrates the impact/ causes of... •*
   > *As you can see from the flow chart ... •*
   > *The arrows show the link between ... •*
   > *... causes / is caused by ... •*
   > *... leads to ... •*
   > *... results from/in ... •*
   > *As a result of ..., ... •*
   > *As a consequence ... •*
   > *Consequently, ...*

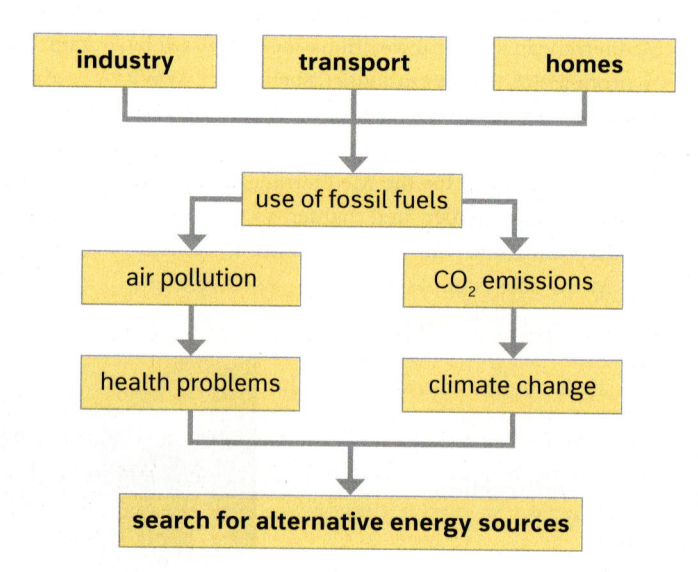

   Flow chart:
   - industry, transport, homes → use of fossil fuels
   - use of fossil fuels → air pollution, CO_2 emissions
   - air pollution → health problems
   - CO_2 emissions → climate change
   - → search for alternative energy sources

2. Now write the following expressions on cards and add further cards if necessary.

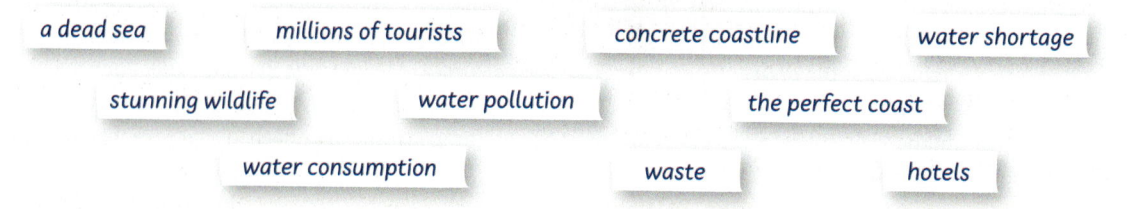

a dead sea	millions of tourists	concrete coastline	water shortage
stunning wildlife	water pollution	the perfect coast	
water consumption	waste	hotels	

3. Organize your cards to explain the impact of mass tourism in the Mediterranean. When you are sure that your arrangement of the cards represents the problem well, glue the cards onto a poster and add arrows to show the relationship between cause and effect.

4. Use the phrases from **1** to present your flow chart to another group. ● *Speaking, p. 132*

5. Give each other feedback. ● *Speaking, p. 133*

4 The perfect getaway

B5 — WB B2, B3, p. 60, B4, p. 61

You are looking for an eco-friendly holiday in Portugal and have found two advertisements online.
Work with a partner. Compare the advertisements on pages 85/86 to decide which option best fits your idea of a good holiday.

Consider …
- the location,
- the size of the hotel,
- the activities on offer,
- the hotel's green policies.

Discuss the pros and cons of both destinations.

Reading, p. 136, Speaking, p. 134

- For me the … sounds promising, but …
- … would be the better choice because …
- I would prefer to … • I would much rather …
- Actually, a hotel in/at/near … might be more/less …
- The activities they offer are quite …
- When I go on holiday, I really expect to …
- I must admit I'm not so/really keen on …, so …

| World Destinations | Countries | Advanced search: |

SUSTAINABLE PORTUGAL: QUINTA DE CÁVADO

Welcome to Quinta de Cávado, on the doorstep of the Peneda-Gerês National Park! An hour and a half's journey from Porto and just outside Portugal's national park, Quinta de Cávado is the ideal destination for the environmentally conscious traveller.

High in the mountains, above the pretty villages of Cova and Ventosa, Quinta de Cávado has stunning views over the Cávado River and the vivid wilderness of the Peneda-Gerês National Park. Far from the noise and stress of the city, you'll be able to leave the modern world and relax to the sights and sounds of nature.

Explore the beauty of Peneda-Gerês any way you choose. Go on a hike in the mountains and enjoy the view. Walk through the woods and discover the local wildlife. Cycle far and wide along the park's cycle paths or canoe along the Cávado River – the choice is yours! Why not experience local culture by visiting peaceful mountain villages and seeing Portuguese traditions and customs first-hand? Portugal's oldest national park has something for everyone.

Stay in a *quinta*, a traditional Portuguese farmhouse, and return to a simpler way of life. Live in harmony with nature and help to protect the environment. All of our electricity is produced by our wind turbine, all of our water is collected from the rain and all of our food waste is recycled and used in our organic garden. Cook your dinner over a fire instead of in a gas oven; keep cool with a mountain breeze instead of with air conditioning. Enjoy the greenest holiday Portugal has to offer!

PRICES
September–March: €240 per week
April–August: €350 per week

FACILITIES
3 flats, each with room for up to five people
Shared bathroom and kitchen

ACTIVITIES
Canoeing, cooking, cultural exchange, cycling, hiking, nature trails, wildlife spotting

GREEN POLICIES
Electricity: 100% renewable energy from our wind turbine. Only basic electrical appliances, low-energy lights.

Water: All water collected from rain. Waste water used for our garden.

Rubbish: Paper, plastic, metal and glass recycled separately. Organic waste used as compost for garden.

Other: Green info packs included for all guests.
Member of Portugal's Society for Sustainable Tourism.
Cooperation with Peneda-Gerês National Park to protect local wildlife.
Eco-friendly bus transfer to and from airport available.

INTERNET
No internet available.

Our stunning views  • *Cook over a fire*  • *Hike through the park*  • *Quinta de Cávado*

4 The perfect getaway

| World Destinations | Countries | Advanced search: |

ECO-HOTEL PRAIA DE ARRIFANA

At Eco-hotel Praia de Arrifana we believe that luxury shouldn't cost the earth.

We promise our guests a luxury beach holiday in Portugal's stunning Vincentine Coast Natural Park, all at an affordable price. In addition, we think that our guests should be able to relax and enjoy a guilt-free stay, which is why we try to be as environmentally friendly as possible.

Located in the Algarve, one of Portugal's best-known tourist destinations, the Vincentine Coast Natural Park is famous for its scenic coastline, perfect weather, clear blue seas and white, sandy beaches. The recognized Blue Flag beach, Praia de Arrifana, is just a few minutes away from our hotel and we're easy to reach from Faro International Airport.

We are proud to offer a wide range of rooms and facilities to meet the needs of any guest. From singles to suites, all of our rooms are modern, comfortable and can be booked as either full or half board. Our hotel is fully air-conditioned and includes a fitness centre, spa, Michelin-starred restaurant and a private section of Praia de Arrifana beach for the exclusive use of our guests.

Protecting the environment is one of our most important aims and we are always looking for new ways to reduce our impact on the environment. At Eco-hotel Praia de Arrifana we use the very latest green technologies to achieve our ambitious environmental goals. We have also introduced a number of policies to reduce our water and electricity consumption, for example by not having a swimming pool when the beach is so close to the hotel.

PRICES
Half board: Singles €40 per night
Doubles €50 per night
Suites €75 per night

Full board: Singles €55 per night
Doubles €70 per night
Suites €100 per night

FACILITIES
Restaurant, Bar, Spa, Fitness Centre, Private Beach

30 Single Rooms, 60 Double Rooms, 15 Suites

ACTIVITIES
Beach, swimming, surfing, sailing, sunbathing, cycling, hiking, massages

GREEN POLICIES
Electricity: Solar panels and wind turbines, energy-saving technologies.

Water: Consumption reduced. No swimming pool at the hotel, guests asked to reuse towels to reduce waste water.

Restaurant: We use organic ingredients from the local area and offer both vegan and vegetarian meals.

Other: We offer our guests bicycles so they can travel around and explore the local area without using a car.
We are an active member of the Portuguese Society for Sustainable Tourism.

INTERNET
Type: Wireless
Available in all guest rooms and public areas, including on our private beach.

Leave your stress behind in our spa

Try organic food in our restaurant

Enjoy our peaceful private beach

The perfect getaway 4

B6

a) Scan the advertisements on pages 85/86 and add more words and phrases to your graphic organizer from B3a).

b) 👥 Work with a partner. Look at each other's graphic organizers and suggest additions or improvements (e.g. suggest a different way of arranging the vocabulary). • *Speaking, p. 133*

B7 Target task   ❖   • P6   ✂ Project   📄 Portfolio   🎯 *Need help? Look at pp. 95/96.*

Choose:

a) Write a personal account of your holiday experience at one of the eco-friendly destinations in Portugal (see B5) for the website from B1.

1. Study the advertisement for your holiday and collect information that you can use in your account, e.g. about the location, activities and facilities.

2. Use the information from the article on page 83 as a starting point and outline your experience of sustainable tourism. Use the checklist on the right and include the following aspects in your text:
   - Give reasons why you chose an eco-friendly holiday.
   - Refer to previous holidays that you have had and compare them to your eco-friendly holiday experience.
   - Use the information from the advertisement and comment on your eco-friendly holiday experience.
   - Come to a conclusion in which you give some advice to young tourists.

   • *Writing, p. 142*   • *Wordbank Travel, p. 189*

> **Checklist: personal account** ✔
>
> **Introduction**
> ✓ Start with a paragraph that introduces what you have experienced and what is interesting or meaningful about it.
> ✓ Alternatively, you can leave out an introduction and start describing your experience immediately.
>
> **Main part**
> ✓ Describe your experience in a lively way (e.g. by using adjectives and adverbs, exclamations and questions).
> ✓ Include details that are relevant to the message of your account.
> ✓ Use informal/colloquial language to appeal to people in your age group.
> ✓ Look at your grid from B1b) for more ideas on how to address your readers directly and make your text more lively.
>
> **Conclusion**
> ✓ Give your personal opinion and recommendation.

OR:

b) Write a personal account of a holiday experience that you had for the website from B1.
Use the checklist and include the following aspects in your text:
   - Give reasons why you chose this kind of holiday.
   - Explain what you liked/didn't like about your holiday.
   - Consider to what extent your holiday qualified as 'eco-friendly'.
   - Come to a conclusion in which you give some advice to young tourists.

   • *Writing, p. 142*   • *Wordbank Travel, p. 189*

Support ·············
Use your graphic organizer from B3a) for help.

4 Speak English and you'll be understood?

C1 Viewing: Global English   WB C2, C3, p. 63

a) Watch the video and say what it is about.

Support

fully-fledged – *fully developed*
to pilfer – *to steal*
to decipher – *to work out the meaning*

b) Read the following statements. Decide whether you think the statements are true or false.

1 The English language has stayed almost the same since the Romans left Britain.
2 The English alphabet and spelling make it easy for people to pronounce English words.
3 In total, 1.5 billion people speak English – a quarter of them as a native language and another quarter as a second language.
4 There are different varieties of English, e.g. Chinglish.
5 The English language is still very closely related to England.
6 It might be time to think of a new name for English.

c) Now watch the video again and change your answers if necessary. If you think a statement is false, correct the sentence. Compare your answers in class.

d) Work with a partner. Consider the information from the video and look at the infographic below. Say what you find most interesting or surprising. • *Wordbank Statistics, p. 189*   WB C4, p. 64

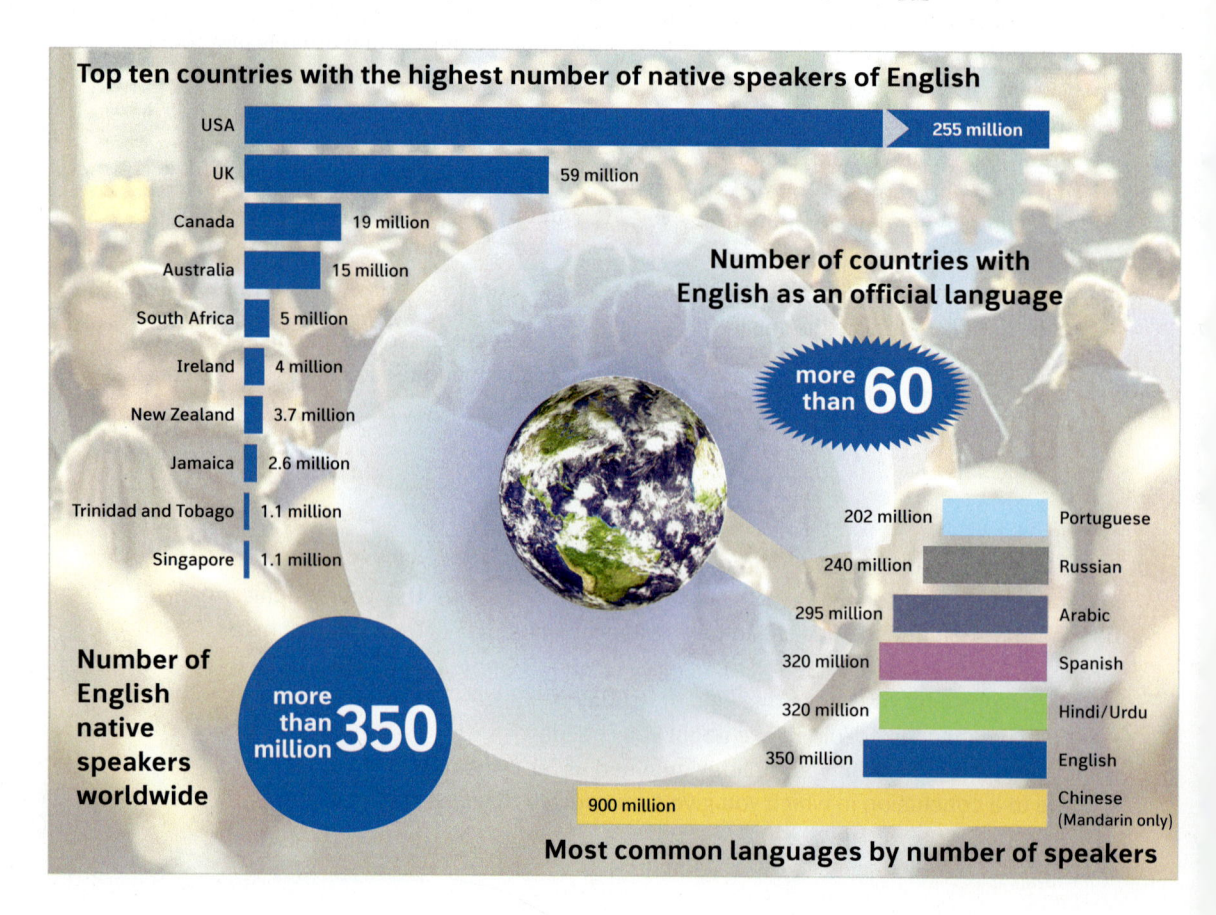

Top ten countries with the highest number of native speakers of English

Country	Native speakers
USA	255 million
UK	59 million
Canada	19 million
Australia	15 million
South Africa	5 million
Ireland	4 million
New Zealand	3.7 million
Jamaica	2.6 million
Trinidad and Tobago	1.1 million
Singapore	1.1 million

Number of countries with English as an official language: more than 60

Number of English native speakers worldwide: more than 350 million

Most common languages by number of speakers

Language	Speakers
Portuguese	202 million
Russian	240 million
Arabic	295 million
Spanish	320 million
Hindi/Urdu	320 million
English	350 million
Chinese (Mandarin only)	900 million

Speak English and you'll be understood? 4

C2 • Speaking, p. 134   WB C5, p. 65

a) 👥 Group work (4): Each year, thousands of German students take part in school exchanges and go abroad to English-speaking countries. Discuss which of the countries on the right (or any other country) you would like to go to on a school exchange. Give reasons for your choice.

b) Class survey: Find out the top three destinations in class and why they are so popular. Check if anyone has chosen a particularly 'exotic' destination.

Favourite destinations of German students

1. USA
2. Canada
3. New Zealand
4. Australia

C3 ( )

Read this article from the *Frankfurter Allgemeine Zeitung*, or *FAZ*, and explain in English the problems that Maria and Barbara experienced when they went abroad.

„Es war so anders als hier"

von Carina Meyer

„Ich würd's auf jeden Fall noch mal machen." In diesem Punkt sind sich Maria Kleinemas und Barbara Zeyer einig. Das, was sie jederzeit wiederholen würden, ist ein Schüleraustausch.

Die 18-jährige Maria hat ein Jahr in Kanada verbracht und kommt aus dem Schwärmen gar nicht mehr heraus: „Es war so anders als hier. Man lebte in einer wunderschönen großen Stadt, die sowohl Berge als auch Meer zu bieten hat." Ihre Heimat für ein Jahr war Vancouver. „Hier in Deutschland lebe ich wirklich in einem Kaff", sagt Maria über ihren Heimatort. Ähnlich sieht es die 17-jährige Barbara, die in dem kleinen Ort Bösel in der Nähe lebt. Allerdings war das Ziel ihrer Austauschreise ebenfalls ein Dorf, das die Größe Bösels sogar unterbot.

Während Maria in einer Gesamtschule in Vancouver viele, vor allem deutsche Austauschschüler um sich hatte, fühlte sich Barbara in Wongaling im australischen Queensland oft alleine. „Ich hatte niemanden, mit dem ich richtig über meine Probleme sprechen konnte, da sie einfach niemand nachvollziehen konnte. Ich war die einzige Austauschschülerin weit und breit. Ich hatte ganz am Anfang und etwa in der Hälfte des Aufenthaltes schlimmes Heimweh und wollte nur noch weg."

Maria informierte sich über Austauschorganisationen: „Abgesehen von vielen Formularen war das eine einfache Angelegenheit. Ich habe mich dann für Kanada entschieden. Das hat den Vorteil, dass man sich dort die Gastfamilien bis zu einem gewissen Grad noch aussuchen kann."

So wie bei Barbara, die die Familie wechseln wollte, da sie sich von der Gastmutter nie wirklich angenommen gefühlt hat: Sie habe Barbara mehr als Au Pair gesehen und als Haushaltshilfe genutzt. „Sie hielt Deutschland für ein Land voller Hinterwäldler und fragte mich tatsächlich, ob wir zu Hause einen Kühlschrank hätten", klagt die 17-Jährige. Mit ihrem Gastvater und Gastbruder kam sie sehr gut klar. „Ein Wechsel hätte sich aber nicht gelohnt, da ich ja nur für drei Monate in Australien war."

Maria hingegen hat in ihrem Auslandsjahr nach einem halben Jahr die Familie gewechselt. „Meine erste Gastfamilie war recht streng, erwartete viel Disziplin und blieb auf Distanz. Des Weiteren wohnte sie sehr weit von meiner Schule entfernt. Viele Schüler sind nur für sechs Monate in Kanada, und daher wurden nach diesem Zeitraum viele Familien wieder frei. Somit war es kein Problem, die Gastfamilie zu wechseln. Meine zweite Familie war super. Sie wohnt nur fünf Minuten von der Schule entfernt und ist sehr nett."

Maria fand die Freizeitangebote besonders toll. „Wenn man wollte, konnte man Ski und Kanu fahren, was ich auch oft getan habe." Auch den Unterricht fand sie gut: „Ich hatte bei meinen insgesamt acht Kursen drei mit dem Thema Kunst." Barbara empfand die Schule ebenfalls als sehr angenehm. „Das Schulleben ist viel entspannter als hier. Die Umstellung war witzig, da einem hier die Schulstunden viel kürzer vorkamen."

4 Speak English and you'll be understood?

C4 • P7, P8, P9   📖 WB C6, p. 66

a) When you are abroad, you will sometimes have to explain in English something that you have read in German, or the other way round.
Read tasks 1–3 carefully so that you understand them in detail.

Task 1:
You are taking part in a project day called 'Go global! Young people abroad' with students from your school's Finnish exchange programme. Your task is to prepare a presentation for the German and Finnish exchange partners about German students' experiences abroad. Use the article from the *FAZ* on page 89 to write a script for your presentation.
Include information on …
- how young Germans organize their exchange trips,
- where they go to,
- what problems they can experience.

Task 2:
Maria, from the article from the *FAZ* on page 89, is a student at your school. You have been asked to write an article about her for the 'English Corner' of your school magazine.
Using the headline 'Vancouver – a home away from home?', write a short article focusing on …
- what Maria liked about her year in Canada,
- how her planning and organizational skills helped her avoid negative experiences.

Task 3:
Your mother has a friend, Mrs Dixon, who lives near Vancouver. Mrs Dixon is thinking of hosting a German student and has asked your mother for some advice. Your mother has asked you to …
- tell Mrs Dixon what German students of your age might like about Canada or Vancouver,
- explain what problems students and host families might experience.

Write an email to Mrs Dixon using information from the article from the *FAZ* on page 89.

b) Study the grid, then copy and complete it with information from the three tasks above.
👥 Work with a partner. Compare your results.

	Task 1	Task 2	Task 3
Author (What is your role when writing your text?)	student taking part in a project day for a German-Finnish exchange group	…	…
Context (What is the situation?)	…	writing an article in English for your German school magazine	…
Target audience (Who is your text for?)	…	…	Mrs Dixon from Vancouver, your mother's friend
Type of text	…	article	…
Content (What is your main focus?)	organization, destinations, possible problems	…	…

Speak English and you'll be understood? 4

c) Now read the English text below and match it to one of the tasks in C4a). Discuss how well the text covers …
- the relevant checklist for the text type (see below right),
- the information on the task in your grid for C4b).

● *Speaking, p. 134*

Hello, everyone. Today I'd like to talk to you about German students and school exchanges.
Now, people usually go on an exchange trip during the 'Oberstufe', so in the last two or three years at
5 school, and the exchange can be just a few months long or even a whole year. The most popular destination for German students is the US, but Canada and Australia are also popular choices. Although there are lots of forms to fill in, there
10 are plenty of organizations whose job is to help students find host families and schools. In some countries, students also have some influence over the choice of host family.
Most exchange students really enjoy their time
15 abroad and learn a lot from being in a completely new environment. However, there can sometimes be problems. Firstly, you might not feel welcome in your host family. Some family members might be prejudiced against your home country, or they
20 could treat you like an au pair and expect you to do a lot of housework. If you're on a longer exchange, you could consider switching host family – many exchange students leave after a few months, so new host families can become available. Another
25 problem is that you might be the only exchange student at your school. You might have language difficulties and want someone to talk to if you get homesick. Finally, you might not like your host town.
30 But don't worry – most people have a great time on their school exchange!

Checklist: article ✓
- ✓ headline ('Vancouver – a home away from home?')
- ✓ introduction: create interest, keep the 5 Ws in mind (who, what, when, where, why)
- ✓ main part: provide the relevant information for the task
- ✓ conclusion: close the article, possibly answer the question in the headline or refer to Maria's general opinion
- ✓ direct speech can be included
- ✓ rather formal register (choice of words, use of participle constructions/subordinate clauses)

Checklist: presentation
- ✓ introduction: address your audience, say what your presentation is about
- ✓ main part: present the required information in a structured way
- ✓ conclusion: sum up the main ideas
- ✓ use words to link the different parts of your presentation
- ✓ generally formal language, but this depends on the audience

Checklist: email
- ✓ start a formal email with "Dear Mr/Mrs …"
- ✓ say why you are writing in the first paragraph
- ✓ use formal or informal language depending on the audience
- ✓ end by offering further help

C5

a) ❖ **Choose:** Choose one of the other mediation tasks from C4a) and write the text as required. Use the checklist from C4c) and the relevant information from your grid from C4b).
● *Mediation, p. 151*

b) 👥 Group work (3-4): Get together with pupils who worked on the same task as you. Exchange your texts, give feedback and choose the text that best fulfils the task.
● *Speaking, p. 133*

c) Present the best versions in class. Discuss what makes these versions good mediation texts.
● *Speaking, p. 132*

4 Speak English and you'll be understood?

C6 ❖ **Extra: Viewing: South Australian schools** 🎥

a) Watch the following video and say …
- who the video is addressed to,
- who produced the video,
- what the purpose of the video is.

b) Watch the video again and note down information that is relevant for students who are interested in a school exchange in South Australia.

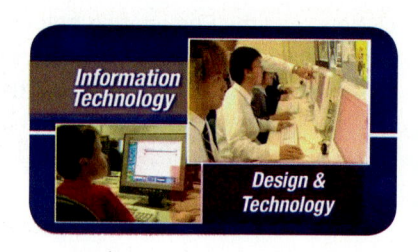

c) 👥 Work with a partner. Discuss whether the video includes all of the necessary information for students interested in a school exchange in South Australia.
● *Speaking, p. 134*

d) Think back to your favourite destination for a school exchange (C2a). Explain whether or not you would be interested in a school exchange in South Australia.

C7 Target task ❖ 📄 Portfolio ● P10, P11, P12 📖 WB C1, p. 62 🎯 *Need help? Look at pp. 96/97.*

Write an email to a host family in Australia using information from the German blog on page 93. ● *Mediation, p. 151*

a) Use what you have learnt in C4 and C5 to work on the following mediation task:

> You are preparing for a school year in Australia and you have started to exchange emails with your future host family in Australia. Your host parents, John and Nicole, have asked you what Germans typically associate with Australia and Australians. While doing some research online, you have found Lara's blog entry (page 93).
>
> Write an email replying to John and Nicole and use information from Lara's blog to tell them about what Germans consider typically Australian.

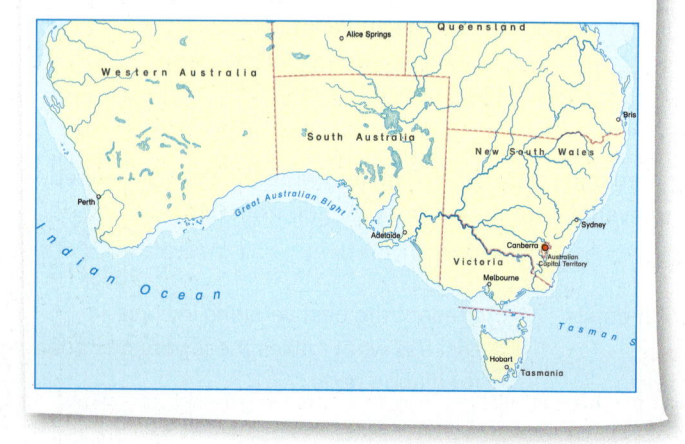

Support
- Make sure that you understand what the task requires in detail.
- Collect relevant information from the blog entry.
- Use a checklist for the text type (see C4).
- Use an appropriate register for the audience and context.

b) 👥 Peer editing: Exchange your email with a partner. Make suggestions to improve the email where necessary. Don't forget to check the spelling and the grammar.
● *Writing, p. 143, Proofreading, p. 150*

Speak English and you'll be understood? 4

| SANDY | + Message | Archiv | | Home | Links | Einstellungen | Logout |

Welcome To South Australia

Hallo allerseits, es ist lange her, dass ich was geschrieben habe, wollte aber erstmal etwas abwarten, bevor ich Sachen schreibe, die sich doch noch ändern […] Ich fühle mich hier sehr wohl. Australien ist mein zweites Zuhause geworden und ich verstehe mich sehr gut mit meiner Gastmum. Sie erzählt sehr viel, ist sehr herzlich und fragt mich immer wieder, ob ich denn auch genug gegessen hätte :D […] Es ist schon anders hier, aber wie schon gesagt, mein zweites Leben. Die ersten Tage waren zwar der Horror, ich hatte nichts zu tun, da die Schule noch nicht losging, dachte so immer an Familie, Zuhause und Freunde. Außerdem, kannte ich hier keinen, meine Gastschwester war nie da, und viele Sachen waren einfach ungewohnt. Es wurde dann besser. An alle, die ins Ausland gehen: Wartet etwas ab und dann wird das! […]

Die Leute sind hier so nett. Als Wendys Freundin uns besuchte, umarmte sie mich sofort. Die andere gab mir gleich ihre Telefonnummern, falls mal was sein sollte, und ich Wendy nicht erreichen sollte. Der „Aussie-Lifestyle" ist auf jeden Fall viel lockerer. Natürlich habe ich auch schon „unfreundliche" Australier kennen gelernt, die ganz untypisch nicht auf der Straße grüßen. :D

Was ich auch von anderen gehört habe, kann natürlich aber hauptsächlich von meinen eigenen Erfahrungen sprechen, dass hier in Australien durchgehend der Fernseher läuft. Egal, ob man auch gerade kurz nicht zuhause ist, er wird angelassen. Ansonsten läuft er auch so gut wie immer. Hier wird nicht zusammen gegessen. Jeder nimmt sich, wann er will. Wenn die Familie kommt, nehmen sich alle einfach Essen und gucken zusammen Fernsehen. Die Wäsche wird kalt gewaschen und dann im Wohnzimmer auf Wäscheständer gehängt. Gebügelt? Pustekuchen :D Hier wird fast jeden Tag Fleisch gegessen, Chicken oder Beef hauptsächlich, denn das ist hier halt billig. […] Manchmal, wenn keiner zuhause ist, werden die Türen trotzdem nicht verschlossen, was für mich Deutsche echt ganz komisch ist. Es gibt auch keine Klingel. Wenn man also vor der Tür steht, weiß man nicht, was man machen soll, denn nach deutschen Gewohnheiten geht man ja nicht einfach in fremde Häuser rein, ohne sich bemerkbar zu machen …

Die Häuser sind hier meistens auch nur 1-Stock-Häuser und sind so schlecht isoliert! Bei mir in Adelaide ist es wirklich „kalt" im Winter. Das Wetter ist so, wie der deutsche Herbst. Wenn man dann morgens zitternd im Zimmer steht, weil die Luft durchs Fenster kommt, die eine Heizung im Wohnzimmer in der Nacht nicht läuft und man ja auch nicht durchgehend die Tür offen lassen möchte, ist das manchmal schon etwas „unpraktisch". Eine Freundin von mir lief sogar im Haus mit Mütze und Handschuhen rum. So schlimm ist es bei mir nicht, aber ich dachte, die Australier frieren schnell, da sie Wärme gewöhnt sind, aber eher das Gegenteil ist der Fall. Ich liebe, dass man so oft, so viele Orangen- oder Zitronenbäume sieht, die so lecker aussehen (Von einem bestimmten Baum sind die Riesen-Mandarinen die besten, die ich je gegessen habe!). Hier in Australien sind auch einfach überall Rasenflächen mit öffentlichen Grillplätzen, mega cool! Der Linksverkehr ist allerdings echt verwirrend. Ich habe mich zwar schon langsam daran gewöhnt, dass die Autos links fahren, aber ich steige jedes mal auf der falschen Seite ein …

Hier sind so viele Sachen anders, aber diese Kleinigkeiten alle aufzuzählen würde ewig dauern … Das Leben ist hier irgendwie anders, aber ich liebe es!

A | B | **C** | Personal Trainer | Intercultural photo page | Optional • Skills • LiF • Words

4 Personal Trainer

Prepare your target task A4:

P1 Words: talking about holidays

a) Match the verbs on the left to the phrases on the right.

1	do	A	a route around the country
2	take off	B	new food
3	book	C	on the beach
4	pack	D	a guidebook
5	plan	E	your foreign language skills
6	relax	F	a hotel room
7	try	G	a sightseeing tour
8	study	H	your bags
9	spend	I	from the airport
10	brush up	J	time with friends and family

b) Fill in verbs to complete reasons why people like to travel.

calm • challenge • follow • forget • gain • get to know • leave • look • party

- to [1] the locals
- to [2] about your problems
- to [3] for adventure
- to [4] new experiences
- to [5] down after stress at work
- to [6] in the footsteps of famous people
- to [7] in the sun
- to [8] your everyday life behind
- to [9] yourself

P2 Speaking: the story behind the photo • Wordbank Pictures, p. 190

Work with a partner.

Step 1: Describe a photo in detail to your partner.

Step 2: Your partner continues by explaining what the story behind the photo could be (e.g. Why did the people go there? What do they like to do? What kind of trip were they on?).
Your partner then picks a new photo and starts with Step 1. Take turns until you have covered all the photos. You can use some of the words from P1.

Personal Trainer | 4

P3 Listening: Why do you like to travel? 🎧 S 6, L 1/12

a) Listen to Jeremy's podcast about why he likes to travel and complete the sentences below.

1 Jeremy's friends ask why he likes travelling so much because they …
2 Some of his friends say that they like travelling because they want …
3 What connects all the statements about travelling is that everyone wants to …
4 Jeremy compares the sound of foreign languages to …
5 Being by the sea or in the mountains makes Jeremy feel …
6 Jeremy wants to travel as much and as long as possible because he is afraid of …
7 Travelling is not just about seeing beautiful parts of the world, it is also about …
8 Jeremy says interesting places that can create special moments can be just …

b) Choose one photo from P2 that you think Jeremy would take for his social media profile. Explain why.

Prepare your target task B7:

P4 Register: formal or informal?

When you talk or write to family or friends, you use an informal register. Colloquial phrases are a typical feature of informal registers.
Match the formal expressions with the colloquial phrases.

1 hello everyone
2 boys
3 friends
4 spend a lot of money
5 ask sb for ideas
6 get sth approved
7 happy, excited

A mates
B throw it out to sb
C chuffed
D break the bank
E lads
F get the go-ahead
G hey guys

P5 Reading

Read the article 'A Concrete Coastline?' on page 83, then use the conjunctions on the right to link the sentence halves. Write down which line(s) in the text contain the relevant information for each sentence. 🔵 *Reading, p. 136*

as • because • if • that (2 x) • despite • which (2 x) • but

1 During the tourist season the number of people living by the Mediterranean doubles
2 There are at least 700 species of animals
3 The Mediterranean ecosystem is diverse
4 The Med is so popular with tourists
5 The Costa del Sol is known as Spain's 'second biggest city'
6 Tourists produce a lot of waste
7 A lot of water is used for pools and golf courses
8 Only 5% of the Mediterranean coastline is currently a protected area
9 The Mediterranean will end up as a lifeless swimming pool

A it is also very sensitive to the effects of mass tourism.
B eventually pollutes the sea.
C increased environmental awareness and campaigns by WWF Mediterranean.
D the coastline is so overdeveloped.
E live in and around the Mediterranean Sea.
F is a serious problem in areas with less rain.
G millions of tourists are attracted by the sunny weather and beautiful coastline.
H we don't adopt more environmentally sustainable forms of tourism.
I 350 million tourists are expected in 2030.

4 Personal Trainer

P6 Reading

a) Read the personal account of a holiday in Spain. Use the checklist on page 87 to see which features have been used.

b) Scan the text for sentences and phrases that you can use for your own personal account.

[1] carbon footprint – the level of CO_2 created by a certain individual or activity

> These days everybody is talking about carbon footprints[1] and how they affect the environment. And of course, that made me wonder about my own holiday. But I had dreamt about a beach holiday in Spain for ages. Saved up and everything.
>
> 5 I got a really cheap flight, too. Now, I think that was OK – at least that's what I learnt from a carbon footprint calculator. Sure, a plane needs loads more fuel than a car, but then it transports hundreds of tourists at once. And I was going to stay for two weeks, which is much better than just doing a long weekend, you know.
>
> 10 I kept thinking about my carbon footprint going through the list. Travelling? I wouldn't need to travel much, since I was practically on the beach. Water consumption? Well, you need the odd shower, don't you, especially when it's soooo hot. But I was determined to go swimming in the sea … That's why I'd chosen a hotel without a pool.

Prepare your target task C7:

P7 Grammar: verbs with infinitive or gerund

a) It is important to find the right words to express the idea of a German sentence in English. Choose the right verb for each sentence.

1 Ich *entschied mich*, mich um einen Platz in Neuseeland zu bewerben.
   A *consider*   B *choose*   C *suggest*

2 Ich *stellte mir vor*, bei einer Familie in der Nähe des Strands zu wohnen und täglich im Meer zu schwimmen.
   A *imagine*   B *remind*   C *expect*

3 Ich *bat* die Organisation, mich in einem Ort in der Nähe der Küste unterzubringen.
   A *beg*   B *ask*   C *allow*

4 Meine Eltern *schlugen vor*, mich nach Neuseeland zu begleiten.
   A *intend*   B *threaten*   C *suggest*

5 Ich *erwartete*, dass meine Gasteltern mich am Flughafen begrüßen würden.
   A *prefer*   B *consider*   C *expect*

6 Die Organisation *entschied* aber, alle Gastschüler erst zu einem Begrüßungswochenende nach Christchurch zu schicken.
   A *decide*   B *deny*   C *advise*

7 Ich *verbrachte* viel Zeit damit, die anderen Gastschüler kennenzulernen.
   A *spend*   B *bring*   C *waste*

8 Ich *hoffte*, eine schöne Zeit auch mit meiner Gastfamilie zu haben.
   A *expect*   B *hope*   C *like*

b) Use the verbs to translate sentences **1-8** into English. Before you write your English versions, make sure that you know whether the verbs you have chosen in a) take …
- an *infinitive* → e.g. *I promised to call at least once a week*.
- or a *gerund* → e.g. *I couldn't help falling in love with her*.

● LiF 18R c: Gerund or infinitive, p. 184

P8 Mediation: Life at a school in Australia

a) Read the task. Then complete a checklist for the points on the right.

- ✓ Author (What is your role?): …
- ✓ Context (What is the situation?): …
- ✓ Audience (Who are you writing to?): …
- ✓ Type of text: …
- ✓ Type of language: …

Task:
Your class is taking part in an international project about education around the world. The aim of the project is for students from different countries to create a website that …
- shows how different education can be in different countries,
- explains how students experience these differences,
- gives an overview of education in schools today.

You have chosen to work on Australia and have found the extract below, which is taken from a long report by a German exchange student about her experiences. As part of your page for the website, write an informative text on the differences that German students see between the German and Australian school systems. Concentrate on the teaching and social interactions.

b) Look at the notes **A-R** which have been taken from the German text below. Pick the points that definitely need to be included in your mediation text.

- **A** very lively school
- **B** no homework
- **C** no bullying
- **D** small classes
- **E** going to school with a smile on one's face
- **F** feeling like part of a family
- **G** lessons less focused on the teacher's instructions
- **H** community spirit
- **I** fascinated by good relationships between pupils and teachers
- **J** no sense of competition in class
- **K** teachers not strict, close relationship to pupils
- **L** respect, tolerance and mutual support are important values
- **M** aim to bring all pupils up to the same level
- **N** take the time to improve each pupil's abilities individually
- **O** wonderful experience of feeling part of a whole
- **P** surprised by school uniforms
- **Q** looked like a tree in the uniform
- **R** uniform makes everyone look equal

c) Use your checklist from a) and the notes from b) to write your mediation text. ● *Mediation, p. 151*

Meine australische Schule sprühte vor Leben. Es gab keine Hausaufgaben, keine strengen Lehrer, keinen kontinuierlichen Frontalunterricht, keine Streitigkeiten und kein Mobbing innerhalb der Klassen, denn die Schulgemeinschaft war wie eine riesengroße Familie. Den Schülern wurde Respekt, Akzeptanz und gegenseitige Unterstützung vermittelt, und ich lernte, was es heißt, morgens gerne aufzustehen und mit
5 einem Lachen zur Schule zu gehen. Die Kurse waren meist klein und die Schüler hatten ein geradezu freundschaftliches Verhältnis zu ihren Lehrern. Als Austauschschüler faszinierte mich besonders diese Beziehung zwischen dem Lehrer und jedem einzelnen seiner Schüler. Es gab keinen Konkurrenzdruck untereinander, stattdessen wurde darauf geachtet, dass sich möglichst alle einer Klasse auf dem gleichen Niveau befanden. Die Lehrer nahmen sich Zeit, auf jeden individuell einzugehen und jeden so zu fördern,
10 dass dieser seine eigenen Grenzen erreichen und erweitern konnte. In Australien lernte ich, was es heißt, als Gemeinschaft zu agieren, ein entscheidender Teil von etwas Ganzem zu sein und als der Mensch geschätzt zu werden, der man ist – eine wundervolle Erfahrung!
Doch eine Sache machte mich zunächst stutzig, und das waren die typischen, altmodischen Schuluniformen. Fast ein Jahr lang hatte ich aufgrund meiner braun-grünen Uniform täglich das Gefühl, wie ein
15 Baum auszusehen. Doch nach einer Weile merkte ich, dass es völlig egal war, wie „doof" man in den eigenen Augen aussieht, wenn jeder Einzelne an der Schule genau das Gleiche trägt.

4 Personal Trainer

Extra language training:

P9 Words: false friends

Find the word in each sentence that does not fit the context. Replace this word with a more appropriate choice and rewrite the sentence. Use a dictionary if necessary.

• *False friends, p. 160*

Example: *1 Could I please have a prescription for my hay fever medicine?*

1. At the doctor's: "Could I please have a recipe for my hay fever medicine?"
2. In a restaurant: "I'd like to become a steak."
3. At a café: "Where have I put my handy?"
4. At a clothes shop: "The rock is really beautiful, but I think it's just too expensive for me."
5. During a placement in a British company: "Is this the chef's office?"
6. In the school cafeteria: "Mrs Clayborne seems to be a sympathetic teacher. I like her."
7. To a friend: "Don't mention Claire's dead hamster. She's very sensible."

P10 Revision: relative clauses • *LiF 17R: Relative clauses, p. 182*

> ❖ **Can you do it?**
> 1. Combine the sentences using relative clauses. Several solutions are possible.
>
>   Adelaide is the capital of South Australia. It has a population of over 1.25 million people. The *Tour Down Under* bicycle race takes place in the area around Adelaide. It is the first cycling race of the season.
>
> 2. You can check your answers on p. 272.
> 3. **You need help?** → Do a), then b).
>   **You can do it?** → Do b).

a) Write down the sentences using the correct relative pronouns.

1. The first Australian gold rush, **???** occurred in 1851, took place in New South Wales.
2. Steve Irwin, **???** was also known as the Crocodile Hunter, was a famous Australian wildlife expert.
3. The company **???** built Sydney Harbour Bridge is based in Middlesbrough, England.
4. The person **???** heads the Australian government is the Prime Minister of Australia.

b) Link the sentences using a relative pronoun.

1. Kylie Minogue first became famous as an actress. She is now a well-known singer.
2. The Australian Museum of Childhood is in Port Adelaide. It has a collection of toys that were made in Australia.
3. Chris Hemsworth is a famous Australian actor. He has two brothers called Luke and Liam.
4. Melbourne is the second largest city in Australia. It has more than 4 million inhabitants.

Personal Trainer **4**

P11 Defining and non-defining relative clauses ● LiF 17R: Relative clauses, p. 182

Read the following sentences and decide whether the relative clauses are defining or non-defining. Copy the sentences and add commas where necessary.

1. Australian football / which is similar to rugby / is played in over 50 countries around the world.
2. The only aboriginal athlete / who won a medal at the 2000 Sydney Olympics / was Cathy Freeman.
3. Jervis Bay Territory / which is the smallest Australian territory / has less than 400 inhabitants.
4. The animals / which kill the most people per year in Australia / are horses.
5. South Australian wine / which some people say is the best Australian wine / is one of the state's most important products.
6. Cate Blanchett / who was born in Melbourne / won an Academy Award for her role as Katharine Hepburn in *The Aviator*.
7. Adelaide / which is famous for its festivals / is considered to be a very lively city.
8. The sight / which many people associate with Sydney / is the Sydney Opera House.

Extra skills training:

P12 Translation

a) Compare the following two texts. One is the original German text and the other is an English version from an online translation programme. Spot the mistakes and correct them.

Translation | Home | Settings | Logout |

German Kim: „Die Städte hier in den USA sehen völlig anders aus als zuhause in Deutschland. Es gibt beispielsweise keine Fußgängerzonen und viel weniger kleine Geschäfte als bei uns. Richtige Innenstädte kennt man eigentlich nur in Großstädten. Das Auto wird auch viel häufiger verwendet als in Deutschland. Und die Autos hier in Amerika sind größer. Praktisch finde ich in Deutschland den guten öffentlichen Nahverkehr."

English Kim: "The cities here in the US look completely in a different way than home in Germany. There is, for example, no pedestrian zones and much less small shops than us. One knows correct city centres really only in major cities. The car is also used much more frequently than in Germany. And the cars here in America are greater. Practically I think in Germany the good public transport."

b) Translate the following passage into English.
Maya: „Was ist typisch deutsch? Diese Frage finde ich schwer zu beantworten. Natürlich gibt es die bekannten Klischees über die Deutschen, die als pünktlich gelten, als sehr korrekt, als etwas langweilig und so weiter. Aber ehrlich gesagt kenne ich viele Deutsche, auf die diese Beschreibung überhaupt nicht passen würde. Meiner Meinung nach hat es deshalb keinen Sinn zu versuchen, typische Eigenschaften zu finden, die auf die Mehrheit der Deutschen zutreffen."

4 Intercultural photo page

Australia

1

👥 Work with a partner.
- Take turns to describe the Australian words on the right. Use these categories: animal, person, place, device, tradition.
  Example: *… is a tradition in which …; … is a person who …*
- Look up any words that you do not know in the dictionary.
  ● Working with dictionaries, p. 148

Aborigine • kangaroo • outback • boomerang • pom • Dreamtime • koala • walkabout • didgeridoo • kookaburra • wombat • bush

2 Viewing: The Top 10 Tourist Destinations 🎥

Look at the map of Australia and watch the video clip.
1 Write down the names of the places mentioned in the video.
2 Watch the video again. Add important information about each place.

3

a) Name the places, people, animals etc you can see in the photos on pages 100/101.

b) Choose one or more adjectives from below to describe your impression of Australia from the video and photos. Give reasons.

attractive • exotic • familiar • frightening • laid-back • striking • positive • relaxed • strange • unappealing • unexpected • varied

4

👥 Work with a partner. Think back to the video and discuss …
- whether you would like to spend an exchange year in Australia,
- which places you might like to visit in Australia and why.

5 🎧 S 7, L 1/13 ● Listening, p. 130

1 Now listen to an interview with 16-year-old Carmen, who is spending her junior year of high school in Australia. Say …
   - what aspects of everyday life in Australia she describes,
   - what surprises you most.
2 👥 Think about your decision in 4 again. Tell your partner whether you have changed your mind and if so, explain why.

6

You are a travel photographer and took one of the photos on pages 100/101. Write a short blog explaining where you were, what you were doing and why you took this photo. ● Writing, p. 142

100 A | B | C | Personal Trainer | **Intercultural photo page** | Optional • Skills • LiF • Words

2
4 5

4 Optional

Travel writing

O1

a) Look at the photos. Choose which of the two destinations you would rather visit and explain why.

b) Find out more about one of these places online and note down what you can do and see there.

Sylvan Beach, NY, USA

Dijon, France

O2

To plan a trip, you might look at a guidebook or at travel websites. Another way to learn about places you would like to visit is to read travel literature – books or essays in which authors who have travelled to various places describe their experiences.
Look at the following elements you might find in travel writing. Identify which of the points you would most like to read about in a piece of travel writing, and list at least four of them.

A how the author experiences new customs and traditions, e.g. how the locals expect tourists to behave, what they eat
B what motivates the author to go on the trip
C how the author gets along with the locals with the help of his/her language skills and cultural knowledge
D how easy or difficult a trip is, e.g. finding a place to sleep, finding something to eat, how locals help you when your car breaks down
E what kinds of activities the author takes part in, e.g. lying on the beach, sports, sightseeing
F how personal relationships influence the travel experience, e.g. travelling with friends or family, meeting someone you know, making new friends
G how the situation on the trip compares to the author's life back home
H how the author feels and what he learns about himself/herself on the trip

O3

a) Read the following essays that were honoured as outstanding texts in a travel writing competition for US teens.
For each text, choose one of the photos from page 102 that you would use to illustrate the content of the essay.
● Reading, p. 136

A Lillian Holmes ■ Pardon My French:
The Art of Making Mistakes and Trying Anyway

France in the summer is lovely. I remember the buildings of yellow stone, ancient beyond belief to my American eyes; the canals whose water lilies inspired Monet; the countryside, passing in a blur of fertile green as I peered out the window of a high-speed train. I spent two weeks visiting Paris and the region of Franche-Comté, and I couldn't get enough of the scenery or the people.

It was the second-to-last day of my exchange trip. Nineteen other American students and I were visiting Dijon without our host families. I sat in a park with my friend Jasmine, eating a cheese baguette. We had just walked Dijon's Parcours de la Chouette – the Owl's Trail – and again I saw my favorite things about France: cobblestones, cafés, historic architecture. I couldn't believe that in twenty-four short hours we would leave.

As Jasmine and I chatted, a little boy walked up. He was nine or ten and, like most French children, dressed in very chic clothing.

"Hello," he said in heavily-accented English. "How are you?"

"I'm doing well," I said.

He ran away.

Jasmine and I chuckled. After two weeks of complete immersion in French – which we spoke scarcely better than the boy spoke English – we recognized that urge to run away. It's terrifying to speak another language when you know exactly how bad you sound. But over our two weeks, Jasmine and I mastered the art of Making Mistakes and Trying Anyway. If my host mother didn't understand me, I tried a different phrase. If my host father spoke too fast, I asked him to slow down. I spoke confidently even when I felt completely unsure of myself. And generally, people understood. Soon the boy was back, this time with friends. A little girl (in a stylish skirt and leggings) stepped forward as the unofficial spokesperson.

"Where are you from?" she asked us in French. I said that we were from California. Jasmine explained that we were exchange students staying with French host families. And the children understood us, despite our awful accents. The girl asked how we liked France, and told us that her class was visiting the park to celebrate the end of school. Her friends clustered around, wide-eyed. As another girl passed, the boy called out to her, saying something in rapid-fire French that I didn't comprehend. But I caught her response quite clearly:

"Americans who speak French well?" she said. "Ce n'est pas possible!" (It's not possible!)

That moment proved to me the value of Making Mistakes and Trying Anyway. Children everywhere are infamous for sharing their "unfiltered" thoughts, with sometimes hurtful results, but to me, the girl's astonishment was a true compliment. Her unguarded disbelief proved that we exceeded expectations.

It is also a reminder of a valuable lesson: no matter how bad we are at something, we owe it to ourselves to overcome our fear of failure and just try. Some of my friends spent the entire trip smiling mutely because they were afraid to speak French and be wrong. I discovered that making the effort is worth the embarrassment. The world didn't end when I forgot words and messed up verb tenses; by letting myself make mistakes, I connected with French culture in a way I couldn't have otherwise. The same is true of anything, from playing an instrument to speaking a new language: the important thing, the rewarding thing, is to swallow your pride and try.

Source: FamilyTravelForum.com

4 Optional

B Mary Wester ■ Relaxing to Roller Coasters: The Perfect Day in Sylvan Beach

After a stressful school year filled with crammed study sessions and all-nighters, only one place can take my mind off it all – Sylvan Beach, New York. Decades ago, my great-great grandparents
5 discovered this beach town on Oneida Lake in Central New York, and it's been a tradition to visit every summer since.

"Anything to drink, hun?" a cheery waitress asks as I peruse the Flashback Café menu. Sipping my
10 coffee in the wrought-iron chairs on the café patio, I watch Sylvan Beach awaken – a well-tanned vacationer drags a laundry bag to the Beachy Clean Laundromat, the owner of the What's the Scoop ice cream window wipes down his plastic tables and
15 yellow umbrellas, and the employee at the Beachcomber gift shop hangs up colorful inner-tubes. The perfect beach day doesn't require any intense planning, all it takes is a leisurely breakfast. First, my family and I slip into bathing suits and
20 walk down to the beach. The tractor that comes by every morning has recently raked the sand, and each step down to the water is soft and satisfying. After we set up umbrellas and lay out towels, I sit in my beach chair and watch the waves lap up onto
25 the sand, like tubes of wrapping paper rolling across the floor. The soft breeze and bright sun is perfect for reading a book or splashing in the lake.

The water can be intimidating at first, as it is filled with clumps of algae and bundles of lake-grass. But
30 it doesn't take long to get used to, and soon the green clusters are hardly noticeable. We continue the day with my favorite beach activities. Everyone participates in a lively game of cornhole, and we end the afternoon with a friendly handstand
35 competition in the lake.

When we're finished at the beach, my family and I walk around the block to Eddie's Restaurant for some pie. My favorite is coconut cream, because one slice is as big as my face and thick as a dictionary. The pie is paired nicely with a Shirley Temple, which is manufactured at the local Saranac brewery in Utica.

After refueling at Eddie's, we head to the historic
45 Sylvan Beach Amusement Park. It's right between the Erie Canal and Oneida Lake, and only a two minute walk from the shores of the beach. My favorite ride is called Laffland, a haunted train ride through two old bath houses that used to be opera-
50 tional right down the road at the beach. Next to Laffland are the arcades. Walking by I hear the shrill sirens from the skeeball machines and the soft voice of an employee at the prize counter tallying up tickets.
55 We grab a slice of pizza for dinner as a pack of little boys run to the Galaxi, one of the tallest roller coasters in Central New York. Many ride the coaster for its thrilling track, but I enjoy the breathtaking views at the top. As the sun sets the coaster car
60 begins its ascent up a hill, and I look out to the left at the glistening lake and the sinking pink and yellow sun.

As dusk sets in, the park gets brighter – lights from the rides flash and swirl and dance, a mini Times
65 Square in the hush of Central New York.

As the park begins to close, so does our perfect beach day. The restaurants lock their doors and cars packed with damp towels and tired children make their way back to normal life. The town slowly falls
70 asleep, preparing for another day of laughter, fun, and memories.

Source: FamilyTravelForum.com

b) Match the statements to the essays and briefly explain your choices. Not every statement can be matched to one of the essays.

1 The author experiences what it means to be brave and try out what you have learnt.
2 The author's travel experience is mainly about relaxing.
3 The author's motivation to travel to that particular place is family-related.
4 The author experiences city life for the first time.
5 The author feels torn as she cannot communicate properly, but feels connected to the people at the same time.

Optional **4**

O4

a) Choose one of the two essays.

1. Explain how the author starts her essay. Here are some suggestions. The essay starts by …
   - describing an event that is happening at the destination, making you want to read on;
   - presenting the background of the trip and explaining why the person is going on it;
   - describing some basic facts about the trip so that you know who is going where;
   - …

2. Read the main part of the essay you have chosen. Work out which strategies are used to keep the reader interested in the story and note down some examples. Here are some suggestions of what the author may do:
   - use adjectives and adverbs that make it easier to imagine what the places, people and activities are like;
   - concentrate on one anecdote, not all the different things someone does;
   - include direct speech to make the text more interesting to read;
   - express thoughts and feelings about the travel experience;
   - make comments on the experiences;
   - …

3. Read the ending of the essay. Describe how it ends. Here are some suggestions of what the author may do:
   - state what she has learnt from the trip;
   - describe how this trip has changed the author as a person;
   - …

b) Compare your notes for O4a) with those of a classmate who has worked on the same essay. Add to or change your notes according to what you may have learnt from your partner.

O5 Portfolio

Write about a special trip you went on or a special experience you had while travelling.

Writing, p. 142

Support
- Write a beginning, a main part and an ending.
- Use some of the strategies you identified in O4.
- Use adjectives and adverbs to create atmosphere.

O6

Put up the travel stories in class and read them. Choose the best story in your class.

After this Theme you can …
- ✓ prepare and present a collage
- ✓ organize information from an article in a flow chart
- ✓ discuss the pros and cons of different holiday destinations
- ✓ write a personal account of a holiday experience
- ✓ work on mediation tasks considering all the aspects that are relevant to the task

WB Portfolio-Fragebogen Theme 4

5 Great expectations

Jobs, jobs, jobs

A1 📖 WB A1, A2, p. 75

Milling around:
You are thinking of spending some time abroad either in Year 10 or after school.

Talk to at least five people and tell each other …
- where you would like to go and why,
- what you would like to do,
- what you might gain from living in a different country.

● *Milling around, p. 153*

A2 📖 WB A3, p. 75

a) Read the website *Student jobs 4 you* on page 107 carefully and decide which jobs you could imagine applying for. Give reasons for your choice.

b) Study the website again, then copy the grid and fill it in.
● *P1*

job	personal qualities/ abilities you need	skills/knowledge/ experience you can gain	perks that come with the job
teen news reporter	enjoy working in a team	…	…
…	…	…	…

A3 🎧 L 2/1   ( )   ● P11   📖 WB A4, p. 76

An exchange student from your American partner school has come across this German radio clip, but he doesn't quite understand what it is about. Listen to the clip. Explain in English …
- what the organization offers,
- what abilities/qualities are required to work for the organization,
- what young people can gain from joining the organization.   ● *Mediation, p. 151*

A4 Target task ❖   🎧 L 2/2   📄 Portfolio   📖 WB A5, p. 76

Write about your worst summer job experience for a radio phone-in.

1. Listen to a radio programme on the worst summer jobs ever. List the jobs mentioned and take notes on what went wrong and why they were the worst summer jobs.   ● P2

2. 👥 Work with a partner. Tell each other which of the summer jobs you would have hated most and why. Use some of these adjectives and their comparative or superlative forms: *bad, disgusting, revolting, embarrassing, tedious, hard, nasty, horrible, smelly, enormous, dull.*   ● *LiF 10R: Comparison, p. 175*

🎯 *Need help? Look at p. 116.*

Support

pipe – Rohr
to shovel – schaufeln
slippery – rutschig
rubber boots – Gummistiefel
contract – Vertrag
droppings – Tierexkremente
bait – Angelköder

3. You want to phone in and tell the radio show about your worst summer job. Decide what your worst summer job might be. Write down what you would say. Include the following points:
   - what you expected to gain from the job
   - what went wrong
   - what you learnt from the experience

4. ❖ **Extra:** 👥 Group work (4): Record a radio show with conversations between three callers and a radio host. Play your radio show to another group and then listen to theirs. Give feedback.

Jobs, jobs, jobs 5

STUDENTS JOBS 4 YOU | SEARCH JOBS | SUMMER JOBS | PART-TIME JOBS

Teen News Reporter
Company: Teen Times of Toronto
Location: Toronto, Ontario
Benefits: C$13 per hour
Start: August   Duration: 10 months

The *Teen Times of Toronto* is looking for teenagers interested in reporting on news and current events for an internet television news show aimed at other teens.
This job also offers you the unique opportunity to gain insights into the modern media world and to learn about reporting. Plus you can go to major media and sports events and use our great cafeteria for free.
Your English language skills should be good, but you do not have to be a native speaker. It is enough if you enjoy working with language, are good with words, can speak well and like writing texts.
You also need to enjoy working in a team and be able to communicate with all age groups, as you will be working with teens as well as with professional adults.   more …

Water Sports Camp Staff
Company: Camp Chippewa
Location: Sheboygan, Wisconsin
Benefits: $200 per month, food and accommodation included
Start: May   Duration: 5 months

So you're over 16 and enjoy boating/canoeing/sailing/windsurfing/water-skiing and want to have an unbelievable summer? Do you also love working with children and want to spend the summer working outdoors? Then this is for you! Come and join the camp staff at our summer camps for kids in the USA.
What's more:
- Once your placement is over, your visa allows you plenty of time for travel so you can visit more of the US.
- You'll make friends for life – from all over the world.
- You'll learn about different cultures and improve your leadership, time management and communication skills.   more …

Au Pair
Company: Poppin's AuPairs
Location: London, UK
Benefits: individual arrangements with the family
Start: August
Duration: one year

Being an au pair opens up a wide range of life and work experiences. The opportunity to discover the United Kingdom, while at the same time enjoying the comfort and security of family life, is uniquely rewarding. This is a good opportunity to learn and build essential skills as well as to have great fun!
In most cases you need to be between the ages of 17 and 27, and single. Your motivations for travelling to the UK should be to live with a British family, to learn English and also to gain experience and understanding of the British way of life and culture.
You will assist with childcare in the home and help out with housework.   more …

Rugby/Football/Tennis Coach
Company: Kickstarters
Location: Scarborough or Leeds
Benefits: good salary + full board accommodation
Start: June-August
Duration: 1 or 2 months

The job involves working with young people from abroad, organizing activities for them, being responsible for their general welfare and entertaining the students in the evenings. You will also be in charge of planning your own sports sessions with the students.
You will be working as part of a large, international team and should be a sociable person. If you enjoy working with young people and sharing your passions and have an outgoing personality, this is the job for you! And in your spare time you can use all our facilities for free.   more …

A | B | C | Personal Trainer | Intercultural photo page | Optional • Skills • LiF • Words   107

5 Doing a good job

B1 🎧 L 2/3 • Listening, p. 130 • P3 📖 WB B1, p. 78

a) When you are applying for a job or an internship, there are several steps you need to bear in mind. Copy the grid below and decide which of the following steps belong to which category.
👥 Work with a partner. Compare your results.

> write a covering letter • look at job adverts • have an application photo taken (if a photo is required) • find out background information about the company where you are applying • write a CV • fill in an application form • put together certificates and other documents • prepare for a job interview • ask for a letter of recommendation • consider the dress code • make a list of your skills

What to do …

… before applying for a job/an internship	… when putting together an application	… when you are invited to a job interview
…	…	…

b) Listen to Jonathan Baker's podcast. He gives advice on how to apply for a job. Highlight the steps in your grid from a) that he deals with in detail.

c) Listen again and write a list of dos and don'ts for the highlighted points that you should bear in mind when applying for a job.

B2 🎧 L 2/4 • Listening, p. 130 • P4

a) Jonathan Baker describes soft skills as an important part of a job application. Listen to another part of his podcast and note down what hard and soft skills are.

b) Look at the skills below and decide which are hard skills and which are soft skills. Note them down in a T-chart.

> responsibility • knowledge of a foreign language • fast at typing • patience • repairing bikes • integrity • experience of managing a youth club's finances • knowledge of computer programming • teamwork • being good at babysitting • friendliness • leadership • used to working independently • high self-esteem

c) 👥 Work with a partner. Compare your results and add more skills to your T-charts.

B3 • P5 📖 WB B2, p. 79, B3, p. 80

a) 👥 Work with a partner. Look at your T-chart from B2b) and the attributes below.
• Write down eight skills/attributes that you think apply to you.
  Then start a second list with eight characteristics that apply to your partner.
• Don't show your lists to each other or talk about them until you have finished writing them down.

> ambitious • communicative • confident • conscientious • copes well under pressure • creative • dedicated • diligent • diplomatic • dynamic • efficient • enjoys a challenge • enthusiastic • flexible • friendly • helpful • honest • is a good listener • motivated • organized • outgoing • patient • practical • punctual • reliable • responsible • sensitive • tactful • trustworthy • works well in a team

b) 👥 Compare your lists and identify where they overlap. Highlight these skills and attributes. If you chose very similar points (e.g. *dedicated* and *motivated*), you can still highlight them as well.

c) Look at the job adverts below and on page 107. Choose the one that you find most attractive and note down which hard and soft skills are required or could be useful for the job. ● *Reading, p. 136*

d) 👥 Work with a partner. Compare the requirements in c) to your results from b) and discuss with your partner if you are really suitable for the job. If not, decide which job would suit your personality best.

| STUDENTS | EMPLOYERS | ABOUT STUDENTJOBS | CONTACT |

STUDENT JOBS

SIGN UP
FAQ
LOGIN

Summer Special: Volunteer in South Africa

Students between the ages of 16 and 19 who would like to work abroad and help people who are less privileged than themselves should look no further. Our placement in Durban, South Africa, might make your next summer holidays the most memorable experience of your life. Staying with host families and working with volunteers from all over the world, you will help children at day care centres under the supervision of professional staff. Your jobs will include playing educational games with the children, helping to run a soup kitchen, cleaning and renovation work. Placements last two to four weeks and include food, accommodation and insurance, as well as the chance to enjoy Durban's stunning beaches.

National Park Volunteer

Banff National Park is the oldest National Park in Canada. International volunteers will get to know the park through their involvement with group activities and special park events, as well as their daily responsibilities. They will also act as park representatives and will often be in contact with visitors. Hiking the trails to observe, record and report their conditions and any wildlife sightings is another important aspect of the job. ■ All volunteers receive comprehensive training and introduction to the park. They work five eight-hour shifts per week, usually between Wednesdays and Sundays, as the weekends are the busiest times for us. We are looking for candidates with strong interpersonal skills and the ability to work in a team or independently. Ideal volunteers have good problem-solving skills, are willing to work hard and remain flexible and positive regardless of ever-changing project work, locations and unpredictable weather. Volunteers must be energetic and physically capable of hiking in mountain areas.

'Goal for Hope' Volunteer

Goal for Hope is a holiday project with a group of international volunteers in the form of a football tournament in various towns in Cameroon. Volunteers will help organize the tournament and take part in training programs in subjects such as IT. As well as courses and matches, volunteers will inform local players about the problems of HIV/Aids, drugs and malaria.
We are seeking highly motivated volunteers who are very enthusiastic about sport, especially football, to take part in this extraordinary program. Excellent communication skills are required because volunteers will speak in public to educate football players and supporters about health issues and drug problems. In addition, volunteers should also be able to teach courses in subjects such as music, photography, IT, design and art. All in all, the project will cover four weeks and volunteers will be expected to work 30-40 hours a week, Monday to Friday.

5 Doing a good job

B4

Read the tips on how to write a good CV and covering letter.
Find words or phrases from the texts that mean the following:

1. a person who is offering a job
2. an adjective that means that you need to have something
3. to check a text for mistakes
4. information that the employer needs or probably would like to know
5. a part of a text, it can be separated from other parts of a text with an empty line
6. a person who has applied for a job
7. a position that a company is trying to hire someone for

How to write a good CV
A well-written CV allows you to show the employer that you have the necessary skills to do the job.
It is important that you make your CV stand out from the rest in order to be invited for an interview.
- Your CV must be easy to read, with good spelling and grammar. Have it proofread by someone who is good at editing.
- Keep your CV short – no longer than two sides of A4.
- Be honest and include as much relevant information as possible, but don't get lost in detail.
- Organize your CV clearly with headings for each section.
- If a portrait photo is required, have it taken by a professional photographer.

How to write a good covering letter
This letter is your chance to introduce yourself to your potential employers. It lets them find out a little bit more about who you are, what you have done so far and why you are the perfect candidate for the job. Your letter should …
- be precise with 3-4 paragraphs on one side of A4,
- explain why you are writing the letter,
- explain why the job interests you,
- explain why you are the right candidate for the job by describing any relevant skills that you have gained from jobs, education, training or hobbies,
- use formal language and no short forms (e.g. "I would" instead of "I'd"),
- include your full name, address, phone number and email address,
- use a clear font to make it look professional and easy to read,
- finish with "I look forward to hearing from you" or "I would be happy to discuss any vacancies with you at your earliest convenience" so that the person reading your letter feels encouraged to contact you,
- end with "Yours faithfully" (if your letter is addressed "Dear Sir or Madam") or with "Yours sincerely" (if you have used the person's name at the beginning).

B5 Grammar card: *let, make* and *have something done*   ● P10   📖 WB B4, p. 81

In the tips you can find various sentences which would include the verb *lassen* if translated into German (e.g. "It is important that you make your CV stand out …"
→ Es ist wichtig, dass du deinen Lebenslauf hervorstechen lässt …).
Find more examples and note them down.
Explain when you can use *let*, when *make*, and when you use *have something done*.
Check LiF 16 on page 182 for help.

Doing a good job 5

B6 • P6

Tim Schäfer has applied for the volunteering project *Goal for Hope*. Read his covering letter and describe your first impression of Tim as an applicant.

• Reading, p. 136

Support

What makes him a good candidate/only an average candidate is … •
He seems/doesn't seem to be well-suited to the project, as he … •
Although he may …, he lacks … •
I (don't) think he will attract the organization's attention because … •
The representatives of the foundation will probably approve of …, but might have a problem with …

Jahnplatz 27
33602 Bielefeld
Germany

Goal for Hope
23 Charlotte Road
London EC2A 3PB
United Kingdom

16 April 2016

Dear Sir or Madam,

I would like to apply for a position as a volunteer in your 'Goal for Hope' team in Cameroon, as advertised on your organization's website. I enclose my CV.

As you will see from my CV, I am currently in my last year at school and I'm quite optimistic that I will have passed my Abitur exam (equivalent of A levels) by the end of June.
Although my English is alright after twelve years, I would like to improve it even further and also practise my French. Since English and French are the two official languages of Cameroon, I'm sure that taking part in the 'Goal for Hope' project would offer a wide variety of opportunities to put my language skills to good use.
Football has been my favourite sport for as long as I can remember and I've been a member of my local football club for ten years. As I have been coaching a team of 8-year-olds in my local football club for the past year, I've already gained some insight into the demands of working as a coach.
In addition, I'm also the head of the graduation ball committee, which means that I'm used to organizing big events and coordinating different duties and co-workers.
Furthermore, I can work well under pressure and I enjoy the challenge of meeting new guys and adapting to new situations. I believe these skills and my work experience would provide an excellent basis for being a member of your team.
I will follow up my application with a phone call within the next week to make sure you have received everything and to find out if you'll give me the job.
I look forward to hearing from you.

Yours faithfully,
Tim Schäfer

5 Doing a good job

B7

a) Look at Tim Schäfer's covering letter on page 111 again and check if it …
- follows the tips from B4,
- covers all the points mentioned in the job advert in B3,
- mentions both hard and soft skills.

Goal for Hope
23 Charlotte Road
London EC2A 3PB
UNITED KINGDOM

b) Read the covering letter again and decide …
- what Tim did well in his covering letter,
- what he should improve (e.g. add information, improve language, …),
- whether you find his covering letter convincing enough to invite him for a job interview.

Work with a partner. Compare your findings and then discuss the results in class.   ● *Speaking, p. 134*

c) Go through the letter again and note down phrases you could use for your own covering letter.

B8 Target task   ✦   ✂ Project   📄 Portfolio   📖 WB B5, p. 82   🎯 Need help? Look at pp. 117/118.

Write an application for one of the jobs on either page 107 or page 109.
Choose either your favourite job or the one you found out you were best suited to in B3.

1 Write a CV. Follow the tips in B4 and on the skills page.
   ● *Writing, p. 147*   ● *Wordbank Jobs, p. 187*

2 Write a covering letter. Make sure you follow the tips in B4 and on the skills page.
   Use some of the phrases you collected in B7c).
   ● *Writing, p. 146*   ● *Wordbank Jobs, p. 187*

3 Peer editing: Swap your CV and covering letter with a partner. Check them for …

- content:
  - does it include all the relevant information?
  - does it refer to all the requirements of the job advert?

- language:
  - spelling
  - grammar
  - choice of words

Give tips on how to improve your partner's application, then improve your own.
   ● *Writing, p. 143, Proofreading, p. 150*

4 Type up your covering letter and make it anonymous (no name, no address).
- Collect all the covering letters in class and put them into piles – one for each job.
- Group work: Form one group for each job. Look at all the applications and choose the two that you consider best for the job. Give reasons for your choice.

Support

That covering letter is not as well-structured/well-written/convincing as this one. •
I think the applicant should have included some more information about … •
In this letter the candidate comes across as very reliable/enthusiastic/mature. •
This covering letter gives/offers an excellent explanation of …

Making a difference

C1

a) 👥 Work with a partner. Look at these slogans and talk about possible causes which they might be used for. ● *Speaking, p. 135*

> Make a difference   Right the wrongs   Get involved   Stand up for your rights

b) Milling around: Think about a cause that you personally care about. Walk around the classroom and talk to your classmates in order to find people with similar ideas.
● *Milling around, p. 153*

c) 👥 Group work (4-6): Form a group with classmates who have similar ideas and agree on a common cause. Give your cause a name and collect ideas about what you could do to take action.

C2 👥 📖 *WB C1, p. 83*

a) Work in your group from C1c) and study the leaflet of the *Goal for Hope* foundation where Tim Schäfer has applied for a job (see page 111). Collect words and phrases that are used to encourage people to join their cause.

Example: *Become a member of our group …*

b) Study the leaflet again and say what other means the foundation uses to make people join their cause. Consider layout and rhetorical devices.
● *Rhetorical devices, p. 138*

c) Design your own leaflet to encourage people to join your group's cause (see C1c). Use your results from a) and b) and some of the words and phrases below.

> to show commitment to … •
> to do voluntary work •
> to campaign for/against … •
> to volunteer to … •
> to fight for/against … •

d) Gallery walk: Present your leaflets in class. Decide …
- which leaflets you find most attractive,
- which causes or projects you would like to join.
Give reasons for your choice.
● *Gallery walk, p. 153*

Goal for Hope

Do you love football? Do you want to make a real difference? Then get involved! Become a member of our group of international volunteers in Cameroon. Join our campaign now!

As one of our volunteers you will …
- meet and get in touch with local young people,
- organize and take part in the football tournament,
- coordinate training programmes,
- inform local football players about the problems of HIV/AIDS, drugs and malaria.

If you want to fight for a good cause, become a volunteer in this extraordinary programme that will also provide you with many amazing experiences. If you love communicating with people and are good at speaking in public, this is the right cause for you. If you can teach courses in music, photography, computing, design, or arts and culture, you are an ideal volunteer.

Goal for Hope – committed to helping young people by offering training opportunities that they can use in daily life and in future jobs.

5 Making a difference

C3 Viewing: Preparing for an interview

Goal for Hope has invited Tim Schäfer for an interview, which he now has to prepare for.

a) Watch the video by career expert Cara Hall on how to prepare for an interview. Divide the class into two groups:
- group 1 notes down the advice for the categories in the yellow boxes,
- group 2 notes down the advice for the categories in the green boxes.

Cara Hall – Career expert

Yellow boxes	Green boxes
Put the interview into perspective	Be clear
Give examples	Never assume
Prepare at least three questions	Listen
Don't talk too much	Do your research

b) Group work (4):
- Form a mixed group with two experts on the yellow categories and two experts on the green categories from the list in a).
- Present your notes to each other and complete your lists of tips.

c) In your group talk about which advice you consider particularly relevant for Tim Schäfer and his job interview and which you see as less important for this job.

C4 S 8, L 2/5 • Listening, p. 130 WB C2, p. 83, C3, p. 84

a) Listen to Tim Schäfer's job interview. Use your notes from C3 as a checklist and note down how well Tim follows each of the tips.

b) Think – pair – share: Discuss and decide whether you would give Tim Schäfer the job.
• Think – pair – share, p. 153

c) Give advice to Tim on what he could/should do differently next time. • LiF 8R: Modal verbs, p. 173

d) Listen to the interview again and note down useful phrases for the roles of the interviewer and applicant.

interviewer	job applicant
…	…

Checklist:
✓ …
✓ …
✓ …
✓ …
✓ …

5 Making a difference

C5 Target task ❖ ✂ Project 📖 WB C4, p. 84, C5, p. 85 🎯 *Need help? Look at pp. 119/120.*

You have sent an application to the organization that appealed to you most in C2d) and they have invited you for a job interview. Prepare for the interview and then act it out:

1 Prepare for your role as an applicant:
- Carefully study your classmates' leaflet and find out what the job requires and which qualifications (hard and soft skills) you have for that job.
- Study the employer's and the applicant's role cards. Note down what you are going to say and ask in the interview as the applicant.
- Make sure you bear in mind the tips from C3. ● *P8, P9*

Employer:
- welcome the applicant
- tell the applicant why you invited him/her for the interview
- ask the applicant what he/she can tell you about his/her background etc

What three things are most important to you in a job?
How would you work under pressure?
Do you like working in a team or do you prefer working on your own? Why is that?
In what ways do you think you'll contribute to our company?
What qualifications would make you successful in this job?
What are your general interests and hobbies?

Applicant:
- talk about your knowledge of English and other languages
- ask questions about the kind of work you would be doing, when you are supposed to start working, working hours etc
- thank the employer for his/her time and interest in you

I'm good at …
I will be leaving school in …
The position you're offering is just what I'm looking for.
I enjoy working with …
I would be happy to work for your company and look forward to hearing from you.

2 Prepare for your role as an employer:
👥 Work with a partner. Study your partner's job advertisement as well as the employer's role card and think of additional questions to ask him/her in the interview. Consider …
- what kind of person you want according to the job advertisement,
- which qualifications (hard and soft skills) you are looking for,
- how you want to find out whether the applicant is the right person for the job (e.g. which questions you would like to ask, how you could try to test the candidate's nerves, how you could surprise him/her with an unexpected question). ● *P8, P9*

3 Act out the job interviews:
👥 Group work (4): Find another pair and take turns acting out your job interviews.
- Pair 1: Act out both of your job interviews. Use your notes from **1** and **2**.
  Pair 2: Observe pair 1 and take notes. After each interview give feedback on how convincing the applicant and employer were in their roles. Tell the applicant whether you would give him/her the job and give advice on what he/she could do better next time.
- After pair 1 has acted out both interviews, pair 2 acts out their interviews and pair 1 observes.
  ● *Speaking, p. 133* ● *P7*

A | B | C | Personal Trainer | Intercultural photo page | Optional • Skills • LiF • Words

5 Personal Trainer

Prepare your target task A4:

P1 Words: jobs

Copy and complete the sentences below by filling in the most suitable word or phrase from the list.

> improve your time management skills • complete a task • develop • gain a new perspective on • offer a unique opportunity • learn and build essential skills • gain experience • develop emotionally

1. Team sports help young people to ??? as well as physically.

2. The ability to ??? on time and meet all customer requirements is essential for many jobs.

3. The 'Internationaler Freiwilligenservice' believes that the exchange experience helps young people to ??? their understanding of other cultures.

4. By working for the 'Internationaler Freiwilligenservice', young people can ??? and learn new skills without feeling like they are in school.

5. Being part of this organization is a great opportunity to get to know another country, to ??? your own country and to improve your language abilities.

6. The European Union in Brussels is ready to ??? to anyone interested in a career in politics or diplomacy in the form of its internship programme.

7. Experiencing daily working life is a good way to ??? and to discover what kind of work you enjoy.

8. Being part of a large organization, even for a short amount of time, will enable young people to ??? for their future careers.

P2 Revision: comparison of adjectives ● LiF 10R: Comparison, p. 175

Copy the grid and fill it in.

adjective	comparative	superlative
bad	worse	worst
disgusting	...	...
revolting	...	...
embarrassing	...	...
tedious	...	...
hard	...	...
nasty	...	...
horrible	...	...
smelly	...	...
enormous	...	...
dull	...	...

Prepare your target task B8:

P3 Words: applying for a job

a) Match the verbs on the left to the phrases on the right.

1	to decide	A	a letter of recommendation
2	to practise for	B	your reports and certificates
3	to put together	C	a covering letter
4	to photocopy	D	job adverts online and in newspapers
5	to choose	E	your strengths and weaknesses
6	to become aware of	F	what kinds of jobs you are interested in
7	to ask for	G	an application
8	to look at	H	the company where you want to apply for a job
9	to contact	I	a job interview
10	to write	J	a suitable outfit for a job interview

b) Use these phrases to write tips for a successful application process.

Step 1: …
Step 2: …
…

P4 Words: soft skills

a) Decide which of the following are soft skills.

> punctual • familiar with database software • reliable • good manners • confident •
> able to speak Spanish • familiar with telephone systems • able to cope well with stress •
> good at teamwork • tolerant • fond of travelling • detailed knowledge of modern literature •
> ambitious • flexible • able to play the piano • good at logical thinking • diligent

b) Match the following examples/situations/activities to the soft skill they illustrate. Add more examples yourself.

Example: *confident – no problem speaking in front of a lot of people and expressing your opinion as a leading member of the student council*

A no problem speaking in front of a lot of people and expressing your opinion as a leading member of the student council
B taking part in a school exchange with a US high school
C always attending lessons, apart from rare cases of being ill
D being sent to special maths and science events by your school
E taking evening classes in Italian
F helping out in your family's business by proofreading letters and emails

c) Work with a partner. Compare your solutions and explain your choices.

5 Personal Trainer

P5 **Words: What do you need for a summer job?**

a) Name the part-time jobs/summer jobs you can see in the photos.

> shop assistant • office help • lifeguard • gardener • tutor • tour guide • babysitter • waiter/waitress • receptionist • pizza delivery boy/girl • cleaner

b) Look at the list of adjectives in B3 again. For each job, choose three qualities that the ideal candidate should have. Explain your decision.

Example: *A pizza delivery boy should definitely be friendly because he has to communicate directly with customers. I think he also needs to be honest, as he collects money from customers. And finally, he ought to be punctual as customers will not want to wait for their pizzas for too long.*

1
2
3
4
5
6

P6 **Writing: register – covering letter** • *Varying expression, p. 159*

a) It is important to use the right register in a covering letter, namely, formal English. Identify the phrases that are not formal English or that would be inappropriate for an application.

> *I am looking forward to hearing from you … • Oh, and I've also added my references. • My classmates describe me as … • As your company enjoys an excellent reputation, … • I would love to gain experience by working with you. • Don't worry, I'm never stressed out. • I can't work Sundays, hope that's OK! • I honestly want that job so that I can learn something about looking after kids. • One of my strengths is my ability to … • Please write back soon! • It would be fantastic if you invited me for an interview. • I would be very grateful if you … • As described in the job advertisement, … • It sounds like a fun job. • I'm a little maths genius. • The guys at school say I'm always on time. • Please find my CV enclosed. • I am available to work during the summer, except for a two-week holiday. • Your company seems really cool and good for summer camps. • Having studied Spanish for four years, I am able to speak the language quite fluently.*

b) Look at the informal phrases again. Write down formal/neutral expressions that have the same meaning. Use the formal phrases above as a guide. • *Wordbank Jobs, p. 187*

Example: *I'm a little maths genius. → Having studied maths for three years, I am very good with figures.*

Prepare your target task C5:

P7 Speaking: giving advice • *LiF 8R: Modals verbs, p. 173, 12R b: Conditional clauses, type 2, p. 177*

Study the different constructions you can use to give advice.
Work with a partner. Using the phrases below, give advice about whether or not …

- to buy a new mobile phone,
- to skip school,
- to apply for a summer job,
- to go to the party at the weekend.

Should
This is probably the most common of the structures for giving advice.
You should dress up.
We shouldn't cheat.

It is common to use "I think …" and "I don't think …" with *should*:
I think you should put the answers back.
She doesn't think they should use them.

If I were you
This version of the second conditional is often used to give advice, especially in spoken English.
Note the use of *were* with *I* in the first clause.
In the second clause, we use *would* – contracted to *'d* – and *wouldn't*.
If I were you, I'd give them back to the teacher.
If I were you, I wouldn't use the answers.

Had better
This structure is common in spoken English and it is mainly used in the contracted form:
You'd better return the answers to the teacher.
You'd better not tell anyone that you stole them.

Ought to
This is the most formal of the structures used for giving advice, and so it isn't very common.
You ought to contact the police.
You ought not to cheat in exams.

P8 Speaking: register – job interview

Read the statements below. Explain which ones would be appropriate to use as an applicant in a job interview.

A Good afternoon. The train was late – again! I hope I will be on time on my first day here. Just joking. Thanks for inviting me.

B As I wrote in my covering letter, I'm going to take my final exams next year and would like to make up my mind about what to do after school. There are different university courses and career options that seem attractive to me and in order to get a better idea of what might really interest me, I decided to apply for an internship at your company.

C Good afternoon. Thanks, some water would be great. No, I didn't have any problems on the way here. Thank you very much again for inviting me to this interview.

D I have said it all in my covering letter. However, one point that I did not mention is that a friend of mine, Sarah Holden, did an internship here two years ago. She recommended your company and said that you make sure your interns really benefit from their work experience.

5 Personal Trainer

P9 **Reading**

In a magazine for students and young job seekers you come across a test on the most common questions asked in job interviews. Take the test and decide which of the possible answers the interviewer would find best.

QUIZ — Going to an interview — Work

1 "How would you describe yourself?"
   a) You give a detailed overview of your life so far.
   b) You give the interviewer an idea of who you are as a person.
   c) You tell the interviewer briefly about some of your experiences and achievements that are relevant to the job.

2 "What are your strengths?"
   a) You mention a lot of different qualities to show how good you are in many different areas.
   b) You concentrate on strengths specifically relevant to the job and back this up with examples.
   c) You state your strengths briefly and to the point.

3 "What are your weaknesses?" Choose the worst answer here.
   a) You mention weaknesses that can be interpreted positively, e.g. "I can be quite impatient and sometimes I work so hard that I forget about everything else around me."
   b) You mention a weakness that you have managed to overcome, e.g. "I used to have problems with spelling when I was younger, but I worked hard to overcome this, although I still keep a dictionary at hand to check if necessary."
   c) You say, "I don't have any weaknesses."

4 "Why should we give the job to you?"
   a) You emphasize the strengths you have (education, abilities etc) that might make you stand out from the rest.
   b) You are modest. Nobody likes someone who is too self-confident.
   c) You emphasize the strengths you have (education, abilities etc) that might help you make the company more successful, profit from your work etc.

5 "Have you ever had a serious conflict with an employer/teacher/professor?"
   a) You say that you have never had any conflicts with superiors.
   b) You mention a conflict, but it should be over something insignificant and you should not blame your superior.
   c) You mention a conflict, but make it clear that it was not your fault, but the teacher's/employer's/…

Personal Trainer 5

Extra language training:

P10 **Let, make, have sth done** for German 'lassen' • LiF 16: English equivalents for 'lassen', p. 182

The following photos show what Gemma did last week.
Use the verbs *let*, *make* and *have sth done* (German: 'lassen') to describe what she did.
Often there is more than one solution.

Example: *1. Gemma's mother made her clean her room.*

1. clean room
2. cut hair 
3. dry-clean dress 
4. repair bike 
5. use computer to look for jobs 
6. proofread CV 

Extra skills training:

P11 Mediation ( )

Larissa Müller is doing an internship at PQTB, an international bank in Frankfurt. One of her jobs is to answer telephone calls for members of staff, in this case Thomas Johansson, a Swedish bank clerk who has recently moved to Frankfurt and cannot speak much German.
Use Larissa's notes to tell him in English what the caller said.
• Mediation, p. 151

Telefonnotiz
Für: Thomas Johansson

Anruf von: Tobias Göllner
Bankhaus Linde, Berlin

Tel.: 030-31672899-44
E-Mail: t.goellner@bh-linde.de
Datum: 24. Juli 2016
Uhrzeit: 15.47 Uhr

Bitte Rückruf/Fax/Ruft selbst zurück
Ruft morgen selbst zurück oder freut sich über Rückruf

Betreff:
– Terminfindung für ein Treffen zur Besprechung der Kooperation beider Banken
– Einladung zur 150-Jahr-Feier des Bankhauses in Berlin (zwei Karten für Festveranstaltung mit Musik und Tanz)
– Würde gern über die Vor- und Nachteile von Geschäften mit chinesischen Banken sprechen
– Hat eine große Firma als Kunden, die für einen Teil ihres internationalen Geschäfts gern mit der PQTB zusammenarbeiten würde

A | B | C | **Personal Trainer** | Intercultural photo page | Optional • Skills • LiF • Words

5 Intercultural photo page

The world of work

1

1. Look at the photos and note down the jobs you can identify.
2. Decide which of the jobs you would be interested in and give reasons.

2

a) Read the text below and match the photos to information from the text.

b) Make a word web about the world of work using words and phrases from the text.

fields of work, qualifications, WORLD OF WORK, workplace, working conditions, globalization

c) Use the words and phrases you have collected to write a caption for each of the photos.
   • Wordbank Jobs, p. 187

Around the world people work in thousands of different industries and under very different working conditions. People have jobs in agriculture, in manufacturing, in services, in the
5 arts and in IT.
In the digital age, computers have transformed the workplace. Fewer workers are needed and, with the speed of computer communication, work has sometimes become more stressful. On
10 the other hand, work is no longer confined to an office or workshop; laptops and tablets allow people, especially in creative jobs, to work from home, or from any other place that might inspire them.
15 The workforce itself is also very varied and is made up of unskilled workers, skilled workers and academics. Unskilled workers haven't had any professional training, whereas skilled workers have learnt a craft and are qualified to
20 provide a variety of services. Academics will have studied at university to obtain higher professional qualifications.
With growing competition around the world, companies try to organize work as efficiently
25 and as cheaply as possible. Outsourcing factory work to low-wage countries means higher profits, as workers are paid less money. But cheap labour is not the only reason to move production abroad. Health and safety regulations
30 are often ignored, meaning that employees have to work long hours and under bad conditions, with poor lighting and no ventilation.
In developing coutries, even children are made to work to support their family. Child labour is a
35 huge problem, as working children cannot attend school and so have no chance to leave poverty behind.
Workers frequently leave home to work in another country, where they hope to earn more money.
40 These migrant workers help harvest the fields, take care of elderly people or work in the building industry, especially on huge building sites. Often they are exploited, as without a work permit they cannot protest against inhumane working
45 conditions or unpaid wages.
With global competition, it is important to give up the idea of typically male or female jobs. In several countries, 'Girls' Day' has been introduced to motivate girls to begin a career in engineering,
50 science and research. New job opportunities offer the chance to use your skills and talents, and companies are interested in giving young people an insight into their future job by offering work experience or internships.

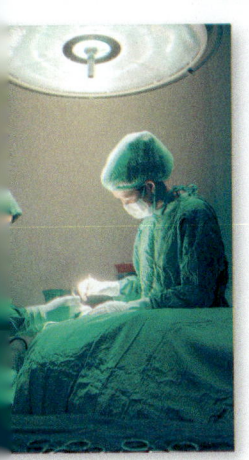

3 🎧 S 9, L 2/6

a) Listen to a radio programme about young migrants working in the UK.
Note down the advantages and disadvantages the speakers mention in a T-chart.   • Listening, p. 130

b) 👥 Work with a partner. Discuss what you found most interesting about working in the UK.

c) ❖ Choose a job that you would like to do and research it. Think of the necessary qualifications, working hours, responsibilities, creative or technical abilities needed etc and write a job profile.

Choose: Give a one-minute presentation to advertise your job at a job fair.   • Speaking, p. 132

Or: Present the job profile as a poster.   • Writing, p. 142

5 Optional

Anya Reiss: Forty-Five Minutes

O1

a) Think of situations that put you under pressure, e.g. a tight deadline you had to meet, or a train you had difficulty catching.
- How did you feel?
- How did you react to the pressure?

👥 Work with a partner. Compare what you experienced and how you reacted to the situation.

● *Wordbank Feelings, p. 186*

b) 1 Before you read the first extract of Anya Reiss' play *Forty-Five Minutes*, make sure you are familiar with the meaning of the following terms relating to the British education system. Use a dictionary or research them online if necessary.

2 Read the first extract and outline the problem that puts the protagonists under pressure.

| A level • grades A-E • sixth form • Year 10 • GCSE • UCAS |

c) Describe the atmosphere.
- Find words, quotations or passages in the extract that reflect the atmosphere.
- Discuss how you could create that atmosphere on stage with props, stage design or other effects (e.g. music, lighting).

d) Imagine you had to meet a deadline at school – e.g. to hand in project work, an essay, or a report – but you couldn't finish it in time. Invent plausible and convincing explanations or excuses as to why you couldn't possibly have met the deadline.
Milling around: Exchange your ideas with your classmates.

● *Milling around, p. 153*

Characters
Nathan, sixth form
Darrel, sixth form
Alex, sixth form
Georgie, sixth form
Trent, sixth form
Lara, sixth form
Louise, year ten

Setting
The school's computer room

Nathan and **Darrel** *are sitting together at two computers,* **Alex** *separately on another.*

Nathan	Read it out then.
Darrel	All of it?
5 **Nathan**	No the key points bit
Alex	Can you please shut up?
Nathan	It'll help you too
Alex	I know what it says
Darrel	Why can't you just read it to yourself?
Nathan	Read it out loud
Alex	Don't Darrel
Nathan	Ignore her
Alex	Oh fuck you
Nathan	Read it out Darrel
Darrel	'Explain why you want to study the course you are applying for. If you mention your personal interests and hobbies, try to link them to the skills and experiences required for the course.'
Alex	Oh 'cause you didn't know that?
Nathan	Shut up. Go on
Darrel	'The personal statement could be used as the basis for an interview, so be prepared to answer questions on it. This may be your only written work that the course tutor sees before making a decision …'

Nathan	Fuck		**Nathan**	You're Sixth Form
Darrel	'Make sure it is organized and literate.'		**Alex**	They don't listen, the new kids
Alex	Oh what a surprise		**Nathan**	Course they will
Nathan	What is the matter with you?		**Darrel**	Nah it's true Nath' this lot just don't give a fuck
Alex	You're talking		**Nathan**	Get Miss Barrett to chuck them off then
Nathan	About the form, we're talking about the form		**Alex**	I don't have time to go to the library, we've got forty-five minutes!
Darrel	'Get the grammar, spelling and punctuation right.'		**Darrel**	I swear it was next week
Alex	Oh my God		**Nathan**	Darrel, if you say it again, if you say that again …
Darrel	That is a stupid thing to put up there		**Darrel**	I told you, I'm sorry. I thought it was next week, I thought it was midnight next week!
Nathan	What?			
Darrel	That is a stupid thing to put up there, you're not going to try and get it wrong are you?		**Alex**	Oh my God please just be quiet
Nathan	You got to do it on a computer anyway Darrel		**Nathan**	Go to the library!
Darrel	So?		**Alex**	It's too loud in the library
Nathan	So obviously you're gonna get spelling and everything right		**Darrel**	What?
			Alex	Miss Barrett's always shouting at everyone to shut up, she's more annoying than you
Darrel	Not all words are on a computer		**Nathan**	If you care so much, why did you leave it till now?
Nathan	Yeah well not like swearing and names and stuff			
Darrel	They have swearing		**Alex**	Because I've been off sick!
Nathan	No they don't		[…]	
Darrel	Yeah they do		*Georgie, Lara and Trent come in. Lara's in tears,*	
Nathan	No they don't, the red line comes up		*Georgie slams down at a computer and turns it on.*	
Darrel	No, they have it in the dictionary, they just don't offer it to you on spell-check suggestions		[…]	
			Georgie	I thought the deadline was next week, she said she said didn't she, Lara?
Nathan	No they don't		**Lara**	She said
Darrel	Look, I'll show you		**Darrel**	I knew it! I told you it wasn't my fault
Alex	We have forty-five minutes and you are doing that?		**Nathan**	What? He did say the deadline was next week then?
Nathan	Why do you care? Just do your UCAS		**Georgie**	They all said it was for next week, all of them, they said we should give it in at the end of this week and school would check them first then it was deadline next week
Alex	I'm doing my UCAS			
Darrel	*(about the computer)* Look, well they don't have 'shite' but they have everything else, see?		**Darrel**	She told me I got it wrong and screamed at me for telling Nathan the wrong thing
Nathan	Someone must have added them		**Nathan**	And screamed at me for not checking
[…]			**Darrel**	The bitch
Alex	Can you shut up!		**Georgie**	I know she is such a bitch
Nathan	Go to the library if we're annoying you		**Trent**	Yeah alright guys, alright but we still got forty-five minutes whoever's fault it is, we've all got to do it
Alex	It'll be full by now			

5 Optional

	Nathan	I thought you guys weren't in today
	Trent	We were late for class, she said she'd let you lot off to do it too
	Darrel	Lara sit down and do the thing don't just stand there crying
120		
	Lara	There's no point
	Alex	You can't miss the deadline Lara
	[...]	
	Darrel	Lara fucking open your UCAS
125	Lara	There's no point! They read my statement said it was terrible, said I did it all wrong and Miss Hall would do it with me next week!
	Alex	You haven't finished your statement!
130	Nathan	Yeah nor have me or Darrel
	Trent	Mine's still fucked up
	Alex	How can you not have done them!
	Nathan	I got some bullet points
	Alex	Oh my God
135	Nathan	If you've done it, why are you here?

	Alex	To finish the form I hadn't put my results in and stuff. I'd done my statement!
	Nathan	They don't care really about statements, they know the teachers have done them
140	Lara	They haven't done mine!
	Georgie	In Cambridge they throw them in the bin
	Alex	Yeah well lucky I'm not trying for Cambridge then isn't it?
	Darrel	Why didn't you fill in your results and stuff before, that's the easy bit
145	Alex	Don't have internet at home
	Nathan	What?
	Darrel	What?
	Trent	You don't have internet at home!?
	Georgie	What the hell Alex? How do you do your homework?
150		
	Alex	Er I dunno like every person before the millennium
	Trent	(seeing she still hasn't started) Lara!

O2

a) Read the second extract on pages 126-128 and explain the dispute between Nathan and Lara.

b) Collect information about the different characters from the first and second extracts.
Choose quotations from or about the characters and write down how they can be interpreted in a grid. Explain what this reveals about the characters. Leave space to add more information later.
● Reading, p. 137

character	quotation	interpretation
Lara	"It's no good" (l. 155), "I can't do it" (l. 157), "But it's all wrong" (l. 164)	is insecure, not very confident
	"What! What why can't I say 'always'? What the hell, why can't I say 'always'?" (ll. 231/232)	gets upset quickly when things don't go her way
	...	...

155	Lara	It's no good
	Trent	Be fine just stop crying and do it
	Lara	I can't do it
	Georgie	Alex why don't you help Lara?
	Nathan	She's helping me!
160	Trent	Yeah but she's crying man
	Nathan	You want me to cry? I'll fucking cry if you want me to mate at least she's done hers, she's got words on a screen

	Lara	But it's all wrong she said it was all wrong
	Alex	I bet it's not
	Lara	No it's all wrong I didn't even get the pack I only just borrowed Beth's now
	Georgie	Her 'pack'?
	Lara	All the stuff with what you're not allowed to say, Miss Hall said I'd done everything you weren't supposed to
	Darrel	Then shut up and change it

Lara	I can't! I don't know any words	
Darrel	Well I haven't done mine either	
Lara	Georgie?	175
Georgie	I can't help you babe I'm shit with words as well	
Lara looks to **Trent**.		
Trent	No I'm doing my statement too	
Lara	Please	180
Trent	I'm applying for Sports Science I can't help you	
Darrel	Fuck off you are	
Trent	Yeah	
Darrel	Why you doing that?	185
Trent	Because I want to be a Scientist of Sport	
Darrel	What?	
Trent	I want to be a sports teacher	
Darrel	Why?	
Trent	What are you doing?	190
Darrel	Management and Leisure … what? What?	
Trent	Nothing man. You knock yourself out folding bed sheets	
Darrel	It's not like that	
Lara	Alex please	195
Nathan	She's helping me!	
Lara	But she's the only one any good at English	
Nathan	She is helping me for fuck's sake. She is helping me!	
Lara	But like okay Alex, just tell me another word for 'and' okay?	200
Alex	What?	
Nathan	She is helping me! I got like eighty words okay.	
Lara	Another word for 'and'?	205
Alex	'Also'	
Lara	I've used that	
Alex	'In addition to'	
Lara	I used that like fifty times	
Alex	Oh um …	210
Louise	'Furthermore'	
Lara	What?	
Louise	'Furthermore'	
Georgie	I thought you weren't going to speak	
Lara	[…]	215
Louise	Fine okay I won't help	
Lara	No please how do I say 'I've always had a passion for France and the language has always fascinated me'?	
Georgie	Why you talking about France?	220
Lara	For background interest stuff	
Louise	What's wrong with that?	
Lara	Wrong with what?	
Louise	What you just said	
Lara	I'm not allowed to use the word 'passion' or 'fascinate'	225
Trent	Or 'always'	
Lara	What!	
Trent	You're not allowed to say 'always' look at the list	230
Lara	What! What why can't I say 'always'? What the hell, why can't I say 'always'?	
Darrel	Can you shut up Lara! Use the thesaurus on the computer	
Lara	But why can't I say it?	235
Darrel	Just look it up man	
Alex is typing for **Nathan** by now and they have swapped seats.		
Nathan	That's really good	
Lara	See Alex why won't you help me!	240
Nathan	Lara look it up on the computer	
Lara	But I don't see why I can't say 'always'. What's wrong with 'always'?	
Nathan comes over to her computer and leans over using it. **Lara** is looking at the list.		245
Lara	And 'mistake'! I'm not allowed to say 'mistake' or 'hate' or 'nothing'! What the hell! What the hell! Why can't I say the word 'nothing'? What is wrong with the word 'nothing'?	250
She puts her head on her desk.		
Nathan (reading from the computer) 'For ever, for all time, for eternity, for the end of time' …		
Trent	What you saying?	
Nathan	Other words for 'always'. Lara. Lara	255
Lara	What?	
Nathan	Here are other words for always: 'for ever, for all time, for eternity, for the end of time' …	
Lara	I can't use them	260
Nathan	Why not?	
Lara	'I've for eternity had a passion for France and the language has for the end of time fascinated me'	
Nathan	Alright fine but I'm saying there's a thesaurus on the computer so stop trying to steal Alex	265
Lara	I'm not trying to steal her! I just need some help okay, she's writing yours for you! She's not allowed to do that	270

	Alex	I'm not writing it for him	**Nathan**	Like what?
	Nathan	What are you doing then?	**Alex**	Like your GCSE grades
	Alex	I'm writing some bits you got to put it together yourself	**Nathan**	I can't put them down
			Alex	You had to in the form
275	**Nathan**	Alex I don't have time for this, okay? You can't play jigsaw with it and test me	**Nathan**	Yeah but I'm not going to draw attention to them am I? They were all like Cs and Ds
	Alex	Yeah but I don't know everything about you. I can't put all the personal stuff in		

O3

a) Read the final extract and describe what happens. Discuss Lara's reasons for choosing accountancy.
 • Speaking, p. 134

b) Add more information about the characters to your grid from O2.

285	**Georgie**	You've not filled out your employment anyway		**Darrel**	No. I hate this shit it's none of their business where I've worked or if I have or haven't, makes no difference to whether I can do my course
	Darrel	What?			
	Georgie	On the form, you can't even send that			
	Darrel	Why do I have to put that down? Why do they care where I've worked? I'm going to study, not work there		**Trent**	Well if you'd worked in a hotel or something –
290				**Darrel**	Is that another crack about my course?
	Alex laughs, the others ignore.			**Trent**	No but I mean shows you want to do it, you know what I mean
	Trent	It's so they can see what kind of person you are		**Darrel**	No this is fucked! This is just like when you're little and the teachers make you draw pictures of your family and describe your bedroom and shit, they're just nosy
295	**Darrel**	What?			
	Trent	Like hard working, 'done work experience' that kind of thing			
	Darrel	It's none of their business!		**Alex**	Darrel I don't think they read the UCAS like it's *Heat* Magazine
	Georgie	Get over it Darrel			
300	**Darrel**	Nah 'cause I'm a kid okay and they're already judging me on everything I've done. What they're not going to take me because I haven't worked at Pizza Hut or something?		[...]	
				Lara	What do you want to be?
				Alex	Journalist
				Nathan	Yeah so you got to get your English degree, please stop screwing around and help me
305	**Georgie**	It's not like that		**Alex**	No, but I don't need a degree
	Lara	I've never worked at Pizza Hut		**Nathan**	Then why did you apply?
	Alex	Oh God's sake shut up Lara and do your statement		**Alex**	Because my parents made me
				Darrel	Aw your parents made you
	Lara	I never worked anywhere except at my mum's salon		**Trent**	Alex shut up
310				**Alex**	Fine, okay do your work
	Darrel	Yeah well exactly		**Trent**	No I mean shut up about your parents made you and you don't want to go, you obviously do
	Lara	And she didn't pay me so that doesn't count			
	Nathan	You've worked Darrel		**Georgie**	Human resources officer, charity fundraiser, youth worker
315	**Darrel**	No. I'm not filling that bit out			
	Trent	Don't be stupid man		**Alex**	I don't

	Georgie	Probation officer		have really good employment graduate history for accountancy
50	Alex	But you know you want to be a sports coach?	Alex	And that's why you picked it!
	Trent	Yeah	Lara	Yeah
	Alex	Exactly and you have to go to uni, you're fine it makes sense for you	Alex	But you don't want to be an accountant?
			Lara	I dunno, maybe
55	Georgie	Like loads of options	Louise	And you are writing about France in your statement?
	Alex	Like Trent you're fine		
	Lara	I don't know what I want to be	Nathan	I know what I want to do Alex, does that mean you'll write my fucking statement please?
	Alex	That's probably why your personal statement is bad		
60	Georgie	What? Of course you know what you want to be	Alex	What do you want to do?
			Nathan	Get into uni!
	Lara	No	Alex	Oh my God
	Georgie	Then why the hell are you applying for accountancy if you don't want to be an accountant?	Nathan *pushes her out of the way and starts on the computer himself.*	
65			Alex	Why did you apply?
	Darrel	You're applying for accountancy!	Lara	I dunno, everyone else was
	Lara	Because I told Ted I want to make a lot of money and he said 'cause I got an A for maths I could take it for A level and then when I saw him again he said universities	Trent	Right, done
			Georgie	Really?
			Trent	Whatever. Can't concentrate with all this, I'm going to send it
70				

Line numbers: 375, 380, 385, 390

O4

a) 👥 Group work: Choose one of the scenes and prepare a dramatic reading or a freeze frame. Make clear how the different characters react to the crisis.
   ● *Dramatic reading, p. 154, Freeze frame, p. 154*

Support
Use your grid from O2 to help you decide how to present a character.

b) Perform your reading/your freeze frame to another group and ask for feedback.
   ● *Speaking, p. 133*

c) Put the different scenes together and perform them in class.

After this Theme you can …
✓ collect information about student jobs from a website
✓ listen to a podcast and note down specific advice on how to apply for a job
✓ read a website with job adverts and note down the hard and soft skills required for a job
✓ use the verbs *let*, *make* and *have* for the German word 'lassen'
✓ talk about how well-suited an applicant is to a job
✓ write an application, including a CV and a covering letter
✓ design a leaflet
✓ watch a video and note down advice on how to prepare for a job interview
✓ prepare for and act out a job interview

📖 *WB Portfolio-Fragebogen Theme 5*

Skills

Listening

1 Before listening: prepare yourself

To prepare yourself for a listening task think about the following aspects:
- **Task:** Have you understood the task? What have you been asked to find out?
- **Topic:** What could the topic of the listening text be? What do you already know about it? Think about the context of what you are talking about in class – for example, consider photos that go with the task etc.
- **Type of text:** What type of text is it? A song, an interview, a dialogue, …?
- **Expectations:** What do you expect to hear? Which keywords might come up?
- **Message:** Do you expect the text to have a message? What could it be?

speaker/language: female expert, therefore probably formal language, maybe with Northern Irish accent

B12
a) Listen to Margaret Tinsley, the human resources manager for a major company in Northern Ireland. Take notes on the dos and don'ts you should keep in mind when applying for a job.
b) Check your results with a partner.
Example: *Margaret Tinsley says that young people applying for a job shou…*

type of text: probably a short talk / presentation with advice

topic: job application (covering letter, CV, job interview)

task/expectations: tips on what to do and not to do in the context of applications (possibly ideas from the theme or other subjects; notes best taken in a grid)

2 While listening: know what to listen for

Listening for gist:
- If you want to catch the main ideas (= the gist) of a text, listen out for **keywords**. They can also help you identify the different parts of the listening text.
- Pay attention to **background noise** if there is any – it suggests where people are.

Listening for detail:
There are many clues which can help you to understand a text better.
1 Very often, the **choice of words** can help you to guess how the text will go on.

Choice of words	might suggest
I'm afraid … • I'm sorry, but …	refusal
Excuse me, do you think you could … • Can you please …?	request
If I were you, I would … • Wouldn't it be better to …?	advice
I think your talk was a bit too … • It's a shame that …	criticism
I'm sorry about … • It's really sad that …	regret
… probably, … • Maybe it's because …	speculation
First, … but then … • On the one hand … On the other hand …	contrast

Study and communication skills **Listening**

2 To understand a text better, focus not only on the words but also on the way something is said. **Emphasis** and **intonation** provide clues as to what the text is about.

WHO told you about this party? (= The party was supposed to be kept secret, but it no longer is. So the question is: who couldn't keep his mouth shut?)

Who told YOU about this party? (= The person who arrives at the party is someone people did not expect at this party, maybe did not even want at that party.)

3 **Taking notes** while listening will give you a better understanding of what has been said. Use abbreviations and symbols to note down information quickly.

4 When you are listening to a song, it is not only the words but also the **melody** and the overall **atmosphere** of the song that can give you clues as to what the song is about.

3 After listening: check your findings

- After listening to the text and collecting information, look at your findings again and **complete your notes** if necessary.

- To check if you have collected all the important facts and have understood the main points, **compare your findings** with a partner's.

4 Dealing with difficulties

- There are many different accents, colloquial forms and slang words in English. Australian English sounds very different to Indian English. It is normal to take a while to get used to understanding people who speak these different forms of English.

- In real-life conversations or when working with films, you don't just listen to someone, but you usually see them as well. Therefore, you may use other – non-verbal – clues to understand this person better, for example his/her **body language** and **facial expressions**.

- When you are talking (and listening) to someone in real life, you cannot listen to what the person says again and again, which you can do with a CD. Therefore, **ask people to speak more slowly**, **to repeat** what they have said or **to use different words to explain** what they are saying.

5 Improving your listening skills

- You can listen to English-speaking radio shows and podcasts from all over the world on the Internet. It may be a bit difficult to understand all of it at first, but you will get used to it if you listen regularly.

- Listen to songs and focus on the melody and the atmosphere, then concentrate on the words to find out what the song is about.

- Watching films (first with subtitles and later without) and TV shows in English can also help you to practise your listening skills.

Skills • **LiF** • **Words**

Speaking

Study and communication skills

1 Preparing and giving a presentation

1. Structuring your presentation
Organize your presentation into three parts:
- **Introduction:** Introduce your topic and let the audience know what you are going to tell them.
- **Main part:** Give your facts, reasons and opinions.
- **Conclusion:** Go over your main points again, briefly and without repeating any examples. Make a good closing statement – you could give a recommendation, ask a question or give your opinion.

Language help: structuring a presentation	
Introduction:	What I'd like to present to you is … • I'm going to talk about … • My talk is divided into … parts. • Let me begin by saying … • You can ask questions at any time. • Please save your questions until the end.
Main part:	The first/second/…/next part of my talk is about … • Now let's look at … • Another important aspect/point is … • I would also like to mention … • As you can (all) see … • Let me show you how statistics … • If you look at …, you'll see …
Conclusion:	To sum up my key points, … • Let me finish by saying … • I'd like to conclude by saying … • If you are interested in further aspects of this topic, I would … • Now I can answer questions from the audience, if you have any.

2. Preparing material for your presentation
Make notes or cards that you can use during your presentation to help you speak clearly and freely.
- Use a variety of sources and present the information in your own words.
- Prepare visuals (slides with main points, photos, maps, statistics etc) to make your presentation livelier and more interesting.
- Make sure the pictures and the writing are big enough.
- Say what your visual is about before going into detail.
- You should always point to the visual that you are talking about.
- If your visual includes key points of your presentation, you shouldn't just read out the same sentences that people can already see on the wall/screen/handout. Instead, you should explain them in more detail.

> Rosa Parks (1913-2005)
> • often called "the First Lady of Civil Rights"
> • famous for her bus boycott in Montgomery, Alabama (USA) in 1955
> → bus boycott: African Americans refusing to give up their seats in the "colored" section of a bus for white people

3. Practising your presentation
You should practise your presentation out loud at least three times before giving it. Time yourself when practising to make sure your presentation is not too long or too short.

4. Giving your presentation
- Use the material you have prepared.
- Keep track of the time you have for your presentation.
- Pay attention to your body language. Make sure you look at the audience and keep eye contact.
- Don't look at your notes all the time or turn your back to the audience.

Study and communication skills Speaking

2 Giving feedback

To improve your language skills, it is important that you give each other feedback on your work:

- Listen or read carefully.
- Look at the task. Check that all the task requirements have been covered (a checklist may help).
- Always remember to start with a positive comment.
- Make suggestions on how to improve the text or presentation. Your tips will help the other pupils and the class to improve.
- Explain in a friendly way what could or should be changed.

I liked the main part because …

Your feedback on a presentation, for example, can refer to different aspects:

Content:
You presented the information clearly.
The information was correct.
The presentation dealt with the relevant points.
You were able to answer questions.
…

Language:
The language was easy to understand.
You explained the difficult words.
Your grammar was OK.
You used an appropriate register.
…

Presentation skills:
You spoke slowly and clearly.
You made eye contact with the audience.
You spoke freely.
You used visuals to help explain difficult points.
…

You can use a feedback sheet to make sure that your feedback covers all the relevant points.

Feedback sheet

Content:	☺	😐	☹
You presented the information clearly.			
The information was correct.			
The presentation dealt with the relevant points.			
You were able to answer questions.			

Language help: feedback	
Positive feedback:	*What I liked about your … was that …* • *I liked the beginning/main part/… because …* • *You explained/presented/… very clearly/… how …* • *The part about … was particularly interesting/easy to understand/…* • *Your visuals were very helpful because …*
Suggestions:	*I'm not quite sure why you mentioned … because your topic was …* • *I think your presentation was a bit too long.* • *I don't think it was very well-structured because …* • *Maybe next time you could …* • *It would be a good idea to …*

Skills • LiF • Words

Speaking   Study and communication skills

3 Having a conversation/discussion

There are some basic rules that help you understand each other and give each other the chance to take part in a conversation/discussion:

- **Take turns**: Give the other person the chance to give his/her opinion, to react to what you have said, etc. This also includes you showing that you have listened to what your partner has said, e.g. by repeating something he/she has said or clearly referring to one of his/her statements.

- **Ask for clarification**: If you don't understand what the other person is trying to tell you, e.g. because he/she does not speak clearly or uses words that you don't know, you should ask for clarification so that communication is possible.

- **Use paraphrases**: If your partner does not understand what you say, you should speak slowly and clearly and use paraphrases, i.e. explain something in other words.

Before a discussion:
- Prepare your arguments carefully and make sure it is clear what you want to say.
- Think of arguments that might be used against you and try to find ways to answer them.
- Collect phrases to express your opinion.

During a discussion:
- Listen carefully to the other people and make sure you understand their arguments.
- Don't interrupt another speaker, but let him/her finish before you start.
- If you don't understand, ask the speaker to explain.
- Express your own opinion – you might not always agree, but stay polite and friendly.
- You can support your opinion by quoting other people or statistics.
- Try to stick to the topic – don't introduce another topic.
- Be aware of your body language. Finger-pointing can appear aggressive, for example.

Language help: having a conversation/discussion	
Turn-taking:	*That sounds interesting/difficult/…* • *So you think that …* • *Really? I haven't heard that before.* • *What do you think about it?* • *Oh, what a great idea!* • *Now that you mention it, I see that …*
Asking for clarification:	*I don't quite understand what you mean.* • *Do you mean that …?* • *Are you saying that …?* • *What exactly do you mean by …?* • *Please say it again. I didn't understand what you said.* • *Could you repeat that, please?* • *Could you speak up a little, please?*
Paraphrasing:	*What I mean is …* • *What I'm trying to say is …* • *Let me express it another way: …*

Study and communication skills — Speaking

Language help: having a conversation/discussion	
Expressing an opinion:	As far as I can see … • I think … • I suppose … • I would say … • I believe … • I'm sure … • Let me add … • Basically, … • I'm convinced that … • I strongly believe …
Assuming/speculating:	I think … • I suppose … • I imagine … • I assume … • It could be … • It would appear to be … • It seems likely/unlikely … • Perhaps, … • Possibly, … • If …
Agreeing:	That's just what I think, too. • You're right about that. • You're absolutely right. • I think that's a good/an important point. • … has my full support for his/her argument that … • … is completely right in saying …
Disagreeing:	Well, I don't think so. • I'm not sure about that. • What I can't understand about your point is … • I see your point, but … • You don't really mean that, do you? • You may be right, but on the other hand … • I'm afraid I don't agree with your view at all.

Language help: hosting a panel discussion	
Introducing the topic:	Good morning/afternoon, my name is … and today we will be talking about/discussing the topic of … • Our topic for this morning/afternoon is … • I'm here with …/Today we will be talking to …
Keeping the discussion going:	Does anyone have anything else to add? • That's a very interesting point, but what do you think? • Could you expand on that? • I'm not sure I understand what you mean by … • Does everyone here agree? • What about if we look at this from another angle? Has anyone thought about …? • We've not heard much from … • Would you like to reply to that? • Where do you stand?
Summing up and closing the discussion:	I'm afraid that's all we've got time for today. • We've covered some very important themes during this discussion, including … • The main point we have all agreed on throughout this debate is … • It's been a fascinating insight into … for me. • Thank you all very much for participating.

Reading

Study and communication skills

1 Reading techniques and strategies

Before you read a text, consider what you want to find out. Then decide on your reading strategy.
The following reading techniques can be useful when working with texts:

Skimming – reading for gist

> If there are any photos or illustrations, look at them carefully.

A Concrete Coastline?
Mediterranean Sea threatened by excessive tourism.

From Greece to Italy, France to Spain, and Turkey to Tunisia, the Mediterranean is surrounded by holiday hotspots. The beautiful coastline, sunny weather and clear, blue sea have always attracted people to the Mediterranean Sea. Today, over 150 million people live along the coast and during the tourist season that number almost doubles.

At the same time the Mediterranean is one of the most diverse natural regions in the world with more than 700 species of dolphins, whales, turtles and fish.

However, this fantastic biodiversity is under threat. Over recent years, the need to protect the Mediterranean's natural wealth has been stressed by environmental organizations, such as WWF Mediterranean and the Union for the Mediterranean.

Speaking on *Our Threatened World*, Lorenzo Imperio from the Union for the Mediterranean explains: "It's becoming harder and harder to ignore the negative effects of the booming tourist industry. The Med's ecosystem is incredibly sensitive and it just can't cope with the pressure caused by so many tourists. [...] structure. Even a UN plan to prevent overdevelopment and protect the last areas of natural coastline has failed to stop developers.

Waste not, want not?

And tourism can cause other problems. A typical tourist will use twice as much water each day as the average local; hotels and businesses need millions of litres of water for swimming pools, parks and golf courses. In countries such as Greece, Spain and Tunisia the tourism industry is wasting far too much water in a region that simply doesn't get enough rain.

Another serious consequence of the booming tourism industry is waste. Tourists create huge amounts of sewage and in some areas this goes into the sea after only minimal treatment. This sewage, combined with rubbish left on beaches by lazier tourists, is a major danger for local wildlife.

Of course, the region's natural beauty is also threatened by pollution – as is the region's [...]

> Read the headings, subheadings and any captions. They will give you clues as to what a text is about before you read it.

> Read through the text quickly and in one go – don't stop to look up any new words, and concentrate on the gist, not the details.

After skimming the text, you can summarize in one or two sentences what it is about.

Scanning – reading for specific information
1. Make sure you have understood the task and decide what information you are looking for.
   Go through the text slowly and note down the keywords.
2. Read the sentences with the keywords. If they have additional information you need, take notes.
3. Don't worry about new words. Try to understand them from the context. Check whether you know part of the word (e.g. un**excuse**d) or think of similar words you might know from French, Latin or German (e.g. *acceptable*). But beware of false friends ('Handy' = *mobile phone ≠ handy*)!
   - *False friends, p. 160*

Reading for detail
1. If you are asked to find detailed information in a text, first identify the part of the text you need to concentrate on.
2. Try to understand as many details as possible. You may have to read the text more than once.
3. You might also need to look up words in a dictionary.
   - *Working with dictionaries, p. 148*

Study and communication skills — Reading

2 Literary analysis

When looking at fictional texts closely, these literary terms help you to describe certain elements:

What happens in the story?	When summarizing the events and the reasons for certain actions, you describe the **plot**.
Where/when does the story take place?	The **setting** is the time and place of the story.
Who tells the story and what is his/her point of view?	The voice the author chooses to tell the story is the **narrator**. The narrator can be a character in or outside the story. A narrator may just tell the story or comment on characters and events.
What is the story about?	The **theme** is the central idea of the story. This is often a matter of interpretation and not everyone will agree on it.
Who is the story about?	A person in a story is called a **character**. The way the author presents a character is called **characterization**. When you write a characterization of one or more characters, you give your interpretation of their personalities.
How is the story written?	The author's **style** of writing is defined by his/her choice of words, the way he/she uses them and the sentence length. The **tone** of the text describes its general character (e.g. melancholic, ironic).

Reading between the lines to collect information on a character

Often, the narrator shows the reader indirectly (= implicitly) what kind of person the character is. This means that it can be necessary to read between the lines to collect more information on a character. Study the text closely and look for clues you can use to draw conclusions about a character:
- appearance: Is there any information on his/her looks? What does this suggest about his/her character?
- attitudes: What does the character say and think?
- actions: How does he/she behave?

Narrative techniques and point of view

- Check whether the story is told in the first person ("I") or the third person ("he/she").
- If the story is told in the third person: look to observe whether the point of view is limited (the story is told from the point of view of only one character) or omniscient (the narrator knows everything about each character).
- Analyse how the narrator tells the story: an objective narrator tells a story without any comment or explanation, while an intrusive narrator comments on characters and actions.

Language help: talking about fictional texts	
The extract is from … It deals with … • *The story is set in … •* *The description of the setting creates a/an … atmosphere. •* *The story takes place in the 1980s.*	*The language the writer uses helps to create a/an … atmosphere. •* *The story is told from the point of view of … •* *The main character seems/appears to be … •* *His/Her behaviour suggests that … •* *From the way he/she acts/behaves we can assume that …*

Reading

3 Rhetorical devices

A rhetorical device is a technique to give a certain meaning, idea or feeling to a text.

Rhetorical device	Definition	Example
alliteration	words beginning with the same sound	"the sweet smell of success" "jump for joy"
anaphora	two or more sentences starting with the same word	"I spoke with Eliza Ramirez. I spoke with Reggie Banks."
climax	words/phrases that increase in importance or emphasis	"It was the best part, the most interesting part – the climax of the celebration!"
ellipsis	incomplete sentence used to focus a reader's attention on what is being said	"You feeling weird?" "Front page. Washington Post. Tomorrow."
enumeration	listing of words and phrases	"He admired her hair, her eyes and her lips."
exaggeration	an extreme statement that makes something seem better, worse, …	"I nearly died laughing." "I tried a thousand times."
metaphor	an indirect comparison without the words *as* or *like*, used to emphasize qualities which are similar	"the river of life"
parallelism	repetition of similar or identical words or constructions	"Tell me and I forget. Teach me and I may remember. Involve me and I will learn."
repetition	repetition of words	"high, high above"
rhetorical question	a question which expects no answer	"Can't you listen?"
simile	comparison	"A man like a bear."
use of inclusive *we*	use of *we* to make the listener/reader feel included	"We need to do something now."
use of superlatives	using superlative forms of adjectives or adverbs	"the highest mountain"

Viewing

Study and communication skills

Knowing how a film works can be helpful for understanding a film you are watching. It can be a much more satisfying experience if you analyse what made a film brilliant or boring. Here are some tips on how to view a film critically. You can apply many of these tips to watching a video clip, too.

1 Before viewing

- One of the first things you notice about a film is the film poster or the DVD cover. Both can give you a lot of information about the film, e.g. genre, plot and actors.
- Like film posters or DVD covers, trailers are made to promote the film, so they give you some information about it. Pay attention to the music, sound effects and what is said.
- The genre of the film you are going to watch tells you a lot about what to expect.

2 While viewing

- To understand the plot you don't have to understand every single word.
- It is not only important what the characters say, but also how they say it. Emphasis and intonation can give you clues to how the characters feel.
- Pay attention to the characters' facial expressions and their body language as well to find out about their mood and what to expect.
- It is important to watch the characters to find out what a film is about. But there are also many other things that can give you valuable clues, e.g. setting, lighting, colours, music and camera work.

Setting
The time, place and situation of a film make up its setting. Studying the setting closely can give you a lot of information about the characters.

Lighting
The kind of light used can provide you with information on the atmosphere of a scene. Shadows and darkness, for example, can convey a dangerous atmosphere. But watch out! It is often the combination of lighting, colours and music that creates an overall atmosphere.

Colours
Like lighting, colours are important when creating a particular atmosphere for a scene or a film. Bright colours can create a happy, positive effect, while dark or extremely bright colours can convey a dramatic atmosphere.

Music
Music emphasizes or intensifies a certain atmosphere in a film. Light-hearted, cheerful music can make a scene funnier, while loud, dramatic music can evoke suspense even if you don't see anything dangerous going on. Music can also be used to characterize people.

Camera work

Like the setting, lighting, colours and music, camera work also contributes to the telling of the story. Depending on what field size, camera angles, camera movement etc are used, the audience can get further information on the characters and the plot.

Field size
The field size describes the distance between the camera and the object. Depending on what type of camera shot is used, the viewer gets specific information about the plot and the characters.

A **long shot** gives a view of the setting, putting the action taking place in context.

A **medium long shot** shows a person or people in interaction with their surroundings.

A **full shot** gives a view of a figure's entire body, e.g. to show action and/or a constellation of characters.

A **medium shot** shows a person down to his/her waist, e.g. to show two people in conversation. It makes the viewer feel included in the scene.

A **close-up** draws the viewer's attention to someone or something, e.g. to show the emotions on someone's face.

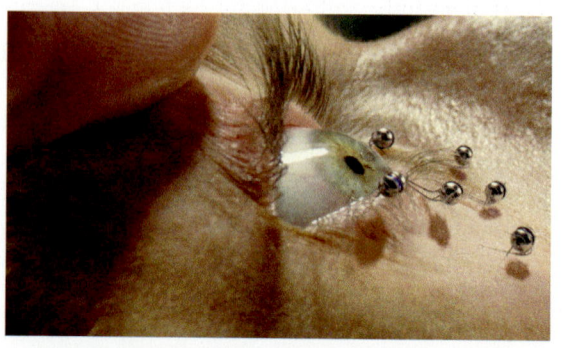

An **extreme close-up** focuses on a detail. It creates suspense or a feeling of disorientation.

Study and communication skills   **Viewing**

Camera movement
Like the field size, the movement of the camera contributes to giving information on the plot:
- A **static shot** shows what is happening from a neutral point of view.
- A **panning shot** provides the viewer with a feeling of orientation by moving the camera from left to right across the picture.
- A **tracking shot** follows a moving object/person by moving the camera along the object/person.
- A **zoom** focuses on important details.

Camera angle
Camera angle means the perspective from which an object is viewed. Depending on what kind of angle is used, it can say something about the person shown.

A **high-angle** shot can make a person seem smaller, helpless and less important.

An **eye-level** shot expresses an objective point of view.

A **low-angle** shot can make people seem more important and powerful, but can also make people look ridiculous.

Language help: talking about films

The character's facial expression shows how frightened/scared/sad/happy he/she is. •
His/Her body language shows his/her attitude towards … It reflects his/her feelings about … •
When analysing the setting you can see that … •
The character's room suggests that … •
The scene is shot from …'s point of view. It is seen from the perspective of … •
The camera is at a great distance from … •
The camera is very close to … •

Language help: talking about a film's message

The lighting and colours create an atmosphere of … •
Dark/bright lighting reflects the negative/positive aspects of … •
The film's background music is used to emphasize … •
The director achieves a certain effect by … He/She uses … to underline/emphasize … •
The … shot/angle is used to show/focus attention on … •
This shot is taken from a high/low angle to show/underline … •
Close-ups of … highlight the importance of … •
By showing clips of …, the video shows how … •

● *Wordbank Film, p. 188*

Writing

Study and communication skills

The different types of text you may have to write all have their special characteristics. Whatever kind of text you write, you should still follow the basic principles of text writing. These include the following phases:
- **A planning phase** – collecting and organizing ideas for the task.
- **A drafting phase** – outlining and writing a first draft.
- **An editing phase** – correcting and improving your first draft.

Make sure you leave yourself enough time at the end for the editing phase.

1 Planning

For example:

> **B6 Target task**   ● P5   WB B4, B5, p. 26   *Need help? Look at pp. 47-49.*
> Write a comment on the following statement:
> "Advertising agencies should not be limited in their choice of pictures or language."

- Before you start planning, it might be helpful to re-read that material and to note down useful ideas and thematic vocabulary and phrases you can use.

- Collect your ideas on the topic and organize them visually in a graphic organizer:

  A T-chart is a useful tool for collecting and classifying arguments.

arguments in favour of …	arguments against …
…	…

  A mind-map is a good way of collecting a variety of different ideas connected to your topic and showing how they relate to each other.

  (mind-map: advertising — Internet, TV, media, …, audience (students, children, …))

- If you use information from books or the Internet, note down your sources.
  Use a variety of sources and present the information in your own words.

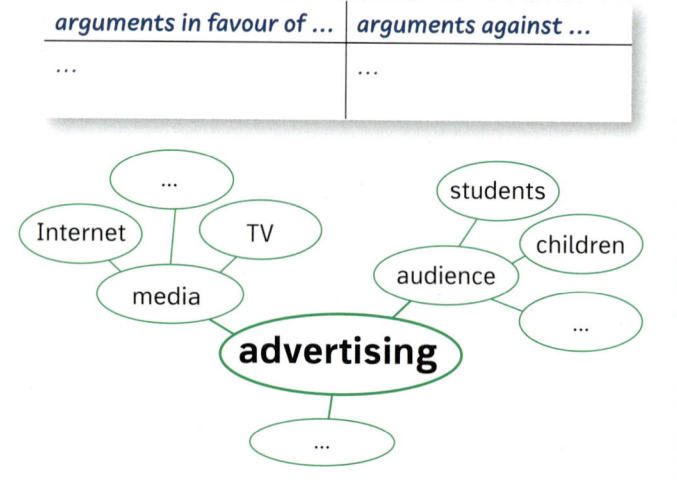

2 Drafting

- Structure your ideas, e.g. add numbers to decide on the sequence. You can also write a list on your computer – then it's easy to change the order of your notes.

- Write a brief outline for your text using your notes from the planning phase. Consider the structure of the type of text. Use the checklists and information on pp. 144-147.

- Keep in mind who you are writing for. Some texts are likely to be more formal than others and you need to choose your words carefully.
  Words like *receive, demonstrate, appear* are more formal than *get, show* and *seem*.
  Long forms *(They will not survive)* are more formal than short forms *(They won't survive)*.

- Write your first draft based on your outline.

Study and communication skills   **Writing**

3 Editing

Check the content:

1 Check whether you have fulfilled the task. You may have been asked to come to a conclusion. Make sure you have done it.

2 Be precise and clear. Leave out information that is not important and clarify any points if necessary.

Check the language:

1 Check your work for mistakes.   • *Proofreading, p. 150*

2 Make sure you have paraphrased any information from the material you have used instead of quoting directly from the text.

3 Vary your language:
Use interesting words and not too many 'overused' words like *really, very, nice, good* or *bad*.
Vary your sentence structure.   • *Varying sentence structure, p. 155*

4 Improve the flow of your writing by using sentence adverbials and conjunctions.

Language help: structuring your text using conjunctions and adverbials	
Expressing time:	*after • as long as • as soon as • when • whenever • while • After that … • Afterwards … • Before that … • Finally … • Meanwhile … • In the meantime … • Suddenly …*
Comparing and contrasting:	*although • even though • whereas • while • However … • At the same time … • Nevertheless … • On the one hand … On the other hand … • In the same way … • By comparison …*
Expressing cause and result:	*so • because • since • due to • Therefore … • As a result … • That's why … • Due to this … • For that reason … •*
Clarifying and expressing opinion:	*Personally … • As far as I'm concerned … • Actually … • In other words … • In fact … • That is to say …*
Adding information and ordering points:	*as well as • in addition to • Firstly … • Furthermore … • In addition … • Finally*
Summarizing and concluding:	*To sum up … • All in all … • In conclusion … • On the whole …*

Writing

Study and communication skills

Comment

Dos ✔

1. **Structure your text:**
   - Structure your comment to include the following parts:
     Introduction – refers to the topic/question.
     Main part – identifies and weighs up arguments and presents your own opinion.
     Conclusion – sums up your arguments and comes to a logical conclusion.
   - Organize your text coherently using paragraphs linked with connectives, e.g. sentence adverbials.
2. **Present your arguments/case:**
   - Present your own point of view clearly.
   - Include both arguments for and against your point of view.
   - Support your own arguments and weaken counter-arguments by including evidence (expert opinions, statistics etc).

Don'ts ✘

- Don't begin writing before you have noted down your ideas and written an outline.
- Don't use informal language, e.g. short forms, colloquial language.

Language help: comment	
Introduction	Today, more and more people are beginning to ask whether … • The issue of … is more important than ever before.
Main part	Personally, … • As I see it, … • I absolutely agree/disagree with the idea/concept … • Unlike the author/environmentalists, I strongly oppose/support … • On the one hand … On the other hand … • Furthermore, it is important to consider … • Another important point is … • It may be argued that … but … • Whereas some people believe that …, I do not agree because …
Conclusion	All in all, I must conclude that … • Having taken all the arguments into consideration, I believe …

Characterization

Dos ✔

1. Note down information on the character you want to write about:
   - What does he/she look like?
   - What can you find out about his/her life?
   - How does he/she behave?
   - What can you find out about his/her relationship to others?
2. You may have to read between the lines to find out about somebody.

Language help: characterization
He seems/appears to be … • You can assume … • From this you could conclude … • It would appear that … • Her behaviour suggests that … • From what he/she says, it can be assumed that …

Don'ts ✘

Don't include information that you can't back up with evidence from the text.

Study and communication skills Writing

Summary

Dos ✔

1 **Before writing**
   - Read the text carefully and highlight keywords and/or sentences.
   - Divide the text up into parts and find your own keywords to summarize each part.
2 **Structure**
   - **Introduction:** Write an introductory sentence. Include the name of the author, the type of text and the topic of the text.
   - **Main part:** Use your keywords and sentences to summarize the text. Only include relevant information.
3 **Language**
   - Use your own words.
   - Use the present tense.
   - Use formal language.

Don'ts ✘
- Don't use the present progressive tense.
- Don't give your opinion.
- Don't analyse the text.

Language help: summary	
Introductory sentence	*The article/story/extract from the novel, …, written by … deals with/is about …*
Main part	*The author believes/states/ points out …* • *The article/story illustrates the problem/topic of …*

Formal letter

Dos ✔

1 **Layout**
   - Follow the rules for the layout of a formal letter (see the example of a covering letter on p. 146).
   - Choose a more formal font (e.g. Times New Roman, Arial) if you write the letter on a computer.
2 **Introduction**
   - Say why you are writing the letter in the first paragraph/sentence.
   - Refer to any letters you have received or written before.
3 **Main part**
   - Organize your information into paragraphs.
   - Keep to the point and avoid unnecessary details.
4 **Conclusion**
   - Say what reaction/reply you expect to get.
   - Type your full name and sign the letter by hand.

Don'ts ✘
- Don't write your name above the address.
- Don't use informal language (e.g. short forms, colloquial expressions).

Language help: formal letter	
Introduction	Say why you are writing: *I am writing this letter in response to …* • *I am writing this letter to apply for …* • *I wish to inquire about the possibility of …* • *Unfortunately, I am forced to complain about …*
Conclusion	Say how you expect the person to react: *I look forward to hearing from you soon.* • *Please accept my thanks for your help.* • *I do hope you will consider my application.*

Writing

Study and communication skills

If you wish to apply for a job, you will usually be expected to write a covering letter and include a recent CV – a curriculum vitae or résumé, as it is called in the US. The way these documents are written could mean the difference between getting the job and being turned down. Take time to write them carefully, paying attention to both layout and wording. Before sending off your application, ask someone to proofread it.

Covering letter

A covering letter is a letter of application which highlights your qualifications for the position you are applying for. In many respects it follows the rules of a formal letter.

Write your address in the top right-hand corner.

> 152, Summerlee Gardens
> East Finchley
> London N2 9QS
> Great Britain

Leave a line and write the date.

> 21 January 2017

Then give the contact details of the person you are writing to.

> Margaret Clegg
> The Manager
> Butlin's Holiday Camp
> Bognor Regis
> West Sussex PO21 1JJ

Dear Mrs Clegg,

Introduction:
Include information on the job you are applying for and say why you are applying.

> In response to your advertisement in the Bognor Regis Observer on Saturday, January 10th I would like to apply for a summer job in your holiday camp. I am a first-year student at Sussex University and I am looking for employment during the holidays. My examinations will have finished by the middle of June so I will be available to start work then.

Main part:
Include information about any experience and qualifications you have which are relevant to the job.

> I would very much like to work for your organisation during the summer. You are advertising for summer jobs as waitresses and as children's nannies and I have had experience in both of these fields. While I was at school I worked for several years as a babysitter, and during my work and travel gap year I served drinks and meals in several different restaurants and cafes in Europe and Australia.
>
> I very much enjoy working with children and was a hockey coach at my club for the under-11s team for one year in my last year at school. Furthermore, I speak both French and some German so that I can communicate successfully with guests who speak those languages.

Conclusion:
Thank the person for considering your application.

> I have attached my CV and would be glad to provide you with any other information you might require, such as references. Thank you for considering my application. I look forward to hearing from you soon.

End the letter in an appropriate way. Sign and print your name.

> Yours sincerely,
> *H. Mason*
> Hazel Mason

Study and communication skills   Writing

CV/Résumé

A CV (curriculum vitae) gives a summary of different aspects of your life so far. It should include information about your education, qualifications and skills. It should enable the potential employer to assess your suitability quickly.

> Don't send a photo with your CV and covering letter when applying in the UK or US!

Hazel Mason

152, Summerlee Gardens, London N2 9QS
Mobile: 07840097725, Email: hmason@hqhlnet.com

> Contact details including your address, email address and phone number.

EDUCATION

2015-2016	Undergraduate student at Sussex University. BA Honours course in History
2007-2014	Camden School for Girls
A Levels 2014	History A* English A Latin B
GCSEs 2012	8 GCSEs: History, English, Maths, Latin, German, French, Art and Music
2001-2007	East Finchley Primary School

> Use block capitals for different categories.

> Dates and details of school examination results in reverse chronological order, i.e. the most recent ones first.

WORK EXPERIENCE

2014-2015	Work and travel gap year: wide variety of jobs as a waitress in France, Germany, Switzerland and Australia – gained great deal of ==experience working under pressure==.
2012-2013	Under-11s team hockey coach. Most successful season for team.
2011-2013	==Regular and reliable== babysitter for neighbour's children.

> Use words that create a strong impression.

INTERESTS
- Sport: Enjoy many team sports including netball and hockey. Also a strong swimmer.
- Music: Play the guitar and enjoy singing.

> Focus on interests and skills relevant to the application.

SKILLS
- Languages: GCSE German (B1), GCSE French (B1)
- Computer: Competent in Word, PowerPoint and Excel

References available

> Bullet points are an effective way to emphasise key skills and interests.

> The ideal CV should be one or two pages long. Always have your CV proofread for grammar and spelling errors.

Working with dictionaries

Study and communication skills

1 Before you use a dictionary

When you read an English text, there may be several words you don't know. Note down the words while you are reading so that you can check them later. But before you start looking up the words in an English-German dictionary, think of the strategies you already know:
- Try and work out the meaning from the context.
- Check whether you already know parts of the new word
  (e.g. un**excused**, **head**gear).
- Think of similar words you might know from French, Latin or German (e.g. *acceptable*).
  But beware of false friends (German 'Handy' = *mobile phone ≠ handy*)!   ● *False friends, p. 160*

Look up the word in your dictionary if you could not work out its meaning using the strategies described above.

2 Working with an English-German dictionary

- When looking up a word, you should first make sure that you are looking at the right type of word (noun, verb, adjective etc). For example, *doubt* can be a verb or a noun.
- Scan the dictionary entry for different meanings to find the one that fits your context best.
- Use the abbreviations, symbols and examples to learn how and when to use a word.
- Some words are more difficult to find than others. For example, some dictionaries may not have an entry for *went* or *knives*. In this case you need to look at the entry for *go* or *knife*.
- Most dictionaries have their own entries for phrasal verbs like *look after*, *point out* or *try on*. When you can't find the combination of verb and preposition you are looking for, you should remember to check if it is a phrasal verb.

The headword helps you to find the word more easily.

The phonetic transcription shows you how to pronounce a word correctly. It not only reflects the sound but also gives you the stress of a word, which may be different depending on the function of the word (e.g. pre'sent v – 'present n).

chest [tʃest] n 1. *(torso)* Brust *f*, Brustkorb *m*; **to fold one's arms across one's ~** die Arme vor der Brust verschränken – 2. *(trunk)* Truhe; *(box)* Kiste – 3. *(treasury)* Schatzkästchen

n, vi, vt, adj tell you what type of word it is (noun, verb etc). If there are abbreviations you don't understand, check the explanations in the dictionary.

Expressions in **bold letters** give you examples of how to use the word correctly in typical phrases or idioms.

The different meanings of a word are listed under numbers. Make sure that you read the whole entry to find the meaning that fits the context.

Study and communication skills | Working with dictionaries

3 Working with an English (monolingual) dictionary

When you are writing a text, a German-English dictionary would seem to be the first choice. However, using an English, or monolingual, dictionary can help to explain the exact differences between similar words or to show how words are used in context.

Here are some tips for working with an English dictionary:
1 The abbreviations in the introduction to your dictionary give you important information about the use of a word, e.g. for *uncountable noun (U), adjective (adj), American English (AE)* etc.
2 The dictionary can help you to improve your texts by making them more interesting or by avoiding mistakes. You can find synonyms for words that come to mind quickly but are not very precise, for example (e.g *bad, nice, happy, sad*). You can also find the correct spelling, the irregular forms of verbs, the correct preposition to use with a word and how you use a word correctly in context.
3 English dictionaries also show collocations – words that are often used in combination with other words. For example, you commonly use the words *follow* or *give* with the word *advice*, and you can only *commit a crime*.
4 As well as the categories *formal* and *informal*, most dictionaries use style labels such as *spoken, literary, impolite, offensive, humorous*. If a word doesn't have one of these labels, it is neutral as far as style is concerned and it is safe for you to use it. If you write a formal text, for example, you should avoid words with the style label *informal* or *offensive*.
5 An idiom is an expression whose meaning is different from the meaning of the individual words. You should know that dictionaries list idioms as their first important word.

example sentence

cook /kʊk/ verb ★★★ 1 [I/T] to prepare food and heat it so that it is ready to eat: *Cook the apple slowly until it is soft.* • **cook sth for sb** *Joe's cooking dinner for me tonight.* • **cook sb sth** *He offered to cook me lunch.* **1a.** [I] when food cooks, it is heated so that it is ready to eat: *The potatoes need to cook for about 20 minutes.* **2** [T] *informal* to change information dishonestly: *They cooked the scripts to make Adams look stupid.* **2a. cook the books** to change accounts and figures dishonestly, usually in order to get money **be cooking** *spoken* to be happening or being planned, often secretly: *I'll try and find out what's cooking.* **cook sb's goose** *informal* to cause a lot of problems for someone or spoil their plans.

— idiom
— style label
— idiom

4 Working with online dictionaries

On the Internet there are various dictionaries to help you. Here are some tips for using them properly:
1 Don't use only one online dictionary, but instead search for several dictionaries that show how words are used in sentences/in context and bookmark them.
2 If you want to find the English for a German word, don't use the first word that the online dictionary gives you because it might be wrong in the context you want to use it in. Therefore, you need to check the word in a dictionary that also gives you example sentences. Only then can you see how the word is used correctly in context.
3 Online dictionaries are often not as extensive as printed dictionaries. Therefore, it is always advisable to check the results. Look them up in another online dictionary or use a printed dictionary to find out if the word fits in your context.
4 Most online dictionaries also let you listen to the pronunciation of a word. Listen several times to be able to pronounce a word correctly.

Proofreading your texts

Study and communication skills

What is proofreading?

Proofreading is primarily about checking your written texts to spot and correct errors in spelling, punctuation, grammar, the use of language, style and format.

Editing is what you do after finishing the first draft of a written text. It involves checking the content of your text to ensure that the ideas are expressed clearly and form a coherent and meaningful whole.

1 General proofreading strategies

- Take a break! Allow yourself some time between writing and proofreading. The goal is to return with a fresh mind, as proofreading requires your full concentration.
- Always read through your writing slowly to give your eyes sufficient time to spot errors.
- Read your text silently, one word at a time. Reading word by word ensures that you don't miss anything. Errors can be difficult to spot.

2 Personalize your proofreading

Personalizing your proofreading to suit your needs will help you proofread more effectively. You should find out what your typical problem areas are and look for each type of error individually:

1. Find out what errors you typically make: Review your written texts and your teacher's or peers' comments and corrections of your writing. Identify and collect your most frequent and typical errors. Write them down by categorizing them according to the kind of error they are. Here is an example:

My personal checklist: typical errors and mistakes

error/mistake	date	correct version	my mistake
spelling	4.9.2017	which, which, which	w!ich
		their dog, their dog, their dog	there → dort
tenses	4.9.2017	She has lived in London since 2012.	She lives in London since 2012. → present perfect with since and for
prepositions		He was looking for a job.	He was looking after a job. to look after → auf … aufpassen

2. Ask your teacher what you can do to avoid those errors in future. In order to help you to avoid them, it might also be useful to do some grammar exercises.
3. Use your personal checklist to check your written texts for your typical mistakes.
4. Memorize your frequently misspelled and misused words.

3 Check for the most common mistakes

- Adjective or adverb? *He is a quick learner*; but: *He learns quickly*.
- If-clauses: No *will/would* in an if-clause. These sentences might help you to remember the rules: '*If*' and '*would*' is no good; '*If*' and '*will*' makes me ill.
- *He, she, it* – das „s" muss mit!
- Tenses: mixing past and present tenses throughout a piece of text; using present continuous instead of simple present.
- Confusing similar words, such as *affect* and *effect*.
- Beware of contractions and apostrophes: *their* and *they're*, *its* and *it's*, *your* and *you're*.
- Words with similar spelling or pronunciation but different meanings, such as *where*, *were*, *we're*, *wear*.

Mediation

Study and communication skills

1 Understanding the task

Before you start working on a mediation task, you need to make sure that you understand the task, namely …
- who you 'are' and what your role is,
- where and why you need to explain things in the other language,
- what aspects of the content you should concentrate on,
- who you talk/write to (audience),
- what type of text you have to produce.

This is true for both English → German and German → English mediation tasks, as the following examples show:

English → German	German → English
Your grandparents offer to finance an internship in the UK for you when you are 16. They ask you to look for a job that you are interested in. You look at advertisements for internships in the UK and like the following one. Write an email to your grandparents. Tell them about what company it is and where, what you can do there and what you need to qualify for the job.	You take part in a school exchange with a British school. You are asked to give short presentations on life at German schools. Your topic is how your school organizes work experience in Year 10 and you take your school's info sheet as a basis. Write down a script for your presentation in front of a class of British pupils. Concentrate on when and where you do your work experience, why you do it and what kinds of jobs you should look for.

2 Finding relevant information and preparing your text

- When you work on a mediation text, you have to find the relevant information as you mustn't translate the whole text.

- Read the text to understand its gist. Texts in English may include words you don't know. Try to understand as much as possible. Then decide if the words/passages you don't understand are relevant to your task. If they are, use the context, a dictionary and other strategies to work out a sentence's meaning. ● *Working with dictionaries, p. 148*

- Watch out for keywords that are related to what you should concentrate on and, if possible, highlight key sentences/phrases.

- Take notes on the points you need for your text production. Be careful:
  1. In some texts, the same ideas are repeated again and again. Don't do the same.
  2. Don't get lost in the details, but concentrate on the general ideas.
  3. If you don't know how to say it in English/German, …
     - use paraphrases, e.g. "the person who looks after the school's equipment" (*Hausmeister* = school caretaker/janitor),
     - use a less complex sentence structure,
     - use synonyms and antonyms.
  4. Structure your notes with your task in mind (see example), not just in the order in which the points are mentioned in the original text.

Mediation   **Study and communication skills**

- when? first two weeks of second term in Year 10 (= first two weeks of February)
- where? in our town or in places up to 30 km from the school; possible to go abroad for work experience if school says it's OK
- why?

Das Schülerbetriebspraktikum (SBP)

Das Schülerbetriebspraktikum (SBP) findet alljährlich in den ersten zwei Wochen des zweiten Halbjahrs der 10. Klasse statt, also üblicherweise in den ersten beiden Februarwochen. Die Vorbereitung darauf erfolgt im Rahmen des Berufsorientierungsprojekts in Klasse 9 sowie dem Politikunterricht im zweiten Halbjahr der Klasse 9. Hier lernst du bereits deine eigenen beruflichen Interessen besser kennen und kannst über Besuche im Informationszentrum der Arbeitsagentur und eine Stärken-Schwächen-Analyse für dich geeignete Berufsbereiche entdecken.

Das SBP ist ein wichtiger Bestandteil des schulischen Programms zur Studien- und Berufsorientierung. Es soll dir ganz allgemein ermöglichen, einen unmittelbaren Eindruck von der Berufs- und Arbeitswelt zu bekommen, z. B. wie der Tagesablauf eines Berufstätigen aussieht. Zugleich geht es aber auch darum, Erfahrungen in einem bestimmten Beruf oder Berufsfeld zu sammeln, das dir interessant erscheint bzw. in der Stärken-Schwächen-Analyse empfohlen worden ist.

Um diese Verknüpfung deiner Stärken und Interessen mit deiner Praktikumsstelle sicherzustellen, ist es nötig, dass du dir selbst einen Praktikumsbetrieb suchst. Damit du ihn auch erreichen kannst, sollte er sich vor Ort oder aber im Umfeld von bis zu max. 30 km befinden. So kann sichergestellt werden, dass der dich betreuende Lehrer dich auch im Praktikumsbetrieb besuchen kann. Auf schriftlichen Antrag bei der Schulleitung ist auch ein Praktikum im Ausland möglich.

3 Writing your mediation text

Before you start writing your mediation text with the help of your notes, you should look at the task again to check that you have covered all the task requirements (see **1 Understanding the task**).

What you should keep in mind at this point is:
- The audience (who the text is for): for example, the style of your text must be a bit more formal when presenting something in class and can be less formal when writing an email to a friend.
- The type of text: remember what is typical of this type of text (e.g. in an email you need a beginning and an end).
- If you notice that something in your text is typically English/German and your audience does not know what it is, you must explain that in your text (e.g. *Abitur* – the exam with which you finish school after 12 or 13 years, like A-levels in Britain).

Finally, don't forget that a mediation task is not a translation. A translation requires you to go through the text word for word without changing the structure of the text. A mediation requires you to choose relevant information and use it to write a completely new text.

Good morning, Sir, good morning, everyone,
Thank you very much for inviting me to your lesson so that I can tell you a little bit about our school back home in Germany. When you think of school, you usually think of teachers, subjects, lessons and tests. But at our school – and practically every other school in Germany, there are times when we don't go to school because we do work experience at a company. At my school, it is in the first two weeks of the second term, or the first two weeks of February. You do it in Year 10 when pupils are about 15 or 16 years old.

Methods

Study and communication skills

1 Think – pair – share
To understand a topic better, you and your classmates can use this method:
1. *Think*: Think about the topic in question and write down your ideas.
2. *Pair*: Get together with a partner and discuss your ideas. Add new ideas to your notes.
3. *Share*: With another pair, talk to each other about all your ideas.

think

pair

share

2 Milling around
This is an easy way to exchange ideas in class:
1. Walk around the classroom quietly.
2. When your teacher says "stop", talk to the classmate in front of you. Exchange your ideas.
3. Take notes on what your partner says and then find someone new to share your ideas with.

3 Gallery walk
Gallery walks are a good way of presenting the results of your group work to the class:
1. Each group puts up their poster, story ending etc in different corners of the classroom.
2. Then form new groups. Each member should come from a different group so that there is one expert in each group who can explain the poster to the others.
3. The groups should walk around the gallery and look at each poster. The poster expert can tell you all about it while everyone else makes notes and asks questions.

4 Buzz groups
You can collect ideas or exchange information in groups:
1. Get together in groups of three or four.
2. Discuss the topic for a few minutes, but keep your voices down. One of you takes notes.
3. Choose a member of your group to present your ideas to the class.

5 Placemat
A placemat helps you to collect ideas and agree on the most important ones in a group:
1. In groups of four, fold a big piece of paper twice. Draw a rectangle in the middle.
2. Each of you writes their ideas in one corner of the paper.
3. Turn the paper round until everyone has read their neighbours' ideas.
4. Decide on the most important ideas as a group and write them in the middle.
5. One of you presents the results to the class.

6 Bus stop
This method is an ideal option whenever a phase of working on your own has partner work as a follow-up. Around the classroom there are 'bus stops'. Students who have finished their work go to one of the bus stops to wait for any other student who has completed his or her work. As soon as a partner arrives, you can continue your work without waiting for the whole group to finish. You can …
- exchange your ideas,
- compare your work and peer-edit it,
- explain your results or the content of different texts to each other.

On the other hand, if you need more time, you can work on your assignment until you are happy with the result and then go to one of the bus stops.

Skills • LiF • Words

7 Freeze frame

This method helps you to understand the relationships between the characters of a story.
1 After reading the text, get together in groups. Talk about the different characters and their relationships to each other.
2 Think about how to present their relationships by arranging the characters in class.
3 Choose one person to be the "director", who arranges the characters.
   The others act as the characters. They are not allowed to talk or move.
4 After your classmates have commented on the scene, the group explains their reasons for the arrangement.

8 Jigsaw

This is a good method for working on different texts in small groups:
1 In groups each of you chooses one text (or a different part of a text). Read it carefully. Note down important details and information.
2 Next find the other pupils in class who have worked on the same text (or part of a text) as you. Compare your notes and discuss the text. Help each other get as much important information as possible.
3 Then go back to your first group and present the information about your text to the others. Make notes on the texts that you have not read yourself.
4 In the end, each of you should know about all of the texts (or the whole text).

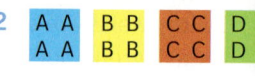

9 Dramatic reading

You can use this method to present a character or a poem in class.
1 First read your character's role or the poem in a low voice.
2 Think about how to perform your role or poem, e.g. which words you want to stress, whether you want to use a low or a loud voice, or if you want to express emotions.
3 Find a partner and read out your role/poem to them, but try to look up while reading it out.
4 Perform your role/poem in class without looking at the text and use facial expressions and gestures to support your performance.

10 Four corners

This method is a good way to collect ideas about a new topic and then discuss them in more detail.
1 Put up a statement in each of the four corners of the classroom.
2 Walk around the classroom quietly and decide which statement you agree with most.
3 Work alone and make notes about why you agree with this statement.
4 Go to the corner of the classroom with your statement and talk to the other students in the corner about why you agree with this statement. You can make notes about what the other students say.
5 Choose one member of the group to explain to the other corners why you chose this statement.

11 Round robin

This method is the perfect way to share your opinion in a group, without feeling under pressure.
1 Write a topic on the board.
2 Consider how you feel about the topic.
3 Sit in a circle.
4 One after the other, say how you feel about the topic in one sentence.
   Don't comment on what the other students say.

Varying sentence structure

Language skills

1 Participles

LS 1

a) Participles are often used in written English. Read the following extract to see how participle constructions are used to vary the sentence structure.

> They caught Micky almost straight away, still **trying** to find Holly. He claimed that it wasn't his fault, **blaming** Bob entirely for what had happened. Finally, **having given** the police Bob's address, he was taken down to the station and put in a cell for the night. The police arrested Bob before the night was over.
>
> It was all over for Holly, too. Safely **squeezed** between Mum and Dad she was driven home in a police car.
> 5 **Relaxing** on the couch, she told Mum and Dad how she had lost her way and how Micky and Bob had driven her to the house, where she had been kept a prisoner. **Holding** both their hands, she cried with relief that she was now back at home. Afterwards they all sat down to a special dinner, **made** by Gran. She promised them all never to wander off on her own again. **Tucked up** in bed at last, she fell asleep almost immediately.

Look at the participles and sort them according to their function.
You can use participles to:

- shorten adverbial clauses of time or reason
- shorten a relative clause in the active or passive voice
- combine information

b) How can you say the sentences from a) differently?

    Example: He claimed that it wasn't his fault, <u>blaming</u> Bob entirely for what had happened.
          • Function: combine information
          • Said differently: *He claimed that it wasn't his fault. He <u>blamed</u> Bob entirely for what had happened.*

c) Use participles to combine or shorten the following sentences:
  1 When they spotted a good place for a picnic, they stopped the car.
  2 The film which was shown at the local cinema got very bad reviews.
  3 When they heard the mother had lost her son, many people went and looked for him.
  4 Since he had come home late yesterday, he decided to leave work early.
  5 Lou owns a fantastic pair of glasses. The glasses were worn by Elton John at one of his concerts.
  6 The young woman who is coming out of that shop is wanted by the police.
  7 She was cleaning her room and listening to music.
  8 He was very angry because he had had to wait in the rain for nearly half an hour.

d) Summarize the information on participles on a grammar card. Include …
  • how they are formed,
  • when they are used,
  • example sentences.

Varying sentence structure

Language skills

2 Connectives, conjunctions and adverbs

LS 2

If you write something well, people will enjoy reading it. Writing well is not just a question of using the right words and getting your grammar right. A good piece of writing will also use a variety of structures and vocabulary so that the reader doesn't lose interest. It is very boring to read the same kind of sentence over and over again.
Look at this text for example:

> I have time in the morning. That morning I was late. I got up and then I cleaned my teeth. I got dressed and had breakfast. Then I put on my shoes and coat and I ran to the bus stop. The bus was late. I caught it and I met my friends and we went to school together.

Although the content of this short piece of writing is not terribly exciting, it is still possible to make it sound more interesting. For example:

> Generally I have enough time in the morning. That morning, however, I was late. Having got up, I cleaned my teeth quickly. I actually had breakfast while I was getting dressed. As soon as I had put on my shoes and coat, I ran to the bus stop. I caught the bus just in time because, luckily, it was late. So I met my friends and we all went to school together.

a) Decide what makes the second text more interesting.
   Then make a list of the connectives/conjunctions and adverbs that are used.

b) Read the email below and rewrite it making it sound more interesting.

Dear Rachel,
You won't believe what happened to me during my holiday in Spain. I went to the beach a lot. It was very hot and sunny. I went to dinner with my parents and my sister every
5 evening. One evening we were all having a good time. We went back to our rooms at about midnight. I discovered that I had left my hotel key in the room. My sister and I couldn't get in. We went into my parents' room, which was next door. We climbed onto the balcony outside our room. We had left
10 a small window open. My sister is smaller than me. She had to climb in through the window. It was difficult. It was very dark. Then it was very light. The hotel manager was shining a torch at us. He said that he was going to call the police. We tried to explain. His German wasn't very good and our
15 Spanish wasn't very good. We tried to convince him that we were the guests. He believed us. We went to bed at 2 o'clock. We were very tired. How were your holidays? Did you have any exciting adventures? I'm sending you some photos. You can see our hotel in one of them!
20 See you soon!
Sam

Varying expression

Language skills

1 Using synonyms

When you write a text or talk to someone, it is often your aim to express yourself as clearly as possible, be entertaining or show that you are an expert on a topic. In order to do so, it is important that you vary your expression. Otherwise, you will sound vague and boring, as the following – slightly exaggerated – examples illustrate.

A Holidays in California are nice. You can see a lot of nice places, go shopping and see the nice countryside. The weather is usually nice, too, with sunshine for most of the year. Last year my parents and I stayed in a very nice hotel in Ventura, not far from Los Angeles.

B I think that you are a bit young for an internship abroad when you are 15 or 16. I think that you can still do that when you're older. It's more important, I think, to do an internship in a company here in Germany, in your home town. You should find out about the jobs you could apply for here because I think that most of us will go to university and work here in Germany.

LS 3
Usually, you already know a number of synonyms (= words that mean more or less the same) for *nice* or *think*. Add more words to the lists below and use some of those words to rewrite A and B.

nice: beautiful, great, …
think: in my opinion, believe, …

Support
Sometimes you can change the sentence structure as well (e.g. *in my opinion* for *I think*). If you can't think of words that have a similar meaning (e.g. *nice – fine*), you can also use opposites and negate them (e.g. *nice – not bad*).

LS 4
In order to have these synonyms at hand, you could start a folder with words that are often used.
You may organize them in the form of lists or a word web, for example.
Copy the word web and add more words to it.

- say
  - tell
  - …
  - general
  - whisper
  - how you use your voice
  - …
  - emphasis on the function of what you say
  - describe
  - …

LS 5
In the following example, you cannot simply make a list of words that mean the same and use those words to replace *get* as *get* can have a lot of different meanings depending on the context.
Look at each use of *get*, and rewrite the text by replacing *get* with another expression.

When I get up in the morning, I get my mobile to see how many messages I have got. On the bus to school, I try to get a quiet place to sit so that I get the time and space to send my friends some messages. When I get to school, I have to turn my mobile off. But sometimes I get it out of my bag during the breaks and get in touch with my friends.

S Varying expression — Language skills

2 Paraphrasing

There are many situations in which you may have to paraphrase what you would like to say, i.e. to explain an idea in other words. Situations in which you typically have to do that are:

A when you are asked to repeat what you have said in other words because someone has not understood what you are trying to say,

B when you have to talk about an idea several times and do not want to repeat the same words again and again, e.g. in a presentation or an essay,

C when you cannot think of one English word or expression that sums up what you are trying to say, e.g. because you have forgotten/don't know the word or it is something typically German, for example, for which there is not an English expression (e.g. 'Schützenfest', 'Schulkonferenz').

LS 6
Look at the examples of situations in which paraphrasing is necessary.
Say which type of situation (A-C) they stand for.

1
"My brother could really concentrate on driving on the left and we didn't have to look at all the street signs all the time. Our rental car had a good sat nav."
"A what?"

2
"I'm sorry, it would be great to have you here that weekend, but I won't be free. It's my sister's *Abi-Ball* and I won't have any time then."
"What is that? A sports match?"
"No, no. Well, how can I explain that …"

3
In the US, many people still have a lot of prejudices against African Americans. In recent years, the police were criticized for having prejudices against young black men. African Americans are often stopped and searched and there were also some cases in which they were shot, although they were not dangerous. But the prejudice that many blacks, especially young black men, are criminals lives on.

4
Internships can be a very rewarding experience. You get to know a certain job that you might find interesting for your career in the future. If the company is pleased with your internship, they may invite you to come back – for another internship or a proper job or training. And it is always good if you can include an internship on your CV.

5
"I really love dystopian novels. I think the *Hunger Games* books are still my favourite. It is very interesting to see what our world could look like in the future."
"Dysto-what?"
"Dystopian. Wait, let me explain …"

LS 7
Match the following example of paraphrasing to one of the examples (1-5) above. Look closely at how the idea is explained in different words.

It means that the society in which the story takes place has developed in a negative way. People usually have no freedom to do what they want and are controlled by the state, often with the help of modern technology.

LS 8
Use paraphrasing for the other examples above.

Language skills
Varying expression

3 Style and register

You can express the same thing in many ways. Very often, this is not just a question of different words, but also of style and register.

If you feel annoyed by someone who will not stop talking, you can say "Please, be quiet!" or you can say "Shut up!" Both mean basically the same, but there is a clear difference in style and register. "Please, be quiet!" is polite and more formal than the colloquial and rude "Shut up!" "Shut up!" may be OK among friends, but it would not be OK if you were a guest in a lesson at a US high school.

LS 9
Look at the following examples and find the sentences that are particularly informal.
Use a dictionary if you are not sure what one of the phrases means.
Then concentrate on the informal sentences and write a formal alternative that means the same.

1 "It came as quite a surprise when she invited me to stay at her place for the summer."

2 "Look at that shirt. I wouldn't be seen dead in it!"

3 "I'm gonna, like, ask my mum to give me some cash so that I can buy those cool shoes."

4 "I would tell her to leave me alone if she said anything like that to me."

5 "It's kinda boring to hang out with those kids all the time. My sis and her friends are just nine."

Unless you write an informal kind of text (e.g. a diary entry, a dialogue between teenagers), your texts in the English classroom are supposed to be neutral or formal in style. Here are some important tips to remember:
- Avoid short forms (e.g. *don't, wouldn't, he's*) in written texts.
- Do not use colloquial expressions from spoken English (e.g. *wanna, kids, guys*).

LS 10
a) Look at the following situations. Rank them from formal to informal.

1 You are in a clothes shop and want to know if a T-shirt is available in a different size.
2 You meet a classmate and his/her parents, who you have never met before.
3 Your teacher wants to talk to you after class because you forgot your homework for the third time.
4 You have been invited to a job interview at an international company and now are talking to the chief of personnel.

formal ⟷ informal

b) Choose one of the situations or invent a situation that you consider very formal or informal. Write a short dialogue using inappropriate register/language.

c) Work with a partner. Swap your dialogues and rewrite them using the correct style and register.

False friends and cultural mistakes

Language skills

1 False friends

The use of English words and expressions in German is becoming more widespread. However, some of these words may be confusing because they in fact have very different meanings in English. Native English speakers who know no German will not understand you if you use them in the wrong (German) context. Here are some common 'false friends':

English word	German translation	False friend	English translation
actual	tatsächlich	aktuell	topical, up-to-date
also	auch	also	so
to become	werden	bekommen	to get
to blame sb	jemandem die Schuld geben	sich blamieren	to make a fool of oneself
brave	mutig	brav	well-behaved
chance	Zufall, Glück	Chance	opportunity
critic	Kritiker	Kritik	criticism
engaged	verlobt; besetzt (Telefon, WC)	engagiert	committed
familiar	bekannt	familiär	family
gift	Geschenk	Gift	poison
ground	(Erd)boden	Grund	reason
mark	Note; Zensur	Marke	brand
note	Notiz	(Schul-)Note	mark
programme *(TV)*	Sendung	Programm *(TV)*	channel
public viewing	öffentliche Leichenaufbahrung	public viewing	public screening
sensible	vernünftig	sensibel	sensitive
to spend	ausgeben *(Geld)* verbringen *(Zeit)*	spenden	donate
sympathetic	mitfühlend	sympathisch	nice, likeable
wellness	Wohlbefinden	Wellnesshotel	Spa, health farm

Tips on how to avoid 'false friends':
1 Be aware that not all of the English-sounding words in the German language are 'true friends' and learn which ones are 'false friends'.
   e.g. The word *homepage* refers only to the first page of a website in English-speaking countries. In Germany the word is often synonymous with website. Similarly, the word *(USB) stick* will not always be understood, because it is usually called *flash drive*, especially in American English.
2 Check your dictionary before using a German word which sounds English if you are not absolutely sure of the translation, e.g. 'Fitnessstudio' = *gym, fitness club* (NOT *fitness studio*).
3 Beware of compound words. It is easy to make mistakes when translating them word for word.
   e.g. 'Hochschule' does not mean *high school*, but *college* or *university*.
   'Überall' does not mean *overall*, but *everywhere*.

Language skills   **False friends and cultural mistakes**

LS 11
Look at the following cartoon and explain what went wrong in the communication.

LS 12
Work with a partner: Write a dialogue in which false friends lead to a misunderstanding.

Man: "Excuse me, please. May I become your handy for a moment?"
Woman: "What are you talking about?"

2 Cultural mistakes

Cultural mistakes arise because there are different customs and ways of dealing with people and situations in different countries. Language often plays an important role. It is not *what* you say but *how* you say it that can make a difference. Choice of words and also politeness are important. In English-speaking countries people are not usually so direct. They prefer to modify criticism and to use less strong adjectives so as not to offend.

Choice of words

LS 13   L 2/7
a) Read this conversation and say why Woody reacts the way he does.

b) Listen to another version of the dialogue and note down the different ways of expressing criticism in the two conversations. Explain why Woody reacts differently.

Woody: So what did you think of my new film?
Alan: I suppose the storyline was OK but the actors were terrible – the female leading actress was really weak – I can't understand how she got the part. And as for the camera work – it was appalling. You know the scene where the two lovers were supposed to be in a spaceship on their way to Mars – it was so unrealistic, I could have done it better myself.
Woody: So you didn't think much of it?
Alan: That isn't what I said.
Woody: Really? Well, I certainly won't give you tickets for my next premiere.

Politeness

LS 14   L 2/8
a) People are likely to react in an unfriendly way in English-speaking countries if you do not observe the rules of politeness. Read this conversation and characterize the woman in it.

b) Work with a partner: Rewrite the conversation convincingly so that the woman gets the help she needs. Then listen to a 'polite version' of the conversation.

Woman: You must help me!
Man: Why should I do that?
Woman: Because I've got a serious problem. I don't know where I am and my car has broken down. You must drive me somewhere in your car.
Man: What do you mean *must*? I don't have to do anything.
Woman: But I've got to be in Derby at 3 o'clock for a lecture. It's extremely important that I get there on time. I'm the expert.
Man: And it's extremely important that I go home and have a cup of tea. Goodbye.

Language in Focus

LiF steht für *Language in Focus*. Das ist der Grammatikteil von *Camden Town*, in dem die englische Sprache genauer unter die Lupe genommen wird. Du findest in LiF die grammatischen Regeln. Wenn vorne im Buch zum Beispiel ● *LiF 13R: Reported speech, p. 178* steht, kannst du in LiF unter Nummer 13R die passenden Regeln nachschlagen. Das „R" hinter der Nummer steht für *revision* (Wiederholung). So gekennzeichnete Regeln kennst du bereits aus den Jahren davor.
Außerdem findest du unter In short die wichtigsten Regeln auf Englisch kurz zusammengefasst.

Auf dieser Seite findest du die grammatischen Begriffe auf Englisch und auf Deutsch.

Grammatical terms

Englisch	LiF	Deutsch	Beispiel
adjective	10R	Adjektiv	a sad story, a talented girl
adverb	11R	Adverb	
adverb of degree		Gradadverb	absolutely, extremely, slightly, …
adverb of frequency		Häufigkeitsadverb	often, sometimes, never, …
adverb of manner		Adverb der Art und Weise	Carlos plays the guitar beautifully.
sentence adverb		Satzadverb	honestly, luckily, clearly, …
clause		Halbsatz, Satz	
adverbial clause	7 b	adverbialer Nebensatz	When I was walking home, I met Tim.
clause of comparison	10R d	Vergleichssatz	Jeff runs as fast as Tim.
conditional clause, type 1	12R a	Bedingungssatz, Typ 1	If you miss the bus, you will be late.
conditional clause, type 2	12R b	Bedingungssatz, Typ 2	If I were rich, I would fly to New York.
conditional clause, type 3	12R c	Bedingungssatz, Typ 3	If Ben had got up earlier, he could have had breakfast.
if-clause	12R	*if*-Satz	If I had the money, I would go skiing.
main clause	7, 12R, 17R	Hauptsatz	If I had more time, I would learn to play the piano.
defining relative clause	17R	notwendiger Relativsatz	This is the man who helped me.
non-defining relative clause	17R	nicht-notwendiger Relativsatz	My football coach, who is also our neighbour, is very nice.
comparison		Vergleich	
comparison of adjectives	10R	Steigerung von Adjektiven	New York City is bigger than Chicago.
comparison of adverbs	11R	Steigerung von Adverbien	Greg runs faster than his brother.
emphatic 'do'	19		I do believe you're right.
future		Futur (Zukunft)	
going to future	2R b	Futur mit *going to*	She's going to buy a CD.
will future	2R a	Futur mit *will*	I'm sure she will be a pop star.
present progressive with future meaning	2R c	Verlaufsform der Gegenwart mit Zukunftsbedeutung	Are you leaving early tomorrow?
simple present with future meaning	2R d	einfache Gegenwart mit Zukunftsbedeutung	The museum closes at five o'clock this evening.
gerund	18R	Gerundium *(wie ein Nomen gebrauchte ing-Form des Verbs)*	Running is not my thing. I like living in the city.
infinitive		Infinitiv (Grundform)	(to) walk, (to) go, (to) read, …
infinitive with *to*	18 R c	Infinitiv mit *to*	Sam prefers to go by bus.
infinitive without *to*	16 a, 19	Infinitiv ohne *to*	Please let me go to the party!
passive infinitive	5R	Infinitiv des Passivs	Lynn hopes to be chosen for the team.
perfect infinitive	9R	Infinitiv Perfekt	You should have come with us.
modal verb	4R, 5R, 8R, 9R, 12R a, 13R a	Modalverb	can, must, need, should, …

Grammatical terms

English	Ref	German	Example
noun		Nomen (Hauptwort, Substantiv)	
collective noun		Sammelname	family, team, group, …
countable noun		zählbares Nomen	song, child, car, dog, …
uncountable noun		nicht zählbares Nomen	milk, hair, homework, information, …
object		Objekt	
direct object	4R, 16 b	direktes Objekt	I've got a bike.
indirect object	4R	indirektes Objekt	We bought my grandmother a bike.
participle		Partizip	
present participle	6 a, 7	Partizip Präsens	going, driving, drinking, …
past participle	1R, 4R, 5R, 6 b, 7, 12R, 16	Partizip Perfekt	eaten, gone, started, …
perfect participle	7		having gone, having left, …
passive (voice)	4R, 5R	Passiv	The bag was stolen. The bag was found by the police.
personal passive	4R	persönliches Passiv	Karl was given the key.
past perfect	1R g	Plusquamperfekt (Vorvergangenheit)	He didn't bring his homework because the dog had eaten it.
past perfect progressive	1R h	Verlaufsform des Plusquamperfekts	They had been playing cards for hours before Molly arrived.
past tense		Vergangenheitsform	
simple past	1R c	einfache Vergangenheit	They played basketball yesterday.
past progressive	1R d	Verlaufsform der Vergangenheit	Jayden was talking to Kate when his mum called.
possessive determiner		Possessivbegleiter	my, your, his, her, its, our, their
preposition	4R, 18R b	Präposition	about, after, at, for, in, into, on, to, …
present perfect	1R e	Perfekt	David has cleaned the kitchen.
present perfect progressive	1R f	Verlaufsform des Perfekts	I have been waiting for you since three o'clock!
present tense		Präsens (Gegenwart)	
simple present	1R a	einfache Gegenwart	I often walk to school.
present progressive	1R b	Verlaufsform der Gegenwart	It is raining.
pronoun		Pronomen (Fürwort)	
object pronoun		Objektpronomen	me, you, him, her, it, us, them
personal pronoun		Personalpronomen	I, you, he, she, it, we, they
possessive pronoun		Possessivpronomen	mine, yours, hers, …
reciprocal pronoun		reziprokes Pronomen	each other
reflexive pronoun		Reflexivpronomen	myself, yourself, themselves, …
relative pronoun	7 a, 17R	Relativpronomen	who, which, that, …
reported imperative	15	indirekter Aufforderungssatz	Jules told her to go back.
reported question	14R	indirekter Fragesatz	They asked what I wanted for my birthday.
reported speech	13R	indirekte Rede	She says that she likes to read.
subject	7, 18R	Subjekt	Our school is great. Jo and I like football.
substitute form	8R	Ersatzform	They won't be able to come.
tense	1R, 2R	Zeitform, Tempus	
verb		Verb	
regular / irregular		regelmäßig / unregelmäßig	(to) look, (to) walk / (to) meet, (to) see
transitive / intransitive		transitiv / intransitiv	(to) take, (to) buy / (to) sleep
stative verb	3R	Zustandsverb	(to) hate, (to) like, (to) love, …

LiF 1R Gegenwarts- und Vergangenheitsformen (Present and past tenses)

Die verschiedenen Zeitformen eines Verbs *(tenses)* helfen dir auszudrücken, wann etwas im Ablauf der Zeit *(time)* passiert. Außerdem sagen die verschiedenen Zeitformen etwas über Gewohnheiten und Zustände aus.
Grundsätzlich werden die einfache *(simple form)* und die Verlaufsform *(progressive form)* einer Zeitform unterschieden. Die Verlaufsform legt den Schwerpunkt auf den Verlauf einer Handlung. Sie drückt aus, dass eine Handlung gerade im Gange ist (oder war), dass sie noch nicht abgeschlossen ist (oder war) bzw. dass es um vorübergehende Zustände geht. Die einfache Zeitform hingegen legt den Schwerpunkt auf den Zeitpunkt einer Handlung. Außerdem beschreibt sie gewohnheitsmäßige Handlungen und Zustände. Zustandsverben *(stative verbs)*, die z. B. ein Gefühl oder eine Sinneswahrnehmung bezeichnen, stehen in der Regel nur in der einfachen Zeitform (→ LiF 3R).

a) Die einfache Gegenwart (The simple present)

Das *simple present* verwendest du, ...

- um über Gewohnheiten oder regelmäßige Handlungen zu sprechen:

  *My brother **goes** to football training **every Thursday**.*

- um aufeinander folgende Handlungen zu beschreiben:

  *First you **change** into your sports clothes. Then you **warm up**. After that you **talk** to the coach.*

- um über Zustände zu sprechen, die längere Zeit andauern oder allgemein gültig sind:

  *Leanne and Jamie **live** in Nottingham.*

Wenn du über Gewohnheiten im *simple present* sprichst, kannst du diese Wörter verwenden, um auszudrücken, wie häufig etwas stattfindet: *never, sometimes, usually, often, always, every day.*

b) Die Verlaufsform der Gegenwart (The present progressive)

Das *present progressive* verwendest du, um Handlungen zu beschreiben, die im Augenblick des Sprechens ablaufen:

*Andrew **is reading** a magazine.*
*Fiona **is doing** her homework **at the moment**.*
*Lindsay and Ben **are just talking** to Mrs Pullman.*

Mit dem *present progressive* kannst du diese Wörter verwenden, um besonders herauszustreichen, dass dies nur eine momentane Tätigkeit ist, auf die etwas anderes folgen wird: *at the moment, just, now.*

c) Die einfache Vergangenheit (The simple past)

Das *simple past* verwendest du, um über abgeschlossene Handlungen in der Vergangenheit zu sprechen:

*Last year, Isabel **celebrated** Thanksgiving with her best friend.*
*I **read** an article about peer pressure **yesterday**.*
*The members of the marching band **met last Tuesday**.*

Mit dem *simple past* kannst du diese Wörter verwenden, um auszudrücken, dass Handlungen in der Vergangenheit abgeschlossen wurden: *last week/month/year, two days ago, yesterday.*

! Wie du weißt, gibt es im Englischen unregelmäßige Verben, die für das *simple past* eigene Formen haben. Eine Liste mit unregelmäßigen Verben findest du auf S. 268/269.

d) Die Verlaufsform der Vergangenheit (The past progressive)

were/was + ing [handwritten]

Das *past progressive* drückt aus, dass eine Handlung in der Vergangenheit im Gang war, als eine zweite Handlung einsetzte. Die zweite Handlung steht im *simple past*:

> *We **were making** dinner **when** the phone rang.*

Mit diesen Wörtern kannst du beide Handlungen miteinander verknüpfen: *while, when*.

> *While she **was taking** pictures, a man took her bag.*

e) Das Perfekt (The present perfect)

Das *present perfect* verwendest du, …
- wenn Handlungen oder Ereignisse, die schon stattgefunden haben, noch Auswirkungen in die Gegenwart hinein haben:
- wenn ein Vorgang, der in der Vergangenheit begonnen hat, bis in die Gegenwart andauert:

> *Oh, no! Oliver **has forgotten** to feed the cats for the third time. His dad is talking to him right now.*
>
> *Please wait a minute. I **haven't finished** my breakfast yet.*

Mit dem *present perfect* kannst du diese Wörter verwenden, um auszudrücken, dass die vergangene Handlung in die Gegenwart hineinwirkt: *already, never, ever, yet, so far*.

Unregelmäßige Verben haben ein unregelmäßiges Partizip Perfekt *(past participle)*.
Eine Liste mit unregelmäßigen Verben findest du auf S. 268/269.

f) Die Verlaufsform des Perfekts (The present perfect progressive)

has been ing [handwritten]

Du verwendest die Verlaufsform des Perfekts *(present perfect progressive)*, um über eine Handlung zu sprechen, die in der Vergangenheit begonnen hat und immer noch andauert.
Meistens handelt es sich um eine vorübergehende Handlung.

> *She **has been watching** TV for over three hours.*

g) Das Plusquamperfekt (The past perfect)

had [handwritten]

Das *past perfect* drückt aus, dass eine Handlung vor einer anderen Handlung in der Vergangenheit stattgefunden hat. Die zweite Handlung steht im *simple past*. Beide Handlungen sind abgeschlossen:

> *Claire ordered two hamburgers because she **hadn't eaten** since yesterday evening.*
>
> *After the rain **had stopped**, they went to the beach.*

Unregelmäßige Verben haben ein unregelmäßiges Partizip Perfekt *(past participle)*.
Eine Liste mit unregelmäßigen Verben findest du auf S. 268/269.

h) Die Verlaufsform des Plusquamperfekts (The past perfect progressive)

[handwritten above title: had been]

Die Verlaufsform des Plusquamperfekts *(past perfect progressive)* verwendest du, um über eine Handlung zu sprechen, die vor einer anderen Handlung stattgefunden hat. Die neu eintretende Handlung steht im *simple past*. Im Vergleich zum *past perfect* wird mit dem *past perfect progressive* die Dauer einer Handlung betont.

Zeitangaben wie *for, since, all day/week/month* werden oft zusammen mit dem *past perfect progressive* verwendet.

> When they finally arrived, the other members of their team **had** already **been talking** about their tactics for half an hour.

LiF 2R Die Wiedergabe der Zukunft (Future tenses)

Die grammatischen Zeitformen *(tenses)* entsprechen nicht immer der Zeit in der Wirklichkeit. So werden nicht nur die Zukunftsformen *will future* und *going to future* verwendet, um die Zukunft wiederzugeben, sondern auch die einfache Gegenwart *(simple present)* und die Verlaufsform der Gegenwart *(present progressive)*.

a) Das Futur mit *will* (The *will* future)

Du verwendest das *will future*, um über Vorhersagen und Vermutungen über die Zukunft zu sprechen:

> *Maybe* it **will rain** tomorrow.
> I **won't tell** anyone about the surprise party.

Diese Wörter bestimmen den zukünftigen Zeitpunkt näher, an dem etwas voraussichtlich stattfinden wird: *tonight, tomorrow, next year*.

Mit diesen Wörtern kannst du ausdrücken, dass du dir nicht sicher bist, ob ein Ereignis eintreten wird: *perhaps, maybe*.

b) Das Futur mit *going to* (The *going to* future)

Du verwendest das *going to future*, um über Absichten und Pläne für die Zukunft zu sprechen:

> We**'re going to fly** to Poland **in July**, but we haven't bought any tickets yet.

Diese Wörter werden oft zusammen mit dem *going to future* verwendet:
in January/February/March/..., I think, I'm sure.

Mit dem *going to future* kannst du auch ausdrücken, dass du glaubst, etwas wird gleich passieren (weil es deutliche Hinweise darauf gibt):

> Look at those black clouds, I think it**'s going to rain**.

c) Die Verlaufsform der Gegenwart mit Zukunftsbedeutung
   (The present progressive with future meaning)

Möchtest du über feste persönliche Pläne und Vorhaben sprechen, kannst du dazu das *present progressive* benutzen. Aus dem Kontext oder durch Zeitangaben wie *tomorrow, next week, this afternoon*, etc. wird deutlich, dass es sich um die Zukunft und nicht die Gegenwart handelt:

*I'm definitely **meeting** my friend tomorrow.*
***Are** you **spending** the day with Grandma?*

d) Die einfache Gegenwart mit Zukunftsbedeutung
   (The simple present with future meaning)

Sprichst du über feststehende Termine, die in der Zukunft liegen, verwendest du dafür wie im Deutschen auch die einfache Gegenwart. Vor allem im Zusammenhang mit Fahrplänen, Programmen oder Öffnungszeiten wird das *simple present with future meaning* gebraucht:

*The plane from Edinburgh **arrives** at seven o'clock.*
*When **does** the film 'Thor' **start**?*

In short: Future tenses

- You can use the *will* future to talk about events in the future that you think may happen:
  I'm sure they **will win** the game. – Really? Their team captain is ill so I think they **will lose**.
- You can use the *going to* future to talk about plans for the future. Moreover, you can use it for when you think that something may happen and there are sure signs for it:
  I'm going to take the car tomorrow. – But there **is going to be** a traffic jam. There is one every morning.
- You can use the present progressive to talk about events in the future that you have already planned:
  What **are you doing** this afternoon? – **I'm taking care** of my little sister.
- You use the simple present to talk about events in the future that are fixed:
  My train **leaves** at 5 o'clock in the evening.

LiF 3R Zustandsverben (Stative verbs)

Stative verbs, also Verben, die einen länger andauernden Zustand beschreiben (z. B. ein Gefühl, ein Haltung oder eine Sinneswahrnehmung), werden normalerweise nur in der Grundform und nicht in der Verlaufsform verwendet.
Hier sind einige der gängigsten Zustandsverben:
to agree, to believe, to belong, to doubt, to hate, to hear, to imagine, to know, to like, to love, to mean, to need, to prefer, to recognize, to remember, to see, to seem, to sound, to surprise, to taste, to understand, to want.

*He **loves** the mountains.*

LiF 4R Das Passiv (The passive)

- Aktivsätze sagen uns, wer oder was handelt. Wenn es aber nicht wichtig oder klar ist, wer etwas tut oder getan hat, kannst du das Passiv verwenden. In diesen Fällen steht die Handlung im Vordergrund.
- Das Passiv bildest du aus einer Form von *be + past participle*:

simple present	am/is/are + past participle	Bags **are** often **stolen** at the market.
simple past	was/were + past participle	A red bag **was stolen** at the market yesterday.
present perfect	has/have been + past participle	Don't worry, the red bag **has been found**.
will future	will be + past participle	The bag **will be given** back.
going to future	am/is/are going to be + past participle	The pickpocket **is going to be sent** to prison.
Modalverben	can/must/may/ … be + past participle	He **must be kept** in prison for many days.

- Wie bei Aktivsätzen gibt es auch im Passiv sowohl eine einfache *(simple form)* als auch eine Verlaufsform *(progressive form)*. Passive Verlaufsformen verwendest du wie aktive (LiF 1R b und d). Das Passiv von Verlaufsformen bildest du aus einer Form von *be + being + past participle*:

present progressive	am/are/is being + past participle	You **are being taught** English as you read this book.
past progressive	was/were being + past participle	I **was being told** to be quiet when my phone rang.

- Wenn du in einem Passiv-Satz die handelnde Person oder die Ursache für etwas nennen willst, hängst du sie mit **by** („von", „durch") an den Satz an:
 *The hockey game will be watched **by** many people.* • *The stadium was damaged **by** a storm.*

- Bei Verben mit zwei Objekten wird im Englischen häufig das *personal passive* verwendet. Dabei wird das indirekte Objekt eines Aktivsatzes zum Subjekt des Passivsatzes:

	Subjekt	Verb	Indirektes Objekt	Direktes Objekt
Aktivsatz:	Somebody	showed	William	an old watch.
personal passive:	William	was shown		an old watch.

- Wie in Aktivsätzen, werden in Passivsätzen Verben und Präpositionen nicht voneinander getrennt:

		Verb + Präposition	
Aktivsatz:	Lizzy	looks after	the horses.
Passivsatz:	The horses	are looked after	by Lizzy.

In short: The passive

You use the passive to show that you think the action is more important than the person or thing who does it: *The tickets **were given** away for free.*
- If you want to use the passive and say who or what does something, you use **by**: *The tickets were given away **by** the musicians.*
- If the **verb has two objects**, you can use the **personal passive: *The fans** were given the tickets.*

LiF 5R — Der Infinitiv des Passivs (The passive infinitive)

- In Passivsätzen mit Modalverben *(modal verbs)*, verwendest du den Infinitiv des Passivs *(passive infinitive)* ohne *to*: *The medicine **should be taken** three times a day.*

Bei Modalverben und ihren Ersatzformen mit *to* (→ LiF 8R), bleibt das *to* im Passivsatz erhalten:

*Cats **have to be fed** every day.* – Katzen müssen jeden Tag gefüttert werden.
*The fee **ought to be paid** immediately.* – Die Gebühr sollte sofort bezahlt werden.

- Nach Verben wie *to ask, to expect, to hope, to like, to hate, to love, to want* verwendest du den Infinitiv des Passivs mit *to*. Er wird gebildet aus *to be* + *past participle*:

	Verb	Infinitiv des Passivs mit *to*		
Carlos	hoped	to be shown	how to find a girlfriend.	... hoffte, dass ihm gezeigt werden würde, wie man eine Freundin findet.
The geeks	didn't want	to be seen	as weird.	... wollten nicht ... angesehen werden.
Nobody	expects	to be given	presents for Thanksgiving.	... erwartet ... zu bekommen.
Megan	asked	to be chosen	for the parade.	... bat darum ... ausgewählt zu werden.

LiF 6 — Partizipien *(Participles)*

a) Das Partizip Präsens (Present participle)

Das Partizip Präsens *(present participle)* wird zur Konstruktion der Verlaufsformen der Zeiten *(progressive forms)* verwendet:

*Zoe is **reading** a book at the moment.*

b) Das Partizip Perfekt (Past participle)

Das Partizip Perfekt *(past participle)* wird für Perfekt-Zeitformen wie das *present perfect* verwendet:

Vorsicht *false friend*:
Partizip Perfekt = *past participle* ≠ *perfect participle*

*Joe has not yet **finished** his homework.*

Language in Focus

LiF 7 Partizipialkonstruktionen (Participle constructions)

Du kannst Partizipien verwenden, um die Satzstruktur zu variieren.

a) Partizipien anstelle von Relativsätzen (Participles in place of relative clauses)

Du kannst mithilfe von Partizipien Relativsätze ersetzen. Voraussetzung dafür ist, dass das Relativpronomen Subjekt des Relativsatzes ist. Ein *present participle* ersetzt dann einen Relativsatz im Aktiv, ein *past participle* einen Relativsatz im Passiv:

active	
sentence with relative clause	sentence with **present participle**
The DVD which is playing right now was a present from my brother.	The DVD **playing** right now was a present from my brother.
My cousin who lives in Canada speaks perfect French.	My cousin **living** in Canada speaks perfect French.
Is there anybody who is listening to me?	Is there anybody **listening** to me?

passive	
sentence with relative clause	sentence with **past participle**
Cars which are parked here will be taken away.	Cars **parked** here will be taken away.
Clothes which have been left in the gym can be picked up in room 221.	Clothes **left** in the gym can be picked up in room 221.
Have all the photos which were taken on the trip already been printed out?	Have all the photos **taken** on the trip already been printed out?

b) Partizipien anstelle von adverbialen Nebensätzen (Participles in place of adverbial clauses)

Du kannst mithilfe von Partizipien auch einige adverbiale Nebensätze ersetzen. Dies betrifft vor allem adverbiale Nebensätze der Zeit und des Grundes. Voraussetzung dafür ist, dass das Subjekt des Hauptsatzes auch Subjekt des adverbialen Nebensatzes ist. Ein *present participle* ersetzt dann einen Nebensatz im Aktiv, ein *past participle* einen Nebensatz im Passiv:

sentence with adverbial clause	sentence with **participle**
Tim lost his mobile phone when he was coming home from school.	Tim lost his mobile phone **coming** home from school.
When I looked up, I saw my friend Andy.	**Looking up**, I saw my friend Andy.
She never goes to rock concerts because she doesn't like loud music.	**Not liking** loud music, she never goes to rock concerts.
The dog couldn't run away because he was chained to the tree.	**Chained** to the tree, the dog couldn't run away.

Möchtest du ausdrücken, dass eine Handlung vor einer anderen geschehen ist, kannst du dafür das *perfect participle* verwenden. Es wird gebildet aus *having* und dem *past participle* des Verbs. Das *perfect participle* ersetzt dann adverbiale Nebensätze im Aktiv:

sentence with adverbial clause	sentence with **perfect participle**
Lisa expected good results in her exam because she had worked really hard.	**Having worked** really hard, Lisa expected good results in her exam.
After he had eaten two bowls of ice cream, Ben felt very sick.	**Having eaten** two bowls of ice cream, Ben felt very sick.
Now that we have seen all the sights, we can go shopping.	**Having seen** all the sights, we can now go shopping.

Das *perfect participle* gibt es auch im Passiv. Es wird gebildet aus *having* + *been* + *past participle* des Verbs. Es ersetzt adverbiale Nebensätze, die im Passiv stehen:

sentence with adverbial clause	sentence with **perfect participle**
After they had been greeted by their friends, they entered the house.	**Having been greeted** by their friends, they entered the house.
The shoes are very cheap because they have been worn before.	**Having been worn** before, the shoes are very cheap.

Vorsicht *false friend*: Partizip Perfekt = *past participle* ≠ *perfect participle*

c) Verbinden von zwei Hauptsätzen mit Partizipien (Using participles to join two sentences)

Du kannst mithilfe von Partizipien auch zwei Hauptsätze miteinander verbinden, wenn beide Sätze das gleiche Subjekt haben und beide Handlungen zur gleichen Zeit ablaufen. Ein *present participle* ersetzt dann einen Satz im Aktiv, ein *past participle* einen Satz im Passiv:

two separate sentences	sentence with **participle** construction
The players left the field. They thought the match was over.	The players left the field **thinking** the match was over.
Jamie looked into the fridge. He hoped to find some ice cream.	Jamie looked into the fridge **hoping** to find some ice cream.
The text was written in a hurry. It was full of mistakes.	**Written** in a hurry, the text was full of mistakes.

d) Partizipien nach bestimmten Verben (Participles after certain verbs)

- Mithilfe des *present participle* kannst du Verben der Ruhe und Bewegung *(verbs of rest and motion)* näher beschreiben. Zu diesen Verben gehören u. a. *to sit, to stand, to come, to go*:
  *Karen just **sits holding** the letter in her hands.* – Karen sitzt nur da und hält den Brief in ihren Händen.
  *Mike **came asking** for the money.* – Mike kam und fragte nach dem Geld.

- Du weißt, dass du nach Verben der Sinneswahrnehmung *(verbs of perception)*
  Objekt + Infinitiv ohne *to* verwenden kannst:
  *I **watched them carry** the boxes into the house.*
  *Tom **heard the phone ring** but didn't have time to answer it.*
  Bei dieser Konstruktion wird der Fokus auf die Abgeschlossenheit des Geschehens gelegt.

  Möchtest du den Moment betonen, in dem ein Geschehen wahrgenommen wird, verwendest du *present participle* anstelle des Infinitivs ohne *to*:
  *Do you **see those children crossing** the street?*
  *When we walked past the garden, we could **hear John singing** his favourite song.*

*When I looked out of the window, I **saw Keiran running** up the stairs.*

In short: Participle constructions

- You can use participle constructions to replace relative clauses and adverbial clauses if they have the same subject as the main clause. Moreover, you can use participle constructions to link two main clauses if they share a subject and the two actions happen at the same time. For active clauses, you use the present participle, for passive clauses, you use the past participle:
  Going home, she noticed that her purse was gone.
  Founded in 2008, the school still looked very new.

- If one action happens before the other, you can use the perfect participle, either in the active or the passive voice:
  Having boarded the plane, she suddenly felt scared.
  Having been awarded to women for three years in a row, the Oscar for best director went to a man this year.

- You can use the present participle after **verbs of rest and motion** and after **verbs of perception + object**:
  *Don't just **stand** waiting for a reaction!*
  *I can **hear you** talking about my sister. That's not very nice.*

LiF 8R Modalverben und ihre Ersatzformen (Modal verbs and their substitute forms)

Modalverben geben zum Beispiel an, ob etwas erlaubt oder notwendig ist.
Die meisten Modalverben haben nur Formen für das *simple present*.
Für andere Zeitformen musst du deshalb Ersatzformen *(substitute forms)* verwenden.

a) Fähigkeit (Ability)

Wenn du sagen willst, dass jemand in der Lage oder fähig ist, etwas zu tun, verwendest du *can* und die Ersatzform *be able to*:
Im *simple past* kannst du auch *could/couldn't* benutzen: *I **couldn't** go to school because I was ill.*

*I **can** read.*
*She **was able to** answer all the questions.*

b) Erlaubnis (Permission)

Mit *may, can* und der Ersatzform *be allowed to* kannst du ausdrücken, dass etwas erlaubt ist:

May/Can I open the window?
*Jo **will be allowed to** go to the party next week.*

Mit *may not, can't* und der Ersatzform *not be allowed to* kannst du ausdrücken, dass etwas nicht erlaubt ist:

*Sorry, but you **may not/can't** leave your bike here.*
*Lynn **hasn't been allowed to** go to the concert.*

Im *simple present* kannst du auch *must not* oder die Kurzform *mustn't* benutzen, um auszudrücken, dass jemand etwas nicht darf. Es ist etwas strenger als *may not/can't*:

❗ *Must not* und die Kurzform *mustn't* klingen wie im Deutschen „muss nicht", heißt aber „etwas nicht dürfen".

*You **mustn't** write notes to your classmates.*

c) Notwendigkeit (Necessity)

Mit *must* und der Ersatzform *have to* kannst du ausdrücken, dass etwas getan werden muss:

*You **must** be careful in national parks.*
*Joanna **has had to** go home. She didn't feel well.*

Wenn du sagen willst, dass jemand etwas nicht zu tun braucht, benutzt du *needn't* und die Ersatzform *don't have to*:

*We **needn't** buy milk. There's enough in the fridge.*
*You **didn't have to** buy me a present.*

❗ *Needn't* hat die gleiche Bedeutung wie *don't have to*, ist aber etwas förmlicher.

d) Möglichkeit (Possibility)

- Mit *may/may not* kannst du ausdrücken, dass etwas möglicherweise geschieht bzw. nicht geschieht:

  *It **may** rain today.*
  *Ann **may not** come to basketball practice today.*

! *May not* ist nicht eindeutig. Es kann sowohl *wird möglicherweise nicht* als auch *darf nicht* heißen.

- Statt *may/may not* kannst du auch *might/might not* verwenden:

  *Kim has been cycling all day long. She **might** be tired.*
  *Ed just called. He **might not** be able to join us tonight.*

e) Empfehlung (Advice)

- Mit *should/shouldn't* drückst du aus, dass etwas deiner Ansicht nach passieren bzw. nicht passieren sollte:

  *You **should** leave now if you want to catch the bus.*
  *You **shouldn't** walk home on your own.*

- *Ought to/ought not to* (Kurzform: *oughtn't*) hat die gleiche Bedeutung wie *should/shouldn't,* ist aber weniger gebräuchlich und wirkt etwas strenger:

  *You **ought to** do more exercise.*
  *You **ought not to** eat so much fast food.*

- Mit *had better* und *could* kannst du auch Empfehlungen aussprechen. *Could* ist am wenigsten streng und gleicht einem Vorschlag:
  *You **had better** tell her that you're sorry.* – Du sagst ihr besser, dass es dir leidtut.
  *You **could** give him a call.* – Du könntest ihn anrufen.

f) Vorschlag/Angebot (Suggestion/offer)

Wenn du einen Vorschlag oder ein Angebot machen möchtest, kannst du *shall* verwenden. Es taucht in Form einer Frage auf:
***Shall** I help you with the bags?* – Kann/Soll ich dir mit den Taschen helfen?
*When **shall** we all meet for dinner?* – Wann sollen wir uns alle zum Abendessen treffen?

g) Pflicht (Obligation)

Wenn du ausdrücken möchtest, dass es die Pflicht ist, etwas zu tun oder zu lassen, verwendest du *to be supposed to/to be not supposed to*:
*You **are supposed to** take off your shoes before you go into the gym.* –
Man soll seine Schuhe ausziehen, bevor man in die Turnhalle geht.
*Luke **was not supposed to** tell his father about the birthday surprise.* –
Luke sollte seinem Vater nichts von der Geburtstagsüberraschung erzählen.

LiF 9R — Modalverben mit dem Infinitiv Perfekt (Modal verbs with the perfect infinitive)

Um auszudrücken, dass etwas in der Vergangenheit hätte passieren können, sollen oder müssen, verwendest du Modalverben mit dem Infinitiv Perfekt *(perfect infinitive)*.
Der Infinitiv Perfekt wird gebildet aus *have + past participle*:

	Modalverb	Infinitiv Perfekt		
You	should	have seen	the view from our hotel room!	*Du hättest die Aussicht von unserem Hotelzimmer sehen sollen.*
Tourists	may	have caused	the damage.	*Vielleicht haben Touristen den Schaden verursacht.*
He	couldn't	have kept	all three puppies.	*Er hätte nicht alle drei Welpen behalten können.*
The trip to Colorado	must	have been	interesting.	*Die Reise nach Colorado muss interessant gewesen sein.*

LiF 10R — Die Steigerung von Adjektiven (The comparison of adjectives)

Mit Adjektiven lassen sich Personen oder Sachen näher beschreiben. Willst du Personen oder Sachen miteinander vergleichen, steigerst du die Adjektive. Die Steigerungsformen heißen *comparative* (Komparativ) und *superlative* (Superlativ).

a) Regelmäßige Steigerung (Regular comparative/superlative forms)

Einsilbige Adjektive werden durch das Anhängen von *-er* und *-est* gesteigert:
cheap, cheaper, cheapest
Diese Regel gilt auch für zweisilbige Adjektive, die auf *-y* enden.
Dabei wird aus dem *-y* ein *-i-*: *pretty, prettier, prettiest*

! Bei manchen Adjektiven ändert sich die Schreibweise: *hot, hotter, hottest*

b) Unregelmäßige Steigerungsformen (Irregular comparative/superlative forms)

Es gibt auch unregelmäßige Steigerungsformen, die du wie Vokabeln lernen musst:
good   better   (the) best
bad   worse   (the) worst

c) Steigerung mit *more* und *most* (Comparison with *more* and *most*)

Die Steigerungsform von Adjektiven mit mehr als zwei Silben bildest du mit *more* und *most*.
Diese Art der Steigerung ist auch bei vielen zweisilbigen Adjektiven möglich, die nicht auf *-y* enden:
*interesting   **more** interesting   (the) **most** interesting*
*polite   **more** polite   (the) **most** polite*

d) Vergleichssätze (Clauses of comparison)

- Für den Vergleich von Dingen und Personen verwendest du den Komparativ gefolgt von *than*:
  The scarf is **cheaper than** the T-shirt.

- Sind die Eigenschaften gleich, verwendest du *as ... as*:
  Sarah is **as** tall **as** Anne.

In short: Comparison of adjectives

- The comparative and superlative of one-syllable adjectives are formed by adding *-er* and *-est*: **short, shorter, shortest**.
  The same is true of two-syllable adjectives ending in *-y*. However, for the comparative and the superlative, the *-y* changes to *-i-*: **easy, easier, easiest**.
- The comparative and superlative of other two-syllable adjectives and those with more syllables are formed using *more* and *most*: **surprising, more surprising, most surprising**.
- Some adjectives have irregular comparative and superlative forms: **good, better, best**.

LiF 11R Die Steigerung von Adverbien (The comparison of adverbs)

Für die Steigerung von Adverbien gelten die gleichen Regeln wie für die Steigerung von Adjektiven.

- Einsilbige Adverbien steigerst du, indem du *-er* und *-est* anhängst:
  Kadhija runs **faster** than the other girls.
  Olivia's team trained the **hardest** of all.

- Adverbien, die auf *-ly* enden, steigerst du mit *more* und *most*:
  Football players earn money **more easily** than hockey players.
  Of all my friends, Ellen can sing the **most beautifully**.

- Es gibt auch unregelmäßige Steigerungsformen der Adverbien, die du wie Vokabeln lernen musst:

adverb	comparative	superlative
well	better	best
badly	worse	worst

*Kadhija runs **faster** than the other girls.*

In short: Comparison of adverbs

- The comparative and superlative of one-syllable adverbs are formed by adding *-er* and *-est*: **fast, faster, fastest**.
- For adverbs ending in *-ly*, *more* and *most* are used: **easily, more easily, most easily**.
- Some adverbs have irregular comparative and superlative forms: **badly, worse, worst**.

LiF 12R Bedingungssätze (Conditional clauses)

a) Bedingungssätze, Typ 1 (Conditional clauses, type 1)

Der Bedingungssatz, Typ 1 *(conditional clause, type 1)*, besteht aus einem *if*-Satz *(if-clause)* und einem Hauptsatz *(main clause)*:
- Der *if*-Satz nennt eine Bedingung. Der Hauptsatz drückt aus, was passiert, wenn die Bedingung erfüllt ist.
- Im *if*-Satz steht das *simple present*, im Hauptsatz das *will future*.
  Im Hauptsatz kannst du auch Modalverben (z. B. *can, must*) oder den Imperativ verwenden:

if-Satz (Bedingung)	Hauptsatz (Folge)
If you **miss** the bus,	you **will be** late.
If the weather **is** nice,	we **can** go hiking.
If you **need** help,	**ask** Alyssa.

Beginnst du mit dem Hauptsatz, steht kein Komma vor dem *if*-Satz:
They won't go to the beach if it rains.

b) Bedingungssätze, Typ 2 (Conditional clauses, type 2)

Mit dem Bedingungssatz, Typ 2 *(conditional clause, type 2)*, drückst du aus, was unter einer nur gedachten Bedingung passieren würde oder könnte. Dabei geht es um Ereignisse, die unwahrscheinlich oder unmöglich sind.
Im *if*-Satz steht das *simple past*, im Hauptsatz *would* oder *could* vor dem Infinitiv:

*If I **lived** in Britain, I **would eat** scones every day.*
*If I **were** rich, I **could help** a lot of people.*

if-Satz (nur gedachte Bedingung)	Hauptsatz (Folge)
If I **had** to spend my vacation in the wilderness,	I **would try** to make the best of it.
If Steve **behaved** better,	he **could get on** really well with his classmates.

Üblicherweise sagt man "If I were …", aber im gesprochenen Englisch ist auch "If I was …" erlaubt.
*If I **were** rich, I could help a lot of people.*
*If I **was** really good at basketball, I would try for a sports scholarship.*

Denke daran: Im *if*-Satz verwendest du nie *would*!

c) Bedingungssätze, Typ 3 (Conditional clauses, type 3)

Mit dem Bedingungssatz, Typ 3 *(conditional clause, type 3)*, spekulierst du darüber, was in der Vergangenheit hätte passieren können, aber nicht passiert ist. Die Bedingung im *if*-Satz ist nicht mehr erfüllbar. Du kannst Bedingungssätze vom Typ 3 verwenden, um über verpasste Möglichkeiten zu sprechen.

Bei dieser Art von Bedingungssätzen steht im *if*-Satz das *past perfect*.
Im Hauptsatz steht *would/could/might* + *have* + *past participle*:

if-Satz (nicht mehr erfüllbare Bedingung)	Hauptsatz (Folge)	
If Coleman **had won** the competition,	he **would have been** the youngest champion ever.	Wenn Coleman den Wettbewerb gewonnen hätte, wäre er der jüngste Meister aller Zeiten gewesen.
If Hailey **had not broken** every school rule,	she **could have stayed** in her class until the end of the year.	Wenn Hailey nicht jede Schulregel gebrochen hätte, hätte sie bis zum Jahresende in ihrer Klasse bleiben können.
If Jason **had not been** in the shower,	he **might have heard** the telephone ring.	Wenn Jason nicht unter der Dusche gewesen wäre, hätte er vielleicht das Telefon klingeln hören.

Wenn du darüber sprechen möchtest, wie die Gegenwart wäre, wenn etwas in der Vergangenheit stattgefunden oder nicht stattgefunden hätte, verwendest du *would/wouldn't* + Infinitiv im Hauptsatz:
If Brandon had apologized earlier, he **would** still **be** good friends with Julia.
If I had eaten breakfast, I **wouldn't be** hungry now.

In short: Conditional clauses

You use the conditional clause, type 1, when you think that the condition is likely:
- In the **if-clause** you use the **simple present**. In the **main clause** you usually use the **will future**: If the weather **is** nice tomorrow, we **will go** for a walk.

You use the conditional clause, type 2, when you think that the condition is unlikely or imaginary:
- In the **if-clause** you use the **simple past**. In the **main clause** you normally use **would**/**could** + infinitive: If the weather **was** nicer, we **could** go for a walk.
- Remember: You can't use *would* in the if-clause.

You use the conditional clause, type 3, to speculate what could or might have happened:
- In the **if-clause** you use the **past perfect**. In the **main clause** you normally use **would**/**could** + **have** + past participle: If the weather **had been** nicer yesterday, we **could have** gone for a walk.

LiF 13R Indirekte Rede (Reported speech)

Wenn du berichten willst, was jemand gesagt hat, verwendest du die indirekte Rede *(reported speech)*:

Direkte Rede	**Indirekte Rede**	
	Begleitsatz	Wiedergegebene Aussage
Callum: "I'm fourteen." →	*Callum says (that)*	*he is fourteen.*

Die indirekte Rede besteht aus einem Begleitsatz und der wiedergegebenen Aussage.
Beide Satzteile können durch *that* verbunden werden, man kann es aber auch weglassen.

a) Zeitverschiebung (Backshift of tenses)

Steht das Verb im Begleitsatz in der Vergangenheit, erfolgt in der wiedergegebenen Aussage eine Zeitverschiebung *(backshift of tenses)*: Die Zeitform der wiedergegebenen Aussage rückt gegenüber der direkten Rede sozusagen eine Stufe weiter in die Vergangenheit:

Language in Focus

Direkte Rede (direct speech)	Indirekte Rede (reported speech)
simple present June to Johnny: "Rob **is** nice."	→ *simple past* June told Johnny (that) Rob **was** nice.
present progressive Tim: "Laura, you **are getting** on my nerves!"	→ *past progressive* Tim told Laura (that) she **was getting** on his nerves.
simple past Samantha: "I **saw** a swan yesterday."	→ *past perfect* Samantha said (that) she **had seen** a swan the day before.
past progressive Elaine: "I **was waiting** for Jerry when George arrived."	→ *past perfect progressive* Elaine said (that) she **had been waiting** for Jerry when George arrived.
present perfect Denzel to Ron: "I**'ve just been** to the dentist."	→ *past perfect* Denzel told Ron (that) he **had just been** to the dentist.
present perfect progressive Lisa: "I**'ve been making** biscuits all day.	→ *past perfect progressive* Lisa said (that) she **had been making** biscuits all day.
past perfect History teacher: "After they **had moved** west, many settlers started their own farms."	→ *past perfect* The history teacher said (that) many settlers started their own farms after they **had moved** west.
past perfect progressive John: "I **had been seeing** patients for three hours when Linda arrived."	→ *past perfect progressive* John said (that) he **had been seeing** patients for three hours when Linda arrived.
will Anita to Sinead: "I **will miss** you!"	→ *would* Anita told Sinead (that) she **would** miss her.
is/are going to Jordan to Taylor: "I**'m going to leave** Cleveland."	→ *was/were going to* Jordan told Taylor (that) he **was going to leave** Cleveland.
can/must/may Al to Nick: "I **can't** play football." Nick to Al: "You **must** come and watch me play." Al: "I **may** come tomorrow."	→ *could/had to/might* Al told Nick (that) he **couldn't** play football. Nick told Al (that) he **had to** come and watch him play. Al said (that) he **might** come the next day.

would/could/should/might bleiben unverändert:
James: "I **should** go." → James said that he **should** go.

Wenn die Aussage, die du wiedergibst, noch von Bedeutung oder allgemeingültig ist, erfolgt kein *backshift of tenses*:
Caroline: "Girls and boys **can** be just friends." → Caroline said that girls and boys **can** be just friends.

b) Weitere Anpassungen in der indirekten Rede (Further changes in reported speech)

Personalpronomen und Possessivbegleiter verändern sich, damit der wiedergegebene Satz Sinn ergibt:

		direct speech		reported speech
I	→ she, he	Mrs Hughes: "I'm going to write a book."	→	Mrs Hughes told me that she was going to write a book.
you	→ I, me, we, us	Patrick: "Sushmita saw you at the supermarket."	→	Patrick said Sushmita had seen us at the supermarket.
we	→ they	Lisa and Luke: "We had a great time at the party."	→	Lisa and Luke said they had had a great time at the party.
my	→ her, his	Molly: "My father has gone away."	→	Molly said her father had gone away.
our	→ their	Mr and Mrs Parr: "Our dog was ill."	→	The Parrs said their dog had been ill.
me	→ him, her	Robert: "She doesn't like me."	→	Robert said that she didn't like him.
us	→ them	Susie: "He took us to the zoo."	→	She said he had taken them to the zoo.

Auch Orts- und Zeitangaben müssen angepasst werden, je nachdem wann und wo du den Satz wiedergibst:

Oct 2nd, at the restaurant: Claire to Paul: "Let's meet here for lunch tomorrow."
Oct 2nd, at home: Paul to his father: "Claire said that we should meet there for lunch tomorrow."
Nov 1st, at the restaurant: Paul to Wayne: "She said that we should meet here for lunch the next day."

So kannst du Orts- und Zeitangaben je nach der Situation anpassen:

here	→ there		
today	→ that day	yesterday	→ the day before
tomorrow	→ the next day	three days ago	→ three days before/earlier
next year	→ the following year	last week/year	→ the week/year before

In short: Reported speech

You use reported speech when you want to report what someone said:
- You begin with a **main clause** followed by a **subclause**:
  He said (that) she was the most beautiful girl in the world.
- If the verb in the main clause is in the past tense, the tense in the subclause usually takes a step back in time. This is called a backshift of tenses.
- You also have to change other words, such as personal pronouns, so that the reported sentence makes sense: Alison: "I often go to the movies." → Alison said she often went to the movies.

LiF 14R Indirekte Fragesätze (Reported questions)

Wenn du eine Entscheidungsfrage wiedergeben willst, benutzt du *if* oder *whether*:

direct speech	reported question
"Have you seen the film?"	→ She asked me **whether I had seen the film**. *Sie fragte mich, ob ich den Film gesehen hätte.*
"Will you be here for Christmas?"	→ We wanted to know **if they would be here for Christmas**. *Wir wollten wissen, ob sie an Weihnachten hier sein würden.*
"Did Duane go to the party?"	→ I asked **whether Duane had gone to the party**. *Ich fragte, ob Duane zu der Party gegangen sei.*
"Would you like some tea?"	→ He asked **whether she would like some tea**. *Er fragte, ob sie gern etwas Tee hätte.*
"Can I open the window?"	→ She asked **if she could open the window**. *Sie fragte, ob sie das Fenster öffnen dürfe.*

Wenn die Frage mit einem Fragewort eingeleitet wird, übernimmst du das Fragewort.
Why do you like being a movie star? → He asked her **why** she liked being a movie star.

- Die **Satzstellung** in indirekten Fragesätzen ist genauso wie in Aussagesätzen:

Direkter Fragesatz:	Indirekter Fragesatz:	Aussagesatz:
"Where is the post office?"	He asked her where the post office was.	The post office was closed.

- Wie bei indirekten Aussagesätzen rückt auch bei indirekten Fragesätzen die Zeitform der wiedergegebenen Rede eine Stufe weiter in die Vergangenheit als die direkte Rede (*backshift of tenses*) (→ LiF 13R a).
- Wenn die Frage, die du wiedergibst, jetzt noch von Bedeutung oder allgemeingültig ist, erfolgt kein *backshift of tenses*:
  Karen: "**Are** smartphones expensive?" → Karen asked if smartphones **are** expensive.

LiF 15 Indirekte Aufforderungssätze (Reported imperatives)

Der Imperativ wird in der indirekten Rede mit dem Infinitiv mit *to* wiedergegeben. Verneinte Aufforderungssätze werden in der indirekten Rede aus *not* + Infinitiv + *to* gebildet.

direct speech	reported imperative
"Put the books back on the shelf."	→ She told me **to put** the books back on the shelf. *Sie verlangte von mir, die Bücher ins Regal zurückzustellen.*
"Don't take them out again."	→ She told me **not to take** them out again. *Sie forderte mich auf, sie nicht wieder herauszunehmen.*

Da auf das Verb im Begleitsatz der Infinitiv folgt, gibt es bei indirekten Aufforderungssätzen kein *backshift of tenses*.

LiF 16 Ausdrucksmöglichkeiten für das deutsche „lassen" (English equivalents for 'lassen')

a) *Let/Make* + Objekt + Infinitiv ohne *to*

Die Verben *let* und *make*, nach denen der Infinitiv ohne *to* und ein direktes Objekt steht, kennst du bereits. Beide werden üblicherweise mit „lassen" übersetzt. Allerdings unterscheiden sie sich in ihrer Bedeutung: *let* meint zulassen/erlauben, während *make* veranlassen/zwingen bedeutet. Vergleiche:

I let him use my mobile phone.	→ Ich habe ihn mein Handy benutzen lassen. Ich habe ihm erlaubt, mein Handy zu benutzen.
My mother made me clean the kitchen.	→ Meine Mutter hat mich die Küche putzen lassen. Meine Mutter hat mich gezwungen/dazu gebracht, die Küche zu putzen.

b) Have something done

Möchtest du ausdrücken, dass jemand etwas von jemand anderem machen lässt, so kannst du dafür *have something done* verwenden:

Subjekt	Form von *have*	Objekt	Partizip Perfekt		
I	have	my bike	repaired	by a friend.	*Ich lasse mein Fahrrad von einem Freund reparieren.*
She	had	her blood pressure	checked.		*Sie hat ihren Blutdruck untersuchen lassen.*

! Achte darauf, dass du *have something done* nicht mit dem *present perfect* oder *past perfect* verwechselst. Beim *present* und *past perfect* steht das **Objekt** nach dem **Partizip Perfekt**, bei *have something done* davor. Vergleiche:
Present perfect: I have **checked** **my blood pressure**. → Ich habe meinen Blutdruck überprüft.
have something done: I have **my blood pressure** **checked**. → Ich lasse meinen Blutdruck untersuchen.

LiF 17R Relativsätze (Relative clauses)

Um eine Person oder eine Sache genauer zu beschreiben, verwendest du Relativsätze *(relative clauses)*. Sie beginnen in der Regel mit einem Relativpronomen *(relative pronoun)*. Die Relativpronomen *who*, *which* und *that* verwendet man im Singular und im Plural. Dabei verwendet man *who* für Personen, *which* für Dinge und *that* sowohl für Personen als auch für Dinge.
Es gibt zwei Arten von Relativsätzen: Notwendige Relativsätze *(defining relative clauses)* und nicht-notwendige Relativsätze *(non-defining relative clauses)*.

- Notwendige Relativsätze bestimmen das Wort näher, auf das sie sich beziehen. Sie können nicht weggelassen werden – der Hauptsatz ergäbe sonst keinen Sinn:
  *Janet is the girl **who is sitting next to your brother**.*
  *'La La Land' is the film **which everybody is talking about**.*
  *Philadelphia is a city **that I have always wanted to visit**.*

- Nicht-notwendige Relativsätze liefern zusätzliche Informationen über eine Person oder Sache im Hauptsatz. Sie könnten weggelassen werden, da der Hauptsatz auch ohne sie verständlich bliebe. Nicht-notwendige Relativsätze sind vom Hauptsatz durch Kommas getrennt:
  *This is my friend Katie, **who is on exchange from America**.*
  *These books, **which I bought yesterday**, are about African American history.*

Das Relativpronomen *that* wird im nicht-notwendigen Relativsatz nicht verwendet.
Es kann nur im notwendigen Relativsatz stehen: *The idea **that I just had** was absolutely brilliant.*

Das Relativpronomen *whose* wird verwendet, um die Zugehörigkeit für Personen, Tiere und Dinge zu zeigen. Es kann sowohl in notwendigen als auch in nicht-notwendigen Relativsätzen stehen:
  *John lives in the only house on his street **whose door is red**.*
  *Julien, **whose family come from Switzerland**, can speak both German and French.*

LiF 18R Das Gerundium (The gerund)

a) Das Gerundium als Subjekt oder Objekt (The gerund as subject or object)

- *Gerund* nennt man ein Verb, das wie ein Nomen verwendet wird.
  Im Englischen hängst du dafür ein *-ing* an den Infinitiv des Verbs:
  ***Boxing** is a sport.*

- Das *gerund* kann Subjekt eines Satzes sein: ***Reading** can be fun.*
  ***Watching television** is his favourite hobby.*

- Als Objekt eines Satzes steht das *gerund* häufig nach bestimmten Verben, wie *to enjoy, to like, to love, to hate: I don't like **swimming**.*

Reading can be fun.

b) Das Gerundium nach Präpositionen (The gerund after prepositions)

Das *gerund* wird auch nach einigen Adjektiven und Verben verwendet, die zusammen mit einer Präposition auftreten:

	Adjektiv + Präposition	*gerund*	
I'm	keen on	seeing	the Statue of Liberty.
Leanne isn't	crazy about	shopping	in New York City.
Robert is	interested in	visiting	Ellis Island.
Mr Andrews is	afraid of	losing	the girls in the crowd.
Mrs Andrews is	used to	taking	the subway every day.

	Verb + Präposition	*gerund*	
Nicola	dreams of	visiting	New York City.
Sinead didn't	look forward to	meeting	her cousin.
The girls	feel like	going	to the zoo.
They	talk about	seeing	a show on Broadway.

c) Gerundium oder Infinitiv (Gerund or infinitive)

- Nach *to begin, to start, to continue, to like, to love, to hate, to prefer* kannst du wahlweise **entweder** das *gerund* oder den Infinitiv mit *to* verwenden. Es besteht praktisch kein Bedeutungsunterschied:

  It **started raining** two hours ago.
  It **started to rain** two hours ago.
  ⟶ Es hat vor zwei Stunden angefangen zu regnen.

! - Nach *to remember, to stop, to try, to mean* und *to forget* macht es einen Unterschied, ob du das *gerund* oder den Infinitiv verwendest:

Remember to buy some milk! *(daran denken)*	I **remember going** to the market every Saturday when I was a child. *(sich an etw erinnern)*
He **stopped to think** about it. *(mit etw aufhören, um etw zu tun)*	He **stopped thinking** about it. *(aufhören, etw zu tun)*
She **tried to find** her key, but she couldn't. *(versuchen, etw zu tun)*	She **tried playing** the piano, but she didn't like it. *(etw ausprobieren)*
He **meant to buy** milk but then forgot. *(beabsichtigen, etw zu tun)*	It **will mean coming** home late. *(etw bedeuten)*
She **forgot to turn off** the light. *(nicht daran denken, etw zu tun)* → man tut es nicht)	She **has** totally **forgotten going** there last year. *(sich nicht daran erinnern können, etw getan zu haben)* → man hat es getan)

- Nach einigen Verben ist **nur das *gerund* oder nur der Infinitiv mit *to* bzw. ein direktes Objekt und der Infinitiv mit *to*** üblich. Am besten lernst du die jeweilige Kombination wie eine Vokabel:

Verben, auf die das *gerund* folgt:
to spend/waste time • to imagine •
to suggest • to recommend •
to enjoy • to consider

*Marie **spent time helping** Arthur with his homework.*
*My grandpa **recommends eating** two apples a day.*

Verben, auf die der Infinitiv mit *to* folgt:
to decide • to hope •
to choose • to offer •
to promise • to threaten

*Our neighbours **offered to lend** us their car.*
*When will you **decide to apply** for that job?*

Verben, auf die ein direktes Objekt und der Infinitiv mit *to* folgen:
to teach (how) • to invite •
to force • to tell •
to persuade • to remind

*Unfortunately nobody **had reminded** Tom **to buy** tickets for the concert.*

Auf *to ask* und *to expect* kann der Infinitiv mit *to* oder ein **direktes Objekt** und der Infinitiv mit *to* folgen:

I **asked to speak** to the boss.	Ich bat darum, mit der Chefin zu sprechen.
I **asked you to speak** to the boss.	Ich bat dich darum, mit der Chefin zu sprechen.
I **expect to be treated** fairly.	Ich erwarte, fair behandelt zu werden.
I **expect him to be treated** fairly.	Ich erwarte, dass er fair behandelt wird.

In short: The gerund

The **gerund** is a verb form that you can use as a noun:
- It can be the subject of a sentence: **Running** is fun.
- It can also function as the object of a sentence: I enjoy **swimming**.
- The gerund is used after **adjectives + prepositions** and certain **verbs + prepositions**:
  Becky is **good at** playing football.
  Max **is looking forward to** organizing the party.
- Some verbs can be followed both by a gerund and an infinitive with *to* with a difference in meaning:
  I'll remember **to go** to the shop. *(daran denken)*
  In ten years, I won't remember **going** to the shop today. *(sich an etw erinnern)*
- Some verbs can only be followed by a gerund and some only by an infinitive with *to*:
  She suggested **going out** for lunch.
  I didn't expect the plane **to be** on time.

LiF 19 Das *emphatic 'do'* (The emphatic 'do')

Möchtest du auf einen Gegensatz aufmerksam machen oder deiner Meinung Nachdruck verleihen, kannst du das *emphatic 'do'* verwenden. Es wird aus **do/does/did** + **Infinitiv ohne *to*** gebildet und hebt das Verb im Infinitiv hervor. Im Deutschen würdest du Wörter wie „doch", „ja", „wirklich", „tatsächlich" benutzen. Im Englischen genügt das *do*, das du beim Aussprechen aber besonders betonst.

Why didn't you do your homework?
I **did do** it – I just forgot to bring it to school with me. – Ich habe sie **doch** gemacht – ich habe nur vergessen, sie mit in die Schule zu bringen.
Sorry, but you **do look** silly in that T-shirt! – Tut mir leid, aber du siehst **wirklich** albern in dem T-Shirt aus.

Um zu betonen, dass etwas tatsächlich eingetreten ist, das du erwartet oder dir erhofft hast, kannst du ebenfalls das *emphatic 'do'* verwenden:
I thought he would win, and he **did run** faster than everyone else. – Ich habe mir gedacht, dass er gewinnen würde, und er ist **tatsächlich** schneller als alle anderen gelaufen.

Words

In den Wordbanks findest du die wichtigsten Wörter zu einem Thema zusammengefasst. Wenn vorne im Buch zum Beispiel ● *Wordbank Jobs, p. 187* steht, findest du in der *Wordbank Jobs* auf Seite 187 zu diesem Thema passende Wörter.

Wordbank Feelings

Talking about feelings

I feel upset about …
I find it strange/annoying that …
It makes me happy/furious to see that …
I am horrified/furious/worried about … because …
They feared that it would …
It breaks my heart.
I can let off some steam when I am angry.

anger • compassion • confidence • desire • despair • disappointment • disbelief • enthusiasm • fear • happiness • hate • love • rejection • safety • shock

You can be/feel …

angry • annoyed • anxious • careless • confused • defeated • depressed • deserted • determined • disappointed • excited • frightened • frustrated • furious • gloomy • hopeful • horrified • ignored • isolated • lonely • mad • motivated • nervous • patient • proud • relieved • shocked • sad • shy • stupid • terrified • tired • unsure • upset • worried

Wordbank People and relationships

Describing people

ambitious • arrogant • athletic • attractive • boring • brave • choosy • communicative • confident • conscientious • creative • dedicated • diligent • diplomatic • dynamic • efficient • friendly • generous • hard-working • honest • independent • intellectual • modest • motivated • organized • outgoing • patient • poor • practical • pretty • proud • punctual • reliable • responsible • selfish • sensible • sensitive • smart • sociable • strict • strong • stunning • successful • talented • tough • trustworthy

Talking about groups at school

Preps/Preppies tend to be …
Emos want to be …
Popular girls will be …
Geeks are more likely to have …
Goths will most often be …
Jocks will typically …

Relationships

to abandon
to appeal to sb
to assist (in/with)
to attack
to attract
to care for
to challenge
to disapprove of
to fear
to fit in
to force
to gossip
to host

to impress
to influence
to judge
to look after
to prefer
to make fun of
to motivate
to respect
to request
to separate
to share
to support
to trust

Wordbanks p. 186 | Word lists p. 192 | English-German dictionary p. 230

Wordbank People and relationships • Wordbank Jobs

Talking about peer pressure

Many people give in to peer pressure because … • Despite peer pressure, …
Most people would … if their friends encouraged them.
For people not to give in to peer pressure, they need to be/have …
No matter what their friends said, I don't think people would …
It is not always easy to resist peer pressure because …
If you feel pressured into something you don't want to do, it might be a good idea to talk to someone you trust.
Many people try to fit in/influence sb/impress sb.

gossip
bullying
reputation
judgement
influence
popularity

Wordbank Jobs

Applying for a job

to apply for a job as …
to apply for a placement (BE)/internship (AE)
to look at job adverts
to put together an application
to photocopy certificates and other documents
to write a CV (BE)/résumé (AE)
to write a covering letter
to ask for a letter of recommendation
to prepare for a job interview
to receive a job offer

Having a job interview

I'm good at …

I will be leaving school in …

The position you're offering is just what I'm looking for.

I enjoy working with …

I would be happy to work for your company and look forward to hearing from you.

The perfect applicant should be …

communicative • conscientious •
creative • dedicated • diligent •
diplomatic • dynamic • efficient •
enthusiastic • flexible • friendly •
hard-working • helpful • honest •
motivated • organized • outgoing •
patient • practical • punctual •
reliable • responsible • sensitive •
tactful • trustworthy

Job skills

commitment
responsibility
experience of …
patience
integrity
leadership skills
knowledge of computer
    programming
teamwork

In a job you may need to …

have experience with … • work well in a team • be good at … •
speak Spanish/French/English fluently • be good at maths/science/… •
be fast at typing • be used to working independently • be able to cope
well under pressure • enjoy a challenge • show commitment to …

to have a full-time/part-time job
to work abroad
to work in an office
to work in a factory
qualification • staff • salary

Wordbank Film

Talking about a film/video

> The extract from ..., by ..., deals with ...
> The extract mainly shows ...
> The film is based on real events.
> It takes place in ... • The plot is ...
> The film follows .../tells the story of ...
> The opening sequence shows ...
> The main characters ... are played by ...
> I would recommend the film because ...

> amusing • clever • detailed • dramatic • dull • eerie • enjoyable • exaggerated • exciting • extraordinary • fascinating • fast-moving • historically accurate • humorous • ironic • moving • offensive • particular • powerful • realistic • sad • satisfying • scary • sentimental • silly • skilful • striking • surprising • tedious • tense • thrilling • true • unexpected • uplifting

Genres

> action film
> comedy
> crime series
> documentary
> drama
> reality show
> romance
> soap opera
> thriller

People

> actor/actress
> director
> film-maker
> cameraman
> cinema-goer

Directing, camera and casting

> ... has made a powerful film.
> ..., one of the greatest directors of our time, shot the film in ...
> She directs simply and achieves maximum effect.
> She creates a ... atmosphere by using ...
> Her camera work is skilful/admirable/...
> The actors and actresses were well/poorly chosen.
> Cinematic devices such as ... are used to ...

> director • directing • cinematic devices • cast • camera movement • camera work • camera angle • field size • atmosphere • use of lighting and colour • use of music and sound • special effects • soundtrack

Acting

> ... plays his part effectively.
> His performance is totally convincing.
> ... does a excellent job of conveying ...
> body language
> facial expression

Wordbank Songs

Talking about the music

> The music conveys a feeling of ...
> The song's mood is soothing/relaxing/exciting/... because ...
> The singer/rapper stresses ... to create a rhythm.
> The rhythm is achieved by ...

Talking about the lyrics

> The phrase "..." suggests that ... ...
> The passage from line ... to line ... shows that ...
> It becomes clear that ...
> By the using the phrase ... the rapper addresses the audience directly.

188 Wordbanks p. 186 | Word lists p. 192 | English-German dictionary p. 230

Wordbank Statistics

Talking about statistics

The diagram provides information about … • *It is clear that there are more people who …, than …* • *The diagram shows how many people …* • *The statistics illustrate that …* • *According to the figures …* • *I found the statistic that … surprising, because …* • *The fact that … was interesting, as …*

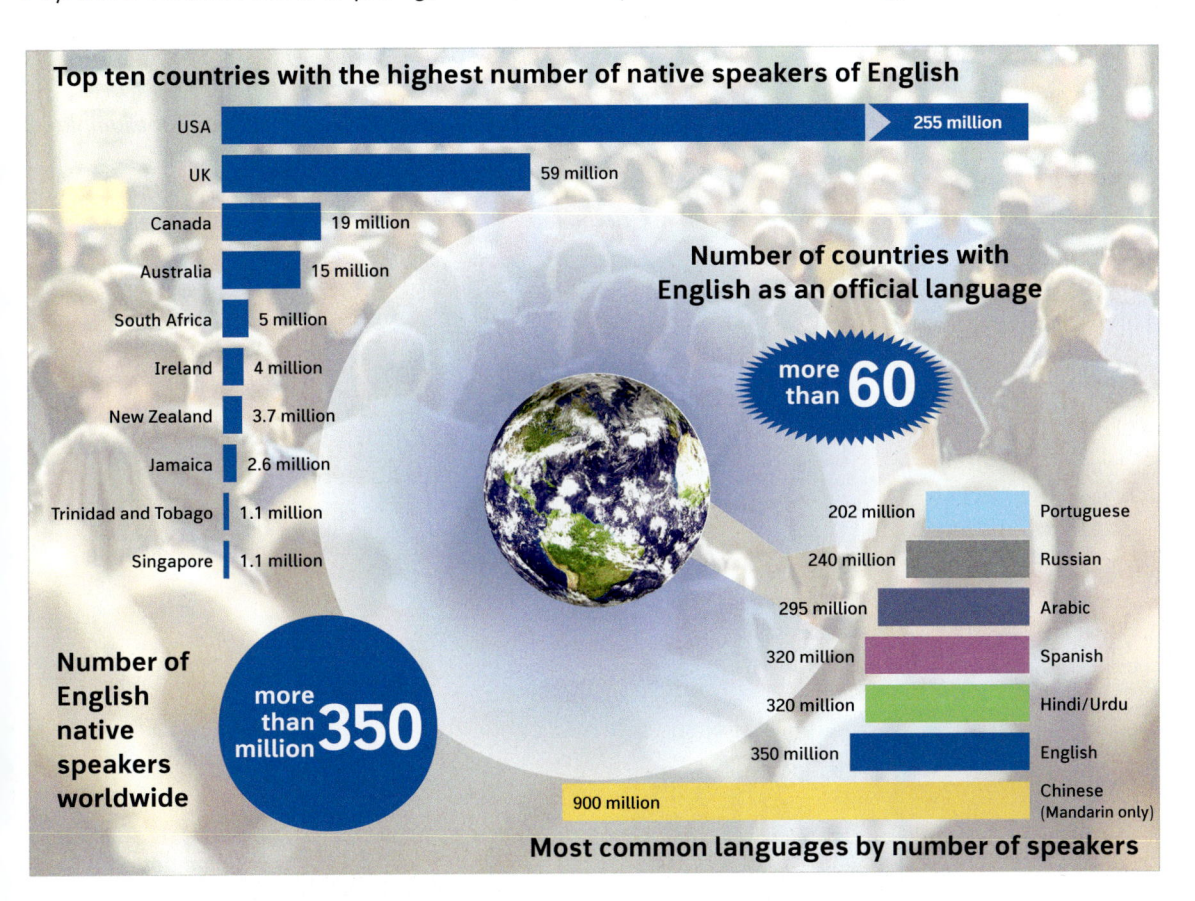

Top ten countries with the highest number of native speakers of English

- USA — 255 million
- UK — 59 million
- Canada — 19 million
- Australia — 15 million
- South Africa — 5 million
- Ireland — 4 million
- New Zealand — 3.7 million
- Jamaica — 2.6 million
- Trinidad and Tobago — 1.1 million
- Singapore — 1.1 million

Number of English native speakers worldwide: more than 350 million

Number of countries with English as an official language: more than 60

Most common languages by number of speakers

- Portuguese — 202 million
- Russian — 240 million
- Arabic — 295 million
- Spanish — 320 million
- Hindi/Urdu — 320 million
- English — 350 million
- Chinese (Mandarin only) — 900 million

Wordbank Travel

Accommodation

bed and breakfast
camping
holiday flat/home
hotel
motel
youth hostel
single room
double room
suite
full board
half board

Tourism and the environment

eco-friendly • environmetally conscious • green policies • recycling • renewable • sustainable • wildlife

A serious consequence of the tourism industry is …
… can't cope with the pressure caused by so many tourists.
The region's natural beauty is also threatened by …
We are looking for new ways to reduce our impact on the environment.
… has introduced a number of policies to reduce …
Looking an eco-friendly holiday, I felt that … would be the best choice because …

Names p. 264 | Class instructions p. 267 | Irregular verbs p. 268

Wordbank Pictures

Describing pictures

In the middle of the picture you can see …
At the top/bottom of the picture there is …
In the foreground/background there are …
In the top/bottom left-hand corner you can see …
The picture is set in …

Comparing pictures

The picture showing … is similar to …
In comparison with/In contrast to …, …
The pictures illustrate the different …
There's a sharp/striking contrast between …
… contrasts with …
The most noticeable difference is …
There are striking similarities, for example …

- in the top left-hand corner
- at the top
- in the top right-hand corner
- in the background
- on the left
- in the middle
- on the right
- in the foreground
- in the bottom left-hand corner
- at the bottom
- in the bottom right-hand corner

The atmosphere a photo conveys might be …

- calm
- depressing
- eerie
- gloomy
- happy
- horrifying
- melancholy
- peaceful
- relaxed
- serious
- shocking

Interpreting pictures

The photo is open to different interpretations, but I would guess that ...
The fact that ... makes me wonder whether the photo is about ...
The ... suggests that this may be ...
The way ... makes me think that ...
The picture illustrates ...
The caption of the photo suggests ...

Describing a poster

The use of colour makes the poster seem ...
The poster's layout/structure helps to ...
By including pictures, the poster ...
Different fonts are used in order to ...
The viewer's attention is drawn to ...
The slogan sticks in the reader's mind.

Wordbank Texts

Talking about a literary text

The author writes in the first/third person.
The author seems to be talking to the reader.
The author uses formal/informal/colloquial/ precise/direct language.
The style of writing is extremely vivid/dramatic/ original/...
The author appears to approve/disapprove of ...
The author seems to have a critical/neutral attitude towards ... because ...
The phrase "..." suggests that ...
The passage from line ... to line ... shows that ...
It becomes clear that ...
The novel "...", pubished in 2017, deals with the issue of ...

chapter
character
content
extract
narrative
narrator
plot
register
section
setting
style
theme
tone
topic

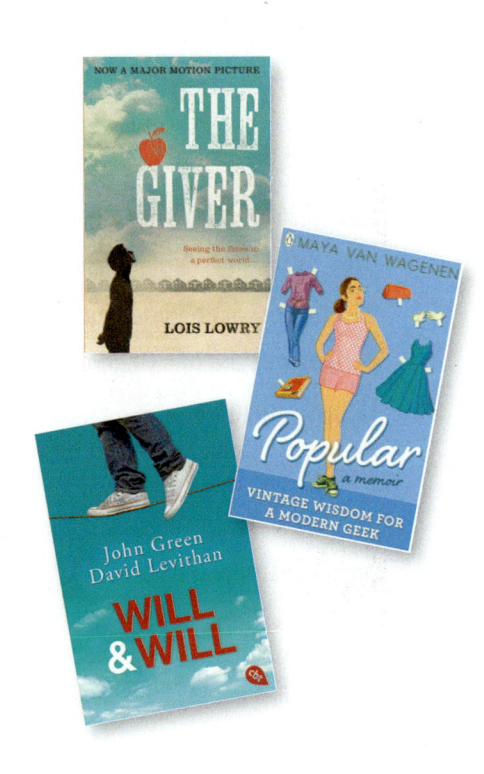

Giving your personal opinion

This book doesn't appeal to me at all because ...
The concept of this book sounds interesting but/ because ...
The cover would put me off reading this book because ...
It could be quite exciting to find out ...
I prefer to read ...
Personally, I find this subject ...
The story makes me angry/sad/thoughtful because ...
I find the story quite interesting/entertaining/ exciting/dramatic/moving because ...

Language and style

colloquial
direct
dramatic
humorous
ironic
light-hearted
matter-of-fact
moving
original
precise
vivid

Rhetorical devices

alliteration
anaphora
climax
ellipsis
enumeration
exaggeration
metaphor
parallelism
quotation
repetition
rhetorical question
simile

● *Rhetorical devices, p. 138*

So funktionieren die Wortlisten

Es gibt Wortlisten nach *Themes* und eine alphabetische Wortliste *(English-German dictionary)*.

Wortlisten nach *Themes*
In den Wortlisten nach *Themes* ab Seite 193 findest du die Wörter in der Reihenfolge, in der sie in den *Themes* vorkommen.
Am Ende der Wortliste zu jedem *Theme* steht *Say it in English*, eine Liste mit nützlichen Redewendungen.

English-German Dictionary
Im *English-German dictionary* ab Seite 230 kannst du nachschlagen, wenn du die Bedeutung von einem englischen Wort aus dem Buch wissen möchtest.

So kannst du die Wortlisten nach *Themes* und das *English-German dictionary* benutzen:

Fett gedruckte Wörter solltest du dir merken.	**approximately** /əˈprɒksɪmətli/
Die /Lautschrift/ zeigt an, wie man ein Wort ausspricht.	to **behave** /bɪˈheɪv/
! weist auf wichtige Besonderheiten hin.	! to **add**ress – *ad*ressieren
↔ bedeutet „ist das Gegenteil von".	to **disapprove** ↔ to approve
In den gelb hinterlegten Kästen stehen Wörter, die du dir merken solltest, Tipps und Hinweise.	**Woods vs wood** Ein **wood** ist für gewöhnlich ein kleines, klar umgrenztes Areal. Dementsprechend kommt **wood** häufig in Ortsna... vor. **Woods** sind größere G...
(informal) bedeutet: Dieses Wort ist umgangssprachlich.	**guy** *(informal)* /gaɪ/
(pl media) bedeutet: Dieses Wort hat einen unregelmäßigen Plural *(media)*.	**medium** *(pl **media**)* /ˈmiːdiəm, ˈmiːdiə/
(no pl) bedeutet: Dieses Wort hat keinen Plural.	**worth** *(no pl)* /wɜːθ/
(only pl) bedeutet: Dieses Wort wird nur oder gewöhnlich im Plural benutzt.	**looks** *(only pl)* /lʊks/
° bedeutet: Dieses Wort ist nur für einen bestimmten Text wichtig. Du brauchst es nicht zu lernen.	° petty theft /ˌpeti ˈθeft/
(irr) bedeutet: Dieses Verb ist unregelmäßig. Auf Seite 268/269 kannst du *irregular verbs* nachschlagen.	to **make up for** *(irr)* /ˌmeɪk ˈʌp fɔː/
° armored *(AE = armoured BE)* bedeutet: Im *American English (AE)* schreibt man *armored*, im *British English (BE) armoured*.	° armored *(AE = armoured BE)* /ˈɑːmərd/
CV *(BE = résumé AE)* bedeutet: Im *British English (BE)* verwendet man *CV*, im *American English (AE) résumé*.	**CV** (= **curriculum vitae**) *(BE = résumé AE)* /ˌsiː ˈviː, kəˌrɪkjʊləm ˈviːtaɪ/
Folgende Abkürzungen werden noch verwendet:	sb = somebody sth = something	jdm / jdn = jemandem / jemanden etw = etwas

Word lists

Theme 1: Knowing me, knowing you

> Wenn du ein englisches Wort aus dem Buch in den Wortlisten nach *Themes* nicht findest, kannst du es im *English-German dictionary* ab Seite 230 nachschlagen.

unique /juːˈniːk/	einzigartig		p. 10
drums *(only pl)* /drʌmz/	Schlagzeug		
to **define** /dɪˈfaɪn/	definieren, festlegen	A dictionary **defines** the meanings of words.	

In anderen Sprachen

To **define** kommt vom lateinischen Wort **definire** (definieren), vgl. französisch **définir**, spanisch **definir** und italienisch **definire**.

familiar /fəˈmɪliə/	vertraut; vertraulich		
survey /ˈsɜːveɪ/	Umfrage		
Mexican /ˈmeksɪkən/	Mexikaner/in; mexikanisch		
upcoming /ˈʌpˌkʌmɪŋ/	bevorstehend, kommend		
return /rɪˈtɜːn/	Rückkehr, Heimkehr	On his **return** he took a different route.	
practice *(no pl)* /ˈpræktɪs/	Übung; *hier:* Training		
shoulder /ˈʃəʊldə/	Schulter	She wore her bag over one **shoulder**.	
to hang out with sb *(informal)* /ˌhæŋ ˈaʊt wɪð/	Zeit mit jdm verbringen		
° mariachi /ˌmæriˈɑːtʃi/	*Form mexikanischer Volksmusik*		
treat /triːt/	(Extra)vergnügen		
guy *(informal)* /gaɪ/	Kerl, Typ, Bursche	I like Tom. He's a nice **guy**.	
to fit the bill /ˌfɪt ðə ˈbɪl/	der/die/das Richtige sein		
extent *(no pl)* /ɪkˈstent/	Größe, Ausdehnung, Umfang, Ausmaß	The **extent** of the damage wasn't clear at first.	p. 11
to **differ** (**from**/**in**) /ˈdɪfə frɒm/ɪn/	sich unterscheiden (von/in)	Opinions **differ** on this controversial topic.	
purpose /ˈpɜːpəs/	Grund, Absicht, Ziel, Zweck	The **purpose** of an umbrella is to keep you dry.	
to **influence** /ˈɪnfluəns/	beeinflussen	The weather **influences** what clothes you wear.	
to choose to do sth /ˌtʃuːz tə ˈduː/	es vorziehen, etw zu tun		
to **take turns** (BE) /ˌteɪk ˈtɜːnz/	sich abwechseln	Karl and Keira **took turns** choosing TV programmes.	
character /ˈkærɪktə/	Charakter, Figur; *hier:* Zeichen	A tweet may have up to 140 **characters**.	
to **take sth into account** /ˌteɪk ˌsʌmθɪŋ ˌɪntʊ əˈkaʊnt/	etw berücksichtigen	Always **take** the weather **into account** when planning a trip.	
precise /prɪˈsaɪs/	genau, präzise, sorgfältig	A definition should be **precise**.	
to **suggest** /səˈdʒest/	vorschlagen; *hier:* andeuten, (darauf) hinweisen	Theo is not saying much, which **suggests** that he is in a bad mood.	p. 12

Word lists

Theme 1: Knowing me, knowing you

theme /θiːm/	Thema(tik), Motto	The **theme** for the party was 'Beauty and the Beast'.
B2 half (*pl* halves) /hɑːf, hɑːvz/	Hälfte	
gay /ɡeɪ/	Homosexuelle(r), Schwule(r); homosexuell, schwul	Richard is **gay**. His boyfriend is called Shaun.
° **straight** /streɪt/	gerade(aus), direkt, ordentlich, hetero(sexuell)	
stereotype /ˈsteriəˌtaɪp/	Stereotyp, Klischee, Vorurteil	Germans are always on time. – That's a **stereotype**.
° **preconceived** /ˌpriːkənˈsiːvd/	vorgefasst	
sex /seks/	Geschlecht	Traditionally there were two **sexes**: male and female.
characteristic /ˌkærɪktəˈrɪstɪk/	(charakteristisches) Merkmal; typisch, charakteristisch	Charlotte had all the **characteristics** of a good student.
° **to cure** /kjʊə/	heilen	
treatment /ˈtriːtmənt/	Behandlung	
to fear /fɪə/	(be)fürchten	Emmy **fears** the dark.
to progress /prəʊˈɡres/	Fortschritte machen, vorankommen	Arsenal **progress** into the next round after beating Chelsea.
° **veil** /veɪl/	Schleier	
cause /kɔːz/	Grund, Ursache, Anlass; *hier:* (gute) Sache	They had a football match to raise money for a good **cause**.
hateful /ˈheɪtf(ə)l/	hasserfüllt, abscheulich	People who try to hurt others are deliberately **hateful**.
certificate /səˈtɪfɪkət/	Urkunde, Bescheinigung	A **certificate** is an official piece of paper.
to solve /sɒlv/	lösen	Think about the problem and you might find a way to **solve** it.
° **to strip away** /ˌstrɪp_əˈweɪ/	entfernen, abstreifen	
° **underneath** /ˌʌndəˈniːθ/	unter, darunter, untere(r, s)	
patient /ˈpeɪʃ(ə)nt/	geduldig	The queue for tickets is extremely long. You'll have to be very **patient**.
passage /ˈpæsɪdʒ/	(Text)passage, Abschnitt	This **passage** is one of the most exciting from the whole book.
B4 **tolerance** /ˈtɒlərəns/	Toleranz	Accepting people of all races, genders, and ages shows **tolerance**.
° **anthem** /ˈænθəm/	Hymne	
B5 **to date sb** (AE) /ˈdeɪt/	mit jdm gehen	I heard that Sharon is **dating** Graham.
to be/feel lovesick /ˌbiː/ˌfiːl ˈlʌvˌsɪk/	Liebeskummer haben	Tony is always daydreaming. He must **be lovesick**.
to pay sb a compliment /ˌpeɪ ˌsʌmbədi_ə ˈkɒmplɪmənt/	jdm ein Kompliment machen	I **paid him a compliment** about his lovely beard.
false /fɔːls/	falsch	If a statement is not true, then it must be **false**.
° **to stand a chance of doing sth** /ˌstænd_ə ˌtʃɑːns_əv ˈduːɪŋ/	Aussichten haben, etw zu tun	
fairly /ˈfeəli/	ziemlich, recht	**fairly** easy ↔ rather difficult
pressure /ˈpreʃə/	Druck, Stress, Belastung	Pupils at our school feel a lot of **pressure** to do well.
date /deɪt/	Verabredung, Rendezvous, Date; *hier:* Partner/in	I'm going out tonight. I have a **date**.

Theme 1: Knowing me, knowing you — Word lists

practice *(no pl)* /ˈpræktɪs/	*hier:* Gewohnheit, Sitte	
couple /ˈkʌp(ə)l/	Paar	Sadie and Pippa have been a **couple** for over three years now.

> Um das Textverständnis zu erleichtern, wird Wortschatz aus Originaltexten in Auswahl auch in den Wortlisten nach *Themes* aufgeführt. Wortschatz, der hier nicht aufgeführt ist, findet sich zum Nachschlagen im *English-German dictionary* ab Seite 230.

° breath /breθ/	Atem(zug)		*p. 14*
° tray /treɪ/	Tablett, Servierbrett		
° to peer /pɪə/	spähen		
° beneath /bɪˈniːθ/	unter, nach unten, darunter		
° frayed /freɪd/	ausgefranst		
° hood /hʊd/	Kapuze, Maske, Haube		
° to garnish /ˈgɑːnɪʃ/	garnieren		
° condiment /ˈkɒndɪmənt/	Gewürz		
° counter /ˈkaʊntə/	(Laden)theke, Schalter		
° to giggle /ˈgɪg(ə)l/	kichern		
° to swarm /swɔːm/	(um)schwärmen		
° mixture /ˈmɪkstʃə/	Mischung		
had better do sth /həd ˌbetə ˈduː ˌsʌmθɪŋ/	*drückt aus, dass jd etw tun soll*	You **had better** do your homework before class!	
difficulty /ˈdɪfɪk(ə)lti/	Mühe; Schwierigkeit; Problem	Craig had **difficulty** concentrating.	*p. 15*
as well /æz ˈwel/	auch	Ellie has two dogs and a cat **as well**!	
extract /ˈekstrækt/	Auszug	An **extract** is a small part of a text.	

Wortbildung – Konversion

Eine Möglichkeit, neue Wörter zu bilden, ist es, die Wortart zu ändern. Nomen können zum Beispiel oft als Verben verwendet werden oder umgekehrt:

return	→	**to return**	**extract**	→	**to extract**	**date**	→	**to date** sb
Rückkehr		*zurückkehren*	*Auszug*		*(heraus)ziehen*	*Verabredung*		*mit jdm gehen*

awkward /ˈɔːkwəd/	schwierig, unangenehm, peinlich	The arrival of his ex-wife made Alex feel **awkward**.
° to intervene /ˌɪntəˈviːn/	einschreiten; *hier:* sich einmischen	
° stiff /stɪf/	steif, hart	
° to loom /luːm/	(drohend) auftauchen	
° to stare (at sb/sth) /ˈsteər ˌæt/	(jdn/etw an)starren	
° throat /θrəʊt/	Rachen, Hals, Kehle	
° expenses *(only pl)* /ɪkˈspensɪz/	Spesen	
° to let sb off /ˌlet ˌsʌmbədi ˈɒf/	jdn davonkommen lassen	
° to flick out /ˌflɪk ˈaʊt/	(her)ausfahren	
° Gay-Straight Alliance /ˌgeɪ ˌstreɪt əˈlaɪəns/	*Bündnis von Menschen unterschiedlicher sexueller Orientierung*	
° to crawl /krɔːl/	krabbeln, kriechen	
° to dab /dæb/	(be)tupfen	
° to wipe /waɪp/	(ab)wischen	
° sleeve /sliːv/	Ärmel	
° mustard /ˈmʌstəd/	Senf	
° dude *(informal, AE)* /duːd/	Typ, Kerl, Mann	
° to groan /grəʊn/	(auf)stöhnen, ächzen	
° to spin, spun, spun /spɪn, spʌn/	drehen	

° to glance /glɑːns/	(flüchtig) schauen	
° bud (= buddy) (informal, AE) /bʌd, ˈbʌdi/	Kumpel	
° to scrunch (up) /ˌskrʌntʃ ˈʌp/	zerknüllen; hier: verziehen	
° forward(s) /ˈfɔːwədz/	nach vorn(e), weiter, vorn(e)	
° bone /bəʊn/	Knochen	
° uneasy /ʌnˈiːzi/	besorgt, unangenehm, unwohl	
to set, set, set /set/	festsetzen, festlegen	
supportive /səˈpɔːtɪv/	unterstützend	
suspicious /səˈspɪʃəs/	verdächtig, misstrauisch, argwöhnisch	He became **suspicious** of her strange behaviour.
intention /ɪnˈtenʃ(ə)n/	Absicht	Although his **intentions** were good, the results were not.
to behave /bɪˈheɪv/	sich verhalten, sich benehmen	Roger's dog always **behaves** well.
B8 to base /beɪs/	basieren, beruhen, stützen sich auf	You must **base** your conclusions on the findings of your research.
content /ˈkɒntent/	Inhalt	The **content** of this website is suitable for all ages.
style /staɪl/	Stil, Art	The painting was in the **style** of Van Gogh.
to correspond with/to sth /ˌkɒrɪˈspɒnd wɪð/tʊ/	mit etw übereinstimmen, etw entsprechen	Oh dear, your answers don't **correspond to** mine at all.
narrative /ˈnærətɪv/	Erzählung, Schilderung	
in terms of /ɪn ˈtɜːmz_əv/	hinsichtlich, was … angeht	
key /kiː/	Schlüssel(-), Taste; hier: Haupt-	Underline **key** phrases in the text.
issue /ˈɪʃuː/	Thema, Angelegenheit; hier: Problem, (Streit)frage	One **issue** that many teenagers face is peer pressure.
finding /ˈfaɪndɪŋ/	Entdeckung, Ergebnis	
B9 to establish /ɪˈstæblɪʃ/	gründen, einführen, schaffen	The teachers **established** a link between the schools.
to overcome (irr) /ˌəʊvəˈkʌm/	bewältigen, meistern	

> **Unregelmäßige Verben**
> Wie du weißt, haben unregelmäßige Verben unregelmäßige Formen: für das *simple past* und auch für das Partizip Perfekt. Diese Formen solltest du wie Vokabeln lernen, z. B. für *to do*: *did* (*simple past*) und *done* (Partizip Perfekt). Du findest die Formen in der Liste der unregelmäßigen Verben (S. 268/269).
> Sie werden immer so angegeben: to do, did, done.
>
>   **Infinitiv**   *simple past*   **Partizip Perfekt**

to demand /dɪˈmɑːnd/	verlangen, fordern	The crowd **demanded** that animals should be treated better.
° tank /tæŋk/	Panzer	
° armored (AE = armoured BE) /ˈɑːməd/	gepanzert, bewaffnet	
° hard-ass (informal, AE) /ˈhɑːdæs/	abwertende Bezeichnung für eine autoritäre Person	
° cannonlike /ˈkænənlaɪk/	wie eine Kanone	
° to order /ˈɔːdə/	anordnen, bestellen, ordnen; hier: auffordern	
° to seize /siːz/	ergreifen	
° to assure /əˈʃɔː/	zusichern	
° peeved /piːvd/	verärgert	
° to brace /breɪs/	(ab)stützen	

Theme 1: Knowing me, knowing you

Word lists

° to furrow one's brow /ˌfʌrəʊ wʌnz ˈbraʊ/	die Stirn runzeln	
° trench /trentʃ/	(Schützen)graben	
° to resonate with sth /ˈrezəneɪt wɪð/	etw ausstrahlen	
° to condone /kənˈdəʊn/	(stillschweigend) dulden	
° immorality (no pl) /ˌɪməˈræləti/	Unmoral, Sittenlosigkeit	
° to harass /həˈræs/	schikanieren, belästigen	
° the rear /ðə ˈrɪə/	der hintere Teil; *hier:* hinten	
° to deny /dɪˈnaɪ/	abstreiten, verweigern, vorenthalten; *hier:* ablehnen	**In anderen Sprachen** **Deny** kommt vom lateinischen Wort **denegare** (verweigern), vgl. französisch **dénier** und spanisch **denegar**.
° to involve /ɪnˈvɒlv/	beinhalten, umfassen, betreffen, beteiligen	
° to intercede /ˌɪntəˈsiːd/	vermitteln	
° queer *(informal)* /kwɪə/	Schwule/r, Lesbe, schwul	
° racial /ˈreɪʃ(ə)l/	rassisch, Rassen-, rassistisch	
° religious /rəˈlɪdʒəs/	religiöse(r, s), Religions-, religiös	
° to appreciate /əˈpriːʃieɪt/	schätzen, zu schätzen wissen	
° concern /kənˈsɜːn/	Anliegen, Sorge, Besorgnis	
° previously /ˈpriːviəsli/	zuvor, vorher, früher	
° disruptive /dɪsˈrʌptɪv/	störend	
° to squirm /skwɜːm/	sich (vor Verlegenheit) winden	
approximately /əˈprɒksɪmətli/	ungefähr, etwa, circa	The time now is **approximately** 5 o'clock. *p. 18*
intervention /ˌɪntəˈvenʃ(ə)n/	Eingreifen	
to **judge** /dʒʌdʒ/	(be)urteilen, schätzen	Don't **judge** a book by its cover.
contribution /ˌkɒntrɪˈbjuːʃ(ə)n/	Beitrag, Spende	
to stay true to the original /ˌsteɪ ˌtruː tə ðiˌəˈrɪdʒ(ə)nəl/	sich an das Original halten	
to **be in character** /ˌbi ɪn ˈkærɪktə/	typisch sein	I won't believe Tom cheated – it wouldn't **be in character** for him!
to **interfere with** /ˌɪntəˈfɪə wɪð/	stören, eingreifen in	I don't want to **interfere with** your plans. *p. 19*
once /wʌns/	sobald	
to **commit** /kəˈmɪt/	begehen	The prisoner **committed** a crime.
obvious /ˈɒbviəs/	deutlich, offensichtlich	The answer is **obvious** if you read the question.
to strike sb as … /ˈstraɪk ˌsʌmbədi ˌəz/	jdm … scheinen	
essential /ɪˈsenʃ(ə)l/	unverzichtbar, wesentlich	Water and air are **essential** for life.
in my view /ɪn ˈmaɪ ˌvjuː/	meiner Meinung nach	**In my view**, animals are dirty and smelly.
to **identify** /aɪˈdentɪfaɪ/	identifizieren, feststellen	The police are trying to **identify** the body.
facial expression /ˌfeɪʃ(ə)l ɪkˈspreʃ(ə)n/	Gesichtsausdruck	*p. 20*
° to be sure to do sth /ˌbi ˈʃɔː tə ˈduː/	daran denken, etw zu tun	
to **depict** /dɪˈpɪkt/	darstellen, beschreiben	This photo **depicts** a pupil at a British school.
to **imply** /ɪmˈplaɪ/	andeuten	James didn't actually say that the film was bad, but he **implied** it.
to **avoid** /əˈvɔɪd/	(ver)meiden, ausweichen	George **avoids** talking to his sister.
eye contact *(no pl)* /ˈaɪ ˌkɒntækt/	Blickkontakt	
look /lʊk/	Blick, Gesichtsausdruck	I knew that Evie was unhappy from the **look** on her face.

	to **gesture** /ˈdʒestʃə/	deuten	It is a stereotype that Italians **gesture** a lot with their hands.
	stance (no pl) /stæns/	Haltung, Standpunkt, Einstellung	
	as though /æz ˈðəʊ/	als ob	Joy looked **as though** she had seen a ghost.
C4	**involved** /ɪnˈvɒlvd/	betroffen, beteiligt, verwickelt	
	present /ˈprez(ə)nt/	derzeitig, jetzig, gegenwärtig	
	emotional state /ɪˌməʊʃ(ə)nəl ˈsteɪt/	Gefühlszustand	
	to **pick** /pɪk/	aussuchen, auswählen	Can you **pick** your favourite super hero?
	mind /maɪnd/	Geist, Verstand; hier: Kopf	Have you lost your **mind**?! That's crazy!
	reference /ˈref(ə)rəns/	Verweis, Anspielung, Erwähnung, Bezugnahme	Clare made a **reference** to her favourite film in her presentation.
	past /pɑːst/	vergangen, frühere(r, s)	We should learn from **past** mistakes.
	to **reflect** /rɪˈflekt/	spiegeln, zeigen, reflektieren; hier: zum Ausdruck bringen	This song **reflects** my feelings.
C5	**giver** /ˈɡɪvə/	Geber/in, Spender/in	
	summary /ˈsʌməri/	Zusammenfassung	Please write a one-page **summary** of the article.
	plot /plɒt/	Handlung	This book's **plot** was so exciting that George couldn't put it down!
	° **sameness** (no pl) /ˈseɪmnəs/	Gleichheit, Gleichförmigkeit	
	to **remove** /rɪˈmuːv/	entfernen; hier: aus der Welt schaffen	
	prejudice /ˈpredʒʊdɪs/	Vorurteil	I don't understand why you have a **prejudice** against blondes.
	to **eliminate** /ɪˈlɪmɪneɪt/	beseitigen, ausschließen	We need to **eliminate** possible risks.
	entirely /ɪnˈtaɪəli/	ganz, total, völlig	I'm so sorry! I **entirely** forgot!
	to **determine** /dɪˈtɜːmɪn/	entscheiden, ermitteln, bestimmen	Where you go to school can **determine** who your friends are.
	convenient /kənˈviːniənt/	praktisch, günstig, bequem	The location of my new home is very **convenient**.
	° **elder** /ˈeldə/	Ältere/r, ältere(r, s)	
	unit /ˈjuːnɪt/	Einheit, Abteilung, Teil	The soldiers formed a very close **unit**.
	° to **assign** /əˈsaɪn/	zuweisen, übertragen, belegen	
	° **birth mother** /ˈbɜːθ ˌmʌðə/	biologische Mutter	
	° to **nurture** /ˈnɜːtʃə/	aufziehen, großziehen, fördern	
	to **release** /rɪˈliːs/	freilassen, entlassen	When it was safe, we **released** the eagle into the wild.
	apart from sth/sb /əˈpɑːt frɒm/	von etw/jdm abgesehen	She doesn't like anyone, **apart from** Jerry.
	° to **conform to/with sth** /kənˈfɔːm tʊ/ wɪð/	etw entsprechen, mit etw übereinstimmen	
	ceremony /ˈserəməni/	Zeremonie, Feier, Feierlichkeiten	Graduation is an important **ceremony** for students in the USA.
	° **assignment** /əˈsaɪnmənt/	Aufgabe, Auftrag	
	whose /huːz/	dessen, deren	It was Jodie **whose** car was stolen, not Joyce.
	to **select** /sɪˈlekt/	aussuchen, auswählen	Please **select** the correct option.
	future /ˈfjuːtʃə/	zukünftig	That's a great story for your **future** children.

Theme 1: Knowing me, knowing you — Word lists

° receiver /rɪˈsiːvə/	Hörer, Receiver, Empfänger	
to **preserve** /prɪˈzɜːv/	erhalten, bewahren	I **preserved** all your letters in good condition.
knowledge (no pl) /ˈnɒlɪdʒ/	Kenntnisse, Wissen, Kenntnis	It is common **knowledge** that a tomato is a fruit.
to bear /beə/	(er)tragen	
wise /waɪz/	weise, klug, vernünftig	Early to bed, early to rise, makes you healthy, wealthy and **wise**.
to **place** /pleɪs/	stellen, setzen, legen	Mandy carefully **placed** the cake on the table.
° overwhelming /ˌəʊvəˈwelmɪŋ/	überwältigend, riesig	
emotionless /ɪˈməʊʃ(ə)nləs/	gefühllos, ausdruckslos, gleichgültig	His face was blank and **emotionless**.
script /skrɪpt/	Drehbuch, Skript, Regiebuch	*p. 23*
to **outline** /ˈaʊtlaɪn/	(kurz) umreißen, skizzieren	Paul quickly **outlined** his plans.
to **analyse** /ˈænəlaɪz/	analysieren, untersuchen	Please **analyse** your results and explain what they mean.
relation /rɪˈleɪʃ(ə)n/	Verbindung, Bezug, Beziehung	
to **quote** /kwəʊt/	zitieren	Ian thinks he's clever because he can **quote** Shakespeare plays.
to suit sb/sth /suːt/	zu jdm/etw passen	*p. 24*
dystopian /dɪsˈtəʊpiən/	dystopisch *(ein pessimistisches Zukunftsbild malend)*	
fiction (no pl) /ˈfɪkʃ(ə)n/	Erzählliteratur	George Orwell's *1984* is a famous example of dystopian **fiction**.
to **warn** /wɔːn/	warnen	Tierney **warned** her friends not to smoke because it is dangerous.
to involve /ɪnˈvɒlv/	beinhalten, umfassen, betreffen, beteiligen	*p. 25*
concept /ˈkɒnsept/	Vorstellung, Idee, Konzept	The **concept** of evolution is difficult to explain.
altogether /ˌɔːltəˈgeðə/	völlig, ganz, insgesamt	
panel discussion /ˈpæn(ə)l dɪˌskʌʃ(ə)n/	Podiumsdiskussion	
to **reject** /rɪˈdʒekt/	ablehnen, zurückweisen, abweisen	She always **rejects** my ideas.
host /həʊst/	Gastgeber/in; *hier:* Moderator/in	Lorraine is the new **host** of 'The World at One'.
respective /rɪˈspektɪv/	jeweilig	
to prove one's point /ˌpruːv wʌnz ˈpɔɪnt/	beweisen, dass jemand recht hat	
to anticipate /ænˈtɪsɪpeɪt/	erwarten, rechnen mit, vorhersehen	
criticism (no pl) /ˈkrɪtɪˌsɪz(ə)m/	Kritik	
to refute /rɪˈfjuːt/	widerlegen, entkräften	
guidance /ˈgaɪd(ə)ns/	Beratung, (An)leitung, Führung	
to **respect** /rɪˈspekt/	respektieren	I **respect** your opinion, but I also disagree.
frequent /ˈfriːkwənt/	häufig, regelmäßig	I enjoy our **frequent** chats.
to **neglect** /nɪˈglekt/	vernachlässigen	You shouldn't have a pet if you're only going to **neglect** it.
to **take** sth **seriously** /ˌteɪk ˌsʌmθɪŋ ˈsɪəriəsli/	etw ernst nehmen	Bill always **takes** his piano lessons **seriously**.

Word lists

Theme 1: Knowing me, knowing you

overprotective /ˌəʊvəprəˈtektɪv/	überfürsorglich	
guidelines *(only pl)* /ˈɡaɪdˌlaɪnz/	Richtlinien, Leitlinien	
to **witness** /ˈwɪtnəs/	beobachten, Zeuge/Zeugin sein, miterleben	I have **witnessed** some very important historical events.
failure *(no pl)* /ˈfeɪljə/	Scheitern	Not working hard enough often leads to **failure**.
representative /ˌreprɪˈzentətɪv/	(Stell)vertreter/in	Politicians are **representatives** for the people.
to **participate (in)** /pɑːˈtɪsɪpeɪt_ɪn/	(an etw) teilnehmen, sich (an etw) beteiligen	She doesn't like to **participate in** class discussions.
observer /əbˈzɜːvə/	Beobachter/in, Zuschauer/in	
balanced /ˈbælənst/	ausgewogen	
agreement /əˈɡriːmənt/	Übereinstimmung, Zustimmung	The wedding will never take place without Mary's **agreement**.
disagreement /ˌdɪsəˈɡriːmənt/	Uneinigkeit, Meinungsverschiedenheit	After hours of arguing, Mary and Tyra are still in **disagreement**.
to **introduce** /ˌɪntrəˈdjuːs/	vorstellen; *hier:* vorbringen	Sarah **introduced** a new argument.

Say it in English – Theme 1

So kannst du ...

über ein Foto spekulieren	The ... suggests that this may be ... The way ... makes me think that ... The photo is open to different interpretations, but I would guess that ... The fact that ... makes me wonder whether the photo is about ...
über einen Liedtext sprechen	The phrase "..." suggests that many people still ... The passage from line ... to line ... shows that ... It becomes clear that ...
über eigene Erfahrungen sprechen	In my experience ...
Erwartungen formulieren	I would prefer my parents to ... As far as I'm concerned ...
Einschätzungen abgeben	What I find (un)necessary/most annoying/helpful is ... For me it's obvious that ... It seems to me that ...
die Ansichten deiner Gruppe wiedergeben	Our group agrees that ... Our general feeling is that ... What seems most relevant/essential is that ... According to most members of the group ...
Körpersprache und Mimik interpretieren	They are smiling/laughing, which implies ... His body language is tense, which suggests ... She is turning away from/avoiding eye contact with ... From the look on his face, I can tell that ... The mother is gesturing with her hands to show that ...
Teilnehmern einer Diskussion Feedback geben	The discussion was (not) very balanced. ... could have used more ... You presented your views/opinion very clearly/convincingly/... Next time you could try to support your view with relevant examples. If I were you, I would have used more phrases of agreement/disagreement to introduce your statements.

Theme 2: Life through a lens

lens /lenz/	Linse, Objektiv	p. 36
① advert *(BE)* (= **advertisement**) /ˈædvɜːt, ədˈvɜːtɪsmənt/	Werbung, Reklame, Anzeige, Inserat	Ben was annoyed that there were so many **adverts** on TV.
to fulfil /fʊlˈfɪl/	erfüllen, nachkommen, verwirklichen	
to entertain /ˌentəˈteɪn/	unterhalten	
sympathy /ˈsɪmpəθi/	Mitleid, Mitgefühl	I have a lot of **sympathy** for that family – their dog just died.
② to pick /pɪk/	aussuchen, auswählen	Can I **pick** which film to watch tonight?
striking /ˈstraɪkɪŋ/	bemerkenswert, auffallend	Layla's outfit is very colourful and rather **striking**.
to post /pəʊst/	posten *(einen Beitrag/Artikel online stellen)*	
to alter /ˈɔːltə/	ändern, bearbeiten	My trousers don't fit, can you **alter** them?
to identify /aɪˈdentɪfaɪ/	identifizieren, feststellen	We **identified** six differences between these two pictures.
alteration /ˌɔːltəˈreɪʃ(ə)n/	Änderung, Bearbeitung	The text sounded better once Terry had made some **alterations** to it.
③ section /ˈsekʃ(ə)n/	Teil, Abschnitt, Abteilung	Only a small **section** of the castle was open to the public.
caption /ˈkæpʃ(ə)n/	Überschrift, Titel, Bildunterschrift	Tim had to read the **caption** before he could understand the cartoon.
to manipulate /məˈnɪpjʊleɪt/	beeinflussen, manipulieren	It is wrong to **manipulate** someone into doing something for you.
public /ˈpʌblɪk/	öffentlich	The best way to get around London is by using **public** transport.
④ to formulate /ˈfɔːmjʊleɪt/	ausarbeiten, formulieren	
guidelines *(only pl)* /ˈɡaɪdˌlaɪnz/	Richtlinien, Leitlinien	
to select /sɪˈlekt/	aussuchen, auswählen	Bianca **selected** a dress to wear to dinner this evening.
° to cover up /ˌkʌvərˈʌp/	bedecken, verdecken	
selection /sɪˈlekʃ(ə)n/	Auswahl	There was a **selection** of fine wines to choose from at dinner.
condition /kənˈdɪʃ(ə)n/	Zustand, Bedingung; *hier:* Umstand	I'll help you on the **condition** that you clean the bathroom.

> **In anderen Sprachen**
>
> Das englische Wort **condition** ist mit dem französischen **condition**, dem spanischen **condición** und dem italienischen **condizione** verwandt.

regarding /rɪˈɡɑːdɪŋ/	bezüglich	
① advertisement /ədˈvɜːtɪsmənt/	Werbung, Reklame, Anzeige, Inserat	Sara read the **advertisements** in her local paper. p. 38
to make an impression on sb /ˌmeɪk_ən_ɪmˈpreʃ(ə)n_ɒn/	auf jdn Eindruck machen, jdn beeindrucken	Auntie Debbie **made a** strong **impression on** Kyle. Now he copies everything she does.
② headline /ˈhedˌlaɪn/	Schlagzeile; *hier:* Überschrift	The **headline** of Ben's report was "Teachers steal biscuits!"
entry /ˈentri/	Eintrag	Cheryl writes a new **entry** in her diary every day.

Word lists

Theme 2: Life through a lens

to not see the wood for the trees (informal, BE) /nɒt siː ðə ˌwʊd fə ðə ˈtriːz/	den Wald vor lauter Bäume nicht sehen	
flatmate (BE) /ˈflætˌmeɪt/	Mitbewohner/-in	
° to fall victim to sb/sth /ˌfɔːl ˈvɪktɪm tʊ/	jdm/etw zum Opfer fallen	
convinced /kənˈvɪnst/	überzeugt	Tony was **convinced** the figures at *Madame Tussauds* were real.
twice /twaɪs/	zweimal	
° thrice /θraɪs/	dreimal	
advertising (no pl) /ˈædvəˌtaɪzɪŋ/	Werbung, Reklame	**Advertising** is important because it tells people about a product.
at some point /æt ˈsʌm pɔɪnt/	irgendwann	Bob couldn't work all the time – he needed a break **at some point**.
brand /brænd/	Marke	Supermakets offer many different **brands** of the same product.
to trust /trʌst/	vertrauen	Macbeth was so paranoid that he didn't **trust** anyone.
daily /ˈdeɪli/	täglich, jeden Tag	Richard reads the newspaper **daily**.
milk (no pl) /mɪlk/	Milch	Beth drinks her tea with **milk** and two sugars.
bar /bɑː/	Stange, Stab; *hier:* Riegel	
packaging (no pl) /ˈpækɪdʒɪŋ/	Verpackung(smaterial)	It's better for the environment to buy products with less **packaging**.
ad (= advertisement) (informal) /æd, ədˈvɜːtɪsmənt/	Werbung, Reklame, Anzeige, Inserat	I saw an **ad** in the newspaper for green trainers.
drums (only pl) /drʌmz/	Schlagzeug	
Tell me about it! (informal) /ˈtel mi ə baʊt ɪt/	Wem sagst du das!	
to tempt sb to do/into doing sth /ˌtempt ˌsʌmbədi tə ˈduː, ˌɪntə ˈduːɪŋ/	jdn dazu verleiten/verführen, etw zu tun	
B3 article /ˈɑːtɪk(ə)l/	Artikel	I read a great **article** in *TIME Magazine* yesterday.
to summarize /ˈsʌməraɪz/	zusammenfassen, resümieren	Ellen **summarized** the text at the start of her essay.
guide /gaɪd/	Leitfaden, Ratgeber	
connection /kəˈnekʃ(ə)n/	Verbindung, Beziehung, Zusammenhang	Ollie couldn't hear Lisa on the phone as the **connection** was bad.
typically /ˈtɪpɪkli/	normalerweise, in der Regel	The British **typically** go on holiday where it is warm and sunny.
to associate /əˈsəʊsiˌeɪt/	in Verbindung bringen	
wealth (no pl) /welθ/	Reichtum, Vermögen, Fülle	It is better to have health than **wealth**.
mind /maɪnd/	Geist, Verstand; *hier:* Kopf	Jeff couldn't get Lady Gaga's new song out of his **mind**.
fluffy /ˈflʌfi/	flaumig (weich), flauschig	
subtle /ˈsʌt(ə)l/	fein(sinnig), subtil	Josh asked Ryan for help **subtly**, so the teacher wouldn't notice.
° to loosen /ˈluːs(ə)n/	(sich) lockern; *hier:* erleichtern	
wallet /ˈwɒlɪt/	Brieftasche, Portemonnaie	The pickpocket stole Simon's **wallet** and all the money that was in it!
° to skyrocket /ˈskaɪˌrɒkɪt/	in die Höhe schießen	
divorce /dɪˈvɔːs/	Scheidung	People who aren't happy with their marriage get a **divorce**.

Theme 2: Life through a lens — Word lists

case /keɪs/	Fall	Helen doesn't like blue? In that **case**, buy her a red cap.
tempting /ˈtemptɪŋ/	verlockend	Max was so tired, it was **tempting** to just stay in bed all day.
effective /ɪˈfektɪv/	fähig, wirksam, wirkungsvoll	Using *Camden Town* is an **effective** way to learn English.
essential /ɪˈsenʃ(ə)l/	unverzichtbar, wesentlich	A raincoat is **essential** in bad weather.
power /ˈpaʊə/	Macht, Kraft, Stärke	The US President has much more **power** than the Prime Minister.
to borrow /ˈbɒrəʊ/	(aus)leihen	
popularity (no pl) /ˌpɒpjʊˈlærəti/	Beliebtheit, Popularität	The **popularity** of electric cars has grown in the last ten years.
celebrity /səˈlebrəti/	Berühmtheit, Star	**Celebrities** are famous people.
endorsement /ɪnˈdɔːsmənt/	Billigung, Befürwortung, Unterstützung	Andrew wouldn't give the product an **endorsement** until he was paid.
to exploit /ɪkˈsplɔɪt/	ausbeuten, (aus)nutzen	Scrooge **exploited** his staff and didn't pay them well.
a touch of /ə ˈtʌtʃ əv/	ein wenig	
desirable /dɪˈzaɪrəb(ə)l/	erstrebenswert, begehrt	A seat close to the fire is **desirable** when it's cold outside.
peer pressure /ˈpɪə ˌpreʃə/	Gruppenzwang	**Peer pressure** is when your friends force you to do something.
instead of /ɪnˈsted əv/	(an)statt	
to leave out, left out, left out /ˌliːv ˈaʊt, ˌleft ˈaʊt/	ausschließen	
to pressure sb into doing sth /ˌpreʃə ˌsʌmbədi ˌɪntʊ ˈduːɪŋ/	jdn dazu drängen, etw zu tun	
as well /æz ˈwel/	auch	Esther went for a walk and took her dog, Tessa, **as well**.
to range /reɪndʒ/	schwanken, sich bewegen, reichen	
to stick, stuck, stuck /stɪk, stʌk/	kleben; *hier:* bleiben	
cinematic /ˌsɪnəˈmætɪk/	Film-; filmisch	
atmosphere /ˈætməsˌfɪə/	Atmosphäre, Stimmung	We all like each other so the **atmosphere** was very relaxed.
ASA (= Advertising Standards Authority) /ˌeɪ ˌes ˈeɪ, ˌædvəˌtaɪzɪŋ ˌstændədz ɔːˈθɒrəti/	Behörde zur Überwachung der Werbung in Großbritannien	*p. 40*
to ensure /ɪnˈʃɔː/	sicherstellen, garantieren	
legal /ˈliːg(ə)l/	legal, gesetzlich (vorgeschrieben)	Following the rules will keep your activities **legal** and safe.

In anderen Sprachen

Denk an das deutsche Wort **legal**. Sowohl das englische Wort als auch das deutsche stammen vom lateinischen **legalis** ab, was wiederum auf das lateinische Wort **Lex** (Gesetz) zurückgeht.

decent /ˈdiːs(ə)nt/	anständig, ordentlich, nett	Dave is a **decent** person. He's always on time and friendly.
truthful /ˈtruːθf(ə)l/	wahr, ehrlich	
to state /steɪt/	aussprechen, erklären, darlegen	Please **state** your name and reason for visiting.
communications /kəˌmjuːnɪˈkeɪʃ(ə)nz/	(Tele)kommunikation	

to **prepare** /prɪˈpeə/	vorbereiten, erstellen; *hier:* versehen (werden)	We **prepare** all our own meals at home.
responsibility /rɪˌspɒnsəˈbɪləti/	Verantwortung, Verantwortlichkeit, Zuständigkeit; *hier:* Verantwortungsgefühl	Having children is a very big **responsibility**.
consumer /kənˈsjuːmə/	Verbraucher/in, Konsument/in	
materially /məˈtɪəriəli/	wesentlich	
to mislead *(irr)* /mɪsˈliːd/	täuschen, verleiten	
widespread /ˈwaɪdˌspred/	weitverbreitet, von beachtlichem Ausmaß	
offence /əˈfens/	Straftat, Beleidigung, Vergehen	People only go to prison for serious **offences**, like stealing.
to **take care** /ˌteɪk ˈkeə/	aufpassen	Goodbye, **take care** of yourself!
to **avoid** /əˈvɔɪd/	(ver)meiden, ausweichen	Gary **avoids** PE lessons because he doesn't like playing sport.
on the grounds of /ɒn ðə ˈgraʊndz əv/	aufgrund, hinsichtlich	
gender /ˈdʒendə/	Geschlecht(sidentität)	**Gender** is more complicated than just male or female.
sexual orientation *(no pl)* /ˌsekʃuəl ˌɔːriənˈteɪʃ(ə)n/	sexuelle Veranlagung	
disability /ˌdɪsəˈbɪləti/	Unfähigkeit, Behinderung, Benachteiligung	Being blind is an example of a **disability**.
distress *(no pl)* /dɪˈstres/	Schmerz, Leid, Kummer, Not	
justifiable /ˈdʒʌstɪˌfaɪəb(ə)l/	berechtigt, gerechtfertigt	
to **justify** /ˈdʒʌstɪfaɪ/	rechtfertigen	It is hard to **justify** their children's terrible behaviour.

Wortbildung – Suffixe

Mit einem Suffix kann man die Wortart verändern.
Einige Suffixe wie **-ify**, und **-ise/-ize** bilden Verben:
  just → to just**ify**
  advert → to advert**ise**

Andere Suffixe wie **-able**, und **-ive** bilden Adjektive:
  to justify → justifi**able**
  offence → offens**ive**

excessive /ɪkˈsesɪv/	übermäßig	
marketer /ˈmɑːkɪtə/	Marketingleiter/in, Werbekampagnegestalter/in	
claim /kleɪm/	Behauptung, Forderung, Anspruch; *hier:* Werbeslogan	
merely /ˈmɪəli/	nur, bloß	
to attract /əˈtrækt/	anziehen	
in close proximity /ɪn ˌkləʊs prɒkˈsɪməti/	in unmittelbarer Nähe	
substance /ˈsʌbstəns/	Substanz, Stoff	
supervision /ˌsuːpəˈvɪʒ(ə)n/	Beaufsichtigung, Aufsicht	
to **ban** /bæn/	verbieten	Our school has **banned** listening to music in class.
to **smoke** /sməʊk/	rauchen	In Germany you have to be 18 years old to be allowed to **smoke**.
° bacon /ˈbeɪkən/	(Schinken)speck	
° processed /ˈprəʊsest/	industriell verarbeitet	
° dead *(informal)* /ded/	*hier:* sehr, total	
° shape up or ship out! *(informal)* /ʃeɪp ˌʌp ɔː ˌʃɪp ˈaʊt/	entweder ihr bringt euch in Form oder ihr dampft ab!	

Theme 2: Life through a lens — Word lists

° miracle /ˈmɪrək(ə)l/	Wunder	
to **get along** (**with sb**) /ˌget_əˈlɒŋ wɪð/	sich (mit jdm) verstehen	Joe **gets along** well **with** his brother, but he argues a lot with his sister.
in my view /ɪn ˈmaɪ ˌvjuː/	meiner Meinung nach	**In my view**, animals are dirty and smelly.
to **violate** /ˈvaɪəleɪt/	verstoßen (gegen), brechen, verletzen	If you **violate** the agreement, it will be cancelled.
presentation /ˌprez(ə)nˈteɪʃ(ə)n/	Präsentation; *hier:* Darstellung	The film's **presentation** of cowboys in the film was funny.
untruthful /ʌnˈtruːθf(ə)l/	unwahr, unaufrichtig	
inadequate /ɪnˈædɪkwət/	unzureichend; *hier:* unangemessen	The school hall was **inadequate** for so many people.
irresponsible /ˌɪrɪˈspɒnsəb(ə)l/	unverantwortlich, verantwortungslos	Bonnie's actions were **irresponsible** and people got hurt.
agency /ˈeɪdʒ(ə)nsi/	Agentur, Behörde	*p. 41*
pros and cons *(only pl)* /ˌprəʊz_ən ˈkɒnz/	Für und Wider, Pro und Kontra	
introductory /ˌɪntrəˈdʌkt(ə)ri/	vorbereitend, einleitend	
importance *(no pl)* /ɪmˈpɔːt(ə)ns/	Bedeutung, Wichtigkeit	This email is of high **importance**.
counter(-) /ˈkaʊntə/	Gegen(-)	
to **weaken** /ˈwiːkən/	schwächer werden, (ab)schwächen; *hier:* entkräften	
to **impress** /ɪmˈpres/	beeindrucken, imponieren	Charlie hoped to **impress** everyone with his football skills. *p.42*
series /ˈsɪəriːz/	(Fernseh)serie, Reihe, Folge	
bling /blɪŋ/	Klunker; glamourös, aufgedonnert	
thief *(pl* **thieves***)* /θiːf, θiːvz/	Dieb/in	The **thief** stole a handbag from a tourist.
to **strike, struck, struck** /straɪk|strʌk|strʌk/	(zu)schlagen	
obsession /əbˈseʃ(ə)n/	Besessenheit, Zwangsvorstellung	My gran's **obsession** with video games is unhealthy!
fame *(no pl)* /feɪm/	Ruhm	The Beatles achieved **fame** during the 1960s.
viewer /ˈvjuːə/	(Fernseh)zuschauer/in, Filmbetrachter/in	
to **appeal to sb/sth** /əˈpiːl tʊ/	jdn/etw reizen, jdn/etw ansprechen	Jim didn't want to see *Les Miserables* as musicals don't **appeal to** him.
plot /plɒt/	Handlung	The film's **plot** was so complicated, Leo didn't understand it at all!
setting /ˈsetɪŋ/	Einstellung; *hier:* Umgebung, Schauplatz	The **setting** of the *Harry Potter* novels is a school for magic.
extract /ˈekstrækt/	Auszug	An **extract** is a small part of a text.
director /daɪˈrektə/	Direktor/in, Regisseur/in	A **director** is someone who makes films.
to **release** /rɪˈliːs/	freilassen, entlassen; *hier:* veröffentlichen	
° **cast** /kɑːst/	Besetzung, Ensemble	
look /lʊk/	Blick, Gesichtsausdruck	I knew that Evie was unhappy from the **look** on her face.

Word lists — Theme 2: Life through a lens

gossip *(no pl)* /ˈgɒsɪp/	Klatsch(-), Tratsch	A conversation about unimportant things, especially about other people's lives, is called **gossip**.
to **place** /pleɪs/	stellen, setzen, legen	After reading "Hamlet", Juliet **placed** the book back on the bookshelf.
self-expression *(no pl)* /ˌself_ɪkˈspreʃ(ə)n/	Selbstdarstellung, Selbstausdruck	
self-absorption *(no pl)* /ˌself_əbˈzɔːpʃ(ə)n/	Ichbezogenheit	
sensitive /ˈsensətɪv/	sensibel, verständnisvoll, empfindlich	Don't joke about his new shirt – Fred can be very **sensitive** sometimes.
to **stress** /stres/	betonen	Daphne **stressed** that she would only go for a walk if it didn't rain.
to **be aware of sth** /ˌbi_əˈweər_əv/	sich einer Sache bewusst sein	Velma **wasn't aware of** her surprise birthday party.
issue /ˈɪʃuː/	Thema, Angelegenheit; *hier:* Problem, (Streit)frage	Climate change is one of the biggest **issues** affecting our society.
° keyword /ˈkiːˌwɜːd/	Schlüsselwort, Stichwort	
quotation /kwəʊˈteɪʃ(ə)n/	Zitat	"To be, or not to be," that is a **quotation** from Shakespeare.
review /rɪˈvjuː/	Überprüfung, Kritik, Rezension	The **reviews** for the new James Bond film were bad.
rather than /ˈrɑːðə ðæn/	anstelle, (und) nicht	
fortune *(no pl)* /ˈfɔːtʃən/	Vermögen, Schicksal, Glück; *hier:* Reichtum	
to **drive** *(irr)* /draɪv/	fahren; *hier:* treiben, bewegen	Chloe's need to help people **drove** her to become a nurse.
terrifying /ˈterəˌfaɪɪŋ/	entsetzlich, Angst erregend, Furcht einflößend	I don't like spiders – I think they're **terrifying**.
° to be hooked (on sth) /ˌbi_ˈhʊkt_ɒn/	(von etw) abhängig/begeistert sein	
° rush /rʌʃ/	Eile; *hier:* Rausch	
° petty theft /ˌpeti ˈθeft/	Bagatelldiebstahl	
casual /ˈkæʒuəl/	zufällig, gelegentlich, beiläufig, lässig	Steve wears **casual** clothes at work.
° purse /pɜːs/	Portemonnaie, Geldbörse	
further /ˈfɜːðə/	weiter(e, er, es), noch mehr, (noch) weiter	Ann had walked much **further** than she thought.
° fixated (on) /fɪkˈseɪtɪd_ɒn/	fixiert (auf)	
luxury /ˈlʌkʃəri/	Luxus(-)	Mrs Hicks has just bought an expensive **luxury** car.
goods *(only pl)* /gʊdz/	Waren, Güter	
worth /wɜːθ/	wert; *hier:* im Wert von	
including /ɪnˈkluːdɪŋ/	einschließlich	
° to track /træk/	verfolgen	
° to swan around *(informal, BE)* /ˌswɒn_əˈraʊnd/	herumtrödeln	
item /ˈaɪtəm/	Artikel, Gegenstand	Lily bought several **items**, including a new hairbrush.
to **direct** /daɪˈrekt/	Regie führen	Clint Eastwood **has directed** many films.
° to loot /luːt/	plündern	
worth *(no pl)* /wɜːθ/	Wert	My teddy bear has no real **worth**, but I love him.

Theme 2: Life through a lens — Word lists

In anderen Sprachen

Worth ist germanischen Ursprungs und ist mit dem deutschen **Wert**, dem niederländischen **waarde** sowie dem schwedischen **värde** verwandt.

° to dub /dʌb/	nennen	
effort /ˈefət/	Mühe, Anstrengung, Bemühung	
° to cover one's tracks /ˌkʌvə wʌnz ˈtræks/	seine Spuren verwischen	
to **vary** /ˈveəri/	variieren	The British weather can **vary** wildly from one day to the next.
jewellery *(no pl)* /ˈdʒuːəlri/	Schmuck	
theft /θeft/	Diebstahl	
careless /ˈkeələs/	unvorsichtig, leichtsinnig, unbedacht, unbekümmert	Bruce was **careless** on his moped and broke his arm.
key /kiː/	Schlüssel(-), Taste	
to photograph /ˈfəʊtəˌɡrɑːf/	fotografieren	
to brag (about sth) /ˈbræɡ‿əˌbaʊt/	(mit etw) angeben/prahlen	
boredom *(no pl)* /ˈbɔːdəm/	Langeweile	*p. 45*
moral value /ˌmɒrəl ˈvæljuː/	Moralvorstellung	
superficial /ˌsuːpəˈfɪʃ(ə)l/	oberflächlich, äußerlich	The model wasn't as **superficial** as the public had expected.
desire /dɪˈzaɪə/	Wunsch	He is so lazy. He has no **desire** to work.
thrilling /ˈθrɪlɪŋ/	aufregend, packend	The action film was so **thrilling** that Caleb couldn't stop watching it.
wish /wɪʃ/	Wunsch	When you see a falling star at night, you can make a **wish**.
peer /pɪə/	*jemand, der der gleichen Gruppe angehört*	
content /ˈkɒntent/	Inhalt	The **content** of Tarantino's latest film was not suitable for children.
cinematic device /ˌsɪnəˌmætɪk dɪˈvaɪs/	filmisches Stilmittel	
burglary /ˈbɜːɡləri/	Einbruch(diebstahl)	
summary /ˈsʌməri/	Zusammenfassung	Please write a one-page **summary** of the article.
to display /dɪˈspleɪ/	aushängen, (an)zeigen	
to **boast** (**about sth**) /ˈbəʊst‿əˌbaʊt/	prahlen/angeben (mit etw)	It isn't very nice to **boast about** your grades.
shot /ʃɒt/	Schuss; *hier:* Aufnahme, Einstellung	
besides /bɪˈsaɪdz/	außerdem	
subsequently /ˈsʌbsɪkwəntli/	später, danach	
to capture /ˈkæptʃə/	festnehmen; *hier:* auf Film festhalten	
to **arrest** /əˈrest/	verhaften	The police **arrested** five people for stealing.

In anderen Sprachen

Arrest kommt vom lateinischen Wort **arrestare** (zum Halten bringen), vgl. französisch **arrêter** und niederländisch **arresteren**.

rating /ˈreɪtɪŋ/	Einschätzung, Bewertung	
to **carry out** /ˌkæriˈaʊt/	durchführen, ausführen	The doctors **carried out** a lot of tests to find out why Quinn was sick.

survey /ˈsɜːveɪ/	Umfrage	The news reporter took a **survey** of the public's opinion on the story.

Say it in English – Theme 2

So kannst du …

darüber sprechen, ob Werbung verboten werden sollte	In my view the ad should be banned because … In my opinion the ad violates the rules because … The presentation of … is offensive/untruthful/irresponsible because … The presentation of … is inadequate for … because … The ad is (not) likely to offend … The ad might have a negative influence on … The ad could be seen as …
die Satzstruktur durch Verwendung von Partizipialkonstruktionen variieren	Already hooked on the rush of petty theft, Rebecca decides to take it a step further. Based on true events, the film follows a gang of wealthy teens fixated on 'celebrity' glamour.
über einen Film sprechen	The film …, by director …, was released in … Based on true events, the film follows … Directed by …, the film tells the story of …
über einen Filmausschnitt sprechen	The extract from …, by …, deals with …

Theme 3: Go with the flow

to go with the flow *(informal)* /ˌgəʊ wɪð ðə ˈfləʊ/	mit dem Strom schwimmen		p. 58
in /ɪn/	in, angesagt		
the in-crowd /ðiˈɪn kraʊd/	Insider-Clique		
to **pick** /pɪk/	aussuchen, auswählen	In a restaurant you look at the menu and **pick** what you want to eat.	
to **appeal to** sb/sth /əˈpiːl tʊ/	jdn/etw reizen, jdn/etw ansprechen	Shopping for clothes has never really **appealed to** Darrell.	
movie *(AE)* /ˈmuːvi/	(Kino)film	Linda likes watching **movies** on TV.	
stereotype /ˈsteriəˌtaɪp/	Stereotyp, Klischee, Vorurteil	**Stereotypes** are generally negative and unhelpful.	
prep(pie)/**preppy** *(AE)* /ˈprep(i)/	privilegierter junger Mensch, der großen Wert auf gute Kleidung und das äußere Erscheinungsbild legt		
to **tend to do** sth /ˌtend tə ˈduː/	zu etw neigen; dazu neigen, etw zu tun	Matt **tends to** shower late in the evening.	
typically /ˈtɪpɪkli/	normalerweise, in der Regel	November is **typically** wet and windy.	
to **be concerned with** sth /ˌbi: kənˈsɜːnd wɪð/	sich um etw Gedanken machen		
outgoing /ˌaʊtˈgəʊɪŋ/	kontaktfreudig; (aus)scheidend; ausgehend		
involved /ɪnˈvɒlvd/	betroffen, beteiligt, verwickelt	The students were **involved** in a special group project.	
council /ˈkaʊns(ə)l/	Rat; *hier:* Vertretung		
privileged /ˈprɪvəlɪdʒd/	privilegiert, bevorrechtigt	Harry and William had very **privileged** childhoods.	
as long as … /æz ˈlɒŋ æz/	solange …, sofern …	Charles will wait for **as long as** it takes to become king.	
jock *(informal, AE)* /dʒɒk/	Sportfanatiker/in	In US highschools, **jocks** can be found playing American football.	
muscly *(informal)* /ˈmʌsli/	muskulös		
entire /ɪnˈtaɪə/	gesamt, ganz, vollständig		
to **revolve around** /rɪˈvɒlv əˌraʊnd/	sich drehen um		
to **demand** /dɪˈmɑːnd/	verlangen, fordern	I **demand** to speak to the manager!	
extremely /ɪkˈstriːmli/	äußerst, höchst	Christie wasn't angry, but she was **extremely** irritated.	
despite /dɪˈspaɪt/	trotz		
pressure /ˈpreʃə/	Druck, Stress, Belastung	Pupils at our school feel a lot of **pressure** to do well.	
intellectual /ˌɪntəˈlektʃuəl/	Intellektuelle/r; intellektuell, geistig	**Intellectual** people are very clever.	
looks *(only pl)* /lʊks/	Aussehen	A good personality is more important than good **looks**.	
to **lack** /læk/	nicht haben, fehlen	Terry wanted to be a pop star, but he **lacked** the ability to sing.	
brains /breɪnz/	(Ge)hirn		
to **make up for** *(irr)* /ˌmeɪk ˈʌp fɔː/	ausgleichen, wettmachen	I'm sorry I hurt you. How can I **make up for** it?	
to **gossip** /ˈgɒsɪp/	tratschen, schlecht reden	Stop **gossiping** about the new boy in class!	
cruelty /ˈkruːəlti/	Grausamkeit, Quälerei	**Cruelty** to animals is never acceptable.	

Word lists
Theme 3: Go with the flow

to be the order of the day (with sb) /ˌbi: ðiˌɔːdər əv ðə ˈdeɪ wɪð/	(bei jdm) an der Tagesordnung sein	
beastliness (no pl) /ˈbiːstlɪnəs/	Widerwärtigkeit, Gemeinheit, Niedertracht	
bullying (no pl) /ˈbʊliɪŋ/	Mobbing	**Bullying** is not tolerated at this school.
geek (informal) /giːk/	Computerfreak	Timmy is a total **geek** – he does nothing but play video games.
to separate /ˈsepəreɪt/	trennen, abspalten; (sich) scheiden (lassen)	When a couple stop living together they **separate**.
brainy (informal) /ˈbreɪni/	gescheit, aufgeweckt	
rank /ræŋk/	Position, Stellung, Rang, Reihe	
popularity (no pl) /ˌpɒpjʊˈlærəti/	Beliebtheit, Popularität	Justin Bieber enjoys great **popularity** among young people.
casual /ˈkæʒuəl/	zufällig, gelegentlich, beiläufig, lässig	Steve wears **casual** clothes to work.
appearance /əˈpɪərəns/	Erscheinen, Aussehen, Auftreten	Tony made a dramatic **appearance** by jumping through the window.

> ### In anderen Sprachen
> Das Wort **appearance** ist verwandt mit den französischen Worten **apparition** und **apparence**, sowie dem spanischen Wort **aparición**.

whereas /weərˈæz/	während, wo(hin)gegen	
Goth /gɒθ/	Anhänger/in der Gothic-Kultur	
emo /ˈiːməʊ/	Anhänger/in des Emo, einer Subkultur mit Wurzeln im Hardcore-Punk	
several /ˈsev(ə)rəl/	einige, ein paar	There are **several** different flavours of ice cream to choose from.
to dye /daɪ/	färben	
streak /striːk/	Streifen, Strahl, Strähne	
as well /æz ˈwel/	auch	Cricket is a British sport and rugby is **as well**.
chain /tʃeɪn/	Kette	
attitude /ˈætɪˌtjuːd/	Haltung, Einstellung	**Attitudes** towards women in business have changed.
A3 rhetorical device /rɪˌtɒrɪk(ə)l dɪˈvaɪs/	rhetorisches Stilmittel, Stilfigur	**Rhetorical devices** are used to persuade or excite the reader.
repetition /ˌrepəˈtɪʃ(ə)n/	Wiederholung	**Repetition** is when the same thing happens again and again.
exaggeration /ɪgˌzædʒəˈreɪʃ(ə)n/	Übertreibung	I've seen this film at least 50 times. – That's an **exaggeration**!
A4 to characterize /ˈkærɪktəraɪz/	kennzeichnen, charakterisieren	Jocks are typically **characterized** by their talent for sport.
tone /təʊn/	Klang, Ton	
light-hearted /ˌlaɪt ˈhɑːtɪd/	sorglos, heiter; hier: mit einem Augenzwinkern	
humorous /ˈhjuːmərəs/	humorvoll, lustig, witzig	This film was quite **humorous**.
ironic /aɪˈrɒnɪk/	ironisch, (leicht) spöttisch	When you say the opposite of what you mean, you are being **ironic**.
critical /ˈkrɪtɪk(ə)l/	kritisch	Tracey was always very **critical** of everything her daughter did.
matter-of-fact /ˌmætər əv ˈfækt/	sachlich, nüchtern	

Theme 3: Go with the flow — **Word lists**

subject /'sʌbdʒɪkt/	(Schul)fach; *hier:* Thema	Politics is a **subject** that one shouldn't discuss with friends.
to **approve of** /ə'pruːv ɒv/	genehmigen, billigen	Nena's parents didn't **approve of** her new boyfriend.
to **disapprove of** /ˌdɪsə'pruːv ɒv/	dagegen sein, missbilligen, ablehnen	Georgia's dad **disapproved of** her short skirt.

Wortbildung – Präfixe

Mit einem Präfix kann man die Bedeutung eines Wortes verändern. Negierende Präfixe wie **dis-**, **im-/in-/ir-** und **un-** sind besonders häufig.

to **dis**approve ↔ to approve **in**tolerant ↔ tolerant **un**important ↔ important
impersonal ↔ personal **ir**relevant ↔ relevant

attribute /'ætrɪˌbjuːt/	Eigenschaft, Merkmal	Ed's best **attribute** was his sense of humour.
to what extent /tə ˌwɒt ɪk'stent/	inwieweit	**To what extent** can one really know a person?
survival guide /sə'vaɪv(ə)l gaɪd/	Überlebensratgeber	*p. 59*
to **fit in** /ˌfɪt 'ɪn/	dazupassen	Larry felt that he didn't really **fit in** with the rest of the football team.
to **exist** /ɪg'zɪst/	existieren, bestehen, leben, vorkommen	
to be meant to be sth /ˌbi: 'ment tə biː/	etw sein sollen	*p. 60*
surely /'ʃɔːli/	sicher(lich), bestimmt, doch	
blurb /blɜːb/	Klappentext	
memoir(s) /'memˌwɑːz/	(Lebens)erinnerungen, Memoiren	
vintage /'vɪntɪdʒ/	erlesen	
wisdom *(no pl)* /'wɪzdəm/	Weisheit, Klugheit	
ladder /'lædə/	(Stufen)leiter	
concept /'kɒnsept/	Vorstellung, Idee, Konzept	
to **put off** *(irr)* /ˌpʊt 'ɒf/	verschieben, abschrecken, abhalten	
personally /'pɜːs(ə)nəli/	persönlich; *hier:* ich für meinen Teil	**Personally**, I would rather learn French than English.
chapter /'tʃæptə/	Kapitel	Novels are divided into **chapters**.
to **make friends (with sb)** /ˌmeɪk 'frendz wɪð/	(mit jdm) Freundschaft schließen	
extract /'ekstrækt/	Auszug	An **extract** is part of a larger text.
to **advise** /əd'vaɪz/	(be)raten	
to **abandon** /ə'bændən/	verlassen, zurücklassen, aufgeben	They had to **abandon** ship in the storm. *p. 61*
outcast /'aʊtˌkɑːst/	Ausgestoßene/r, Geächtete/r	
to **pluck up (the) courage (to do sth)** /ˌplʌk ˌʌp ðə ˌkʌrɪdʒ/	allen Mut zusammennehmen(, um etw zu tun)	
to **impress** /ɪm'pres/	beeindrucken, imponieren	Charlie hoped to **impress** everyone with his football skills.
guy *(informal)* /gaɪ/	Kerl, Typ, Bursche	Shaun is a really cool **guy**.
nearby /ˌnɪə'baɪ/	in der Nähe (gelegen), nahe gelegen	In Britain, there's always a pub **nearby**.
section /'sekʃ(ə)n/	Teil, Abschnitt, Abteilung	A train has two **sections**; first class and second class.
summary /'sʌməri/	Zusammenfassung	A **summary** of a text has the same message, but uses less words. *p. 62*

opening /ˈəʊp(ə)nɪŋ/	Öffnen, Öffnung, Eröffnung(s-), Anfang(s-)	
to **introduce** /ˌɪntrəˈdjuːs/	vorstellen; *hier:* einleiten	The first sentence of a text should **introduce** the topic.
to **analyse** /ˈænəlaɪz/	analysieren, untersuchen	Please **analyse** your results and explain what they mean.
B6 **incident** /ˈɪnsɪd(ə)nt/	(Vor)fall, Zwischenfall, Ereignis, Begebenheit, Geschehen	The **incident** happened at 9:37 on 14th March.
drunk /drʌŋk/	betrunken	
B7 **criticism** *(no pl)* /ˈkrɪtɪˌsɪz(ə)m/	Kritik; *hier:* kritische Anmerkung	Giving constructive **criticism** helps people to correct their mistakes.
counter(-) /ˈkaʊntə/	Gegen(-)	
B8 to **complain (about)** /kəmˈpleɪn əˌbaʊt/	sich beklagen (über)	Zoe always **complains about** the weather.
to **turn into** /ˈtɜːn ˌɪntʊ/	(ver)wandeln	Each month, when the moon was full, Pete **turned into** a werewolf!
old-fashioned /ˌəʊld ˈfæʃ(ə)nd/	altmodisch, traditionsverbunden	
reputation /ˌrepjʊˈteɪʃ(ə)n/	Ruf, Renommee, Ansehen	Jake didn't have a good **reputation** for being early.
to beg /beg/	betteln, bitten, anflehen	
to **reply** /rɪˈplaɪ/	antworten, erwidern	"Are you coming to the cinema?" said Rosie. "I can't wait!" **replied** Jim.
what on earth ... *(informal)* /ˌwɒt ˌɒn ˈɜːθ/	was um alles in der Welt ...	
B9 **rhythm** /ˈrɪðəm/	Rhythmus, Takt	This song has got a good **rhythm**. You can really dance to it.
tone of voice /ˌtəʊn əv ˈvɔɪs/	Ton(fall)	Mum's **tone of voice** was serious. She wasn't joking.
to relate to /rɪˈleɪt tʊ/	eine Beziehung/Zugang finden zu, sich beziehen (auf)	
to **stress** /stres/	betonen	Mr Harris **stressed** the importance of this summer's exams.
to **address** /əˈdres/	adressieren, (sich) wenden an, ansprechen	**!** to a**ddress** – *adressieren*
to **bear sth in mind** /ˌbeə ˌsʌmθɪŋ ɪn ˈmaɪnd/	etw (mit)berücksichtigen	John **bore** Myra's suggestions **in mind** as he wrote his next essay.
rhyming /ˈraɪmɪŋ/	Reim-	
facial expression /ˌfeɪʃ(ə)l ɪkˈspreʃ(ə)n/	Gesichtsausdruck	
B10 **theme** /θiːm/	Thema(tik), Motto	Our school disco had a 70s **theme**.
rhyme /raɪm/	Reim(vers), Reimwort	
scheme /skiːm/	Plan, Projekt; *hier:* Schema	
movement /ˈmuːvmənt/	Bewegung	Protest **movements** have become more and more popular recently.
to post /pəʊst/	posten *(einen Beitrag/Artikel online stellen)*	
° post /pəʊst/	*online veröffentlichter Beitrag/Artikel/ Eintrag*	
° to pass /pɑːs/	geben, (herüber)reichen	
° therefore /ˈðeəfɔː/	deshalb, deswegen, daher	
unkind /ʌnˈkaɪnd/	unfreundlich; *hier:* unhöflich, grob	

Theme 3: Go with the flow — Word lists

as far as /æz ˈfɑːr_æz/	soweit	**As far as** I know, the plans haven't changed.
basically /ˈbeɪsɪkli/	im Wesentlichen, im Grunde, eigentlich	**Basically**, Abby told Liam that she didn't want to see him again.
I see your point. /aɪ ˌsiː jə ˈpɔɪnt/	Ich verstehe, was du sagst.	
spot /spɒt/	Fleck, Stelle; *hier:* Ort	*p. 66*
peer pressure /ˈpɪə ˌpreʃə/	Gruppenzwang	Mike was affected by **peer pressure**.
exercise /ˈeksəsaɪz/	Übung, Aufgabe; *hier:* Bewegung	Dogs need a lot of **exercise**.
to get *(irr)* /get/	erhalten, bekommen; *hier:* kapieren	I **don't get** what you've written. It doesn't make sense.
peer /pɪə/	*jemand, der der gleichen Gruppe angehört*	
to pressure sb into doing sth /ˌpreʃə ˌsʌmbədi ˌɪntʊ ˈduːɪŋ/	jdn dazu drängen, etw zu tun	
to give in *(irr)* /ˌgɪv ˈɪn/	nachgeben, aufgeben	Charlie was scared, but he didn't **give in** to Simon's bullying. *p. 67*
no matter ... /ˌnəʊ ˈmætə/	egal(,) ...	
article /ˈɑːtɪk(ə)l/	Artikel	I read a great **article** in *TIME Magazine* yesterday.
to influence /ˈɪnfluəns/	beeinflussen	The news **influences** public opinion.
to avoid /əˈvɔɪd/	(ver)meiden, ausweichen	Pip tries to **avoid** going to the doctor.
broad /brɔːd/	breit; *hier:* groß	David has a **broad** vocabulary but doesn't always use it correctly.
to trust /trʌst/	vertrauen	Paranoid people don't **trust** anyone.
counselor *(AE = counsellor BE)* /ˈkaʊnsələr/	Berater/in; *hier:* psychologischer Betreuer/psychologische Betreuerin	
obvious /ˈɒbviəs/	deutlich, offensichtlich	The answer is **obvious** if you read the question.
uncommon /ʌnˈkɒmən/	selten, ungewöhnlich	
habit /ˈhæbɪt/	Gewohnheit	It isn't easy to give up bad **habits**.
unlikely /ʌnˈlaɪkli/	unwahrscheinlich	It's **unlikely** that Andy will lose his next tennis match.
to smoke /sməʊk/	rauchen	Tim doesn't **smoke**. He doesn't like how cigarettes smell.
individually /ˌɪndɪˈvɪdʒuəli/	einzeln, für sich, individuell	
out of place /ˌaʊt_əv ˈpleɪs/	fehl am Platz	A zebra would be rather **out of place** on most farms.
unsure /ʌnˈʃʊə/	unsicher, ungewiss	Harry was **unsure** whether or not to ask Sally out.
adolescent /ˌædəˈles(ə)nt/	Jugendliche/r; heranwachsend, jugendlich	Teenagers are also called **adolescents**.
addiction (to) /əˈdɪkʃ(ə)n tʊ/	Abhängigkeit (von), Sucht (nach)	Ben has an **addiction to** sugar.
conviction /kənˈvɪkʃ(ə)n/	Verurteilung; Überzeugung	A life of crime can lead to a criminal **conviction**.
dependent /dɪˈpendənt/	abhängig	Alistair was **dependent** on his parents for everything.
to move on to sth /ˌmuːv_ˈɒn tʊ/	zu etw übergehen	
harm *(no pl)* /hɑːm/	Schaden, Verletzung	One more sweet won't do any **harm**.
to behave /bɪˈheɪv/	sich verhalten, sich benehmen	Roger's dog always **behaves** well.
enormous /ɪˈnɔːməs/	enorm, riesig, gewaltig	The Titanic was an **enormous** ship.
power /ˈpaʊə/	Macht, Kraft, Stärke	The Queen doesn't have any **power** over politics any more.

Word lists

Theme 3: Go with the flow

to **commit** /kəˈmɪt/	begehen	The prisoner had **committed** a serious crime.
offence /əˈfens/	Straftat, Beleidigung, Vergehen	
responsibility /rɪˌspɒnsəˈbɪləti/	Verantwortung, Verantwortlichkeit, Zuständigkeit	People should take **responsibility** for their actions.
to **value** /ˈvæljuː/	schätzen	
to **resist** /rɪˈzɪst/	sich wehren, widerstehen, Widerstand leisten	Georgia could never **resist** having a second piece of cake.
to **manage** /ˈmænɪdʒ/	leiten, führen, managen; *hier:* zurechtkommen mit	Ralph **managed** without food for six days in the desert!
calm /kɑːm/	ruhig, gelassen	After the storm, all was **calm**.
to **gain** /ɡeɪn/	bekommen, erreichen, gewinnen	Dan **gained** so much from his school exchange to France.
confidence *(no pl)* /ˈkɒnfɪd(ə)ns/	(Selbst)vertrauen, Zuversicht	Mark had no **confidence** in himself.
to **judge** /dʒʌdʒ/	(be)urteilen, schätzen	Don't **judge** a book by its cover.
to **respect** /rɪˈspekt/	respektieren	I **respect** your opinion, but I also disagree.
atmosphere /ˈætməsˌfɪə/	Atmosphäre, Stimmung	The **atmosphere** was very tense.
struggle (for) /ˈstrʌɡ(ə)l fɔː/	Kampf (um)	The **struggle for** power was too much for Henry, so he gave up.
C4 to **summarize** /ˈsʌməraɪz/	zusammenfassen, resümieren	Ellen **summarized** the text at the start of her essay.
C5 **horrified** /ˈhɒrɪfaɪd/	entsetzt	Grant was **horrified** by the news.
to **disappoint** /ˌdɪsəˈpɔɪnt/	enttäuschen	Glenn didn't want to **disappoint** his parents.
responsible /rɪˈspɒnsəb(ə)l/	verantwortlich, zuständig; *hier:* verantwortungsvoll	Jake is so **responsible**. He always babysits his little sister.
to **rely on sb/sth** /rɪˈlaɪ ɒn/	sich auf jdn/etw verlassen	Tom is always there for Jill. She can **rely on** him.
greeting /ˈɡriːtɪŋ/	Begrüßung	
to **be aware of sth** /ˌbɪ ə'weər əv/	sich einer Sache bewusst sein	Most smokers **are aware of** the dangers of smoking.
to **request** /rɪˈkwest/	bitten um, (sich) wünschen	I would like to **request** a meeting with the President.
to **repeat** /rɪˈpiːt/	wiederholen; *hier:* wiedergeben, erzählen	Could you **repeat** the story please, I didn't hear it the first time.
hopefully /ˈhəʊpf(ə)li/	hoffnungsvoll, hoffentlich	**Hopefully** my brother will visit soon.
to **take turns** *(BE)* /ˌteɪk ˈtɜːnz/	sich abwechseln	Karl and Keira **took turns** choosing TV programmes.
eye contact /ˈaɪ ˌkɒntækt/	Blickkontakt	
gesture /ˈdʒestʃə/	Handbewegung, Geste	Tony made a **gesture** to emphasize his point.
to **refuse** /rɪˈfjuːz/	ablehnen, verweigern	Jenny **refused** to speak to Darren.
clarification /ˌklærəfɪˈkeɪʃ(ə)n/	Klarstellung, (Ab)klärung	I need some **clarification** as to what happened.
to **interrupt** /ˌɪntəˈrʌpt/	unterbrechen	You mustn't **interrupt** the teacher when she is speaking.
to **make a/your point** /ˌmeɪk ə/jə ˈpɔɪnt/	etwas ansprechen, (s)ein Argument einbringen, mit etwas recht haben	
connection /kəˈnekʃ(ə)n/	Verbindung, Beziehung, Zusammenhang	There is a good train **connection** between London and Bristol.

Say it in English – Theme 3
So kannst du …

über verschiedene Jugendgruppen sprechen	I chose/decided on/picked this group because … I think this group has similar interests/clothes to me, for example … This group appealed to me the most because … I could not imagine joining any of the other groups because …
Mutmaßungen anstellen	It seems to me … • It seems likely that … I assume … • Wouldn't you agree that …?
ausdrücken, was für eine Gruppe typisch ist	Preps tend to be … • Expect to see people like them … Popular girls will be at the top of the social ladder … Geeks are more likely to have … Goths will most often be …
über die Haltung eines Autors sprechen	The author appears to approve/disapprove of … The author seems to have a critical/neutral attitude towards school groups because …
die Ernsthaftigkeit/Nützlichkeit einer Sache bewerten	You can/can't really take any/most of the tips seriously because … The tip about … is quite useful/is meant seriously because … In general, I think you can learn a lot about … Surely you don't think … I really don't believe …
Interesse oder Desinteresse an einem Buch formulieren	This book doesn't appeal to me at all because … The concept of this book sounds interesting but/because … The cover would put me off reading this book because … It could be quite exciting to find out … I prefer to read … Personally, I find this subject …
über einen Rap, Song oder ein Musikvideo sprechen	The rapper stresses … to convey his emotions. The rhythm is achieved by … The rapper exaggerates … By using the phrase … the rapper addresses the audience directly. When … speaks, the rapper …
deine Meinung ausdrücken	As far as I can see … Personally, … Basically, … I would say …
Zustimmung äußern	You're absolutely right. That's just how I see it, too. That's exactly what I think.
eine gegenteilige Meinung äußern	I see your point but … • I see it differently. You don't really mean that, do you?
bewerten, wie realistisch etwas ist	The examples are quite true to life because … I can't imagine that … The examples seem quite unrealistic to me because …
über Gruppenzwang sprechen	Many people give in to peer pressure because … Most people would … if their friends encouraged them. Despite peer pressure, … For people not to give in to peer pressure, they need to be/have … No matter what their friends said, I don't think people would …
nachfragen	Are you saying that …? Do you mean …?

Theme 4: One world?

	to hit the road *(informal)* /ˌhɪt ðə ˈrəʊd/	sich auf den Weg machen	
A1	survey /ˈsɜːveɪ/	Umfrage	Dan answered a **survey** about his family.
	youth hostel /ˈjuːθ ˌhɒst(ə)l/	Jugendherberge	
	to cluster /ˈklʌstə/	(lose) zusammenstellen, sammeln	
	briefly /ˈbriːfli/	kurz (gesagt), knapp	
A2	caption /ˈkæpʃ(ə)n/	Überschrift, Titel, Bildunterschrift	**Captions** can explain what is happening in a picture.
	to be related to /ˌbi rɪˈleɪtɪd_tʊ/	verwandt sein (mit); *hier:* in Beziehung stehen (zu)	
	to appreciate /əˈpriːʃiˌeɪt/	*hier:* schätzen lernen	
	to de-stress /diːˈstres/	(sich) entstressen (Wortneuschöpfung)	
	overall /ˌəʊvərˈɔːl/	Gesamt-, allgemein, insgesamt	The expert criticized some choices, but her **overall** view was positive.
A3	recent /ˈriːs(ə)nt/	kürzlich; *hier:* neu(e)ste	Our shop is really cool. We sell all the **recent** trends.
	to **motivate** /ˈməʊtɪveɪt/	motivieren, veranlassen	Rita's dream of being a doctor **motivates** her to work hard.
	to **interest sb** /ˈɪntrəst/	jdn interessieren	History really **interests me**, I love learning about the Romans.
	local /ˈləʊk(ə)l/	Ortsansässige/r, Einheimische/r	
	industry /ˈɪndəstri/	Industrie, Branche	
	the present /ðə ˈprez(ə)nt/	die Gegenwart	
	° **voluntourism** /ˈvɒlən,tʊərɪz(ə)m/	Freiwilligenarbeit in Kombination mit Urlaub	
	finding /ˈfaɪndɪŋ/	Entdeckung, Ergebnis	
A4	carefree /ˈkeəˌfriː/	sorgenfrei, unbekümmert	
	custom /ˈkʌstəm/	Brauch, Sitte, Gewohnheit	It's a British **custom** to wear paper crowns at Christmas.
	flavour /ˈfleɪvə/	(Wohl)geschmack	
	to **interpret** /ɪnˈtɜːprɪt/	deuten, auslegen, wiedergeben	We had different answers because we **interpreted** the question differently.
	cue card /ˈkjuː kɑːd/	Stichwortkarte	
	to **take turns** *(BE)* /ˌteɪk ˈtɜːnz/	sich abwechseln	Karl and Keira **took turns** choosing TV programmes.
	in terms of /ɪn ˈtɜːmz_əv/	hinsichtlich, was … angeht	Can you explain that **in terms of** how much money we've lost?
B1	getaway *(informal)* /ˈgetəˌweɪ/	Trip, Ausflug	
	entry /ˈentri/	Eintrag	I wrote a new blog **entry** yesterday, did you read it?
	to occur /əˈkɜː/	geschehen, sich ereignen; *hier:* auftreten	When did the accident **occur**?
	quotation /kwəʊˈteɪʃ(ə)n/	Zitat	*"Ich bin ein Berliner"* is a famous **quotation** from John F. Kennedy.
	abroad /əˈbrɔːd/	im/ins Ausland	Klaus has never been on holiday **abroad** – only in Germany.
	guys *(only pl, informal)* /gaɪz/	Leute	
	GCSE (= General Certificate of Secondary Education) /ˌdʒiː siː_es_ˈiː/	Abschlussprüfung der Sekundarstufe 1	

Theme 4: One world? — Word lists

a couple of ... /ə ˈkʌp(ə)l_əv/	einige ..., ein paar ...	
° mate *(informal, BE)* /meɪt/	Freund/in, Kumpel	
° to give/get the go-ahead *(informal)* /ˌgɪv/ˌget ðə ˈgəʊəˌhed/	grünes Licht geben/erhalten	
somewhere /ˈsʌmweə/	irgendwo	Benji was sure he'd seen Lorna **somewhere** before – but where?
Let's face it *(informal)* /ˌlets ˈfeɪs_ɪt/	Machen wir uns (doch) nichts vor	
° chuffed *(informal, BE)* /tʃʌft/	froh, begeistert	
rowdy /ˈraʊdi/	laut, rüpelhaft	
lad *(informal, BE)* /læd/	Junge	
° to throw it out to sb *(informal)* /ˌθrəʊ_ɪt_ˈaʊt_tʊ/	jdn um Ideen/Input bitten	
° to rough it *(informal)* /ˈrʌf_ɪt/	(ganz) primitiv leben	
° kinda (= kind of) *(informal, AE)* /ˈkaɪndə, ˈkaɪnd_əv/	irgendwie	
point /pɔɪnt/	*hier:* Zweck, Sinn	
nearby /ˌnɪəˈbaɪ/	in der Nähe (gelegen), nahe gelegen	Charlie was hungry, so he went to a **nearby** supermarket to get pizza.
tight *(informal)* /taɪt/	*hier:* knausrig	
° or anything *(informal)* /ɔːr_ˈeniθɪŋ/	oder so was	
° to break the bank *(informal)* /ˌbreɪk ðə ˈbæŋk/	verschwenderisch sein	
Spain /speɪn/	Spanien	
cost /kɒst/	Preis, Kosten	
low /ləʊ/	niedrig, gering, tief	Customers are always happy when they see **low** prices.
° pretty *(informal)* /ˈprɪti/	ziemlich	
Denmark /ˈdenmɑːk/	Dänemark	
peaceful /ˈpiːsf(ə)l/	friedlich, ruhig	
° probs (= probably) *(informal)* /ˈprɒbz, ˈprɒbəbli/	wahrscheinlich	
outdoors /ˌaʊtˈdɔːz/	draußen, im Freien	Some shops ask customers to leave their pets **outdoors**.
to **address** /əˈdres/	adressieren, (sich) wenden an, ansprechen	The prime minister **addressed** her supporters in Parliament.
colloquial /kəˈləʊkwiəl/	umgangssprachlich	Never use **colloquial** phrases in an essay.
incomplete /ˌɪnkəmˈpliːt/	unvollständig, unfertig	This information is **incomplete**. Please provide your full name.
address /əˈdres/	Adresse, Anschrift; *hier:* Anrede	"Mate" and "bro" are informal forms of **address**.
to post /pəʊst/	posten *(einen Beitrag/Artikel online stellen)*	
headline /ˈhedˌlaɪn/	Schlagzeile; *hier:* Überschrift	The newspaper's **headline** was "Man bites dog".
subhead(ing) /ˈsʌbˌhedɪŋ/	Untertitel	
article /ˈɑːtɪk(ə)l/	Artikel	Did you see that **article** about penguins on *Spiegel Online*?
to **summarize** /ˈsʌməraɪz/	zusammenfassen, resümieren	Mary **summarized** the novel *Frankenstein*: Don't play God.
concrete /ˈkɒŋkriːt/	Beton(-)	
coastline /ˈkəʊstˌlaɪn/	Küste(nlinie)	

Wortbildung – Komposition

Die deutsche Sprache kennt viele Zusammensetzungen wie Angsthase oder Schadenfreude.
Im Englischen gibt es auch Zusammensetzungen, die aber getrennt-, zusammen- oder mit Bindestrich geschrieben werden können:

head + line = **headline**
coast + line = **coastline**
wild + life = **wildlife**
go + ahead = **go-ahead**
youth + hostel = **youth hostel**
hot + spot = **hot spot**

the **Mediterranean** (**Sea**) /ðə ˌmedɪtəˌreɪniən ˈsiː/	das Mittelmeer	Isobel went on holiday to the south of France, on the **Mediterranean**.
excessive /ɪkˈsesɪv/	übermäßig	
° **hot spot** /ˈhɒt spɒt/	Krisenherd, *hier:* angesagter Ort	
to **attract** /əˈtrækt/	anziehen	Berlin **attracts** more tourists than any other German city.
° **species** /ˈspiːʃiːz/	Art, Spezies	
biodiversity (*no pl*) /ˌbaɪəʊdaɪˈvɜːsəti/	Artenvielfalt	
recent /ˈriːs(ə)nt/	kürzlich, *hier:* jüngst …/letzt …	Winters have become warmer and warmer in **recent** years.
wealth (*no pl*) /welθ/	Reichtum, Vermögen, Fülle	After years as a teacher, Mr Jones had a **wealth** of experience.
to **stress** /stres/	betonen	Percy spoke slowly and **stressed** every single word.
the **Med** (*informal, BE*) /ðə ˈmed/	das Mittelmeer	
ecosystem /ˈiːkəʊˌsɪstəm/	Ökosystem	
sensitive /ˈsensətɪv/	sensibel, verständnisvoll, empfindlich	Heidi gets very **sensitive** when people criticize her.
pressure /ˈpreʃə/	Druck, Stress, Belastung	Sam always felt under **pressure** to do well at school.
under construction /ˌʌndə kənˈstrʌkʃ(ə)n/	im Bau	
popularity (*no pl*) /ˌpɒpjʊˈlærəti/	Beliebtheit, Popularität	Madonna and Michael Jackson achieved **popularity** in the 1980s.
decline /dɪˈklaɪn/	Rückgang, Verschlechterung, Niedergang	**In anderen Sprachen** **Popularity** kommt vom lateinischen **popularis** (vom Volk) und ist mit **popular**, **population** und **people** verwandt.
° **on the contrary** /ɒn ðə ˈkɒntrəri/	ganz im Gegenteil	
entire /ɪnˈtaɪə/	gesamt, ganz, vollständig	
to **cover** /ˈkʌvə/	bedecken	The clouds have **covered** the sky.
to **warn** /wɔːn/	warnen	In a library people are **warned** not to speak too loudly.
to **fail** /feɪl/	versagen, scheitern, missglücken	Although she tried, Elaine **failed** to give up eating cake.
° **developer** /dɪˈveləpə/	Entwickler, *hier:* Bauunternehmer	
twice /twaɪs/	zweimal	
° **sewage** (*no pl*) /ˈsuːɪdʒ/	Abwasser	
treatment /ˈtriːtmənt/	Behandlung	
wildlife (*no pl*) /ˈwaɪldˌlaɪf/	die (natürliche) Tier- und Pflanzenwelt	The world's natural **wildlife** needs to be protected from humans.
once /wʌns/	sobald	

Theme 4: One world? — Word lists

cause /kɔːz/	Grund, Ursache, Anlass	Having a birthday is alway a **cause** for celebration!
to **gain** /kɔːz/	bekommen, erreichen, gewinnen	Eugene was so nice to Arthur that he quickly **gained** a new friend.
yet /jet/	(und) doch, (und) trotzdem	
sustainable /səˈsteɪnəb(ə)l/	haltbar, nachhaltig	Spending more money than you earn is not **sustainable**.
to **relate to** /rɪˈleɪt‿tʊ/	eine Beziehung/Zugang finden zu, sich beziehen (auf)	*p. 84*
unsure /ʌnˈʃʊə/	unsicher, ungewiss	
graphic organizer /ˌɡræfɪk‿ˈɔːɡəˌnaɪzə/	*grafische Darstellungsform*	
to **outline** /ˈaʊtlaɪn/	(kurz) umreißen, skizzieren	The minister **outlined** his policies.
mass /mæs/	Masse, Massen-, Menge	Factories have enabled the **mass** production of clothes and cars.
flow chart /ˈfləʊ tʃɑːt/	Flussdiagramm	
consumption *(no pl)* /kənˈsʌmpʃ(ə)n/	Verbrauch, Konsum	
impact /ˈɪmpækt/	Auswirkung	Drinking too much alcohol will have a negative **impact** on your health.
arrow /ˈærəʊ/	Pfeil	
to **result from** /rɪˈzʌlt frəm/	aus etw resultieren	Many problems **result from** smoking cigarettes.
consequently /ˈkɒnsɪkwəntli/	folglich, infolgedessen	Tia went to bed late. **Consequently**, she was tired the next day.
fossil fuel /ˌfɒs(ə)l ˈfjuːəl/	fossiler Brennstoff	
search /sɜːtʃ/	Suche	Velma's **search** for her lost glasses wasn't easy, as she couldn't see!
source /sɔːs/	Quelle, Informationsquelle	Money is the **source** of all evil.
further /ˈfɜːðə/	weiter(e, er, es), noch mehr, (noch) weiter	You've made an interesting point, can you explain it **further**?
shortage /ˈʃɔːtɪdʒ/	Knappheit, Mangel	
arrangement /əˈreɪndʒmənt/	Abmachung, Vereinbarung; *hier:* Anordnung	
to **represent sb/sth** /ˌreprɪˈzent/	jdn/etw repräsentieren, jdn vertreten; *hier:* etw wiedergeben	This poem **represents** the author's feelings.
to **glue** /gluː/	kleben	
eco-friendly /ˌiːkəʊ ˈfrendli/	umweltfreundlich	Modern cars are more **eco-friendly** than older ones *p. 85*
advertisement /ədˈvɜːtɪsmənt/	Werbung, Reklame, Anzeige, Inserat	There was an **advertisement** in the paper selling a car.
offer /ˈɒfə/	Angebot	Our bar has many different drinks on **offer**.
policy /ˈpɒləsi/	Programm, Strategie, Grundsatz, Politik	
pros and cons *(only pl)* /ˌprəʊz‿ən ˈkɒnz/	Für und Wider, Pro und Kontra	
promising /ˈprɒmɪsɪŋ/	viel versprechend	
environmentally conscious /ɪnˌvaɪrənˌment(ə)li ˈkɒnʃəs/	umweltbewusst	
traveller /ˈtræv(ə)lər/	Reisende/r	The two young **travellers** bought their tickets at the train station.
wood(s) /wʊdz/	(kleiner) Wald	A **wood** is a small forest.

Word lists

Theme 4: One world?

Wood vs woods

Ein **wood** ist für gewöhnlich ein kleines, klar umgrenztes Areal. Dementsprechend kommt **wood** häufig in Ortsnamen vor. **Woods** sind größere bewaldete Gebiete, oft ohne klar definierbare Grenzen.

° path /pɑːθ/	Weg, Pfad, Bahn	
the choice is yours /ðə ˌtʃɔɪs ɪz ˈjɔːz/	Sie haben die Wahl	
wind turbine /ˈwɪnd ˌtɜːbaɪn/	Windkraftanlage	
organic /ɔːˈɡænɪk/	organisch, Bio-	
instead of /ɪnˈsted əv/	(an)statt	
air conditioning *(no pl)* /ˈeə kənˌdɪʃ(ə)nɪŋ/	Klimatisierung, Klimaanlage	Bridget wished her school had **air conditioning** in the summer.
facilities *(no pl)* /fəˈsɪlətiz/	Einrichtungen, Anlagen	Expensive hotels often claim to have better **facilities** than other hotels.
hiking *(no pl)* /ˈhaɪkɪŋ/	Wandern	Arnie went **hiking** in the mountains.
° trail /treɪl/	Weg, Pfad, Spur	
° wildlife spotting *(no pl)* /ˈwaɪldlaɪf ˌspɒtɪŋ/	Naturbeobachtung	
renewable /rɪˈnjuːəb(ə)l/	erneuerbar	Solar energy is **renewable**, oil isn't.
luxury /ˈlʌkʃəri/	Luxus(-)	Expensive cars and holidays abroad are **luxuries** not all can afford.
° to cost the earth *(informal)* /ˌkɒst ði ˈɜːθ/	ein Vermögen kosten	
° affordable /əˈfɔːdəb(ə)l/	erschwinglich	
guilt-free /ˌɡɪltˈfriː/	ohne schlechtes Gewissen	
scenic /ˈsiːnɪk/	landschaftlich (schön)	The British countryside is **scenic**.
° Blue Flag /ˌbluː ˈflæɡ/	Blaue Flagge *(Gütezeichen im Bereich des nachhaltigen Tourismus)*	
range /reɪndʒ/	Reichweite, Bereich, *hier:* Angebot	
to **meet, met, met** /miːt|met|met/	*hier:* erfüllen, entsprechen	Fred's last holiday **met** all his expectations.
single /ˈsɪŋɡ(ə)l/	Single, *hier:* Einzelzimmer	
full board *(no pl)* /ˌfʊl ˈbɔːd/	(mit) Vollpension	
half board *(no pl)* /ˌhɑːf ˈbɔːd/	Halbpension(-)	
spa /spɑː/	(Heil)bad, Wellness-Bereich	
section /ˈsekʃ(ə)n/	Teil, Abschnitt, Abteilung	Katie only read a **section** of the book, not the whole thing.
goal /ɡəʊl/	Ziel, Tor	
double /ˈdʌb(ə)l/	Doppelte(r), *hier:* Doppelzimmer	
° sailing *(no pl)* /ˈseɪlɪŋ/	Segeln	
sunbathing *(no pl)* /ˈsʌnˌbeɪðɪŋ/	Sonnenbaden	
solar panel /ˌsəʊlə ˈpæn(ə)l/	Sonnenkollektor	
energy-saving /ˈenədʒi ˌseɪvɪŋ/	energiesparend	
to **reuse** /riːˈjuːz/	wiederverwenden, wiederverwerten	Peter doesn't throw away plastic bottles, he **reuses** them instead.
wireless /ˈwaɪələs/	drahtlos, *hier:* WLAN-	
public /ˈpʌblɪk/	öffentlich	Libraries, schools and hospitals are all **public** places.
including /ɪnˈkluːdɪŋ/	einschließlich	

In anderen Sprachen
Wie das deutsche **Sektion** kommt **section** vom lateinischen **sectio** (Abschnitt). Vgl. französisch **section** und spanisch **sección**.

Theme 4: One world? — Word lists

addition (to) /əˈdɪʃ(ə)n tʊ/	Ergänzung (zu), Zusatz (zu)	In **addition to** singing, Ellie also plays the piano and guitar.	p. 87
improvement /ɪmˈpruːvmənt/	Verbesserung	The new school bus is definitely an **improvement** on the old one.	
account /əˈkaʊnt/	Bericht	The **accounts** that Colin and Paula gave the police were the same.	
previous /ˈpriːviəs/	vor(her)ig, vorhergehend	Mike's **previous** boyfriend was taller.	
to come to a conclusion /ˌkʌm tʊ ə kənˈkluːʒ(ə)n/	zu einem Schluss kommen/gelangen	We have to look at all the facts before we **come to a conclusion**.	
to what extent /tə ˌwɒt ɪkˈstent/	inwieweit	**To what extent** are wolves and dogs the same?	
to qualify /ˈkwɒlɪfaɪ/	(sich) qualifizieren; klassifiziert werden, gelten	Hippos do not **qualify** as 'small pets'.	
alternatively /ɔːlˈtɜːnətɪvli/	als Alternative, stattdessen	Give me the keys. **Alternatively**, I can break down the door.	
exclamation /ˌekskləˈmeɪʃ(ə)n/	Ausruf	Alex's **exclamation** of excitement could be heard next door.	
to appeal to sb/sth /əˈpiːl tʊ/	jdn/etw reizen, jdn/etw ansprechen	The idea of a week abroad **appealed to** Jim in the winter.	
recommendation /ˌrekəmenˈdeɪʃ(ə)n/	Empfehlung	What is your **recommendation** for a story about zombies?	
false /fɔːls/	falsch	Try to work out if these facts are true or **false**.	p. 88
the Romans /ðə ˈrəʊmənz/	die Römer		
in total /ɪn ˈtəʊt(ə)l/	insgesamt	Liam, Nathan and Adam scored one goal each, or three **in total**.	
billion /ˈbɪljən/	Milliarde		
native language /ˌneɪtɪv ˈlæŋɡwɪdʒ/	Muttersprache	We all understood each other, even though English wasn't our **native language**.	
variety /vəˈraɪəti/	Art, Varietät		
Chinglish /ˈtʃɪŋɡlɪʃ/	vom Chinesischen beeinflusste Variante des Englischen		
native speaker /ˌneɪtɪv ˈspiːkə/	Muttersprachler/in	Petra's accent is so good, she sounds like a **native speaker**.	
worldwide /ˌwɜːldˈwaɪd/	weltweit		
official /əˈfɪʃ(ə)l/	offiziell		
speaker /ˈspiːkə/	Redner/in, Sprecher/in	Everyone listened politely to the **speaker's** presentation in class.	
° **Portuguese** /ˌpɔːtʃʊˈɡiːz/	Portugiese/Portugiesin, Portugiesisch; portugiesisch		
° **Russian** /ˈrʌʃ(ə)n/	Russe/Russin, Russisch; russisch		
° **Arabic** *(no pl)* /ˈærəbɪk/	Arabisch; arabisch		
° **Spanish** /ˈspænɪʃ/	Spanisch; spanisch		
° **Hindi** *(no pl)* /ˈhɪndi/	Hindi *(Amtssprache in Indien)*		
° **Urdu** *(no pl)* /ˈʊəduː/	Urdu *(Amtssprache in Pakistan)*		
° **Chinese** /ˌtʃaɪˈniːz/	Chinese/Chinesin, Chinesisch *(Sprache)*; chinesisch		
° **Mandarin** *(no pl)* /ˈmændərɪn/	Mandarin *(chinesische Hochsprache)*		
the other way round /ðɪ ˌʌðə weɪ ˈraʊnd/	umgekehrt	Sometimes Jo is faster than Kate but often it's **the other way round**.	p. 90
script /skrɪpt/	Drehbuch, Skript, Regiebuch		

to **avoid** /əˈvɔɪd/		(ver)meiden, ausweichen	Keesha never speaks in class, she **avoids** answering questions.
to **host** /həʊst/		ausrichten, präsentieren, moderieren; *hier:* als Gast aufnehmen	
audience /ˈɔːdiəns/		*hier:* Leser(schaft)	*The Giver* and *Twilight* were both written for a teenage **audience**.

Collective nouns

Ein *collective noun* ist ein Wort, das sich auf eine Gruppe von Menschen bezieht. Einige der häufigsten englischen *collective nouns* sind:
    audience, band, class, company, crowd, family, government, group, (political) party, public, staff, team
Im britischen Englisch steht das zum *collective noun* gehörende Verb manchmal im **Singular** und manchmal im **Plural**. Wenn das Verb im **Singular** steht, wird die Einheit des *collective noun* als Gruppe betont. Steht das Verb im **Plural**, dann werden die einzelnen Mitglieder der Gruppe des *collective noun* betont.
    The audience **was** amused.   Das (ganze) Publikum war erfreut.
    The audience **are** laughing.   (Einige) Zuschauer lachen.
! Das englische Wort *police* bildet eine Ausnahme. Das dazu gehörende Verb muss immer im Plural stehen!
    The police **are** searching for a young man.   Die Polizei sucht einen jungen Mann.

content /ˈkɒntent/		Inhalt	The **content** of the magazine was boring.
to **cover** /ˈkʌvə/		bedecken; *hier:* sich befassen mit, behandeln	*Camden Town 5* **covers** a wide range of topics.
form /fɔːm/		Formular	
whose /huːz/		dessen, deren	Italy, **whose** flag is green, white and red, is on the Mediterranean Sea.
prejudiced /ˈpredʒʊdɪst/		voreingenommen	
housework *(no pl)* /ˈhaʊsˌwɜːk/		Hausarbeit	Reece's parents often ask him to help with the **housework**.
to **switch** /swɪtʃ/		wechseln	
difficulty /ˈdɪfɪk(ə)lti/		Mühe; Schwierigkeit; Problem	Kerry passed the test with **difficulty**.
to **be/feel homesick** /ˌbiː/ˌfiːl ˈhəʊmˌsɪk/		Heimweh haben	Verity misses her mum. She **is homesick**.
to **keep in mind** /ˌkiːp ɪn ˈmaɪnd/		nicht vergessen	Be polite, you must **keep in mind** how scary this is for Evie.
possibly /ˈpɒsəbli/		möglicherweise; *hier:* gegebenenfalls	We might **possibly** need our passports at the border.
register /ˈredʒɪstə/		Register, Verzeichnis; *hier:* Sprachebene	You can use an informal **register** when talking to your friends.
generally /ˈdʒen(ə)rəli/		normalerweise, im Allgemeinen, allgemein, generell	Judy **generally** spends about an hour a day doing sport.
C5	to **fulfil** /fʊlˈfɪl/	erfüllen, nachkommen, verwirklichen	p.
C7	**future** /ˈfjuːtʃə/	zukünftig	I will name my **future** children Emily and Richard. p.
Australian /ɒˈstreɪliən/		Australier/in; australisch	
to **reply** /rɪˈplaɪ/		antworten, erwidern	Kate was still waiting for Will to **reply** to her text message.

Say it in English – Theme 4

So kannst du ...

über Urlaubserfahrungen sprechen	Most of the time I travel by car or by bus. I have been on a few family holidays to ... and one school exchange. I usually stay with other people – the host family in ... and my grandparents or aunts and uncles.
über verschiedene Urlaubsziele diskutieren	For me the ... sounds promising, but ... ... would be the better choice because ... I would prefer to ... I would much rather ... Actually, a hotel in/at/near ... might be more/less ... The activities they offer are quite ... When I go on holiday, I really expect to ... I must admit I'm not so/really keen on ..., so ...
über einen Schüleraustausch sprechen	I'd like to talk you about German students and school exchanges. The exchange can be just a few months long or even a whole year. Although there are lots of forms to fill in, there are organizations whose job is to help students find host families and schools. In some countries, students also have some influence over the choice of host family. Most exchange students really enjoy their time abroad and learn a lot from being in a completely new environment. If you're on a longer exchange, you could consider switching host family – many exchange students leave after a few months, so new host families can become available.

Theme 5: Great expectations

A1	**abroad**	/əˈbrɔːd/	im/ins Ausland	They always go on holiday **abroad**.
	to **gain**	/geɪn/	bekommen, erreichen, gewinnen; *hier:* Nutzen ziehen	Dan **gained** so much from his school exchange to France.
A2	**current**	/ˈkʌrənt/	jetzig, gegenwärtig, aktuell	People watch the news for information on **current** events.
	unique	/juːˈniːk/	einzigartig	
	insight	/ˈɪnsaɪt/	Einsicht, Einblick	The reporter provided great **insight** into the latest news stories.
	medium (*pl* **media**)	/ˈmiːdiəm, ˈmiːdiə/	(Informations)medium	Newspapers aren't the only **medium** used to spread news.
	major	/ˈmeɪdʒə/	bedeutend, wichtig, schwer	All of the **major** newspapers publish their articles online.
	native speaker	/ˌneɪtɪv ˈspiːkə/	Muttersprachler/in	Even **native speakers** make mistakes sometimes.
	to **communicate**	/kəˈmjuːnɪkeɪt/	kommunizieren, Kontakt haben	People can also **communicate** without language.
	accommodation (*no pl*)	/əˌkɒməˈdeɪʃ(ə)n/	Unterkunft	Our **accommodation** in Spain was right next to the beach.
	to **sail**	/seɪl/	(auf dem Wasser) fahren/reisen, segeln	We **sailed** from France to Italy. It was a great boat trip.
	windsurfing (*no pl*)	/ˈwɪndˌsɜːfɪŋ/	Windsurfen	
	water-skiing (*no pl*)	/ˈwɔːtəˌskiːɪŋ/	Wasserski	
	unbelievable	/ˌʌnbɪˈliːvəb(ə)l/	unglaublich, sagenhaft	Everyone was shouting. The noise was **unbelievable**.
	outdoors	/ˌaʊtˈdɔːz/	draußen, im Freien	It is very good for children to spend lots of time **outdoors**.
	once	/wʌns/	sobald	
	placement (*BE*)	/ˈpleɪsmənt/	Praktikum, vorübergehende Beschäftigung	Joey needed work experience, so he found a **placement** in London.
	to **make friends** (**with sb**)	/ˌmeɪk ˈfrendz wɪð/	(mit jdm) Freundschaft schließen	
	leadership (*no pl*)	/ˈliːdəʃɪp/	Führung, Leitung; *hier:* Führungsqualitäten	The group all felt that Freddie's **leadership** was effective.
	arrangement	/əˈreɪndʒmənt/	Abmachung, Vereinbarung	
	range	/reɪndʒ/	Reichweite, Bereich; *hier:* Angebot	
	uniquely	/juːˈniːkli/	besonders	
	rewarding	/rɪˈwɔːdɪŋ/	befriedigend, lohnend	
	essential	/ɪˈsenʃ(ə)l/	unverzichtbar, wesentlich	It is **essential** that people learn to swim.
	case	/keɪs/	Fall	Please check your answers carefully, in **case** you've made a mistake.
	understanding (*no pl*)	/ˌʌndəˈstændɪŋ/	Verständnis, Übereinkunft	
	to **assist** (**in/with**)	/əˈsɪst ɪn/wɪð/	(mit)helfen (bei)	I'm sorry sir, is there anything I can **assist** you **with**?
	childcare (*no pl*)	/ˈtʃaɪldˌkeə/	Kinderbetreuung	
	housework (*no pl*)	/ˈhaʊsˌwɜːk/	Hausarbeit	Claire hates doing **housework**, especially the hoovering.
	full board (*no pl*)	/ˌfʊl ˈbɔːd/	(mit) Vollpension	

Theme 5: Great expectations — Word lists

to **involve** /ɪnˈvɒlv/	beinhalten, umfassen, betreffen, beteiligen	Jill didn't know what the job would **involve** until she started working.
welfare *(no pl)* /ˈwelfeə/	Wohlergehen	
to **entertain** /ˌentəˈteɪn/	unterhalten	John **entertains** his classmates with his jokes.
to **be in charge** (**of**) /ˌbi_ɪn ˈtʃɑːdʒ_əv/	verantwortlich/zuständig sein (für)	The headteacher **is in charge of** the whole school.
session /ˈseʃ(ə)n/	Sitzung, Stunde, Session	
sociable /ˈsəʊʃəb(ə)l/	gesellig, freundlich, umgänglich	Leo was not very **sociable**; he didn't talk to Frank or Carl all evening.
outgoing /ˌaʊtˈɡəʊɪŋ/	kontaktfreudig, (aus)scheidend, ausgehend	
spare time *(no pl)* /ˌspeə ˈtaɪm/	Freizeit	
facilities *(only pl)* /fəˈsɪlətiz/	Einrichtungen, Anlagen	Our school has amazing **facilities** – we've got a huge swimming pool!
quality /ˈkwɒləti/	Qualität, Art, Eigenschaft, Merkmal	The **quality** of our school's facilities is stunning.
ability /əˈbɪləti/	Fähigkeit, Talent, Begabung	Sheila's **ability** to remember dates is most impressive.
knowledge *(no pl)* /ˈnɒlɪdʒ/	Kenntnisse, Wissen, Kenntnis	**Knowledge** is power.
perk /pɜːk/	Vergünstigung, Vorteil	
to **come across** *(irr)* /ˌkʌm_əˈkrɒs/	begegnen, stoßen auf	Have you **come across** the new kid yet? He started last week.
phone-in *(BE)* /ˈfəʊn_ɪn/	Anrufsendung	
disgusting /dɪsˈɡʌstɪŋ/	empörend, widerlich, widerwärtig	Liam's **behaviour** was disgusting. He should be ashamed!
revolting /rɪˈvəʊltɪŋ/	abstoßend, widerlich	
tedious /ˈtiːdiəs/	langweilig, fad	Reading a dictionary can be a rather **tedious** task.
nasty /ˈnɑːsti/	scheußlich, schlimm, ekelhaft	Bullies at school can be very **nasty**.
smelly /ˈsmeli/	stinkend, übel riechend	I don't like **smelly** cheeses.
enormous /ɪˈnɔːməs/	enorm, riesig, gewaltig	That slice of cake is **enormous**!
dull /dʌl/	langweilig, eintönig, matt, trüb(e)	The history lesson was incredibly **dull**.
internship *(AE)* /ˈɪntɜːnʃɪp/	Praktikum	Joel's **internship** in New York helped him to gain work experience. *p. 108*
several /ˈsev(ə)rəl/	einige, ein paar	Myra gave John **several** suggestions on how to improve his work.
to **bear sth in mind** /ˌbeə ˌsʌmθɪŋ_ɪn ˈmaɪnd/	etw (mit)berücksichtigen	John **bore** Myra's suggestions **in mind** he wrote his next essay.
covering letter *(BE)* /ˌkʌvərɪŋ ˈletə/	Anschreiben	Writing a good **covering letter** is essential when applying for a job.
job ad(vert)/job advertisement /ˈdʒɒb_ˌædvɜːt/ˈdʒɒb_əd,vɜːtɪsmənt/	Stellenanzeige	
to **have sth done** /ˌhæv ˌsʌmθɪŋ ˈdʌn/	etw tun lassen	Some people hate **having their hair cut**.
CV (= **curriculum vitae**) (*BE* = **résumé** *AE*) /ˌsiː ˈviː, kəˌrɪkjʊləm ˈviːtaɪ/	Lebenslauf	A **CV** contains information about your work experience and qualifications.
form /fɔːm/	Formular	The **form** I had to fill in at the doctor's was much too long.

Word lists

Theme 5: Great expectations

certificate /səˈtɪfɪkət/	Urkunde, Bescheinigung	Dom was given a **certifcate** to show that he had been on the course.
job interview /ˈdʒɒb ˌɪntəˌvjuː/	Bewerbungsgespräch, Vorstellungsgespräch	Ellen was very nervous about her latest **job interview**.
letter of recommendation /ˌletər_əv ˌrekəmenˈdeɪʃ(ə)n/	Empfehlungsschreiben	
B2 soft skills /ˌsɒft ˈskɪlz/	Soft Skills *(soziale oder emotionale Kompetenz)*	**Soft skills** are the skills needed to work well with other people.
hard skills /ˌhɑːd ˈskɪlz/	Hard Skills *(rein fachliche Qualifikation)*	Certificates highlight your **hard skills**.
responsibility /rɪˌspɒnsəˈbɪləti/	Verantwortung, Verantwortlichkeit, Zuständigkeit; *hier:* Verantwortungsgefühl	Having chidren is a very big **responsibility**.
typing *(no pl)* /ˈtaɪpɪŋ/	Maschineschreiben, Tippen, Tipp-	
patience *(no pl)* /ˈpeɪʃ(ə)ns/	Geduld	You must have **patience** when standing in a queue.
to **repair** /rɪˈpeə/	reparieren, (wieder) in Ordnung bringen	After the accident my bike needed to be **repaired**.
integrity *(no pl)* /ɪnˈtegrəti/	Integrität, Anständigkeit	
programming *(no pl)* /ˈprəʊˌgræmɪŋ/	Programmieren	Computer **programming** is very complicated.
friendliness *(no pl)* /ˈfrendlinəs/	Freundlichkeit	Joanna's **friendliness** meant that she was very popular.
self-esteem *(no pl)* /ˌself_ɪˈstiːm/	Selbstwertgefühl	
B3 characteristic /ˌkærɪktəˈrɪstɪk/	(charakteristisches) Merkmal; typisch, charakteristisch	Long skirts and big hair were **characteristic** of the 1980s.
communicative /kəˈmjuːnɪkətɪv/	mitteilsam, kommunikationsfreudig	Toby was quite shy and not particularly **communicative**.
conscientious /ˌkɒnʃiˈenʃəs/	gewissenhaft, pflichtbewusst	They are **conscientious** and hard-working students.
pressure /ˈpreʃə/	Druck, Stress, Belastung	Pupils at our school feel a lot of **pressure** to do well.
dedicated /ˈdedɪˌkeɪtɪd/	engagiert	
diligent /ˈdɪlɪdʒ(ə)nt/	fleißig, sorgfältig, gewissenhaft	Timothy was not a very **diligent** student.
diplomatic /ˌdɪpləˈmætɪk/	diplomatisch, taktvoll	
dynamic /daɪˈnæmɪk/	Dynamik; dynamisch	Nancy had a **dynamic** personality.
efficient /ɪˈfɪʃ(ə)nt/	leistungsstark, effizient	Many people expect Germans to be **efficent** and hard-working.
listener /ˈlɪs(ə)nə/	Zuhörer/in	
motivated /ˈməʊtɪˌveɪtɪd/	motiviert	It's hard to feel **motivated** on a Monday morning.
organized /ˈɔːgənaɪzd/	(gut) organisiert	Jonny isn't very **organized**, he loses things all the time.
patient /ˈpeɪʃ(ə)nt/	geduldig	Claire was very **patient** when teaching her brother to read.
practical /ˈpræktɪk(ə)l/	praktisch, auf die Praxis bezogen	
punctual /ˈpʌŋktʃuəl/	pünktlich	
reliable /rɪˈlaɪəb(ə)l/	verlässlich, zuverlässig	Patrick has never been **reliable** at school – he is always late.

Theme 5: Great expectations — Word lists

responsible /rɪˈspɒnsəb(ə)l/	verantwortlich, zuständig; *hier:* verantwortungsvoll	Jake is so **responsible**. He always babysits his little sister.
sensitive /ˈsensətɪv/	sensibel, verständnisvoll, empfindlich	It is important to be **sensitive** to other people's feelings.
trustworthy /ˈtrʌstˌwɜːði/	vertrauenswürdig, zuverlässig	
to identify /aɪˈdentɪfaɪ/	identifizieren, feststellen	The police are trying to **identify** the body.
as well /æzˈwel/	auch	Bill likes Jill and Jill likes Bill **as well**.
volunteer /ˌvɒlənˈtɪə/	Ehrenamtler/in, Freiwillige/r	
subject /ˈsʌbdʒɪkt/	(Schul)fach; *hier:* Thema	Politics is a **subject** that one shouldn't discuss with friends.
requirement /rɪˈkwaɪəmənt/	Voraussetzung, Erfordernis	Rhiannon was perfect for the job. She met all of our **requirements**.
to suit sb/sth /suːt/	zu jdm/etw passen	
❹ **employer** /ɪmˈplɔɪə/	Arbeitgeber/in	When writing a CV, you have to impress potential **employers**. *p. 110*
to separate /ˈsepəreɪt/	trennen, abspalten, (sich) scheiden (lassen)	When a couple stops living together they **separate**.
to hire /ˈhaɪə/	einstellen, beauftragen	
to proofread *(irr)* /ˈpruːfriːd/	Korrektur lesen	
section /ˈsekʃ(ə)n/	Teil, Abschnitt, Abteilung	The sports **section** is my favourite part of a newspaper.
candidate /ˈkændɪdeɪt/	Kandidat/in, Bewerber/in	
precise /prɪˈsaɪs/	genau, präzise, sorgfältig	Follow the recipe **precisely**, don't change anything!
font /fɒnt/	Schriftart	
vacancy /ˈveɪkənsi/	freie Stelle	There is a teaching **vacancy** now, as we need a new history teacher.
at your earliest convenience /æt jərˌɜːliəst kənˈviːniəns/	möglichst bald	

Yours faithfully und *Yours sincerely*

Yours faithfully und *Yours sincerely* werden als Schlussfloskeln für formelle Briefe verwendet. Auf Deutsch können sie mit *Mit freundlichen Grüßen* übersetzt werden.
- *Yours sincerely* /jɔːzˈsɪnsɪəli/ verwendet man, wenn man den Brief mit einer persönlichen Anrede begonnen hat, z. B. *Dear Mr Rogers, …*
- *Yours faithfully* /jɔːzˈfeɪθf(ə)li/ *(BE)* verwendet man dagegen, wenn man den Brief mit *Dear Sir or Madam, …* begonnen hat.

to address /əˈdres/	adressieren, (sich) wenden an, ansprechen	The teacher **addressed** the class.
Dear Sir or Madam /dɪəˌsɜːrˌɔːˈmædəm/	Sehr geehrte Damen und Herren	
❺ **various** /ˈveəriəs/	verschieden	
to translate /trænsˈleɪt/	übersetzen	You sometimes have to **translate** texts from English into German.
to stand out *(irr)* /ˌstændˈaʊt/	hervorragen, sich abheben	
❻ **goal** /gəʊl/	Ziel, Tor	*p. 111*
applicant /ˈæplɪkənt/	Bewerber/in	They had 50 **applicants** for the job.

	to **lack** /læk/	nicht haben, fehlen	Luke didn't get the job as he **lacked** the necessary qualifications.
	to **attract** /ə'trækt/	anziehen	Big Ben and Buckingham Palace **attract** many tourists to London.
	to **approve of** /ə'pruːv ɒv/	genehmigen, billigen; *hier:* für gut halten	Nena's parents didn't **approve of** her new boyfriend.
B7	to **cover** /'kʌvə/	bedecken; *hier:* sich befassen mit, behandeln	Susanna's university course **covered** many different subjects.
	finding /'faɪndɪŋ/	Entdeckung, Ergebnis	
B8	**content** /'kɒntent/	Inhalt	The **content** of Beth's essay was good, but her grammar was not.
	explanation /ˌekspləˈneɪʃ(ə)n/	Erklärung, Erläuterung	What do you think? Write a short **explanation** about your answer.
C1	**cause** /kɔːz/	Grund, Ursache, Anlass; *hier:* (gute) Sache	The students decided to raise money for a good **cause**.
	to **right a wrong** /ˌraɪt ə 'rɒŋ/	ein Unrecht wiedergutmachen	
	involved /ɪn'vɒlvd/	betroffen, beteiligt, verwickelt	Everybody wanted to be **involved** in the school play.
	personally /'pɜːs(ə)nəli/	persönlich	I **personally** can't agree with your opinion.
	to **take (immediate) action** /ˌteɪk ɪˌmiːdiət 'ækʃ(ə)n/	(augenblicklich) handeln	
C2	**foundation** /faʊn'deɪʃ(ə)n/	Fundament, Basis; *hier:* Stiftung	
	to **get in touch (with sb)** /ˌget ɪn 'tʌtʃ wɪð/	(mit jdm) in Kontakt treten	Jo had wanted to **get in touch with** Sue for ages, so she rang her up.
	tournament /'tɔːnəmənt/	Turnier	
	to **coordinate** /kəʊ'ɔːdɪneɪt/	koordinieren, aufeinander abstimmen	We will need to **coordinate** our timetables to arrange a meeting.
	to **inform** /ɪn'fɔːm/	informieren, benachrichtigen, mitteilen	Matthew **informed** the police that his wallet had been stolen.
	extraordinary /ɪk'strɔːd(ə)n(ə)ri/	außerordentlich, ungewöhnlich	A crocodile is an **extraordinary** pet.
	in public /ɪn 'pʌblɪk/	in der Öffentlichkeit, öffentlich	It is rude to discuss private matters **in public**.
	committed /kə'mɪtɪd/	verpflichtet, gebunden, engagiert	Freya came to every meeting. She was very **committed** to her work.
	training *(no pl)* /'treɪnɪŋ/	Training; *hier:* Ausbildung, Schulung	
	daily life /ˌdeɪli 'laɪf/	Alltag(sleben)	
	rhetorical device /rɪˌtɒrɪk(ə)l dɪ'vaɪs/	rhetorisches Stilmittel, Stilfigur	**Rhetorical devices** are used to persuade or excite the reader.
	commitment /kə'mɪtmənt/	Engagement, Verpflichtung	Being part of a sports team takes a lot of **commitment**.
	voluntary /'vɒlənt(ə)ri/	freiwillig, ehrenamtlich	Once a week Freddie does **voluntary** work at an old people's home.
	to **campaign for/against sth** /kæm'peɪn fɔː/əˌgenst/	für etw eintreten/gegen etw kämpfen	
C3	to **put sth in(to) perspective** /ˌpʊt ˌsʌmθɪŋ ˌɪntə pə'spektɪv/	etw in die richtige Perspektive rücken	
	to **assume** /ə'sjuːm/	annehmen; *hier:* eine vorgefasste Meinung haben, vorschnell Schlüsse ziehen	One should never **assume** the worst. It is better to hope for the best.
C5	to **appeal to sb/sth** /ə'piːl tʊ/	jdn/etw reizen, jdn/etw ansprechen	A big piece of chocolate cake always **appeals to** Britta. Delicious!

Theme 5: Great expectations   **Word lists**

to **contribute** /kənˈtrɪbjuːt/	beisteuern, beitragen	Rose was asked what she could **contribute** to the company.
working hours *(only pl)* /ˈwɜːkɪŋ ˌaʊəz/	Arbeitszeit	
additional /əˈdɪʃ(ə)nəl/	zusätzlich	**Additional** information can be found on our website.
nerves /nɜːvz/	Nerven; *hier:* Nervenstärke	
to **take turns** *(BE)* /ˌteɪk ˈtɜːnz/	sich abwechseln	Tennis players **take turns** to hit the tennis ball.
to **observe** /əbˈzɜːv/	beobachten, bemerken; *hier:* zuschauen	The children **observed** the animals at the zoo.

Say it in English – Theme 5

So kannst du ...

über eine Bewerbung sprechen	What makes him a good candidate/only an average candidate is ... He seems/doesn't seem to be well-suited to the project, as he ... Although he may ..., he lacks ... I (don't) think he will attract the organization's attention because ... The representatives of the foundation will probably approve of ..., but might have a problem with ... That covering letter is not as well-structured/well-written/convincing as this one. I think the applicant should have included some more information about ... In this letter the candidate comes across as very reliable/enthuasiastic/mature. This covering letter gives/offers an excellent explanation of ...
ein Anschreiben für eine Bewerbung verfassen	I would like to apply for a position as ... I enclose my CV. As you will see from my CV, I am currently ... I believe these skills and my work experience would provide an excellent basis for being a member of your team. I look forward to hearing from you. Yours faithfully, .../Yours sincerely, ...
in einem Bewerbungsgespräch über dich selbst sprechen	I'm good at ... I will be leaving school in ... The position you're offering is just what I'm looking for. I enjoy working with ... I would be happy to work for your company and look forward to hearing from you.
für eine Sache werben	Become a member of our group of ... Join our campaign now! If you want to fight for a good cause, ... If you love ..., this is the right cause for you. If you can ..., you are an ideal volunteer.

English-German dictionary

Hier findest du die Wörter, die in deinem Buch vorkommen.
- Die **fett gedruckten** Wörter solltest du dir merken.
- Wörter mit einem ° sind nur für einen bestimmten Text wichtig. Du brauchst sie nicht zu lernen.
- 1B1 bedeutet: Dieses Wort kommt in *Theme 1*, Aufgabe B1 vor.
- I bedeutet: Dieses Wort kommt in Band 1 (5. Klasse) vor. Entsprechend steht II, III und IV für die Bände 2, 3 und 4.
- Folgende Abkürzungen werden noch verwendet:
  P = *Personal Trainer*   PP = *Intercultural photo page*   O = *Optional*

A

a/an /ə/ən/ ein(e) I
  a bit /ə ˈbɪt/ ein bisschen; ein wenig II
  ° **a bunch (of …)** *(informal, AE)* /ə ˈbʌntʃ_əv/ einen Haufen (…) 1B2
  a couple of … /ə ˈkʌp(ə)l_əv/ einige … ; ein paar … 4B1
  a few /ə ˈfjuː/ einige; wenige II
  ° **A level** /ˈeɪ ˌlev(ə)l/ *entspricht dem deutschen Abitur* 5B6
  a lot (of) /ə ˈlɒt_əv/ viel(e); eine Menge I
  ° **a number of** /ə ˈnʌmbər_əv/ einige; eine Reihe (von) 1B5
  a small one /ə ˈsmɔːl ˌwʌn/ ein(e) kleine(s, r) II
  a touch of /ə ˈtʌtʃ_əv/ ein wenig 2B3
  ° **a whole/the whole** /ə ˈhəʊl/ðə ˈhəʊl/ ein Ganzes/das Ganze 4P8
to abandon /əˈbændən/ verlassen; zurücklassen; aufgeben 3B4
ability /əˈbɪləti/ Fähigkeit; Talent; Begabung 5A2
  ° **to the best of one's ability** /tʊ ðə ˌbest_əv wʌnz_əˈbɪləti/ so gut jd kann 1C7
° **aboriginal** /ˌæbəˈrɪdʒ(ə)n(ə)l/ Aboriginal *(australische/r Ureinwohner/in)*; der Aboriginals 4P11
° **Aborigine** /ˌæbəˈrɪdʒəni/ australischer Ureinwohner/australische Ureinwohnerin 4PP1
about /əˈbaʊt/ über; von I; wegen; an; zu II
  ° **about time** /əˌbaʊt ˈtaɪm/ wird/wurde aber auch (langsam) Zeit! 1B2
above /əˈbʌv/ über III
abroad /əˈbrɔːd/ im/ins Ausland 4B1, 5A1
° **abrupt** /əˈbrʌpt/ abrupt; plötzlich; schroff 3P10
absolutely /ˈæbsəluːtli/ absolut; völlig IV
abuse /əˈbjuːs/ Missbrauch; Verletzung; Beschimpfung(en) IV
° **academic** /ˌækəˈdemɪk/ akademisch; wissenschaftlich; *hier:* Lehrkraft an der Universität 5PP2

° **Academy Award** /əˌkædəmi_əˈwɔːd/ offizieller Name des amerikanischen Filmpreises „Oscar" 4P11
° **accent** /ˈæks(ə)nt/ Akzent 3P2
to accept /əkˈsept/ annehmen; akzeptieren III
acceptable /əkˈseptəb(ə)l/ akzeptabel; hinnehmbar IV
accident /ˈæksɪd(ə)nt/ Unfall II
accommodation *(no pl)* /əˌkɒməˈdeɪʃ(ə)n/ Unterkunft 5A2
according to /əˈkɔːdɪŋ ˌtuː/ nach; laut; gemäß; entsprechend IV
account /əˈkaʊnt/ Bericht 4B7
° **accountancy** *(no pl)* /əˈkaʊntənsi/ Buchhaltung; Rechnungswesen 5O3
° **accountant** /əˈkaʊntənt/ Buchhalter/in 5O3
to ache /eɪk/ schmerzen; wehtun III
to achieve /əˈtʃiːv/ erreichen; erlangen; erzielen III
° **achievement** /əˈtʃiːvmənt/ Leistung; Errungenschaft 2PP1
to acknowledge /əkˈnɒlɪdʒ/ zugeben; anerkennen; bestätigen IV
across /əˈkrɒs/ über I; jenseits; gegenüberliegend II
to act /ækt/ handeln; vorgehen; schauspielern II
  ° **to act out** /ˌækt ˈaʊt/ ausleben; *hier:* (nach)spielen 3C5
° **acting** *(no pl)* /ˈæktɪŋ/ Schauspielerei(-) 3P7
action /ˈækʃ(ə)n/ Handlung; Tat III
activity /ækˈtɪvəti/ Aktivität; Tätigkeit I
actor /ˈæktə/ Schauspieler II
actress /ˈæktrəs/ Schauspielerin II
actually /ˈæktʃuəli/ eigentlich; wirklich III
ad (= advertisement) *(informal)* /æd, ədˈvɜːtɪsmənt/ Werbung; Reklame; Anzeige; Inserat 2B2
° **to adapt (to)** /əˈdæpt_tʊ/ anpassen (an) 5B6
to add (sth to sth) /æd/ (etw etw) hinzufügen I
addiction (to) /əˈdɪkʃ(ə)n tʊ/ Abhängigkeit (von); Sucht (nach) 3C3
addition (to) /əˈdɪʃ(ə)n tʊ/ Ergänzung (zu); Zusatz (zu) 4B6

additional /əˈdɪʃ(ə)nəl/ zusätzlich 5C5
address /əˈdres/ Adresse; Anschrift; Anrede 4B1
to address /əˈdres/ adressieren; (sich) wenden an; ansprechen 3B9, 4B1, 5B4
° **adequate** /ˈædɪkwət/ ausreichend; angemessen 1P9
to admit /ədˈmɪt/ zugeben II
adolescent /ˌædəˈles(ə)nt/ Jugendliche/r; heranwachsend; jugendlich 3C3
° **to adopt** /əˈdɒpt/ adoptieren; annehmen 2O4
adult /ˈædʌlt/ Erwachsene/r I
advantage /ədˈvɑːntɪdʒ/ Vorteil IV
adventure /ədˈventʃə/ Abenteuer; Erlebnis I
advert (BE) (= advertisement) /ˈædvɜːt, ədˈvɜːtɪsmənt/ Werbung; Reklame; Anzeige; Inserat; Werbeanzeige 2A1
to advertise /ˈædvətaɪz/ werben; Werbung machen für; in Umlauf geben IV
advertisement /ədˈvɜːtɪsmənt/ Werbung; Reklame; Anzeige; Inserat 2B1, 4B5
advertising *(no pl)* /ˈædvəˌtaɪzɪŋ/ Werbung; Reklame; Werbe- 2B2
advice *(no pl)* /ədˈvaɪs/ Rat; Tipp II
to advise /ədˈvaɪz/ (be)raten 3B3
to affect /əˈfekt/ sich auswirken auf; beeinflussen IV
to afford sth /əˈfɔːd/ sich etw leisten; etw bieten III
° **affordable** /əˈfɔːdəb(ə)l/ erschwinglich 4B5
to be afraid (of) /bɪ_əˈfreɪd_əv/ Angst haben/sich fürchten (vor) I
I'm afraid /ˌaɪm_əˈfreɪd/ leider I
African American /ˌæfrɪkən_əˈmerɪkən/ Afroamerikaner/in; afroamerikanisch IV
after /ˈɑːftə/ nach I; nachdem III
after all /ˌɑːftər ˈɔːl/ schließlich; zumindest II
after that /ˌɑːftə ˈðæt/ danach I
° **afterlife** *(no pl)* /ˈɑːftəˌlaɪf/ Leben nach dem Tod 1O4
afternoon /ˌɑːftəˈnuːn/ Nachmittag I

English-German dictionary

in the afternoon /ˌɪn ðiˈɑːftəˌnuːn/ am Nachmittag I
afterward(s) /ˈɑːftəwədz/ später; danach; anschließend IV
again /əˈgen/ wieder; noch einmal I
against /əˈgenst/ gegen II
age /eɪdʒ/ Alter II; Zeitalter, Ära III
agency /ˈeɪdʒ(ə)nsi/ Agentur; Behörde 2B6
ages (pl, informal) /ˈeɪdʒɪz/ eine Ewigkeit; Ewigkeiten III
ago /əˈgəʊ/ vor II
to **agree (on)** /əˈgriː ˌɒn/ zustimmen I; sich einigen (auf) II
agreement /əˈgriːmənt/ Übereinstimmung; Zustimmung 1C10
° **agriculture** (no pl) /ˈægrɪˌkʌltʃə/ Landwirtschaft 2P8
° **ahead of** /əˈhed əv/ vor(aus) 1B6
aim /eɪm/ Ziel; Absicht III
to **aim** /eɪm/ zielen; anstreben; sich vornehmen III
air (no pl) /eə/ Luft IV
air conditioning (no pl) /ˈeə kənˌdɪʃ(ə)nɪŋ/ Klimatisierung; Klimaanlage 4B5
° **akin to sth** /əˈkɪn tʊ/ ... ähnlich 1C7
° **alarmed** /əˈlɑːmd/ beunruhigt; besorgt 2C3
all /ɔːl/ alle(s) I
° **all in all** /ˌɔːl ɪn ˈɔːl/ alles in allem 5B3
° **all of a sudden** /ˌɔːl əv ə ˈsʌd(ə)n/ (ganz) plötzlich 1B8
° **all sorts of** /ˌɔːl ˈsɔːts əv/ alle möglichen 3A2
all summer /ˌɔːl ˈsʌmə/ den ganzen Sommer I
all the time /ˌɔːl ðə ˈtaɪm/ die ganze Zeit I
to **allow** /əˈlaʊ/ erlauben; ermöglichen III
almost /ˈɔːlməʊst/ fast; beinahe II
alone /əˈləʊn/ allein I
along /əˈlɒŋ/ entlang II
already /ɔːlˈredi/ schon; bereits I
° **alright** /ɔːlˈraɪt/ in Ordnung 5B6
also /ˈɔːlsəʊ/ auch I
to **alter** /ˈɔːltə/ ändern; bearbeiten 2A2
alteration /ˌɔːltəˈreɪʃ(ə)n/ Änderung; Bearbeitung 2A2
alternatively /ɔːlˈtɜːnətɪvli/ als Alternative; stattdessen 4B7
although /ɔːlˈðəʊ/ obwohl II
altogether /ˌɔːltəˈgeðə/ völlig; ganz; insgesamt 1C10
always /ˈɔːlweɪz/ immer I
am (= ante meridiem) /ˌeɪ ˈem, ˌænti məˈrɪdiəm/ morgens; vormittags (nur hinter Uhrzeit zwischen Mitternacht und 12 Uhr mittags) I
amazed /əˈmeɪzd/ erstaunt; verblüfft IV
amazing /əˈmeɪzɪŋ/ erstaunlich; toll I

ambition /æmˈbɪʃ(ə)n/ Ehrgeiz; Ambition(en); (angestrebtes) Ziel III
ambitious /æmˈbɪʃəs/ ehrgeizig II
(American) Indian /əˌmerɪkənˈɪndiən/ Indianer/in; indianisch; amerikanische/r Ureinwohner/in IV
° **amid(st)** /əˈmɪdst/ (in)mitten; bei 1P3
° **amnesia** (no pl) /æmˈniːziə/ Gedächtnisschwund 1O4
among(st) /əˈmʌŋst/ unter; inmitten von IV
° **amount** /əˈmaʊnt/ Menge; Betrag; Spanne 5P1
amused /əˈmjuːzd/ amüsiert III
amusing /əˈmjuːzɪŋ/ amüsant; unterhaltsam III
to **analyse** /ˈænəlaɪz/ analysieren; untersuchen 1C7, 3B5
and /ænd/ und I
anger (no pl) /ˈæŋgə/ Ärger; Wut 1B8
angle /ˈæŋg(ə)l/ (Blick)winkel; Perspektive 2C4
angry /ˈæŋgri/ verärgert; zornig; wütend I
animal /ˈænɪm(ə)l/ Tier I
ankle /ˈæŋk(ə)l/ (Fuß)knöchel III
annoyed /əˈnɔɪd/ verärgert II
annoying /əˈnɔɪɪŋ/ ärgerlich IV
° **anonymous** /əˈnɒnɪməs/ anonym; ungenannt 3O4
another /əˈnʌðə/ noch eine(r, s) I; ein(e) andere(r) II
answer /ˈɑːnsə/ Antwort I
to **answer** /ˈɑːnsə/ (be)antworten I
to **answer the phone** /ˌɑːnsə ðə ˈfəʊn/ ans Telefon gehen I
anthem /ˈænθəm/ Hymne 1B4
to **anticipate** /ænˈtɪsɪpeɪt/ erwarten; rechnen mit; vorhersehen 1C10
anvil /ˈænvɪl/ Amboss 1O3
anxious /ˈæŋkʃəs/ besorgt IV
any /ˈeni/ (irgend)ein(e); jede(r, s) I
anyone /ˈeniˌwʌn/ (irgend)jemand II
anything /ˈeniθɪŋ/ (irgend)etwas; (irgend)was II
anyway /ˈeniweɪ/ sowieso; jedenfalls; ohnehin II
apart from sth/sb /əˈpɑːt frɒm/ von etw/jdm abgesehen 1C5
to **apologize (to/for)** /əˈpɒlədʒaɪz tʊ/ fɔː/ sich entschuldigen (bei/für) III
apology /əˈpɒlədʒi/ Entschuldigung; Bedauern III
° **appeal (for)** /əˈpiːl fɔː/ Aufruf (zu/r); Appell (für) 1C7
to **appeal to sb/sth** /əˈpiːl tʊ/ jdn/ etw reizen; jdn/etw ansprechen 2C2, 3A1, 4B7, 5C5
appealing /əˈpiːlɪŋ/ attraktiv; verlockend; ansprechend IV
to **appear** /əˈpɪə/ erscheinen; auftauchen; scheinen III
appearance /əˈpɪərəns/ Erscheinen; Aussehen; Auftreten 3A2

apple /ˈæp(ə)l/ Apfel I
° **appliance** /əˈplaɪəns/ (Haushalts)gerät 4B5
applicant /ˈæplɪkənt/ Bewerber/in 5B6
application /ˌæplɪˈkeɪʃ(ə)n/ Bewerbung; Antrag; Anwendung IV
to **apply for sth** /əˈplaɪ fɔː/ sich um etw bewerben; etw beantragen IV
to **apply to sb/sth** /əˈplaɪ tʊ/ für jdn/ etw gelten; jdn/etw betreffen IV
to **appreciate** /əˈpriːʃieɪt/ schätzen; zu schätzen wissen; *hier:* schätzen lernen 4A2
° to **approach** /əˈprəʊtʃ/ sich nähern; zukommen auf 1C7
appropriate /əˈprəʊpriət/ angemessen; angebracht; passend IV
to **approve of** /əˈpruːv ɒv/ genehmigen; billigen 3A4; für gut halten 5B6
approximately /əˈprɒksɪmətli/ ungefähr; etwa; circa 1B10
April /ˈeɪprəl/ April I
° **Arabic** (no pl) /ˈærəbɪk/ Arabisch 4C1
area /ˈeəriə/ Gebiet; Region; Gegend II
to **argue (about)** /ˈɑːgjuː əˌbaʊt/ sich streiten (wegen) II; verfechten III
to **argue for/against sth** /ˈɑːgjuː fɔː, əˈgenst/ für/gegen etw argumentieren IV
argument /ˈɑːgjʊmənt/ Auseinandersetzung; Argument II
arm /ɑːm/ Arm I
to **break one's arm** /ˌbreɪk wʌnz ˈɑːm/ sich den Arm brechen II
° **armored** (AE = armoured BE) /ˈɑːməd/ gepanzert; bewaffnet 1B9
army /ˈɑːmi/ Armee; Heer I
around /əˈraʊnd/ umher; um; rund um; um ... herum II
to **arrange** /əˈreɪndʒ/ arrangieren; (an)ordnen; vereinbaren, organisieren IV
arrangement /əˈreɪndʒmənt/ Abmachung; Vereinbarung; Anordnung 4B4
to **arrest** /əˈrest/ verhaften 2C9
° **arrival** /əˈraɪv(ə)l/ Ankunft 1O6
to **arrive** /əˈraɪv/ ankommen; da sein I
arrogant /ˈærəgənt/ arrogant II
arrow /ˈærəʊ/ Pfeil 4B4
art /ɑːt/ Kunst(unterricht) I
article /ˈɑːtɪk(ə)l/ Artikel 2B3, 3C3, 4B2
artist /ˈɑːtɪst/ Künstler/in III
as /æz/ weil; da; als; wie II; während III
as ... as: so ... wie II
as a result of sth /æz ə rɪˈzʌlt əv/ als Folge einer Sache IV
as far as /æz ˈfɑːr æz/ soweit 3B10
as far as sb is concerned /æz ˌfɑːr æz ˈsʌmbədi ɪz kənˈsɜːnd/ was jdn anbelangt/betrifft IV

Words

English-German dictionary

° **as far as sth goes** /æz ˌfɑːrˌæzˈsʌmθɪŋˌgəʊz/ was etw angeht 3A2
as if /æzˌɪf/ als ob III
as long as ... /æzˈlɒŋˌæz/ solange ...; sofern ... 3A2
as soon as /əzˈsuːnˌəz/ sobald; als, in dem Moment, als ... III
as though /æzˈðəʊ/ als ob 1C3
° **as to** /ˈæz tʊ/ bezüglich; *hier:* darüber, dafür 5O1
° **as usual** /æzˈjuːʒəl/ wie üblich 1B8
as well /æzˈwel/ auch 1B7, 2B3, 3A2, 5B3
as well as /æzˈwelˌæz/ sowohl ... als auch ... IV
ASA (= Advertising Standards Authority) /ˌeɪˌesˈeɪ, ˌædvəˌtaɪzɪŋ ˌstændədzˌɔːˈθɒrəti/ *Behörde zur Überwachung der Werbung in Großbritannien* 2B4
Asia /ˈeɪʒə/ Asien III
° **aside from** /əˈsaɪd frəm/ abgesehen von 1O2
to ask /ɑːsk/ fragen I
to ask (for sth) /ˈɑːsk fə/ (um etw) bitten II
° **to assign** /əˈsaɪn/ zuweisen; übertragen; belegen 1C5
° **assignment** /əˈsaɪnmənt/ Aufgabe; Auftrag 1C5
to assist (in/with) /əˈsɪstˌɪn/wɪð/ (mit)helfen (bei) 5A2
to associate /əˈsəʊsiˌeɪt/ in Verbindung bringen 2B3
to assume /əˈsjuːm/ annehmen; eine vorgefasste Meinung haben, vorschnell Schlüsse ziehen 5C3
° **assuming (that)** /əˈsjuːmɪŋ ðət/ angenommen, (dass) 1C7
° **to assure** /əˈʃɔː/ zusichern 1B9
at /æt/ auf; an; in; bei; um I
at all /ætˈɔːl/ überhaupt II
at first /ætˈfɜːst/ zuerst I
° **at hand** /ætˈhænd/ nah; griffbereit 5P9
at home /ætˈhəʊm/ zu Hause I
at last /ætˈlɑːst/ endlich III
at least /ætˈliːst/ mindestens; wenigstens; zumindest II
at night /ætˈnaɪt/ nachts I
° **at once** /ætˈwʌns/ sofort; auf einmal 4P6
at some point /ætˈsʌm pɔɪnt/ irgendwann 2B2
at the moment /ætˈðə ˈməʊmənt/ im Moment I
at your earliest convenience /æt jərˌɜːliəst kənˈviːniəns/ möglichst bald 5B4
athlete /ˈæθliːt/ Athlet/in III
° **athletic** /æθˈletɪk/ sportlich; athletisch 3A2

athletics (only pl, AE) /æθˈletɪks/ *Sport und andere Arten von körperlicher Betätigung* IV
atmosphere /ˈætməsˌfɪə/ Atmosphäre; Stimmung 2B3, 3C3
attack /əˈtæk/ Angriff; Anfall IV
to attack /əˈtæk/ angreifen III
to attend /əˈtend/ besuchen; gehen auf III
attention (no pl) /əˈtenʃ(ə)n/ Aufmerksamkeit; Achtung III
to pay attention /ˌpeɪ əˈtenʃ(ə)n/ Acht geben; aufpassen III
° **attention span** /əˈtenʃ(ə)n spæn/ Konzentrationsvermögen 2C5
attitude /ˈætɪˌtjuːd/ Haltung; Einstellung 3A2
to attract /əˈtrækt/ anziehen 2B5, 4B2, 5B6
attraction /əˈtrækʃ(ə)n/ (Touristen)attraktion II
attractive /əˈtræktɪv/ attraktiv; verlockend I
attribute /ˈætrɪˌbjuːt/ Eigenschaft; Merkmal 3A4
audience /ˈɔːdiəns/ Publikum; Besucher; Zuschauer II; Leser(schaft) 4C4
August /ˈɔːɡəst/ August I
aunt /ɑːnt/ Tante I
Australian /ɒˈstreɪliən/ Australier/in; australisch 4C7
° **Australian (Rules) football** (no pl) /ɒˌstreɪliən ˌruːlz ˈfʊtˌbɔl/ *australische Art des Football mit 18 Spielern* 4P11
autumn /ˈɔːtəm/ Herbst I
available /əˈveɪləb(ə)l/ verfügbar; erhältlich IV
average /ˈæv(ə)rɪdʒ/ (im) Durchschnitt; durchschnittlich III
° **aviator** /ˈeɪviˌeɪtə/ Flieger/in 4P11
to avoid /əˈvɔɪd/ (ver)meiden; ausweichen 1C3, 2B5, 3C3, 4C4
° **avoidable** /əˈvɔɪdəb(ə)l/ vermeidbar 1O2
awareness (no pl) /əˈweənəs/ Bewusstsein III
away /əˈweɪ/ weg I
awesome (informal, AE) /ˈɔːsəm/ spitze; super IV
awful /ˈɔːf(ə)l/ furchtbar; schrecklich I
awkward /ˈɔːkwəd/ schwierig; unangenehm; peinlich 1B7

B

back /bæk/ (wieder) zurück I; Rücken; Rückseite II; der hintere Teil IV
° **back door** /ˌbæk ˈdɔː/ Hintertür 1O2
° **to back out** /ˌbækˈaʊt/ einen Rückzieher machen 1P3
° **to back up** /ˌbækˈʌp/ (unter)stützen; bestätigen 2O3

background /ˈbækˌɡraʊnd/ Hintergrund; Herkunft III
backpack (AE) /ˈbækˌpæk/ Rucksack(-) IV
° **bacon** /ˈbeɪkən/ (Schinken)speck 2B5
bad /bæd/ schlecht; schlimm I
bag /bæɡ/ Tasche I; Tüte II
to pack one's bags /ˌpæk wʌnz ˈbæɡz/ die Koffer packen II
to bake /beɪk/ backen II
balanced /ˈbælənst/ ausgewogen 1C10
° **balls** (only pl, informal) /bɔːlz/ Eier; Mumm; Mut 3B4
to ban /bæn/ verbieten 2B5
banana /bəˈnɑːnə/ Banane I
° **Baptist** /ˈbæptɪst/ Baptist/in; Baptisten- 1B9
bar /bɑː/ Stange; Stab; *hier:* Riegel 2B2
barbecue /ˈbɑːbɪˌkjuː/ Grill; Grillparty II
to base /beɪs/ basieren; beruhen; sich stützen auf 1B8
basement /ˈbeɪsmənt/ Untergeschoss; Keller II
basic /ˈbeɪsɪk/ grundlegend; Grund-; (sehr) einfach IV
basically /ˈbeɪsɪkli/ im Wesentlichen; im Grunde; eigentlich 3B10
bathroom /ˈbɑːθˌruːm/ Bad(ezimmer) II
° **bathroom** (AE) /ˈbæθˌrum/ Toilette 1P5
battery /ˈbæt(ə)ri/ Batterie II
battle /ˈbæt(ə)l/ Kampf; Gefecht; Schlacht III
to be (irr) /biː/ sein I
to be able to do sth /ˌbiːˌeɪbl tə ˈduː/ etw tun können II
to be afraid (of) /ˌbiːəˈfreɪd əv/ Angst haben/sich fürchten (vor) I
to be allergic to sth /ˌbiːəˈlɜːdʒɪk tʊ/ auf etw allergisch reagieren; gegen etw allergisch sein III
to be allowed to do sth /ˌbiːəˌlaʊd tə ˈduː/ etw tun dürfen II
to be angry with sb /ˌbiːˈæŋɡri wɪð/ sich über jdn ärgern I
to be ashamed (of) /ˌbiːəˈʃeɪmd əv/ sich schämen (für) IV
to be asleep /ˌbiːəˈsliːp/ schlafen I
° **to be attached to sb/sth** /ˌbiːəˈtætʃt tʊ/ an jdm/etw sehr hängen 1C7
to be aware of sth /ˌbiːəˈweər əv/ sich einer Sache bewusst sein 2C3, 3C5
° **to be based** /ˌbiːˈbeɪst/ seinen Sitz haben 4P10
to be based on /ˌbiːˈbeɪst ɒn/ basieren auf; beruhen auf IV
to be called /ˌbiːˈkɔːld/ genannt werden; heißen I

English-German dictionary

° to **be capable of doing sth** /ˌbiː ˌkeɪpəb(ə)l_əv ˈduːɪŋ/ in der Lage sein, etw zu tun 5B3
to **be concerned with sth** /ˌbiː kənˈsɜːnd wɪð/ sich um etw Gedanken machen 3A2
° to **be confined to sth** /ˌbiː kənˈfaɪnd_tʊ/ auf etw beschränkt sein 5PP2
to **be crazy about sb/sth** /ˌbiː ˈkreɪzi_əˌbaʊt/ nach jdm/etw verrückt sein IV
to **be expected to do sth** /ˌbiː_ɪkˌspektɪd_tə ˈduː/ von jdm erwarten, dass er etw tut IV
° to **be fond of sb/sth** /ˌbiː ˈfɒnd_əv/ jdn/etw gerne mögen 5P4
to **be free** /ˌbiː ˈfriː/ frei haben/sein; Zeit für etw haben I
to **be friends (with sb)** /ˌbiː ˈfrendz wɪð/ (mit jdm) befreundet sein III
to **be fun** /ˌbiː ˈfʌn/ Spaß machen I
to **be good at** /ˌbiː ˈɡʊd_ət/ gut in ... sein I
to **be/feel homesick** /ˌbiː/ˌfiːl ˈhəʊmˌsɪk/ Heimweh haben 4C4
° to **be hooked (on sth)** /ˌbiː ˈhʊkt_ɒn/ (von etw) abhängig/begeistert sein 2C5
° to **be in** /ˌbiːˌˈɪn/ da sein 5O1
to **be in character** /ˌbi_ɪn ˈkærɪktə/ typisch sein 1B10
to **be in charge (of)** /ˌbi_ɪn ˈtʃɑːdʒ_əv/ verantwortlich/zuständig sein (für) 5A2
° to **be in sb's shoes** /ˌbi_ɪn ˌsʌmbədiz ˈʃuːz/ in jds Haut stecken; an jds Stelle sein 3C3
to **be in touch (with sb)** /ˌbi_ɪn ˈtʌtʃ wɪð/ (mit jdm) in Kontakt sein III
to **be into sb/sth** (informal) /ˌbi_ˈɪntu:/ an jdm/etw interessiert sein III
to **be interested (in)** /ˌbi_ˈɪntrəstɪd_ɪn/ sich interessieren (für); interessiert sein (an) I
to **be keen on sb/sth** (informal) /ˌbiː ˈkiːn_ɒn/ auf jdn/etw scharf sein; versessen sein auf III
to **be keen to do sth** /ˌbiː ˌkiːn tə ˈduː/ etw unbedingt tun wollen III
to **be left** /ˌbiː ˈleft/ übrig bleiben III
to **be located** /ˌbiː ləʊˈkeɪtɪd/ sich befinden; gelegen sein IV
to **be/feel lovesick** /ˌbiː/ˌfiːl ˈlʌvˌsɪk/ Liebeskummer haben 1B5
to **be lucky** /ˌbiː ˈlʌki/ Glück haben I
to **be meant to be sth** /ˌbiː ˈment_tə biː/ etw sein sollen 3B1
° to **be missing** /ˌbiː ˈmɪsɪŋ/ fehlen I
to **be over** /ˌbiːˌˈəʊvə/ vorbei sein I
° to **be plagued by sth** /ˌbiː ˈpleɪɡd baɪ/ von etw geplagt/heimgesucht werden 1B2
° to **be present** /ˌbiː ˈprez(ə)nt/ vorkommen; auftreten 3C3

to **be related to** /ˌbiː rɪˈleɪtɪd_tʊ/ verwandt sein (mit); in Beziehung stehen (zu) 4A2
to **be right** /ˌbiː ˈraɪt/ recht haben I
to **be set** /ˌbiː ˈset/ liegen; spielen III
° to **be/get sick** /ˌbiː/ˌɡet ˈsɪk/ sich erbrechen 3B4
° to **be stressed (out)** /ˌbiː ˌstrest_ˈaʊt/ gestresst sein 5P6
to **be (not) supposed to do sth** /ˌbiː ˌnɒt səˌpəʊzd_tə ˈduː/ etw (nicht) tun sollen IV
to **be sure** /ˌbiː ˈʃɔː/ sicher sein I
° to **be sure to do sth** /ˌbiː ˌʃɔː tə ˈduː/ daran denken, etw zu tun 1C3
° to **be the centre of attention** /ˌbiː ðə ˌsentər_əv_əˈtenʃ(ə)n/ im Mittelpunkt/Zentrum des Interesses stehen 3P7
to **be the order of the day (with sb)** /ˌbiː ði_ˌɔːdər_əv ðə ˈdeɪ wɪð/ (bei jdm) an der Tagesordnung sein 3A2
to **be thirsty** /ˌbiː ˈθɜːsti/ Durst haben; durstig sein III
° to **be tied to** /ˌbiː ˈtaɪd_tʊ/ gebunden sein an 1O4
to **be tired of (doing) sth** /ˌbiː ˌtaɪəd_əv ˈduːɪŋ/ es satt haben (etw zu tun); einer Sache überdrüssig sein IV
° to **be torn** /ˌbiː ˈtɔːn/ hin- und hergerissen sein 1O2
to **be upset (about sth)** /ˌbiː ʌpˈset_əˌbaʊt/ (über etw) traurig/aufgebracht sein II
to **be used to doing sth** /ˌbiː ˌjuːst_tuː ˈduːɪŋ/ gewohnt sein, etw zu tun III
to **be worried about** /ˌbiː ˈwʌrid_əˌbaʊt/ sich Sorgen machen um IV
to **be wrong** /ˌbiː ˈrɒŋ/ nicht stimmen; sich irren I
beach /biːtʃ/ Strand I
bear /beə/ Bär IV
° to **bear** (irr) /beə/ (er)tragen 1C5; gebären 1P9
to **bear sth in mind** /ˌbeə ˌsʌmθɪŋ_ɪn ˈmaɪnd/ etw (mit)berücksichtigen 3B9, 5B1
beastliness (no pl) /ˈbiːstlinəs/ Widerwärtigkeit; Gemeinheit; Niedertracht 3A2
to **beat** (irr) /biːt/ schlagen; übertreffen II
beautiful /ˈbjuːtəf(ə)l/ schön I
beauty (no pl) /ˈbjuːti/ Schönheit III
because /bɪˈkɒz/ weil; da I
because of /bɪˈkɒz_əv/ wegen IV
to **become** (irr) /bɪˈkʌm/ werden II
bed /bed/ Bett I
to **go to bed** /ˌɡəʊ tə ˈbed/ ins Bett gehen I
bedroom /ˈbedruːm/ Schlafzimmer II

before /bɪˈfɔː/ bevor; ehe; zuvor; vorher; vor II
to **beg** /beɡ/ betteln; bitten; anflehen 3B8
to **begin** (irr) /bɪˈɡɪn/ anfangen; beginnen I
beginning /bɪˈɡɪnɪŋ/ Anfang; Beginn II
to **behave** /bɪˈheɪv/ sich verhalten; sich benehmen 1B7, 3C3
behaviour (no pl) /bɪˈheɪvjə/ Benehmen; Verhalten; Betragen II
behind /bɪˈhaɪnd/ hinter I
belief (pl **beliefs**) /bɪˈliːf, bɪˈliːfs/ Glaube; Überzeugung; Ansicht IV
to **believe** /bɪˈliːv/ glauben I
° **bell** /bel/ Glocke 1B8
to **belong** /bɪˈlɒŋ/ (dazu)gehören III
to **belong to sb** /bɪˈlɒŋ tə/ jdm gehören II
below /bɪˈləʊ/ unter; unterhalb II
° **beneath** /bɪˈniːθ/ unter; nach unten; darunter 1B6
° **benefit** /ˈbenɪfɪt/ Nutzen; Vorteil; Verdienst 5A2
° to **benefit** /ˈbenɪfɪt/ profitieren; Nutzen ziehen 5P8
besides /bɪˈsaɪdz/ außerdem 2C8
best /best/ beste(r, s) I; am liebsten/am meisten II
to **bet** (irr) /bet/ wetten III
° to **betray** /bɪˈtreɪ/ verraten; untreu sein; betrügen 1O4
better /ˈbetə/ besser II
between /bɪˈtwiːn/ zwischen I
° **beyond belief** /bɪˌjɒnd bɪˈliːf/ (einfach) unglaublich 4O3
bicycle /ˈbaɪsɪk(ə)l/ Fahrrad III
big /bɪɡ/ groß I
bike (informal) /baɪk/ (Fahr)rad I
° **bikeport** /ˈbaɪkˌpɔːt/ Fahrradstellplatz 1C7
billion /ˈbɪljən/ Milliarde 4C1
bin /bɪn/ Mülleimer; Mülltonne II
biodiversity (no pl) /ˌbaɪəʊdaɪˈvɜːsəti/ Artenvielfalt 4B2
biology (no pl) /baɪˈɒlədʒi/ Biologie II
bird /bɜːd/ Vogel I
° **birth** /bɜːθ/ Geburt; Abstammung; Herkunft 2C3
birthday /ˈbɜːθdeɪ/ Geburtstag I
° **birth mother** /ˈbɜːθ ˌmʌðə/ biologische Mutter 1C5
biscuit (BE) /ˈbɪskɪt/ Keks; Biskuit III
bit /bɪt/ Stück; Teil II
to **bite** (irr) /baɪt/ beißen II
black /blæk/ schwarz I
to **blame** /bleɪm/ beschuldigen IV
° to **blend** /blend/ vermischen 1B9
bling /blɪŋ/ Klunker; glamourös; aufgedonnert 2C1
to **block** /blɒk/ blockieren III
blond(e) /blɒnd/ blond I
° **blood** (no pl) /blʌd/ Blut 3B4
blue /bluː/ blau I

Words

English-German dictionary

° **Blue Flag** /ˌbluː ˈflæɡ/ Blaue Flagge *(Gütezeichen im Bereich des nachhaltigen Tourismus)* 4B5
blurb /blɜːb/ Klappentext 3B2
board /bɔːd/ Brett; Tafel I
to **board** /bɔːd/ (ein Flugzeug oder Schiff) besteigen; an Bord gehen IV
boarding school /ˈbɔːdɪŋ skuːl/ Internat III
to **boast (about sth)** /ˈbəʊst ˌəˌbaʊt/ prahlen/angeben (mit etw) 2C8
boat /bəʊt/ Boot; Schiff I
° **boating** *(no pl)* /ˈbəʊtɪŋ/ Bootfahren 5A2
° **body language** /ˈbɒdi ˌlæŋɡwɪdʒ/ Körpersprache 1C3
bold /bəʊld/ mutig; kräftig; forsch 3B4
° **bone** /bəʊn/ Knochen 1B7
book /bʊk/ Buch I
to **book** /bʊk/ reservieren; buchen II
° to **boom** /buːm/ dröhnen 1B9; boomen 4B2
boot /buːt/ Stiefel I
border /ˈbɔːdə/ Grenze; Begrenzung IV
° to **bore sb** /bɔː/ jdn langweilen 3P1
bored /bɔːd/ gelangweilt II
boredom *(no pl)* /ˈbɔːdəm/ Langeweile 2C8
boring /ˈbɔːrɪŋ/ langweilig II
born /bɔːn/ geboren III
to **borrow** /ˈbɒrəʊ/ (aus)leihen 2B3
bossy /ˈbɒsi/ herrschsüchtig; herrisch II
both /bəʊθ/ beide II
  both ... and ... /ˈbəʊθ ænd/ sowohl ... als auch ... IV
to **bother** /ˈbɒðə/ beunruhigen; stören IV
bottle /ˈbɒt(ə)l/ Flasche I
bottom /ˈbɒtəm/ Boden; (unteres) Ende III; untere(r, s) IV
box /bɒks/ Kiste; Schachtel I
boy /bɔɪ/ Junge I
boyfriend /ˈbɔɪˌfrend/ Freund III
° to **brace** /breɪs/ (ab)stützen 1B9
° **bracket** /ˈbrækɪt/ Klammer 3P7
to **brag (about sth)** /ˈbræɡ ˌəˌbaʊt/ (mit etw) angeben/prahlen 2C7
° **brain** /breɪn/ Gehirn; Verstand 2C3
brains /breɪnz/ (Ge)hirn 3A2
brainy *(informal)* /ˈbreɪni/ gescheit; aufgeweckt 3A2
brand /brænd/ Marke 2B2
brave /breɪv/ tapfer; mutig III
bread /bred/ Brot(sorte) IV
break /breɪk/ Pause III
to **break** *(irr)* /breɪk/ (zer)brechen; verstoßen gegen; neu aufstellen II
to **break down** /ˌbreɪk ˈdaʊn/ stehen bleiben; versagen; zusammenbrechen III
to **break one's arm** /ˌbreɪk wʌnz ˈɑːm/ sich den Arm brechen II
° to **break the bank** *(informal)* /ˌbreɪk ðə ˈbæŋk/ verschwenderisch sein 4B1
breakfast /ˈbrekfəst/ Frühstück I
  to **have breakfast** /ˌhæv ˈbrekfəst/ frühstücken I
breast /brest/ Brust IV
° **breath** /breθ/ Atem(zug) 1B6
° **breeze** /briːz/ Brise; (leichter) Wind 4B5
bridge /brɪdʒ/ Brücke III
briefly /ˈbriːfli/ kurz (gesagt); knapp 4A1
° **brilliant** *(informal, BE)* /ˈbrɪljənt/ toll, klasse II
to **bring** *(irr)* /brɪŋ/ (mit)bringen I
Britain /ˈbrɪt(ə)n/ Großbritannien I
British /ˈbrɪtɪʃ/ britisch II
broad /brɔːd/ breit; groß 3C3
° to **broadcast** /ˈbrɔːdˌkɑːst/ senden; übertragen 2C3
brochure /ˈbrəʊʃə/ Broschüre; Katalog I
brother /ˈbrʌðə/ Bruder I
brown /braʊn/ braun I
° to **brush up** /ˌbrʌʃ ˈʌp/ auffrischen 4P1
° **bud** (= buddy) *(informal, AE)* /bʌd, ˈbʌdi/ Kumpel 1B7
to **build** *(irr)* /bɪld/ bauen III
building /ˈbɪldɪŋ/ Gebäude II
  ° **building:** hier: Bau- 5PP2
° **bullet point** /ˈbʊlɪt pɔɪnt/ Aufzählungspunkt 5O1
° **bully** /ˈbʊli/ Rüpel; Schläger 1P2
to **bully** /ˈbʊli/ tyrannisieren; mobben II
bullying *(no pl)* /ˈbʊliɪŋ/ Mobbing 3A2
burglary /ˈbɜːɡləri/ Einbruch(diebstahl) 2C8
to **burn** *(irr)* /bɜːn/ (ab)brennen; verbrennen III
° to **burst out** *(irr)* /ˌbɜːst ˈaʊt/ herausplatzen 1P3
° **bush** /bʊʃ/ Busch; Gebüsch; Wildnis 4PP1
business /ˈbɪznəs/ Handel; Geschäft(s-); Unternehmen; Firma; Betrieb IV
  ° **business:** Sache, Angelegenheit 1B9
busy /ˈbɪzi/ beschäftigt; arbeitsreich; ereignisreich II
but /bʌt/ aber I
butter /ˈbʌtə/ Butter I
to **buy** *(irr)* /baɪ/ kaufen I
by /baɪ/ von II; mit III; bis (spätestens) IV
  by bike /ˌbaɪ ˈbaɪk/ mit dem (Fahr)rad II
  by bus /ˌbaɪ ˈbʌs/ mit dem Bus II
  °**by chance** /ˌbaɪ ˈtʃɑːns/ zufällig 1O2
  by heart /ˌbaɪ ˈhɑːt/ auswendig II
  by the sea /ˌbaɪ ðə ˈsiː/ am Meer III
bye *(informal)*/**goodbye** /baɪ, ɡʊdˈbaɪ/ tschüss I

C

cage /keɪdʒ/ Käfig I
cake /keɪk/ Kuchen I
° **calculator** /ˈkælkjʊˌleɪtə/ Rechner 4P6
calendar /ˈkælɪndə/ Kalender I
° **call** /kɔːl/ (Telefon)anruf 2B5
to **call** /kɔːl/ rufen; nennen; anrufen I
  ° to **call for sth** /ˈkɔːl fɔː/ (nach) etw verlangen 3A2
° **caller** /ˈkɔːlə/ Anrufer/in 5A4
calm /kɑːm/ ruhig; gelassen 3C3
to **calm down** /ˌkɑːm ˈdaʊn/ sich beruhigen I
camera /ˈkæm(ə)rə/ Kamera; Fotoapparat I
° **Cameroon** /ˌkæməˈruːn/ Kamerun 5B3
camp /kæmp/ (Zelt)lager III
campaign /kæmˈpeɪn/ Kampagne; Aktion IV
to **campaign for/against sth** /kæmˈpeɪn fɔː/əˌɡenst/ für etw eintreten/gegen etw kämpfen 5C2
camping *(no pl)* /ˈkæmpɪŋ/ Camping; Zelten III
can /kæn/ können I
  ° **cannot/can't help sth** /ˌkænɒt, ˌkɑːnt ˈhelp/ nicht anders können, als etw zu tun 4P7
cancer /ˈkænsə/ Krebs(geschwulst) IV
candidate /ˈkændɪdeɪt/ Kandidat/in; Bewerber/in 5B4
candle /ˈkænd(ə)l/ Kerze II
° **cannonlike** /ˈkænənlaɪk/ wie eine Kanone 1B9
canoe /kəˈnuː/ Kanu; Paddelboot III
° to **canoe** /kəˈnuː/ paddeln; Kanu fahren 4B5
canoeing *(no pl)* /kəˈnuːɪŋ/ Kanufahren III
° **captain** /ˈkæptɪn/ (Mannschafts)kapitän/in; Hauptmann 1B9
caption /ˈkæpʃ(ə)n/ Überschrift; Titel; Bildunterschrift 2A3, 4A2
to **capture** /ˈkæptʃə/ festnehmen; auf Film festhalten 2C8
car /kɑː/ Auto I
card /kɑːd/ Karte I
to **care (about)** /ˈkeər əˌbaʊt/ sich etw machen (aus) I
  to **care for** /ˈkeə fɔː/ sich kümmern um IV
career /kəˈrɪə/ Beruf; Karriere; Werdegang III
carefree /ˈkeəˌfriː/ sorgenfrei; unbekümmert 4A4
careful /ˈkeəf(ə)l/ vorsichtig II; sorgfältig III
careless /ˈkeələs/ unvorsichtig; leichtsinnig; unbedacht; unbekümmert 2C7
carpet /ˈkɑːpɪt/ Teppich I

English-German dictionary

to **carry** /ˈkæri/ tragen II
  to **carry out** /ˌkæriˈaʊt/ durchführen; ausführen 2C9
° **carrying basket** /ˈkæriɪŋ ˌbɑːskɪt/ Tragekorb 1C7
case /keɪs/ Fall 2B3, 5A2
° **cast** /kɑːst/ Besetzung; Ensemble 2C2
castle /ˈkɑːs(ə)l/ Burg; Schloss III
casual /ˈkæʒuəl/ zufällig; gelegentlich; beiläufig; lässig 2C5, 3A2
cat /kæt/ Katze I
to **catch** (irr) /kætʃ/ fangen I; treffen II
catchy /ˈkætʃi/ eingängig; einprägsam III
cathedral /kəˈθiːdrəl/ Kathedrale; Dom; Münster III
cause /kɔːz/ Grund; Ursache; Anlass; (gute) Sache 1B2, 4B2, 5C1
to **cause** /kɔːz/ verursachen III
  to **cause sb to do sth** /ˌkɔːzˌsʌmbədi təˈduː/ jdn veranlassen, etw zu tun IV
to **celebrate** /ˈseləˌbreɪt/ feiern II
celebration /ˌseləˈbreɪʃ(ə)n/ Feier II
celebrity /səˈlebrəti/ Berühmtheit; Star 2B3
center (AE = **centre** BE) /ˈsentər/ Zentrum; Mitte IV
° to **center on/(a)round** /ˈsentərˌɒn/ ˌəˈraʊnd/ sich drehen um 3C5
central /ˈsentrəl/ zentral; Haupt- IV
centre /ˈsentə/ Zentrum; Mitte I
century /ˈsentʃəri/ Jahrhundert II
ceremony /ˈserəməni/ Zeremonie; Feier; Feierlichkeiten 1C5
certain /ˈsɜːt(ə)n/ sicher; gewiss; bestimmt II
certificate /səˈtɪfɪkət/ Urkunde; Bescheinigung 1B2, 5B1
chain /tʃeɪn/ Kette 3A2
chair /tʃeə/ Stuhl I
challenge /ˈtʃælɪndʒ/ Herausforderung III
to **challenge** /ˈtʃælɪndʒ/ herausfordern III
challenging /ˈtʃælɪndʒɪŋ/ (heraus)fordernd III
change /tʃeɪndʒ/ (Ver)änderung; Wechsel; Umstellung; Wandel; Umstieg II
to **change** /tʃeɪndʒ/ (ver)ändern II; umsteigen III
  to **change one's mind** /ˌtʃeɪndʒ wʌnz ˈmaɪnd/ es sich anders überlegen; seine Meinung ändern II
the Channel /ðə ˈtʃæn(ə)l/ der Ärmelkanal III
chapter /ˈtʃæptə/ Kapitel 3B3
character /ˈkærɪktə/ Charakter; Figur; Zeichen 1A5
characteristic /ˌkærɪktəˈrɪstɪk/ (charakteristisches) Merkmal; typisch; charakteristisch 1B2, 5B3

to **characterize** /ˈkærɪktəraɪz/ kennzeichnen; charakterisieren 3A4
° **charity fundraiser** /ˈtʃærəti ˌfʌndˌreɪzə/ Spendenbeschaffer/in für wohltätige Zwecke 5O3
to **chat** (**to sb**) /ˈtʃætˌtə/ (mit jdm) plaudern; chatten III
cheap /tʃiːp/ billig; preiswert I
° to **cheat** /tʃiːt/ täuschen; betrügen 1P5
to **cheer** /tʃɪə/ jubeln I
  to **cheer up** /ˌtʃɪərˈʌp/ aufmuntern II
cheerful /ˈtʃɪəf(ə)l/ fröhlich; vergnügt; heiter II
cheese /tʃiːz/ Käse I
chef /ʃef/ Koch; Köchin IV
° **chest** /tʃest/ Brust(korb) 1P3
° **chewing gum** (no pl) /ˈtʃuːɪŋˌɡʌm/ Kaugummi 3B4
chicken /ˈtʃɪkɪn/ Huhn I
child (pl **children**) /tʃaɪld, ˈtʃɪldrən/ Kind I
childcare (no pl) /ˈtʃaɪldˌkeə/ Kinderbetreuung 5A2
childhood (no pl) /ˈtʃaɪldˌhʊd/ Kindheit III
° **Chinese** /ˌtʃaɪˈniːz/ Chinese/ Chinesin; Chinesisch (Sprache); chinesisch 4C1
Chinglish /ˈtʃɪŋɡlɪʃ/ vom Chinesischen beeinflusste Variante des Englischen 4C1
chocolate (no pl) /ˈtʃɒklət/ Schokolade I
choice /tʃɔɪs/ Wahl; Auswahl III
  the choice is yours /ðə ˌtʃɔɪs ɪz ˈjɔːz/ Sie haben die Wahl 4B5
to **choose** (irr) /tʃuːz/ (aus)wählen I
  to **choose to do sth** /ˌtʃuːz təˈduː/ es vorziehen, etwas zu tun 5A2
choosy /ˈtʃuːzi/ wählerisch; heikel III
Christmas /ˈkrɪsməs/ Weihnachten II
° to **chuck** (informal) /tʃʌk/ schmeißen 5O1
° **chuffed** (informal, BE) /tʃʌft/ froh; begeistert 4B1
church /tʃɜːtʃ/ Kirche II
cinema /ˈsɪnəmə/ Kino I
cinematic /ˌsɪnəˈmætɪk/ Film-; filmisch 2B3
  cinematic device /ˌsɪnəˌmætɪk dɪˈvaɪs/ filmisches Stilmittel 2C8
circle /ˈsɜːk(ə)l/ Kreis IV
circus /ˈsɜːkəs/ Zirkus I
° **citizen** /ˈsɪtɪz(ə)n/ (Staats)bürger/in 1P9
city /ˈsɪti/ (Groß)stadt(-); städtisch II
claim /kleɪm/ Behauptung; Forderung; Anspruch; Werbeslogan 2B5
to **claim** /kleɪm/ behaupten; Anspruch erheben auf III
° **clamor** (no pl, AE = clamour BE) /ˈklæmər/ Lärm 1P3

° to **clap** /klæp/ klatschen 3P3
clarification /ˌklærɪfɪˈkeɪʃ(ə)n/ Klarstellung; (Ab)klärung 3C5
class /klɑːs/ (Schul)klasse I
classmate /ˈklɑːsˌmeɪt/ Klassenkamerad/in; Mitschüler/in I
classroom /ˈklɑːsˌruːm/ Klassenzimmer I
to **clean** (**up**) /ˌkliːnˈʌp/ sauber machen; reinigen; putzen I; abbauen, eindämmen III
° **cleaner** /ˈkliːnə/ Putzhilfe; Putzfrau 5P5
clear /klɪə/ klar; deutlich; eindeutig II
° to **clench one's fist** /ˌklentʃ wʌnz ˈfɪst/ die Faust ballen 1B8
° **clerk** /klɑːk/ (Büro)angestellte/r 5P11
climate (no pl) /ˈklaɪmət/ Klima III
to **climb** (**up**) /ˌklaɪmˈʌp/ (hinauf) steigen; klettern (auf); besteigen I
clock /klɒk/ Uhr I
close /kləʊs/ nah(e) III
to **close** /kləʊz/ schließen; zumachen II
clothes (pl) /kləʊðz/ Kleider; Kleidung I
clothing (no pl) /ˈkləʊðɪŋ/ (Be)kleidung IV
cloud /klaʊd/ Wolke I
to **cluster** /ˈklʌstə/ (lose) zusammenstellen; sammeln 4A1
coach /kəʊtʃ/ Trainer/in I; (Omni)bus; Reisebus II
° to **coach** /kəʊtʃ/ trainieren 5B6
coast /kəʊst/ Küste I
coastline /ˈkəʊstˌlaɪn/ Küste(nlinie) 4B2
coat /kəʊt/ Mantel I
coffee /ˈkɒfi/ Kaffee III
cold /kəʊld/ kalt I
° to **collapse** /kəˈlæps/ zusammenbrechen; einstürzen 1P3
° **collar** /ˈkɒlə/ Kragen 1P3
to **collect** /kəˈlekt/ sammeln; aufheben; einsammeln II
° **collection** /kəˈlekʃ(ə)n/ Sammlung 4P10
college /ˈkɒlɪdʒ/ Gymnasium; Hochschule IV
colloquial /kəˈləʊkwiəl/ umgangssprachlich 4B1
colour /ˈkʌlə/ Farbe I
combination /ˌkɒmbɪˈneɪʃ(ə)n/ Kombination; Verbindung III
to **combine** /kəmˈbaɪn/ verbinden; kombinieren III
to **come** (irr) /kʌm/ kommen I; werden II
  to **come across** /ˌkʌm əˈkrɒs/ begegnen; stoßen auf 5A3
  ° to **come across**: herüberkommen; wirken 5B8
  Come on! (informal) /ˌkʌmˈɒn/ Komm(t) jetzt!; Mach(t) schon! I

Words

English-German dictionary

to **come to a conclusion** /ˌkʌm tʊ ə kənˈkluːʒ(ə)n/ zu einem Schluss kommen/gelangen 4B7
° to **come up** /ˌkʌmˈʌp/ hochkommen; auftauchen 5O1
° to **come up with sth** /ˌkʌmˈʌp wɪð/ auf etw kommen; sich etw einfallen lassen 1B8
comedy /ˈkɒmədi/ Comedy(show); humoristische Sendung; Komödie IV
comfort (no pl) /ˈkʌmfət/ Komfort; Behaglichkeit; Trost IV
to **comfort** /ˈkʌmfət/ trösten III
comfortable /ˈkʌmftəb(ə)l/ behaglich; bequem; komfortabel III
° **comforting** /ˈkʌmfətɪŋ/ beruhigend; tröstlich; ermutigend 1O4
° to **command** /kəˈmɑːnd/ Befehl geben; befehlen 1B9
comment /ˈkɒment/ Kommentar; Bemerkung III
to **comment (on)** /ˈkɒment ɒn/ kommentieren II
commercial /kəˈmɜːʃ(ə)l/ Werbespot; Fernseh-/Radiowerbung IV
to **commit** /kəˈmɪt/ begehen 1C1, 3C3
commitment /kəˈmɪtmənt/ Engagement; Verpflichtung 5C2
committed /kəˈmɪtɪd/ verpflichtet; gebunden; engagiert 5C2
° **committee** /kəˈmɪti/ Ausschuss; Komitee 1C7
common /ˈkɒmən/ üblich; weit verbreitet; gemeinsam; gemeinschaftlich (genutzt) IV
° **commotion** (no pl) /kəˈməʊʃ(ə)n/ Theater; Chaos; Aufruhr 1C7
to **communicate** /kəˈmjuːnɪkeɪt/ kommunizieren; Kontakt haben 5A2
communications /kəˌmjuːnɪˈkeɪʃ(ə)nz/ (Tele)kommunikation 2B5
communicative /kəˈmjuːnɪkətɪv/ mitteilsam; kommunikationsfreudig 5B3
community /kəˈmjuːnəti/ Gemeinde; Gemeinschaft IV
° **community spirit** /kəˌmjuːnəti ˈspɪrɪt/ Gemeinschaftssinn 4P8
company /ˈkʌmp(ə)ni/ Firma IV
to **compare** /kəmˈpeə/ vergleichen II
comparison /kəmˈpærɪs(ə)n/ Vergleich IV
° **compassionate** /kəmˈpæʃ(ə)nət/ mitfühlend; voller Mitgefühl 1O4
to **compete** /kəmˈpiːt/ wetteifern; antreten; kämpfen III
competition /ˌkɒmpəˈtɪʃ(ə)n/ Wettbewerb II
competitive /kəmˈpetətɪv/ konkurrierend; kampfbereit II
to **complain (about)** /kəmˈpleɪn əˌbaʊt/ sich beklagen (über) 3B8

to **complete** /kəmˈpliːt/ vervollständigen; ausfüllen II
completely /kəmˈpliːtli/ völlig III
° **complex** /ˈkɒmpleks/ komplex; kompliziert; verwickelt 3P6
° **complicated** /ˈkɒmplɪkeɪtɪd/ kompliziert; schwierig III
° **comprehensive** /ˌkɒmprɪˈhensɪv/ umfassend 5B3
° **computing** (no pl) /kəmˈpjuːtɪŋ/ EDV 5C2
to **concentrate** /ˈkɒns(ə)n,treɪt/ (sich) konzentrieren III
concept /ˈkɒnsept/ Vorstellung; Idee; Konzept 1C10
° **concern** /kənˈsɜːn/ Anliegen; Sorge; Besorgnis 1B9
° **concerned** /kənˈsɜːnd/ betroffen; besorgt; beunruhigt 1O3
concert /ˈkɒnsət/ Konzert II
conclusion /kənˈkluːʒ(ə)n/ Abschluss; Schluss; Schlussfolgerung IV
to **come to a conclusion** /ˌkʌm tʊ ə kənˈkluːʒ(ə)n/ zu einem Schluss kommen/gelangen 4B7
concrete /ˈkɒŋkriːt/ Beton(-) 4B2
° **condiment** /ˈkɒndɪmənt/ Gewürz 1B6
condition /kənˈdɪʃ(ə)n/ Zustand; Bedingung; Umstand 2A4
° to **condone** /kənˈdəʊn/ (stillschweigend) dulden 1B9
confidence (no pl) /ˈkɒnfɪd(ə)ns/ (Selbst)vertrauen; Zuversicht 3C3
confident /ˈkɒnfɪd(ə)nt/ zuversichtlich; selbstsicher; selbstbewusst II
conflict /ˈkɒnflɪkt/ Konflikt; Kampf; Zusammenstoß III
° to **conform to/with sth** /kənˈfɔːm tʊ/ wɪð/ etw entsprechen; mit etw übereinstimmen 1C5
° to **confront** /kənˈfrʌnt/ begegnen; konfrontieren 1P2
confused /kənˈfjuːzd/ verwirrt; durcheinander; verworren III
Congratulations! /kənˌɡrætʃəˈleɪʃ(ə)nz/ Gratuliere!; Glückwunsch! II
to **connect** /kəˈnekt/ verbinden; anschließen II
connection /kəˈnekʃ(ə)n/ Verbindung; Beziehung; Zusammenhang 2B3, 3C5
° **connotation** /ˌkɒnəˈteɪʃ(ə)n/ Konnotation (assoziative [Neben] bedeutung) 1P3
to **conquer** /ˈkɒŋkə/ erobern; besiegen; bezwingen III
° **conscientious** /ˌkɒnʃiˈenʃəs/ gewissenhaft; pflichtbewusst 5B3
consequence /ˈkɒnsɪkwəns/ Folge; Konsequenz II
consequently /ˈkɒnsɪkwəntli/ folglich; infolgedessen 4B4
° **conservative** /kənˈsɜːvətɪv/ Konservative(r); konservativ 1B2

to **consider** /kənˈsɪdə/ nachdenken; betrachten; ansehen (als); berücksichtigen III
considerate /kənˈsɪd(ə)rət/ rücksichtsvoll; aufmerksam IV
° **constantly** /ˈkɒnstəntli/ ständig 1B9
° to **construct** /kənˈstrʌkt/ bauen 2O2
under construction /ˌʌndə kənˈstrʌkʃ(ə)n/ im Bau 4B2
consumer /kənˈsjuːmə/ Verbraucher/in; Konsument/in 2B5
consumption (no pl) /kənˈsʌmpʃ(ə)n/ Verbrauch; Konsum 4B4
to **contact sb** /ˈkɒntækt/ sich mit jdm in Verbindung setzen IV
to **contain** /kənˈteɪn/ enthalten IV
to **contaminate** /kənˈtæmɪneɪt/ verschmutzen; verunreinigen; verseuchen IV
° **cont'd** (= continued) /kənˈtɪnjuːd/ fortgesetzt; Fortsetzung 1C7
content /ˈkɒntent/ Inhalt 1B8, 2C8, 4C4, 5B8
context /ˈkɒntekst/ Kontext; (Satz)zusammenhang IV
to **continue doing sth/to do sth** /kənˌtɪnjuː/ weiter(hin) etw tun III
° **contract** /ˈkɒntrækt/ Vertrag 2O2
° to **contract** /kənˈtrækt/ schrumpfen; verkürzen, zusammenziehen 5P7
° **on the contrary** /ˌɒn ðə ˈkɒntrəri/ ganz im Gegenteil 4B2
to **contribute** /kənˈtrɪbjuːt/ beisteuern; beitragen 5C5
contribution /ˌkɒntrɪˈbjuːʃ(ə)n/ Beitrag; Spende 1B10
control (no pl) /kənˈtrəʊl/ Kontrolle; Gewalt; Herrschaft III
to **control** /kənˈtrəʊl/ kontrollieren; steuern; beherrschen III
convenient /kənˈviːniənt/ praktisch; günstig; bequem 1C5
conversation /ˌkɒnvəˈseɪʃ(ə)n/ Gespräch; Unterhaltung II
to **convey** /kənˈveɪ/ (r)überbringen; vermitteln IV
conviction /kənˈvɪkʃ(ə)n/ Verurteilung; Überzeugung 3C3
to **convince** /kənˈvɪns/ überzeugen II
convinced /kənˈvɪnst/ überzeugt 2B2
convincing /kənˈvɪnsɪŋ/ überzeugend II
to **cook** /kʊk/ kochen I
cooking /ˈkʊkɪŋ/ Kochen I
to **coordinate** /kəʊˈɔːdɪneɪt/ koordinieren; aufeinander abstimmen 5C2
to **cope with** /ˈkəʊp wɪð/ zurechtkommen mit; bewältigen IV
to **copy** /ˈkɒpi/ abschreiben; niederschreiben; kopieren II
corner /ˈkɔːnə/ Ecke II
to **correct** /kəˈrekt/ korrigieren III
to **correspond with/to sth** /ˌkɒrɪˈspɒnd wɪð/tʊ/ mit etw übereinstimmen; etw entsprechen 1B8

English-German dictionary — Words

cost /kɒst/ Preis; Kosten 4B1
to **cost** *(irr)* /kɒst/ kosten IV
  ° to cost the earth *(informal)* /ˌkɒst ðiˈɜːθ/ ein Vermögen kosten 4B5
costume /ˈkɒstjuːm/ Kostüm II
cottage /ˈkɒtɪdʒ/ Landhaus; Hütte III
couldn't (= could not) /ˈkʊdnt, kəd ˈnɒt/ Vergangenheitsform von „can't" I
council /ˈkaʊns(ə)l/ Rat; Vertretung 3A2
counselor *(AE = counsellor BE)* /ˈkaʊnsələr/ Berater/in; psychologischer Betreuer/ psychologische Betreuerin 3C3
° to **count** /kaʊnt/ (ab)zählen; mitzählen; auszählen 5O3
  ° to count on sb to do sth /ˌkaʊnt ɒn ˌsʌmbədi tə ˈduː/ sich darauf verlassen, dass jd etw tut 3A2
° **counter** /ˈkaʊntə/ (Laden)theke; Schalter 1B6
° to **counter** /ˈkaʊntə/ kontern; dagegenhalten 1B9
counter(-) /ˈkaʊntə/ Gegen(-) 2B6, 3B7
country /ˈkʌntri/ Land II
countryside *(no pl)* /ˈkʌntriˌsaɪd/ Land; Landschaft III
couple /ˈkʌp(ə)l/ Paar 1B5
° **courage** /ˈkʌrɪdʒ/ Mut 1B8
courageous /kəˈreɪdʒəs/ mutig; tapfer IV
course /kɔːs/ Kurs IV
  ° course (= of course) *(informal)*: natürlich 5O1
of course /əv ˈkɔːs/ natürlich I
cousin /ˈkʌz(ə)n/ Cousin; Cousine I
to **cover** /ˈkʌvə/ bedecken 4B2; *hier:* sich befassen mit, behandeln 4C4, 5B7
  ° to cover one's tracks /ˌkʌvə wʌnz ˈtræks/ seine Spuren verwischen 2C5
  to cover up /ˌkʌvərˈʌp/ bedecken; verdecken 2A4
covering letter *(BE)* /ˌkʌvərɪŋ ˈletə/ Anschreiben 5B1
cow /kaʊ/ Kuh I
° **co-worker** /ˌkəʊ ˈwɜːkə/ Mitarbeiter/ in; Kollege/Kollegin 5B6
° **crack** /kræk/ Riss; *hier:* Witz 5O3
° to **crack up** *(informal)* /ˌkrækˈʌp/ lachen müssen 3B7
° **craft** /krɑːft/ Handwerk 5PP2
° to **crawl** /krɔːl/ krabbeln; kriechen 1B7
crazy /ˈkreɪzi/ verrückt I
  to **be crazy about sb/sth** /ˌbiː ˈkreɪziˌəˌbaʊt/ nach jdm/etw verrückt sein IV
to **create** /kriˈeɪt/ erschaffen; erstellen IV
creative /kriˈeɪtɪv/ kreativ; schöpferisch III
creature /ˈkriːtʃə/ Kreatur; Lebewesen; Geschöpf III

° **creep** *(informal)* /kriːp/ Mistkerl; Fiesling 1B7
crime /kraɪm/ Verbrechen IV
° **crisis** *(pl crises)* /ˈkraɪsɪs, ˈkraɪsiːz/ Krise 5O4
crisps *(pl, BE)* /krɪsps/ Chips II
critical /ˈkrɪtɪk(ə)l/ kritisch 3A4
criticism *(no pl)* /ˈkrɪtɪˌsɪz(ə)m/ Kritik; kritische Anmerkung 3B7
to **criticize** /ˈkrɪtɪsaɪz/ kritisch beurteilen; kritisieren IV
to **cross** /krɒs/ überqueren II
crowd /kraʊd/ (Menschen)menge; Zuschauermenge IV
crowded /ˈkraʊdɪd/ überfüllt IV
crown /kraʊn/ Krone III
° **cruel** /ˈkruːəl/ grausam; gemein 3P5
cruelty /ˈkruːəlti/ Grausamkeit; Quälerei 3A2
to **cry** /kraɪ/ weinen; schreien I
cue card /ˈkjuːˌkɑːd/ Stichwortkarte 4A4
culture /ˈkʌltʃə/ Kultur IV
cup /kʌp/ Tasse; Becher; Pokal II
cupboard /ˈkʌbəd/ Schrank I
° to **cure** /kjʊə/ heilen 1B2
current /ˈkʌrənt/ jetzig; gegenwärtig; aktuell 5A2
currently /ˈkʌrəntli/ zurzeit; gegenwärtig; momentan IV
custom /ˈkʌstəm/ Brauch; Sitte; Gewohnheit 4A4
customer /ˈkʌstəmə/ Kunde/Kundin I
to **cut** *(irr)* /kʌt/ schneiden I
° **cute** /kjuːt/ süß; niedlich 1C7
CV (= curriculum vitae) *(BE = résumé AE)* /ˌsiː ˈviː, kəˌrɪkjʊləm ˈviːtaɪ/ Lebenslauf 5B1
to **cycle** /ˈsaɪk(ə)l/ Rad fahren; radeln II
° **cycling** *(no pl)* /ˈsaɪklɪŋ/ Radfahren; Radeln 4B5
cyclist /ˈsaɪklɪst/ Radfahrer/in III

D

° to **dab** /dæb/ (be)tupfen 1B7
dad *(informal)* /dæd/ Papa; Vati I
daily /ˈdeɪli/ täglich; jeden Tag 2B2
  daily life /ˌdeɪli ˈlaɪf/ Alltag(sleben) 5C2
damage *(no pl)* /ˈdæmɪdʒ/ Schaden; (Be)schädigung III
° **damn(ed)** *(informal)* /dæmd/ verdammt 1B2
° to **dampen** /ˈdæmpən/ befeuchten; dämpfen 1P3
dance *(no pl)* /dɑːns/ Tanz II
to **dance** /dɑːns/ tanzen I
danger /ˈdeɪndʒə/ Gefahr IV
dangerous /ˈdeɪndʒərəs/ gefährlich I
dark /dɑːk/ dunkel I
° to **dart** /dɑːt/ flitzen; sausen; schießen; werfen 1P3

° **database** /ˈdeɪtəˌbeɪs/ Datenbank(-) 5P4
date /deɪt/ Verabredung; Rendezvous; Date; *hier:* Partner/in 1B5; Datum I
to **date sb** *(AE)* /ˈdeɪt/ mit jdm gehen 1B5
° **dated** /ˈdeɪtɪd/ veraltet; überholt 3B2
daughter /ˈdɔːtə/ Tochter I
day /deɪ/ Tag I
  ° **day care centre** *(BE)* /ˈdeɪ keəˌsentə/ Kindertagesstätte; Altentagesstätte 5B3
dead /ded/ tot II
  ° **dead** *(informal)*: sehr; total 2B5
to **deal with** *(irr)* /ˈdiːl wɪð/ sich befassen mit IV
Dear ..., /dɪə/ Sehr geehrte(r) ...; Liebe(r, s) ... I
  Dear Sir or Madam /dɪə ˌsɜːr ɔː ˈmædəm/ Sehr geehrte Damen und Herren 5B4
death *(no pl)* /deθ/ Tod; Ende III
debate /dɪˈbeɪt/ Debatte; Diskussion IV
° **decade** /ˈdekeɪd/ Jahrzehnt 4O3
December /dɪˈsembə/ Dezember I
decent /ˈdiːs(ə)nt/ anständig; ordentlich; nett 2B4
to **decide** /dɪˈsaɪd/ entscheiden; bestimmen I
decision /dɪˈsɪʒ(ə)n/ Entscheidung; Entschluss III
to **declare** /dɪˈkleə/ verkünden; erklären III
decline /dɪˈklaɪn/ Rückgang; Verschlechterung; Niedergang 4B2
to **decorate** /ˈdekəreɪt/ dekorieren II
to **decrease** /diːˈkriːs/ abnehmen; zurückgehen IV
dedicated /ˈdedɪˌkeɪtɪd/ engagiert 5B3
defeat /dɪˈfiːt/ Niederlage IV
to **defeat** /dɪˈfiːt/ besiegen; schlagen III
to **define** /dɪˈfaɪn/ definieren; festlegen 1A1
definitely /ˈdef(ə)nətli/ eindeutig; definitiv III
° **degree** /dɪˈɡriː/ Grad; Abschluss 5O3
° **dejected** /dɪˈdʒektɪd/ niedergeschlagen 1O4
° to **delete** /dɪˈliːt/ löschen; streichen 1P5
delicious /dɪˈlɪʃəs/ köstlich; lecker II
delighted /dɪˈlaɪtɪd/ hocherfreut; begeistert I
° **delivery boy/girl** /dɪˈlɪv(ə)ri bɔɪ/ɡɜːl/ Austräger/in; Fahrer/in 5P5
° **demand** /dɪˈmɑːnd/ (An)forderung 1P2
to **demand** /dɪˈmɑːnd/ verlangen; fordern 1B9, 3A2
° **democratization** /dɪˌmɒkrətaɪˈzeɪʃ(ə)n/ Demokratisierung 4A3
Denmark /ˈdenmɑːk/ Dänemark 4B1

W — Words — English-German dictionary

° to **deny** /dɪˈnaɪ/ abstreiten; verweigern; vorenthalten; ablehnen 1B9
° **Department of Justice** /dɪˌpɑːtmənt_əv ˈdʒʌstɪs/ Justizministerium 1C5
department store /dɪˈpɑːtmənt stɔː/ Kaufhaus IV
departure /dɪˈpɑːtʃə/ Abreise; Abflug; Abfahrt III
to **depend (on)** /dɪˈpend_ɒn/ abhängen (von) II
dependent /dɪˈpendənt/ abhängig 3C3
to **depict** /dɪˈpɪkt/ darstellen; beschreiben 1C3
depressed /dɪˈprest/ deprimiert III
° **depressing** /dɪˈpresɪŋ/ deprimierend 1O4
to **describe** /dɪˈskraɪb/ beschreiben II
description /dɪˈskrɪpʃ(ə)n/ Beschreibung III
° **descriptive** /dɪˈskrɪptɪv/ beschreibend 1O6
deserted /dɪˈzɜːtɪd/ verlassen IV
desirable /dɪˈzaɪrəb(ə)l/ erstrebenswert; begehrt 2B3
desire /dɪˈzaɪə/ Wunsch 2C8
° to **desire** /dɪˈzaɪə/ wünschen; begehren 3P6
desk /desk/ Schreibtisch I
desperate /ˈdesp(ə)rət/ verzweifelt III
despite /dɪˈspaɪt/ trotz 3A2
dessert /dɪˈzɜːt/ Nachtisch IV
destination /ˌdestɪˈneɪʃ(ə)n/ (Reise)ziel; Bestimmungsort III
to **de-stress** /diːˈstres/ (sich) entspannen (Wortneuschöpfung) 4A2
to **destroy** /dɪˈstrɔɪ/ zerstören; vernichten IV
° **destruction** (no pl) /dɪˈstrʌkʃ(ə)n/ Zerstörung 1O4
detail /ˈdiːteɪl/ Detail; Einzelheit II
detailed /ˈdiːteɪld/ detailliert; genau; ausführlich III
determination (no pl) /dɪˌtɜːmɪˈneɪʃ(ə)n/ Entschlossenheit; Entschiedenheit; Bestimmung III
to **determine** /dɪˈtɜːmɪn/ entscheiden; ermitteln; bestimmen 1C5
determined /dɪˈtɜːmɪnd/ entschlossen II
° **devastated** /ˈdevəˌsteɪtɪd/ am Boden zerstört 1O4
° **devastating** /ˈdevəˌsteɪtɪŋ/ vernichtend 1O4
to **develop** /dɪˈveləp/ entwickeln; entstehen; erarbeiten III
° **developer** /dɪˈveləpə/ Entwickler; hier: Bauunternehmer 4B2
development /dɪˈveləpmənt/ Entwicklung III
° **device** /dɪˈvaɪs/ Gerät; Vorrichtung; Apparat 4PP1

dialogue /ˈdaɪəlɒg/ Gespräch; Dialog I
diary /ˈdaɪəri/ Tagebuch I
dictionary /ˈdɪkʃən(ə)ri/ Wörterbuch II
° **didgeridoo** /ˌdɪdʒəriˈduː/ röhrenförmiges Blasinstrument australischer Ureinwohner 4PP1
to **die (of)** /daɪ_əv/ sterben (an) II
° **dieting** (no pl) /ˈdaɪətɪŋ/ Diät halten 3B2
to **differ (from/in)** /ˈdɪfə frɒm/ɪn/ sich unterscheiden (von/in) 1A4
difference /ˈdɪfrəns/ Unterschied; Verschiedenheit; Abweichung III
different /ˈdɪfrənt/ anders; andere(r, s); verschieden II
difficult /ˈdɪfɪk(ə)lt/ schwierig; schwer I
difficulty /ˈdɪfɪk(ə)lti/ Mühe; Schwierigkeit; Problem 1B7, 4C4
diligent /ˈdɪlɪdʒ(ə)nt/ fleißig; sorgfältig; gewissenhaft 5B3
° **dimple** /ˈdɪmp(ə)l/ Grübchen; Delle 1O4
dinner /ˈdɪnə/ Abendessen; Mittagessen I
° **diplomacy** (no pl) /dɪˈpləʊməsi/ Diplomatie; Verhandlungsgeschick 5P1
diplomatic /ˌdɪpləˈmætɪk/ diplomatisch; taktvoll 5B3
direct /dɪˈrekt/ direkt; unmittelbar III
to **direct** /daɪˈrekt/ Regie führen 2C5
direction /dɪˈrekʃ(ə)n/ Richtung II
director /daɪˈrektə/ Direktor/in; Regisseur/in 2C2
dirty /ˈdɜːti/ dreckig; schmutzig II
disability /ˌdɪsəˈbɪləti/ Unfähigkeit; Behinderung; Benachteiligung 2B5
disadvantage /ˌdɪsədˈvɑːntɪdʒ/ Nachteil IV
to **disagree** /ˌdɪsəˈgriː/ nicht übereinstimmen; nicht einverstanden sein II
disagreement /ˌdɪsəˈgriːmənt/ Uneinigkeit; Meinungsverschiedenheit 1C10
° to **disappear** /ˌdɪsəˈpɪə/ verschwinden 3B4
to **disappoint** /ˌdɪsəˈpɔɪnt/ enttäuschen 3C5
disappointed /ˌdɪsəˈpɔɪntɪd/ enttäuscht I
disappointment /ˌdɪsəˈpɔɪntmənt/ Enttäuschung III
to **disapprove of** /ˌdɪsəˈpruːv_ɒv/ dagegen sein; missbilligen; ablehnen 3A4
disaster /dɪˈzɑːstə/ Katastrophe; Unglück III
to **discover** /dɪˈskʌvə/ herausfinden; entdecken III
to **discuss** /dɪˈskʌs/ besprechen; diskutieren I
disgusting /dɪsˈgʌstɪŋ/ empörend; widerlich; widerwärtig 5A4

dishwasher /ˈdɪʃˌwɒʃə/ Geschirrspülmaschine I
to **load the dishwasher** /ˌləʊd ðə ˈdɪʃˌwɒʃə/ die Spülmaschine einräumen I
disillusioned /ˌdɪsɪˈluːʒ(ə)nd/ desillusioniert; enttäuscht IV
to **dislike** /dɪsˈlaɪk/ nicht mögen II
° to **dismiss** /dɪsˈmɪs/ wegschicken; abweisen 3P10
° **(You're) dismissed!** /jɔː dɪsˈmɪst/ Weggetreten! 1B9
to **display** /dɪˈspleɪ/ aushängen; (an)zeigen 2C8
° **dispute** /ˈdɪspjuːt/ Debatte; Streit 5O2
° **disruptive** /dɪsˈrʌptɪv/ störend 1B9
distance /ˈdɪstəns/ Strecke; Entfernung IV
distant /ˈdɪstənt/ fern; (weit) entfernt III
distress (no pl) /dɪˈstres/ Schmerz; Leid; Kummer; Not 2B5
° **distressed** /dɪˈstrest/ bekümmert; erschüttert 3P5
diverse /daɪˈvɜːs/ vielfältig; breit gefächert; unterschiedlich III
to **divide into** /dɪˈvaɪd_ˌɪntʊ/ (auf)teilen in III
divorce /dɪˈvɔːs/ Scheidung 2B3
divorced /dɪˈvɔːst/ geschieden III
to **do** (irr) /duː/ machen; tun I
to **do research** /ˌduː rɪˈsɜːtʃ/ (er)forschen; recherchieren II
to **do sightseeing** /ˌduː ˈsaɪtˌsiːɪŋ/ eine Besichtigungstour machen I
documentary /ˌdɒkjʊˈment(ə)ri/ Dokumentation; Dokumentarfilm IV
dog /dɒg/ Hund I
door /dɔː/ Tür I
° **doormat** /ˈdɔːmæt/ Fußmatte; Fußabstreifer 2C7
dorm (= **dormitory**) (informal) /dɔːm, ˈdɔːmɪtri/ Schlafsaal III
° **dos and don'ts** (only pl) /ˌduːz_ən ˈdəʊnts/ Verhaltensregeln 3P1
double /ˈdʌb(ə)l/ doppelt; Doppel- III
double: Doppelte(r); hier: Doppelzimmer 4B5
doubt /daʊt/ Zweifel; Bedenken III
to **doubt** /daʊt/ misstrauen; bezweifeln IV
down /daʊn/ hinunter; herunter I
downtown (AE) /ˈdaʊnˌtaʊn/ Innenstadt(-) IV
° **down under** (no pl, informal) /ˌdaʊn_ˈʌndə/ Australien; Neuseeland 4P10
° to **drag** /dræg/ ziehen; schleifen 3B4
drama (no pl) /ˈdrɑːmə/ Schauspielerei; Drama; Theater- III
° to **draw** (irr) /drɔː/ zeichnen 1B2; hier: (an)ziehen; lenken 2PP1
dream /driːm/ Traum IV
to **dream (of)** (irr) /ˈdriːm_əv/ träumen (von) IV

English-German dictionary — Words — W

° Dreamtime /ˈdriːmˌtaɪm/ *zentraler Begriff der Aborigine-Mythologie* 4PP1
° to drench /drentʃ/ durchnässen 1P3
dress /dres/ Kleid III
to dress /dres/ sich anziehen III
° to dress up /ˌdresˈʌp/ sich herausputzen 5P7
drink /drɪŋk/ Getränk II
drink *(no pl)* /drɪŋk/ Trinken I
to drink *(irr)* /drɪŋk/ trinken I
to drive *(irr)* /draɪv/ fahren; treiben, bewegen 2C5
drug /drʌg/ Medikament; Droge; Rauschgift IV
drums *(only pl)* /drʌmz/ Schlagzeug 1A1, 2B2
drunk /drʌŋk/ betrunken 3B6
dry /draɪ/ trocken IV
° to dry-clean /ˈdraɪˌkliːn/ chemisch reinigen 5P10
° to dub /dʌb/ nennen 2C5
duck /dʌk/ Ente I
° dude *(informal, AE)* /dud/ Typ; Kerl; Mann 1B7
due to /ˈdjuːtu/ wegen IV
dull /dʌl/ langweilig; eintönig; matt; trüb(e) 5A4
° dumb *(informal)* /dʌm/ dumm; blöd; doof 3B4
° dumb-ass *(informal, AE)* /ˈdʌmˌæs/ dumm; blöd 1O3
° dunno (= don't know) *(informal)* /dəˈnəʊ/ weiß nicht 5O1
duration *(no pl)* /djʊˈreɪʃ(ə)n/ Dauer; Länge III
during /ˈdjʊərɪŋ/ während II
duty /ˈdjuːti/ Pflicht; Verpflichtung; Aufgabe IV
° dwelling /ˈdwelɪŋ/ Wohnung 1C7
to dye /daɪ/ färben 3A2
dynamic /daɪˈnæmɪk/ Dynamik; dynamisch 5B3
dystopian /dɪsˈtəʊpiən/ dystopisch *(ein pessimistisches Zukunftsbild malend)* 1C8

E

each /iːtʃ/ jede(r, s) I
each other /ˌiːtʃˈʌðə/ einander; gegenseitig II
ear /ɪə/ Ohr I
early /ˈɜːli/ früh; zeitig II
to earn /ɜːn/ verdienen III
earth *(no pl)* /ɜːθ/ Erde III
east /iːst/ Osten; östlich; Ost- III
easy /ˈiːzi/ leicht; einfach I
to eat *(irr)* /iːt/ essen; fressen I
to eat out /ˌiːtˈaʊt/ auswärts essen; essen gehen IV
° to echo /ˈekəʊ/ (wider)hallen 1P3
eco-friendly /ˌiːkəʊˈfrendli/ umweltfreundlich 4B5
economic /ˌiːkəˈnɒmɪk/ ökonomisch; Wirtschafts-; wirtschaftlich IV
economy /ɪˈkɒnəmi/ Wirtschaft IV
ecosystem /ˈiːkəʊˌsɪstəm/ Ökosystem 4B2
to edit /ˈedɪt/ redigieren; bearbeiten III
° to educate /ˈedjʊkeɪt/ unterrichten; ausbilden; erziehen; aufklären 1P2
educated /ˈedjʊˌkeɪtɪd/ gebildet; kultiviert III
education /ˌedjʊˈkeɪʃ(ə)n/ Bildung; Ausbildung III
° educational /ˌedjʊˈkeɪʃ(ə)nəl/ Bildungs-; pädagogisch 5B3
eerie /ˈɪəri/ unheimlich II
effect /ɪˈfekt/ Wirkung; Effekt; Auswirkung II
effective /ɪˈfektɪv/ fähig; wirksam; wirkungsvoll III
efficient /ɪˈfɪʃ(ə)nt/ leistungsstark; effizient 5B3
effort /ˈefət/ Mühe; Anstrengung; Bemühung 2C5
e.g. /ˌiːˈdʒiː/ z. B. *(zum Beispiel)* II
egg /eg/ Ei I
eight /eɪt/ acht I
either … or … /ˌaɪðəˈɔː/ entweder … oder … III
elbow /ˈelbəʊ/ Ell(en)bogen III
° elder /ˈeldə/ Ältere/r; ältere(r, s) 1C5
° elderly /ˈeldəli/ ältere(r, s) 1C5
° electrical /ɪˈlektrɪk(ə)l/ elektrisch; Elekto- 4B5
electronic /ˌelekˈtrɒnɪk/ elektronisch IV
elephant /ˈelɪfənt/ Elefant I
eleven /ɪˈlev(ə)n/ elf I
to eliminate /ɪˈlɪmɪneɪt/ beseitigen; ausschließen 2B3
else /els/ sonst (noch) II
° elsewhere /elsˈweə/ woanders; anderswo 1C5
° to embark on /ɪmˈbɑːkˌɒn/ in Angriff nehmen; anfangen 3B2
embarrassed /ɪmˈbærəst/ verlegen; peinlich berührt II
embarrassing /ɪmˈbærəsɪŋ/ peinlich; unangenehm II
to embrace /ɪmˈbreɪs/ umarmen; übernehmen; aufgreifen 2O2
to emigrate /ˈemɪgreɪt/ auswandern; emigrieren IV
emo /ˈiːməʊ/ *Anhänger/in des Emo, einer Subkultur mit Wurzeln im Hardcore-Punk* 3A2
emotion /ɪˈməʊʃ(ə)n/ Gefühl; Emotion II
emotional /ɪˈməʊʃ(ə)nəl/ emotional; gefühlvoll II
emotional state /ɪˌməʊʃ(ə)nəlˈsteɪt/ Gefühlszustand 1C4
emotionless /ɪˈməʊʃ(ə)nləs/ gefühllos; ausdruckslos; gleichgültig 1C5
° emphasis /ˈemfəsɪs/ Betonung; Schwerpunkt 1O2
to emphasize /ˈemfəsaɪz/ betonen; hervorheben IV
employee /ɪmˈplɔɪiː/ Angestellte/r; Mitarbeiter/in; Beschäftigte/r IV
employer /ɪmˈplɔɪə/ Arbeitgeber/in 5B4
° employment /ɪmˈplɔɪmənt/ Beschäftigung; Anstellung; Tätigkeit 5O3
empty /ˈempti/ leer; frei III
° to enable /ɪnˈeɪb(ə)l/ ermöglichen 5P1
° to enclose /ɪnˈkləʊz/ einschließen; beifügen 5B6
to encourage /ɪnˈkʌrɪdʒ/ ermutigen; ermuntern; dazu bewegen IV
end /end/ Ende; Schluss II
in the end /ɪnˌðiˈend/ letzten Endes; schließlich; zum Schluss I
to end /end/ beenden; zu Ende bringen; enden II
° to end up /ˌendˈʌp/ enden 1A2
ending /ˈendɪŋ/ Ende; Schluss III
endorsement /ɪnˈdɔːsmənt/ Billigung; Befürwortung; Unterstützung 2B3
enemy /ˈenəmi/ Feind/in III
° energetic /ˌenəˈdʒetɪk/ voller Energie 5B3
energy *(no pl)* /ˈenədʒi/ Energie; Kraft II
energy-saving /ˈenədʒiˌseɪvɪŋ/ energiesparend 4B5
engineer /ˌendʒɪˈnɪə/ Ingenieur/in IV
English /ˈɪŋglɪʃ/ Englisch; englisch I
English-speaking /ˈɪŋglɪʃˌspiːkɪŋ/ englischsprachig II
to enhance /ɪnˈhɑːns/ verbessern; hervorheben IV
to enjoy /ɪnˈdʒɔɪ/ genießen I; gefallen IV
enjoyable /ɪnˈdʒɔɪəb(ə)l/ angenehm; nett; unterhaltsam III
enormous /ɪˈnɔːməs/ enorm; riesig; gewaltig 3C3, 5A4
enough /ɪˈnʌf/ genügend; ausreichend; genug I
to ensure /ɪnˈʃɔː/ sicherstellen; garantieren 2B4
to enter /ˈentə/ eingeben; eintragen; (herein)kommen IV
to entertain /ˌentəˈteɪn/ unterhalten 5A2
entertaining /ˌentəˈteɪnɪŋ/ unterhaltsam II
entertainment /ˌentəˈteɪnmənt/ Unterhaltung II
enthusiastic /ɪnˌθjuːziˈæstɪk/ enthusiastisch; begeistert II
entire /ɪnˈtaɪə/ gesamt; ganz; vollständig 3A2, 4B2
entirely /ɪnˈtaɪəli/ ganz; total; völlig 1C5
entry /ˈentri/ Eintrag 2B2, 4B1
environment *(no pl)* /ɪnˈvaɪrənmənt/ Umwelt II

Words — English-German dictionary

environmental /ɪnˌvaɪrən'ment(ə)l/ Umwelt-; die Umwelt betreffend; ökologisch III
environmentally conscious /ɪnˌvaɪrənˌment(ə)li 'kɒnʃəs/ umweltbewusst 4B5
equality (no pl) /ɪ'kwɒləti/ Gleichberechtigung; Gleichheit IV
° **equivalent** /ɪ'kwɪvələnt/ Entsprechung; Gegenstück 5B6
° **error** /'erə/ Fehler; Irrtum 2O4
° **to escalate** /'eskəleɪt/ eskalieren; sich ausweiten; stark zunehmen 2C3
escalator /'eskəˌleɪtə/ Rolltreppe III
to escape /ɪ'skeɪp/ fliehen; flüchten III
especially /ɪ'speʃ(ə)li/ besonders; insbesondere IV
° **essay** /'eseɪ/ Aufsatz 5O1
essential /ɪ'senʃ(ə)l/ unverzichtbar; wesentlich 1C1, 2B3, 5A2
to establish /ɪ'stæblɪʃ/ gründen; einführen; schaffen 1B9
° **to estimate** /'estɪmeɪt/ (ein)schätzen 2P5
° **eternity** (no pl) /ɪ'tɜ:nəti/ Ewigkeit 5O2
ethnic /'eθnɪk/ ethnisch; Volks- IV
° **Europe** /'jʊərəp/ Europa 4B2
European /ˌjʊərə'pi:ən/ Europäer/in; europäisch IV
  ° **the European Union** /ðə ˌjʊərəˌpi:ən 'ju:niən/ die Europäische Union 5P1
even /'i:v(ə)n/ selbst; sogar I; noch III
  even though /ˌi:v(ə)n 'ðəʊ/ obwohl IV
evening /'i:vnɪŋ/ Abend I
  in the evening /ˌɪn ðɪ 'i:vnɪŋ/ am Abend I
eventually /ɪ'ventʃuəli/ schließlich IV
ever /'evə/ jemals II
  ° **ever-changing** /ˌevə 'tʃeɪndʒɪŋ/ ständig wechselnd 5B3
  ever since /ˌevə 'sɪns/ seitdem IV
every /'evri/ jede(r, s) I
everybody /'evriˌbɒdi/ alle; jede/r I
° **everyday life** /ˌevriˌdeɪ 'laɪf/ Alltagsleben 4P1
everyone /'evriˌwʌn/ jede/r; alle zusammen II
everything /'evriθɪŋ/ alles I
everywhere /'evriˌweə/ überall I
° **evidently** /'evɪd(ə)ntli/ (ganz) offensichtlich 2P8
evil /'i:v(ə)l/ Übel; das Böse; böse IV
to evoke /ɪ'vəʊk/ hervorrufen IV
exactly /ɪg'zæktli/ genau I
° **to exaggerate** /ɪg'zædʒəreɪt/ übertreiben IV
° **exaggeration** /ɪgˌzædʒə'reɪʃ(ə)n/ Übertreibung 3A3
exam /ɪg'zæm/ Prüfung I
° **examination** /ɪgˌzæmɪ'neɪʃ(ə)n/ Prüfung; Untersuchung 3O4
example /ɪg'zɑ:mp(ə)l/ Beispiel I
excellent /'eksələnt/ ausgezeichnet II
except /ɪk'sept/ außer III
  ° **except for ...** /ɪk'sept fɔ:/ außer ...; bis auf ... 5P6
excessive /ɪk'sesɪv/ übermäßig 2B5, 4B2
exchange /ɪks'tʃeɪndʒ/ (Aus)tausch III
to exchange /ɪks'tʃeɪndʒ/ austauschen; umtauschen; wechseln IV
excited /ɪk'saɪtɪd/ aufgeregt I
exciting /ɪk'saɪtɪŋ/ aufregend; spannend I
exclamation /ˌeksklə'meɪʃ(ə)n/ Ausruf 4B7
° **to exclude** /ɪk'sklu:d/ ausschließen 1P4
° **excuse** /ɪk'skju:s/ Entschuldigung; Grund; Ausrede 5O1
to execute /'eksɪˌkju:t/ hinrichten III
exercise /'eksəsaɪz/ Übung; Aufgabe; Bewegung 3C1
  exercise book /'eksəsaɪz ˌbʊk/ Heft I
exhausted /ɪg'zɔ:stɪd/ erschöpft; aufgebraucht III
exhausting /ɪg'zɔ:stɪŋ/ anstrengend III
to exist /ɪg'zɪst/ existieren; bestehen; leben; vorkommen 3A5
to expect /ɪk'spekt/ erwarten; rechnen III
expectation /ˌekspek'teɪʃ(ə)n/ Erwartung IV
° **expenses** (onyl pl) /ɪk'spensɪz/ Spesen 1B7
expensive /ɪk'spensɪv/ teuer I
experience (no pl) /ɪk'spɪəriəns/ Erfahrung; Erlebnis I
to experience /ɪk'spɪəriəns/ erleben; erfahren; stoßen auf IV
° **to experiment (with sth)** /ɪk'sperɪˌment wɪð/ (mit etw) experimentieren; (etw) ausprobieren 3C3
to explain (sth to sb) /ɪk'spleɪn/ (jdm etw) erklären I
explanation /ˌeksplə'neɪʃ(ə)n/ Erklärung; Erläuterung 5B8
° **to explode** /ɪk'spləʊd/ explodieren; sprengen 1C5
to exploit /ɪk'splɔɪt/ ausbeuten; (aus)nutzen 2B3
to explore /ɪk'splɔ:/ erforschen; untersuchen II
to express /ɪk'spres/ ausdrücken; aussprechen II
expression /ɪk'spreʃ(ə)n/ Ausdruck; Äußerung III
° **ext. (= exterior)** /ɪk'stɪəriə/ Außenseite; Außenaufnahme 1C7
extent (no pl) /ɪk'stent/ Größe; Ausdehnung; Umfang; Ausmaß 1A3
extract /'ekstrækt/ Auszug 1B7, 2C2, 3B3

extracurricular /ˌekstrəkə'rɪkjʊlə/ außerhalb des Stundenplans; Wahl- III
extraordinary /ɪk'strɔ:d(ə)n(ə)ri/ außerordentlich; ungewöhnlich 5C2
extremely /ɪk'stri:mli/ äußerst; höchst 3A2
eye /aɪ/ Auge I
  eye contact (no pl) /'aɪ ˌkɒntækt/ Blickkontakt 1C3, 3C5

F

fabulous /'fæbjʊləs/ fabelhaft; sagenhaft II
face /feɪs/ Gesicht I
to face sth /feɪs/ sich etw gegenübersehen; etw gegenüberstehen IV
facial expression /ˌfeɪʃ(ə)l ɪk'spreʃ(ə)n/ Gesichtsausdruck 1C3, 3B9
facilities (only pl) /fə'sɪlətiz/ Einrichtungen; Anlagen 4B5, 5A2
fact /fækt/ Wirklichkeit; Tatsache II
° **faction** /'fækʃ(ə)n/ (Splitter)gruppe; Fraktion 3B4
factory /'fæktri/ Fabrik IV
to fail /feɪl/ versagen; scheitern; missglücken III
failure (no pl) /'feɪljə/ Scheitern 1C10
  ° **failure** (no pl): Unterlassung 1O2
° **fair** /feə/ Jahrmarkt; Messe 5PP2
fairly /'feəli/ ziemlich; recht 1B5
to fall (irr) /fɔ:l/ (um)fallen; stürzen I
to fall asleep /ˌfɔ:l ə'sli:p/ einschlafen III
to fall down /ˌfɔ:l 'daʊn/ hin(unter)fallen; (ein)stürzen IV
to fall in love (with sb) /ˌfɔ:l ɪn 'lʌv wɪð/ sich (in jdn) verlieben III
to fall victim to sb/sth /ˌfɔ:l 'vɪktɪm tʊ/ jdm/etw zum Opfer fallen 2B2
false /fɔ:ls/ falsch 1B5, 4C1
fame (no pl) /feɪm/ Ruhm 2C1
familiar /fə'mɪliə/ vertraut; vertraulich 1A2
family /'fæm(ə)li/ Familie I
famous /'feɪməs/ berühmt II
° **fanatical** /fə'nætɪk(ə)l/ fanatisch; besessen; unbelehrbar 3A2
fantastic (informal) /fæn'tæstɪk/ fantastisch I
far /fɑ:/ weit III
fare /feə/ (Fahr)preis III
farm /fɑ:m/ Bauernhof I
° **farmhouse** /'fɑ:mˌhaʊs/ Bauernhaus 4B5
° **fascinated (by/with)** /'fæsɪneɪtɪd baɪ/ wɪð/ fasziniert (von) 4P8
fascinating /'fæsɪneɪtɪŋ/ faszinierend I
fashion /'fæʃ(ə)n/ Mode III
° **fashionista** /ˌfæʃə'ni:stə/ *sehr modebewusste Frau* 2C3
fast /fɑ:st/ schnell II

English-German dictionary

father /ˈfɑːðə/ Vater I
fault /fɔːlt/ Schuld; Fehler III
favourite /ˈfeɪv(ə)rət/ Lieblings- I
fear (no pl) /fɪə/ Angst; Furcht; Befürchtung IV
to **fear** /fɪə/ (be)fürchten 1B2
feature /ˈfiːtʃə/ Merkmal; Kennzeichen; Besonderheit IV
° **featuring** ... /ˈfiːtʃərɪŋ/ zeigt an, welcher Künstler/welche Künstlerin in einem Film, Lied, Album usw. (noch) vorkommt 1B1
February /ˈfebruəri/ Februar I
fee /fiː/ Gebühr; Beitrag; Entgelt III
to **feed** (irr) /fiːd/ (zu) essen geben; füttern I
to **feel** (irr) /fiːl/ (sich) fühlen; halten von II
to **feel like doing sth** /ˌfiːl ˈlaɪk ˈduːɪŋ/ Lust haben, etw zu tun III
to **feel lost** /ˌfiːl ˈlɒst/ sich verloren fühlen III
to **feel sick** /ˌfiːl ˈsɪk/ schlecht sein; sich schlecht fühlen III
to **feel sorry** /ˌfiːl ˈsɒri/ bedauern; leidtun III
to **feel up to sth** /ˌfiːl ˈʌp tə/ sich etw gewachsen fühlen; Lust haben auf IV
feeling /ˈfiːlɪŋ/ Gefühl I; Meinung III
° **female** /ˈfiːmeɪl/ weiblich 5PP2
festival /ˈfestɪv(ə)l/ Fest II
fiction (no pl) /ˈfɪkʃ(ə)n/ Erzählliteratur 1C8
field /fiːld/ Wiese; Feld; Spielfeld IV
° field: hier: Gebiet; Bereich 2O4
° **field size** /ˈfiːld saɪz/ Einstellungsgröße 2C4
fight /faɪt/ Kampf; Streit III
to **fight** (irr) /faɪt/ (be)kämpfen II
figure /ˈfɪɡə/ Gestalt; Figur; Zahl, Wert IV
file /faɪl/ (Akten)ordner; Unterlagen; Datei III
to **fill in** /ˌfɪl ˈɪn/ (aus)füllen; eintragen II
° **final** /ˈfaɪn(ə)l/ letzte(r, s); End-; entscheidend; endgültig 1P3
finally /ˈfaɪn(ə)li/ schließlich; endlich I
° **finances** (only pl) /ˈfaɪnænsɪz/ Finanzen; Finanzlage 5B2
to **find** (irr) /faɪnd/ finden I
to **find out** /ˌfaɪnd ˈaʊt/ herausfinden II
finding /ˈfaɪndɪŋ/ Entdeckung; Ergebnis 1B8
fine /faɪn/ in Ordnung; gut III
to **finish** /ˈfɪnɪʃ/ (be)enden; aufhören I; abschließen II
° **Finnish** /ˈfɪnɪʃ/ Finnisch; finnisch 4C4
fire /ˈfaɪə/ Feuer; Brand IV
fireworks (pl) /ˈfaɪəˌwɜːks/ Feuerwerk II
first /fɜːst/ erste(r, s) I; zuerst; als Erstes II

° **first-hand/firsthand** /ˌfɜːstˈhænd/ aus erster Hand 4B5
firstly /ˈfɜːstli/ erstens III
fish (pl **fish** or **fishes**) /fɪʃ, fɪʃ, fɪʃɪz/ Fisch I
fish and chips (no pl, BE) /ˌfɪʃ ən ˈtʃɪps/ fritierter Fisch mit Pommes frites III
° **fist** /fɪst/ Faust 1P3
to **fit** /fɪt/ passen I
to **fit in** /ˌfɪt ˈɪn/ dazupassen 3A5
to **fit the bill** /ˌfɪt ðə ˈbɪl/ der/die/ das Richtige sein 1A2
five /faɪv/ fünf I
° **fixated (on)** /fɪkˈseɪtɪd ɒn/ fixiert (auf) 2C5
° **fixation** /fɪkˈseɪʃ(ə)n/ Fixierung 2C3
flat (BE) /flæt/ (Etagen)wohnung; Mietwohnung III
flat /flæt/ flach; eben IV
flatmate /ˈflætmeɪt/ Mitbewohner/ -in 2B2
flavour /ˈfleɪvə/ (Wohl)geschmack 4A4
° to **flick out** /ˌflɪk ˈaʊt/ (her)ausfahren 1B7
flight /flaɪt/ Flug III
° **float** /fləʊt/ Floß 3B4
floor /flɔː/ Boden I; Stock(werk) II
to **sweep the floor** /ˌswiːp ðə ˈflɔː/ den Boden fegen I
flow chart /ˈfləʊ tʃɑːt/ Flussdiagramm 4B4
flower /ˈflaʊə/ Blume I
° **fluent** /ˈfluːənt/ fließend; flüssig 5P6
fluffy /ˈflʌfi/ flaumig (weich); flauschig 2B3
to **fly** (irr) /flaɪ/ fliegen I
to **focus** /ˈfəʊkəs/ sich konzentrieren; fokussieren II
° **focus(s)ed** /ˈfəʊkəst/ fokussiert; konzentriert 1P8
to **fold** /fəʊld/ (zusammen)falten; verschränken 5O2
to **follow** /ˈfɒləʊ/ folgen I
° to **follow in sb's footsteps** /ˌfɒləʊ ɪn ˌsʌmbədiz ˈfʊtˌsteps/ in jds Fußstapfen treten 4P1
° to **follow sth up with sth** /ˌfɒləʊ ˈʌp wɪð/ etw etw folgen lassen 5B6
following /ˈfɒləʊɪŋ/ folgende(r, s) III
° **follow-up** /ˈfɒləʊ ˌʌp/ Fortsetzung(s-); Nach-; Anschluss- 3C5
font /fɒnt/ Schriftart 5B4
food (no pl) /fuːd/ Essen; Nahrung; Futter I
foot (pl **feet**) /fʊt, fiːt/ Fuß I
football /ˈfʊtˌbɔːl/ Fußball I
football (= American football) (AE) /ˈfʊtˌbɔːl, əˌmerɪkən ˈfʊtˌbɔːl/ Football (in Amerika aus dem Rugby entwickelte Ballsportart) IV
for /fɔː/ für I; seit II
for example /fər ɪɡˈzɑːmp(ə)l/ zum Beispiel I

for free (informal) /fə ˈfriː/ gratis; umsonst II
° **for God's sake** (informal) /fə ˌɡɒdz ˈseɪk/ um Himmels willen 5O3
° **for life** /fə ˈlaɪf/ lebenslang 5A2
° **for that matter** /fə ˈðæt ˌmætə/ eigentlich 3B4
to **force** /fɔːs/ zwingen IV
° **foreground** /ˈfɔːˌɡraʊnd/ Vordergrund; Mittelpunkt III
foreign /ˈfɒrɪn/ ausländisch; fremd IV
forest /ˈfɒrɪst/ Wald II
forever /fərˈevə/ ewig; ständig II
to **forget** (irr) /fəˈɡet/ vergessen I
to **forget about sth/sb** /fəˈɡet əˌbaʊt/ etw/jdn vergessen III
fork /fɔːk/ Gabel I
form /fɔːm/ Formular 5B1
form (BE) /fɔːm/ Klasse; Jahrgangsstufe III
to **form** /fɔːm/ formen; bilden II
formal /ˈfɔːm(ə)l/ formell; förmlich; offiziell III
former /ˈfɔːmə/ ehemalige(r, s); frühere(r, s) IV
to **formulate** /ˈfɔːmjʊleɪt/ ausarbeiten; formulieren 2A4
fortune (no pl) /ˈfɔːtʃən/ Vermögen; Schicksal; Glück; Reichtum 2C5
° **forward(s)** /ˈfɔːwədz/ nach vorn(e); weiter; vorn(e) 1B7
fossil fuel /ˌfɒs(ə)l ˈfjuːəl/ fossiler Brennstoff 4B4
foundation /faʊnˈdeɪʃ(ə)n/ Fundament; Basis; Stiftung 5C2
° **fountain pen** /ˈfaʊntɪn ˌpen/ Füllfederhalter 1C7
four /fɔː/ vier I
France /frɑːns/ Frankreich III
° **frayed** /freɪd/ ausgefranst 1B6
free /friː/ frei IV
free time /ˌfriː ˈtaɪm/ Freizeit I
freedom (no pl) /ˈfriːdəm/ Freiheit IV
° to **freeze** (irr) /friːz/ gefrieren; erstarren 3B4
French /frentʃ/ Französisch I; Französisch(-); französisch III
frequent /ˈfriːkwənt/ häufig; regelmäßig 1C10
fresh /freʃ/ neu; ungebraucht; frisch IV
Friday /ˈfraɪdeɪ/ Freitag I
fridge (informal) /frɪdʒ/ Kühlschrank I
friend /frend/ Freund/in I
friendliness (no pl) /ˈfrendlinəs/ Freundlichkeit 5B2
friendly /ˈfrendli/ freundlich I
° **friendship** /ˈfrendʃɪp/ Freundschaft 2O3
frightened /ˈfraɪt(ə)nd/ verängstigt II
frightening /ˈfraɪt(ə)nɪŋ/ Furcht erregend; beängstigend IV
from /frɒm/ von; aus I; vor III

W

Words — English-German dictionary

fruit (no pl) /fruːt/ Frucht; Obst I
frustrated /frʌˈstreɪtɪd/ frustriert II
° **fuel** /ˈfjuːəl/ Brennstoff; Benzin; Kraftstoff 4P6
to fulfil /fʊlˈfɪl/ erfüllen; nachkommen; verwirklichen 2A1, 4C5
full /fʊl/ voll; überfüllt II
full board (no pl) /ˌfʊl ˈbɔːd/ (mit) Vollpension 4B5, 5A2
fun (no pl) /fʌn/ Spaß I
to be fun /ˌbiː ˈfʌn/ Spaß machen I
° **to function** /ˈfʌŋkʃ(ə)n/ funktionieren 2P5
funny /ˈfʌni/ lustig; witzig; komisch I
° **furious** /ˈfjʊəriəs/ (sehr) wütend; heftig; stürmisch 1P4
furniture (no pl) /ˈfɜːnɪtʃə/ Möbel I
° **to furrow one's brow** /ˌfʌrəʊ wʌnz ˈbraʊ/ die Stirn runzeln 1B9
further /ˈfɜːðə/ weiter(e, er, es); noch mehr; (noch) weiter 2C5, 4B4
° **furthermore** /ˈfɜːðəˌmɔː/ außerdem; ferner 5B6
future /ˈfjuːtʃə/ zukünftig 1C5, 4C7; Zukunft II
° **futuristic** /ˌfjuːtʃəˈrɪstɪk/ futuristisch 1C5

G

to gain /ɡeɪn/ bekommen; erreichen; gewinnen 3C3, 4B2; Nutzen ziehen 5A1
° **to gallop** /ˈɡæləp/ galoppieren 1P3
game /ɡeɪm/ Spiel I
garden /ˈɡɑːd(ə)n/ Garten I
° **gardener** /ˈɡɑːd(ə)nə/ Gärtner/in; Gartenarbeiter/in 5P5
° **to garnish** /ˈɡɑːnɪʃ/ garnieren 1B6
° **gas oven** /ˈɡæsˌʌv(ə)n/ Gasherd 4B5
gas station (AE = **petrol station** BE) /ˈɡæsˌsteɪʃ(ə)n/ Tankstelle IV
° **to gather** /ˈɡæðə/ (sich ver)sammeln 1P7
° **to gawk** (informal) /ɡɔːk/ glotzen 3B4
gay /ɡeɪ/ Homosexuelle(r); Schwule(r); homosexuell; schwul 1B2
° **Gay-Straight Alliance** /ˌɡeɪˌstreɪt əˈlaɪəns/ Bündnis von Menschen unterschiedlicher sexueller Orientierung 1B7
GCSE (= General Certificate of Secondary Education) /ˌdʒiː siː es ˈiː/ Abschlussprüfung der Sekundarstufe 1 4B1
° **gee** (informal, AE) /dʒiː/ Wahnsinn; wow 1O3
geek (informal) /ɡiːk/ Computerfreak 3A2
gender /ˈdʒendə/ Geschlecht(sidentität) 2B5
general /ˈdʒen(ə)rəl/ allgemein; generell IV

generally /ˈdʒen(ə)rəli/ normalerweise; im Allgemeinen; allgemein; generell 4C4
generous /ˈdʒenərəs/ großzügig; freigebig III
° **genius** /ˈdʒiːniəs/ Genie; Genialität 5P6
geography /dʒiˈɒɡrəfi/ Erdkunde; Geografie I
German /ˈdʒɜːmən/ Deutsche/r; deutsch; Deutsch(unterricht) I
gesture /ˈdʒestʃə/ Handbewegung; Geste 3C5
to gesture /ˈdʒestʃə/ deuten 1C3
to get (irr) /ɡet/ erhalten; bekommen; holen I; werden; geraten II; kapieren 3C1
° **to get along (with sb)** /ˌɡet əˈlɒŋ wɪð/ sich (mit jdm) verstehen 2B5
to get away /ˌɡet əˈweɪ/ fortkommen; flüchten I
to get back /ˌɡet ˈbæk/ zurückkommen I
to get dressed /ˌɡet ˈdrest/ sich anziehen I
to get into /ˌɡet ˌɪntə/ einsteigen in II
to get in touch (with sb) /ˌɡet ɪn ˈtʌtʃ wɪð/ (mit jdm) in Kontakt treten 5C2
to get lost /ˌɡet ˈlɒst/ sich verirren; sich verlaufen II
to get married /ˌɡet ˈmærɪd/ heiraten III
to get off /ˌɡet ˈɒf/ aussteigen; runterkommen II
to get on (with sb) /ˌɡet ˈɒn wɪð/ sich (mit jdm) verstehen III
° **to get over** /ˌɡet ˈəʊvə/ hinter sich bringen 3B7
to get scared /ˌɡet ˈskeəd/ sich (anfangen zu) fürchten II
to get to /ˌɡet tə/ erreichen I
° **to get to do sth** /ˌɡet tə ˈduː/ die Möglichkeit haben, etw zu tun 3A2
to get to know sb /ˌɡet tə ˈnəʊ/ jdn kennenlernen III
to get up /ˌɡet ˈʌp/ aufstehen I
to get upset /ˌɡet ʌpˈset/ sich aufregen IV
to get used to /ˌɡet ˈjuːst tə/ sich gewöhnen an I
getaway (informal) /ˈɡetəˌweɪ/ Trip; Ausflug 4B1
ghost /ɡəʊst/ Geist; Gespenst I
° **to giggle** /ˈɡɪɡ(ə)l/ kichern 1B6
° **ginormous** (informal, BE) /dʒaɪˈnɔːməs/ enorm 1O4
girl /ɡɜːl/ Mädchen I
° **girlfriend** /ˈɡɜːlˌfrend/ Freundin 1B7
to give (irr) /ɡɪv/ geben I
to give in /ˌɡɪv ˈɪn/ nachgeben; aufgeben 3C2
° **to give sb shit** (informal) /ˌɡɪv ˌsʌmbədi ˈʃɪt/ jdm das Leben zur Hölle machen 1B7

to give up /ˌɡɪv ˈʌp/ aufgeben; resignieren II
giver /ˈɡɪvə/ Geber/in; Spender/in 1C5
° **glad** /ɡlæd/ glücklich; dankbar; froh III
° **glance** /ɡlɑːns/ Blick 1B8
° **to glance** /ɡlɑːns/ (flüchtig) schauen 1B7
° **to glare** /ɡleə/ (an)starren 1C7
glass (no pl) /ɡlɑːs/ Glas II
° **globalization** (no pl) /ˌɡləʊbəlaɪˈzeɪʃ(ə)n/ Glaobalisierung 5PP2
° **gloomy** /ˈɡluːmi/ trostlos; düster 1O4
° **to glower at** /ˈɡlaʊə/ zornig anstarren 1B9
glue (no pl) /ɡluː/ Klebstoff I
to glue /ɡluː/ kleben 4B4
to go (irr) /ɡəʊ/ gehen; fahren I
to go camping /ˌɡəʊ ˈkæmpɪŋ/ zelten gehen I
° **to go down well/badly (with sb)** /ˌɡəʊ ˌdaʊn ˈwel/ˈbædli wɪð/ (bei jdm) gut/schlecht ankommen 3P1
to go for a walk /ˌɡəʊ fər ə ˈwɔːk/ einen Spaziergang machen III
to go on /ˌɡəʊ ˈɒn/ weitergehen; weitermachen I; passieren II
° **to go on a hike** /ˌɡəʊ ˌɒn ə ˈhaɪk/ wandern gehen 4B5
to go on a tour /ˌɡəʊ ˌɒn ə ˈtʊə/ eine Tour machen II
to go on a trip /ˌɡəʊ ˌɒn ə ˈtrɪp/ einen Ausflug/eine Reise machen II
to go on holiday /ˌɡəʊ ɒn ˈhɒlədeɪ/ in Urlaub gehen/fahren I
to go shopping /ˌɡəʊ ˈʃɒpɪŋ/ einkaufen gehen I
to go skiing /ˌɡəʊ ˈskiːɪŋ/ Ski fahren gehen III
to go surfing /ˌɡəʊ ˈsɜːfɪŋ/ surfen gehen I
to go swimming /ˌɡəʊ ˈswɪmɪŋ/ schwimmen gehen I
to go to bed /ˌɡəʊ tə ˈbed/ ins Bett gehen I
to go to the seaside /ˌɡəʊ tə ðə ˈsiːˌsaɪd/ ans Meer fahren I
to go walking /ˌɡəʊ ˈwɔːkɪŋ/ wandern; spazieren gehen I
to go with /ˌɡəʊ wɪð/ zu ... gehören; zu ... passen III
° **to go with the flow** (informal) /ˌɡəʊ wɪð ðə ˈfləʊ/ mit dem Strom schwimmen 3A1
to go wrong /ˌɡəʊ ˈrɒŋ/ schiefgehen III
° **to give/get the go-ahead** /ˌɡɪv/ˌɡet ðə ˈɡəʊəˌhed/ grünes Licht geben/erhalten II
goal /ɡəʊl/ Ziel; Tor 4B5, 5B6
° **God** /ɡɒd/ Gott 1B2
° **golf course** /ˈɡɒlf kɔːs/ Golfplatz 4B2
° **gonna** (= going to) (informal) /ˈɡʌnə, ˈɡəʊɪŋ tə/ werden 1B2

English-German dictionary — Words — W

good /gʊd/ gut I
  to **be good at** /ˌbiː ˈgʊd ət/ gut in ... sein I
° **good-looking** /ˌgʊd ˈlʊkɪŋ/ gut aussehend 3A2
goods (only pl) /gʊdz/ Waren; Güter 2C5
gossip (no pl) /ˈgɒsɪp/ Klatsch(-); Tratsch 2C3
to **gossip** /ˈgɒsɪp/ tratschen; schlecht reden 3A2
Goth /gɒθ/ Anhänger/in der Gothic-Kultur 3A2
° **gotta** (= have got to) (informal) /ˈgɒtə, həv ˈgɒt tə/ müssen 3B7
government /ˈgʌvənmənt/ Regierung(s-) III
grade /greɪd/ Note IV
grade (AE) /greɪd/ Klasse IV
° **graduate** /ˈgrædʒuət/ Absolvent/in (einer [Hoch]schule) 5O3
° **graduation** (no pl) /ˌgrædʒuˈeɪʃ(ə)n/ (Studien)abschluss; Abschlussfeier 5B6
grandfather /ˈgræn,fɑːðə/ Großvater I
grandmother /ˈgræn,mʌðə/ Großmutter I
grandparents (pl) /ˈgræn,peərənts/ Großeltern I
° to **grant** /grɑːnt/ gewähren 1C7
graphic organizer /ˌgræfɪk ˈɔːgəˌnaɪzə/ grafische Darstellungsform 4B3
° **grateful** /ˈgreɪtf(ə)l/ dankbar 5P6
great /greɪt/ groß; riesig; großartig; wunderbar I
green /griːn/ grün I
greeting /ˈgriːtɪŋ/ Begrüßung 3C5
grey /greɪ/ grau I
grid /grɪd/ Gitter(netz); Tabelle II
° to **groan** /grəʊn/ (auf)stöhnen; ächzen 1B7
ground /graʊnd/ (Erd)boden; Erde; Gelände IV
group /gruːp/ Gruppe I
to **grow** (irr) /grəʊ/ wachsen; gedeihen; anbauen III
° to **guarantee** /ˌgærənˈtiː/ garantieren 1C5
guess /ges/ Vermutung; Annahme I
to **guess** /ges/ (er)raten I; annehmen II
guest /gest/ Gast I
guidance /ˈgaɪd(ə)ns/ Beratung; (An)leitung; Führung 1C10
guide /gaɪd/ Führer/in IV
  guide: Leitfaden; Ratgeber 2B3
  ° guide: Richtschnur 5P6
° **guidebook** /ˈgaɪd,bʊk/ Reiseführer 4P1
guidelines (only pl) /ˈgaɪd,laɪnz/ Richtlinien; Leitlinien 1C10, 2A4
° **guilt-free** /ˌgɪltˈfriː/ ohne schlechtes Gewissen 4B5
guitar /gɪˈtɑː/ Gitarre III

gun /gʌn/ (Schuss)waffe; Pistole; Gewehr IV
guy (informal) /gaɪ/ Kerl; Typ; Bursche 1A2, 3B4
  guys (only pl, informal) /gaɪz/ Leute 4B1
gym /dʒɪm/ Turnhalle I

H

habit /ˈhæbɪt/ Gewohnheit 3C3
° to **hack** /hæk/ hacken; illegal eindringen/beschaffen 1O3
had better do sth /həd ˌbetə ˈduː ˌsʌmθɪŋ/ drückt aus, dass jd etw tun soll 1B6
hair (no pl) /heə/ Haare I
° **haircut** /ˈheə,kʌt/ Haarschnitt; Frisur 1B9
half (pl halves) /hɑːf, hɑːvz/ Hälfte 1B2
half /hɑːf/ halb; dreißig Minuten I
  half an hour /ˌhɑːf ən ˈaʊə/ eine halbe Stunde I
  half board (no pl) /ˌhɑːf ˈbɔːd/ Halbpension(-) 4B5
  half past (seven) /ˌhɑːf pɑːst ˈsev(ə)n/ halb (acht) I
hall /hɔːl/ Korridor; Halle; Aula IV
° **hallway** /ˈhɔːl,weɪ/ Korridor; Diele; Flur 1B2
ham /hæm/ Schinken I
hand /hænd/ Hand I
° to **hand in** /ˌhænd ˈɪn/ einreichen; abgeben 5O1
° **handy** /ˈhændi/ praktisch; nützlich; griffbereit 4P9
° to **hang back** (irr) /ˌhæŋ ˈbæk/ sich zurückhalten; zurückbleiben 1B9
  to **hang out with sb** (informal) /ˌhæŋ ˈaʊt wɪð/ Zeit mit jdm verbringen 1A2
  to **hang up** (irr) /ˌhæŋ ˈʌp/ aufhängen; auflegen 4O3
to **happen** /ˈhæpən/ geschehen; passieren I
happiness (no pl) /ˈhæpinəs/ Glück; Zufriedenheit; Fröhlichkeit IV
happy /ˈhæpi/ glücklich; zufrieden; fröhlich I
° to **harass** /həˈræs/ schikanieren; belästigen 1B9
harbor (AE = **harbour** BE) /ˈhɑːbər/ Hafen IV
hard /hɑːd/ hart; schwer; schwierig; fest; kräftig II
  hard skills /ˌhɑːd ˈskɪlz/ Hard Skills (rein fachliche Qualifikation) 5B2
° **hard-ass** (informal) /ˈhɑːdæs/ abwertende Bezeichnung für eine autoritäre Person 1B9
° **hard-jawed** /ˌhɑːd ˈdʒɔːd/ eisern 1P3
hardly /ˈhɑːdli/ kaum II
° **hardship** /ˈhɑːdʃɪp/ Not; Elend; Härte 1P9
° **hard-working** /ˌhɑːd ˈwɜːkɪŋ/ fleißig 5O3

harm (no pl) /hɑːm/ Schaden; Verletzung 3C3
° **harmonious** /hɑːˈməʊniəs/ harmonisch 1C5
° to **harvest** /ˈhɑːvɪst/ (ab)ernten 5PP2
hat /hæt/ Hut I
hate /heɪt/ Hass III
to **hate** /heɪt/ hassen; verabscheuen I
  to **hate to do sth** /ˌheɪt tə ˈduː/ äußerst ungern tun II
hateful /ˈheɪtf(ə)l/ hasserfüllt; abscheulich 1B2
to **have** (irr) /hæv/ haben; essen I
  to **have a look** /ˌhæv ə ˈlʊk/ nachsehen; nachschauen II
  to **have a look at ...** /ˌhæv ə ˈlʊk æt/ sich ... ansehen III
  to **have a party** /ˌhæv ə ˈpɑːti/ eine Party geben II
  to **have/take a shower** /ˌhæv, ˌteɪk ə ˈʃaʊə/ sich duschen II
  to **have breakfast** /ˌhæv ˈbrekfəst/ frühstücken I
  to **have got** /ˌhæv ˈgɒt/ haben I
  to **have lunch** /ˌhæv ˈlʌntʃ/ zu Mittag essen I
  ° to **have sb over** /ˌhæv ˌsʌmbədi ˈəʊvə/ jdn zu Besuch haben; jdn zu sich einladen 3C1
  to **have sth done** /ˌhæv ˌsʌmθɪŋ ˈdʌn/ etw tun lassen 5B1
  to **have sth in common (with sb)** /ˌhæv ˌsʌmθɪŋ ɪn ˈkɒmən wɪð/ etw (mit jdm) gemein haben IV
have to (irr) /ˈhæv tə/ müssen I
° **hay fever** /ˈheɪ ˌfiːvə/ Heuschnupfen 4P9
he /hiː/ er I
head /hed/ Kopf I
  ° head: Leiter/in 5B6
° to **head** /hed/ leiten; anführen 4P10
  ° to **head (for/to)** /ˈhed fɔː, tə/ zusteuern (auf); gehen (zu) 3B7
heading /ˈhedɪŋ/ Überschrift; Titel II
headline /ˈhed,laɪn/ Schlagzeile; Überschrift 2B2, 4B2
headmaster /ˌhedˈmɑːstə/ Schulleiter; Rektor; Direktor III
health (no pl) /helθ/ Gesundheit II
healthy /ˈhelθi/ gesund III
to **hear** (irr) /hɪə/ hören I
heart /hɑːt/ Herz III
° **Heat** /hiːt/ britische Illustrierte 5O3
° **heated** /ˈhiːtɪd/ hitzig; heftig 3P10
heavy /ˈhevi/ schwer IV
hello /həˈləʊ/ hallo! I
help /help/ Hilfe II; Aushilfe, Hilfskraft IV
to **help** /help/ helfen I
helpful /ˈhelpf(ə)l/ hilfsbereit; hilfreich; nützlich III
° **helpless** /ˈhelpləs/ hilflos; machtlos 1P4
° **helpline** (BE) /ˈhelp,laɪn/ Notruf; telefonischer Beratungsdienst 3C3

Words — English-German dictionary

her /hɜ:/ ihr(e); ihr; sie I
here /hɪə/ hier I
° **here goes** *(informal)* /ˌhɪə ˈɡəʊz/ los geht's; dann mal los 3B4
here you are /ˌhɪə juˈɑ:/ Hier, bitte!; Bitte schön! I
hero /ˈhɪərəʊ/ Held III
hers /hɜ:z/ ihre(r, s); ihrs II
herself /həˈself/ sich; (sich) selbst III
to **hide** *(irr)* /haɪd/ (sich) verstecken I
high /haɪ/ hoch I
  high street *(BE)* /ˈhaɪ stri:t/ Haupt(einkaufs)straße III
to **highlight** /ˈhaɪˌlaɪt/ hervorheben; markieren III
highly /ˈhaɪli/ hoch-; ausgesprochen; äußerst IV
hike /haɪk/ Wanderung III
  ° **to go on a hike** /ˌɡəʊˌɒn_əˈhaɪk/ wandern gehen 4B5
to **hike** /haɪk/ wandern III
hiking *(no pl)* /ˈhaɪkɪŋ/ Wandern 4B5
hill /hɪl/ Hügel; Berg II
him /hɪm/ ihm; ihn I
himself /hɪmˈself/ sich; (sich) selbst III
° **Hindi** *(no pl)* /ˈhɪndi/ Hindi *(Amtssprache in Indien)* 4C1
to **hire** /ˈhaɪə/ einstellen; beauftragen 5B4
his /hɪz/ sein(e) I; seine(r, s); seins II
Hispanic /hɪˈspænɪk/ Hispano-amerikaner/in; hispanisch IV
historic /hɪˈstɒrɪk/ historisch IV
historical /hɪˈstɒrɪk(ə)l/ geschichtlich; historisch III
history /ˈhɪst(ə)ri/ Geschichte *(als Schulfach)* I
to **hit** *(irr)* /hɪt/ schlagen; treffen; stoßen (gegen) II
  to hit the road *(informal)* /ˌhɪt ðəˈrəʊd/ sich auf den Weg machen 4A1
to **hold** *(irr)* /həʊld/ halten II
  ° **to hold out** /ˌhəʊldˌˈaʊt/ ausstrecken 1O4
holiday /ˈhɒlədeɪ/ Urlaub; Ferien I; Feiertag IV
  on holiday /ɒn ˈhɒlədeɪ/ im Urlaub; in den Ferien I
  to go on holiday /ˌɡəʊˌɒn ˈhɒlədeɪ/ in Urlaub gehen/fahren I
° **Holy crap!** *(informal)* /ˌhəʊli ˈkræp/ (Du) heilige Scheiße! 3B4
at home /æt ˈhəʊm/ zu Hause I
° **homeroom** /ˈhəʊmru:m/ *Planungs-/Registrierungsstunde* 1P3
homework *(no pl)* /ˈhəʊmwɜ:k/ Hausaufgabe(n) I
° **homosexual** /ˌhəʊməʊˈsekʃuəl/ Homosexuelle/r; homosexuell 1B9
° **homosexuality** *(no pl)* /ˌhəʊməʊsekʃuˈælətɪ/ Homosexualität 1P8
honest /ˈɒnɪst/ ehrlich II

° **honestly** /ˈɒnɪstli/ (ganz) ehrlich (gesagt); wirklich 1O4
° **honoured** /ˈɒnəd/ ehrenvoll 1C5
° **hood** /hʊd/ Kapuze; Maske; Haube 1B6
to **hoover** /ˈhu:və/ staubsaugen I
° to **hop** /hɒp/ hüpfen; springen 3B7
hope /həʊp/ Hoffnung III
to **hope** /həʊp/ hoffen I
hopeful /ˈhəʊpf(ə)l/ zuversichtlich IV
hopefully /ˈhəʊpf(ə)li/ hoffnungsvoll; hoffentlich 3C5
° **hopeless** /ˈhəʊpləs/ hoffnungslos 1O4
horrible /ˈhɒrəb(ə)l/ schrecklich II
° **horrific** /hɒˈrɪfɪk/ entsetzlich; schrecklich 3P6
horrified /ˈhɒrɪfaɪd/ entsetzt 3C5
° **horrifying** /ˈhɒrɪˌfaɪɪŋ/ schrecklich; entsetzlich; grauenhaft 3P6
horse /hɔ:s/ Pferd I
  horse-riding *(no pl)* /ˈhɔ:sˌraɪdɪŋ/ Reiten III
hospital /ˈhɒspɪt(ə)l/ Krankenhaus II
host /həʊst/ Gastgeber/in; Moderator/in 1C10; Gast- IV
to **host** /həʊst/ ausrichten; präsentieren; moderieren; als Gast aufnehmen 4C4
hot /hɒt/ heiß I
  ° **hot: scharf** 1A2
° **hot spot** /ˈhɒt spɒt/ Krisenherd; *hier:* angesagter Ort 4B2
hour /ˈaʊə/ Stunde I
house /haʊs/ Haus I
housework *(no pl)* /ˈhaʊsˌwɜ:k/ Hausarbeit 4C4, 5A2
how /haʊ/ wie I
  How are you? /ˌhaʊˈɑ:ju:/ Wie geht es dir/Ihnen/euch? I
  How many ...? /haʊˈmeni/ Wie viele ...? I
  How much ...? /haʊˈmʌtʃ/ Wie viel ...? I
  How much is/are ...? /ˈhaʊˌmʌtʃˌɪz/ɑ:/ Was kostet/kosten ...? I
  How old are you?: Wie alt bist du? I
however /haʊˈevə/ jedoch II
huge /hju:dʒ/ riesig; riesengroß II
human /ˈhju:mən/ Mensch; menschlich II
° **human resources officer** /ˌhju:mən rɪˈzɔ:sɪzˌɒfɪsə/ Personalleiter/in 5O3
° to **humiliate** /hju:ˈmɪlieɪt/ demütigen; erniedrigen; blamieren 3O1
° **humiliating** /hju:ˈmɪliˌeɪtɪŋ/ erniedrigend 3P5
humorous /ˈhju:mərəs/ humorvoll; lustig; witzig 3A4
hungry /ˈhʌŋɡri/ hungrig I
to **hunt** /hʌnt/ jagen IV
hunter /ˈhʌntə/ Jäger/in 4P10
to **hurry (up)** /ˌhʌriˈʌp/ sich beeilen III
hurt /hɜ:t/ verletzt; verwundet I

to **hurt (sb)** *(irr)* /hɜ:t/ (jdm) wehtun; (jdn) verletzen II
husband /ˈhʌzbənd/ (Ehe)mann I

I

I /aɪ/ ich I
I don't care /ˌaɪ dəʊnt ˈkeə/ Mir ist es egal III
I don't like ...: Ich mag ... nicht. I
I guess ... /aɪ ˈɡes/ Ich schätze ... I
I like: Ich mag I
I see your point. /aɪ ˌsi: jəˈpɔɪnt/ Ich verstehe, was du sagst. 3B10
I'd rather (= I would rather) /aɪd ˈrɑːðə/ ich würde lieber III
I'm afraid /ˌaɪm_əˈfreɪd/ leider I
I'm fine /aɪm ˈfaɪn/ Es geht mir gut. I
I'm from ...: Ich komme aus ... I
(I'm) sorry. /ˌaɪm ˈsɒri/ Entschuldigung!; Tut mir leid. I
I'm ... years old: Ich bin ... Jahre alt. I
ice cream /ˌaɪs ˈkri:m/ Eiscreme; Eis I
ID (= identity) (card) /ˌaɪˈdi: kɑ:d, aɪˈdentɪti kɑ:d/ (Personal)ausweis IV
idea /aɪˈdɪə/ Idee; Einfall I
to **identify** /aɪˈdentɪfaɪ/ identifizieren; feststellen 1C2, 2A2, 5B3
identity /aɪˈdentɪti/ Identität IV
° **i.e.** /ˌaɪˈi:/ d.h. 2P5
if /ɪf/ wenn; falls; ob II
to **ignore** /ɪɡˈnɔ:/ ignorieren; nicht beachten III
ill /ɪl/ krank I
illegal /ɪˈli:ɡ(ə)l/ ungesetzlich; rechtswidrig; illegal IV
to **illustrate** /ˈɪləstreɪt/ illustrieren; verdeutlichen III
image /ˈɪmɪdʒ/ (Eben)bild; Abbild; Vorstellung IV
to **imagine** /ɪˈmædʒɪn/ sich vorstellen II
° to **imitate** /ˈɪmɪteɪt/ imitieren; nachahmen 1O7
immediately /ɪˈmi:diətli/ sofort; gleich; direkt II
immigrant /ˈɪmɪɡrənt/ Einwanderer/in; Immigrant/in IV
to **immigrate** /ˈɪmɪˌɡreɪt/ einwandern; immigrieren IV
immigration /ˌɪmɪˈɡreɪʃ(ə)n/ Einwanderung; Immigration IV
° **immoral** /ɪˈmɒrəl/ unmoralisch 1B9
° **immorality** *(no pl)* /ˌɪməˈrælətɪ/ Unmoral; Sittenlosigkeit 1B9
impact /ˈɪmpækt/ Auswirkung 4B4
impatient /ɪmˈpeɪʃ(ə)nt/ ungeduldig II
to **imply** /ɪmˈplaɪ/ andeuten 1C3
importance *(no pl)* /ɪmˈpɔ:t(ə)ns/ Bedeutung; Wichtigkeit 2B6
important /ɪmˈpɔ:t(ə)nt/ wichtig; wesentlich; bedeutend II

to **impress** /ɪmˈpres/ beeindrucken; imponieren 2B3
impression /ɪmˈpreʃ(ə)n/ Eindruck III
impressive /ɪmˈpresɪv/ beeindruckend IV
to **improve** /ɪmˈpruːv/ (sich) verbessern; besser werden II
improvement /ɪmˈpruːvmənt/ Verbesserung 4B6
in /ɪn/ in; auf I
 in: in; angesagt 3Titel A-Teil
 in a row /ɪn ə ˈrəʊ/ hintereinander IV
 in addition (to) /ɪn əˈdɪʃ(ə)n tʊ/ zusätzlich (zu) III
 in advance /ɪn ədˈvɑːns/ im Voraus; im Vorverkauf IV
 in close proximity /ɪn ˌkləʊs prɒkˈsɪməti/ in unmittelbarer Nähe 2B5
 in conclusion /ɪn kənˈkluːʒ(ə)n/ zum Abschluss; abschließend IV
 in English /ɪn ˈɪŋglɪʃ/ auf Englisch I
° **in fact** /ɪn ˈfækt/ genaugenommen 1O3
 in favor of (AE = **in favour of** BE) /ɪn ˈfeɪvər əv/ für IV
 in front of /ɪn ˈfrʌnt əv/ vor I
 in general /ɪn ˈdʒen(ə)rəl/ im Allgemeinen; generell IV
 in my opinion /ɪn maɪ əˈpɪnjən/ meiner Meinung nach III
 in my view /ɪn maɪ ˌvjuː/ meiner Meinung nach 1C1, 2B5
 in order to do sth /ɪn ˌɔːdə tə ˈduː/ um etw zu tun IV
 in public /ɪn ˈpʌblɪk/ in der Öffentlichkeit; öffentlich 5C2
° **in return for** /ɪn rɪˈtɜːn fɔː/ als Ausgleich/Gegenleistung für 1B9
 in terms of /ɪn ˈtɜːmz əv/ hinsichtlich; was ... angeht 4A4
 in the afternoon /ɪn ði ˌɑːftəˌnuːn/ am Nachmittag I
 in the end /ɪn ði ˈend/ letzten Endes; schließlich; zum Schluss I
 in the evening /ɪn ði ˈiːvnɪŋ/ am Abend I
 in the meantime /ɪn ðə ˈmiːntaɪm/ inzwischen; in der Zwischenzeit IV
 in the morning /ɪn ðə ˈmɔːnɪŋ/ am Morgen I
 in time /ɪn ˈtaɪm/ (gerade noch) rechtzeitig III
 in total /ɪn ˈtəʊt(ə)l/ insgesamt 4C1
 in winter /ɪn ˈwɪntə/ im Winter I
inadequate /ɪnˈædɪkwət/ unzureichend; unangemessen 2B5
° **inappropriate** /ˌɪnəˈprəʊpriət/ ungeeignet; unangebracht; unangemessen 5P6
° **incapable** /ɪnˈkeɪpəb(ə)l/ unfähig 1O2
incident /ˈɪnsɪd(ə)nt/ (Vor)fall; Zwischenfall; Ereignis; Begebenheit; Geschehen 3B6
to **include** /ɪnˈkluːd/ beinhalten; mit einschließen; aufnehmen II

including /ɪnˈkluːdɪŋ/ einschließlich 2C5, 4B5
incomplete /ˌɪnkəmˈpliːt/ unvollständig; unfertig 4B1
inconsiderate /ˌɪnkənˈsɪdərət/ rücksichtslos IV
to **increase** /ɪnˈkriːs/ (an)steigen; stärker werden; zunehmen; wachsen IV
incredible /ɪnˈkredəb(ə)l/ unglaublich IV
 the in-crowd /ði ˌɪn kraʊd/ Insider-Clique 3A1
° **indeed** /ɪnˈdiːd/ in der Tat; allerdings; ja 1B9
independence (no pl) /ˌɪndɪˈpendəns/ Unabhängigkeit IV
independent /ˌɪndɪˈpendənt/ unabhängig; selbstständig III
° **index finger** /ˈɪndeks ˌfɪŋgə/ Zeigefinger 1B7
individual /ˌɪndɪˈvɪdʒuəl/ Einzelne/r; Individuum; einzeln; individuell IV
individually /ˌɪndɪˈvɪdʒuəli/ einzeln; für sich; individuell 3C3
industry /ˈɪndəstri/ Industrie; Branche 4A3
° **inevitable** /ɪnˈevɪtəb(ə)l/ unvermeidlich 3B7
influence /ˈɪnfluəns/ Einfluss III
to **influence** /ˈɪnfluəns/ beeinflussen 1A4, 3C3
° **influential** /ˌɪnfluˈenʃ(ə)l/ einflussreich 2C3
to **inform** /ɪnˈfɔːm/ informieren; benachrichtigen; mitteilen 5C2
informal /ɪnˈfɔːm(ə)l/ informell; locker; zwanglos III
information (no pl) /ˌɪnfəˈmeɪʃ(ə)n/ Information(en); Auskunft I
informative /ɪnˈfɔːmətɪv/ informativ III
° **ingredient** /ɪnˈgriːdiənt/ Zutat; Bestandteil 4B5
° **inhabitant** /ɪnˈhæbɪtənt/ Einwohner/in; Bewohner/in 4P10
° **insecure** /ˌɪnsɪˈkjʊə/ unsicher; instabil; nicht sicher 5O2
° **inside** /ˈɪnˌsaɪd/ innen; drinnen; nach drinnen II
° **inside** (no pl) /ˈɪnˌsaɪd/ Innere; Innenseite 3B4
insight /ˈɪnsaɪt/ Einsicht; Einblick 5A2
° **insignificant** /ˌɪnsɪɡˈnɪfɪkənt/ unbedeutend 5P9
to **insist** /ɪnˈsɪst/ (darauf) bestehen III
° **to inspire** /ɪnˈspaɪə/ inspirieren 1P4
° **instantly** /ˈɪnstəntli/ sofort 1P3
instead /ɪnˈsted/ stattdessen IV
 instead of /ɪnˈsted əv/ (an)statt 2B3, 4B5
° to **instruct** /ɪnˈstrʌkt/ beibringen; anweisen 3P6
° **instruction** /ɪnˈstrʌkʃ(ə)n/ Anweisung; Instruktion 4P8

° to **insult** /ɪnˈsʌlt/ beleidigen 1O3
° **insurance** (no pl) /ɪnˈʃʊərəns/ Versicherung 5B3
° **int.** (= interior) /ɪnˈtɪəriə/ Innere; Innenaufnahme 1C7
integrity (no pl) /ɪnˈtegrəti/ Integrität; Anständigkeit 5B2
intellectual /ˌɪntəˈlektʃuəl/ Intellektuelle/r; intellektuell; geistig 3A2
intelligence (no pl) /ɪnˈtelɪdʒ(ə)ns/ Intelligenz III
° to **intend** /ɪnˈtend/ beabsichtigen 2O4
intention /ɪnˈtenʃ(ə)n/ Absicht 1B7
° to **interact** /ˌɪntərˈækt/ interagieren 5O4
° to **intercede** /ˌɪntəˈsiːd/ vermitteln 1B9
interest /ˈɪntrəst/ Interesse I
to **interest sb** /ˈɪntrəst/ jdn interessieren 4A3
 to **be interested (in)** /ˌbiː ˈɪntrəstɪd ɪn/ sich interessieren (für); interessiert sein (an) I
interesting /ˈɪntrəstɪŋ/ interessant I
to **interfere with** /ˌɪntəˈfɪə wɪð/ stören; eingreifen in 1C1
° **intern** /ˈɪntɜːn/ Praktikant/in 5P8
internship (AE = **placement** BE) /ˈɪntɜːnʃɪp/ Praktikum 5B1
° **interpersonal skills** /ˌɪntəpɜːs(ə)nəl ˈskɪlz/ soziale Kompetenz 5B3
to **interpret** /ɪnˈtɜːprɪt/ deuten; auslegen; wiedergeben 4A4
to **interrupt** /ˌɪntəˈrʌpt/ unterbrechen 3C5
° to **intervene** /ˌɪntəˈviːn/ einschreiten; sich einmischen 1B7
intervention /ˌɪntəˈvenʃ(ə)n/ Eingreifen 1B10
to **interview** /ˈɪntəˌvjuː/ interviewen; befragen II
° **interviewee** /ˌɪntəvjuːˈiː/ Interviewte/r 3C2
° **intimate** /ˈɪntɪmət/ eng; vertraut; intim 1O3
into /ˈɪntuː/ in II
to **introduce** /ˌɪntrəˈdjuːs/ vorstellen; vorbringen 1C10; einleiten 3B5
 ° to **introduce**: einführen 4B5
introduction /ˌɪntrəˈdʌkʃ(ə)n/ Vorstellung; Einleitung IV
introductory /ˌɪntrəˈdʌkt(ə)ri/ vorbereitend; einleitend 2B6
° to **invent** /ɪnˈvent/ erfinden 5O1
invitation /ˌɪnvɪˈteɪʃ(ə)n/ Einladung I
to **invite** /ɪnˈvaɪt/ einladen I
to **involve** /ɪnˈvɒlv/ beinhalten; umfassen; betreffen; beteiligen 5A2
involved /ɪnˈvɒlvd/ betroffen; beteiligt; verwickelt 3A2, 5C1
° **involvement** /ɪnˈvɒlvmənt/ Beteiligung 5B3
ironic /aɪˈrɒnɪk/ ironisch; (leicht) spöttisch 3A4

Words — English-German dictionary

irresponsible /ˌɪrɪˈspɒnsəb(ə)l/ unverantwortlich; verantwortungslos 2B5
irritated /ˈɪrɪˌteɪtɪd/ verärgert; gereizt III
° **irritation** /ˌɪrɪˈteɪʃ(ə)n/ Ärger; Verärgerung 1B9
island /ˈaɪlənd/ Insel I
isolated /ˈaɪsəˌleɪtɪd/ abgelegen; isoliert IV
issue /ˈɪʃuː/ Thema; Angelegenheit; Problem, (Streit)frage 1B8, 2C3
it /ɪt/ es; er/sie/es I
IT (no pl) (= **information technology**) /ˌaɪ ˈtiː, ˌɪnfəˈmeɪʃ(ə)n tekˌnɒlədʒi/ Informationstechnologie I
° **Italian** /ɪˈtæliən/ Italiener/in; Italienisch; italienisch 5P4
item /ˈaɪtəm/ Artikel; Gegenstand 2C5
its /ɪts/ sein(e), ihr(e) I
itself /ɪtˈself/ sich; (sich) selbst III

J

° to **jab** /dʒæb/ stechen; stoßen 1B9
jacket /ˈdʒækɪt/ Jacke I
January /ˈdʒænjuəri/ Januar I
° **jail** /dʒeɪl/ Gefängnis 2C3
° **jargon** /ˈdʒɑːɡən/ (Fach)jargon; Fachchinesisch 3P2
jealous /ˈdʒeləs/ eifersüchtig; neidisch II
jewellery (no pl) /ˈdʒuːəlri/ Schmuck 2C7
Jewish /ˈdʒuːɪʃ/ jüdisch IV
° **jigsaw** /ˈdʒɪɡsɔː/ Puzzle(spiel) 5O2
job ad(vert)/job advertisement /ˈdʒɒbˌædvɜːt/ˈdʒɒbˌədˌvɜːtɪsmənt/ Stellenanzeige 5B1
job interview /ˈdʒɒbˌɪntəˌvjuː/ Bewerbungsgespräch; Vorstellungsgespräch 5B1
° **job seeker** /ˈdʒɒbsiːkə/ Arbeitssuchende/r 5P9
jock (informal, AE) /dʒɑk/ Sportfanatiker/in 3A2
to **join** /dʒɔɪn/ verbinden; sich gesellen II; sich anschließen III
joke /dʒəʊk/ Spaß; Streich; Witz III
to **joke** /dʒəʊk/ scherzen; witzeln; Spaß machen IV
journey /ˈdʒɜːni/ Reise III
to **judge** /dʒʌdʒ/ (be)urteilen; schätzen 1B10, 3C3
° **judg(e)ment** /ˈdʒʌdʒmənt/ Urteil; Ansicht; Meinung 3C3
juice /dʒuːs/ Saft I
July /dʒʊˈlaɪ/ Juli I
to **jump (up)** /ˌdʒʌmpˈʌp/ (auf)springen; (hoch)springen I
June /dʒuːn/ Juni I
jungle /ˈdʒʌŋɡ(ə)l/ Dschungel; Urwald IV

° **junior** (AE) /ˈdʒuːniər/ Oberstufenschüler/in im vorletzten Jahr 4PP5
just /dʒʌst/ nur; bloß; einfach I; gerade II
justifiable /ˈdʒʌstɪˌfaɪəb(ə)l/ berechtigt; gerechtfertigt 2B5
to **justify** /ˈdʒʌstɪfaɪ/ rechtfertigen 2B5

K

° **kangaroo** /ˌkæŋɡəˈruː/ Känguru 4PP1
to **keep** (irr) /kiːp/ behalten; aufbewahren; halten I; lassen, beibehalten III
to **keep in mind** /ˌkiːp ɪn ˈmaɪnd/ nicht vergessen 4C4
to **keep quiet** /ˌkiːp ˈkwaɪət/ ruhig sein IV
to **keep sb up-to-date** /ˌkiːp ˌsʌmbədiˌʌptəˈdeɪt/ jdn auf dem neuesten Stand halten III
° to **keep sth alive** /ˌkiːp ˌsʌmθɪŋ əˈlaɪv/ etw aufrechterhalten 1C10
° **keeper** /ˈkiːpə/ Aufseher/in 1O3
key /kiː/ Schlüssel(-); Taste; Haupt- 1B8
° **key:** wesentlich 5O1
to **kill** /kɪl/ töten; umbringen II
° to **kill time** /ˌkɪl ˈtaɪm/ die Zeit totschlagen 1O2
kind /kaɪnd/ nett; freundlich; liebenswürdig II; Art; Sorte IV
° **kind of** /ˈkaɪnd əv/ irgendwie 1B9
° **kinda** (= kind of) (informal, AE) /ˈkaɪndə, ˈkaɪnd əv/ irgendwie 1O3
king /kɪŋ/ König II
kingdom /ˈkɪŋdəm/ Königreich III
to **kiss** /kɪs/ küssen III
kitchen /ˈkɪtʃən/ Küche III
knife (pl **knives**) /naɪf, naɪvz/ Messer II
° to **knock out** /ˌnɒk ˈaʊt/ herausschlagen; ausschalten; außer Gefecht setzen 5O2
to **know** (irr) /nəʊ/ wissen; kennen I
knowledge (no pl) /ˈnɒlɪdʒ/ Kenntnisse; Wissen; Kenntnis 1C5, 5A2
° **kookaburra** /ˈkʊkəˌbʌrə/ australischer Rieseneisvogel 4PP1

L

° to **label** /ˈleɪb(ə)l/ etikettieren; beschriften; kennzeichnen 1C7
° **labour** (no pl) /ˈleɪbə/ Arbeit 5PP2
lack (of) (no pl) /ˈlæk əv/ Mangel (an) IV
to **lack** /læk/ nicht haben; fehlen 3A2, 5B6
lad (informal, BE) /læd/ Junge 4B1
ladder /ˈlædə/ (Stufen)leiter 3B2
lady /ˈleɪdi/ Frau; Dame I
° **laid-back** (informal) /ˌleɪd ˈbæk/ locker; gelassen 4PP3
lake /leɪk/ See III

lamp /læmp/ Lampe I
language /ˈlæŋɡwɪdʒ/ Sprache II
large /lɑːdʒ/ groß IV
last /lɑːst/ letzte(r, s) I; das letzte Mal; zuletzt III
° to **last (for)** … /ˈlɑːst fɔː/ … (an)dauern; (an)halten 5B3
late /leɪt/ (zu) spät I
later /ˈleɪtə/ später I
latest /ˈleɪtɪst/ jüngste(r, s); letzte(r, s); neueste(r, s) III
to **laugh** /lɑːf/ lachen I
law /lɔː/ Gesetz; Recht IV
to **lay the table** /ˌleɪ ðə ˈteɪb(ə)l/ den Tisch decken I
lazy /ˈleɪzi/ faul; träge II
to **lead** (irr) /liːd/ führen III
° **leader** /ˈliːdə/ Leiter/in; Führer/in 2C5
leadership (no pl) /ˈliːdəʃɪp/ Führung; Leitung; Führungsqualitäten 5A2
° **leading** /ˈliːdɪŋ/ führend 5P4
leaflet /ˈliːflət/ Flyer; Prospekt I
° to **lean** (irr) /liːn/ sich beugen; sich lehnen 1B7
to **learn** (irr) /lɜːn/ lernen I
° **leather** /ˈleðə/ Leder(-) 3A2
to **leave** (irr) /liːv/ verlassen; weggehen; zurücklassen I; lassen II
to **leave out** /ˌliːv ˈaʊt/ auslassen; weglassen III
to **leave out:** ausschließen 2B3
to **leave sb behind** /ˌliːv ˌsʌmbədi bɪˈhaɪnd/ jdn zurücklassen III
left /left/ (nach) links I
left-hand /ˌleft ˈhænd/ linke(r, s) III
leg /leɡ/ Bein I
legal /ˈliːɡ(ə)l/ legal; gesetzlich (vorgeschrieben) 2B4
° **leisure** (no pl) /ˈleʒə/ Freizeit(-) 5O2
lens /lenz/ Linse; Objektiv 2A1
less /les/ weniger II
lesson /ˈles(ə)n/ (Unterrichts)stunde I
to **let** (irr) /let/ lassen I
° to **let go** /ˌlet ˈɡəʊ/ loslassen; aufhören 1B8
° to **let off steam** /ˌlet ɒf ˈstiːm/ Dampf ablassen; sich abreagieren 1A1
° to **let sb down** /ˌlet ˌsʌmbədi ˈdaʊn/ jdn enttäuschen; jdn im Stich lassen 1P2
° to **let sb off** /ˌlet ˌsʌmbədi ˈɒf/ jdn davonkommen lassen 1B7
let's (= **let us**) /lets, ˌlet ʌs/ Lass(t) uns I
Let's face it (informal) /ˌlets ˈfeɪs ɪt/ Machen wir uns (doch) nichts vor 4B1
letter /ˈletə/ Brief I
letter of recommendation /ˌletər əv ˌrekəmenˈdeɪʃ(ə)n/ Empfehlungsschreiben 5B1
level /ˈlev(ə)l/ Niveau; Höhe; Ebene; Stufe IV

English-German dictionary

W — Words

- ° liar /ˈlaɪə/ Lügner/in 1o3
- liberty /ˈlɪbəti/ Freiheit IV
- library /ˈlaɪbrəri/ Bibliothek; Bücherei I
- license (AE = licence BE) /ˈlaɪs(ə)ns/ Genehmigung; Erlaubnis; Lizenz IV
- to lie (irr) /laɪ/ liegen; sich hinlegen I
  - ° to lie (to sb) /ˈlaɪ tʊ/ (jdn be)lügen 1o3
- life (pl lives) /laɪf, laɪvz/ Leben I
- ° lifeguard /ˈlaɪfˌɡɑːd/ Bademeister/in; Rettungsschwimmer/in 5P5
- ° lifeless /ˈlaɪfləs/ lebenslos; tot 4B2
- light /laɪt/ Licht; Lichtquelle; Lampe II
- light-hearted /ˌlaɪt ˈhɑːtɪd/ sorglos; heiter; mit einem Augenzwinkern 3A4
- ° lighting (no pl) /ˈlaɪtɪŋ/ Beleuchtung 2C4
- like /laɪk/ wie I
- to like /laɪk/ mögen I
- likely /ˈlaɪkli/ wahrscheinlich IV
- to limit /ˈlɪmɪt/ einschränken; beschränken; begrenzen IV
- limited /ˈlɪmɪtɪd/ begrenzt; eingeschränkt IV
- line /laɪn/ Linie; Zeile; Reihe; Verbindung, Strecke III
- link /lɪŋk/ Verbindung III
- to link /lɪŋk/ verbinden IV
- lion /ˈlaɪən/ Löwe I
- ° lip /lɪp/ Lippe 1B7
- to list /lɪst/ auflisten III
- to listen to /ˈlɪs(ə)n tə/ zuhören; (an)hören I
- listener /ˈlɪs(ə)nə/ Zuhörer/in 5B3
- ° literate /ˈlɪt(ə)rət/ gebildet 5O1
- literature (no pl) /ˈlɪtrətʃə/ (Fach)literatur; Informationsmaterial 5P4
- little /ˈlɪt(ə)l/ klein(e, er, es) I; wenig II
- to live /lɪv/ leben; wohnen I
- lively /ˈlaɪvli/ lebhaft; lebendig; anschaulich IV
- ° living area /ˈlɪvɪŋ ˌeəriə/ Wohnbereich 1C7
- living room /ˈlɪvɪŋ ˌruːm/ Wohnzimmer I
- to load the dishwasher /ˌləʊd ðə ˈdɪʃˌwɒʃə/ die Spülmaschine einräumen I
- ° loads of (informal) /ˈləʊdz əv/ jede Menge; massenhaft 4P6
- local /ˈləʊk(ə)l/ hiesig; örtlich IV
- local /ˈləʊk(ə)l/ Ortsansässige/r; Einheimische/r 4A3
- location /ləʊˈkeɪʃ(ə)n/ Lage; (Stand)ort IV
- lock /lɒk/ Schloss II
- to lock /lɒk/ (ab)schließen; einschließen II
- ° locker /ˈlɒkə/ Schließfach; Spind 1P3
- ° logical /ˈlɒdʒɪk(ə)l/ logisch; vernünftig 5P4

- lonely /ˈləʊnli/ einsam IV
- long /lɒŋ/ lang I
  - ° long-term /ˌlɒŋ ˈtɜːm/ langfristig; Langzeit(-) 3C3
- look /lʊk/ Blick; Gesichtsausdruck 1C3, 2C3
- to look /lʊk/ aussehen; sehen; schauen I
  - to look after /ˌlʊk ˈɑːftə/ sich kümmern um I
  - to look around /ˌlʊk əˈraʊnd/ sich umsehen II
  - to look at /ˈlʊk æt/ (sich) ansehen; anschauen I
  - to look for /ˈlʊk fɔː/ suchen nach I
  - to look forward to doing sth /ˌlʊk ˌfɔːwəd tə ˈduːɪŋ/ sich darauf freuen, etw zu tun I
  - to look forward to sth /ˌlʊk ˈfɔːwəd tə/ sich auf etw freuen I
  - to look up sth /ˌlʊk ˈʌp/ etw nachschlagen; etw heraussuchen II
- looks (only pl) /lʊks/ Aussehen 3A2
- ° to loom /luːm/ (drohend) auftauchen 1B7
- ° to loosen /ˈluːs(ə)n/ (sich) lockern; hier: erleichtern 2B3
- ° to loot /luːt/ plündern 2C5
- ° the Lord /ðə ˈlɔːd/ (Gott) der Herr 1o4
- to lose (irr) /luːz/ verlieren; aus den Augen verlieren II
  - ° to lose one's nerve /ˌluːz wʌnz ˈnɜːv/ die Nerven verlieren 1P3
  - ° to lose one's temper /ˌluːz wʌnz ˈtempə/ die Geduld verlieren 3P10
  - to lose one's way /ˌluːz wʌnz ˈweɪ/ sich verirren II
- loser /ˈluːzə/ Verlierer/in II
- ° lot (informal, BE) /lɒt/ Trupp; Haufen; Pack 5O1
- a lot (of) /ə ˈlɒt əv/ viel(e); eine Menge I
- lots of (informal) /ˈlɒts əv/ viel(e); eine Menge I
- loud /laʊd/ laut I
- love /lʌv/ Liebe; alles Liebe (Briefschlussformel) II
- to love /lʌv/ lieben; sehr mögen I
- lovely /ˈlʌvli/ schön; hübsch; nett I
- low /ləʊ/ niedrig; gering; tief 4B1
- ° low-wage /ˌləʊ ˈweɪdʒ/ Niedriglohn- 5PP2
- luck (no pl) /lʌk/ Glück II
- lucky /ˈlʌki/ glücklich (Glück habend; Glück bringend) I
  - to be lucky /ˈlʌki/ Glück haben I
- lunch /lʌntʃ/ Mittagessen I
- ° lunchroom /ˈlʌntʃˌruːm/ Speisesaal 3B4
- luxury /ˈlʌkʃəri/ Luxus(-) 2C5, 4B5
- lyrics (pl) /ˈlɪrɪks/ (Lied)text II

M

- machine /məˈʃiːn/ Maschine; Apparat III

- mad /mæd/ wahnsinnig; verrückt II
  - ° mad: wütend 1o3
- ° to be made up of /ˌbiː ˌmeɪd ˈʌp əv/ bestehen aus 5PP2
- magic /ˈmædʒɪk/ magisch; zauberhaft; wundervoll II
- main /meɪn/ Haupt- II
- major /ˈmeɪdʒə/ bedeutend; wichtig; schwer 5A2
  - ° major: groß 4B2
- to make (irr) /meɪk/ machen; erstellen; ausmachen II
  - to make a/your point /ˌmeɪk ə/jə ˈpɔɪnt/ etwas ansprechen; (s)ein Argument einbringen; mit etwas recht haben 3C5
  - to make a promise /ˌmeɪk ə ˈprɒmɪs/ ein Versprechen geben III
  - to make an impression on sb /ˌmeɪk ən ɪmˈpreʃ(ə)n ɒn/ auf jdn Eindruck machen; jdn beeindrucken 2B1
  - to make friends (with sb) /ˌmeɪk ˈfrendz wɪð/ (mit jdm) Freundschaft schließen 3B3
  - to make fun of sb /ˌmeɪk ˈfʌn əv/ sich über jdn lustig machen III
  - to make sb do sth /ˌmeɪk ˌsʌmbədi ˈduː/ jdn zu etwas bringen; jdn etwas tun lassen III
  - to make sth: etw schaffen; etw erreichen IV
  - to make sure (that) /ˌmeɪk ˈʃɔː ðæt/ darauf achten, (dass) II
  - to make the most of sth /ˌmeɪk ðə ˈməʊst əv/ das Beste aus etw machen; das Beste aus etw herausholen III
  - to make up /ˌmeɪk ˈʌp/ erfinden; (sich) ausdenken III
  - to make up for /ˌmeɪk ˈʌp fɔː/ ausgleichen; wettmachen 3A2
  - ° to make up one's mind /ˌmeɪk ˌʌp wʌnz ˈmaɪnd/ sich entscheiden 1B7
- male /meɪl/ männlich III
- ° mall /mɔːl/ (große) Einkaufspassage; (überdachtes) Einkaufszentrum 3B7
- man (pl men) /mæn, men/ Mann I
- to manage /ˈmænɪdʒ/ leiten; führen; managen; zurechtkommen mit 3C3
  - to manage sth /ˈmænɪdʒ/ etw schaffen III
- manager /ˈmænɪdʒə/ Manager/in; Geschäftsführer/in, Leiter/in IV
- ° Mandarin (no pl) /ˈmændərɪn/ Mandarin (chinesische Hochsprache) 4C1
- to manipulate /məˈnɪpjʊleɪt/ beeinflussen; manipulieren 2A3
- manners (only pl) /ˈmænəz/ Manieren; (gutes) Benehmen IV
- ° manufacturing (no pl) /ˌmænjʊˈfæktʃərɪŋ/ Herstellungs-; Fertigung; hier: verarbeitend 5PP2
- many /ˈmeni/ viele I

W Words — English-German dictionary

map /mæp/ (Land)karte; (Stadt)plan I
March /mɑːtʃ/ März I
° **to march** /mɑːtʃ/ marschieren 1B2
° **mariachi** /ˌmæriˈɑːtʃi/ *Form mexikanischer Volksmusik* 1A2
market /ˈmɑːkɪt/ Markt I
marketer /ˈmɑːkɪtə/ Marketingleiter/in; Werbekampagnegestalter/in 2B5
° **marriage** /ˈmærɪdʒ/ Heirat; Trauung; Ehe 1P8
to marry /ˈmæri/ heiraten III
mass /mæs/ Masse; Massen-; Menge 4B3
to match sth to sth /mætʃ/ etw auf etw abstimmen; etw zuordnen III
° **mate** *(informal, BE)* /meɪt/ Freund/in; Kumpel 3O2
materially /məˈtɪəriəli/ wesentlich 2B5
maths *(pl, informal)* /mæθs/ Mathe(unterricht) I
matter /ˈmætə/ Angelegenheit; Sache III
to matter /ˈmætə/ von Bedeutung sein IV
matter-of-fact /ˌmætər_əv_ˈfækt/ sachlich; nüchtern 3A4
° **mature** /məˈtʃʊə/ erwachsen; reif 5B8
° **maturity** *(no pl)* /məˈtʃʊərəti/ Reife 1C7
May /meɪ/ Mai I
may /meɪ/ können; dürfen II; vielleicht III
maybe /ˈmeɪbi/ vielleicht; möglicherweise II
me /miː/ mir; mich I
meal /miːl/ Mahlzeit; Essen II
to mean *(irr)* /miːn/ bedeuten; meinen I
to mean to do sth /ˌmiːn tə ˈduː/ etw tun wollen; etw beabsichtigen III
° **mean** /miːn/ gemein; fies 3O1
meaning /ˈmiːnɪŋ/ Bedeutung III
meaningful /ˈmiːnɪŋf(ə)l/ bedeutsam; wichtig; bedeutungsvoll III
means (of) /ˈmiːnz_əv/ Weg; Mittel; Art III
meanwhile /ˈmiːnwaɪl/ inzwischen; unterdessen; mittlerweile IV
meat *(no pl)* /miːt/ Fleisch IV
the Med *(informal, BE)* /ðə ˌmed/ das Mittelmeer 4B2
° **medal** /ˈmed(ə)l/ Medaille 4P11
the media /ðə ˈmiːdiə/ die Medien IV
medical /ˈmedɪk(ə)l/ medizinisch; ärztlich III
medicine *(no pl)* /ˈmed(ə)s(ə)n/ Medizin; Medikamente II
° **Mediterranean** /ˌmedɪtəˈreɪniən/ mediterran; Mittelmeer- 4B2
the Mediterranean (Sea) /ðə ˌmedɪtəˌreɪniən ˈsiː/ das Mittelmeer 4B2

medium *(pl media)* /ˈmiːdiəm, ˈmiːdiə/ (Informations)medium 5A2
to meet *(irr)* /miːt/ (sich) treffen I; kennenlernen III; erfüllen, entsprechen 4B5
° **to meet a (tight) deadline** /ˌmiːt_ə ˌtaɪt ˈdedˌlaɪn/ einen (knappen) Abgabezeitpunkt einhalten 5O1
melody /ˈmelədi/ Melodie II
member /ˈmembə/ Mitglied II
memoir(s) /ˈmem,wɑːz/ (Lebens)erinnerungen; Memoiren 3B2
° **memorable** /ˈmem(ə)rəb(ə)l/ denkwürdig; unvergesslich 5B3
memory /ˈmem(ə)ri/ Gedächtnis; Andenken; Erinnerung III
to mention /ˈmenʃ(ə)n/ erwähnen II
merely /ˈmɪəli/ nur; bloß 2B5
message /ˈmesɪdʒ/ Nachricht; Botschaft II
Mexican /ˈmeksɪkən/ Mexikaner/in; mexikanisch 1A2
microphone /ˈmaɪkrəˌfəʊn/ Mikrofon II
middle /ˈmɪd(ə)l/ Mitte II
midnight *(no pl)* /ˈmɪdˌnaɪt/ Mitternacht IV
might /maɪt/ könnte III
mile /maɪl/ Meile *(= 1,609 km)* IV
milk *(no pl)* /mɪlk/ Milch 2B2
° **the Millennial generation** /ðə mɪˈleniəl ˌdʒenəˌreɪʃ(ə)n/ *Bezeichnung für die zwischen 1974 und 1995 geborenen Kinder* 2C3
° **millennium** /mɪˈleniəm/ Jahrtausend; *hier:* Jahrtausendwende 5O1
° **to mime** /maɪm/ pantomimisch darstellen; mimen 1P4
mind /maɪnd/ Geist; Verstand; Kopf 1C4, 2B3
mine /maɪn/ meine(r, s); meins III
minute /ˈmɪnɪt/ Minute I
° **miracle** /ˈmɪrək(ə)l/ Wunder 2B5
° **miserable** /ˈmɪz(ə)rəb(ə)l/ unglücklich; elend; armselig III
to mislead *(irr)* /mɪsˈliːd/ täuschen; verleiten 2B5
to miss /mɪs/ vermissen; verfehlen; versäumen; verpassen II
mistake /mɪˈsteɪk/ Fehler; Irrtum; Versehen II
° **misunderstanding** /ˌmɪsʌndəˈstændɪŋ/ Missverständnis; Meinungsverschiedenheit III
° **misunderstood** /ˌmɪsʌndəˈstʊd/ missverstanden 1P4
to mix /mɪks/ (miteinander) (ver)mischen I
mixed /mɪkst/ gemischt III
° **mixture** /ˈmɪkstʃə/ Mischung 1B6
mobile (= mobile phone) /ˈməʊbaɪl, ˌməʊbaɪl ˈfəʊn/ Mobiltelefon; Handy I
modest /ˈmɒdɪst/ bescheiden; zurückhaltend III

mom *(informal, AE = mum BE)* /mɑm/ Mama IV
moment /ˈməʊmənt/ Moment; Augenblick I
monarch /ˈmɒnək/ Monarch/in; Herrscher/in III
Monday /ˈmʌndeɪ/ Montag I
money *(no pl)* /ˈmʌni/ Geld I
to save money /ˌseɪv ˈmʌni/ Geld sparen II
month /mʌnθ/ Monat I
mood /muːd/ Laune; Stimmung III
moon /muːn/ Mond III
moral value /ˌmɒrəl ˈvæljuː/ Moralvorstellung 2C8
more /mɔː/ (noch) mehr; weitere(r, s) I
morning /ˈmɔːnɪŋ/ Morgen I
in the morning /ˌɪn ðə ˈmɔːnɪŋ/ am Morgen I
most /məʊst/ (die) meisten II
° **mostly** /ˈməʊstli/ meistens; größtenteils; hauptsächlich 2C3
mother /ˈmʌðə/ Mutter I
to motivate /ˈməʊtɪveɪt/ motivieren; veranlassen 4A3
motivated /ˈməʊtɪˌveɪtɪd/ motiviert 5B3
motorway *(BE)* /ˈməʊtəˌweɪ/ Autobahn III
mountain /ˈmaʊntɪn/ Berg I
mouse *(pl mice)* /maʊs, maɪs/ Maus I
mouth /maʊθ/ Mund I
° **to mouth** /maʊθ/ lautlos sagen 3B4
to move /muːv/ (sich) bewegen II; (um)ziehen III
to move house/home /ˌmuːv ˈhaʊs, ˈhəʊm/ umziehen III
to move on to sth /ˌmuːv ˈɒn tʊ/ zu etw übergehen 3C3
movement /ˈmuːvmənt/ Bewegung 3B10
° **movement:** *hier:* Führung 2C4
movie *(AE)* /ˈmuːvi/ (Kino)film 3A2
Mr (= Mister) /ˈmɪstə/ Herr *(Anrede)* I
Mrs /ˈmɪsɪz/ Frau *(Anrede)* I
much /mʌtʃ/ viel I
multicultural /ˌmʌltiˈkʌltʃərəl/ multikulturell IV
mum *(informal)* /mʌm/ Mama, Mutti I
muscly *(informal)* /ˈmʌsli/ muskulös 3A2
music /ˈmjuːzɪk/ Musik *(als Schulfach)* I
musical /ˈmjuːzɪk(ə)l/ musikalisch; Musik- III
musician /mjuˈzɪʃ(ə)n/ Musiker/in III
Muslim /ˈmʊzləm/ Muslim/in; muslimisch IV
must *(no pl)* /mʌst/ Muss III
must /mʌst/ müssen I
mustn't (= must not) /ˈmʌsnt, mʌst ˈnɒt/ nicht dürfen I
° **mustard** /ˈmʌstəd/ Senf 1B7

English-German dictionary — Words

° mutual /ˈmjuːtʃuəl/ gegenseitig 4P8
my /maɪ/ mein(e) I
  My favourite ... is /maɪ ˈfeɪv(ə)rət ... ɪz/ Mein Lieblings... ist I
  My name is /ˈmaɪ neɪm ɪz/ Ich heiße I
myself /maɪˈself/ mir; mich; ich (selbst) III

N

° to nag /næg/ (herum)nörgeln; nicht in Ruhe lassen 1B8
name /neɪm/ Name I
to name /neɪm/ (be)nennen III
° namely /ˈneɪmli/ nämlich 5P6
narrative /ˈnærətɪv/ Erzählung; Schilderung 1B8
narrator /nəˈreɪtə/ Erzähler/in IV
narrow /ˈnærəʊ/ eng; schmal II
nasty /ˈnɑːsti/ scheußlich; schlimm; ekelhaft 5A4
national /ˈnæʃ(ə)nəl/ national I
native /ˈneɪtɪv/ Einheimische/r IV
  Native American /ˌneɪtɪv əˈmerɪkən/ amerikanischer Ureinwohner/amerikanische Ureinwohnerin IV
  native language /ˌneɪtɪv ˈlæŋgwɪdʒ/ Muttersprache 4C1
  native speaker /ˌneɪtɪv ˈspiːkə/ Muttersprachler/in 4C1, 5A2
natural /ˈnætʃ(ə)rəl/ natürlich; angeboren; Natur- III
near /nɪə/ nahe; in der Nähe I
nearby /ˌnɪəˈbaɪ/ in der Nähe (gelegen); nahe gelegen 3B4, 4B1
necessary /ˈnesəs(ə)ri/ nötig; notwendig; erforderlich III
° neck /nek/ Hals; Nacken; Genick 1P3
need (no pl) /niːd/ Bedarf; Notwendigkeit; Bedürfnis III
to need /niːd/ müssen; brauchen I
  needn't (= need not) /ˈniːdnt, ˈniːd nɒt/ müssen nicht; brauchen nicht I
negative /ˈnegətɪv/ negativ; ablehnend; verneinend II
to neglect /nɪˈglekt/ vernachlässigen 1C10
neighborhood (AE = neighbourhood BE) /ˈneɪbəˌhʊd/ Nachbarschaft; (Wohn)viertel; Gegend; Umgebung IV
neighbour /ˈneɪbə/ Nachbar/in III
nerves /nɜːvz/ Nerven; Nervenstärke 5C5
nervous /ˈnɜːvəs/ nervös II
never /ˈnevə/ nie(mals) I
  never mind /ˌnevə ˈmaɪnd/ (ist doch) egal IV
° nevertheless /ˌnevəðəˈles/ trotzdem; dennoch; nichtsdestoweniger 1P9
new /njuː/ neu I
  New Year /ˌnjuː ˈjɪə/ Neujahr II

news (pl) /njuːz/ Neuigkeit; Nachricht; Nachrichtensendung II
newspaper /ˈnjuːzˌpeɪpə/ Zeitung(s-) IV
next /nekst/ nächste(r, s); als Nächste(r, s) I
  next to /ˈnekst tə/ neben I
nice /naɪs/ schön; angenehm; nett; freundlich I
nickname /ˈnɪkˌneɪm/ Spitzname; Kosename III
night /naɪt/ Nacht; Abend I
  at night /æt ˈnaɪt/ nachts I
nightmare /ˈnaɪtˌmeə/ Albtraum II
nine /naɪn/ neun I
no /nəʊ/ nein; kein/e I
  ° no longer /nəʊ ˈlɒŋgə/ nicht mehr 5PP2
  no matter ... /ˌnəʊ ˈmætə/ egal(,) ... 3C2
  ° No way! (informal) /ˌnəʊ ˈweɪ/ Ausgeschlossen! 3B7
nobody /ˈnəʊbɒdi/ niemand; keiner III
° to nod /nɒd/ nicken 1P3
noise /nɔɪz/ Geräusch I
  noise (no pl) /nɔɪz/ Lärm; Krach II
noisy /ˈnɔɪzi/ laut II
° none /nʌn/ keine(r, s); niemand 3P7
° nor /nɔː/ und auch nicht; noch 3B7
normal /ˈnɔːm(ə)l/ normal; üblich II
° normally /ˈnɔːm(ə)li/ normalerweise 1C7
north /nɔːθ/ Norden; nördlich; Nord- I
nose /nəʊz/ Nase I
nosy /ˈnəʊzi/ neugierig II
not /nɒt/ nicht I
  not ... anymore /nɒt ˌeniˈmɔː/ nicht mehr II
  not ... either /nɒt ˈaɪðə/ auch nicht III
  ° not exactly /nɒt ɪgˈzæktli/ eigentlich nicht; nicht gerade; nicht ganz 3A2
  not mind doing sth /nɒt ˌmaɪnd ˈduːɪŋ/ nichts gegen etw (einzuwenden) haben III
note /nəʊt/ Notiz; Mitteilung II
to note down /ˌnəʊt ˈdaʊn/ (sich) notieren II
nothing /ˈnʌθɪŋ/ nichts II
to notice /ˈnəʊtɪs/ bemerken; beachten I
novel /ˈnɒv(ə)l/ Roman III
November /nəʊˈvembə/ November I
now /naʊ/ jetzt; nun I
° nowadays /ˈnaʊəˌdeɪz/ heutzutage 2P5
nowhere /ˈnəʊweə/ nirgends; nirgendwo IV
number /ˈnʌmbə/ Zahl; Ziffer; Nummer I
nurse /nɜːs/ (Kranken)schwester; Krankenpfleger IV

° to nurture /ˈnɜːtʃə/ aufziehen; großziehen; fördern 1C5

O

object /ˈɒbdʒekt/ Objekt; Gegenstand III
to observe /əbˈzɜːv/ beobachten; bemerken; zuschauen 5C5
observer /əbˈzɜːvə/ Beobachter/in; Zuschauer/in 1C10
obsession /əbˈseʃ(ə)n/ Besessenheit; Zwangsvorstellung 2C1
° to obtain /əbˈteɪn/ bekommen; erhalten 5PP2
obvious /ˈɒbviəs/ deutlich; offensichtlich 1C1, 3C3
obviously /ˈɒbviəsli/ offensichtlich; deutlich II
to occur /əˈkɜː/ geschehen; sich ereignen; auftreten 4B1
ocean /ˈəʊʃ(ə)n/ Ozean; (Welt)meer III
October /ɒkˈtəʊbə/ Oktober I
° odd /ɒd/ merkwürdig; gelegentlich 4P6
of /əv/ von I
  of course /əv ˈkɔːs/ natürlich I
offence /əˈfens/ Straftat; Beleidigung; Vergehen 2B5, 3C3
offensive /əˈfensɪv/ anstößig IV
offer /ˈɒfə/ Angebot 4B5
to offer /ˈɒfə/ anbieten; bieten I
office /ˈɒfɪs/ Büro; Amt IV
official /əˈfɪʃ(ə)l/ offiziell 4C1
° off sick (BE) /ˌɒf ˈsɪk/ krank(gemeldet) 5O1
often /ˈɒf(ə)n/ oft I
° Oh Lord! /əʊ ˈlɔːd/ Du lieber Himmel! 1O3
oil /ɔɪl/ (Erd)öl IV
old /əʊld/ alt I
old-fashioned /ˌəʊld ˈfæʃ(ə)nd/ altmodisch; traditionsverbunden 3B8
° olive /ˈɒlɪv/ Olive; oliv(farben) 1B7
° Olympics (only pl) /əˈlɪmpɪks/ Olympische Spiele 4P11
° OMG (= oh my God) /ˌəʊ em ˈdʒiː, ˌəʊ maɪ ˈɡɒd/ Oh (mein) Gott!; Großer Gott! 1A2
on /ɒn/ auf I; über; zu II
  on foot /ɒn ˈfʊt/ zu Fuß III
  on holiday /ɒn ˈhɒlədeɪ/ im Urlaub; in den Ferien I
  on one's own /ˌɒn wʌnz ˈəʊn/ (ganz) allein(e) III
  ° on the contrary /ˌɒn ðə ˈkɒntrəri/ ganz im Gegenteil 4B2
  on the grounds of /ɒn ðə ˈɡraʊndz əv/ aufgrund; hinsichtlich 2B5
  on the left /ˌɒn ðə ˈleft/ links; auf der linken Seite III
  on the one hand /ˌɒn ðə ˈwʌn ˌhænd/ einerseits; auf der einen Seite III

on the other hand /ˌɒn ði‿ˈʌðə ˌhænd/ andererseits; auf der anderen Seite III
on the right /ˌɒn ðə ˈraɪt/ rechts; auf der rechten Seite I
° **on time** /ˌɒn ˈtaɪm/ pünktlich 5P1
° **on top of** /ˌɒn ˈtɒp‿əv/ (oben) auf 1B9
once /wʌns/ früher; einst III
once: sobald 1C1, 4B2, 5A2
° once: einmal 2O3
one /wʌn/ eins; ein(e, er, es) I
a small one /ə ˈsmɔːl ˌwʌn/ ein(e) kleine(s, r) II
° **one day** /ˈwʌn deɪ/ eines Tages 3B2
(one) o'clock /ˌwʌn‿əˈklɒk/ (ein) Uhr I
the one /ðə ˈwʌn/ der-/die-/dasjenige II
one-way /ˌwʌn ˈweɪ/ in eine(r) Richtung; einseitig III
° **onlooker** /ˈɒnˌlʊkə/ Zuschauer/in 3B4
° **only** /ˈəʊnli/ nur; einzige(r, s) I; erst II
° **onto** /ˈɒntə/ in; auf 1B9
open (from ... to ...) /ˈəʊpən frəm tʊ/ offen; geöffnet (von ... bis ...) I
to **open** /ˈəʊpən/ öffnen I
opening /ˈəʊp(ə)nɪŋ/ Öffnen; Öffnung; Eröffnung(s-); Anfang(s-) 3B5
° **opera house** /ˈɒp(ə)rə haʊs/ Opernhaus 4P11
opinion /əˈpɪnjən/ Meinung; Ansicht; Standpunkt II
opportunity /ˌɒpəˈtjuːnəti/ Gelegenheit; Chance; Möglichkeit IV
opposite /ˈɒpəzɪt/ gegenüberliegend II
optimistic /ˌɒptɪˈmɪstɪk/ optimistisch I
° **option** /ˈɒpʃ(ə)n/ Wahl; Möglichkeit; Option 5P8
or /ɔː/ oder I
° **or anything** (informal) /ɔːr‿ˈeniθɪŋ/ oder so was 4B1
orange /ˈɒrɪndʒ/ orange; orange(farben) I
° **orchestra** /ˈɔːkɪstrə/ Orchester 3P1
order /ˈɔːdə/ Ordnung; Reihenfolge III
to **order** /ˈɔːdə/ anordnen; bestellen; ordnen IV
° to order: auffordern 1B9
organic /ɔːˈɡænɪk/ organisch; hier: Bio- 4B5
° **organizational** /ˌɔːɡənaɪˈzeɪʃ(ə)nəl/ organisatorisch; Organisations- 3A2
to **organize** /ˈɔːɡənaɪz/ organisieren; ordnen II
organized /ˈɔːɡənaɪzd/ (gut) organisiert 5B3
° **orienteering** (no pl) /ˌɔːriənˈtɪərɪŋ/ Orientierungslauf I
original /əˈrɪdʒ(ə)nəl/ ursprünglich; originell, außergewöhnlich III

originally /əˈrɪdʒ(ə)nəli/ ursprünglich III
other /ˈʌðə/ andere(r, s) I
° other: Sonstiges 4B5
° **the other day** (informal) /ðiˈʌðə ˌdeɪ/ neulich 3B10
the other one /ðiˈʌðə wʌn/ der/die andere I
the other way round /ðiˌʌðə weɪ ˈraʊnd/ umgekehrt 4C4
others (pl) /ˈʌðəz/ andere I
otherwise /ˈʌðəˌwaɪz/ anders; ansonsten; anderweitig IV
ought to do sth /ˈɔːtə ˈduː/ etw tun sollen III
our /aʊə/ unser(e) I
ourselves /aʊəˈselvz/ uns; wir III
out /aʊt/ außen; draußen I
out of place /ˌaʊt‿əv ˈpleɪs/ fehl am Platz 3C3
out of sight /ˌaʊt‿əv ˈsaɪt/ außer Sichtweite IV
° **outback** (no pl) /ˈaʊtˌbæk/ Hinterland (Australiens) 4P P1
outcast /ˈaʊtˌkɑːst/ Ausgestoßene/r; Geächtete/r 3B4
outdoors /ˌaʊtˈdɔːz/ draußen; im Freien 4B1, 5A2
outgoing /ˌaʊtˈɡəʊɪŋ/ kontaktfreudig; (aus)scheidend; ausgehend 3A2
to **outline** /ˈaʊtlaɪn/ (kurz) umreißen; skizzieren 1C7, 4B3
outside /ˌaʊtˈsaɪd/ außen; außerhalb; nach draußen II
° **outside (of)** /ˌaʊtˈsaɪd‿əv/ außerhalb (von) 1C7
outstanding /ˌaʊtˈstændɪŋ/ außergewöhnlich; bemerkenswert; hervorragend II
over /ˈəʊvə/ über II; hinüber; herüber III
over there /ˌəʊvə ˈðeə/ dort drüben I
overall /ˌəʊvərˈɔːl/ Gesamt-; allgemein; insgesamt 4A2
to **overcome** (irr) /ˌəʊvəˈkʌm/ bewältigen; meistern 1B9
° **overdeveloped** /ˌəʊvə(r)dɪˈveləpt/ bevölkerungsreich; stark bebaut 4B2
° to **overlap** /ˌəʊvəˈlæp/ sich überlappen; sich überschneiden 5B3
overprotective /ˌəʊvəprəˈtektɪv/ überfürsorglich 1C10
to **overtake** (irr) /ˌəʊvəˈteɪk/ überholen; einholen II
° **overview (of)** /ˈəʊvəˌvjuː‿əv/ Überblick (über) 4P8
° **overwhelming** /ˌəʊvəˈwelmɪŋ/ überwältigend; riesig 1C5
° **overworked** /ˌəʊvəˈwɜːkt/ überarbeitet 1C10
own /əʊn/ eigene(r, s) I
° **of one's own** /əv wʌnz‿ˈəʊn/ jds eigene(r, s) 2B2

owner /ˈəʊnə/ Besitzer/in; Eigentümer/in IV
° **ownership** /ˈəʊnəʃɪp/ Besitz; Eigentum 3C3

P

° **pack** /pæk/ Gruppe; Rudel; Meute 1B6; Pack(ung); Packet 4B5; Infomappe 5O1
to pack one's bags /ˌpæk wʌnz ˈbæɡz/ die Koffer packen II
packaging (no pl) /ˈpækɪdʒɪŋ/ Verpackung(smaterial) 2B2
page /peɪdʒ/ Seite II
pain /peɪn/ Schmerz(en); Leid IV
° **painting** /ˈpeɪntɪŋ/ Bild; Gemälde, Malerei 2P7
pair /peə/ Paar III
° **pale** /peɪl/ blass; bleich 1C5
panel discussion /ˈpæn(ə)l dɪˌskʌʃ(ə)n/ Podiumsdiskussion 1C10
paper (no pl) /ˈpeɪpə/ Papier I
paragraph /ˈpærəˌɡrɑːf/ Absatz; Abschnitt IV
to **paraphrase** /ˈpærəˌfreɪz/ umschreiben; (mit anderen Worten) wiedergeben IV
parents (pl) /ˈpeərənts/ Eltern I
part /pɑːt/ Teil II
° **part-time** /ˌpɑːtˈtaɪm/ Teilzeit-; Halbtags- 5P5
to **participate (in)** /pɑːˈtɪsɪpeɪt‿ɪn/ (an etw) teilnehmen; sich (an etw) beteiligen 1C10
particular /pəˈtɪkjʊlə/ bestimmt; besondere(r, s); speziell III
particularly /pəˈtɪkjʊləli/ besonders; vor allem II
° **party** /ˈpɑːti/ Partei; Gruppe 2PP1
to have a party /ˌhæv‿ə ˈpɑːti/ eine Party geben I
° to **party** (informal) /ˈpɑːti/ feiern 4P1
to **pass** /pɑːs/ vorbeigehen an; bestehen III
° to pass: geben; (herüber)reichen 3B10
° to **pass on** /ˌpɑːs‿ˈɒn/ fortfahren; weitergeben 1C5
° to **pass over** /ˌpɑːs‿ˈəʊvə/ weitergeben; übermitteln 1P9
passage /ˈpæsɪdʒ/ (Text)passage; Abschnitt 1B2
passion /ˈpæʃ(ə)n/ Passion; Vorliebe; Leidenschaft III
past /pɑːst/ vergangen; frühere(r, s) 1C4; nach I; Vergangenheit; an ... vorbei; hinter II
° **path** /pɑːθ/ Weg; Pfad; Bahn 4B5
patience (no pl) /ˈpeɪʃ(ə)ns/ Geduld 5B2
patient /ˈpeɪʃ(ə)nt/ geduldig 1B2, 5B3
° **to pause for breath** /ˌpɔːz fə ˈbreθ/ eine (kurze) Pause machen, um Luft zu holen 3B3

English-German dictionary — Words — W

to **pay** *(irr)* /peɪ/ (be)zahlen II
  to **pay attention** /ˌpeɪ əˈtenʃ(ə)n/ Acht geben; aufpassen III
  to **pay sb a compliment** /ˌpeɪ ˌsʌmbədi ə ˈkɒmplɪmənt/ jdm ein Kompliment machen 1B5
payment /ˈpeɪmənt/ (Be)zahlung III
PE (= physical education) /ˌpiːˈiː, ˌfɪzɪk(ə)l ˌedjʊˈkeɪʃ(ə)n/ Sport *(als Schulfach)* I
peace *(no pl)* /piːs/ Frieden; Ruhe III
peaceful /ˈpiːsf(ə)l/ friedlich; ruhig 4B1
° **pedestrian** /pəˈdestriən/ Fußgänger/in; Fußgänger- 4P12
peer /pɪə/ jemand, der der gleichen Gruppe angehört 2C8, 3C1
  peer pressure /ˈpɪə ˌpreʃə/ Gruppenzwang 2B3, 3C1
° to **peer** /pɪə/ spähen 1B6
° **peeved** /piːvd/ verärgert 1B9
pen /pen/ Stift I
pencil /ˈpensl/ Bleistift I
  pencil case /ˈpensl ˌkeɪs/ Federmäppchen I
people *(no pl)* /ˈpiːp(ə)l/ Leute; Menschen I
pepper *(no pl)* /ˈpepə/ Pfeffer I
° **per** /pɜː/ pro 4B5
perfect /ˈpɜːfɪkt/ perfekt I
perfectly /ˈpɜːfɪktli/ vollkommen; perfekt III
to **perform** /pəˈfɔːm/ vorführen; aufführen; auftreten II
performance /pəˈfɔːməns/ Vorführung; Darbietung; Vorstellung III
perhaps /pəˈhæps/ vielleicht I
period /ˈpɪəriəd/ Zeitspanne; (Unterrichts)stunde; Zeitraum; Periode III
  ° **period:** Zeiteinheit bei einer Sportart 3B4
perk /pɜːk/ Vergünstigung; Vorteil 5A2
person /ˈpɜːs(ə)n/ Person I
personal /ˈpɜːs(ə)nəl/ persönlich; privat III
personality /ˌpɜːsəˈnæləti/ Persönlichkeit; Charakter IV
personally /ˈpɜːs(ə)nəli/ persönlich 5C1; ich für meinen Teil 3B2
to **persuade** /pəˈsweɪd/ überreden; überzeugen II
pet /pet/ Haustier I
° **petty theft** /ˌpeti ˈθeft/ Bagatelldiebstahl 2C5
phone (= telephone) /fəʊn, ˈtelɪˌfəʊn/ Telefon I
  to **answer the phone** /ˌɑːnsə ðə ˈfəʊn/ ans Telefon gehen I
  phone call (= telephone call) /ˈfəʊn ˌkɔːl, ˈtelɪˌfəʊn ˌkɔːl/ Anruf; Telefongespräch II
  phone-in *(BE)* /ˈfəʊn ˌɪn/ Anrufsendung 5A4

to **phone** /fəʊn/ anrufen; telefonieren II
to **take photos** /ˌteɪk ˈfəʊtəʊz/ fotografieren; Fotos machen I
° to **photocopy** /ˈfəʊtəˌkɒpi/ (foto)kopieren 5P3
to **photograph** /ˈfəʊtəˌɡrɑːf/ fotografieren 2C7
° **photographer** /fəˈtɒɡrəfə/ Fotograf/in 2P2
° **photography** *(no pl)* /fəˈtɒɡrəfi/ Fotografie 5B3
phrase /freɪz/ Satz; Ausdruck II
physical /ˈfɪzɪk(ə)l/ körperlich; physisch III
piano /piˈænəʊ/ Klavier; Piano III
to **pick** /pɪk/ aussuchen; auswählen 1C4, 2A2, 3A1
  ° to **pick:** abheben 1P4
  to **pick up** /ˌpɪk ˈʌp/ aufheben; abholen II
pickpocket /ˈpɪkˌpɒkɪt/ Taschendieb/in I
picture /ˈpɪktʃə/ Bild I
pie /paɪ/ Pastete; Kuchen IV
piece /piːs/ Stück IV
  piece of information /ˌpiːs əv ˌɪnfəˈmeɪʃ(ə)n/ eine Information III
  piece of paper /ˌpiːs əv ˈpeɪpə/ Blatt Papier I
pig /pɪɡ/ Schwein I
° **pile** /paɪl/ Stapel; Haufen 5B8
pink /pɪŋk/ rosa; pink I
pioneer /ˌpaɪəˈnɪə/ Pionier/in IV
place /pleɪs/ Ort; Platz; Stelle I
to **place** /pleɪs/ stellen; setzen; legen 1C5, 2C3
  ° to **place:** fällen, äußern 3C3
placement (BE = internship AE) /ˈpleɪsmənt/ Praktikum; vorübergehende Beschäftigung 5A2
° **placement** /ˈpleɪsmənt/ Platzierung; Vermittlung 1C7
to **plan** /plæn/ planen II
plane /pleɪn/ Flugzeug III
planet /ˈplænɪt/ Planet II
plant /plɑːnt/ Pflanze II
plastic /ˈplæstɪk/ Plastik(-); Kunststoff(-) II
plate /pleɪt/ Teller II
play /pleɪ/ Spiel; (Theater)stück II
to **play** /pleɪ/ spielen I
player /ˈpleɪə/ Spieler/in III
play-offs *(only pl)* /ˈpleɪɒfs/ System von Ausscheidungsspielen IV
° **plea (for)** /ˈpliː fɔː/ Bitte (um); Gesuch (auf/um) 1C7
please /pliːz/ bitte I
° **pleased** /pliːzd/ froh; zufrieden I
° **pledge** /pledʒ/ Versprechen; Zusicherung 1C7
plenty of /ˈplenti əv/ viel III
° to **plop** /plɒp/ platschen; plumpsen 1B9

plot /plɒt/ Handlung 1C5, 2C2
to **pluck up (the) courage (to do sth)** /ˌplʌk ˌʌp ðə ˌkʌrɪdʒ tə ˈduː/ allen Mut zusammennehmen(, um etw zu tun) 3B4
° **plus** /plʌs/ darüber hinaus; zusätzlich; außerdem 5A2
pm (= post meridiem) /ˌpiːˈem, ˌpəʊst məˈrɪdiəm/ nachmittags; abends *(nur hinter Uhrzeit zwischen 12 Uhr mittags und Mitternacht)* I
pocket /ˈpɒkɪt/ Tasche *(an Kleidungsstücken)* I
  pocket knife /ˈpɒkɪt ˌnaɪf/ Taschenmesser II
  pocket money /ˈpɒkɪt ˌmʌni/ Taschengeld II
poem /ˈpəʊɪm/ Gedicht I
point /pɔɪnt/ Punkt; Argument, Standpunkt IV
  point: Sinn, Zweck 4B1
  at some point /æt ˈsʌm pɔɪnt/ irgendwann 2B2
  point of view /ˌpɔɪnt əv ˈvjuː/ Ansicht; Einstellung; Perspektive III
  to **prove one's point** /ˌpruːv wʌnz ˈpɔɪnt/ beweisen, dass jmd recht hat 1C10
  ° **to the point** /tə ðə ˈpɔɪnt/ griffig; prägnant 5P9
to **point (to)** /pɔɪnt/ deuten/zeigen (auf) IV
to **point out** /ˌpɔɪnt ˈaʊt/ hinweisen; deuten; aufmerksam machen III
° to **poke** /pəʊk/ anstoßen 3B4
the police *(no pl)* /ðə pəˈliːs/ die Polizei I
policeman *(pl* **policemen)** /pəˈliːsmən/ Polizist I
policy /ˈpɒləsi/ Programm; Strategie; Grundsatz; Politik 4B5
polite /pəˈlaɪt/ höflich II
politics *(only pl)* /ˈpɒlətɪks/ Politik III
° to **pollute** /pəˈluːt/ verschmutzen 4P5
pollution /pəˈluːʃ(ə)n/ Verschmutzung IV
° **pom (= pommy/pommie)** *(informal)* /pɒm/ in Australien verwendete abwertende Bezeichnung für Briten 4PP1
poor /pɔː/ arm II
  ° **poor:** unzureichend; schlecht 4P5
popular /ˈpɒpjʊlə/ beliebt; populär II
popularity *(no pl)* /ˌpɒpjʊˈlærəti/ Beliebtheit; Popularität 2B3, 3A2, 4B2
population *(no pl)* /ˌpɒpjʊˈleɪʃ(ə)n/ Bevölkerung; Einwohnerzahl III
° **Portuguese** /ˌpɔːtʃʊˈɡiːz/ Portugiese/Portugiesin; Portugiesisch; portugiesisch 4B5
position /pəˈzɪʃ(ə)n/ Platz; Stelle; Position IV
positive /ˈpɒzətɪv/ positiv; bejahend II

Words

English-German dictionary

to **possess** /pəˈzes/ besitzen IV
° **possibility** /ˌpɒsəˈbɪləti/ Möglichkeit 5PP2
possible /ˈpɒsəb(ə)l/ möglich I
possibly /ˈpɒsəbli/ möglicherweise; gegebenenfalls 4C4
° **post** /pəʊst/ online veröffentlichter Beitrag/Artikel/Eintrag 3B10
to **post** /pəʊst/ posten (einen Beitrag/Artikel online stellen) 2A2, 3B10, 4B1
postcard /ˈpəʊstˌkɑːd/ Postkarte I
° **potential** /pəˈtenʃ(ə)l/ potenziell; möglich 5B4
° to **pound** /paʊnd/ hämmern; schlagen; pochen 1P3
poverty (no pl) /ˈpɒvəti/ Armut IV
power /ˈpaʊə/ Macht; Kraft; Stärke 2B3, 3C3
powerful /ˈpaʊəf(ə)l/ mächtig; druckvoll III
practical /ˈpræktɪk(ə)l/ praktisch; auf die Praxis bezogen 5B3
° **practically** /ˈpræktɪkli/ praktisch 3B4
practice (no pl) /ˈpræktɪs/ Übung; Gewohnheit, Sitte 1B5; Training 1A2
to **practice** (AE = to **practise** BE) /ˈpræktɪs/ üben IV
° **precious** /ˈpreʃəs/ wertvoll; kostbar 1C7
precise /prɪˈsaɪs/ genau; präzise; sorgfältig 1A5, 5B4
° **preconceived** /ˌpriːkənˈsiːvd/ vorgefasst 1B2
to **prefer** /prɪˈfɜː/ vorziehen; bevorzugen III
prejudice /ˈpredʒʊdɪs/ Vorurteil 1C5
prejudiced /ˈpredʒʊdɪst/ voreingenommen 4C4
preparation /ˌprepəˈreɪʃ(ə)n/ Vorbereitung; Zubereitung II
to **prepare** /prɪˈpeə/ vorbereiten; erstellen; versehen (werden) 2B5
prep(pie)/preppy (AE) /ˈprep(i)/ privilegierter junger Mensch, der großen Wert auf gute Kleidung und das äußere Erscheinungsbild legt 3A2
° **prescription** /prɪˈskrɪpʃ(ə)n/ Rezept; (Medikamenten)verschreibung 4P9
present /ˈprez(ə)nt/ Geschenk I
the **present** /ðə ˈprez(ə)nt/ die Gegenwart 4A3
present /ˈprez(ə)nt/ derzeitig; jetzig; gegenwärtig 1C4
° **present**: anwesend; vorhanden 1B8
to **present (sth to sb)** /prɪˈzent/ (jdm etw) präsentieren; vortragen I
presentation /ˌprez(ə)nˈteɪʃ(ə)n/ Präsentation; Darstellung 2B5
to **preserve** /prɪˈzɜːv/ erhalten; bewahren 1C1
° to **press** /pres/ (zusammen)drücken; (aus)pressen 1B2
pressure /ˈpreʃə/ Druck; Stress; Belastung 1B5, 3A2, 4B2, 5B3

to **pressure sb into doing sth** /ˌpreʃə ˌsʌmbədi ˌɪntə ˈduːɪŋ/ jdn dazu drängen, etw zu tun 2B3, 3C1
to **pretend** /prɪˈtend/ vorgeben; vortäuschen II
pretty /ˈprɪti/ hübsch; nett II
pretty (informal): ziemlich 4B5
pretty much (informal) /ˌprɪti ˈmʌtʃ/ ziemlich; beinahe 3B2
to **prevent** /prɪˈvent/ verhindern III
previous /ˈpriːviəs/ vor(her)ig; vorhergehend 4B7
° **previously** /ˈpriːviəsli/ zuvor; vorher; früher 1B9
price /praɪs/ Preis I
pride (no pl) /praɪd/ Stolz IV
° **prime minister** /ˌpraɪm ˈmɪnɪstə/ Premierminister/in; Ministerpräsident/in 4P10
° **princess** /ˌprɪnˈses/ Prinzessin 3B4
° **principal** (AE = head teacher BE) /ˈprɪnsəp(ə)l/ Schulleiter/in; Direktor/in 1P2
prison /ˈprɪz(ə)n/ Gefängnis(-); Haft IV
prisoner /ˈprɪz(ə)nə/ Gefangene/r; Häftling III
privileged /ˈprɪvəlɪdʒd/ privilegiert; bevorrechtigt 3A2
° **probably** /ˈprɒbəbli/ wahrscheinlich II
° **probation officer** /prəˈbeɪʃ(ə)n ˌɒfɪsə/ Bewährungshelfer/in 5O3
° **problematic** /ˌprɒbləˈmætɪk/ problematisch; fragwürdig 3P6
° **problem-solving** /ˈprɒbləm ˌsɒlvɪŋ/ Problemlöse(n) 5B3
° **probs** (= probably) (informal) /ˈprɒbz, ˈprɒbəbli/ wahrscheinlich 4B1
° **process** /ˈprəʊses/ Prozess; Verfahren 5P3
° **processed** /ˈprəʊsest/ industriell verarbeitet 2B5
to **produce** /prəˈdjuːs/ herstellen; produzieren II
product /ˈprɒdʌkt/ Produkt; Erzeugnis II
° **profession** /prəˈfeʃ(ə)n/ Beruf 1P9
professional /prəˈfeʃ(ə)nəl/ beruflich; Berufs-; professionell III
to **profit (from/by)** /ˈprɒfɪt frɒm/baɪ/ profitieren (von); Nutzen ziehen (aus) IV
programming (no pl) /ˈprəʊˌɡræmɪŋ/ Programmieren 5B2
progress (no pl) /ˈprəʊɡres/ Vorwärtskommen; Fortschritt III
to **progress** /prəʊˈɡres/ Fortschritte machen; vorankommen 1B2
to **prohibit** /prəʊˈhɪbɪt/ verbieten; verhindern IV
promise /ˈprɒmɪs/ Versprechen IV
to **promise** /ˈprɒmɪs/ versprechen II
promising /ˈprɒmɪsɪŋ/ viel versprechend 4B5

° to **promote** /prəˈməʊt/ (be)fördern; aufsteigen; werben (für) 2P3
to **pronounce** /prəˈnaʊns/ aussprechen II
pronunciation (no pl) /prəˌnʌnsiˈeɪʃ(ə)n/ Aussprache III
proof /pruːf/ Beweis IV
to **proofread** (irr) /ˈpruːfriːd/ Korrektur lesen 5B4
° **prop** /prɒp/ Requisit (für eine Theater- oder Filmszene verwendeter Gegenstand) 5O1
proper /ˈprɒpə/ echt; richtig II
pros and cons (only pl) /ˌprəʊz ən ˈkɒnz/ Für und Wider; Pro und Kontra 2B6, 4B5
to **protect** /prəˈtekt/ (be)schützen II
proud /praʊd/ stolz III
° to **prove** /pruːv/ beweisen; hier: stützen 2O2
° to **prove**: sich erwiesen 2O2
to **prove one's point** /ˌpruːv wʌnz ˈpɔɪnt/ beweisen, dass jmd recht hat 1C10
to **provide** /prəˈvaɪd/ bereitstellen; bieten; liefern III
° **provided (that)** /prəˈvaɪdɪd ðæt/ vorausgesetzt, (dass) 2C6
in close proximity /ɪn ˌkləʊs prɒkˈsɪməti/ in unmittelbarer Nähe 2B5
public /ˈpʌblɪk/ öffentlich 2A3, 4B5
the public /ðə ˈpʌblɪk/ die Öffentlichkeit; die Allgemeinheit IV
° **public transport** (BE) /ˌpʌblɪk ˈtrænspɔːt/ öffentliche Verkehrsmittel 4P12
to **publish** /ˈpʌblɪʃ/ veröffentlichen; herausgeben III
to **pull** /pʊl/ ziehen II
° to **pull a face** /ˌpʊl ə ˈfeɪs/ das Gesicht verziehen 3P3
° to **pull out** /ˌpʊl ˈaʊt/ ausscheren; herausziehen 3B4
punctual /ˈpʌŋktʃʊəl/ pünktlich 5B3
° **punctuation** (no pl) /ˌpʌŋktʃuˈeɪʃ(ə)n/ Zeichensetzung; Interpunktion 5O1
° to **punish** /ˈpʌnɪʃ/ (be)strafen 2C3
pupil /ˈpjuːp(ə)l/ Schüler/in I
to **purchase** /ˈpɜːtʃəs/ kaufen; (käuflich) erwerben IV
purple /ˈpɜːp(ə)l/ violett; lila I
purpose /ˈpɜːpəs/ Grund; Absicht; Ziel; Zweck 1A4
° **purse** /pɜːs/ Portemonnaie; Geldbörse 2C5
to **push** /pʊʃ/ stoßen; schieben II
to **put** (irr) /pʊt/ setzen; legen; stellen I; bringen II
° to **put down** /ˌpʊt ˈdaʊn/ hier: eintragen 5O2
to **put off** /ˌpʊt ˈɒf/ verschieben; abschrecken; abhalten 3B2
° to **put oneself in sb's shoes** /ˌpʊt ˌwʌnˌself ɪn ˌsʌmbədiz ˈʃuːz/ sich in jds Lage versetzen 1P2

English-German dictionary

° to put sth forward /ˌpʊt ˌsʌmθɪŋ ˈfɔːwəd/ etw vorbringen/anführen 1C2
to put sth in(to) perspective /ˌpʊt ˌsʌmθɪŋ ˌɪntʊ pəˈspektɪv/ etw in die richtige Perspektive rücken 5C3
° to put sth into action /ˌpʊt ˌsʌmθɪŋ ˌɪntʊ ˈækʃ(ə)n/ etw in die Tat umsetzen 3B4
° to put sth to good use /ˌpʊt ˌsʌmθɪŋ tə ˌɡʊd ˈjuːs/ gute Verwendung für etw finden können 5B6
to **put up** /ˌpʊt ˈʌp/ aufhängen; hochheben; aufstellen II

Q

qualification /ˌkwɒlɪfɪˈkeɪʃ(ə)n/ Qualifikation; Ausbildung; Abschluss; Kenntnisse IV
to **qualify** /ˈkwɒlɪfaɪ/ (sich) qualifizieren; klassifiziert werden, gelten 4B7
quality /ˈkwɒləti/ Qualität; Art; Eigenschaft; Merkmal 5A2
quarter (past/to) /ˈkwɔːtə/ Viertel (nach/vor) I
  quarter of an hour /ˌkwɔːtər əv ən ˈaʊə/ Viertelstunde I
queen /kwiːn/ Königin II
° **queer** *(informal)* /kwɪə/ Schwule/r; Lesbe; schwul 1B9
question /ˈkwestʃ(ə)n/ Frage I
queue /kjuː/ Schlange; Reihe III
quick /kwɪk/ schnell I
quiet /ˈkwaɪət/ leise; ruhig I
quite /kwaɪt/ ziemlich; ganz II
quotation /kwəʊˈteɪʃ(ə)n/ Zitat 2C5, 4B1
to **quote** /kwəʊt/ zitieren 1C7

R

rabbit /ˈræbɪt/ Kaninchen IV
race /reɪs/ Rennen II; Rasse III
° **racial** /ˈreɪʃ(ə)l/ rassisch; Rassen-; rassistisch 1B9
racist /ˈreɪsɪst/ Rassist/in; rassistisch IV
° **radical** /ˈrædɪk(ə)l/ radikal; *hier:* tiefgreifend 4B2
railway /ˈreɪlweɪ/ Gleise; Schienen; (Eisen)bahn III
rain *(no pl)* /reɪn/ Regen I
to **rain** /reɪn/ regnen I
to **raise** /reɪz/ heben; beschaffen, (ein)sammeln; aufziehen, großziehen III; aufstellen IV
range /reɪndʒ/ Reichweite; Bereich; Angebot 5A2
to **range** /reɪndʒ/ schwanken; sich bewegen; reichen 2B3
rank /ræŋk/ Position; Stellung; Rang; Reihe 3A2

° to **rap** /ræp/ rappen 3B10
° **rare** /reə/ rar; selten 5P4
rarely /ˈreəli/ selten; nicht oft IV
rate /reɪt/ Maß; Menge; Rate, Quote IV
rather /ˈrɑːðə/ ziemlich; recht II
  rather than /ˈrɑːðə ðæn/ anstelle; (und) nicht 2C5
rating /ˈreɪtɪŋ/ Einschätzung; Bewertung 2C9
RE (= religious education) /ˌɑːrˈiː, rəˌlɪdʒəsˌedjʊˈkeɪʃ(ə)n/ Religionslehre I
to **reach** /riːtʃ/ erreichen III
to **react (to sb/sth)** /riˈækt tə/ (auf jdn/etw) reagieren II
to **read** *(irr)* /riːd/ lesen I
reader /ˈriːdə/ Leser/in IV
ready /ˈredi/ fertig; bereit I
real /rɪəl/ wirklich; echt I
realistic /ˌrɪəˈlɪstɪk/ realistisch IV
reality *(no pl)* /riˈæləti/ Realität; Wirklichkeit IV
to **realize** /ˈrɪəlaɪz/ sich einer Sache bewusst sein/werden; bemerken III
really /ˈrɪəli/ wirklich I
° the **rear** /ðə ˈrɪə/ der hintere Teil; hinten 1B9
reason /ˈriːz(ə)n/ Grund II
° **rebel** /ˈreb(ə)l/ Rebell/in; Aufständische/r 3A2
° to **rebuke** /rɪˈbjuːk/ rügen; zurechtweisen 1C7
to **receive** /rɪˈsiːv/ erhalten; bekommen II
° **receiver** /rɪˈsiːvə/ Hörer; Receiver; Empfänger 1C5
recent /ˈriːs(ə)nt/ kürzlich; neu(e)ste 4A3; jüngst.../letzt... 4B2
recently /ˈriːs(ə)ntli/ kürzlich; vor Kurzem; neulich IV
° **receptionist** /rɪˈsepʃ(ə)nɪst/ *jemand, der in der Rezeption arbeitet* 5P5
recipe /ˈresəpi/ Rezept I
° **reckless** /ˈrekləs/ unbesonnen; leichtsinnig; rücksichtslos 2C3
to **recognize** /ˈrekəɡnaɪz/ (wieder) erkennen; anerkennen III
° **recognized** /ˈrekəɡnaɪzd/ anerkannt; zugelassen 4B5
to **recommend** /ˌrekəˈmend/ empfehlen III
recommendation /ˌrekəmenˈdeɪʃ(ə)n/ Empfehlung 4B7
° to **record** /rɪˈkɔːd/ aufzeichnen; aufnehmen 5A4
° **recording** /rɪˈkɔːdɪŋ/ Aufnahme; Aufzeichnen 1A2
to **recycle** /riːˈsaɪk(ə)l/ wiederverwenden II
red /red/ rot I
to **reduce** /rɪˈdjuːs/ verringern; reduzieren III

to **refer (back) to** /rɪˌfɜː ˈbæk tʊ/ (zurück)verweisen auf; sich beziehen auf IV
reference /ˈref(ə)rəns/ Verweis; Anspielung; Erwähnung; Bezugnahme 1C4
° **reference:** (Arbeits)zeugnis; Referenz 5P6
to **reflect** /rɪˈflekt/ spiegeln; zeigen; reflektieren; zum Ausdruck bringen 1C4
to **refuse** /rɪˈfjuːz/ ablehnen; verweigern 3C5
to **refute** /rɪˈfjuːt/ widerlegen; entkräften 1C10
regarding /rɪˈɡɑːdɪŋ/ bezüglich 2A4
° **regardless of sth** /rɪˈɡɑːdləs ˌəv/ trotz etw; ungeachtet etw 5B3
region /ˈriːdʒən/ Region; Gegend III
register /ˈredʒɪstə/ Register; Verzeichnis; Sprachebene 4C4
° **regular** /ˈreɡjʊlə/ regelmäßig 3B3
° to **regulate** /ˈreɡjʊleɪt/ regeln; regulieren 2O4
° **regulation** /ˌreɡjʊˈleɪʃ(ə)n/ Vorschrift; Bestimmung; Regelung; Regulierung 5PP2
to **rehearse** /rɪˈhɜːs/ proben; vorsprechen IV
to **reject** /rɪˈdʒekt/ ablehnen; zurückweisen; abweisen 1C10
° to **rejoin** /ˌriːˈdʒɔɪn/ wiedervereinigen; wiederaufnehmen 3B4
to **relate to** /rɪˈleɪt tʊ/ eine Beziehung/Zugang finden zu; sich beziehen (auf) 3B9, 4B3
relation /rɪˈleɪʃ(ə)n/ Verbindung; Bezug; Beziehung 1C7
relationship /rɪˈleɪʃ(ə)nʃɪp/ Beziehung II
relative /ˈrelətɪv/ Verwandter/ Verwandte III
to **relax** /rɪˈlæks/ entspannen III
relaxed /rɪˈlækst/ entspannt; locker II
to **release** /rɪˈliːs/ freilassen; entlassen 1C5
  to release: *hier:* veröffentlichen 2C2
° **relevance** /ˈreləv(ə)ns/ Relevanz; Bedeutung 2C3
reliable /rɪˈlaɪəb(ə)l/ verlässlich; zuverlässig 5B3
relieved /rɪˈliːvd/ erleichtert III
° **religious** /rəˈlɪdʒəs/ religiöse(r, s); Religions-; religiös 1B9
° to **relinquish** /rəˈlɪŋkwɪʃ/ aufgeben; abgeben 1C7
reluctant /rɪˈlʌktənt/ widerwillig; widerstrebend IV
to **rely on sb/sth** /rɪˈlaɪ ˌɒn/ sich auf jdn/etw verlassen 3C5
° to **remain** /rɪˈmeɪn/ (übrig) bleiben 5B3
° **remark** /rɪˈmɑːk/ Bemerkung; Äußerung 1B8

remarkable /rɪˈmɑːkəb(ə)l/ bemerkenswert; erstaunlich; beachtlich III
to **remember** /rɪˈmembə/ sich erinnern; daran denken II
° to **remind** /rɪˈmaɪnd/ erinnern 4P7
to **remove** /rɪˈmuːv/ entfernen; aus der Welt schaffen 1C5
renewable /rɪˈnjuːəb(ə)l/ erneuerbar 4B5
° **renovation** /ˌrenəˈveɪʃ(ə)n/ Renovierung; Sanierung 5B3
to **repair** /rɪˈpeə/ reparieren; (wieder) in Ordnung bringen 5B2
to **repeat** /rɪˈpiːt/ wiederholen; wiedergeben, erzählen 3C5; nachsprechen II
repetition /ˌrepəˈtɪʃ(ə)n/ Wiederholung 3A3
to **replace (with)** /rɪˈpleɪs wɪð/ ersetzen (durch) III
to **reply** /rɪˈplaɪ/ antworten; erwidern 3B8, 4C7
report /rɪˈpɔːt/ (Zeitungs-)Bericht; (Zeitungs-)Meldung II
° **report** /rɪˈpɔːt/ Zeugnis 5P3
to **report** /rɪˈpɔːt/ berichten; melden; wiedergeben II
reporter /rɪˈpɔːtə/ Reporter/in II
to **represent sb/sth** /ˌreprɪˈzent/ jdn/etw repräsentieren; jdn vertreten; etw wiedergeben 4B4
representative /ˌreprɪˈzentətɪv/ (Stell)vertreter/in 1C10
reputation /ˌrepjʊˈteɪʃ(ə)n/ Ruf; Renommee; Ansehen 3B8
to **request** /rɪˈkwest/ bitten um; (sich) wünschen 3C5
to **require** /rɪˈkwaɪə/ brauchen; verlangen; benötigen IV
requirement /rɪˈkwaɪəmənt/ Voraussetzung; Erfordernis 5B3
to **rescue** /ˈreskjuː/ retten; befreien III
research /ˈriːsɜːtʃ/ (Er)forschung; Untersuchung; Recherche III
to **do research** /duː ˈriːsɜːtʃ/ (er)forschen; recherchieren II
to **research** /rɪˈsɜːtʃ/ erforschen; recherchieren III
reservation /ˌrezəˈveɪʃ(ə)n/ Reservierung; Reservation (den Indianern vorbehaltenes Gebiet in Nordamerika) IV
to **resist** /rɪˈzɪst/ sich wehren; widerstehen; Widerstand leisten 3C3
° **resolve** (no pl) /rɪˈzɒlv/ Entschlossenheit 1P3
° to **resonate with sth** /ˈrezəneɪt wɪð/ etw ausstrahlen 1B9
to **respect** /rɪˈspekt/ respektieren 1C10, 3C3
respective /rɪˈspektɪv/ jeweilig 1C10

° **response** /rɪˈspɒns/ Antwort; Reaktion 1P3
responsibility /rɪˌspɒnsəˈbɪləti/ Verantwortung; Verantwortlichkeit; Zuständigkeit 3C3; Verantwortungsgefühl 2B5, 5B2
responsible /rɪˈspɒnsəb(ə)l/ verantwortlich; zuständig; verantwortungsvoll 3C5, 5B3
restaurant /ˈrestrɒnt/ Restaurant; Gaststätte I
result /rɪˈzʌlt/ Folge; Ergebnis I
to **result from** /rɪˈzʌlt frəm/ aus etw resultieren 4B4
return /rɪˈtɜːn/ Rückkehr; Heimkehr 1A2
return (ticket) (BE) /rɪˌtɜːn ˈtɪkɪt/ Rückfahrkarte III
to **return** /rɪˈtɜːn/ zurückkehren; zurückkommen III
to **reuse** /riːˈjuːz/ wiederverwenden; wiederverwerten 4B5
to **reveal** /rɪˈviːl/ zeigen; enthüllen IV
review /rɪˈvjuː/ Überprüfung; Kritik; Rezension 2C5
revolting /rɪˈvəʊltɪŋ/ abstoßend; widerlich 5A4
to **revolve around** /rɪˈvɒlv əˌraʊnd/ sich drehen um 3A2
rewarding /rɪˈwɔːdɪŋ/ befriedigend; lohnend 5A2
to **rewrite** (irr) /ˌriːˈraɪt/ neu schreiben; überarbeiten; umschreiben III
rhetorical device /rɪˌtɒrɪk(ə)l dɪˈvaɪs/ rhetorisches Stilmittel; Stilfigur 3A3, 5C2
rhyme /raɪm/ Reim(vers); Reimwort 3B10
rhyming /ˈraɪmɪŋ/ Reim- 3B9
rhythm /ˈrɪðəm/ Rhythmus; Takt 3B9
rich /rɪtʃ/ reich III; bedeutend IV
to **ride** (irr) /raɪd/ fahren (mit); reiten I
rider /ˈraɪdə/ Reiter/in; Fahrer/in IV
riding (no pl) /ˈraɪdɪŋ/ Reiten III
right /raɪt/ richtig; (nach) rechts I; Recht IV
to **be right** /ˌbiː ˈraɪt/ recht haben I
right-hand /ˌraɪt ˈhænd/ rechte(r, s) III
right now /ˌraɪt ˈnaʊ/ jetzt (gerade); sofort; gleich III
° **right-wing** /ˌraɪt ˈwɪŋ/ (politisch) rechts 1B2
to **right a wrong** /ˌraɪt ə ˈrɒŋ/ ein Unrecht wiedergutmachen 5C1
to **ring (up)** (irr) /ˌrɪŋ ˈʌp/ anrufen; klingeln; läuten II
to **rise** (irr) /raɪz/ steigen; aufgehen; hochgehen; sich erheben III
risk /rɪsk/ Risiko IV
rival /ˈraɪv(ə)l/ Rivale/Rivalin; Konkurrent/in II
river /ˈrɪvə/ Fluss II

road /rəʊd/ Straße II
° **rock** /rɒk/ Stein; Fels(en) 4P9
rocket /ˈrɒkɪt/ Rakete II
role /rəʊl/ Rolle II
romance /rəʊˈmæns/ Romantik; Romanze; Liebesfilm IV
the **Romans** /ðə ˈrəʊmənz/ die Römer 4C1
room /ruːm/ Zimmer; Raum I
° to **rough it** (informal) /ˈrʌf ɪt/ (ganz) primitiv leben 4B1
the other way round /ðɪ ˌʌðə weɪ ˈraʊnd/ umgekehrt 4C4
° **row** /rəʊ/ Reihe 1C7
rowdy /ˈraʊdi/ laut; rüpelhaft 4B1
rubbish (no pl) /ˈrʌbɪʃ/ Müll I
° **rude** /ruːd/ unhöflich 1C7
to **ruin** /ˈruːɪn/ zerstören; verderben; kaputtmachen IV
rule /ruːl/ Regel I
to **rule** /ruːl/ regieren; (be)herrschen III
ruler /ˈruːlə/ Lineal I; Herrscher/in III
° to **rumble** /ˈrʌmb(ə)l/ rumpeln; knurren 2B2
to **run (away)** (irr) /ˌrʌn əˈweɪ/ (weg)rennen I; laufen II
° to **run** /rʌn/ betreiben 5B3
° to **run out of sth** /ˌrʌn ˈaʊt əv/ etw nicht mehr haben 4P4
° **rush** /rʌʃ/ Eile; Rausch 2C5
° to **rush** /rʌʃ/ eilen; hetzen; strömen 1B2
° **Russian** /ˈrʌʃ(ə)n/ Russe/Russin; Russisch; russisch 4C1

S

sad /sæd/ traurig I
safe /seɪf/ sicher I
to **sail** /seɪl/ (auf dem Wasser) fahren/reisen; segeln 5A2
° **sailing** (no pl) /ˈseɪlɪŋ/ Segeln 4B5
salary /ˈsæləri/ Gehalt IV
salt (no pl) /sɔːlt/ Salz I
the same /ðə ˈseɪm/ der-/die-/dasselbe II
° **sameness** (no pl) /ˈseɪmnəs/ Gleichheit; Gleichförmigkeit 1C5
° **same-sex** /ˌseɪmˈseks/ gleichgeschlechtlich 1P10
° **sandy** /ˈsændi/ sandig; hier: Sand- 4B5
° **sarcasm** (no pl) /ˈsɑːkæz(ə)m/ Sarkasmus 3A2
° **satisfaction** /ˌsætɪsˈfækʃ(ə)n/ Zufriedenheit; Befriedigung; Genugtuung 3O1
° **satisfying** /ˈsætɪsˌfaɪɪŋ/ zufriedenstellend 4O3
Saturday /ˈsætədeɪ/ Samstag I
to **save** /seɪv/ retten; schützen; (be)wahren II
to **save money** /ˌseɪv ˈmʌni/ Geld sparen II

English-German dictionary — W — Words

to **say** (irr) /seɪ/ sagen I
  to **say sorry** /ˌseɪ ˈsɒri/ sich entschuldigen I
to **scan (for)** /skæn/ absuchen (nach); überfliegen; (ein)scannen III
to **scare** /skeə/ Angst machen; erschrecken I
scared /ˈskeəd/ verängstigt I
  to **get scared** /ˌget ˈskeəd/ sich (anfangen zu) fürchten II
scarf /skɑːf/ Schal II
scary /ˈskeəri/ furchterregend I
scene /siːn/ Szene III
scenic /ˈsiːnɪk/ landschaftlich (schön) 4B5
scheme /skiːm/ Plan; Projekt; Schema 3B10
scholarship /ˈskɒləʃɪp/ Stipendium III
school /skuːl/ Schule I
  school bag, schoolbag /ˈskuːl ˌbæɡ/ Schultasche I
science /ˈsaɪəns/ (Natur)wissenschaft I
scissors (only pl) /ˈsɪzəz/ Schere I
to **score (a goal)** /ˌskɔːr ə ˈɡəʊl/ (ein Tor) schießen II
Scotland /ˈskɒtlənd/ Schottland I
° to **scowl** /skaʊl/ mürrisch dreinblicken 1B7
to **scream** /skriːm/ schreien; kreischen I
° **screen** /skriːn/ Leinwand; Bildschirm 5O2
° to **screw around** (informal) /ˌskruː əˈraʊnd/ (he)rummachen; hier: veräppeln 5O3
screwdriver /ˈskruːˌdraɪvə/ Schraubenzieher III
script /skrɪpt/ Drehbuch; Skript; Regiebuch 1C7
° to **scrunch (up)** /ˌskrʌntʃˈʌp/ zerknüllen; verziehen 1B7
sea (no pl) /siː/ Meer; (die) See I
search /sɜːtʃ/ Suche 4B4
seaside (no pl, BE) /ˈsiːˌsaɪd/ (Meeres)küste I
  to **go to the seaside** /ˌɡəʊ tə ðə ˈsiːˌsaɪd/ ans Meer fahren I
season /ˈsiːz(ə)n/ Jahreszeit I
seat /siːt/ (Sitz)platz II
° **sec** (= second) (informal) /sek/ Sek.; Sekunde 1P3
second /ˈsekənd/ zweite(r, s) I
secret /ˈsiːkrət/ Geheimnis; geheim; Geheim- III
° **secretly** /ˈsiːkrətli/ heimlich 1B9
° **section** /ˈsekʃ(ə)n/ Teil; Abschnitt; Abteilung 2A3, 3B4, 4B5, 5B4
security (no pl) /sɪˈkjʊərəti/ Sicherheit II
to **see** (irr) /siː/ sehen I; verstehen II
  See you soon! (informal) /ˌsiː jə ˈsuːn/ bis bald! I
° to **seek** (irr) /siːk/ suchen 5B3

to **seem** /siːm/ scheinen I
° **seemingly** /ˈsiːmɪŋli/ scheinbar 1P7
° to **seize** /siːz/ ergreifen 1B9
to **select** /sɪˈlekt/ aussuchen; auswählen 1C5, 2A4
selection /sɪˈlekʃ(ə)n/ Auswahl 2A4
self-absorption (no pl) /ˌself əbˈzɔːpʃ(ə)n/ Ichbezogenheit 2C3
° **self-confident** /ˌself ˈkɒnfɪd(ə)nt/ selbstsicher; selbstbewusst 5P9
self-conscious /ˌself ˈkɒnʃəs/ gehemmt; verlegen IV
self-esteem (no pl) /ˌself ɪˈstiːm/ Selbstwertgefühl 5B2
self-expression (no pl) /ˌself ɪkˈspreʃ(ə)n/ Selbstdarstellung; Selbstausdruck 2C2
selfish /ˈselfɪʃ/ selbstsüchtig; egoistisch III
° **self-promotion** (no pl) /ˌself prəˈməʊʃ(ə)n/ Selbstdarstellung; Eigenwerbung 2C3
to **sell** (irr) /sel/ verkaufen I
to **send** (irr) /send/ (zu)schicken I
° **Señor** /senˈjɔː/ spanische Bezeichnung für „Herr" 1A2
sense /sens/ Verstand; Sinn III; Gefühl IV
sensible /ˈsensəb(ə)l/ vernünftig; angemessen II
sensitive /ˈsensətɪv/ sensibel; verständnisvoll; empfindlich 2C3, 4B2, 5B3
separate /ˈsep(ə)rət/ getrennt; separat; einzeln III
to **separate** /ˈsepəreɪt/ trennen; abspalten; (sich) scheiden (lassen) 3A2, 5B4
September /sepˈtembə/ September I
series (only pl) /ˈsɪəriːz/ (Fernseh)serie; Reihe; Folge 2C1
serious /ˈsɪəriəs/ ernst II; schwer III
service /ˈsɜːvɪs/ Service; Dienst; Verbindung III; Gottesdienst IV
session /ˈseʃ(ə)n/ Sitzung; Stunde; Session 5A2
° **set** /set/ Satz; Paar; Reihe 1C7
to **set** (irr) /set/ festsetzen; festlegen 1B7
  ° to **set up** (irr) /ˌset ˈʌp/ errichten; einrichten 1P5
setting /ˈsetɪŋ/ Einstellung; hier: Umgebung; Schauplatz 2C2
settler /ˈsetlə/ Siedler/in IV
seven /ˈsev(ə)n/ sieben I
several /ˈsev(ə)rəl/ einige; ein paar 3A2, 5B1
° **severe** /sɪˈvɪə/ schwer; schlimm; heftig 2O4
° **sewage** (no pl) /ˈsuːɪdʒ/ Abwasser 4B2
sex /seks/ Geschlecht 1B2

sexual orientation (no pl) /ˌsekʃuəl ˌɔːriənˈteɪʃ(ə)n/ sexuelle Veranlagung 2B5
shadow /ˈʃædəʊ/ Schatten II
° to **shake** (irr) /ʃeɪk/ schütteln 1O4; zittern 3B4
  ° to **shake one's head** /ˌʃeɪk wʌnz ˈhed/ den Kopf schütteln 3B4
shall /ʃæl/ sollen; werden III
° **shape up or ship out!** (informal) /ˌʃeɪp ˌʌp ɔː ˌʃɪp ˈaʊt/ entweder ihr bringt euch in Form oder ihr dampft ab! 2B5
to **share** /ʃeə/ teilen III
° **sharp** /ʃɑːp/ scharf; spitz; deutlich 1B8
she /ʃiː/ sie I
  ° **She had a point.** /ʃi: hæd ə ˈpɔɪnt/ Sie hatte nicht ganz unrecht. 1B2
  ° **She wasn't moved.** /ʃi: ˌwɒzənt ˈmuːvd/ Das ließ sie kalt. 3B7
sheep (pl sheep) /ʃiːp/ Schaf I
° **sheet** /ʃiːt/ Blatt; Platte; Laken 1B6
shelf (pl shelves) /ʃelf, ʃelvz/ (Regal)brett; Bord I
° **shift** /ʃɪft/ Schicht 5B3
° to **shift** /ʃɪft/ (weg)bewegen 1B9
ship /ʃɪp/ Schiff I
shirt /ʃɜːt/ Hemd II
shocked /ʃɒkt/ schockiert; entsetzt I
shocking /ˈʃɒkɪŋ/ schockierend; schrecklich IV
shoe /ʃuː/ Schuh I
to **shoot** (irr) /ʃuːt/ schießen II; filmen, drehen IV
shop /ʃɒp/ Geschäft; Laden I
  shop assistant /ˈʃɒp əˌsɪst(ə)nt/ Verkäufer/in I
shopping (no pl) /ˈʃɒpɪŋ/ Einkaufen I
  to **go shopping** /ˌɡəʊ ˈʃɒpɪŋ/ einkaufen gehen I
short /ʃɔːt/ kurz I
shortage /ˈʃɔːtɪdʒ/ Knappheit; Mangel 4B4
° to **shorten** /ˈʃɔːt(ə)n/ (ab)kürzen 2C6
shot /ʃɒt/ Schuss; Aufnahme, Einstellung 2C8
should /ʃʊd/ sollen I
shoulder /ˈʃəʊldə/ Schulter 1A2
to **shout (at)** /ʃaʊt ˌæt/ (an)schreien I
° to **shove** /ʃʌv/ schieben; stecken 1P3
to **show** (irr) /ʃəʊ/ zeigen II
  to **show off** /ˌʃəʊ ˈɒf/ angeben; (voller Stolz) zeigen IV
  to **show sb (a)round** /ˌʃəʊ ˌsʌmbədi əˈraʊnd/ jdn herumführen II
° **shower** /ˈʃaʊə/ Schauer; Regen; Dusche 4P6
  to **have/take a shower** /ˌhæv ˌteɪk ə ˈʃaʊə/ sich duschen II
° to **shrug (one's shoulders)** /ˌʃrʌɡ wʌnz ˈʃəʊldəz/ die Achseln zucken 3P3
° to **shuffle** /ˈʃʌf(ə)l/ mischen (von Karten) 1P4
° to **shut** (irr) /ʃʌt/ (ver)schließen 1O4

Words

English-German dictionary

° to shut out /ˌʃʌtˈaʊt/ ausschließen; verdrängen 1O4
° to shut up /ˌʃʌtˈʌp/ zuschließen; den Mund halten 1O2
shy /ʃaɪ/ schüchtern IV
sick /sɪk/ krank I
side /saɪd/ Seite III
sight /saɪt/ Sehenswürdigkeit II
° sighting /ˈsaɪtɪŋ/ Sichtung 5B3
sightseeing (no pl) /ˈsaɪtˌsiːɪŋ/ Besichtigungen; Sightseeing I
to do sightseeing /ˌduː ˈsaɪtˌsiːɪŋ/ eine Besichtigungstour machen I
sign /saɪn/ Zeichen; (Straßen-/Verkehrs)schild II
to sign /saɪn/ unterschreiben; unterzeichnen II
° signature /ˈsɪɡnətʃə/ Unterschrift 1C7
silent /ˈsaɪlənt/ still; ruhig; schweigsam III
silly /ˈsɪli/ albern; dumm I
silver /ˈsɪlvə/ Silber(-); silbern III
similar /ˈsɪmɪlə/ ähnlich II
similarity /ˌsɪməˈlærəti/ Ähnlichkeit IV
simple /ˈsɪmp(ə)l/ einfach III
simply /ˈsɪmpli/ einfach; nur III
since /sɪns/ seitdem; seither; seit II; da; weil III
Sincerely (yours) (AE) /sɪnˈsɪrli jɔːrz/ Mit freundlichen Grüßen IV
to sing (irr) /sɪŋ/ singen I
singer /ˈsɪŋə/ Sänger/in II
single /ˈsɪŋɡ(ə)l/ einzige(r, s); Einzel- III
single: Single; hier: Einzelzimmer 5B3
single (ticket) (BE) /ˌsɪŋɡ(ə)l ˈtɪkɪt/ einfache Fahrkarte; Einzelfahrkarte III
sister /ˈsɪstə/ Schwester I
to sit (irr) /sɪt/ sitzen I
to sit down /ˌsɪtˈdaʊn/ sich (hin)setzen I
site /saɪt/ Stelle; Platz; Ort IV
six /sɪks/ sechs I
size /saɪz/ Größe I
skill /skɪl/ Geschick; Fähigkeit, Fertigkeit III
° skilled /skɪld/ ausgebildet; qualifiziert 5PP2
to skim /skɪm/ streifen; überfliegen III
skin (no pl) /skɪn/ Haut II
° -skinned /skɪnd/ -häutig 1B6
° to skip /skɪp/ hüpfen; auslassen; schwänzen 5P7
skirt /skɜːt/ Rock I
° skull /skʌl/ Schädel 3B4
sky /skaɪ/ Himmel IV
° to skyrocket /ˈskaɪˌrɒkɪt/ in die Höhe schießen 2B3
° to slam down /ˌslæmˈdaʊn/ hinknallen; hier: sich (in einen Sitz) fallen lassen 5O1

slave /sleɪv/ Sklave/Sklavin IV
to sleep (irr) /sliːp/ schlafen I
to sleep late /ˌsliːp ˈleɪt/ lange schlafen; ausschlafen I
° sleeve /sliːv/ Ärmel 1B7
slow /sləʊ/ langsam II
° to smack /smæk/ knallen; schmatzen 3B4
small /smɔːl/ klein I
° smart /smɑːt/ schlau; clever 3B4
° to smear /smɪə/ beschmieren 1B7
to smell (irr) /smel/ riechen; duften I
smelly /ˈsmeli/ stinkend; übel riechend 5A4
smile /smaɪl/ Lächeln III
to smile (at) /ˈsmaɪl ˌæt/ (an)lächeln II
to smoke /sməʊk/ rauchen 2B5, 3C3
snake /sneɪk/ Schlange I
° to snap /snæp/ schnalzen; schnippen 3P3
° to sneak /sniːk/ schleichen 1O3
snow (no pl) /snəʊ/ Schnee II
so /səʊ/ also; deshalb I; so; sehr II
° so far /ˌsəʊ ˈfɑː/ bisher 1P5
soap /səʊp/ Seife II
° to soar /sɔː/ aufsteigen; gleiten, schweben 3B4
sociable /ˈsəʊʃəb(ə)l/ gesellig; freundlich; umgänglich 5A2
social /ˈsəʊʃ(ə)l/ Gesellschaft(s)-; gesellschaftlich; sozial III
social networking site /ˈsəʊʃ(ə)l ˈnetwɜːkɪŋ saɪt/ soziales Netzwerk III
social worker /ˈsəʊʃ(ə)l ˌwɜːkə/ Sozialarbeiter/in IV
society /səˈsaɪəti/ Gesellschaft; die feine Gesellschaft II
soft skills /ˌsɒft ˈskɪlz/ Soft Skills (soziale oder emotionale Kompetenz) 5B2
solar panel /ˌsəʊlə ˈpæn(ə)l/ Sonnenkollektor 4B5
soldier /ˈsəʊldʒə/ Soldat/in III
° solemn /ˈsɒləm/ feierlich; ernst 1C7
° solution /səˈluːʃ(ə)n/ (Auf)lösung 4P10
to solve /sɒlv/ lösen 1B2
some /sʌm/ einige; etwas I; irgendein(e) III
somebody /ˈsʌmbədi/ (irgend)jemand; irgendwer I
someone /ˈsʌmwʌn/ (irgend)jemand; irgendwer II
someone else /ˌsʌmwʌn ˈels/ jemand anders III
something /ˈsʌmθɪŋ/ etwas I
sometimes /ˈsʌmtaɪmz/ manchmal I
° somewhat /ˈsʌmwɒt/ etwas; ein wenig 1C5
somewhere /ˈsʌmweə/ irgendwo 4B1
son /sʌn/ Sohn I
soon /suːn/ bald II
° soothing /ˈsuːðɪŋ/ beruhigend IV
sorry /ˈsɒri/ Entschuldigung!; Tut mir leid. I

to say sorry /ˌseɪ ˈsɒri/ sich entschuldigen I
° sort /sɔːt/ Sorte; Art 1B9
sound /saʊnd/ Geräusch; Klang; Laut I
to sound /saʊnd/ klingen I
° soup /suːp/ Suppe 5B3
° sour /ˈsaʊə/ sauer 1B7
source /sɔːs/ Quelle; Informationsquelle 4B4
south /saʊθ/ Süden; südlich; Süd- III
spa /spɑː/ (Heil)bad; Wellness-Bereich 4B5
space /speɪs/ Raum; Platz III
space (no pl) /speɪs/ Raum; Weltraum III
spaceship /ˈspeɪsʃɪp/ Raumschiff III
Spain /speɪn/ Spanien 4B1
° Spanish /ˈspænɪʃ/ Spanisch; spanisch 4C1
spare time (no pl) /ˌspeə ˈtaɪm/ Freizeit 5A2
to speak (irr) /spiːk/ sprechen I
° to speak out /ˌspiːk ˈaʊt/ seine Meinung deutlich vertreten 1B9
to speak to sb /ˈspiːk tʊ/ mit jdm reden II
° to speak up /ˌspiːk ˈʌp/ seine Meinung sagen 1B9
speaker /ˈspiːkə/ Redner/in; Sprecher/in 4C1
° speaking of … /ˈspiːkɪŋ ˌəv/ apropos …; da wir gerade von … sprechen 3C5
special /ˈspeʃ(ə)l/ besondere(r, s) II
° species /ˈspiːʃiːz/ Art; Spezies 4B2
° specifically /spəˈsɪfɪkli/ speziell; ausdrücklich 5P9
spectacular /spekˈtækjʊlə/ atemraubend; fantastisch II
to speculate (on) /ˈspekjuleɪt ˌɒn/ spekulieren; Vermutungen anstellen (über) II
speed /spiːd/ Geschwindigkeit; Tempo III
° spellchecker /ˈspelˌtʃekə/ Rechtschreibprüfprogramm 5O1
spelling (no pl) /ˈspelɪŋ/ Rechtschreibung III
to spend (irr) /spend/ verbringen (Zeit); ausgeben (Geld) I
° to spin (irr) /spɪn/ drehen 1B7
spirit /ˈspɪrɪt/ Geist; Stimmung; Seele; Einstellung IV
° spiteful /ˈspaɪtf(ə)l/ gehässig 1P8
to split up (irr) /ˌsplɪt ˈʌp/ (auf)teilen; sich trennen III
spoon /spuːn/ Löffel II
° to sport /spɔːt/ tragen 3A2
° sports field /ˈspɔːts ˌfiːld/ Sportplatz 3A2
sports ground /ˈspɔːts ˌɡraʊnd/ Sportplatz I
° sporty /ˈspɔːti/ sportlich 3P2
spot /spɒt/ Fleck; Stelle; Ort 3C1

English-German dictionary

° to spot /spɒt/ entdecken; finden 4P12
to **spread** *(irr)* /spred/ (sich) ausbreiten; (sich) verbreiten IV
spring /sprɪŋ/ Frühling I
square /skweə/ Quadrat(-) IV
° to **squirm** /skwɜːm/ sich (vor Verlegenheit) winden 1B9
° **stack** /stæk/ Stapel; Stoß; Haufen 1B9
stadium /'steɪdɪəm/ Stadion II
staff *(no pl)* /stɑːf/ Belegschaft; Personal; Lehrerkollegium IV
stage /steɪdʒ/ Bühne II
stairs *(pl)* /steəz/ Treppe I
stance *(no pl)* /stæns/ Haltung; Standpunkt; Einstellung 1C3
to **stand** *(irr)* /stænd/ stehen; ertragen, aushalten I
° to **stand a chance of doing sth** /ˌstænd ə ˌtʃɑːns əv 'duːɪŋ/ Aussichten haben, etw zu tun 1B5
to **stand out** *(irr)* /ˌstænd 'aʊt/ hervorragen; sich abheben 5B5
to **stand up** *(irr)* /ˌstænd 'ʌp/ aufstehen II
° to **stand up to sb/sth** /ˌstænd ˈʌp tʊ/ sich jdm/etw widersetzen 1B8
° **star** /stɑː/ Stern 2C9
° to **stare (at sb/sth)** /'steər æt/ (jdn/etw an)starren 1B7
° **starlet** /'stɑːlət/ (Film)sternchen 2C3
start /stɑːt/ Anfang; Beginn II
to **start** /stɑːt/ anfangen I
state /steɪt/ staatlich; Staat(s-); Land; US-Bundesstaat IV
to **state** /steɪt/ aussprechen; erklären; darlegen 2B4
statement /'steɪtmənt/ Äußerung; Aussage II
station /'steɪʃ(ə)n/ Bahnhof; Haltestelle; Station II
statistic(s) /stə'tɪstɪks/ Statistik IV
° the **status quo** /ðə ˌsteɪtəs 'kwəʊ/ Status quo *(gegenwärtiger Zustand)* 3B3
stay /steɪ/ Aufenthalt III
to **stay** /steɪ/ bleiben; sich aufhalten; untergebracht sein I
to **stay true to the original** /ˌsteɪ ˌtruː tə ðɪ əˈrɪdʒ(ə)nəl/ sich an das Original halten 1B10
to **steal** *(irr)* /stiːl/ stehlen I
° to **steel oneself** /'stiːl wʌn self/ sich wappnen; all seinen Mut zusammennehmen 1P3
° to **stem from** /'stem frəm/ zurückzuführen sein auf 1O2
step /step/ Schritt; (Treppen)stufe II
° to **step** /step/ treten; steigen; gehen 1P3
stereotype /'sterɪəˌtaɪp/ Stereotyp; Klischee; Vorurteil 1B2, 3A2
to **stick** *(irr)* /stɪk/ kleben; *hier:* bleiben 2B3

° to **stick with sth** /'stɪk wɪð/ an etw festhalten; bei etw dabei bleiben 3C3
° **stiff** /stɪf/ steif; hart 1B7
still /stɪl/ (immer) noch; noch immer; trotzdem II
° **stomach** /'stʌmək/ Magen; Bauch 2B2
stone /stəʊn/ Stein I
to **stop** /stɒp/ aufhören; beenden; stoppen; (an)halten; aufhalten I
to **stop sb from doing sth:** jdn davon abhalten, etw zu tun IV
store /stɔː/ Laden; Geschäft; Kaufhaus II
storm /stɔːm/ Gewitter; Unwetter; (Protest)sturm III
story /'stɔːri/ Geschichte; Erzählung I
straight /streɪt/ gerade(aus); direkt; ordentlich, hetero(sexuell) 1B2
° **straight:** *hier:* glatt 2B5
strange /streɪndʒ/ sonderbar; merkwürdig; unheimlich I
streak /striːk/ Streifen; Strahl; Strähne 3A2
street /'striːt/ Straße I
strength *(no pl)* /streŋθ/ Kraft; Stärke III
to **stress** /stres/ betonen 2C3, 3B9, 4B2
° to **stress sb (out)** /ˌstres ˌsʌmbədi ˈaʊt/ jdn stressen 3B3
° to **stretch** /stretʃ/ (sich) dehnen; strecken 2O2
strict /strɪkt/ streng; strikt; genau II
to **strike** *(irr)* /straɪk|strʌk|strʌk/ zuschlagen 2C1
to **strike sb as ...** /'straɪk ˌsʌmbədi əz/ jdm ... scheinen 1C1
striking /'straɪkɪŋ/ bemerkenswert; auffallend 2A2
° to **strip away** /ˌstrɪp əˈweɪ/ entfernen; abstreifen 1B2
strong /strɒŋ/ stark; kräftig; fest II
structure /'strʌktʃə/ Struktur; Aufbau III
to **structure** /'strʌktʃə/ strukturieren II
struggle (for) /'strʌg(ə)l fɔː/ Kampf (um) 3C3
to **struggle** /'strʌg(ə)l/ sich abmühen; kämpfen; ringen IV
student /'stjuːd(ə)nt/ Student/in; Schüler/in III
studies *(pl)* /'stʌdiz/ Studium III
to **study** /'stʌdi/ studieren; sich befassen mit; erforschen II; lernen III
stuff *(no pl, informal)* /stʌf/ Zeug; Sachen III
° to **stumble** /'stʌmb(ə)l/ stolpern; straucheln 3B4
stunning /'stʌnɪŋ/ toll; fantastisch; umwerfend II
stupid /'stjuːpɪd/ dumm; blöd I
style /staɪl/ Stil; Art 1B8
subhead(ing) /'sʌbˌhedɪŋ/ Untertitel 4B2

subject /'sʌbdʒɪkt/ (Schul)fach; Thema 3A4, 5B3
subsequently /'sʌbsɪkwəntli/ später; danach 2C8
substance /'sʌbstəns/ Substanz; Stoff 2B5
subtle /'sʌt(ə)l/ fein(sinnig); subtil 2B3
suburb /'sʌbɜːb/ Vorstadt; Vorort IV
to **succeed** /sək'siːd/ Erfolg haben; nachfolgen III
success *(no pl)* /sək'ses/ Erfolg II
successful /sək'sesf(ə)l/ erfolgreich II
such /sʌtʃ/ solch(er/es); so II
° to **suck** *(informal, AE)* /sʌk/ ätzend sein 1O4
suddenly /'sʌd(ə)nli/ plötzlich II
to **suffer (from)** /'sʌfə frɒm/ erleiden; ertragen; leiden (an/unter) IV
sugar /'ʃʊgə/ Zucker I
to **suggest** /sə'dʒest/ vorschlagen; andeuten, (darauf) hinweisen 1B1
suggestion /sə'dʒestʃ(ə)n/ Vorschlag II
suicide /'suːɪsaɪd/ Selbstmord IV
to **suit sb/sth** /suːt/ zu jdm/etw passen 1C8, 5B3
suitable /'suːtəb(ə)l/ geeignet; passend; angemessen III
suitcase /'suːtˌkeɪs/ Koffer I
suited (to) /'suːtɪd tʊ/ geeignet (für) IV
to **sum up** /ˌsʌm 'ʌp/ resümieren; zusammenfassen III
to **summarize** /'sʌməraɪz/ zusammenfassen; resümieren 2B3, 3C4, 4B2
summary /'sʌməri/ Zusammenfassung 1C5, 2C8, 3B5
summer /'sʌmə/ Sommer I
all summer /ˌɔːl 'sʌmə/ den ganzen Sommer I
sun /sʌn/ Sonne I
sunbathing *(no pl)* /'sʌnˌbeɪðɪŋ/ Sonnenbaden 4B5
Sunday /'sʌndeɪ/ Sonntag I
sunglasses *(pl)* /'sʌnˌglɑːsɪz/ Sonnenbrille I
sunny /'sʌni/ sonnig I
° **S'up?** (= **What's up?**) *(informal)* /sʌp, ˌwɒts 'ʌp/ Was geht (ab)? 1P3
superficial /ˌsuːpə'fɪʃ(ə)l/ oberflächlich; äußerlich 2C8
° **superior** /sʊ'pɪərɪə/ Vorgesetzte/r 5P9
supervision /ˌsuːpə'vɪʒ(ə)n/ Beaufsichtigung; Aufsicht 2B5
supply /sə'plaɪ/ Vorrat; Versorgung; Bereitstellung; Angebot IV
support /sə'pɔːt/ Unterstützung; Hilfestellung II
to **support** /sə'pɔːt/ (unter)stützen; für jdn sein III
supporter /sə'pɔːtə/ Unterstützer/in; Anhänger/in; Verfechter/in III
supportive /sə'pɔːtɪv/ unterstützend 1B7

to **suppose** /səˈpəʊz/ annehmen; denken III
° to **suppress** /səˈpres/ unterdrücken; verdrängen 1C5
° the **Supreme Court** (AE) /ðə sʊˌpriːm ˈkɔːt/ Oberstes Bundesgericht 1P10
sure /ʃɔː/ sicher I
  to **be sure** /biː ˈʃɔː/ sicher sein I
surely /ˈʃɔːli/ sicher(lich); bestimmt; doch 3B1
to **go surfing** /ˌɡəʊ ˈsɜːfɪŋ/ surfen gehen I
surprise /səˈpraɪz/ Überraschung I
to **surprise** /səˈpraɪz/ überraschen I
surprised /səˈpraɪzd/ überrascht; erstaunt I
surprising /səˈpraɪzɪŋ/ überraschend III
° to **surround** /səˈraʊnd/ einkreisen 3B4; umgeben 4B2
survey /ˈsɜːveɪ/ Umfrage 2C9, 4A1
survival guide /səˈvaɪv(ə)l ɡaɪd/ Überlebensratgeber 3A5
to **survive** /səˈvaɪv/ überleben III
suspicious /səˈspɪʃəs/ verdächtig; misstrauisch; argwöhnisch 1B7
sustainable /səˈsteɪnəb(ə)l/ haltbar; nachhaltig 4B2
° to **swab** /swɒb/ abtupfen 1B7
° He **swallowed** the lump in his throat. /hiː ˌswɒləʊd ðə ˈlʌmp ɪn hɪz ˌθrəʊt/ Er schluckte den Kloß in seinem Hals hinunter. 1P3
° to **swan around** (informal, BE) /ˌswɒn əˈraʊnd/ herumtrödeln 2C5
to **swap** /swɒp/ (aus)tauschen III
° to **swarm** /swɔːm/ (um)schwärmen 1B6
to **swear** (irr) /sweə/ schwören; fluchen, derbe Schimpfwörter gebrauchen IV
sweat (no pl) /swet/ Schweiß 1P3
° **Swedish** /ˈswiːdɪʃ/ Schwedisch; schwedisch 5P11
to **sweep** (irr) /swiːp/ kehren; fegen I
  to **sweep the floor** /ˌswiːp ðə ˈflɔː/ den Boden fegen I
sweet /swiːt/ süß III
sweets (pl) /swiːts/ Süßigkeiten I
to **swim** (irr) /swɪm/ schwimmen II
swimming /ˈswɪmɪŋ/ Schwimmen I
  to **go swimming** /ˌɡəʊ ˈswɪmɪŋ/ schwimmen gehen I
to **switch** /swɪtʃ/ wechseln 4C4
° **sympathetic** /ˌsɪmpəˈθetɪk/ verständnisvoll; wohlgesonnen 4P9
to **sympathize (with)** /ˈsɪmpəθaɪz wɪð/ mitfühlen (mit) III
sympathy /ˈsɪmpəθi/ Mitleid; Mitgefühl 2A1

T

table /ˈteɪb(ə)l/ Tisch I
  to **lay the table** /ˌleɪ ðə ˈteɪb(ə)l/ den Tisch decken I

° **tactful** /ˈtæktf(ə)l/ taktvoll 5B3
to **take** (irr) /teɪk/ (mit)nehmen; wegnehmen; bringen I; dauern III
  ° to **take a class in sth** /ˌteɪk ə ˈklɑːs ɪn/ einen Kurs in etw belegen 5P4
  to **take a (closer) look at sth** /ˌteɪk ə ˌkləʊsə ˈlʊk æt/ sich etw (genauer) ansehen I
  ° to **take a seat** /ˌteɪk ə ˈsiːt/ sich (hin)setzen 1B9
  to **take care** /ˌteɪk ˈkeə/ aufpassen 2B5
  ° to **take care of** /ˌteɪk ˈkeər əv/ sich kümmern um 5PP2
  to **take ... for a walk** /ˌteɪk fər ə ˈwɔːk/ ... spazieren führen; Gassi gehen mit ... I
  to **take (immediate) action** /ˌteɪk ɪˌmiːdiət ˈækʃ(ə)n/ (augenblicklich) handeln 5C1
  to **take notes** /ˌteɪk ˈnəʊts/ (sich) Notizen machen II
  ° to **take off** /ˌteɪk ˈɒf/ abnehmen; ausziehen; abziehen; abheben 4P1
  to **take out** /ˌteɪk ˈaʊt/ herausnehmen; hinausbringen I
  to **take out the rubbish** /ˌteɪk aʊt ðə ˈrʌbɪʃ/ den Müll hinausbringen I
  to **take part (in)** /ˌteɪk ˈpɑːt ɪn/ teilnehmen (an) I
  to **take photos** /ˌteɪk ˈfəʊtəʊz/ fotografieren; Fotos machen I
  to **take place** /ˌteɪk ˈpleɪs/ stattfinden I
  to **take sth into account** /ˌteɪk ˌsʌmθɪŋ ˌɪntə əˈkaʊnt/ etw berücksichtigen 1A5
  to **take sth seriously** /ˌteɪk ˌsʌmθɪŋ ˈsɪəriəsli/ etw ernst nehmen 1C10
  to **take turns** (BE) /ˌteɪk ˈtɜːnz/ sich abwechseln 1A5, 3C5, 4A4, 5C5
° **tale** /teɪl/ Geschichte; Erzählung; Bericht 1P5
talented /ˈtæləntɪd/ talentiert; begabt III
to **talk (about)** /ˈtɔːk əˌbaʊt/ sprechen (über); reden (über) I
to **talk (to)** /tɔːk/ sprechen; reden (mit) I
  ° to **talk sb out of something** /ˌtɔːk ˌsʌmbədi ˈaʊt əv/ jdn etw ausreden 3P7
tall /tɔːl/ groß; hoch (gewachsen) I
° **tank** /tæŋk/ Panzer 1B9
° to **tap one's feet** /ˌtæp wʌnz ˈfiːt/ mit den Füßen wippen 3P3
task /tɑːsk/ Aufgabe III
to **taste** /teɪst/ schmecken III
tea (no pl) /tiː/ Tee III
to **teach** (irr) /tiːtʃ/ unterrichten; beibringen II
teacher /ˈtiːtʃə/ Lehrer/in I
° **teaching** (no pl) /ˈtiːtʃɪŋ/ Lehren; Unterrichten 4P8
tear /tɪə/ Träne III

technology /tekˈnɒlədʒi/ Technologie; Technik I
tedious /ˈtiːdiəs/ langweilig; fad 5A4
° **teenage** /ˈtiːnˌeɪdʒ/ Teenager-; Jugend- 1B6
telephone /ˈtelɪˌfəʊn/ Telefon I
° **television** /ˈtelɪˌvɪʒ(ə)n/ Fernsehen; Fernseher 2PP1
to **tell** (irr) /tel/ erzählen; sagen I
  ° **Tell me about it!** /ˈtel mi əˌbaʊt ɪt/ Wem sagst du das! 2B2
to **tempt sb to do/into doing sth** /ˌtempt ˌsʌmbədi tə ˈduː, ˌɪntə ˈduːɪŋ/ jdn dazu verleiten/verführen, etw zu tun 2B2
tempting /ˈtemptɪŋ/ verlockend 2B3
ten /ten/ zehn I
to **tend to do sth** /ˌtend tə ˈduː/ zu etw neigen; dazu neigen, etw zu tun 3A2
tense /tens/ Zeitform; Tempus II; angespannt III
tent /tent/ Zelt I
term /tɜːm/ Semester; Periode; (Amts)zeit III
  ° **term:** Ausdruck; Begriff 5O1
terrible /ˈterəb(ə)l/ schrecklich; furchtbar I
° **terrified** /ˈterəfaɪd/ erschrocken; verängstigt 3O3
terrifying /ˈterəˌfaɪɪŋ/ entsetzlich; Angst erregend; Furcht einflößend 2C5
° **territory** /ˈterət(ə)ri/ Gebiet; Revier; Territorium 4P11
to **text** /tekst/ eine SMS senden II
text message /ˈtekst ˌmesɪdʒ/ SMS II
than /ðæn/ als II
° to **thank** /θæŋk/ danken 5C5
thank you /ˈθæŋk juː/ Danke I
thanks /θæŋks/ Danke I
  thanks to /ˈθæŋks tʊ/ dank; wegen IV
that /ðæt/ das; der/die/das I; dass II
  That would be great. /ˌðæt wəd bi ˈɡreɪt/ Das wäre toll. I
  That's none of your business. (informal) /ˌðæts ˌnʌn əv jə ˈbɪznəs/ Das geht dich nichts an. III
  that's why /ˌðæts ˈwaɪ/ deshalb; darum; deswegen II
the /ðə/ der/die/das I
  the ... the: je ..., desto ... II
theater (AE = theatre BE) /ˈθɪətər/ Theater IV
theft /θeft/ Diebstahl 2C7
their /ðeə/ ihr(e) I
theirs /ðeəz/ ihre(r, s); ihrs II
them /ðem/ sie; ihnen I
theme /θiːm/ Thema(tik); Motto 1B1, 3B10
themselves /ðəmˈselvz/ sich; sie selbst; (sich) selbst III
then /ðen/ dann; danach; darauf I
there /ðeə/ dort; da I

English-German dictionary   **Words**

there is/are /ðeər_ˈɪz/ˈɑː/ es gibt, da ist; da sind I
° **There's no point** /ðeəz ˌnəʊ ˈpɔɪnt/ Es hat keinen Zweck/Sinn 5O1
° **therefore** /ˈðeəfɔː/ deshalb; deswegen; daher 3B10
° **thesaurus** /θɪˈsɔːrəs/ Synonymwörterbuch 5O2
these (= *pl of* **this**) /ðiːz/ diese I
° **these days** /ˈðiːz deɪz/ in letzter Zeit; heutzutage; zurzeit 1B5
they /ðeɪ/ sie I
thief (*pl* **thieves**) /θiːf, θiːvz/ Dieb/in 2C1
thing /θɪŋ/ Ding; Gegenstand; Sache I
to **think** (*irr*) /θɪŋk/ denken; glauben; meinen I
to **think about sb/sth** /ˈθɪŋk_əˌbaʊt/ an jdn/etw denken; über jdn/etw nachdenken II
to **think of** /ˈθɪŋk_əv/ denken an; sich ausdenken I; denken an; sich ausdenken; halten von III
third /θɜːd/ dritte(r, s) I
this /ðɪs/ diese(r, s); das I
those (= *pl of* **that**) /ðəʊz/ diese I
though /ðəʊ/ trotzdem; aber II
thought /θɔːt/ Gedanke II
to **threaten** /ˈθret(ə)n/ (be)drohen III
three /θriː/ drei I
° **thrice** /θraɪs/ dreimal 2B2
thrilled /θrɪld/ außer sich vor Freude III
thrilling /ˈθrɪlɪŋ/ aufregend; packend 2C8
° **throat** /θrəʊt/ Rachen; Hals; Kehle 1B7
throne /θrəʊn/ Thron III
through /θruː/ durch II
to **throw (away)** (*irr*) /ˌθrəʊ_əˈweɪ/ (weg)werfen II
° to **throw it out to sb** (*informal*) /ˌθrəʊ_ɪt_ˈaʊt_tʊ/ jdn um Ideen/Input bitten 4B1
° to **throw/shed light on sth** /ˌθrəʊ/ ˌʃed ˈlaɪt_ɒn/ Licht auf etw werfen 3C5
Thursday /ˈθɜːzdeɪ/ Donnerstag I
to **tidy (up)** /ˌtaɪdiˈ_ʌp/ aufräumen I
tight /taɪt/ fest; eng IV
tight (*informal*): *hier:* knausrig 4B1
till (= **until**) /tɪl, ʌnˈtɪl/ bis II
time /taɪm/ Zeit; Uhrzeit I; Mal III
all the time /ˌɔːl ðə ˈtaɪm/ die ganze Zeit I
timetable /ˈtaɪmˌteɪb(ə)l/ Stundenplan I; Fahrplan, Zeitplan, Terminkalender IV
° **tiny** /ˈtaɪni/ winzig 1C7
tired /ˈtaɪəd/ müde II
title /ˈtaɪt(ə)l/ Titel II
to /tʊ/ in; nach; zu; an; vor; bis I
today /təˈdeɪ/ heute I
together /təˈɡeðə/ zusammen I

toilet /ˈtɔɪlət/ Toilette; Klo I
tolerance /ˈtɒlərəns/ Toleranz 1B4
tomato /təˈmɑːtəʊ/ Tomate I
tomorrow /təˈmɒrəʊ/ morgen I
tone /təʊn/ Klang; Ton 3A4
tone of voice /ˌtəʊn_əvˈ_vɔɪs/ Ton(fall) 3B9
tongue /tʌŋ/ Zunge II
tonight /təˈnaɪt/ heute Abend I
° **tons of …** (*informal*) /ˈtʌnz_əv/ Unmengen von …; jede Menge … 3B4
too /tuː/ auch; zu I
too loud /ˌtuːˈlaʊd/ zu laut I
tool /tuːl/ Werkzeug III
tooth (*pl* **teeth**) /tuːθ, tiːθ/ Zahn I
toothbrush /ˈtuːθˌbrʌʃ/ Zahnbürste II
top /tɒp/ oberes Ende; Spitze II; obere(r, s) III
° **on top of** /ɒnˈtɒp_əv/ (oben) auf 1B9
topic /ˈtɒpɪk/ Thema II
° **totally** /ˈtəʊt(ə)li/ völlig; total 1B5
a touch of /əˈtʌtʃ_əv/ ein wenig 2B3
tough /tʌf/ robust; zäh III
tournament /ˈtɔːnəmənt/ Turnier 5C2
toward(s) /təˈwɔːdz/ in Richtung I; gegenüber II
° **towel** /ˈtaʊəl/ Handtuch 4B5
tower /ˈtaʊə/ Turm I
town /taʊn/ Stadt III
toy /tɔɪ/ Spielzeug(-) II
track /træk/ Weg; Pfad; Gleis III
° to **track** /træk/ verfolgen 2C5
traditional /trəˈdɪʃ(ə)l/ traditionell IV
traffic (*no pl*) /ˈtræfɪk/ Verkehr II
traffic jam /ˈtræfɪk dʒæm/ Stau III
tragedy /ˈtrædʒədi/ Tragödie; Trauerspiel IV
° **trail** /treɪl/ Weg; Pfad; Spur 4B5
train /treɪn/ Zug II
to **train** /treɪn/ trainieren II
° to **train:** (*die Augen*) richten auf 1B7
° **trained** /treɪnd/ ausgebildet; geschult 3C3
trainer /ˈtreɪnə/ Trainer/in; Turnschuh II
training (*no pl*) /ˈtreɪnɪŋ/ Training; Ausbildung, Schulung 5C2
° to **transform** /trænsˈfɔːm/ verwandeln 5PP2
° to **translate** /trænsˈleɪt/ übersetzen 5B5
° **translation** /trænsˈleɪʃ(ə)n/ Übersetzung 2P4
° to **transmit** /trænzˈmɪt/ senden; übertragen 1P7
transport (*no pl*) /ˈtrænspɔːt/ Transport; Beförderung II
trap /træp/ Falle 1O3
trash (*no pl, AE*) /træʃ/ Müll; Abfall IV
travel (*no pl*) /ˈtræv(ə)l/ Reisen III
to **travel** /ˈtræv(ə)l/ reisen III
traveller /ˈtræv(ə)lər/ Reisende/r 4B5

travelling /ˈtræv(ə)lɪŋ/ reisend; Reise-; Reisen III
° **tray** /treɪ/ Tablett; Serviertbrett 1B6
treat /triːt/ (Extra)vergnügen 1A2
to **treat** /triːt/ behandeln IV
treatment /ˈtriːtmənt/ Behandlung 1B2, 4B2
tree /triː/ Baum I
° to **trek** /trek/ schleppend gehen 1P3
° **trench** /trentʃ/ (Schützen)graben 1B9
tribe /traɪb/ Stamm; Sippe IV
to **go on a trip** /ˌɡəʊ_ɒn_əˈ trɪp/ einen Ausflug/eine Reise machen II
° **triumphant** /traɪˈʌmfənt/ triumphierend 1B8
trouble (*no pl*) /ˈtrʌb(ə)l/ Schwierigkeiten; Ärger III
trousers (*pl*) /ˈtraʊzəz/ Hose I
true /truː/ wahr I
° **true to life** /ˌtruː təˈ laɪf/ lebensnah 3C1
° **truly** /ˈtruːli/ wirklich; wahrhaftig; ehrlich 3B4
to **trust** /trʌst/ vertrauen 2B2, 3C3
° to **trust:** betreuen 1P7
° **trusted** /ˈtrʌstɪd/ getreu; bewährt 3P6
° **trusting** /ˈtrʌstɪŋ/ vertrauensvoll; zutraulich; leichtgläubig 3P6
trustworthy /ˈtrʌstˌwɜːðɪ/ vertrauenswürdig; zuverlässig 5B3
truth (*no pl*) /truːθ/ Wahrheit IV
truthful /ˈtruːθf(ə)l/ wahr; ehrlich 2B4
to **try** /traɪ/ versuchen; probieren I
to **try on** /ˌtraɪˈ_ɒn/ anprobieren I
Tuesday /ˈtjuːzdeɪ/ Dienstag I
° **Tunisia** /tjuːˈnɪziə/ Tunesien 4B2
° **Turkey** /ˈtɜːki/ Turkei 4B2
to **turn** /tɜːn/ (sich) umdrehen; drehen III
° to **turn:** verwandeln, (ver)ändern 1A2; werden 1B8
° to **turn against sb** /ˌtɜːn_əˈɡenst/ sich gegen jdn wenden 1P2
to **turn away** /ˌtɜːn_əˈweɪ/ sich abwenden; wegrücken III
to **turn into** /ˈtɜːn_ˌɪntʊ/ (ver)wandeln 3B8
to **turn off** /ˌtɜːnˈ_ɒf/ abschalten; ausmachen II
to **turn on** /ˌtɜːnˈ_ɒn/ einschalten; aufdrehen; anmachen III
° to **turn one's back on sb/sth** /ˌtɜːn wʌnz ˈbæk_ɒn/ sich von jdm/etw abwenden 1B2
to **turn right/left** /ˌtɜːnˈ raɪt/ˈleft/ rechts/links abbiegen II
° to **turn to** /ˈtɜːn tʊ/ sich richten auf 1B7
to **turn up** /ˌtɜːnˈ_ʌp/ erscheinen; auftauchen III
° to **turn up one's nose** /ˌtɜːn_ˌʌp wʌnz ˈnəʊz/ die Nase rümpfen 3B7
° **tutor** /ˈtjuːtə/ Nachhilfelehrer/in; Tutor/in 5P5; *hier:* Dozent/in 5O1
° to **tweet** /twiːt/ *eine Nachricht über Twitter verbreiten* 1P6

Words

English-German dictionary

twelve /twelv/ zwölf I
twice /twaɪs/ zweimal 2B2, 4B2
two /tuː/ zwei I
type /taɪp/ Art; Typ; Sorte III
° **to type** /taɪp/ tippen 1O3
typical (of) /ˈtɪpɪk(ə)l_əv/ typisch (für) III
typically /ˈtɪpɪkli/ normalerweise; in der Regel 2B3, 3A2
typing (no pl) /ˈtaɪpɪŋ/ Maschineschreiben; Tippen; Tipp- 5B2

U

ugly /ˈʌgli/ hässlich; scheußlich; übel III
UK (= the United Kingdom) /juːˌkeɪ ðə juːˌnaɪtɪd ˈkɪŋdəm/ Vereinigtes Königreich I
° **the ultimate** /ðɪ_ˈʌltɪmət/ das (Aller)letzte; die Krönung (ironisch) 3B7
umbrella /ʌmˈbrelə/ (Regen)schirm I
° **UN (= United Nations)** /juːˌen, juːˌnaɪtɪd ˈneɪʃ(ə)nz/ Vereinte Nationen 4B2
unacceptable /ˌʌnəkˈseptəb(ə)l/ inakzeptabel; nicht hinnehmbar IV
° **unappealing** /ˌʌnəˈpiːlɪŋ/ unerfreulich; unattraktiv 4PP3
unbelievable /ˌʌnbɪˈliːvəb(ə)l/ unglaublich; sagenhaft 5A2
° **uncertain** /ʌnˈsɜːt(ə)n/ unsicher; ungewiss 1C7
° **uncharacteristically** /ˌʌnˌkærɪktəˈrɪstɪkli/ untypisch(erweise) 3C3
uncle /ˈʌŋk(ə)l/ Onkel I
uncomfortable /ʌnˈkʌmftəb(ə)l/ unbequem; unwohl; unbehaglich III
uncommon /ʌnˈkɒmən/ selten; ungewöhnlich 3C3
unconscious /ʌnˈkɒnʃəs/ bewusstlos II
under /ˈʌndə/ unter I
under construction /ˌʌndə kənˈstrʌkʃ(ə)n/ im Bau 4B2
the Underground (no pl, BE) /ðɪ_ˈʌndəˌgraʊnd/ U-Bahn II
to underline /ˌʌndəˈlaɪn/ unterstreichen IV
° **underneath** /ˌʌndəˈniːθ/ unter; darunter; untere(r, s) 1B2
to understand (irr) /ˌʌndəˈstænd/ verstehen I
understanding (no pl) /ˌʌndəˈstændɪŋ/ Verständnis; Übereinkunft 5A2
° **understanding** /ˌʌndəˈstændɪŋ/ verständnisvoll 1O4
uneasy /ʌnˈiːzi/ besorgt; unangenehm; unwohl 1B7
unemployment (no pl) /ˌʌnɪmˈplɔɪmənt/ Arbeitslosigkeit IV
unexpected /ˌʌnɪkˈspektɪd/ unerwartet IV
° **unfit** /ʌnˈfɪt/ nicht fit; untauglich; ungeeignet 1C5

° **unfortunate** /ʌnˈfɔːtʃ(ə)nət/ unglücklich; unglückselig 1O2
unhappy /ʌnˈhæpi/ unglücklich I
uniform /ˈjuːnɪfɔːm/ Uniform I
unique /juːˈniːk/ einzigartig 1A1
uniquely /juːˈniːkli/ besonders 5A2
unit /ˈjuːnɪt/ Einheit; Abteilung; Teil 1C5
university /ˌjuːnɪˈvɜːsəti/ Universität(s-) II
unkind /ʌnˈkaɪnd/ unfreundlich; unhöflich, grob 3B10
° **the unknown** /ðɪ_ʌnˈnəʊn/ das Unbekannte 4A2
unlikely /ʌnˈlaɪkli/ unwahrscheinlich 3C3
unnecessary /ʌnˈnesəs(ə)ri/ unnötig; überflüssig; verzichtbar III
° **unpredictable** /ˌʌnprɪˈdɪktəb(ə)l/ unvorhersehbar; unberechenbar 5B3
° **unspoken** /ʌnˈspəʊkən/ unausgesprochen 3C1
° **to unstrap** /ʌnˈstræp/ abschnallen 1C7
unsure /ʌnˈʃʊə/ unsicher; ungewiss 3C3, 4B3
until /ʌnˈtɪl/ bis II
untruthful /ʌnˈtruːθf(ə)l/ unwahr; unaufrichtig 2B5
° **unwanted** /ʌnˈwɒntɪd/ unerwünscht; störend 1P4
up /ʌp/ nach oben; hoch I
up to /ˈʌp tuː/ bis (zu) IV
upcoming /ˈʌpˌkʌmɪŋ/ bevorstehend; kommend 1A2
uplifting /ʌpˈlɪftɪŋ/ erbaulich IV
to upload /ˈʌpˌləʊd/ hochladen III
upset /ʌpˈset/ aufgeregt; aufgebracht; bestürzt I
to upset (irr) /ʌpˈset/ in Aufregung versetzen; beunruhigen; aufwühlen III
urban /ˈɜːbən/ (groß)städtisch; urban III
° **Urdu** (no pl) /ˈʊəduː/ Urdu (Amtssprache in Pakistan) 4C1
° **urge** /ɜːdʒ/ Verlangen; Bedürfnis; Drang 1P3
us /ʌs/ uns I
use /juːs/ Verwendung; (Be)nutzung; Gebrauch III
to use /juːz/ benutzen I
° **used to (do sth)** /ˈjuːst_tuː duː/ drückt aus, was man früher (gewohnheitsmäßig) gemacht hat oder war 5P9
useful /ˈjuːsf(ə)l/ nützlich; praktisch IV
username /ˈjuːzəˌneɪm/ Benutzername; Username III
usually /ˈjuːʒʊəli/ gewöhnlich; normalerweise I
° **to utter** /ˈʌtə/ von sich geben; sagen 1B6

V

vacancy /ˈveɪkənsi/ freie Stelle 5B4
vacation (AE = **holiday** BE) /veɪˈkeɪʃ(ə)n/ Urlaub; Ferien IV
valley /ˈvæli/ Tal IV
° **value** /ˈvæljuː/ Wert(vorstellung) 4P8
to value /ˈvæljuː/ schätzen 3C3
vampire /ˈvæmpaɪə/ Vampir/in II
° **varied** /ˈveərɪd/ vielfältig; unterschiedlich 4PP3
variety /vəˈraɪəti/ Art; Varietät 4C1
° **variety** (no pl): Vielfalt; Vielzahl; Auswahl 5B6
various /ˈveərɪəs/ verschieden 5B5
to vary /ˈveəri/ variieren 2C6
vegetable /ˈvedʒtəb(ə)l/ Gemüse II
vegetarian /ˌvedʒəˈteərɪən/ Vegetarier/in; vegetarisch III
° **veil** /veɪl/ Schleier 1B2
verse /vɜːs/ Strophe II
very /ˈveri/ sehr; außerordentlich I
via /ˈvaɪə/ über; per; via III
victim /ˈvɪktɪm/ Opfer II
to fall victim to sb/sth /ˌfɔːl ˈvɪktɪm tə/ jdm/etw zum Opfer fallen 2B2
victory /ˈvɪkt(ə)ri/ Sieg II
view /vjuː/ (Aus)sicht; (Aus)blick II; Ansicht, Meinung III
° **to view** /vjuː/ betrachten; zusehen; ansehen 2C3
viewer /ˈvjuːə/ (Fernseh)zuschauer/in; Filmbetrachter/in 2C1
village /ˈvɪlɪdʒ/ Dorf II
vintage /ˈvɪntɪdʒ/ erlesen 3B2
° **vinyl** /ˈvaɪn(ə)l/ Vinyl(kunststoff) 1B9
to violate /ˈvaɪəleɪt/ verstoßen (gegen); brechen; verletzen 2B5
violence (no pl) /ˈvaɪələns/ Gewalt(tätigkeit); Heftigkeit III
° **visa** /ˈviːzə/ Visum (Ein- oder Ausreiseerlaubnis) 5A2
visit /ˈvɪzɪt/ Besuch III
to visit /ˈvɪzɪt/ besuchen; anschauen I
visitor /ˈvɪzɪtə/ Besucher/in; Gast I
° **visual** /ˈvɪʒʊəl/ visuell; Bild- 1C9
° **vivid** /ˈvɪvɪd/ anschaulich; lebendig; lebhaft 4B5
° **vocabulary** /vəʊˈkæbjʊləri/ Vokabular; Wortschatz; Vokabeln 3B10
° **vodka** /ˈvɒdkə/ Wodka 3C5
voice /vɔɪs/ Stimme II
voluntary /ˈvɒlənt(ə)ri/ freiwillig; ehrenamtlich 5C2
volunteer /ˌvɒlənˈtɪə/ Ehrenamtler/in; Freiwillige/r 5B3
to volunteer /ˌvɒlənˈtɪə/ sich freiwillig melden; ehrenamtlich tätig sein III
° **voluntourism** /ˈvɒlənˌtɔːrɪz(ə)m/ Freiwilligenarbeit in Kombination mit Urlaub 4A3

English-German dictionary

W

° wage(s) /ˈweɪdʒɪz/ Lohn 5PP2
to **wait** /weɪt/ warten I; erwarten II
to **wait for** /ˈweɪt fɔː/ warten auf I
° waiter /ˈweɪtə/ Bedienung; Kellner 5P5
° waitress /ˈweɪtrəs/ Bedienung; Kellnerin 5P5
to **wake up** (irr) /ˌweɪk ˈʌp/ aufwecken; aufwachen II
walk /wɔːk/ Spaziergang III
to **go for a walk** /ˌgəʊ fər ə ˈwɔːk/ einen Spaziergang machen III
to **take ... for a walk** /ˌteɪk fər ə ˈwɔːk/ ... spazieren führen; Gassi gehen mit ... I
to **walk** /wɔːk/ zu Fuß gehen; laufen I
to **walk on** /ˌwɔːk ˈɒn/ weiterlaufen II
to **walk straight on** /ˌwɔːk ˌstreɪt ˈɒn/ immer geradeaus weiterlaufen II
to **walk the dog** /ˌwɔːk ðə ˈdɒg/ den Hund ausführen I
° walkabout /ˈwɔːkəˌbaʊt/ *Aborigine-Ritual* 4PP1
walking (no pl) /ˈwɔːkɪŋ/ Gehen; Spazierengehen III
to **go walking** /ˌgəʊ ˈwɔːkɪŋ/ wandern; spazieren gehen I
wall /wɔːl/ Wand I
wallet /ˈwɒlɪt/ Brieftasche; Portmonnaie 2B3
to **want** /wɒnt/ wünschen; wollen I
to **want sb to do sth:** wollen, dass jd etw tut II
war /wɔː/ Krieg IV
warm /wɔːm/ warm I
° to **warm** /wɔːm/ (er)wärmen 2B3
to **warn** /wɔːn/ warnen 1C8, 4B2
° warning /ˈwɔːnɪŋ/ Warnung 3B4
to **wash** /wɒʃ/ (sich) waschen III
waste (no pl) /weɪst/ Verschwendung; Vergeudung; Abfall II
° waste water /ˈweɪst ˌwɔːtə/ Abwasser 4B5
to **waste** /weɪst/ verschwenden IV
to **watch** /wɒtʃ/ beobachten; zuschauen; anschauen I; aufpassen auf IV
to **watch TV** /ˌwɒtʃ ˌtiː ˈviː/ fernsehen I
water (no pl) /ˈwɔːtə/ Wasser I
water-skiing (no pl) /ˈwɔːtəˌskiːɪŋ/ Wasserski 5A2
° to **wave (at)** /ˈweɪv ˌæt/ (zu)winken 3B4
way /weɪ/ Weg; Art und Weise I; Richtung III
way of life /ˌweɪ əv ˈlaɪf/ Lebensart; Lebensstil IV
we /wiː/ wir I
We're just looking. Wir schauen uns nur um. I

to **weaken** /ˈwiːkən/ schwächer werden; (ab)schwächen; entkräften 2B6
° weakness /ˈwiːknəs/ Schwäche; Schwachstelle 5P3
wealth (no pl) /welθ/ Reichtum; Vermögen; Fülle 2B3, 4B2
wealthy /ˈwelθi/ reich; wohlhabend; vermögend IV
to **wear** (irr) /weə/ tragen; anhaben I
weather /ˈweðə/ Wetter I
wedding /ˈwedɪŋ/ Hochzeit III
Wednesday /ˈwenzdeɪ/ Mittwoch I
week /wiːk/ Woche I
weekend /ˌwiːkˈend/ Wochenende I
° weight /weɪt/ Gewicht 1C7
° to **welcome** /ˈwelkəm/ willkommen heißen; begrüßen 5C5
° welcoming /ˈwelkəmɪŋ/ freundlich 3C3
welfare (no pl) /ˈwelfeə/ Wohlergehen 5A2
well /wel/ nun (ja); tja I
Well done! /ˌwel ˈdʌn/ gut gemacht!; super! I
° well-known /ˌwel ˈnəʊn/ (allgemein) bekannt; berühmt 4P10
° well-structured /ˌwel ˈstrʌktʃəd/ gut strukturiert 5B8
west /west/ Westen; westlich; West- III
wet /wet/ nass II
what /wɒt/ was I; welche(r, s) II
What about ...? (informal) /ˈwɒt əˌbaʊt/ Was ist mit ...?; Wie wäre es mit ...? I
What about you? /ˌwɒt əˈbaʊt juː/ Was ist mit dir? I
What do you like? Was magst du? I
What don't you like? Was magst du nicht? I
to **what extent** /tə ˌwɒt ɪkˈstent/ inwieweit 3A4, 4B7
What is ... about? /ˌwɒt ɪz əˈbaʊt/ Worum geht es in/bei ...? II
what on earth ... (informal) /ˌwɒt ɒn ˈɜːθ/ was um alles in der Welt ... 3B8
° **What the hell ...?** (informal) /ˌwɒt ðə ˈhel/ Was zum Teufel ...? 3B3
What time is it? /ˌwɒt ˌtaɪm ɪz ˈɪt/ Wie spät/Wie viel Uhr ist es? I
What's ... in English? /ˌwɒts ɪn ˈɪŋglɪʃ/ Was bedeutet ... auf Englisch? I
° **What's the matter?** /ˌwɒts ðə ˈmætə/ Was ist los? 5O1
What's the time? /ˌwɒts ðə ˈtaɪm/ Wie spät/Wie viel Uhr ist es? I
° **What's up?** (informal) /ˌwɒts ˈʌp/ Was ist los?; Wie geht's? 3B4
What's wrong with ...? /ˌwɒts ˈrɒŋ wɪð/ Was stimmt nicht mit ...?; Was fehlt ...? I
What's your name? /ˌwɒts jə ˈneɪm/ Wie heißt du? I

° whatever /wɒtˈevə/ was auch immer; egal was 1B2
when /wen/ wann; als; wenn I
° whenever /wenˈevə/ wann (auch) immer 3A2
where /weə/ wo; wohin I
Where are you from? /ˌweər ə juː ˈfrɒm/ Woher kommst du? I
Where is ...? / Where are ...? /ˌweər ˈɪz, ˌweər ˈɑː/ Wo ist ...? / Wo sind ...? I
whereas /weərˈæz/ während; wo(hin)gegen 3A2
whether /ˈweðə/ (egal) ob III
which /wɪtʃ/ welche(r, s); der/die/das II
while /waɪl/ während; als II
to **whisper** /ˈwɪspə/ flüstern II
white /waɪt/ weiß I
who /huː/ wer I; der/die/das II
whole /həʊl/ ganz; gesamt III
whose /huːz/ wessen II; dessen/deren 1C5, 4C4
why /waɪ/ warum I
wide /waɪd/ breit; groß IV
° to **widen** /ˈwaɪd(ə)n/ breiter werden 3B4
widespread /ˈwaɪdˌspred/ weitverbreitet; von beachtlichem Ausmaß 2B5
wife /waɪf/ (Ehe)frau I
wild /waɪld/ wild; in freier Wildbahn lebend I
wilderness /ˈwɪldənəs/ Wildnis; Wüste IV
wildlife (no pl) /ˈwaɪldˌlaɪf/ *die (natürliche) Tier- und Pflanzenwelt* 4B2
° wildlife spotting (no pl) /ˈwaɪldˌlaɪf ˌspɒtɪŋ/ Naturbeobachtung 4B5
° willing /ˈwɪlɪŋ/ bereit; gewillt; willig 1P10
to **win** (irr) /wɪn/ gewinnen I
window /ˈwɪndəʊ/ Fenster I
windsurfing (no pl) /ˈwɪndˌsɜːfɪŋ/ Windsurfen 5A2
wind turbine /ˈwɪnd ˌtɜːbaɪn/ Windkraftanlage 4B5
wine /waɪn/ Wein III
winner /ˈwɪnə/ Gewinner/in; Sieger/in II
winter /ˈwɪntə/ Winter I
in winter /ɪn ˈwɪntə/ im Winter I
° to **wipe** /waɪp/ (ab)wischen 1B7
wireless /ˈwaɪələs/ drahtlos; *hier:* WLAN- 4B5
wisdom (no pl) /ˈwɪzdəm/ Weisheit; Klugheit 3B2
wise /waɪz/ weise; klug; vernünftig 1C5, 2C8
wish /wɪʃ/ Wunsch 2C8
to **wish** /wɪʃ/ wünschen I
wit (no pl) /wɪt/ Witz; Geist; Verstand III
with /wɪð/ mit I

Words

English-German dictionary

° within /wɪðˈɪn/ innerhalb 3C3
without /wɪðˈaʊt/ ohne II
witness /ˈwɪtnəs/ Zeuge/Zeugin II
to witness /ˈwɪtnəs/ beobachten; Zeuge/Zeugin sein; miterleben 1C10
woman (pl women) /ˈwʊmən, ˈwɪmɪn/ Frau I
° wombat /ˈwɒm.bæt/ australisches Beuteltier 4PP1
° wonder /ˈwʌndə/ Wunder 4B2
to wonder /ˈwʌndə/ sich fragen; sich wundern; überrascht sein III
° to wonder about sb/sth /ˈwʌndər_əˌbaʊt/ sich über jdn/etw Gedanken machen 3P6
wonderful /ˈwʌndəf(ə)l/ wunderbar; wundervoll I
wood(s) /wʊdz/ (kleiner) Wald 4B5
° to not see the wood for the trees /nɒt siː ðə ˌwʊd fə ðə ˈtriːz/ den Wald nicht vor lauter Bäume sehen 2B2
word /wɜːd/ Wort I
° word web /ˈwɜːdˌweb/ Wortnetz 3P9
work /wɜːk/ Arbeit I
° work experience (BE) /ˈwɜːk_ɪkˌspɪəriəns/ Praktikum 4P9
° work permit /ˈwɜːk_pɜːmɪt/ Arbeitserlaubnis 5PP2
to work /wɜːk/ arbeiten; funktionieren I
to work out /ˌwɜːk_ˈaʊt/ lösen; verstehen; herausfinden III
° workforce (no pl) /ˈwɜːkˌfɔːs/ Belegschaft; Arbeiterschaft 5PP2
working hours (only pl) /ˈwɜːkɪŋ_ˌaʊəz/ Arbeitszeit 5C5
° workshop /ˈwɜːkˌʃɒp/ Werkstatt 5PP2
world /wɜːld/ Welt I
worldwide /ˌwɜːldˈwaɪd/ weltweit 4C1
worried /ˈwʌrid/ beunruhigt; besorgt I
worry /ˈwʌri/ Sorge III
to worry (about) /ˈwʌri_əˌbaʊt/ sich Sorgen machen (um) I
worth /wɜːθ/ wert; im Wert von 2C5
worth (no pl) /wɜːθ/ Wert 2C5
would like to /wʊd ˈlaɪk tʊ/ würde(n/st/t) gern II
to write (irr) /raɪt/ schreiben I
to write down /ˌraɪt_ˈdaʊn/ aufschreiben; niederschreiben I
writer /ˈraɪtə/ Verfasser/in; Autor/in II
wrong /rɒŋ/ falsch I

Y

° to yank /jæŋk/ zerren 1O4
yard (AE) /jɑːd/ (Vor)garten IV
year /jɪə/ Jahr I; (Schul-)Jahrgang II
yellow /ˈjeləʊ/ gelb I
yes /jes/ ja I
yesterday /ˈjestədeɪ/ gestern I
yet /jet/ bis jetzt; schon; noch II; yet: (und) doch; (und) trotzdem 4B2
you /juː/ du; dich; dir; Sie; Ihnen; ihr; euch I
° (You're) dismissed! /jɔː dɪsˈmɪst/ Weggetreten! 1B9
young /jʌŋ/ jung I
your /jɔː/ dein(e); euer/eure; Ihr(e) I
yours /jɔːz/ deine(r, s); eure(r, s); Ihre(r, s) II
Yours faithfully (BE) /jɔːz ˈfeɪθf(ə)li/ Schlussformel in einem nicht an eine bestimmte Person gerichteten formellen Brief 5B4
Yours sincerely /jɔːz sɪnˈsɪəli/ Schlussformel in einem formellen Brief bei persönlicher Anrede 5B4
yourself (pl yourselves) /jəˈself, jəˈselvz/ dich; dir; (du/Sie) selbst III
youth (no pl) /juːθ/ Jugend(-) IV
youth hostel /ˈjuːθˌhɒst(ə)l/ Jugendherberge 4A1

The English alphabet

a	/eɪ/	h	/eɪtʃ/	o	/əʊ/	u	/juː/
b	/biː/	i	/aɪ/	p	/piː/	v	/viː/
c	/siː/	j	/dʒeɪ/	q	/kjuː/	w	/ˈdʌbljuː/
d	/diː/	k	/keɪ/	r	/aː/	x	/eks/
e	/iː/	l	/el/	s	/es/	y	/waɪ/
f	/ef/	m	/em/	t	/tiː/	z	/zed/
g	/dʒiː/	n	/en/				

English sounds

Im Englischen spricht man Wörter oft anders aus, als man sie schreibt.
Deshalb ist die Lautschrift sehr nützlich: Sie gibt an, wie ein Wort ausgesprochen wird.
Hier ist eine Liste der Lautschriftzeichen zusammen mit Beispielwörtern:

Vokale

/ɑː/	**a**rm
/ʌ/	b**u**t
/e/	d**e**sk
/ə/	**a**, **a**n
/ɜː/	g**i**rl, b**i**rd
/æ/	**a**pple
/ɪ/	**i**n, **i**t
/i/	ever**y**
/iː/	**ea**sy, **ea**t
/ɒ/	**o**range
/ɔː/	**a**ll, st**o**ry
/ʊ/	l**oo**k
/u/	Febr**u**ary
/uː/	f**oo**d

Doppellaute

/aɪ/	**ey**e, b**uy**
/aʊ/	h**ou**se
/eə/	th**ere**
/eɪ/	t**a**ke, th**ey**
/ɪə/	h**ere**
/ɔɪ/	b**oy**
/əʊ/	g**o**, **o**ld
/ʊə/	**you're**

Konsonanten

/b/	**b**ag, clu**b**		/dʒ/	**o**ra**nge**
/d/	**d**uck, car**d**		/ʃ/	**s**ure, Engli**sh**
/f/	**f**ish, lau**gh**		/tʃ/	**ch**ild, **ch**eese
/g/	**g**et, do**g**		/ð/	**th**ese, mo**th**er (weicher Laut)
/h/	**h**ot			
/j/	**y**ou		/θ/	mou**th**, **th**ink (harter Laut)
/k/	**c**an, du**ck**			
/l/	**l**ot, smal**l**		/v/	**v**ery, ha**v**e
/m/	**m**ore, **m**um		/w/	**wh**at, **w**ord
/n/	**n**ow, su**n**			
/ŋ/	so**ng**, lo**ng**			
/p/	**p**resent, to**p**			
/r/	**r**ed, **r**ight			
/s/	**s**ister, cla**ss** (scharfes s)			
/t/	**t**ime, ca**t**			
/z/	no**s**e, dog**s** (weiches s)			
/ʒ/	televi**s**ion			

Betonungszeichen für die folgende Silbe

/ˈ/ Hauptbetonung
/ˌ/ Nebenbetonung

Names

Girls/women
Alison /ˈælɪs(ə)n/
Betty /ˈbeti/
Cara /ˈkɑːrə/
Carlotta /kɑːˈlɒtə/
Carmen /ˈkɑːmen/
Cate /keɪt/
Cathleen /ˈkæθliːn/
Cathy /ˈkæθi/
Chloe /ˈkləʊi/
Claire /kleə/
Cristine /ˈkrɪstiːn/
Emma /emə/
Espie /ˈespi/
Gemma /ˈdʒemə/
Georgie /ˈdʒɔːdʒi/
Janet /ˈdʒænɪt/
Janice /ˈdʒænɪs/
Jennifer /ˈdʒenɪfə/
Jo /dʒəʊ/
Julia /ˈdʒuːliə/
Julien /ˈdʒuːliən/
Katharine /ˈkæθ(ə)rɪn/
Katie /ˈkeɪti/
Katriona /kætriˈəʊnə/
Kenzie /ˈkenzi/
Kim /kɪm/
Kyla /ˈkaɪlə/
Kylie /ˈkaɪli/
Lara /ˈlɑːrə/
Lily /ˈlɪli/
Linda /ˈlɪndə/
Lindsay /ˈlɪndzi/
Lois /ˈləʊɪs/
Mandy /ˈmændi/
Mary /ˈmeəri/
Maura /ˈmɔːrə/
Maya /ˈmeɪə/
Nancy /ˈnænsi/
Nicki /ˈnɪki/
Nicole /nɪˈkəʊl/
Paris /ˈpærɪs/
Rebecca /rɪˈbekə/
Roxana /rɒkˈsɑːnə/
Roxy /ˈrɒksi/
Sandy /ˈsændi/
Sarah /ˈsɑːrə/
Selena /səˈliːnə/
Sofia /səʊˈfiːə/
Tara /ˈtɑːrə/
Taissa /ˈtaɪsə/
Vicky /ˈvɪki/

Boys/men
Aaron /ˈeərən/
Alasdair /ˈæləstə/
Alex /ˈælɪks/
Ben /ben/
Carlos /ˈkɑːlɒs/
Chris /krɪs/
Corey /ˈkɔːri/
Dan /dæn/
Daniel /ˈdænjəl/
Dave /deɪv/
David /ˈdeɪvɪd/
Dylan /ˈdɪlən/
Eugene /ˈjuːdʒiːn/
Holden /ˈhəʊldən/
Isaac /ˈaɪzək/
Israel /ˈɪzreɪəl/
Jay /dʒeɪ/
Jeremy /ˈdʒerəmi/
Joel /ˈdʒəʊ(ə)l/
John /dʒɒn/
Jonas /ˈdʒəʊnəs/
Jonathan /ˈdʒɒnəθ(ə)n/
Josh /dʒɒʃ/
Lee /liː/
Liam /ˈliːəm/
Luke /luːk/
Marc /mɑːk/
Mark /mɑːk/
Mel /mel/
Mike /maɪk/
Nick /nɪk/
Orlando /ɔːˈlændəʊ/
Pablo /ˈpæbləʊ/
Pulga /ˈpʌlgə/
Ralph /rælf/
Ryan /ˈraɪən/
Sal /sæl/
Sam /sæm/
Steve /stiːv/
Thomas /ˈtɒməs/
Timmy /ˈtɪmi/
Tiny /ˈtaɪni/
Tom /tɒm/
Toro /ˈtɒrəʊ/
Trent /trent/
Will /wɪl/
Zayne /zeɪn/

Families
Baker /ˈbeɪkə/
Blanchett /ˈblɑːnʃət/
Bloom /bluːm/
Broussard /ˈbruːsɑːd/
Chang /tʃæŋ/
Clayborne /ˈkleɪbɔːn/
Cooper /ˈkuːpə/
Coppola /ˈkɒpələ/
Cornell /ˌkɔːˈnel/
Dixon /ˈdɪks(ə)n/
Farmiga /fəˈmiːgə/
Freeman /ˈfriːmən/
Gomez /ˈgəʊmez/
Grayson /ˈgreɪs(ə)n/
Green /griːn/
Hall /hɔːl/
Harris /ˈhærɪs/
Hemsworth /ˈhemzwəθ/
Hepburn /ˈhepbɜːn/
Hilton /ˈhɪlt(ə)n/
Irwin /ˈɜːwɪn/
Johansson /ˈjəʊhænsən/
Lambert /ˈlæmbət/
Lauren /ˈlɔːr(ə)n/
Levithan /ˈlevɪθən/
Lewis /ˈluːɪs/
Lohan /ˈləʊhən/
Lowry /ˈlaʊri/
Minogue /mɪˈnəʊg/
Rodriguez /rɒˈdriːgez/
Sales /seɪlz/
Sanchez /ˈsæntʃez/
Sankey /ˈsæŋki/
Smith /smɪθ/
van Wagenen /væn ˈwægənən/
Watson /ˈwɒtsən/
Wood /wʊd/

Other names
Adidas /ˈædɪdæs/
Adolfo Camarillo /əˌdɒlfəʊ ˌkæməˈrɪləʊ/
Aids/AIDS /eɪdz/
Apple /ˈæp(ə)l/
Burger Joint /ˈbɜːgə dʒɔɪnt/
Camp Chippewa /ˌkæmp ˈtʃɪpɪwɑː/
DJ Jazzy Jeff /ˌdiː ˌdʒeɪ ˌdʒæzi ˈdʒef/
Facebook /ˈfeɪsbʊk/
Forbes /fɔːbz/
Gallery Mall /ˌgæləri ˈmɔːl/
HBO /ˌeɪtʃ biː ˈəʊ/
Instagram /ˈɪnstəgræm/
Lone Star High /ˌləʊn ˌstɑː ˈhaɪ/
Macklemore /ˈmæk(ə)lmɔː/
Maîtrise /ˈmeɪtriːz/
PQTB /ˌpiː kjuː tiː ˈbiː/
SPIN /spɪn/
Sydney Harbour Bridge /ˌsɪdni ˌhɑːbə ˈbrɪdʒ/
The Bling Ring /ðə ˈblɪŋ rɪŋ/
Teen Times of Toronto /ˌtiːn ˌtaɪmz ˌəv təˈrɒntəʊ/
TylerMartin /ˌtaɪləˈmɑːtɪn/
Ventura High /venˌtjʊərə ˈhaɪ/
WWF /ˌdʌb(ə)ljuː ˌdʌb(ə)ljuːˈef/

Geographical names
Adelaide /ˈædəleɪd/
Algarve /ælˈgɑːv/
Australia /ɒˈstreɪliə/
Banff /bænf/
Brussels /ˈbrʌs(ə)lz/
CA (= California) /ˌkæləˈfɔːniə/
Camarillo /ˌkæməˈrɪləʊ/
Cameroon /ˌkæməˈruːn/
Canada /ˈkænədə/
Charlotte Road /ˈʃɑːlət rəʊd/
Chicago /ʃɪˈkɑːgəʊ/
Copenhagen /ˌkəʊp(ə)nˈheɪg(ə)n/
Costa del Sol /ˌkɒstə del ˈsɒl/
Denmark /ˈdenmɑːk/
Devon /ˈdev(ə)n/
Durban /ˈdɜːb(ə)n/
England /ˈɪŋglənd/
Europe /ˈjʊərəp/
Faro /ˈfɑːrəʊ/
Georgia /ˈdʒɔːdʒə/
Greece /griːs/
Iraq /ɪˈrɑːk/
Ireland /ˈaɪələnd/
Italy /ˈɪtəli/
Jamaica /dʒəˈmeɪkə/
Jervis Bay Territory /ˌdʒɜːvɪs ˌbeɪ ˈterət(ə)ri/
LA (= Los Angeles) /ˌelˈeɪ, ˌlɒsˈændʒəliːz/
Leeds /liːdz/
London /ˈlʌndən/
Marbella /mɑːˈbeɪə/
Melbourne /ˈmelbən/
Middlesbrough /ˈmɪd(ə)lzbrə/
Nevada /nɪˈvɑːdə/

Names | Words

New South Wales /ˌnjuːˌsaʊθ ˈweɪlz/
New Zealand /njuː ˈziːlənd/
Ontario /ɒnˈteəriəʊ/
Paris /ˈpærɪs/
Port Adelaide /ˌpɔːt ˈædəleɪd/
Portugal /ˈpɔːtʃʊɡ(ə)l/
Scarborough /ˈskɑːbərə/
Sheboygan /ʃɪˈbɔɪɡ(ə)n/
Singapore /ˌsɪŋəˈpɔː/
South Africa /ˌsaʊθ ˈæfrɪkə/
Spain /speɪn/
Sydney /ˈsɪdni/
Toronto /təˈrɒntəʊ/
Trinidad and Tobago /ˌtrɪnɪdæd ən təˈbeɪɡəʊ/
Tunisia /tjuːˈnɪziə/
Turkey /ˈtɜːki/
USA (= United States of America) /ˌjuːesˈeɪ, juːˌnaɪtɪd ˌsteɪts əv əˈmerɪkə/
Vancouver /vænˈkuːvə/
Vincentine Coast /ˌvɪnsəntaɪn ˈkəʊst/
Wisconsin /wɪˈskɒnsɪn/

Wörter, die im Deutschen und Englischen ähnlich sind

Es gibt viele Wörter, die im Englischen und im Deutschen gleich sind. Sie unterscheiden sich oft nur darin, wie sie geschrieben werden. Viele dieser Wörter sprechen wir gleich aus. Diese Wörter stehen nicht in den Wortlisten, weil sie dir ja nicht neu sind. Bei denen, die ein bisschen anders ausgesprochen werden als im Deutschen, ist die Lautschrift farbig hervorgehoben.

A4 /ˌeɪ ˈfɔː/
action (no pl) /ˈækʃ(ə)n/
aftershave /ˈɑːftəʃeɪv/
aggressive /əˈɡresɪv/
album /ˈælbəm/
alcohol (no pl) /ˈælkəˌhɒl/
alien /ˈeɪliən/
Allah /ˈælə/
alliteration /əˌlɪtəˈreɪʃ(ə)n/
alternative /ɔːlˈtɜːnətɪv/
aluminum (no pl) /əˈluːmɪnəm/
animation /ˌænɪˈmeɪʃ(ə)n/
aspect /ˈæspekt/
asphalt (no pl) /ˈæsfælt/
au pair /ˌəʊ ˈpeə/
audio guide /ˈɔːdiəʊ ˌɡaɪd/
author /ˈɔːθə/
baby /ˈbeɪbi/
babysitter /ˈbeɪbiˌsɪtə/
babysitting (no pl) /ˈbeɪbiˌsɪtɪŋ/
ball /bɔːl/
bank /bæŋk/
bar /bɑː/
baseball /ˈbeɪsˌbɔːl/
basis /ˈbeɪsɪs/
beer /bɪə/
bikini /bɪˈkiːni/
blog /blɒɡ/
blogger /ˈblɒɡə/
bomb /bɒm/
café /ˈkæfeɪ/
cafeteria /ˌkæfəˈtɪəriə/
campus /ˈkæmpəs/
cartoon /kɑːˈtuːn/
catalogue /ˈkætəlɒɡ/
category /ˈkætəɡ(ə)ri/
champion /ˈtʃæmpiən/
chance /tʃɑːns/
chaos /ˈkeɪɒs/
chat /tʃæt/
check /tʃek/
checklist /ˈtʃeklɪst/
cheerleader /ˈtʃɪəˌliːdə/
chicken nugget /ˌtʃɪkɪn ˈnʌɡɪt/
clever /ˈklevə/
click /klɪk/
(video) clip /ˈvɪdiəʊ klɪp/
clique /kliːk/
club /klʌb/
CO_2 /ˌsiːˌəʊ ˈtuː/
Coke /kəʊk/
colonial /kəˈləʊniəl/
communication /kəˌmjuːnɪˈkeɪʃ(ə)n/
compost (no pl) /ˈkɒmpɒst/
complex /ˈkɒmpleks/
computer /kəmˈpjuːtə/
concentration /ˌkɒns(ə)nˈtreɪʃ(ə)n/
concert /ˈkɒnsət/
construction /kənˈstrʌkʃ(ə)n/
contact /ˈkɒntækt/
contrast /ˈkɒntrɑːst/
cool /kuːl/
cooperation (no pl) /kəʊˌɒpəˈreɪʃ(ə)n/
correct /kəˈrekt/
cosmos /ˈkɒzmɒs/
cover /ˈkʌvə/
cowboy /ˈkaʊˌbɔɪ/
credit card /ˈkredɪt kɑːd/
crew /kruː/
crocodile /ˈkrɒkədaɪl/
cultural /ˈkʌltʃ(ə)rəl/
deal /diːl/
definition /ˌdefəˈnɪʃ(ə)n/
democratic /ˌdeməˈkrætɪk/
design /dɪˈzaɪn/
designer /dɪˈzaɪnə/
dilemma /dɪˈlemə/
discipline (no pl) /ˈdɪsəplɪn/
discussion /dɪˈskʌʃ(ə)n/
doctor /ˈdɒktə/
document /ˈdɒkjʊmənt/
dollar /ˈdɒlə/
drumstick /ˈdrʌmˌstɪk/
duty-free shop /ˌdjuːti ˈfriː ʃɒp/
elegant /ˈelɪɡənt/
element /ˈelɪmənt/
email /ˈiːmeɪl/
emission /ɪˈmɪʃ(ə)n/
equipment /ɪˈkwɪpmənt/
etc (= et cetera) /et ˈset(ə)rə/
event /ɪˈvent/
exclusive /ɪkˈskluːsɪv/
existence (no pl) /ɪɡˈzɪst(ə)ns/
experiment /ɪkˈsperɪmənt/
expert /ˈekspɜːt/
extra /ˈekstrə/
extreme /ɪkˈstriːm/
factor /ˈfæktə/
fair /feə/
fair play /ˌfeə ˈpleɪ/
fast food (no pl) /ˌfɑːst ˈfuːd/
feedback /ˈfiːdbæk/
film /fɪlm/
finger /ˈfɪŋɡə/
fitness centre /ˈfɪtnəsˌsentə/
flexible /ˈfleksəb(ə)l/
follower /ˈfɒləʊə/
form /fɔːm/
forum /ˈfɔːrəm/
foul /faʊl/
frustration (no pl) /frʌˈstreɪʃ(ə)n/
function /ˈfʌŋkʃ(ə)n/
gang /ɡæŋ/
gangster /ˈɡæŋstə/
generation /ˌdʒenəˈreɪʃ(ə)n/
giraffe /dʒəˈrɑːf/
glamour /ˈɡlæmə/
global /ˈɡləʊb(ə)l/
gold /ɡəʊld/
google /ˈɡuːɡ(ə)l/
gorilla /ɡəˈrɪlə/
graffiti (no pl) /ɡrəˈfiːti/
harmony (no pl) /ˈhɑːməni/
helium (no pl) /ˈhiːliəm/
high school (AE) /ˈhaɪ skuːl/
high society /ˌhaɪ səˈsaɪəti/
HIV /ˌeɪtʃ ˌaɪ ˈviː/

Words

hobby /ˈhɒbi/
hockey /ˈhɒki/
horn /hɔːn/
humour (no pl) /ˈhjuːmə/
hundred /ˈhʌndrəd/
ideal /aɪˈdɪəl/
idiot (informal) /ˈɪdiət/
idol /ˈaɪd(ə)l/
illustration /ˌɪləˈstreɪʃ(ə)n/
image /ˈɪmɪdʒ/
import /ˈɪmpɔːt/
infrastructure /ˈɪnfrəˌstrʌktʃə/
instinct /ˈɪnstɪŋkt/
institution /ˌɪnstɪˈtjuːʃ(ə)n/
intelligent /ɪnˈtelɪdʒ(ə)nt/
intercultural /ˌɪntəˈkʌltʃ(ə)rəl/
international /ˌɪntəˈnæʃ(ə)nəl/
Internet /ˈɪntə(r)ˌnet/
interpretation /ɪnˌtɜːprɪˈteɪʃ(ə)n/
interview /ˈɪntəˌvjuː/
interviewer /ˈɪntəˌvjuːə/
jeans (only pl) /ˈdʒiːnz/
jingle /ˈdʒɪŋg(ə)l/
job /dʒɒb/
journalist /ˈdʒɜːnəlɪst/
kid /kɪd/
kiwi /ˈkiːwiː/
koala /kəʊˈɑːlə/
land /lænd/
layout /ˈleɪaʊt/
leopard /ˈlepəd/
lifestyle /ˈlaɪfˌstaɪl/
link /lɪŋk/
Londoner /ˈlʌndənə/
magazine /ˌmægəˈziːn/
make-up (no pl) /ˈmeɪkˌʌp/
malaria (no pl) /məˈleəriə/
management (no pl) /ˈmænɪdʒmənt/
massage /ˈmæsɑːʒ/
match /mætʃ/
material /məˈtɪəriəl/
meeting /ˈmiːtɪŋ/
mental /ˈment(ə)l/
metal /ˈmet(ə)l/
metaphor /ˈmetəfə/
method /ˈmeθəd/
migration /maɪˈgreɪʃ(ə)n/
million /ˈmɪljən/
mini /ˈmɪni/
minimal /ˈmɪnɪm(ə)l/

minister /ˈmɪnɪstə/
model /ˈmɒd(ə)l/
modern /ˈmɒdən/
moped /ˈməʊped/
motivation (no pl) /ˌməʊtɪˈveɪʃ(ə)n/
museum /mjuːˈziːəm/
must-have /ˈmʌst ˌhæv/
nation /ˈneɪʃ(ə)n/
national park /ˌnæʃ(ə)nəl ˈpɑːk/
nature (no pl) /ˈneɪtʃə/
neon /ˈniːɒn/
nerd (informal) /nɜːd/
neutral /ˈnjuːtrəl/
online /ˌɒnˈlaɪn/
organization /ˌɔːgənaɪˈzeɪʃ(ə)n/
outfit /ˈaʊtfɪt/
parallel /ˈpærəlel/
paranoid /ˈpærˌənɔɪd/
password /ˈpɑːsˌwɜːd/
pause /pɔːz/
perfection (no pl) /pəˈfekʃ(ə)n/
perspective /pəˈspektɪv/
petition /pəˈtɪʃ(ə)n/
photo (= photograph) /ˈfəʊtəʊ, ˈfəʊtəˌgrɑːf/
piercing /ˈpɪəsɪŋ/
pizza /ˈpiːtsə/
plan /plæn/
Plan B /ˌplæn ˈbiː/
platform /ˈplætˌfɔːm/
plus /plʌs/
podcast /ˈpɒdˌkɑːst/
pony /ˈpəʊni/
pool /puːl/
portion /ˈpɔːʃ(ə)n/
portrait /ˈpɔːtrət/
poster /ˈpəʊstə/
privilege /ˈprɪvəlɪdʒ/
problem /ˈprɒbləm/
production /prəˈdʌkʃ(ə)n/
professor /prəˈfesə/
profile /ˈprəʊfaɪl/
program (AE = programme BE) /ˈprəʊˌgræm/
programme /ˈprəʊgræm/
project /ˈprɒdʒekt/
protest /ˈprəʊtest/
quarterback /ˈkwɔːtəˌbæk/
radio /ˈreɪdiəʊ/
rap /ræp/
rapper /ˈræpə/
reaction /riˈækʃ(ə)n/

reality TV /riˈæləti ˌtiːˌviː/
relevant /ˈreləv(ə)nt/
religion /rɪˈlɪdʒ(ə)n/
republic /rɪˈpʌblɪk/
respect /rɪˈspekt/
rest /rest/
revolver /rɪˈvɒlvə/
ring /rɪŋ/
Rolex /ˈrəʊleks/
route /ruːt/
rugby (no pl) /ˈrʌgbi/
sandbank /ˈsændˌbæŋk/
scenario /səˈnɑːriəʊ/
science fiction (no pl) /ˌsaɪəns ˈfɪkʃ(ə)n/
semester /səˈmestə/
sequence /ˈsiːkwəns/
sex /seks/
sexuality (no pl) /ˌsekʃuˈæləti/
shock /ʃɒk/
show /ʃəʊ/
single /ˈsɪŋg(ə)l/
situation /ˌsɪtʃuˈeɪʃ(ə)n/
skateboard /ˈskeɪtˌbɔːd/
ski /skiː/
skyline /ˈskaɪˌlaɪn/
slogan /ˈsləʊgən/
smartphone /ˈsmɑːtfəʊn/
social media /ˌsəʊʃ(ə)l ˈmiːdiə/
social network /ˌsəʊʃ(ə)l ˈnetˌwɜːk/
software /ˈsɒfˌweə/
soundtrack /ˈsaʊndˌtræk/
special /ˈspeʃ(ə)l/
special effects /ˌspeʃ(ə)l ɪˈfekts/
speculation /ˌspekjʊˈleɪʃ(ə)n/
sport /spɔːt/
standard /ˈstændəd/
star /stɑː/
status /ˈsteɪtəs/
strategy /ˈstrætədʒi/
stress /stres/
stunt /stʌnt/
suite /swiːt/
supermarket /ˈsuːpəˌmɑːkɪt/
surfer /ˈsɜːfə/
surfing /ˈsɜːfɪŋ/
symbol /ˈsɪmb(ə)l/
symptom /ˈsɪmptəm/
synapse /ˈsaɪnæps/
system /ˈsɪstəm/
T-shirt /ˈtiː ˌʃɜːt/

tablet /ˈtæblət/
talent /ˈtælənt/
tattoo /tæˈtuː/
team /tiːm/
teamwork (no pl) /ˈtiːmˌwɜːk/
teen /tiːn/
teenager /ˈtiːnˌeɪdʒə/
teleportation (no pl) /ˌtelipɔːˈteɪʃ(ə)n/
tennis (no pl) /ˈtenɪs/
terrorist /ˈterərɪst/
test /test/
ticket /ˈtɪkɪt/
timing /ˈtaɪmɪŋ/
tolerant /ˈtɒlərənt/
tortilla /tɔːˈtiːə/
tour /tʊə/
tourism (no pl) /ˈtʊərɪz(ə)m/
tourist /ˈtʊərɪst/
tradition /trəˈdɪʃ(ə)n/
training (no pl) /ˈtreɪnɪŋ/
transfer /ˈtrænsfɜː/
transport (no pl) /ˈtrænsˌpɔːt/
trend /trend/
tunnel /ˈtʌn(ə)l/
TV (= television) /ˌtiː ˈviː, ˈteliˌvɪʒn/
tweet /twiːt/
unfair /ʌnˈfeə/
union /ˈjuːnjən/
unrealistic /ˌʌnrɪəˈlɪstɪk/
up-to-date /ˌʌp tə ˈdeɪt/
user /ˈjuːzə/
version /ˈvɜːʃ(ə)n/
veto /ˈviːtəʊ/
vision /ˈvɪʒ(ə)n/
volleyball (no pl) /ˈvɒliˌbɔːl/
website /ˈwebˌsaɪt/
wind /wɪnd/
YouTube /ˈjuːtjuːb/

Class instructions

Hier kannst du Arbeitsanweisungen aus deinem Buch nachschlagen.

Add more/new information to …	**Füge** … weitere/neue Informationen **hinzu**.
Check LiF 16 on page 182 for help.	**Sieh** als Hilfe bei LiF 16 auf Seite 182 **nach**.
Choose one of the …	**Wähle** eines/eine der … **aus**.
Collect ideas/reasons …	**Sammle** Idee/Gründe …
Compare your notes with a partner's.	**Vergleiche** deine Notizen mit denen eines Partners.
Consider the following questions:	**Berücksichtige** dabei die folgenden Fragen:
Copy and complete the sentences.	**Übertrage und vervollständige** die Sätze.
Decide if/what/which …	**Entscheide,** ob/was/welche/n/r …
Describe the roles of …	**Beschreibe** die Rollen von …
Discuss how well the text covers …	**Diskutiert darüber,** wie gut der Text … behandelt.
Divide the class in half/into two groups.	**Teilt** die Klasse in zwei Hälften/Gruppen.
Explain your choice.	**Begründe** deine Wahl.
Fill in the grid.	**Fülle** die Tabelle **aus**.
Find more arguments/examples.	**Finde** weitere Argumente/Beispiele.
Find out (more) about …	**Finde** etwas/mehr **heraus** über …
Give (each other) **feedback**.	**Gebt euch Feedback**.
Give reasons for your choice/opinion.	**Begründe** deine Entscheidung/Meinung.
Group work:	**Gruppenarbeit:**
Identify the phrases that …	**Mache** die Ausdrücke **ausfindig,** die …
Imagine …	**Stell dir vor,** …
Listen to …	**Hör dir** … **an**.
Look at … (again).	**Sieh dir** (noch einmal) … **an**.
Make sure (that) you …	**Achte darauf,** dass du …
Match … **and/with** …	**Ordne** … … **zu**.
Note down information about …	**Notiere** Informationen zu …
Pay (particular) **attention to** …	**Achte** (insbesondere) **auf** …
Prepare for your role as …	**Bereite dich auf** deine Rolle als …
Present your results to each other.	**Präsentiert** euch gegenseitig eure Ergebnisse.
Read the article/following statements	**Lies** den Artikel/die folgenden Aussagen.
Refer to the character's body language.	**Beziehe dich auf** die Körpersprache der Figur.
Rewrite the sentences (by) …	**Schreibe** die Sätze **neu/um,** (indem du) …
Scan the article and …	**Überfliege** den Artikel und …
Speculate on …	**Stelle Vermutungen darüber an,** …
Study the advert for your holiday and …	**Sieh dir** die Anzeige für deinen Urlaub **genau an** und …
Summarize … with your own words	**Fasse** mit deinen eigenen Worten … **zusammen**.
Take notes (on …).	**Mach dir Notizen** (zu …).
Talk (to a partner) **about** …	**Sprich** (mit einem Partner/einer Partnerin) **über** …
Tell each other whether/which …	**Erzählt euch gegenseitig,** ob/welche/n/r …
Use the following expressions: …	**Verwende** die folgenden Ausdrücke: …
Watch the video and **say** what it is about.	**Sieh dir** das Video **an** und sag, woran es geht.
Work with a partner.	**Arbeitet mit einem Partner/einer Partnerin**.
Write an email to …	**Schreibe** eine E-Mail an …
Write down …	**Schreibe** … **auf**.

Irregular verbs

infinitive	simple past	participle	German
to be /biː/	was/were /wɒz/wɜː/	been /biːn/	sein
to beat /biːt/	beat /biːt/	beaten /ˈbiːtən/	schlagen
to become /bɪˈkʌm/	became /bɪˈkeɪm/	become /bɪˈkʌm/	werden
to begin /bɪˈgɪn/	began /bɪˈgæn/	begun /bɪˈgʌn/	anfangen
to bet /bet/	bet /bet/	bet /bet/	wetten
to bite /baɪt/	bit /bɪt/	bitten /ˈbɪt(ə)n/	beißen
to break /breɪk/	broke /brəʊk/	broken /ˈbrəʊkən/	brechen
to bring /brɪŋ/	brought /brɔːt/	brought /brɔːt/	(mit)bringen
to build /bɪld/	built /bɪlt/	built /bɪlt/	bauen
to burn /bɜːn/	burnt / burned /bɜːnt, bɜːnd/	burnt / burned /bɜːnt, bɜːnd/	(ab)brennen
to buy /baɪ/	bought /bɔːt/	bought /bɔːt/	kaufen
to catch /kætʃ/	caught /kɔːt/	caught /kɔːt/	fangen
to choose /tʃuːz/	chose /tʃəʊz/	chosen /ˈtʃəʊzən/	(aus)wählen
to come /kʌm/	came /keɪm/	come /kʌm/	kommen
to cost /kɒst/	cost /kɒst/	cost /kɒst/	kosten
to cut /kʌt/	cut /kʌt/	cut /kʌt/	schneiden
to deal with /ˈdiːl wɪð/	dealt with /ˈdelt wɪð/	dealt with /ˈdelt wɪð/	sich befassen mit
to do /duː/	did /dɪd/	done /dʌn/	machen, tun
to draw /drɔː/	drew /druː/	drawn /drɔːn/	zeichnen
to dream /driːm/	dreamt/dreamed /dremt, driːmd/	dreamt/dreamed /dremt, driːmd/	träumen
to drink /drɪŋk/	drank /dræŋk/	drunk /drʌŋk/	trinken
to drive /draɪv/	drove /drəʊv/	driven /ˈdrɪvn/	fahren
to eat /iːt/	ate /et/	eaten /ˈiːt(ə)n/	essen; fressen
to fall /fɔːl/	fell /fel/	fallen /ˈfɔːlən/	(um)fallen
to feed /fiːd/	fed /fed/	fed /fed/	füttern
to feel /fiːl/	felt /felt/	felt /felt/	(sich) fühlen
to fight /faɪt/	fought /fɔːt/	fought /fɔːt/	(be)kämpfen
to find /faɪnd/	found /faʊnd/	found /faʊnd/	finden
to fly /flaɪ/	flew /fluː/	flown /fləʊn/	fliegen
to forget /fəˈget/	forgot /fəˈgɒt/	forgotten /fəˈgɒtən/	vergessen
to get /get/	got /gɒt/	got/gotten /gɒt, ˈgɒtən/	bekommen
to give /gɪv/	gave /geɪv/	given /ˈgɪvən/	geben
to go /gəʊ/	went /went/	gone /gɒn/	gehen; fahren
to grow /grəʊ/	grew /gruː/	grown /grəʊn/	anbauen, wachsen
to hang out /ˌhæŋˈaʊt/	hung out /ˌhʌŋˈaʊt/	hung out /ˌhʌŋˈaʊt/	sich aufhalten, sich herumtreiben
to have /hæv/	had /hæd/	had /hæd/	haben
to hear /hɪə/	heard /hɜːd/	heard /hɜːd/	hören
to hide /haɪd/	hid /hɪd/	hidden /ˈhɪd(ə)n/	(sich) verstecken
to hit /hɪt/	hit /hɪt/	hit /hɪt/	schlagen
to hold /həʊld/	held /held/	held /held/	halten
to hurt /hɜːt/	hurt /hɜːt/	hurt /hɜːt/	schmerzen
to keep /kiːp/	kept /kept/	kept /kept/	aufbewahren
to know /nəʊ/	knew /njuː/	known /nəʊn/	wissen; kennen
to lead /liːd/	led /led/	led /led/	führen
to learn /lɜːn/	learnt/learned /lɜːnt, lɜːnd/	learnt/learned /lɜːnt, lɜːnd/	lernen
to leave /liːv/	left /left/	left /left/	verlassen

Irregular verbs

infinitive	simple past	participle	German
to let /let/	let /let/	let /let/	lassen
to lie /laɪ/	lay /leɪ/	lain /leɪn/	liegen
to lose /luːz/	lost /lɒst/	lost /lɒst/	verlieren
to make /meɪk/	made /meɪd/	made /meɪd/	machen
to mean /miːn/	meant /ment/	meant /ment/	bedeuten
to meet /miːt/	met /met/	met /met/	(sich) treffen
to overcome /ˌəʊvəˈkʌm/	overcame /ˌəʊvəˈkeɪm/	overcome /ˌəʊvəˈkʌm/	bewältigen, meistern
to overtake /ˌəʊvəˈteɪk/	overtook /ˌəʊvəˈtʊk/	overtaken /ˌəʊvəˌteɪkən/	überholen
to pay /peɪ/	paid /peɪd/	paid /peɪd/	(be)zahlen
to proofread /ˈpruːfriːd/	proofread /ˈpruːfred/	proofread /ˈpruːfred/	Korrektur lesen
to put /pʊt/	put /pʊt/	put /pʊt/	setzen, legen, stellen
to read /riːd/	read /red/	read /red/	lesen
to rewrite /ˌriːˈraɪt/	rewrote /ˌriːˈrəʊt/	rewritten /ˌriːˈrɪtən/	überarbeiten, umschreiben
to ride /raɪd/	rode /rəʊd/	ridden /ˈrɪd(ə)n/	fahren (mit); reiten
to ring (up) /ˌrɪŋ ˈʌp/	rang (up) /ˌræŋ ˈʌp/	rung (up) /ˌrʌŋ ˈʌp/	anrufen
to rise /raɪz/	rose /rəʊz/	risen /ˈrɪz(ə)n/	aufgehen; steigen
to run /rʌn/	ran /ræn/	run /rʌn/	rennen
to say /seɪ/	said /sed/	said /sed/	sagen
to see /siː/	saw /sɔː/	seen /siːn/	sehen
to sell /sel/	sold /səʊld/	sold /səʊld/	verkaufen
to send /send/	sent /sent/	sent /sent/	(zu)schicken
to set /set/	set /set/	set /set/	festlegen, festsetzen
to shoot /ʃuːt/	shot /ʃɒt/	shot /ʃɒt/	schießen
to show /ʃəʊ/	showed /ʃəʊd/	shown /ʃəʊn/	zeigen
to sing /sɪŋ/	sang /sæŋ/	sung /sʌŋ/	singen
to sit /sɪt/	sat /sæt/	sat /sæt/	sitzen
to sleep /sliːp/	slept /slept/	slept /slept/	schlafen
to smell /smel/	smelt/smelled /smelt, smeld/	smelt/smelled /smelt, smeld/	duften; riechen
to speak /spiːk/	spoke /spəʊk/	spoken /ˈspəʊkən/	sprechen
to spend /spend/	spent /spent/	spent /spent/	ausgeben; verbringen
to split up /ˌsplɪt ˈʌp/	split up /ˌsplɪt ˈʌp/	split up /ˌsplɪt ˈʌp/	(auf)teilen; sich trennen
to spread /spred/	spread /spred/	spread /spred/	(sich) aus-/verbreiten
to stand /stænd/	stood /stʊd/	stood /stʊd/	stehen
to steal /stiːl/	stole /stəʊl/	stolen /ˈstəʊlən/	stehlen
to stick to sth /ˈstɪk tʊ/	stuck to sth /ˈstʌk tʊ/	stuck to sth /ˈstʌk tʊ/	(sich) an etw halten
to strike /straɪk/	struck /strʌk/	struck /strʌk/	(zu)schlagen
to swear /sweə/	swore /swɔː/	sworn /swɔːn/	fluchen; schwören
to swim /swɪm/	swam /swæm/	swum /swʌm/	schwimmen
to take /teɪk/	took /tʊk/	taken /ˈteɪkən/	(mit)nehmen
to teach /tiːtʃ/	taught /tɔːt/	taught /tɔːt/	unterrichten
to tell /tel/	told /təʊld/	told /təʊld/	erzählen; sagen
to think /θɪŋk/	thought /θɔːt/	thought /θɔːt/	denken, glauben, meinen
to throw /θrəʊ/	threw /θruː/	thrown /θrəʊn/	werfen
to understand /ˌʌndəˈstænd/	understood /ˌʌndəˈstʊd/	understood /ˌʌndəˈstʊd/	verstehen
to upset /ʌpˈset/	upset /ʌpˈset/	upset /ʌpˈset/	beunruhigen
to wake up /ˌweɪk ˈʌp/	woke up /ˌwəʊk ˈʌp/	woken up /ˌwəʊkən ˈʌp/	aufwachen; aufwecken
to wear /weə/	wore /wɔː/	worn /wɔːn/	tragen *(Kleidung)*
to win /wɪn/	won /wʌn/	won /wʌn/	gewinnen
to write /raɪt/	wrote /rəʊt/	written /ˈrɪtən/	schreiben

Quellenverzeichnis

Bildquellen:
alamy images, Abingdon/Oxfordshire: 4 (Andrew McConnell), 4 (Montgomery Martin), 5 (Documentography), 10 (NG Images), 10 (Edwin Remsberg / Stockimo), 10 (JLangridge / Stockimo), 10 (Scott Indermaur / Stockimo), 10 (Scott Indermaur / Stockimo), 10 (Nitish Naharas), 10 (Keith Jefferies / Stockimo), 10 (Marmaduke St. John), 10 (Chris Mackler / Stockimo), 10 (Danny Hooks), 10 (John Crowe), 10 (Pauloo), 10 (david martyn hughes / Stockimo), 10 (Lenscap), 11 (Bloomsbury Photo inc), 11 (Keith Dannemiller), 26 (Zoonar GmbH), 26 (MBI), 26 (MBI), 26 (Bob Daemmrich), 37 (Mike Goldwater), 38, 47 (Photo Researchers, Inc), 53 (brt CIRCUS), 53 (RosaIreneBetancourt 9), 58 (RubberBall), 73 73 (RubberBall), 80 (Andrew McConnell), 101 (robertharding), 102 103 (incamerastock), 102 104 (debra millet), 102 104 (debra millet), 102 104 (Cindy Hopkins), 103 (incamerastock), 104 (debra millet), 104 (debra millet), 104 (Cindy Hopkins), 108 (OJO Images Ltd), 109 (Charles O. Cecil), 109 (Montgomery Martin), 113 (gualtiero boffi), 113 (Documentography), 117 (© Jim Holden), 140 80 (Andrew McConnell), 190 (Extreme Sports Photo); Amy Koerner, Frankfurt am Main: 114 .1; Associated Press, Frankfurt/M.: 36 (Itsuo Inouye); Caro Fotoagentur, Berlin: 65 (Korth), 71 71 (Korth); Colourbox.com, Odense: 75, 156 (Eugen Wais); Cycling Scotland, Glasgow: 41; ddp images GmbH, Hamburg: 39 (SIPA/B. Berbert), 80; dreamstime.com, Brentwood: 18 (Wavebreakmediamicro), 46 (Hdesert), 102 103 (Dabldy), 103 (Dabldy); dsphotos.de, Hamburg: Titel; Eyferth, Konrad, Berlin: 112; fotolia.com, New York: 4 (adisa), 15 (Daniel Ernst), 37 Peter_Nile, iStock: 178890817 (beer5020/montiert in iStockphoto, Peter_Nile), 39 (Ingo Bartussek), 39 (Natallia Vintsik), 41 (sdecoret), 49 (Woodapple), 49 (Gina Sanders), 80 (adisa), 81 (Joshua Resnick), 85 (Dmitry Naumov), 85 (mulveg), 85 (joyt), 86 (BillionPhotos.com), 86 (Gundolf Renze), 86 (Maksim Shebeko), 96 (Yevgen Belich), 100 (Martin Valigursky), 101 (pbardocz), 107 (dmitimaruta), 107 (claudiaveja), 117 (apops), 120 (contrastwerkstatt), 120 (Kaarsten), 121 (Syda Productions), 140 (Antonioguillem), 140 81 (Joshua Resnick), 152 (Marco2811), 189 86 (Gundolf Renze); Frambach, Timo, Braunschweig: 81; Getty Images, München: 10 (Mike Kemp), 10 (Rubberball), 52 (AFP), 53 (Ricardo DeAratanha), 53 (gotpap/Bauer-Griffin), 62 (Ron Galella Collection), 63 (Graham Wiltshire/Redferns), 63 (1972 American Broadcasting Companies, Inc.), 94 (Anadolu Agency), 94 (Simone Joyner), 99 (Doug Pearson/ JAI), 139 139 (Ricardo DeAratanha); Hanus, Pamela, Hamburg: 58, 73 73; Harper Collins Publishers, London: 5 (reprinted by permission of HarperCollins Publishers Ltd © 2017 Lois Lowry), 24 (reprinted by permission of HarperCollins Publishers Ltd © 2017 Lois Lowry), 191 (reprinted by permission of HarperCollins Publishers Ltd © 2017 Lois Lowry); Helga Lade Fotoagenturen GmbH, Frankfurt/M.: 49 (Schulz); Houghton Mifflin Harcourt, Orlando: 24 (Lois Lowry: The Giver); Huber Images, Garmisch-Partenkirchen: 156; Interfoto, München: 140 (Mary Evans / Ronald Grant); iStockphoto.com, Calgary: 4 (DavidCallan), 12 (XiXinXing), 14 (Art-Of-Photo), 15 (asiseeit), 15 (Neustockimages), 15 (Tassii), 20, 28 (monkeybusinessimages), 30 (XiXinXing), 37 (Melle1959), 38 (Ridofranz), 38 (Rinelle), 41 (Samuil_Levich), 41 (gilaxia), 53, 64 (Yuri_Arcurs), 64 (Andrei Kuzmik), 74, 74, 80 (DavidCallan), 85 (vuk8691), 93 (Andrey Moisseyev), 94 (Matej Kastelic), 95, 118, 121, 121, 140 (deimagine); Kathrin Pätzold, Berlin: 141, 141, 141; Kiel James Patrick; www.KJP.com, Rhode Island-Pawtucket: 58, 73, 186 58, 73; mauritius images GmbH, Mittenwald: 68 (Phototake), 130 (Ripp); National Institute on Alcohol Abuse and Alcoholism (NIAAA), Bethesda: 66; Panther Media GmbH (panthermedia.net), München: 88 (David Rajecky), 189 (David Rajecky); Penguin Group (USA) Inc., New York: 32 (John Green, David Levithan: Will Grayson, Will Grayson), 32 (John Green, David Levithan: Will Grayson, Will Grayson); Penguin Random House, New York: 5 ((c) 2014 by Maya Van Wagenen), 22 24 (Lois Lowry: The Giver), 24 (Lois Lowry: The Giver), 54 ((c) 2010 by Allyson Braithwaite Condie), 60 ((c) 2014 by Maya Van Wagenen), 65 ((c) 2014 by Maya Van Wagenen), 191 60, 65 ((c) 2014 by Maya Van Wagenen); PETA Europe Ltd,, London: 41; Picture-Alliance GmbH, Frankfurt/M.: 37 (The Advertising Archives), 107 (dpa/Uwe Zucchi), 111 (eb-stock), 114 (picture-alliance / eb-stock); Richard Mosse - Courtesy of the artist and Jack Shainman Gallery, New York: 4 (Safe From Harm, 2012), 37 (Safe From Harm, 2012); Rieke, Michael, Braunschweig: 99; Shutterstock.com, New York: 4 (photobank.ch), 4 (PhotoSky), 4 (pisaphotography), 4, 4, 5 (michaeljung), 5, 5 (Mandy Godbehear), 5 (Syda Productions), 10, 10 (ittleny), 11 30, 13 (Monkey Business Images), 13 (Suzanne Tucker), 13 (michaeljung), 13 (Dragon Images), 20 (Twin Sails), 20 (threerocksimages), 20 (Monkey Business Images), 20 (Monkey Business Images), 20 (Monkey Business Images), 21 (michaeljung), 21 (threerocksimages), 21 (SpeedKingz), 26, 26, 29 (sianc), 29 .2, 31 (Syda Productions), 39, 41 (Shellydave), 42 (Featureflash Phot), 52 (Leonard Zhukovsky), 58 (Syda Productions), 58 (Mandy Godbehear), 67, 68, 70 (Png Studio Photography), 72 (Antonio Guillem), 73 73 (Syda Productions), 73 73 (Mandy Godbehear), 76 (guteksk7), 83 (Philip Lange), 88 (blvdone), 89 (NikoNomad), 93 (PomInOz), 93 (Lev Kropotov), 93 (kwest), 94 (Banet), 100 (Pete Niesen), 100 (Marco Tomasini), 100, 101 (pisaphotography), 101 (fritz16), 102 103 (Solodovnikova Elena), 103 (Solodovnikova Elena), 109 (PhotoSky), 109 (igor.stevanovic), 118, 118, 118, 118, 118, 119, 121, 121, 121, 122 (Monkey Business Images), 122 (bikeriderlondon), 123 (photobank.ch), 123 (jgolby), 123 (xmee), 123 (Catalin Petolea), 123 (michaeljung), 123 (paul prescott), 123 (Monkey Business Images), 124 (STILLFX), 131 (Thai Soriano), 134 (Zurijeta), 136 (EDHAR), 136 83 (Philip Lange), 140 140 (SpeedKingz), 187 119, 188 (Vacclav), 188 (jgolby), 189 (blvdone), 190 (Diriye Amey); Simon & Schuster Inc., New York: 14 (From GETTING IT by Alex Sanchez. Copyright © 2006 by Alex Sanchez. Reprinted with the permission of Simon & Schuster Books for Young Readers, an imprint of Simon & Schuster Children's Publishing Division. All rights reserved.), 27 27 (From GETTING IT by Alex Sanchez. Copyright © 2006 by Alex Sanchez. Reprinted with the permission of Simon & Schuster Books for Young Readers, an imprint of Simon & Schuster Children's Publishing Division. All rights reserved.); U.S. Air Force: 37 (Lance Cheung, Fotograf Hai: Charles Maxwell); Utmost Adventure Trekking, Thamel/Kathmandu: 4 (Subin Thakuri), 80 (Subin Thakuri); vario images, Bonn: 107; Verlagsgruppe Random

Quellenverzeichnis

House GmbH, München: 5 (cbt: John Green, David Levithan: Will & Will; Übersetzung: Bernadette Ott, Taschenbuch, Broschur, 384 Seiten, ISBN: 978-3-570-30885-1, September 2013), 32 (cbt: John Green, David Levithan: Will & Will; Übersetzung: Bernadette Ott, Taschenbuch, Broschur, 384 Seiten, ISBN: 978-3-570-30885-1, September 2013), 191 32 (cbt: John Green, David Levithan: Will & Will; Übersetzung: Bernadette Ott, Taschenbuch, Broschur, 384 Seiten, ISBN: 978-3-570-30885-1, September 2013); Zwick, Joachim, Gießen: 1, 258; © Government of South Australia: 92; © Open University 2011. Used with permission of DCD Rights Ltd.Vertrag: "Global English (4C1) Lizenz": 88.

Textquellen:

12, 30 „Same Love" written by Mary Lambert, Ryan Lewis and Ben Haggerty
© Published by Inside Passage Music and Macklemore LLC. Administered by Kobalt Music Publishing Limited.

14/15, 17/18, 27 „getting it" Reprinted with permission of DeFiore and Company, on behalf of Alex Sanchez. Copyright © 2006 by Alex Sanchez.

23 „The Giver" (Film Script) © 2008 by Alexander Ramirez, based on the novel "The Giver" © 1993 by Lowis Lowry

31 „Supreme Court rules in favor of gay marriage" Adapted from a PBS NewsHour report © 2015 by NewsHour Productions LLC.

32–35 „Will Grayson, Will Grayson" © John Green and David Levithan, Penguin Books

40 „ASA Advertising and Marketing Guidelines" © Committee of Advertising Practise Ltd.

43 Excerpts from "Nancy Jo Sales On 'The Bling Ring' And The Trouble With Our Fixation On Fame" © Dina Gachman, https://www.forbes.com/sites/dinagachman/2013/05/20/nancy-jo-sales-on-the-bling-ring-and-the-trouble-with-our-fixation-on-fame/#72c78ec97437

51 https://www.welt.de/politik/article143161447/Minister-will-Zigarettenwerbung-komplett-verbieten.html

54–57 Excerpt(s) from MATCHED by Ally Condie, copyright © 2010 by Allison Braithwaite Condie. Used by permission of Dutton Children's Books, an imprint of Penguin Young Readers Group, a division of Penguin Random House LLC. All rights reserved. Any third party use of this material, outside of this publication, is prohibited. Interested parties must apply directly to Penguin Random House LLC directly for permission.

60/61 Excerpt(s) from POPULAR: VINTAGE WISDOM FOR A MODERN GEEK by Maya Van Wagenen, copyright © 2014 by Maya Van Wagenen. Used by permission of Dutton Children's Books, an imprint of Penguin Young Readers Group, a division of Penguin Random House LLC. All rights reserved. Any third party use of this material, outside of this publication, is prohibited. Interested parties must apply directly to Penguin Random House LLC directly for permission.

63 „Parents just don't understand" by Jeffrey Townes, Williard Smith, Peter Brian Harris © Universal Music-Z Tunes LLC, IMAGEM MUSIC GmbH, Berlin.

67/68 Texte zu peer pressure © ReachOut USA, us.reachout.com

76–79 „The Hacktivists" © Ben Ockrent, aus: Connections 2015 New Plays for Young People, S. 365–369; 378/379

89 Carina Meyer: „Es war so anders als hier", www.faz.net, gekürzt

93 http://laraaustralien.auslandsblog.de

97 http://www.weltweiser.de/schueleraustausch/schueleraustausch-gastfamilie-australien.htm

103 „Pardon My French: The Art of Making Mistakes and Trying anyway" by Lillian Holmes
© FamilyTravelForum.com Teen Scholarship sponsored by Allianz Global Assistance

104 „Relaxing to Roller Coasters:
The Perfect Day in Sylvan Beach", by Mary Wester © FamilyTravelForum.com Teen Scholarship sponsored by Allianz Global Assistance

122–127 „Forty-Five Minutes" © Anya Reiss, published in National Theatre Connections 2013. New Plays for Young People, Bloomsbury, p. 489-550.

Lösungen

Lösungen zu *Can you do it?* im Personal Trainer:

Theme 1:
P5 (S. 28):
1 had
2 took
3 didn't/don't
4 were
5 'm not going to/won't start

Theme 2:
P2 (S. 46):
The threatening clouds of a thunderstorm are shown in the photo.

The cloud was designed by a special effects team for a disaster movie.

The photo has been used in posts because people thought it was real.

P7 (S. 50):
Googling his name, Rebecca and Mark find out that Orlando Bloom is currently shooting a movie in New York.

Having learnt that Orlando Bloom and Miranda Kerr are out of town, Rebecca and Mark invite Chloe, Nicki and Sam to break into their house with them.

Theme 3:
P7 (S. 73):
If I had stayed at the party until 4am, my parents would have been angry with me.

My exam results would have been much better if I had been better prepared/had prepared better.

Theme 4:
P10 (S. 98):
Adelaide, which is the capital of South Australia, has a population of over 1.25 million people.
Adelaide, which has a population of over 1.25 million people, is the capital of South Australia.

The *Tour Down Under* bicycle race, which takes place in the area around Adelaide, is the first (cycling) race of the season.
The *Tour Down Under* bicycle race, which is the first (cycling) race of the season, takes place in the area around Adelaide.

The English-speaking world

English-speaking countries

members of the Commonwealth
- official and majority use
- official or semi-official use

non-members of the Commonwealth
- official and majority use
- official or semi-official use

- ● capital
- ○ city

C A N A D A
U N I T E D S T A T E S O F A M E R I C A
M E X I C O
Pacific Ocean
Atlantic Ocean
Gulf of Mexico
WASHINGTON
OREGON
CALIFORNIA
NEVADA
IDAHO
MONTANA
WYOMING
UTAH
COLORADO
ARIZONA
NEW MEXICO
NORTH DAKOTA
SOUTH DAKOTA
NEBRASKA
KANSAS
OKLAHOMA
TEXAS
MINNESOTA
IOWA
MISSOURI
ARKANSAS
LOUISIANA
WISCONSIN
ILLINOIS
MICHIGAN
INDIANA
OHIO
KENTUCKY
TENNESSEE
MISSISSIPPI
ALABAMA
GEORGIA
FLORIDA
SOUTH CAROLINA
NORTH CAROLINA
VIRGINIA
WEST VIRGINIA
MARYLAND
DELAWARE
PENNSYLVANIA
NEW JERSEY
NEW YORK
CONNECTICUT
RHODE ISLAND
MASSACHUSETTS
VER-MONT
NEW HAMPSHIRE
MAINE
BAHAMAS
CUBA
HAITI
Cascade Range
Coast Ranges
Sierra Nevada
Basin Region
Rocky Mountains
Black Hills
Colorado Plateau
Appalachian Mountains
Mount Olympus 2424
Mount Rainier 4392
Mount Hood 3427
Mount Shasta 4317
Lassen Peak 3181
Mount Whitney 4418
Gannet Peak 4202
Harney Peak 2207
Longs Peak 4345
Mount Elbert 4399
Blanca Peak 4372
St. Francisco Peak 3868
Mt. Mitchell 2037
Glacier National Park
Yellowstone National Park
Badlands National Park
Rocky Mountain National Park
Uintah & Ouray Reservation
Canyonlands National Park
Bryce Canyon National Park
Mesa Verde National Park
Great Sand Dunes National Park
Yosemite National Park
Sequoia National Park
Big Bend National Park
Monument Valley
Grand Canyon
Death Valley
Seattle
Olympia
Salem
Boise
Helena
Sacramento
Carson City
San Francisco
San Jose
Las Vegas
Los Angeles
San Diego
Tijuana
Mexicali
Phoenix
Salt Lake City
Great Salt Lake
Cheyenne
Denver
Santa Fé
El Paso
Ciudad Juarez
Bismarck
Pierre
Winnipeg
Lincoln
Topeka
Oklahoma City
Dallas
Austin
San Antonio
Houston
Corpus Christi
Laredo
Nuevo Laredo
Reynosa
Matamoros
Monterrey
Minneapolis
St. Paul
Des Moines
Muscatine
Jefferson City
Springfield
St. Louis
Little Rock
Benton
Memphis
Jackson
Baton Rouge
New Orleans
Madison
Milwaukee
Roselle
Chicago
Lansing
Detroit
Indianapolis
Columbus
Cleveland
Cincinnati
Frankfort
Nashville
Montgomery
Atlanta
Tallahassee
Jacksonville
Cape Canaveral
Lake Okeechobee
Everglades
Miami
Nassau
Habana
Santiago
Columbia
Raleigh
Charleston
Richmond
Washington D.C.
Annapolis
Baltimore
Dover
Philadelphia
Trenton
Pittsburgh
Harrisburg
New York
Hartford
Providence
Boston
Albany
Concord
Montpelier
Augusta
Toronto
Niagara Falls
Ottawa
Montreal
Quebec
Lake Superior
Lake Michigan
Lake Huron
Georgian Bay
L. Erie
Ontario
L. Nippigon
Lake of the Woods
Columbia
Snake River
Missouri
Milk River
Yellowstone
Green River
Colorado
San Juan
Rio Grande
Rio Pecos
Conchos
Gila
Salt River
Humboldt River
Sacramento
S. Joaquin
Platte
Niobrara
James
Red River
Brazos
Sabine
Mississippi
Des Moines
Illinois
Ohio
Tennessee
Cumberland
Savannah
Alabama
St. Lawrence
St. John
Ottawa
Assiniboine
Moose
Albany
Alaska
USA
Hawaii Isl.
Heights in m
0 - 200
200 - 500
500 - 1000
1000 - 2000
> 2000
Washington D.C.
Austin
National capitals
Administrative centres
Cities
Time zones
Time in Germany
12⁰⁰
18⁰⁰
11⁰⁰
10⁰⁰
0 mile 125 250
0 km 250 500